MACROECONOMICS

GARY SMITH
Pomona College

MACROECONOMICS

W. H. FREEMAN AND COMPANY
NEW YORK

Cover art by Kazumasa Nagai, 1981, Tokyo.

LIBRARY OF CONGRESS CATALOGING IN PUBLICATION DATA

Smith, Gary, 1945–
Macroeconomics

Bibliography: p.
Includes index.
1. Macroeconomics. I. Title.
HB172.5.S63 1984 339 84-18690
ISBN: 0-7167-1646-1

Some of the material in this book has been adapted from *Money and Banking* by Gary Smith. © 1982 by Addison-Wesley Publishing Company, Inc. Reprinted by permission.

Printed in the United States of America

1 2 3 4 5 6 7 8 9 0 KP 2 1 0 8 9 8 7 6 5 4

For my parents, Bette and Bill

CONTENTS

FOREWORD

In his *Inquiry into the Nature and Causes of the Wealth of Nations,* published in 1776, Adam Smith sought to explain how whole economies work, what determines affluence and poverty, and what governments can and cannot do to help their countries prosper. Such "macroeconomic" issues have always been, before Smith as well as after, the principal agenda of political economy. (This older term for what we now call economics reveals the discipline's historic focus on national and governmental housekeeping.) These issues engaged the great economists of the nineteenth and early twentieth centuries—among them David Ricardo, the Reverend Thomas Malthus, John Stuart Mill, Karl Marx, Knut Wicksell, Alfred Marshall, Irving Fisher, and Joseph Schumpeter.

Yet in an important sense macroeconomics is quite new. The word itself crept into professional jargon in the years following World War II, along with the now commonplace distinction of "macro" from "micro," which would never have occurred to economists of previous generations. The founder of macroeconomics as a distinct subject was John Maynard Keynes, though he did not use the word and most likely would have abhorred it. The book that did it was his *General Theory of Employment, Interest, and Money* (1936). Its publication revolutionized economic theory and, eventually, also the monetary and fiscal policies of the governments of democratic capitalist countries. This "Keynesian revolution" has dominated macroeconomics for half a century. Subsequent economists have taught, extended, and implemented its ideas or have amended, criticized, and opposed them. Even today, when Keynesian economics is on the defensive both in the economics profession and in the public arena, the counter-revolutions—monetarist, supply-side, new classical—seek to explain in their own ways the same phenomena Keynes was studying.

Keynes's book was written and published during the Great Depression, a decade of mass unemployment. Business cycles were a long-standing feature of capitalist economies, but the severity and duration of the slump of the 1930s were unprecedented. Market capitalism—indeed, democracy and western civilization—barely survived. The world economic collapse of 1929–33 delivered the Weimar Republic of Germany to Hitler, weakened European democracies, and paved the way for the aggression of the Axis powers.

The crisis of capitalism was also a crisis of economic science. Classical economics could neither explain the mass unemployment nor offer a remedy. Standard doctrine relied on adjustments of market prices to eliminate any temporary excess of supply over demand. But in labor markets the process was not functioning. An enormous excess supply persisted—the involuntarily unemployed, in Keynes's words—and cuts in wages, the price of labor, did not eliminate it.

Keynes's insight was to focus on "effective demand": without sufficient demand for goods and services to buy the goods and services labor produces, there simply won't be enough jobs. Put so simply, the insight seems only common sense. But classical theory allowed no room for economy-wide deficiencies of demand, on the grounds that "supply creates its own demand." Keynes originated "demand-side" economics, providing a new understanding not only of the Great Depression but of business cycles in general. Of course, as Keynes himself recognized, long-run growth and progress depend on supply—on labor force, management, productive capital, natural resources, and technology. Fluctuations around the growth trend, however, are mainly movements of aggregate demand.

I was a sophomore at Harvard, just beginning to study economics, when Keynes's book broke upon the scene. It was an exciting time, even for undergraduates. Young teachers and graduate students were quick to grasp the basic message. Most senior professors were skeptical or hostile. A major exception was Harvard professor Alvin Hansen, who, after writing an unfavorable review of Keynes, changed his mind and became the leader of the revolution in America. Those were years of lively controversy and intense inquiry. For many young economists like myself, the challenging research opportunities opened by the new ideas were the happy beginnings of professional careers. The intellectual excitement was suffused with hope. Economics was not just interesting, it was immediately relevant; it could save the world. In Hansen's famous Fiscal Policy seminar, graduate students he had placed in jobs in the Roosevelt Administration returned to Harvard to give papers relating to the implementation of the new macroeconomics in Washington.

FDR's New Deal adopted Keynesian economics only late in the game, after the 1937–38 recession interrupted the recovery that had begun in 1933 and raised the frightening prospect of relapse into deep depression. Soon thereafter, defense and war spending restored full employment, as Keynesian theory would predict; demand deficiencies were supplanted by supply shortages. After World War II Keynesian macroeconomics became the accepted mainstream. In the United States as in other democracies, political leaders were determined not to let the pre-war depression happen again. Governments were committed to use the fiscal and monetary tools of demand management to moderate business fluctuations and maintain high employment.

In my view, this commitment was a major reason why the United States, Canada, and the other economically advanced nations of the free world in Europe and Japan enjoyed unpredecented prosperity and progress.

The high point of macroeconomics occurred in the 1960s, when a synthesis of Keynesian and classical economics attracted broad consensus in the profession. Its policy prescriptions appeared to work in practice and won widespread public and political support. I personally had the gratifying and rewarding experience of putting macroeconomics to work in Washington, serving as a member of President Kennedy's Council of Economic Advisers in 1961–62 and consulting frequently with the Council for several years thereafter. I recommend our *1962 Economic Report of the President* to anyone interested in policy-oriented macroeconomics as it stood in that golden age. Compare it to the 1982 *Report,* which also represents an initial philosophic statement of a new Administration. Of course the economists advising President Reagan have very different ideas from those of the 1962 Council.

Like the Great Depression, the Great Stagflation of the 1970s powerfully altered both professional and public thinking about macroeconomics. Keynesian economics, a revolution matured into orthodoxy, was the target of several counter-revolutions. Milton Friedman's monetarism and "supply-side" economics were the most prominent in the media and the political arena. A more serious basic intellectual challenge has been a revival of the classical tradition against which Keynes was revolting fifty years ago. The new classicals bring modern artillery to the fray, notably the appealing idea of "rational expectations." They question whether government fiscal and monetary policies of demand management can stabilize the economy as Keynesian macroeconomists had hoped, and indeed whether they can have any real effects at all. Reaganomics, like the policies of Mrs. Thatcher in Britain and those of other conservative governments, reflects in varying degrees these several counter-revolutions. So macroeconomics finds itself in another period of ferment—doubtless confusing to the lay public and to students, but exciting and challenging too. As always, macroeconomics is close to real-world events, debates, and policies. As ever, the stakes are high.

Students learning macroeconomics are fortunate to have Gary Smith as their guide. At Yale, where he got his Ph.D. in 1971, he was one of the best graduate students I have taught. He stayed at Yale another seven years as a faculty member. We taught together, did research together, and wrote together. We learned from one another. Gary is a first-rate economist and a marvelous teacher of macroeconomics. In this book he is sharing his talents with a wider audience. As in the classroom, he will guide you through the controversies I described above, introduce you to the analytical tools of the discipline, relate macroeconomics to economic history and to the real world you live in today. Most important, he will prepare you to be your own macroeconomist and invite you to think for yourself.

JAMES TOBIN
Sterling Professor of Economics
Yale University

PREFACE

> The study of economics does not seem to require any specialized gifts of an unusually high order. Is it not, intellectually regarded, a very easy subject compared with the higher branches of philosophy or pure science? An easy subject, at which very few excel!
>
> The paradox finds its explanation, perhaps, in that the master-economist must possess a rare combination of gifts. He must be a mathematician, historian, statesman, philosopher—in some degree. He must understand symbols and speak in words. He must contemplate the particular in terms of the general, and touch abstract and concrete in the same flight of thought.
>
> He must study the present in light of the past for the purposes of the future. No part of man's nature or his institutions must lie entirely outside his regard. He must be purposeful and disinterested in a simultaneous mood; as aloof and incorruptible as an artist, yet sometimes as near the earth as a politician.
>
> JOHN MAYNARD KEYNES

Macroeconomics is a wonderfully interesting and endlessly challenging subject. It is interesting because it is concerned with crucial national—indeed, worldwide—implications of human economic behavior, with how working, spending, and investing decisions affect all our lives. It is challenging because it involves—in addition to economic theory—political science, history, human psychology, and much more.

Macroeconomic policy is debated in national elections and macroeconomic events are reported daily in the news. Households, businesses, and governments continually use and misuse macroeconomic reasoning—the former because it is so important, the latter because the users are too often economically illiterate.

This book aims to leave its readers better equipped to use the lessons of macroeconomics and better able to recognize their misuse. To do so it emphasizes understanding of the important macroeconomic issues of our time and analysis of the macro effects of a variety of economic events. Historical examples and policy issues are used to illustrate and buttress the economic logic. These examples are interwoven into the textual discussion because, in macroeconomics, theory and practice are not distinct, seemingly unrelated, subjects. Intended for a standard intermediate macroeconomics course, this text covers the usual material plus a wide variety of "modern" topics, including the rational expectations viewpoint, supply-side policies, market disequilibria, and Tobin's *q*. No mathematics beyond the most elementary algebra is used, since any economic reasoning that is sensible can be explained in plain English, without a barrage of mathematical pyrotechnics.

The first eleven chapters compose the core material that should be in any intermediate course; the rest can be used selectively, depending on the length of the term and on the course's objectives. These last seven chapters, self-contained extensions of the basic core material that branch in several directions, are never very difficult, but always a bit specialized.

The breadth and flair of the subject are suggested by numerous news items ("In the News . . . ") and by guest essays by authors eminent in the field:

James Tobin, Yale University
George Akerlof and Janet Yellen, University of California at Berkeley
Edward Yardeni, of Prudential-Bache Securities
John Shoven, Stanford University
Dale Henderson, of the Federal Reserve Board

Many of the exercises at the ends of chapters are based on actual events or policy debates, and are designed to give readers an opportunity to apply what they are learning to real-life situations. Such application is essential in learning macroeconomics: One can neither become an able swimmer by watching nor learn economics just by reading; it is essential that the feet get wet—in macroeconomics, by reasoning things out for oneself.

This book has benefited from reviews by many wonderfully conscientious people. Among those who read various drafts were the following:

David Backus, Queens University, Kingston, Ontario
Robert Barry, College of William and Mary
James Barth, George Washington University
Douglas Brown, Georgetown University
Shirley Browning, University of North Carolina at Asheville
John Graham, University of Illinois
Mark Kuperberg, Swarthmore College
Edward McNertney, Texas Christian University
James Rakowski, University of Notre Dame
Jonathan Ratner, State University of New York at Albany
Lloyd Thomas, Kansas State University
Michael Wiseman, University of California, Berkeley
Hiroshi Yoshikawa, Osaka University, Osaka
William Zahka, Widener University

Hundreds of students—in my classes at Pomona College, Rice University, and the University of Houston—read the original manuscript and were cheerfully diligent in pointing out errors and deficiencies. Gail Orozco typed the many drafts, and several people at W. H. Freeman helped turn these drafts into a handsome book; these include James Dodd, Kathleen Dolan, Peter Dougherty, Jill Feldheim, Janet Koenig, Phil Ressner, and Lynne Sheehan.

I welcome your comments and suggestions.

GARY SMITH
August 1984

PART ONE

INTRODUCTION

CHAPTER ONE

THE NATURE AND IMPORTANCE OF MACROECONOMICS

From its earliest days, capitalism has always been as critically ill as it has been intensely alive. "Convulsions" and "revulsions" (as the older political economists called them), "crises" (as Marx identified them), "recessions" and "depressions" (in modern economic language) have been as prominent features of capitalism as its dizzying succession of technical advances, its enormous material productivity, its irresistible global expansion.

ROBERT HEILBRONER[1]

This chapter will briefly define macroeconomics, describe its origins, and trace its recent role in Western economies. It closes with a concise agenda of this book.

THE more doctrinaire of Karl Marx's disciples saw economics as the basis of all forms and aspects of human society, from the way we earn our livings to the institution of marriage to political structures to the subjects and manners of our arts. Not many these days subscribe to so sweeping a view; yet, undeniably, economics, and particularly macroeconomics, underlies and has profound effects on all our lives. Macroeconomics is distinguished from microeconomics primarily in its scope—the latter focusing on ways in which specific markets will be affected by economic events, the former on the broader, overall aspects. Thus, while microeconomics might analyze how an oil embargo will affect the prices of gasoline, cars, and Detroit housing, macroeconomics predicts how that embargo will affect total employment, total output, average wages, average prices, and average interest rates. Macroeconomists let the microeconomists worry about the market for Porsches in Kokomo and Kansas City.

Macroeconomics tries to improve our understanding of recessions, booms, poverty, prosperity, unemployment, inflation. It asks and answers important questions about all these phenomena and many more: interest rates, the stock market, foreign trade, the prospering of some nations while others falter—in sum, almost all major economic issues. These issues are complex, and the relevant features are constantly changing as people's aims and needs change and as societies evolve; hence macroeconomics is as much an art as a science.

Households and businesses are, of course, keenly interested in employment, output, inflation, and interest rates. These all directly affect our lives and many of the working, spending, saving, and investing decisions we must make. Macroeconomic issues are on the front pages of newspapers and on the nightly news—"Unemployment Rises to 9%," "6% Inflation Predicted," "Tax Increase

Urged to Balance Budget." In our elections, we vote not only for individual candidates, but also for the macroeconomic policies (government spending, taxation, monetary policies) they advocate and that they spend much of their campaigns debating and defending.

Macroeconomics, because it deals with the behavior of millions of very different people, each following his or her own logic, intuition, and emotions, cannot be conveniently summarized in concise immutable laws. Moreover, economists cannot make the world stand still while they run economic experiments under controlled laboratory conditions.* Instead, they must make do with "nature's experiments," trying to unravel the effects of ongoing policies in a world in which many things are happening at once: Did the policy cause this, or was it caused by something else? And there is *always* something else.

Microeconomists go to a great deal of trouble to determine how rational people should behave under certain carefully prescribed conditions—on the assumption that most people will behave rationally. (Should theory not agree with actual behavior, then it is assumed that it is people's behavior that is in error.) Macroeconomists tend to be more flexible, being primarily interested in describing the economy we live in, rather than some hypothetical, perfectly rational one. They draw their insights from many disciplines and use logical deduction, mathematical proof, statistical inference, historical anecedote, psychological theory, and a whole lot of common sense.

HISTORICAL BACKGROUND

There is plenty of room in macroeconomics for intelligent, informed, and well-intentioned economists to disagree. And macroeconomics has had some long and memorable disagreements. The classical economics of Adam Smith, David Ricardo, and Leon Walras reigned well into the twentieth century, with only occasional dissent by Thomas Malthus, Karl Marx, and a few other malcontents. The classical economists focused their attention on the efficient deployment of a nation's resources. They argued that market prices equating demands and supplies would, like "an invisible hand," guide each person, machine, and piece of land into its most productive use, providing the products that people want. Those best at farming would be lured by high wages onto farms. The best bakers would make bread and the best tailors, clothes. Whether they made white bread and polyester suits or whole wheat bread and blue jeans would depend on what their customers wanted. In the classical analysis, production, transactions, and prices are determined by demand and supply in the bloodless verdict of the marketplace. There is no need for government intervention or planning. Indeed, markets work best when governments don't meddle in them.

* Although free of these limitations the physical sciences are still subject to constant revision and debate. Recently, scientists heatedly argued about whether or not Vitamin C warded off colds. A while back, there was a frightful debate about whether the accumulation in the atmosphere of carbon dioxide from the burning of fossil fuels would raise the average temperature, melting the polar icecaps and flooding the world. If physical scientists cannot decide whether we will live serenely or die by drowning, is it so astonishing that economists cannot decide whether we should raise or lower taxes?

The classical economists paid little or no attention to the possibility that recessions would leave farmers, bakers, and tailors idle. This neglect of unemployed workers and idle factories became more and more embarassing as industrial economies were staggered by increasingly serious business slumps. In the 1930s, a brilliant Englishman, John Maynard Keynes, argued persuasively in *The General Theory of Employment, Interest, and Money,* which was really the beginning of macroeconomics, that the classical paradigm may be appropriate for some imaginary Robinson Crusoe society, but is a seriously flawed depiction of a modern industrial economy. Equally matched individuals do not gather in a serene environment to trade their perishable produce at whatever price equates demand and supply.* Instead, most prices are set by large institutions with considerable market power but very imperfect information. These prices are seldom at the razor's edge where demand equals supply. They adjust infrequently and imperfectly, amidst recurring changes in demand and supply. The classical economists focused on market equilibrium, arguing that surely, in the long run, prices will equate demand and supply. But Keynes argued that our attention should be on the turmoil of market disequilibria rather than some hypothetical far-distant eventual equilibrium. After all, as Keynes pointed out:

> In the long run we are all dead. Economists set themselves too easy, too useless a task if in tempestuous seasons they can only tell us that when the storm is long past the ocean is flat again.[2]

Keynes saw many economic booms and busts, and he was convinced that markets do not always work—that is, that the private economy does not always provide stable full employment. He advocated aggressive government policies to avoid the social losses and private tragedies of unemployed workers and idle factories. The economics profession accepted Keynes' logic and, by the end of World War II, most economists were Keynesians. The Keynesian revolution routed classical economics and became the conventional wisdom. Keynes argued for active government policies to ensure the full utilization of a nation's resources; Milton Friedman and a handful of other classically oriented economists became the dissenters.

After World War II, the western governments guided their nations through smooth, almost uninterrupted expansion. There were only mild recessions in the United States in the 1950s and none at all in the 1960s. The average standard of living in the United States nearly doubled over these twenty glorious years. And other western nations grew even faster. Governments had apparently learned Keynes' lessons on how to avoid the crippling recessions and depressions of the past. Some enthusiastic economists promised endless prosperity; active government macroeconomic policies had apparently made industrial economies "recession proof." Even Richard Nixon, who had scorned Keynesian economics early in his political career, declared, "We are all Keynesians now."

But the endless prosperity ended in the 1970s, and this brought with it a growing disaffection with Keynesians. There were four recessions between

* Actually, prices were not all that flexible in primitive societies, being usually fixed at some customary level—such as two fish for one coconut—for decades.

JOHN MAYNARD KEYNES

John Maynard Keynes was born in Cambridge, England, in 1883. His father was a lecturer in logic and political economy at Cambridge University, while his remarkable mother was to become mayor of the city. Keynes was an outstanding student, first at Eton College and then at Cambridge University. Although his primary studies were in mathematics and classics, he passed the Civil Service examinations in English composition, logic, psychology, political science, and economics. His lowest mark was in economics. ("The examiners presumably knew less than I did.")

While serving in the India Office of the Civil Service, he finished a dissertation on probability that won him a prize fellowship to King's College at Cambridge University. Alfred Marshall, perhaps the greatest classical economist of his time, was so eager to get Keynes back at Cambridge that he supplemented Keynes' fellowship out of his own pocket. Keynes lectured in economics at Cambridge and was widely regarded as Marshall's protégé and heir-apparent.

During World War I, while still in his early thirties, Keynes was a key official in the British Treasury, where he was in charge of all foreign lending and borrowing involved in financing the war effort. After the war he went to Versailles to help negotiate the armistice and then resigned in protest of the harsh reparations demanded of Germany. His polemic, *The Economic Consequences of the Peace,* predicted (correctly) that an overly punitive treaty would only encourage turmoil in Germany that could terminate in a second world war. This strongly worded mixture of impassioned rhetoric and detailed facts was a runaway best-seller and made Keynes a worldwide celebrity.

In the 1920s, his pamphlet, *The Economic Consequences of Mr. Churchill,* warned (correctly) that Winston Churchill's efforts to reestablish a gold standard, with the British pound set at its prewar value, would lead to a prolonged depression. As early as the 1929 election campaign he argued (correctly) that aggressive government spending programs were needed to ease the Depression. During World War II he again helped the British treasury's war financing. And, as the war ended, he helped design the system of fixed exchange rates that governed international trade until 1971.

Despite his government service, Keynes still found time for personal successes. He married a celebrated Russian ballerina and was a member of the Bloomsbury Circle, with E. M. Forster, Virginia Woolf, Lytton Strachey, and other British writers, artists and intellectuals. His speculations in stocks, bonds, and foreign exchange made him rich, bankrolled the ballet, and multiplied the endowment of King's College by a factor of ten. He even found time to be chairman of several insurance companies, and to run a profitable investment company.

On the academic front, Keynes was an influential teacher, author of several books, and editor, from1911 to 1945, of *The Economic Journal,* one of the most important publishers of scholarly papers.

In recognition of his public and personal successes, he was made a peer, Lord Keynes of Tilton. When asked what in his full life he would have done differently, he answered, "I'd have drunk more champagne."

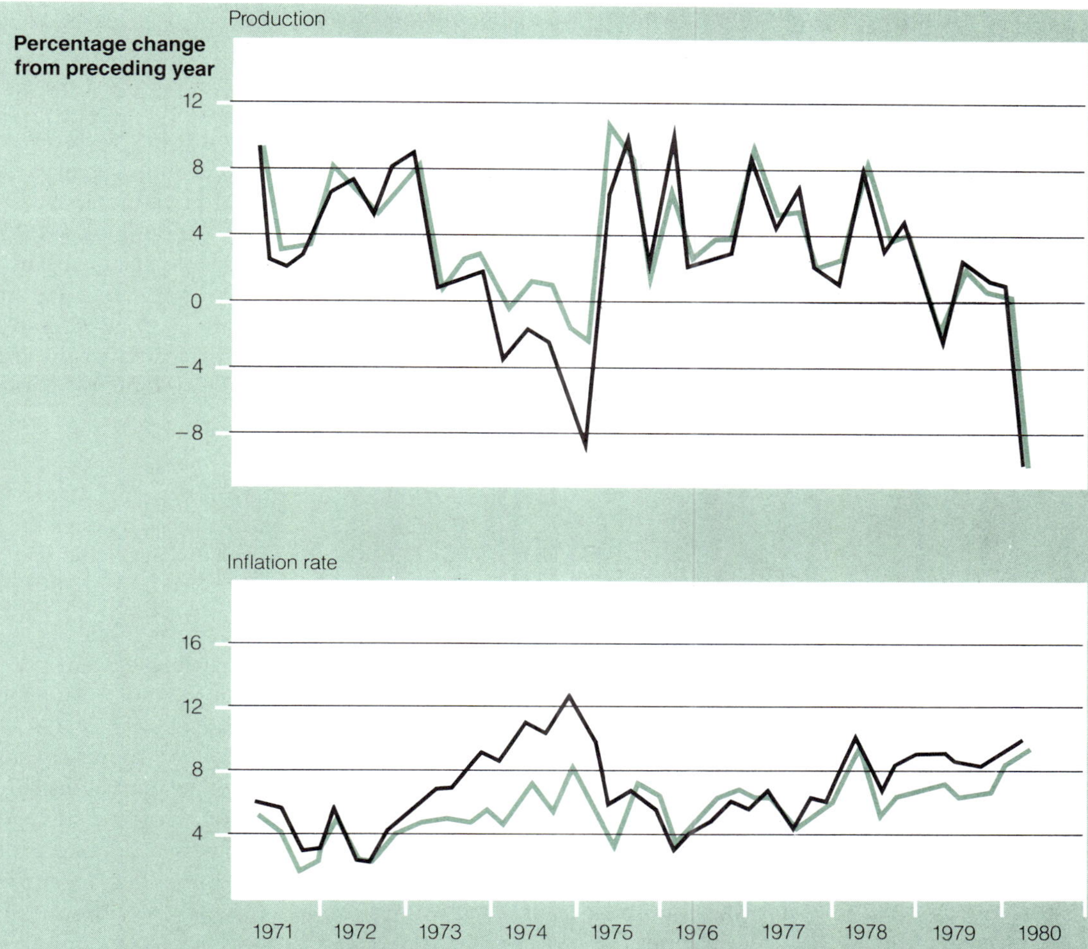

FIGURE 1.1 MACROECONOMICS FORECASTING. **The actual and predicted U.S. production and inflation rate for 1971–80 show exceptionally close correspondence. Sharp excursions and deviations in the 1973–74 period are attributable to the OPEC-precipitated energy crisis of that time. Predictions are the average forecasts of Chase Econometric Forecasting Associates, American Statistical Assn.—National Bureau of Economic Research Survey, and the Bureau of Economic Analysis of the U.S. Department of Commerce. (Source: The Chase *Economic Observer*, Jan/Feb 1981, p. 8.)**

1970 and 1981, with the economy in recession almost as often as it was out. And, yet, despite this recurrent economic weakness, there was also discomforting inflation throughout the 1970s (Figure 1.1)*. This new malaise, an un-

* Macroeconomics actually predicted very well the course of the economy in the 1970s. The figure shows the considerable fluctuations in output and inflation during the 1970s and, except for the extraordinary 1973–74 energy crisis, the impressive accuracy of macroeconomists' predictions. Errors in foreseeing the energy crisis are certainly understandable.

comfortable marriage of economic stagnation and inflation, was given the jarring label "stagflation."

The primary indictment of Keynesian economics was its seeming inability to deliver low unemployment without high inflation. It is not clear to what extent the fault lies with the economists and to what extent it lies with the economy. Some economists concluded that modern industrial economies may, indeed, be unable to sustain low unemployment without rapid price increases. Others argued that the economy would be fine, if only the economists would leave it alone. The academic pendulum swung back toward the classical faith in markets and distrust of government. Keynesian economists were now on the defensive, and today, many economists eschew Keynesian doctrine and embrace the "new classical economics." Ronald Reagan was elected to the presidency promising an economic program based on classical economic principles.

THE MACROECONOMIC CONSENSUS

The controversies described above, which make for lively theatre in academic journals, the popular press, and political contests, also make it easy to exaggerate the differences among economists. The dull truth is that macroeconomists do agree on the great majority of economic issues. Most public arguments are between straw economists—extreme caricatures battling extreme caricatures. The few macroeconomists who profess extreme views and are untroubled by uncertainties are usually engaging in brand-name advertising of the sort practiced by cereal companies. In bright graphics and catchy tunes, consumers are told that the product is new, improved, and altogether marvelous. But a peek inside reveals that it is pretty much the same old stuff. Unfortunately, outsiders sometimes get the impression that macroeconomics is a bit like professional wrestling, where the controversial, flamboyant personalities are more important than the sport itself. That impression is wrong; even without the outspoken celebrities, macroeconomics would still be of profound importance and interest.

The present macroeconomic consensus is not a pure strain running back to any single economist—not to Ricardo, Marshall, Keynes, or anyone else. The tests it has to satisfy are whether or not it is logical, consistent, and useful—not whether it is ideologically faithful to the views of some defunct economist. It is a broad mixture of the best ideas of the best economists. As such, this consensus is a healthy blend of classical and Keynesian economics. In effect, economists are now all Keynesians, but we are also all classical and whatever else has some useful ideas.

THE AGENDA

This book will present the big arguments of economics—and some of the little ones as well. The next chapter will show how output, unemployment,and inflation are actually measured. Part II will present a simple macroeconomic model that can be used to explain economic fluctuations and to predict the consequences of various economic events, including government spending, taxation, and monetary policies. Part III focuses on the dilemma posed by unemployment and inflation and on the government's policy options and will examine why competing policy recommendations are offered by different economists.

The macroeconomic model to be mastered in Part II, purposely simple so that it can be easily understood and manipulated, is too simple to show the fine details that are often of interest to economists, policy makers, and the public. Part IV, therefore, explains the kinds of elaborations and refinements that are put into the detailed empirical models actually used by government and private industry. Part V treats the microeconomic foundations of our subject, and Part VI extends the analysis in two directions: that of international transactions and of long-run growth.

REFERENCES

1. Robert Heilbroner, "Boom and Crash," *New Yorker,* August 28, 1978, p. 52.
2. John Maynard Keynes, *A Tract on Monetary Reform,* London, Macmillan, 1923.

CHAPTER TWO

MEASURING ECONOMIC ACTIVITY

True the statistics are not as good as we want them to be, but what would we do without them?

OSKAR MORGENSTERN[1]

This chapter will explain the measurement of output, employment, and unemployment; draw a crucial distinction between nominal and real magnitudes; and describe the characteristics of economic booms and recessions.

SOME economic analysis deals with abstract, theoretical issues that have no apparent real-world counterparts. Macroeconomics, down-to-earth and practical, discusses the very things that concern all households, businesses, and governments. Macroeconomics, as we have said, deals with booms and recessions, with inflation and unemployment. But how do we gauge booms and recessions? How do we measure inflation and unemployment? Headlines speak of "GNP up 2%" and "Double-digit inflation." What do these terms and figures mean? What does GNP actually measure? Who gets counted as unemployed? (Just those who have lost jobs, or also people who have quit one job and not found another? Are students and people who have never had a job included?) And how is inflation measured? (Some prices go up a lot, some a little, and some even go down. Which are used to measure inflation?)

All the data that are the answers to these questions help describe an economy, explain its past, and anticipate its future. Good data can be used to sort through competing theories and judge which are contradicted by the facts. The congressman who said, "My mind is made up; don't confuse me with the facts," stands in sharp contrast, to the macroeconomist, for whom the challenge is to explain the facts.

Unfortunately, many interesting economic activities go unmeasured and others are measured only approximately. Assembling good numbers is expensive, tedious, and not the least bit glamorous. As a result, not nearly enough resources and effort are expended on data collection, so that macroeconomic data are far from perfect. But this, too, is worth knowing.

There are two major macroeconomic data bases in the United States: the *national income and product accounts,* compiled by the Department of Commerce, and the *flow of funds accounts,* compiled by the Federal Reserve Board. The national income and product accounts were developed at the National Bureau of Economic Research (NBER), a private research organization, in the 1930s in order to measure the nation's total output each year. Flow-of-funds accounts were developed in the 1950s in order to supplement the production data (of the income and product accounts) with data for purely financial transactions (such as the buying and selling of corporate bonds). Because flow-of-funds data give a broad overview of the economy, we begin with them, then examine some of the basic details of measuring production.

FLOW-OF-FUNDS ACCOUNTING

One of the best ways of getting a macroeconomic picture of an economy is to examine a set of flow-of-funds accounts, because it summarizes a nation's economic transactions. Table 2.1 shows a highly condensed set of such accounts for the United States. Economic agents are listed across the top of this table, while the types of transactions are listed along the side, forming a matrix, each cell of which records transactions over some specified period—here the 1983 calendar year. A positive entry indicates that the sector was a net purchaser during the period; a negative, that it was a net seller. The labor row, for example, shows that, in 1983, households raised $1664.4 billion by selling their labor services—that is, by working for a living. Businesses paid $1600.9 billion for this labor and the federal government spent another $63.5 billion. The total amount businesses and government paid is, of course, equal to the amount that households received. The household column shows first, the $1664.4 billion raised from employment ("labor"). The next entry, "interest, dividends, and taxes," includes a variety of payments, the common feature of which is that they are not really purchases or sales. Instead, they represent fulfillment of various financial obligations. Households receive interest and dividends on their saving accounts, bonds, stocks, and so on. They *pay* interest on their mortgages and car loans. They also receive Social Security benefits and pay income taxes, sales taxes, and yet more taxes. On balance, they received $607.3 billion more in net interest, dividends, and other benefits than they paid in taxes in 1983.

Together, wages plus interest and dividends less taxes, provided households with $1664.4 + $607.3, or $2271.7 billion of disposable income. They spent $2158.6 billion of this income on goods and services—food, clothing, haircuts, video games. Households saved the remaining $113.1 billion—$103.8 billion in financial securities, such as savings accounts and Treasury bills, and $9.3 billion in cash.

The business column of the table makes it clear that businesses hire labor; pay interest, dividends, and taxes; and sell goods and services. The goods and services number is actually a net figure. Businesses sold $3246.0 billion, of which $875.7 billion was purchased by other businesses. The net figure ($3246.0 − $875.7 = $2370.3 billion) is the amount sold to households and government. On balance, businesses were creditors in 1983, acquiring $69.8 billion in cash and securities.

TABLE 2.1
United States flow-of-funds accounts for 1983 in billions of dollars.

	Households	Businesses	Government	Sum
Labor	−1664.4	1600.9	63.5	0
Interest, dividends, taxes	−607.3	699.6	−92.3	0
Goods and services	2158.6	−2370.3	211.7	0
Currency	9.3	2.0	−11.3	0
Securities	103.8	−67.8	−171.6	0
Sum	0	0	0	0

SOURCE: Federal Reserve Board *Flow of Funds Accounts*

The next column shows that the federal government was a debtor in 1983. Government spent $275.2 billion for labor and goods and services. Taxes, less Social Security and interest payments on the federal debt, raised only $92.3 billion, leaving a $171.6 billion deficit. This deficit was financed mostly by selling securities and, to a lesser extent, by printing money.

The numbers in Table 2.1 are *flow data,* measuring the volume of transactions over some period. *Stock data,* in contrast, measure the levels at a specific time. For example, the stock of treasury securities outstanding was $991.4 billion on December 31, 1982 and $1163.0 billion on December 31, 1983. The $171.6 billion flow shown in Table 2.1 accounts for the increase in the stock during 1983.

Flows can be measured in units other than the time period to which they apply. Weekly, monthly, and quarterly flow data are often reported at their annual rates. If, for instance, household spending on goods and services is $500 billion during the fourth quarter of the year, this will probably be reported as "an annual rate of $2000 billion during the fourth quarter." Similarly, prices might be described as having increased at an annual rate of 9.0% in October 1981, or increased by 8.6% per year during the 1970s.

Interrelatedness of decisions

One of the main lessons of macroeconomics is that economic decisions are interrelated. Output, employment, wages, prices, and interest rates are determined by the simultaneous interaction of economic agents choosing among alternatives. A flow-of-funds table like Table 2.1 demonstrates some of the fundamental budget and market interrelationships in an economy.

As looking down any column will show, agents face a variety of options, subject to the budget constraint that purchases and sales sum to zero. Budget constraints make economic decisions interdependent. If you buy more of something, then you must buy correspondingly less (or sell more) of something else. There is a trade-off, and any purchase or sale should take the alternatives into account. If you want to accumulate cash, for instance, then you must either work more, buy fewer commodities, or hold fewer securities. Thus the demand for money depends not only on how attractive money is, but also on the attractiveness of the alternatives.

As looking across any row in Table 2.1 shows, the market constraint in an economy operates among economic agents. One person's purchase is another person's sale, so that there are two sides to every exchange, and a transaction requires both a buyer and a seller. Households cannot buy commodities that are not for sale, nor can they sell their labor if employers will not hire them.

An example can clarify these interrelationships and some of the implications of budget and market constraints. Assume that the federal government decides to hire college students for summer jobs planting trees. The project would be subject to a labor market constraint: The government must find students willing to take the jobs. If all of the students who want to work in the summer already have jobs, then the government must lure them away from private jobs. Government employment is at the expense of private employment, so that the composition of national output changes: More trees get planted but there are fewer waiters, waitresses, and lifeguards. If, on the other hand, some students have been unable to find jobs, then government hiring increases total employment and production.

There is also a budget constraint, in that the government must find funds to pay the students. One possibility is to cut back spending elsewhere—on missiles, paper clips, cancer research—in which case the sellers of these goods and services must try to find other buyers. A second possibility is to raise taxes. Here the market constraint says that someone must pay these additional taxes, and the budget constraint says that whoever pays the taxes must cut back somewhere else. A third possibility is for the Treasury to sell government bonds to raise the money to pay the students. If more people buy government bonds, then less money is available for corporate bonds. And, if corporations cannot sell as many bonds, they will have to cut back somewhere.

Economic agents and markets, then, are all enormously intertwined, and, if one is to understand macroeconomic events fully, these interrelationships must be taken into account. This can be done by means of a surprisingly simple model (described in Chapters 3–5) that allows us to analyze all of these interactions simultaneously.

NATIONAL INCOME ACCOUNTING

The data base called the national income and product accounts focuses on the income and spending shown in the first three rows of Table 2.1. Income and spending are a direct reflection of the actual, physical economic activity that produces food, clothing, and shelter, as well as the luxuries of life. Saving and the acquisition of currency and securities are important, but they are more a means to an end, rather than the end itself.

The *gross national product (GNP),* records the market value of the aggregate production of new goods and services—houses, automobiles, haircuts, textbooks. GNP is a flow, measuring the amount produced during some specified period, and it includes goods and services purchased by households, businesses, and government. It can be subdivided into things quickly consumed—ice cream and strawberries—and things that last for decades—factories and apartment buildings and into tangibles—milk, and cookies—and intangibles, such as hairstyling and financial advice.

GNP statisticians have to avoid double-counting or triple-counting goods that pass from hand to hand. This is done by including only the *final* value of

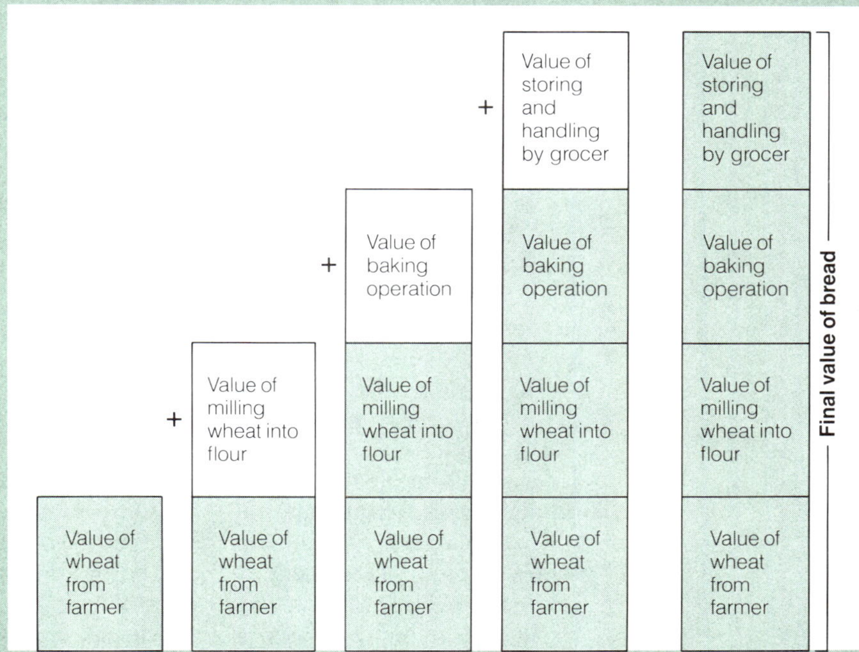

FIGURE 2.1 **AVOIDING DOUBLE COUNTING. For calculating GNP, only the final value of a product (the total of the value added at each stage of production) is counted. Thus, the final value of a loaf of bread is the value of the wheat from the farmer plus the value added by the miller, and so on.**

goods and services or, equivalently, only the value that is added at each stage of production. Thus if the farmer sells wheat to the miller, who sells flour to the baker, who sells fresh bread to the grocer, who sells week-old bread to you and me, it would be a double-counting mistake simply to add up all of the prices paid at each stage. Instead, GNP statistics include only the final store price of the bread, which, as shown in Figure 2.1, is equal to the value of the farmer's wheat (the price paid by the miller) plus the value added by the miller (the price of the flour minus the cost of the wheat) plus the value added by the baker (the price of fresh bread minus the cost of the flour) plus the value added by the grocer (the store price of bread minus the cost from the baker).

Nonmarket activity

The GNP figure is not, in fact, a comprehensive measure of production because data are scarce for economic activities that do not take place in open marketplaces. The GNP data do not, for example, include do-it-yourself and voluntary activities. If you repair your own car, or your neighbor helps you do so, this is not included in GNP; if you pay someone to allegedly fix your car, this does show up in GNP. The same is true of haircuts, lawn mowing, child care, Boy Scout activities, and political campaign work.

An important exception is the value of owner-occupied housing, which does show up in the GNP data, even though no market transactions take place. If you rent an apartment or house, your rental payments are included in the GNP statistics as a purchase of housing services. (You are buying shelter, which is produced by the house you rent.) If you live in your own condominium or house, then you are receiving housing services equal to what you would have paid had you rented, and an estimate of the rental value of your housing is included in the GNP statistics. In contrast, the imputed value of services received from other consumer durable goods (such as cars, washing machines, and televisions) are excluded from the GNP calculations. The data on these other consumer durables and their rental values are just too sketchy to be very useful.

The GNP statistics also exclude data on the value of prostitution, illegal drugs, and other covert activities. In addition, your plumber, barkeep, or waitress may hide some perfectly legal activities from tax authorities and GNP statisticians. This unreported "underground economy" makes GNP an incomplete tabulation of national output.

Government activities are included in GNP at cost. There is some value added by most government activities, but we don't know how much since governments do not (at least openly) sell their services. Congressional salaries, paper clip purchases, and national defense outlays are all included, dollar for dollar, in GNP.

While the GNP attempts to gauge economic activity by measuring the production of new goods and services, there is much more to life, to a nation's well-being, than those things counted by GNP statisticians. Their data entirely ignore the value of unpaid leisure activities such as reading books, going to the beach, hiking in the woods, or all-purpose daydreaming. If you give up 40 hours a week of book-reading, beach-going, hiking, and daydreaming in order to shuffle papers in some dull office, government statisticians will increase GNP by your annual income; you will notice your lost leisure time, but they won't.

Nor do GNP statistics take into consideration the costs of deterioration in the quality of life due to distasteful water, obnoxious fumes, disruptive noises, ugly environments, and unsettling fears of crime and war. Indeed, these unpleasantnesses actually increase GNP to the extent that we spend money to purify our water, cleanse the air, shield our ears, beautify our surroundings, and protect ourselves from domestic criminals and foreign aggressors.

Despite its limitations, GNP is widely used as a barometer of economic activity. Other barometers can be derived by making adjustments to GNP or by studying its components. One such adjustment is a "capital consumption allowance" for wear-and-tear depreciation—the amount of money that would have to be spent each year to maintain in its current state the capital equipment used to produce GNP. The deduction of these depreciation charges from GNP gives *net national product* (NNP).

A second adjustment is to subtract sales taxes, excise taxes, and other indirect taxes that show up in market prices and are consequently included in both GNP and NNP. The latter, minus these indirect taxes, gives *national income.*

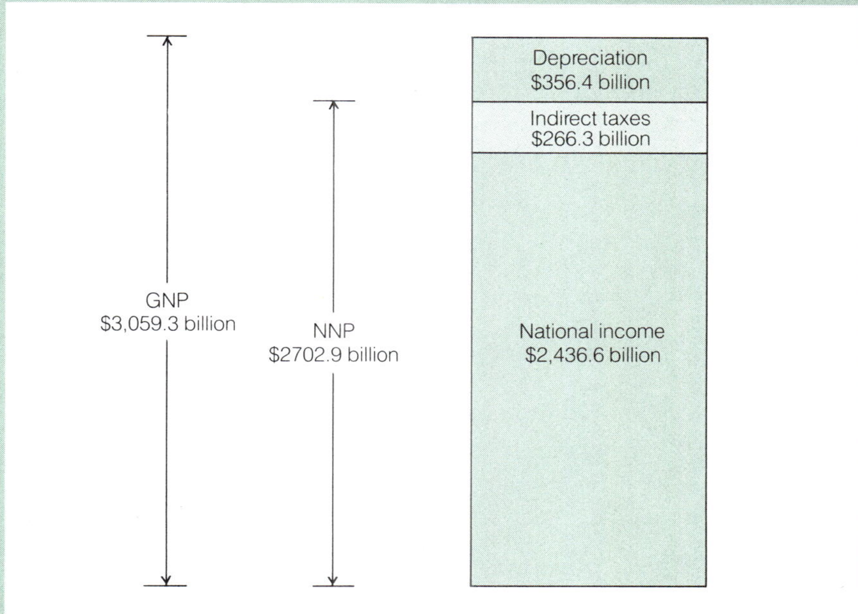

FIGURE 2.2 **THE RELATIONSHIP OF ELEMENTS COMPOSING THE GROSS NATIONAL PRODUCT (GNP). GNP is the final market value of a nation's output. The exclusion of the production needed to replenish the nation's capital stock gives NNP. The further deduction of taxes that are included in market prices gives national income. These particular figures are for 1982, but the relative magnitudes vary little from year to year.**

The relationship between GNP, NNP, and national income is shown in Figure 2.2. National income is a very useful measure of a nation's net output—that is, before sales taxes are added and after depreciation is allowed for.

National income can be viewed from the standpoint of the types of goods and services produced or from that of the types of agents paid for producing them. This dual perspective reflects the accounting identity that every person's expenditure is someone else's income.

Assume a sweater is purchased for $22, of which $1 is sales tax and $1 covers the depreciation of the store and the equipment used to make the sweater. That leaves $20 that is counted as national income, because it does indeed provide income to someone. Some of the $20 goes to the store's employees (as wage income) and some to its owners (as profit income on their investment in the store). If the store premises are rented, then some of the $20 may provide rental income to the building owners. Some of the $20 may go in interest income to those who have loaned the store money; some goes to the supplier of the sweater and for electricity and other utilities. These payments, too, become income to workers or others. Ultimately, every penny of the $20 expenditure

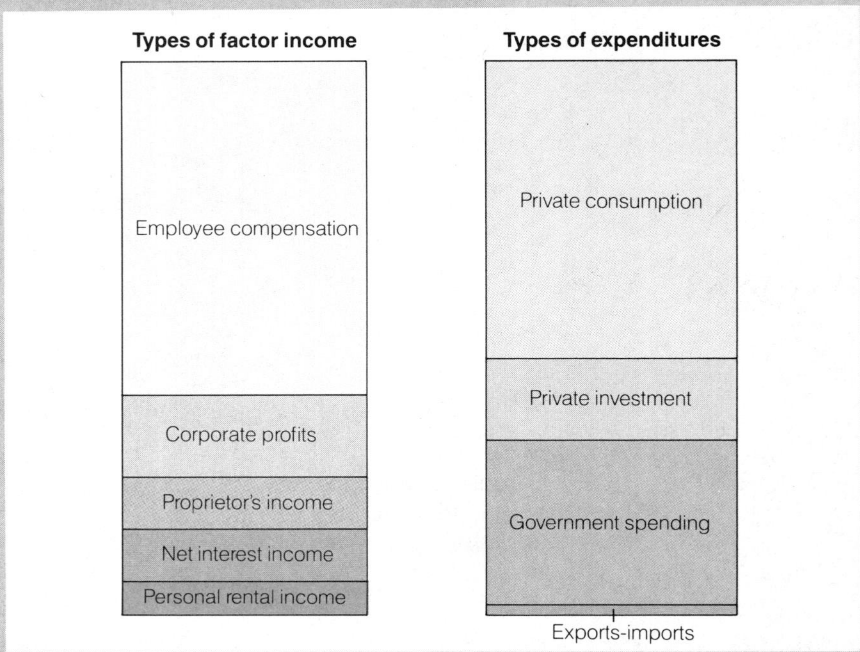

FIGURE 2.3 **TWO VIEWS OF TYPICAL NATIONAL INCOME DISTRIBUTION. Since every expenditure provides income to someone, national income can be divided into different types of income or into different types of expenditures.**

(and of everyone's expenditures) provides income to someone somewhere. This identity can be expressed as: national income *(Y)* equals expenditures *(E)*, or

$$Y = E. \tag{2.1}$$

Since this is the case, national income can be expressed as income *or* as expenditure, as is done in Figure 2.3. On the income side, the figure shows a division of national income into five categories, of which employee compensation (wages and salaries) accounts for about three-fourths. The remaining quarter is divided among corporate profits, proprietor's income (from unincorporated businesses), net interest income, and personal rental income (imputed housing rents, patents, royalties, and such). On the spending side, expenditures can be divided among private consumption *(C)*, private investment *(I)*, government expenditures *(G)*, and exports *(X)* less imports *(Z)*:

$$E = C + I + G + X - Z. \tag{2.2}$$

Although national income accounting is concerned with the nation's production, *C*, *I*, and *G* include expenditures on foreign as well as domestic goods.

Subtracting imports gives $C + I + G - Z$, which is domestic expenditures on domestic goods only. Including exports (foreign expenditures on domestic goods) gives the total expenditures on domestic goods. Figure 2.3 shows that total expenditures in 1982 consisted of roughly 70% private consumption, 20% government spending, and 10% private net investment (not including depreciation replacement and refurbishment). Exports minus imports were about 1% of expenditures, showing that, because the United States exported more than it imported, it produced about 1% more than it spent.

Consumption versus investment

Macroeconomists use the labels "consumption" and "investment" to distinguish between those goods that are used up or "consumed" shortly after they are acquired and those that have longer useful lives. Raspberries are clearly consumption, while a skyscraper is an investment. But there are many borderline cases. A pair of cheap sandals may be consumption, while a good pair of boots is an investment. What about tennis shoes?

Because it's hard to draw a dividing line and even harder to get good applicable data, all household expenditures—except for housing (including the flimsiest mobile homes)—are simply counted as consumption in the aggregate data. Automobiles, washing machines, televisions, and good boots are all considered consumption expenditures. There is, however, a consumption subcategory, "consumer durables," that does include cars, refrigerators, and other obviously durable goods.

Many find it useful to distinguish between the purchase of consumer durables and the actual consumption of the services provided by these durables. This is similar to the imputation, discussed above, of rental income to those who own their homes. When I buy a car, for example, I consume automobile services for as long as the car lasts. These services might be estimated from car rental rates or from the costs of operating the car (including the depreciation in its value). These imputed automobile services can then be put with raspberries and cheap sandals to calculate total household consumption. The GNP data do not make such imputations, so that economists who do have to make estimates and extrapolations from other data.

Business fixed investment and inventories

Business investment can be separated into fixed investment and inventory investment. Fixed investment includes buildings and equipment that are used to produce more goods and services. Inventory investment includes raw materials, goods that are still being processed, and finished goods that have not yet been sold. Much of a firm's inventory accumulation is intentional. It is helpful and prudent to have production materials on hand and to keep a stock of finished goods to meet customer demands. But some inventory accumulation is unplanned and unwanted. When customers stop appearing, unsold goods accumulate. The national income accounts, however, make no distinction between planned and unplanned changes in inventories. Goods unexpectedly unsold are treated as inventory investment, the same as intentionally stockpiled goods. (The accounts are balanced by assuming that the firms have sold these goods to themselves.) The reasoning behind this is that GNP data are an attempt to measure production rather than actual sales. Thus, if sales and income data are to equal output, sales and income figures must be adjusted. For example, if a craftsman produces a chair priced at $200 (including taxes), this production automatically adds $200 to GNP. If the chair is sold right away, then aggregate sales increase by $200, too. And, since sales provide income, national income goes up by $200 (less depreciation and taxes). If the chair is *not* sold, GNP still rises by $200, and the national income accountants pretend that the craftsman bought the chair from himself in order to add to his inventory of finished chairs. Firms with unwanted inventory may reduce production to slow the accumulation or they may try to sell some of their surplus by cutting prices.

In practice, inventory investment data are used by many economists as a barometer of business conditions. An upward jump in inventories often indicates that sales are weak and that production may soon be slowed. A sharp drop in inventories often signals strong sales that may stimulate increased production.

Government spending

The federal government's budget in 1982 was as follows:

Disbursements	**Billions of dollars**
Purchases of goods and services	257.9
Transfer payments to persons	322.2
Grants-in-aid to state and local governments	83.7
Interest on the federal debt	85.0
Subsidies of government enterprises	14.6
	763.4

Receipts	
Personal income taxes	292.4
Social insurance contributions	216.6
Excise and other taxes	57.7
Corporate profit taxes	47.2
	613.9

Thus, in 1982, the budget deficit was 763.4 – 613.9, or $149.5 billion. The government's budget includes purchases of goods and services and also disbursements for such things as Social Security benefits, unemployment compensation, and welfare payments. These latter disbursements are *transfer payments,* in that they are outlays by the government for which the recipients do not have to produce any goods or provide any services. Government taxes are also transfer payments, this time from the citizens to the government. When you pay income taxes to the government, you do not personally receive any goods or services by return mail.

The government expenditure factor (G in Equation 2.2) includes only expenditures on paper clips, Congressional salaries, bombs, and other useful goods and services. (In 1982, 70% was for national defense.) Transfer payments are not included in *G*. If households use their Social Security, unemployment, or welfare payments to purchase food and clothing, then these expenditures will be included in consumption *(C)*.

The government expenditure category includes both government consumption and investment spending. Often, the popular press treats all government purchases as consumption by assuming that only businesses make investments. This is incorrect and misleading. Government expenditures on highways, airports, land reclamation, libraries, education, and research all increase the nation's capacity to produce goods and services. All of these projects should be included in an accounting of a nation's investment and in its stock of productive capital. But the national income accounts do not do this and, so, we make do without it.

NOMINAL AND REAL MAGNITUDES

Much of our economic data record the dollar volume of transactions. Economic numbers that are recorded in dollars are called *nominal data.* If you are paid $5 an hour, that is your nominal wage rate. If you earn $10,000 a year, that is your nominal income. Your nominal net wealth is the market value, in dollars, of the difference between your total assets and liabilities.

People, however, do not work and save solely for the simple pleasures of counting and recounting dollars. Instead, they work and accumulate dollars in order to purchase and enjoy goods and services. Thus, people are keenly aware of how much their dollars will buy. Economic numbers measured in terms of this purchasing power are called *real data.*

For instance, if you are interested in purchasing only loaves of bread, your real income would be determined by dividing your nominal income by the price of bread:

$$\underset{\text{(loaves/year)}}{\text{real income}} = \underset{\text{(\$/year)}}{\text{nominal income}} / \underset{\text{(\$/loaf)}}{\text{price of bread.}}$$

Thus, if you earn $10,000 a year and bread costs $2 a loaf, your real income is 5000 loaves a year. Similarly, $5 an hour is a real wage rate of 2.5 loaves an hour.

The underlying economic principle behind the calculation of real data is that it is real, rather than nominal, magnitudes that affect people's behavior. If choosing between working and playing this summer, you will think about more than the nominal wage rate: Whether $5 an hour is attractive or unattractive depends on what a dollar will buy. Fifty years ago, when a dollar would buy a lot, most people would have jumped at any chance to earn $5 an hour. Now, when a dollar buys little, many people would rather lie on the beach than work for $5 an hour.

Those who think about nominal income and wealth rather than what the dollars will buy suffer from what economists call *money illusion.* Someone who feels financially better off with a rise in nominal income of 3% while prices rise by 8%, is showing definite signs of money illusion.

Price indexes

The same distinction must be made in measuring a nation's real income and expenditures. It is important to know whether a rise of 5% in nominal GNP is an increase in real GNP or just an increase in prices. Similarly it is important to keep track of real consumption, real investment, and real government spending.

The numerical examples above used a single price, the price of bread. However, man lives not by bread alone, but also by wine, meat, clothing, shelter, medical care, haircuts, football tickets, chewing gum, and so on. The purchasing power of our dollars depends on the prices of a vast array of goods and services. Individuals with differing tastes will attach varying importance to different prices. The well-dressed will keep a close eye on clothing prices, while the sickly will monitor medical costs. Those who don't smoke will not watch cigarette prices, while those who dislike football games will ignore the price of football tickets. Purchasing-power calculations will, like tastes, vary from person to person.

To get a representative picture of real income and expenditures, government statisticians monitor the prices of goods and services purchased by "typical" people. These price data are combined into several price indexes, which measure the cost of representative bundles of goods and services.

A price index, *P*, shows the cost of a bundle of goods and services in one year relative to the cost in a given base year:

$$P = \frac{\text{cost of bundle this year}}{\text{cost of bundle in base year.}}$$

Table 2.2 gives a simple three-item example of index arithmetic. Here, the representative bundle contains 10 loaves of bread, 6 pounds of meat, and 2 gallons of milk. The price of bread doubled between 1967 and 1975, the price of meat rose 50% and the price of milk rose 33%. The cost of the bundle of commodities shown in the table was $15 in 1967 and $25 in 1975. Using 1967 as the base year, the price index in 1975 is

$$P = \frac{\text{cost in 1975}}{\text{cost in 1967}} = \frac{\$25}{\$15} = 1.67.$$

This calculation shows that the cost of this bundle of goods rose by 67% between 1967 and 1975.

Price indexes are often scaled by multiplying by an appropriate number so that the index equals 100 in a selected period. Because some sources might scale an index to equal 100 in 1967, while another scales the same index to equal 100 in 1975, it is important to keep this in mind when gathering data. Apart from

TABLE 2.2
Price index calculation for three items

		1967		1975	
	Quantity	Price of one	Cost of bundle	Price of one	Cost of bundle
Loaf of bread	10	$0.60	$ 6.00	$1.20	$12.00
Pound of Meat	6	$1.00	$ 6.00	$1.50	$ 9.00
Gallon of milk	2	$1.50	$ 3.00	$2.00	$ 4.00
TOTAL			$15.00		$25.00

this, the scale of a price index is unimportant; what *is* important is the percentage change in the index—here 67%.

Once we have a price index we can convert nominal data into real data by dividing by P. If nominal income is Y, then real income, y, is Y/P. (Upper-case letters will be used for nominal data, lower case for real data.) Since price indexes are used to measure changes in the cost of a bundle of goods and services, the corresponding real data show the changes in the number of these bundles that can be purchased. For instance, the purchasing power of a family that earned \$15,000 in 1967 and \$30,000 in 1975 (assuming the bundle cost \$15 in 1967 and \$25 in 1975) can be calculated in terms of the number of bundles purchasable:

	Nominal income	Cost of bundle	Number of bundles
1967	\$15,000	\$15	1000
1975	\$30,000	\$25	1200

This family's real income went up by 20%—that is, they could purchase 20% more in 1975 than in 1967.

In practice, we divide by the price index rather than the cost of a bundle:

	Nominal income	Price index	Real income
1967	\$15,000	100	150 (15,000/100)
1975	\$30,000	167	180 (30,000/167)

Again, as with the scale of a price index, the scale of real income data is arbitrary; the real income numbers 150 and 180 do not measure 150 loaves of bread, 150 bundles of commodities, or anything else that is tangible. What matters is changes, over time, in the real income data: In this case the increase from 150 to 180, or 20%, between 1967 and 1975.

Alternate indexes

Because a price index allows us to compare the cost of a certain bundle of commodities to their cost in some base year, an important choice is the components of the commodity bundle used. Government agencies actually calculate many different price indexes, using various bundles of goods and services. The most familiar is the *consumer price index (CPI),* which is calculated and reported monthly by the Department of Labor's Bureau of Labor Statistics.* Each month, some 250 agents call or visit almost 20,000 stores in more than 50 cities to collect price data on a "market basket" of about 400 goods and services purchased by typical urban households. The CPI market basket is based on a detailed survey made in 1972–1973, and includes not only newly produced goods and services, but all sorts of things that consumers spend money on—including used cars, insurance, and sales taxes.

Another major index compiled by the Bureau of Labor Statistics is the *producer price index (PPI).* This index surveys the prices paid by businesses for some 2700 commodities, ranging from raw materials to partially processed

* Actually, the Bureau has a whole family of consumer price indexes. The most widely reported is the CPI (often called the "urban consumer index"), discussed in the text.

IN THE NEWS

Index Decline Could Mean Good News for Consumers

Good news!

The Producer Price Index actually declined in January to 283.6 from 285.1 in December, a drop of 0.53 percent or an annual rate of 6.36 percent before compounding. The index measures the level of prices on merchandise sold to processors for further production. It represents the level of costs to manufacturers and wholesalers of the tangible goods they buy and use to produce the things we buy. . . .

The Consumer Price Index is the measure to watch to see what is happening to consumer prices. This index, which measures the level of prices on goods and services purchased by consumers, stood at 292.4 in December—0.4 percent below the November level (a 4.8 percent annual decline before compounding.)

The indices tell us how much it now costs to purchase the same amount of the goods and services which cost $100 in the base year—1967 for both indices. Thus, it now costs producers $283.60 to buy the same material that cost $100 in 1967, a 183.6 percent increase.

Will the decline in producer prices result in a consumer price decline? To answer this, we must consider two further questions: why is the producer index declining, and is there a relationship between the two indices? A final question to ponder is whether we will all be made better off by the Producer Price Index decline.

What has caused the index to decline? A number of things.

Lower crude oil prices explain part of the decline. Lower prices on other import goods also pay a part. Import prices have fallen partly because of the general malaise in the world economy.

Crude oil prices are falling because the economies of the world are very weak, lessening oil demand. Also, a fairly mild winter in some parts of this country has reduced heating fuel demand. And the tendency of U.S. consumers to buy smaller, fuel efficient cars seems to have eroded demand for gasoline.

One outcome of the world economic malaise has been an increase in the value of the dollar relative to other currencies. The stronger dollar means lower prices on a wide range of import products. A ton of iron ore that costs 150 Bolivares will cost 10 percent less if the dollar is 10 percent stronger. This affects the Producer Price Index since a large portion of our imports are raw materials for domestic production.

Is there a relationship between the producer and consumer indices? Reductions in the producer index will only affect the costs of producing tangible goods. We do not expect any change in the cost of haircuts, greens fees or dry cleaning. The impact on the cost of food products is not clear. Food prices may ease slightly, but this is not certain because farmers spend a great deal on fuel for machinery and transporting goods to market.

A second consideration is the costs of medical care. Rising medical costs have contributed significantly to Consumer Price Index increases. It is doubtful that declining producer prices will mean much to medical costs.

How the producer price change will be reflected in the price of goods will depend on some other market factors. In many cases, it is likely that the lower cost will be absorbed in higher profits, in which case the average consumer will never see the benefit. Thus, we cannot say for sure that declining producer prices will be reflected in declining consumer prices.

Will we all be made better off by this decline in the Producer Price Index? Buyers of goods certainly will, but not sellers. Owners of that somewhat vital resource, oil, are certainly not going to be better off because their income is declining. (Remember: what is a cost to one person is income to another.) The decline could certainly have adverse affects for an area that depends heavily on oil income for its economic growth and development.

One final point: How you recognize the effects in your own budget depends on how you spend your money. If you buy a lot of manufactured goods and few services, the decline might well be very obvious. However, if your budget is heavy on the services side, you may not notice the impact at all. (Richard Waits and Edward M. McNertney, *Fort Worth Star-Telegram,* Feb. 22, 1983) commodities to finished goods ready for retailers. The broadest price index is the Commerce Department's *quarterly GNP implicit price deflator,* covering the prices of all currently produced goods and services that are included in the GNP accounts.

Index flaws

Current or base-year? Price indexes are very useful, but have two inherent difficulties. The first is rooted in the fact that purchases respond to price changes. For example, gasoline consumption fell when its price soared in the 1970s. Should the price index's "typical market basket" reflect the quantities purchased before or after the price change? If before, then the price index will overstate the cost of living, because it ignores the fact that people will substitute less expensive items for more expensive ones or use less of an item when it becomes more costly. If after, then the price index will understate the cost of living, ignoring the ill effects of higher prices on lifestyle.

There is no good answer to this before-or-after question. Some indexes, called Laspeyres indexes, use the quantities purchased in the base period. Others, called Paasche indexes, vary the bundle of goods and services year to year according to spending habits.* Both the CPI and PPI are Laspeyres indexes, while the GNP deflator is a Paasche index.

Which of the two bases is used—base-period or current-year purchases—can make a big difference in the behavior of price indexes, particularly when prices have changed greatly and the base-period survey of spending habits was made several years before. Many economists believe that the fact that the CPI is a Laspeyres index diminished its usefulness in the 1970s. The major CPI surveys were made in 1934–39, 1952, 1961, and 1972–74. The 1961 survey of consumer buying habits was used to compute the CPI until the end of 1977. In 1978 survey data from that year began to be used. Some critics of the CPI argue that consumer buying patterns changed significantly between the early 1960s and late 1970s. The CPI was also criticized for its inclusion of mortgage rates and the prices of homes. For people who already have their homes, such an increase is a benefit rather than a cost. Similarly, an increase in mortgage rates does not raise the expenses of people with old, fixed-rate mortgages. In addition, the CPI neglected the tax deductibility of interest payments and the fact that interest rates are a source of income as well as expense. In 1983, the Bureau of Labor Statistics responded to these criticisms by switching to rental costs as a measure of housing expenses.

An interesting comparison can be made between the CPI and the Commerce Department's deflator for personal consumption (one of various components of GNP). This consumption deflator differs from the CPI in that it (like the GNP deflator) is a Paasche index (that is, weighted to reflect changes in spending habits). It covers rural as well as urban households and it has always used rents

* Since the Paasche weights vary year to year, changes in the index reflect quantity as well as price changes. Thus a Paasche index can rise or fall even when all prices are constant! An intermediate approach is a "chain index," in which each period's computations use the market basket from the immediately preceding period. In an annual chain index, for example, a calculation of the average change in prices in 1980 would be based on 1979 spending habits, while the 1981 calculation would use 1980 spending habits. The Commerce Department computes Paasche, Laspeyres, and chain GNP price indexes.

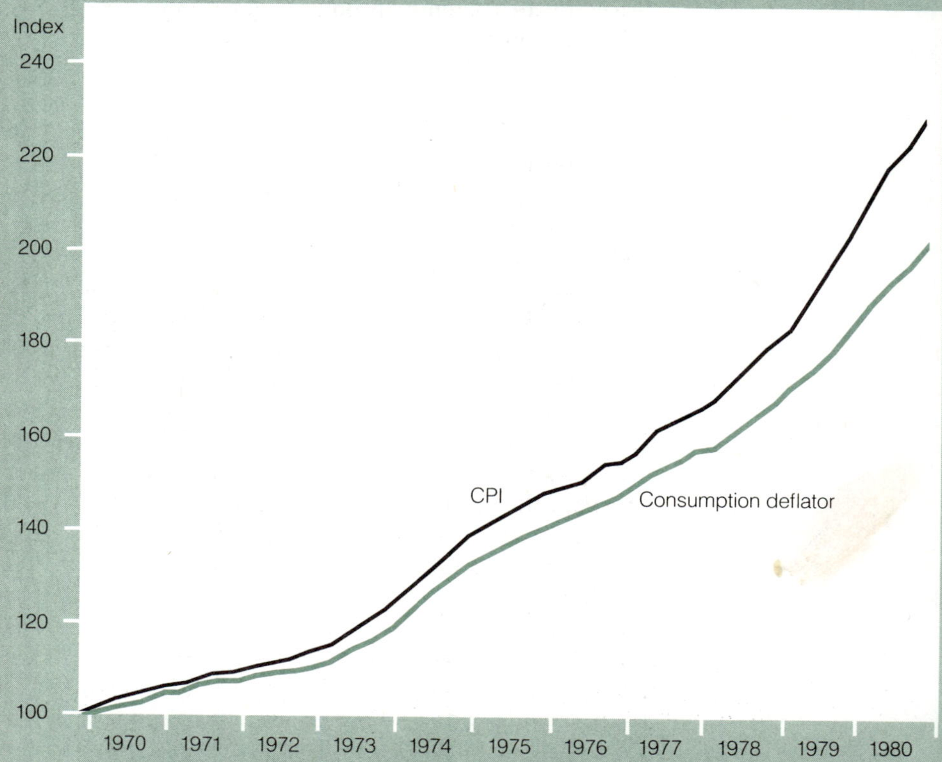

FIGURE 2.4 CONSUMPTION DEFLATOR AND CPI, 1970–83. **Both indexes equaled 100 in the fourth quarter of 1969. The CPI increased faster than the consumption deflator during the 1970s because the CPI included housing prices and mortgage rates.**

to estimate housing costs. Figure 2.4 shows the consumption deflator and the CPI for the years 1970 to 1980. Both indexes are scaled to equal 100.0 in the fourth quarter of 1969. As can be seen from the figure, the CPI increased by about 130% over the period indexed, while the consumption deflator went up by 100%. The average annual percentage increases over the 11 years were 7.8% for the CPI and 6.7% for the consumption deflator. There was inflation, no matter how you look at it, but how you look at it does affect estimates of the inflation's severity.

Quality adjustments The second inherent difficulty with price indexes is that the quality of many items varies as time passes. However, when the price goes up 10%, and it says "new, improved" on the box, should we believe it? If the quality has in fact improved 10%, then there has really been no inflation; it is as if one has bought a 10% larger size, and simply paid more to get more. But how do you measure quality? Volkswagen Rabbits are very different from Beetles—they are roomier, more fuel-efficient, and have many additional features, but what percentage change in their quality do these features represent? Many consumer goods, such as personal computers, didn't even exist ten years ago, or, in another example, medical doctors use medicines and equipment that didn't exist 20 years ago. They are also much more expensive and don't make house calls. What, then, is the percentage change in the quality of doctor services?

The other side of this coin is "candy bar inflation." For years, candy bar prices were constant, while the bars gradually became smaller and smaller. Makers of the penny gum ball have been especially inventive in holding down prices as costs have risen. The size of the gumball has shrunk, while the inside has been progressively hollowed out. These thin shells now weigh as little as a third of what they weighed 35 years ago. In addition, inexpensive synthetic materials have been substituted for chicle and natural flavorings, while corn syrup has replaced some of the sugar. Statisticians devising price indexes try to deal with such cases, but making quality adjustments is difficult and subjective. In the 1960s many economists argued that quality improvements were underestimated to the extent that the reported annual increase in the CPI was 1 to 2% too high.

In the 1970s, another quality issue emerged when state and federal governments began to legislate environmental protection measures. The costs of complying with the new regulations showed up in higher prices for automobiles, electricity, and other products. But the benefits were not counted in any market basket. We paid more, but the price indexes did not show that we were also getting more—better air, water, and so on.

It is difficult to say how price indexes can be adjusted to reflect these sorts of changes in the quality of living and working environments. Most environmental phenomena are public goods—air that is clean for me is clean for you—which cannot be bought and sold to individuals in supermarkets. There are some benefits (such as reduced medical expenses and longer life expectancies) that might be given a rough monetary value; but these benefits typically will not become evident for many years. All we can really say is that failure to include some quantification of environmental quality changes caused price indexes to understate inflation in the 1960s and to overstate inflation in the 1970s. Since price indexes are used to compute real magnitudes, an overestimate of inflation implies an underestimate of real wages, real income, and so on. Thus the understatement of inflation in the 1960s means that our prosperity was exaggerated somewhat. Correspondingly, the overstatement of inflation in the 1970s means that the economy was a bit healthier than reported.

OUTPUT

The amount of goods and services produced in an economy—what national income accounts tell us—depends on the amount of resources utilized and the productivity of these resources. An efficient blend of fertile land, useful equipment, and skillful people can produce an amazing quantity of goods and services. A nation's output can also be disappointingly low when resources are lacking, misused, or left unused. It is particularly distressing when available resources are squandered, with potentially productive factories and people left idle. Data on business capacity utilization and labor unemployment can be used to gauge this unfortunate waste.

Utilization of capacity

Apart from the obvious effect of economic booms and of economic recessions on utilization of productive capacity, businesses routinely build slack into their operations. Frenetic all-out production reduces the efficiency of machines and of the people who operate them. In addition, firms like to leave a little room to expand production so that surges in customer demand can be accommodated quickly. (It can take years to construct new plant and equipment, and impatient customers can be snared by competing businesses.)

Thus, most plant and equipment ("capital") are normally operated at only 85 to 90% of capacity. Some equipment may be used at less than maximum speed. Some may be used only part of each day, rather than in continuous 24-hour operation. Some equipment, buildings, and land may sit idle for days or months while being refurbished and replenished.

In economic booms, as the demand for output increases, more capital is used, and used harder. A nation's capital may be used at 90, 95, or close to 100% of capacity. For brief periods, capital could even be said to be used at greater than 100% capacity—beyond limits that could be sustained permanently.

In economic recessions, capital is left idle and output declines. Shifts are discontinued and plants are closed. Part of the nation's capital is left idle or refurbished in anticipation of the next boom. In such times capital utilization may be at a rate of only 85, 80, or even 75%.

The Federal Reserve Board, in its *capacity utilization* data, attempts to measure how fully capital is being utilized. These data are graphed in Figure 2.5, which also shows the recessionary periods as identified by the NBER, unofficial arbiter of booms and recessions. Recessions are periods of economic slack and declining GNP (traditionally, for at least two consecutive quarters). Booms are periods of rapid growth in real GNP. The NBER uses a variety of criteria to label the beginning and end of a recession. Not surprisingly, the figure shows that capacity utilization drops during recessions and rises during booms. In economic recessions, some capital is left partly or totally idle. In booms, capital is put back into production and pushed hard to produce more output.

Utilization of labor

The utilization of labor as well as capital varies over the business cycle. In booms, more people have jobs and work longer and harder hours. In recessions, people become unemployed, and even those who keep their jobs can work fewer hours and have less to do.

Measures of employment One proxy measure of labor utilization is the *employment ratio,* which is the proportion of the noninstitutionalized working-age (16 years or older) population that is actually employed to that not employed. This is a simple body count—number of persons employed divided

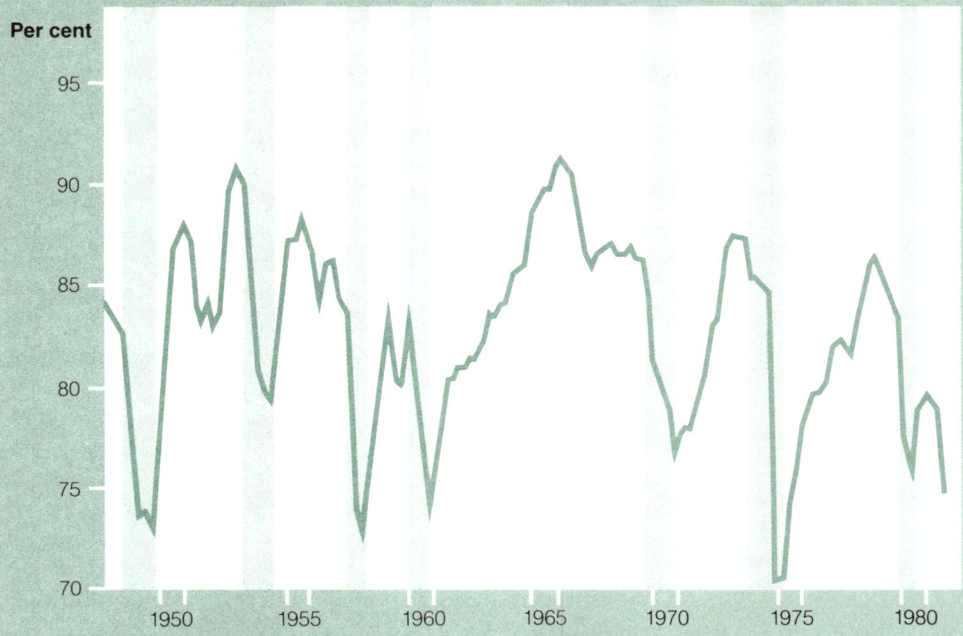

FIGURE 2.5 FEDERAL RESERVE BOARD CAPACITY UTILIZATION DATA. **Shaded areas indicate periods of economic recession. Capacity utilization drops during recessions and rises during economic booms.**

by number of persons of working age. It does not take into account variations in the number of hours people work or how hard they work. Like capital, a person may typically work at only 87.5% of capacity.

The *unemployment rate* is a more widely known barometer of the extent to which labor resources are being underutilized. These data attempt to separate nonworkers into those who do and do not want jobs. To make this separation, the Census Bureau conducts a monthly survey of about 55,000 households to estimate what part of the working-age population is neither working nor looking for work. These nonworkers who are not looking for jobs include homemakers, students, the retired, and people who simply will not work. Subtracting these from the working-age population leaves the available civilian *labor force*—people who are ready, able, and willing to work. The labor force "participation rate" is the ratio of the labor force to the working-age population.

People who have paid jobs of any sort (full time or part time, glamorous or menial) are counted as employed.* The remaining people in the labor force

* These include people with jobs who are not actually at work because of vacation, illness, natural disasters, bad weather, or labor disputes. Similarly, the unemployed include those who are temporarily ill, but would otherwise have been looking for work. For more details on employment and unemployment data, see Reference 2.

who do not have jobs are labeled unemployed. The dividing line between the unemployed who are included in the labor force and the homemakers, students, and bums, who are excluded, is that the former told the census interviewer that they are waiting for recall from a temporary layoff or that they actively looked for a job during the preceding four weeks. The Bureau of Labor Statistics uses these data to estimate an overall *unemployment rate*, which is the ratio of the number of unemployed to the civilian labor force. The Bureau also compiles a large number of detailed unemployment rates for specific segments of the population. The overall unemployment rate differs from the employment ratio in that it considers only the presently available labor force, rather than the total working-age population. It seems reasonable to use a measure of labor capacity utilization that excludes those who are unable or unwilling to work.

In practice the monthly Census Bureau surveys may give a misleading count of the number of people available for work. The survey questions on active seeking of work are particularly vague and subjective. Embarrassment (or fear of losing unemployment insurance) undoubtedly prompts some who are not really interested in work to pretend that they are. And some people have frankly unrealistic job hopes, half-heartedly looking for pleasant jobs with short hours and high pay. (Should I be counted as unemployed if I am sitting by my pool, drinking beer, and waiting for the Yankees to call?) In addition, a significant number of the unemployed are students, homemakers, and retirees looking for part-time jobs. Should they be counted in the same way as a family's primary breadwinner, who is desperately looking for a full-time job? Finally, some unemployed are temporarily so—while they gather and evaluate job offers and information about prospective employers in order to make the best choice.

On the other hand, some wasteful unemployment does not appear in the unemployment statistics. People wanting full-time jobs but forced to settle for temporary part-time employment are counted as fully employed. So are people who have jobs for which they are overqualified. Both a history Ph.D. waiting on tables and an auto worker pumping gas are counted as fully employed. And people who have become so discouraged that they have quit looking for work are not counted as unemployed; instead, they are no longer included in the labor force. In December 1982, with the unemployment rate at 10.8%, the Bureau of Labor Statistics estimated the number of such discouraged workers to be almost two million. Had they been counted as unemployed, the unemployment rate would have been almost two percentage points higher.

Movements in and out of the labor force may cause misleading short-term changes in unemployment data. During recessions, the reported unemployment rate sometimes drops for a month or two, not because more people find jobs, but because more people stop looking for jobs. In such cases, both the employment ratio and the unemployment rate decline! Similarly, the unemployment rate occasionally increases in the midst of an economic boom when many people enter the labor force looking for the jobs that they have heard are plentiful. When this happens, both the employment ratio and the unemployment rate increase.

There are also longer-term changes in labor force participation that cause the employment ratio and unemployment rate to give different signals of labor utilization. Figure 2.6 shows some historical data on labor force participation,

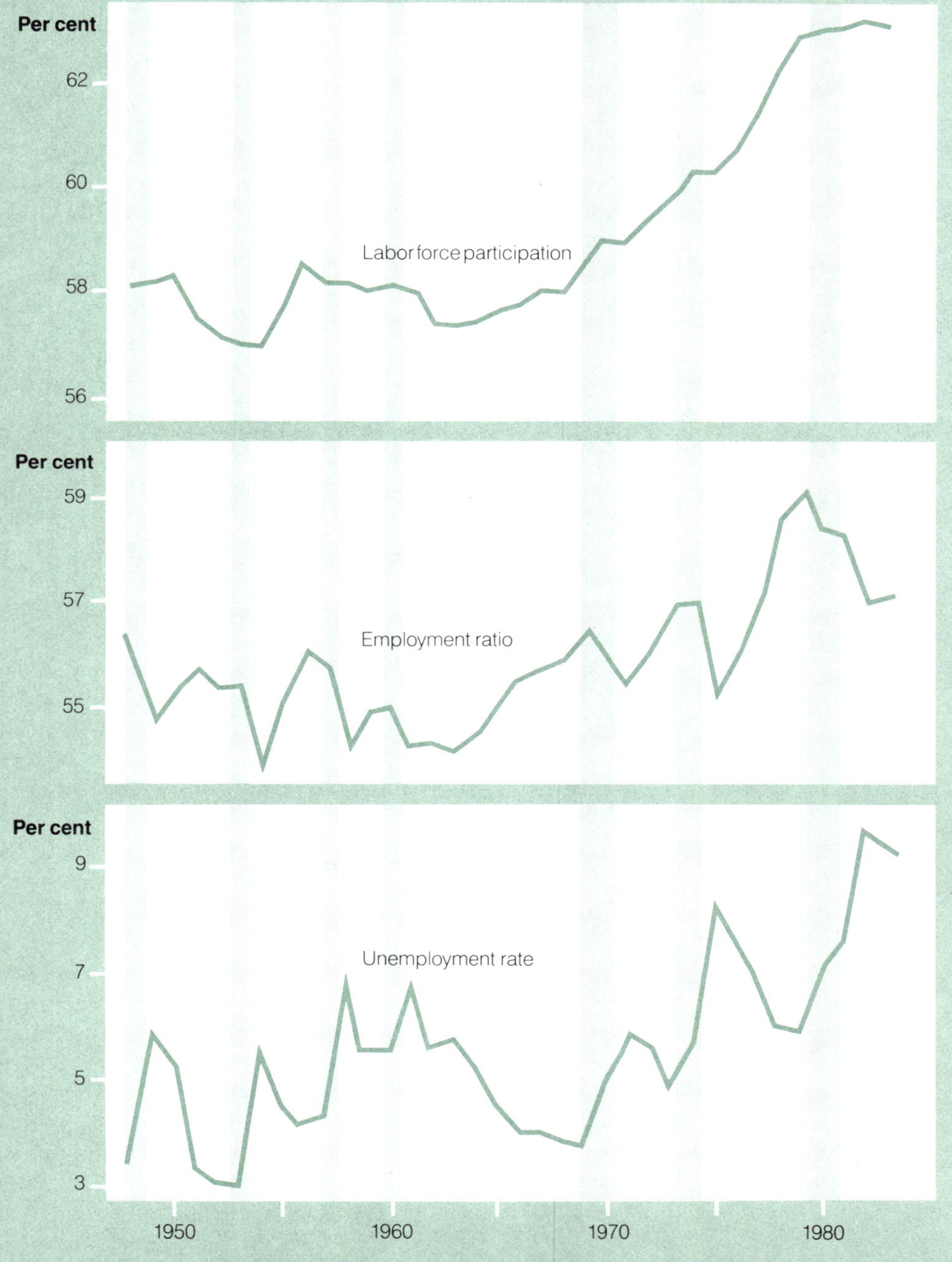

FIGURE 2.6 LABOR FORCE PARTICIPATION, EMPLOYMENT, AND UNEMPLOYMENT, 1948–83. **During a recession, the unemployment rate rises while the employment ratio and the participation rate usually fall. But the dramatic upward surge in labor force participation during the 1960s and 1970s pulled the employment ratio up, even while the unemployment rate was very high. Shaded areas represent periods of economic recession.**

the employment ratio, and the unemployment rate. It is clear from the data that labor force participation tends to sag in recessions and perk up in booms.

The figure also reveals a dramatic longer-run increase in labor force participation. Those born in the post-World War II baby boom reached working age in the late 1960s and the 1970s. The high participation rates for this age-bulge pushed up the overall labor force participation rate. The second, and more important, factor has been the large increase in females working outside of the home. Women are marrying later, getting divorced more often, having fewer children, and choosing, more frequently than in earlier years, to work outside the home when married.

This growth in the labor force relative to the population increases the employment ratio associated with a given unemployment rate, as can be seen from the following identity:

$$\text{Employment ratio} = \frac{(1 - \text{unemployment rate})\,(\text{labor force})}{\text{population}}$$

In 1949 the unemployment rate was 5.9%, and 55% of the working-age population had jobs. In 1978–79 the unemployment rate was again 5.9%, but now 60% of the working age population had jobs. Which figure gives a better measure of labor utilization? Should we say that, since in both cases 94.1% of the labor force had jobs, there was equal slack in labor utilization? Or should we conclude that, because 60% of the population was working in 1978–79, labor was more fully utilized and the economy was operating closer to capacity than in 1949? Put another way, did the historically high unemployment rates in the 1970s mean that there was considerable unused labor available, or did the historically high employment ratios in the same period mean that labor was pretty much fully utilized? This issue has been hotly debated by economists and will be referred to in later chapters.

POTENTIAL OUTPUT

In the early 1960s, Arthur Okun first constructed *potential output* data to estimate what could be produced if capital and labor were fully utilized. These potential output data are not intended to measure the maximum amount that could be produced in an all-out, around-the-clock mobilization of all of a nation's resources. Potential output is, instead, an estimate of how much would be produced with a voluntary, normal utilization of resources. The concept of potential output recognizes that, under normal circumstances, there will be (as discussed above) some built-in excess capacity and some unemployment.

There are, of course, difficulties in defining "normal" capacity utilization and "normal" unemployment. When Arthur Okun and the President's Council of Economic Advisors (CEA) first estimated potential output in the early 1960s, they looked for levels of production where resource constraints caused prices to increase greatly. Similarly, in the 1980s, Ronald Reagan's CEA defined full employment as the "inflationary threshold." (Rapidly rising prices suggest resource bottlenecks, which make it difficult to increase output further. In addition, political realities argue against stimulating the economy past the point where prices begin rising rapidly.) Looking at the historical data from several angles, Okun and the CEA settled on a 4% unemployment rate as a benchmark for potential output. They were especially influenced by the years 1955–57, when the unemployment rate fell to around 4% and several signs of economic strain surfaced. Economists have since quibbled about potential output in other years, but virtually all agree that the economy was operating at close to normal, full-resource utilization in the years 1955–57. Potential output in 1955–57, then, was roughly equal to the actual output.

There are a couple of ways to estimate potential output in years when the economy has not operated at normal capacity. One, called the benchmark approach, requires finding another period, such as 1965–66, when the unemployment rate was around 4% and the economy again seemed to be fully utilizing available resources. Potential output in 1965–66 is then set equal to actual output, and with this and the estimates for 1955–57 as benchmarks or points of reference, potential output in other years can be estimated by interpolating and extrapolating, as shown in Figure 2.7. Note that the figure shows actual output exceeding potential output in 1952–53 (when the unemployment rate was around 3%) and again in 1968–69 (when the unemployment rate was about 3.5%); thus potential output is not necessarily maximum output.

A second approach to measuring potential output is based on the long-run determinants of output growth. The output equation can be written:

$$\text{output} = \left(\frac{\text{output}}{\text{hour}}\right)\left(\frac{\text{hours}}{\text{worker}}\right)\left(\frac{\text{workers}}{\text{population}}\right)(\text{population}) \qquad (2.3)$$

That output is the product of output per hour, hours per worker, the employment ratio, and total population implies that the percentage change in output is equal to the sum of the percentage changes in these four factors and that, therefore, output growth depends upon the growth rates of these factors. Data from several years can be used to smooth out fluctuations and to estimate these long-run growth rates and, hence, the long-run growth rate of output. This output growth rate can then be extrapolated from a benchmark potential output (1955–57, for instance) to estimate the long-run path of potential output. In the early 1960s, the CEA estimated that potential output was growing by about 3.5% a year.

These two separate approaches—two benchmarks and the long-run determinants—give quite similar estimates of potential output. The estimates have, however, been adjusted a number of times as new data have become available. The CEA benchmark potential-output unemployment rate has been steadily revised upward from 4% in 1955–57, and was considered to be 5.1% by the late 1970s. Inflation was so high in the early 1980s—even while unemployment was high—that some economists now consider 6 or even 7% unemployment to be a reasonable target. One possible explanation for these upward revisions is the increased labor force participation of youths and women, two groups with traditionally high unemployment rates. As the benchmark unemployment rate has crept upward, potential output estimates have been revised downward.

Similarly, CEA estimates of long-run growth were raised to 4% in the mid-1960s, but have since been reduced to 3.5 and 3% in the 1970s. The recent 3% estimated growth in potential output is composed of the following percentage

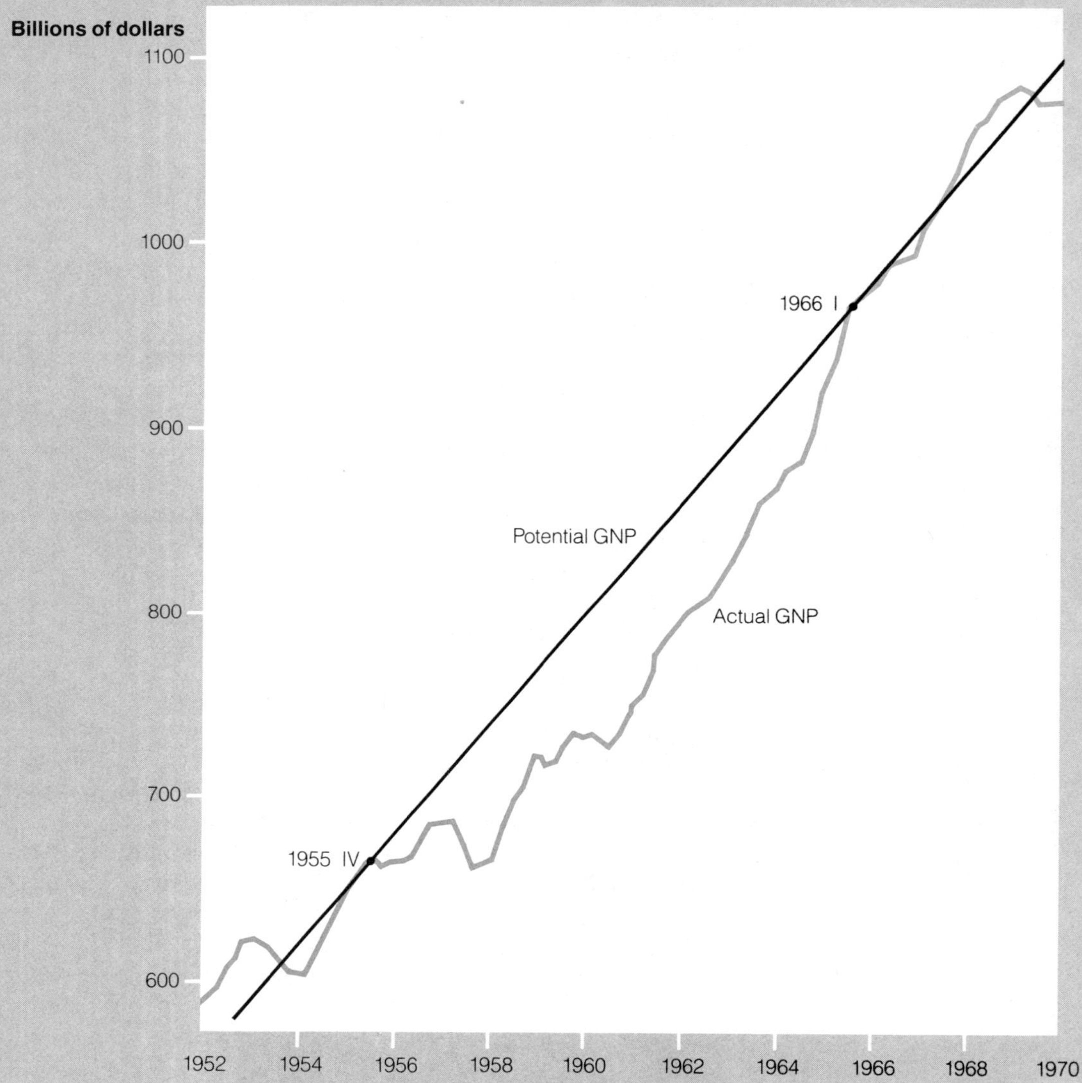

FIGURE 2.7 **THE BENCHMARK APPROACH TO ESTIMATING POTENTIAL GNP. In this method, two full-employment periods are selected as benchmarks, and potential GNP in other periods is then estimated by interpolation and extrapolation. The two periods used in this case are the fourth quarter of 1955 and the first quarter of 1966.**

changes in the four output factors (Equation 2.3): output per hour, + 1.50; hours per worker, − 0.50; employment ratio, + 0.75; and population, + 1.25. Considerable attention has focused on the modest 1.5% estimated growth in labor productivity (output per hour). Over the 20-year period 1948–68, output per hour grew by slightly more than 3% per year. This halving of productivity growth is the infamous "productivity slowdown" that has worried politicians, businesses, and households.

A 1.5% decline in productivity growth may not seem like much, but those small numbers do add up when continued year after year. A productivity increase of 3% a year (instead of 1.5%) for 20 years would result in an output 34% higher. We could enjoy 34% more goods and services or have correspondingly more leisure time.

Productivity and the business cycle

Output per hour in the United States increased at an annual average rate of 3.1% between 1948 and 1968, but by only 1.3% per year between 1968 and 1980. This slowing of productivity gains is worrisome; note, though, that the CEA is anticipating a 1.5% annual increase in productivity for the 1980s, rather than the 1.3% per year that was actually experienced between 1968 and 1980. The reason is that there were three recessions in the 12 years 1968–80, and measured productivity tends to fall during recessions. In the Great Depression output per hour fell by 8.5%. In the most severe recession since then, 1973–75, output per hour fell by 2.5%—instead of showing the usual annual increase of 2–3%.

We have already seen how capital utilization moves procyclically—that is, increasing in booms and decreasing in slumps. General Motors does not auction off all its excess capacity during recessions. Instead, some structures and equipment are allowed to sit idle, waiting for the next boom. The same is true of valuable, hard-to-replace workers, who are really very much like a firm's fixed plant and equipment and are viewed as a fixed cost of doing business. Skilled employees are very expensive to find and train. They have proven their ability and learned how to do their specific jobs and how to mesh with other employees. The secretary with the mysterious filing system, the accountant with the cryptic books, the scientist with the secret formula, and the president with the safe full of indiscretions are all popular caricatures for the simple truth that many employees are, in fact, largely irreplaceable. Thus, businesses do not myopically fire everybody in sight when sales slump; instead, they practice *labor hoarding.* These hoarded employees chat more, take longer lunches and coffee breaks, reorganize their files and desks, take paid vacations, and wait for the next boom.

When sales dip, labor and capital utilization fall while the fixed costs remain. Measured productivity consequently slumps, too. In booms, the reverse occurs: People and equipment work harder so that output rises faster than paid employment, and measured productivity increases. This procyclical tendency of productivity makes it difficult to separate business cycle fluctuations from long-run trends. To what extent was the lackluster productivity performance in the 1970s due to the recessions of the same period? And to what extent did it reflect a genuine longer-run slowing of productivity improvements? Undoubtedly, as the CEA has concluded, it was some of each. Productivity improvements have slowed, but not by as much as the recession-filled 1970s suggest. Later chapters will discuss some theories as to why productivity gains have diminished and whether this deterioration is likely to continue or to be reversed.

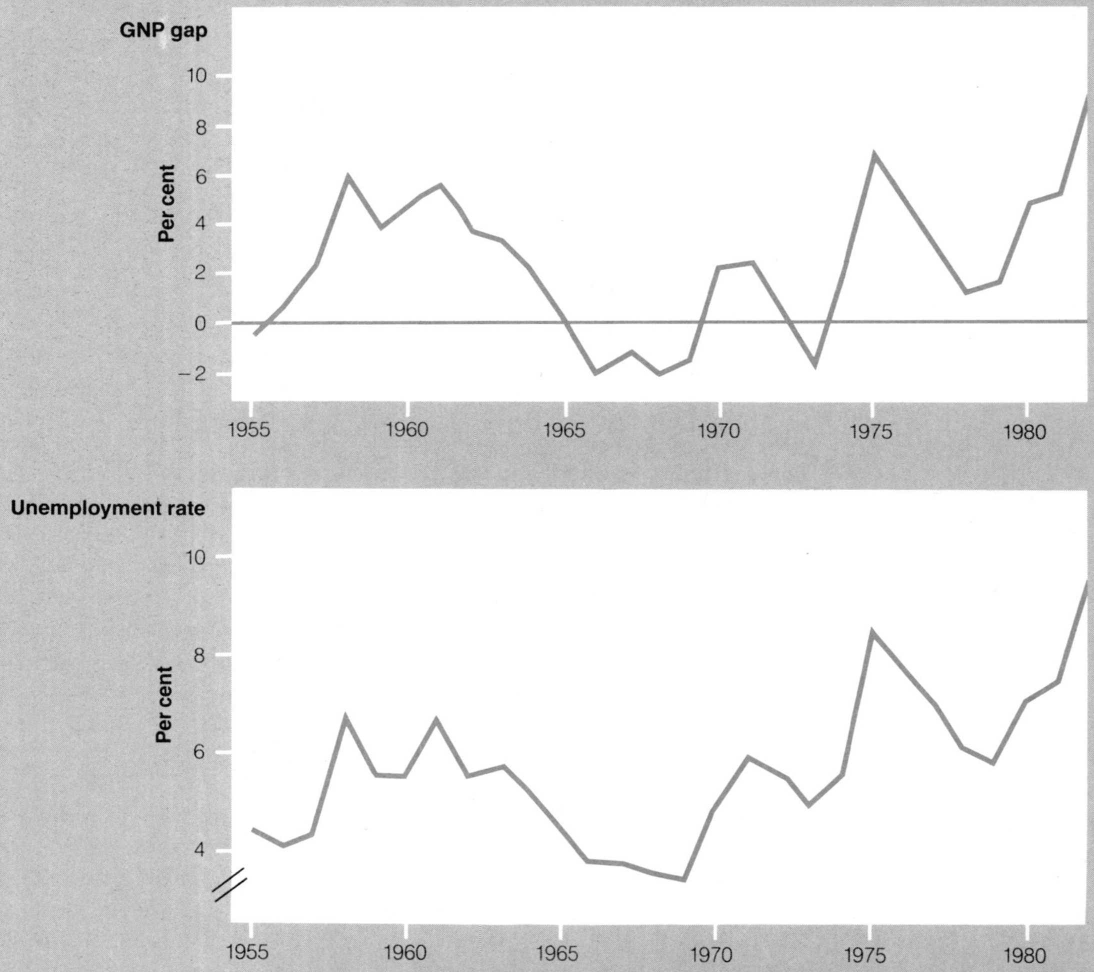

FIGURE 2.8 THE GNP GAP IN RELATION TO THE UNEMPLOYMENT RATE, 1955–82. **When the unemployment rate increases, the gap between actual and potential output widens. This gap represents the output that these unemployed could have produced but did not.**

Okun's law

As we have noted, a nation's output may fall far short of its potential. Arthur Okun estimated potential GNP in order to estimate the macroeconomic cost of idle resources. Figure 2.8 shows the GNP gap and the unemployment rate in the United States since 1955. (The difference between potential and actual GNP is the "GNP gap—the output that could have been, but wasn't.) During recessions, the capacity utilization rate declines, the unemployment rate rises, and the GNP gap increases; during booms, the reverse occurs. (In some years, the GNP gap is negative, in that the economy temporarily produces beyond normal full-resource utilization.) In 1982, with a 9.7% unemployment rate, the GNP gap reached a staggering 9.5% of potential GNP. In the early 1960s, Okun devised the following simple rule of thumb, which expresses the relationship between the unemployment rate and the GNP gap and has become known as *Okun's law:*

$$\frac{y_p - y}{y} = 3.2\ (u - u_f) \tag{2.4}$$

where y is real GNP: y_p, real potential GNP; u, unemployment rate; and u_f, the full-employment unemployment rate.

When the economy is at full employment, which Okun originally considered to be a 4% unemployment rate ($u_f = 0.04$), actual GNP is equal to potential GNP. Every percentage point increase in the unemployment rate is associated with a 3.2% increase in the GNP gap. (Because of labor hoarding, declines in average hours worked, and the exodus of discouraged workers from the labor force, GNP decreases much more than the unemployment rate increases.)

Okun's law can be used to estimate the GNP loss associated with various unemployment rates and also the increase in GNP needed to bring the economy to full employment. In recent years,[3] changes in the labor force and in productivity have increased estimates of the full-employment unemployment rate (to 5, 6, or even 7%) and have reduced potential-output projections. The Okun's law coefficient has been reduced from 3.2 to about 2.0 or 2.5. Increases in the unemployment rate apparently do not increase the GNP gap as much now as in the 1960s or, looked at the other way around, the unemployment rate is now more sensitive to GNP fluctuations.

GNP fluctuations in the United States have been relatively mild since World War II. Annual real GNP in 1908 was 8% less than in 1907, in 1915 was 5% less than in 1913, in 1921 was 16% less than 1918, and in 1933 was 30% less than in 1929. The biggest recessions in the post-World War II period occurred in 1973–75, when real GNP fell by less than 5%, and in 1981–82, when real GNP fell by 3%.

While recessions have been relatively mild, they are still costly. Real GNP in 1975 was estimated to be about $100 billion below potential GNP. In 1982, the unemployment rate averaged 10%. If the unemployment rate had been four percentage points lower, Okun's law tells us, real GNP would have been some 8 to 10% higher. In a three-trillion-dollar economy, that amounts to nearly $300 billion in additional output. Buildings, equipment, and people sat idle, and $300 billion in goods and services were not produced that year. An extra $300 billion would have gone a long way toward feeding and clothing the poor, constructing modern factories, repairing roads, rebuilding cities, rearming our military, and toward fulfilling whatever else is on the national agenda.

Evenly spread throughout society, that $300 billion loss would be $1500 less per person. The loss is, however, not evenly distributed. It is felt most keenly, of course, by the unemployed and by the owners of idle capital. Their losses are psychological as well as financial. Unemployed workers lose self-esteem and resent both employers and those who still have jobs. They have diminished re-

IN THE NEWS

Ghosts of Unemployment Haunt Victims for Years

WASHINGTON—"The American dream always said that if you worked hard, you'd get ahead," Claude Williams lamented.

Reared in Detroit's black ghetto, Williams, 32, earned a masters degree in industrial relations and earned $45,000 a year as a foreman for Ford Motor Co. But the nation's economic doldrums forced production cuts and sent him back to the assembly line. Then last August, as the current recession deepened, Williams lost that job too.

"What happened to the American dream?" he asked.

For economic forecasters and policy-makers, recessions are the bottom side of the business cycle, regarded by some as a necessary evil to combat inflation. In the modern world, nearly all the economic indicators that head downward during a recession bounce back up when recovery comes.

But for Claude Williams and millions of others, recessions are also the stuff of American tragedies. Behind the dips and dives of the economic statistics are the human costs that do not go away when the leading indicators rebound—costs that can haunt and hobble individuals and families for years.

Nearly 9.5 million Americans are out of work, more than at any time since 1939. Some will lose their homes. Others will see plans for education deferred or dashed, ventures into small business destroyed, autos repossessed.

Beyond these material costs, scholars have found that recessions and the accompanying unemployment inflict deep emotional wounds. Layoffs not only take away a worker's livelihood, they threaten his sense of identity and self-esteem, leaving behind shattered hopes and twisted lives.

"I don't want to have any children," said Greg Youngblood, a factory worker idled in Detroit, where the economy was still struggling to recover from the city's 1980 economic difficulties when it was crippled by the current slump. "I don't want my kids to come into the world to suffer."

The psychological impact of unemployment is not limited to its immediate victims. Reinforced by memories of the Great Depression of the 1930s, recessions send spasms of anxiety across American society, undermining confidence in political leadership and in the country's institutions.

Andrew Kohut, president of the Gallup Poll organization, said: "Nothing dampens the mood of America as much as the prospect of rising unemployment."

One reason for the pervasive distress is that unemployment represents a betrayal of some fundamental articles of faith that have been cherished since the birth of the nation.

Claude Williams recently found another job, in a federally funded retraining program for the unemployed. But he is making less money and he expects this job to be eliminated in May because of cutbacks in federal funding.

Although Williams has been more successful than some in scrambling for work, this sort of experience can impose psychological strains, according to Louis A. Ferman, research director of the University of Michigan's Institute of Labor and Industrial Relations.

"What we're finding is that job loss in many cases is only mildly traumatic compared to what follows —searching for new jobs, dashing of hopes that the old employer will call again, being rebuffed by new prospective employers. These are the events that try the patience and sanity of most workers."

Adding to the burden of unemployment is the shame many workers feel at their predicament. Hannah Levin, a psychology professor who studied jobless New Yorkers during the 1975 recession, wrote: "Many of the men we interviewed stayed off the street during the day in their neighborhood because they felt a sense of embarrassment at having lost status. Two choose the role of being sick as a preferable substitute to unemployment." . .

Wherever the blame is placed, unemployment creates resentment among the unemployed and their families and uneasiness among other workers who worry that their own jobs may be in jeopardy. . . .

One indication of the concern about unemployment is provided by Gallup Polls over the last 20 years. They show that rises in unemployment are accompanied by substantial declines in presidential popularity, ranging from 9 to 29 percentage points.

Other surveys show a link between unemployment and loss of public confidence in such institutions as Congress, big business, the military, education and organized labor. . . .

On an individual level, recessions also set off a vicious circle. As Louis Ferman of the University of Michigan points out, the emotional and physical toll of unemployment can make it harder for some victims to find jobs in the future. Other workers, forced to accept lower-paying and less-skilled work, find themselves on a dead-end street.

"In both cases," Ferman warned, "there is the danger of developing 'unemployment careers' that can last a substantial part of one's life."

Unemployment insurance and welfare payments help alleviate some of the economic hardships. But they do little to make up for the psychic loss suffered by the unemployed. Psychoanalyst Sigmund Freud and others have said what common sense confirms—that a job is an individual's strongest link to reality and his most essential means of defining himself in relation to the rest of society.

In a 1976 study for the Joint Economic Committee of Congress, M. Harvey Brenner of Johns Hopkins University showed that over more than 30 years, increases in the unemployment rate were accompanied by increases in suicide, mental illness, homicide and deaths from strokes and heart and kidney disease.

"This study reveals that unemployment has a striking potent impact on society," wrote the late Sen. Hubert H. Humphrey (D-Minn.), then chairman of the Joint Economic Committee. "Even a 1% increase in unemployment, for example, creates a legacy of stress, of aggression and of illness affecting society long into the future."

Although the emotional strain of unemployment is hard to gauge precisely on a national level, it is often quite clear in individual cases.

"I get cranky and irritable just sitting at home," said Williams, whose wife, Linda, calls him a "workaholic."

For Youngblood, who has been unable to find work since July, 1980, and whose unemployment benefits ran out last February, the tensions are more severe. His bitterness has soured his marriage; his wife, Debra, left him last February.

Although she returned a few months later, the Youngbloods—who spend much of their time in his father's home—still find it hard to get along. "We're together too much," he said. "We're constantly at each other's throats. It tears up my father." (Robert Shogan, *Los Angeles Times,* Jan. 11, 1982. Copyright, 1982, by *Los Angeles Times.* Reprinted by permission.)

spect for government and lowered confidence in society. Family relations are strained, particularly for breadwinners who can no longer satisfactorily provide for their families.

There is considerable stress on both the unemployed and on those who are fearful of becoming unemployed. Alcohol and drug abuse increase during recessions. Diets deteriorate, and health problems are left untreated. Heart disease, suicides, murders, auto accidents, and even infant mortality all rise in recessions. It has been estimated that a one-point increase in the unemployment rate causes 37,000 deaths over the succeeding six years.[4] Most of the mental and physical pains of recessions are less tragic, but still quite real.

One of the primary objectives of macroeconomics is to understand the swings in economic activity from recession to boom and back again. Once understood, these business fluctuations may be predictable and even controllable.

Early economists often accepted booms and recessions as interesting but unavoidable characteristics of industrial economies. These economists were primarily interested in identifying and cataloguing statistical regularities in the persistent business cycles. The private tragedies and social waste during recessions spurred other economists, including Keynes, to advocate active government policies to moderate business fluctuations. Some such policies were instituted, and recessions have been milder since the 1940s. By the 1960s, some economists declared that business cycles were dead. The period February 1961 to December 1969 was, in fact, recession free, but the business cycle was resurrected in the 1970s. Recessions have not been eradicated, and economists are again debating the causes of business cycles and the role of government. These are the central questions of macroeconomics, questions that we will begin answering in the next chapter.

IMPORTANT TERMS AND CONCEPTS

- National income and product accounts
- Flow-of-funds data
- Stock data
- Flow data
- Gross national product (GNP)
- Net national product (NNP)
- Depreciation
- National income
- Transfer payments
- Nominal data
- Real data
- Money illusion
- Consumer price index (CPI)
- Producer price index (PPI)
- Capacity utilization
- Labor force
- Employment ratio
- Unemployment rate
- Potential output
- Labor hoarding
- Okun's law

A flow-of-funds table shows the fundamental budget and market interrelationships in an economy. Budget constraints link markets, while market constraints link agents.

Gross national product, net national product, and national income are important measures of aggregate economic activity. We will focus mainly on national income (GNP minus depreciation and indirect taxes) as a measure of output. National income can be viewed from either the expenditure or income side, since every expenditure is someone else's income.

Nominal data are measured in dollars. Real data are measured in terms of purchasing power. Real wage rates, real income, and real wealth are equal to nominal wage rates, nominal income, and nominal wealth divided by the price level. Price indexes are used to gauge changes in the prices of bundles of goods and services.

During economic recessions, output falls below potential output, capacity utilization dips, the employment ratio falls, and the unemployment rate rises. An increase of one percentage point in the unemployment rate is associated with about a 2 or $2\frac{1}{2}$% decrement of real GNP below potential GNP.

EXERCISES

1. Which of the following are stocks and which flows?
   a. General Motors car sales this year
   b. Robin Yount's batting average
   c. The population of the United States
   d. The number of births in the United States this year
   e. The amount of money in your checking account
   f. The rate of inflation
   g. GNP
   h. The government's budget deficit
   i. The government debt
   j. Oil imports this year

2. Why do the national income accounts look only at the production of new goods and services and exclude the nation's endowment of houses, factories, offices, machines, roads, and so on?

3. Why do the national income accounts exclude do-it-yourself projects?

4. How would the following be designated—consumption, investment, or neither—in the national income accounts?
   a. The production of strawberries
   b. The construction of a new office building
   c. The purchase of 10 shares of IBM stock
   d. The production of new Chrysler cars
   e. The production of new Hondas in Japan
   f. The sale of new Chryslers that were produced last year
   g. The construction of a new federal dam in Oregon

5. A new house is built in 1980 and sold in 1981 for $100,000. The owner rents it out for three years at $500 a month. The house is then sold to someone who lives in it until it burns down in 1988. Describe how the annual national income accounts would be affected by this house.

6. Workers nationwide successfully campaign for a 25-hour work week. GNP drops by a third. Does this show a depression, a drop in national well-being, or something else?

7. What is the difference between nominal GNP and real GNP? What was the percentage slump in real GNP between 1929 and 1932, when national GNP fell from $104 billion to $58.5 billion, while the CPI dropped from 59.7 to 47.6?

8. Mr. Bunker lives on beer and pretzels. In 1970, he bought 1000 six-packs of beer at $1.00 each and 500 bags of pretzels at $0.50 each. In 1980, Bunker's beer cost $1.50 and his pretzels cost $1.00.
   a. One way to calculate the rate of inflation in Bunker's case is

$$\frac{\text{cost of 1000 6-packs and 500 bags in 1980}}{\text{cost of 1000 6-packs and 500 bags in 1970}}$$

What was the percentage increase in Bunker's cost of living from 1970 to 1980? If we calculated a Bunker Price Index (BPI) and scaled this BPI to equal 100 in 1970, what would be the 1980 value of the BPI?

b. Another way to calculate Bunker's rate of inflation is

$$\begin{pmatrix}\text{\% increase in}\\ \text{price of beer}\end{pmatrix}\begin{pmatrix}\text{fraction of 1970 budget}\\ \text{spent on beer}\end{pmatrix}$$
$$+\begin{pmatrix}\text{\% increase in}\\ \text{pretzel prices}\end{pmatrix}\begin{pmatrix}\text{fraction of 1970 budget}\\ \text{spent on pretzels}\end{pmatrix}$$

What was Bunker's inflation rate using this approach?

c. Bunker earned $2 an hour in 1970 and $3 an hour in 1980. What was the percentage change in his nominal wage rate? in his real wage rate?

9. The CPI increased at an average annual rate of 8.1% during the five years 1975 through 1979. During these years, the home ownership component of the CPI had a weight of one-twelfth and the "price" of home ownership increased at an average annual rate of 10%. What was the rate of inflation for the remaining components of the CPI?

The personal consumption deflator data used an estimate of 6.1% for the annual percentage increase in the "price" of home ownership from 1975 through 1979. If the CPI index had used this 6.1% figure, rather than 10%, what would have been the overall CPI inflation rate for 1975–79?

10. *Business Conditions Digest* reported the following CPI data:

	CPI ($P = 100.0$ in 1967)
1975	161.2
1976	170.5
1977	181.5

The United Nations *Statistical Bulletin* reported these CPI data:

	CPI ($P = 100.0$ in 1975)
1978	121.2
1979	135.1
1980	153.1

How much did prices increase between 1977 and 1978? Putting all six years of data together on the same scale ($P = 100.0$ in 1967), recalibrate these data so that $P = 100.0$ in 1980. Which of the following CPI facts are the most important: levels, first differences, or ratios?

11. It has been alleged that statisticians do not fully take into account quality improvements in what we buy. If so, will their estimates of inflation be too high or too low? Will their estimates of real income be too high or too low?

12. Under what circumstances would you expect to find a significant difference between Laspeyres and Paasche price indexes? Which index would increase more in the circumstances summarized by the following data?

	Nominal GNP ($ billions)	**CPI (Average level during year)**	**Food prices (Average level during year)**
1980	2626.1	246.8	254.6
1981	2924.8	272.5	274.6

13. On the basis of the recent U.S. economic data shown above, and using the CPI to calculate real data:

a. What was the percentage increase in nominal GNP between 1980 and 1981?

b. What was the percentage increase in real GNP between 1980 and 1981?

c. What was the percentage increase in the real price of food between 1980 and 1981? What does "the real price of food" mean?

14. The Council of Economic Advisers estimated that, in 1975, real potential GNP was $1302.1 billion, while full employment was at a 5.1% unemployment rate. Actual real GNP in 1975 was $1202.1 billion, and the actual unemployment rate was 8.5%. Using only these data, estimate the Okun's law coefficient for 1975.

	GNP	Unemployment rate
1980	$2632	7.1
1981	$2954	7.6
1982	$3073	9.7
1983	$3310	9.6

15. For the GNP and the unemployment rate data above use Okun's law to estimate potential GNP and the GNP gap in each of these years, assuming a full-employment unemployment rate of 6%. How much total output was lost over these four years? (For simplicity, ignore the distinction between nominal and real GNP.)

16. Okun's law implicitly reports that output fluctuations are proportionately much larger than changes in the unemployment rate. Give the economic logic behind the following explanations for that phenomenon.

a. Labor hoarding
b. Changes in average hours worked
c. The exodus of discouraged workers from the labor force.

REFERENCES

1. O. Morgenstern, "Qui Numerare Incipit Errare Incipit," *Fortune,* October 1963.

2. U.S. Department of Labor, Bureau of Labor Statistics, *How the Government Measures Unemployment,* Washington, D.C.: U.S. Government Printing Office, 1977.

3. See *Economic Report of the President,* 1979, Washington, D.C.: U.S. Government Printing Office, p. 74.

4. M. H. Brenner, A Study for the Joint Economic Committee of Congress, reported in Gerald F. Seib, "Recessions Cause Death Rate to Rise, As Pressures of Coping Take Hold," *Wall Street Journal,* August 25, 1980.

SUGGESTIONS FOR FURTHER READING

Flow-of-funds modeling is discussed in David Backus, William Brainard, Gary Smith, and James Tobin, "A Flow of Funds Model of U.S. Financial Markets," *Journal of Money, Credit, and Banking* (May 1980), pp. 259–83. An excellent discussion of the CPI is given in Robert J. Gordon, "The CPI: Measuring Inflation and Causing It," *The Public Interest* (Spring 1981), pp. 112–34. Arthur Okun's "Potential GNP: Its measurement and Significance" (1962) is reprinted in his book *The Political Economy of Prosperity,* New York: Norton, 1970. For an attempt to gauge the human costs of unemployment, see Barry Bluestone and Bennett Harrison, *The Deindustrialization of America,* New York: Basic Books, 1982, ch. 3. The annual editions of the *Economic Report of the President* contain good, readable discussions of recent business cycles and lots of economic data. More data can be found in the monthly *Business Conditions Digest,* Washington: U.S. Government Printing Office, and *Federal Reserve Bulletin,* Washington: Publications Services, Federal Reserve System.

PART TWO

MACROECONOMIC MODELS

CHAPTER THREE

MACRO MODELING: A FIRST STEP

The theory of economics does not furnish a body of settled conclusions immediately applicable to policy. It is a method rather than a doctrine, an apparatus of the mind, a technique of thinking, which helps its possessor to draw correct conclusions.

JOHN MAYNARD KEYNES[1]

This chapter will distinguish between market equilibria and disequilibria and examine the interaction of income and spending. It will also introduce two important macroeconomic concepts—automatic stabilization and the full-employment surplus.

IN the not too distant past, macroeconomics was very descriptive and intuitive. Economists would strip way what they felt were the unimportant secondary effects, and concentrate on simple chains of reasoning. Macroeconomics consisted mostly of separate, seemingly unrelated theories: A nation's output is determined by its resources; the interest rate is determined by investment and saving; and the price level is determined by the money supply. But, beyond these generalities, economic reasoning was not very precise and many, even within the profession, were unsure of the underlying logic. There was no coherent framework for economic analysis. Instead, macroeconomics consisted largely of the secret idiosyncrasies of individual economists, who seemed to be more than a little mystical.

Fundamental to the scientific revolution that engulfed economics in the twentieth century was adoption of the use of explicit models. A model is a group of equations describing the interrelationships between such variables as output, employment, and government spending. The virtues of an explicit model are threefold. It reveals an author's assumptions, permits verification of the logical deductions, and allows application by others. As Paul Samuelson has declared:

. . . science is public knowledge, reproducible knowledge. When Robert Adams wrote an MIT thesis on the accuracy of different forecasting models, he found that "being Sumner Slichter" was apparently one of the best methods known at the time. This was a scientific fact, but a *sad* scientific fact. For Slichter could not and did not pass on his art to an assistant or to a new generation of economists. It died with him, if indeed it did not slightly predecease him. What we hope to get by scientific breakthrough is a way of substituting for men of genius men of talent and even run-of-the-mill men. This is the sense in which science is public, reproducible knowledge.[2]

These days mystics are a small but noisy minority, and models have the upper hand in macroeconomics. Explicit theoretical models are used to deduce the qualitative effects of economic events, and explicit empirical models are used to predict the quantitative effects.

Most macroeconomic forecasting models are large and complex. Many contain hundreds of equations and are much too complicated to be analyzed by mental gymnastics alone. Even their creators are occasionally puzzled by the implications of the models. In order to apply these models and accurately determine their predictions, it is invariably necessary to use the memory and computational skills of large computers. In fact, it is the advances in computer technology that fueled the growth of formal macroeconomic models.

For theoretical work and classroom exposition, economists rely on greatly simplified models. In the next few chapters, a standard condensed macroeconomic model is described and analyzed. This model is a rich and yet tractable vehicle for sketching the broad determinants of aggregate economic activity.

We will begin in this chapter with an unadorned multiplier model that is, in many ways, the ideal first model for showing how national income is determined. Multiplier models are readily accessible yet rich enough to yield many basic macroeconomic concepts. These models are the back-of-the-envelope equations that were first used to explain business cycles and to formulate stabilization policies. Today, multiplier models are still the starting point of large, sophisticated macroeconomic models.

BASIC CONCEPTS

Demand and supply

The following material is necessary to the understanding of models. Demand and supply curves are the bread and butter of economics. They show the amounts people want to purchase and the amounts they want to sell: they describe desired transactions. The terms demand and supply are often prefaced by the phrases *ex ante* (before the fact) or *ex post* (after the fact). Thus "*ex ante* demand" and "*ex ante* supply" remind us that these are the amounts that people want to trade, *before* transactions actually take place. The actual amount bought must equal the amount sold. This is simply an accounting identity. But the amount bought need not equal the amount demanded: Some demanders may not find willing sellers. Similarly, the amount sold need not equal the amount supplied: Some suppliers may not find willing buyers. Thus, actual transactions need not equal desired transactions. It is to emphasize this distinction that purchases and sales are sometimes preceded by the phrase *ex post*. *Ex post* purchases and sales must be equal to each other, but they need not be equal to *ex ante* demand and supply.

Figure 3.1 shows typical demand and supply curves, giving the quantities demanded and supplied at various prices. The so-called "laws of demand and supply" state that, as drawn, increases in price reduce demand and increase the amount supplied. (The word "demand" is sometimes used to mean the specific

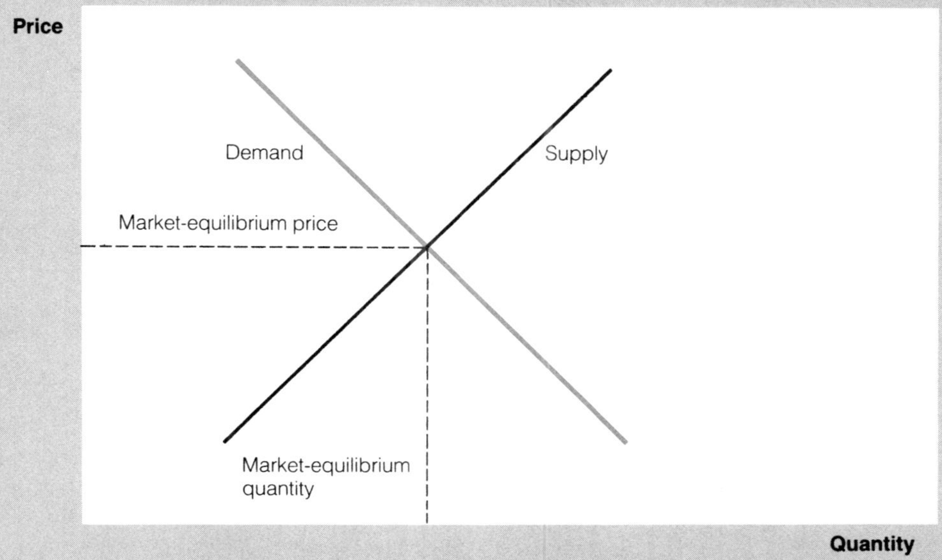

FIGURE 3.1 DEMAND AND SUPPLY CURVES SHOWING A MARKET EQUILIBRIUM. **Market equilibrium price and quantity are determined by the intersection of the demand and supply curves.**

quantity demanded at a particular price and, at other times, to signify the complete demand curve. Where the context leaves one meaning ambiguous, we should use "quantity demanded" or "the demand curve" for clarity; in other cases the shorthand "demand" can be used. The same applies to "supply," of course.)

Equilibrium and disequilibrium

Absolutely crucial to understanding macroeconomics is recognition of the equilibrium-disequilibrium phenomena. The *equilibrium price* (shown in the figure) is that price at which the quantities demanded and supplied are just equal. Here, and only here, will *ex post* purchases and sales equal *ex ante* demand and supply. Leon Walras (1834–1910), the great French economist who analyzed theoretical equilibrium models, described a hypothetical auction mechanism by which equilibrium prices might be determined. In what is called a *tatonnement* process, a mythical auctioneer announces tentative prices for all items. People then report their (truthful, but tentative) demands and supplies at these preliminary prices, and the auctioneer checks to see if demand equals supply in every market. If so, then these are the equilibrium prices, and transactions take place. If not, then the auctioneer tries a new set of prices and solicits new demand and supply offers. This trial-and-error process continues until equilibrium prices are found. Economists have proven (at considerable expense) that such an equilibrium does exist, but few have volunteered to serve as the Walrasian auctioneer who tries to find it.

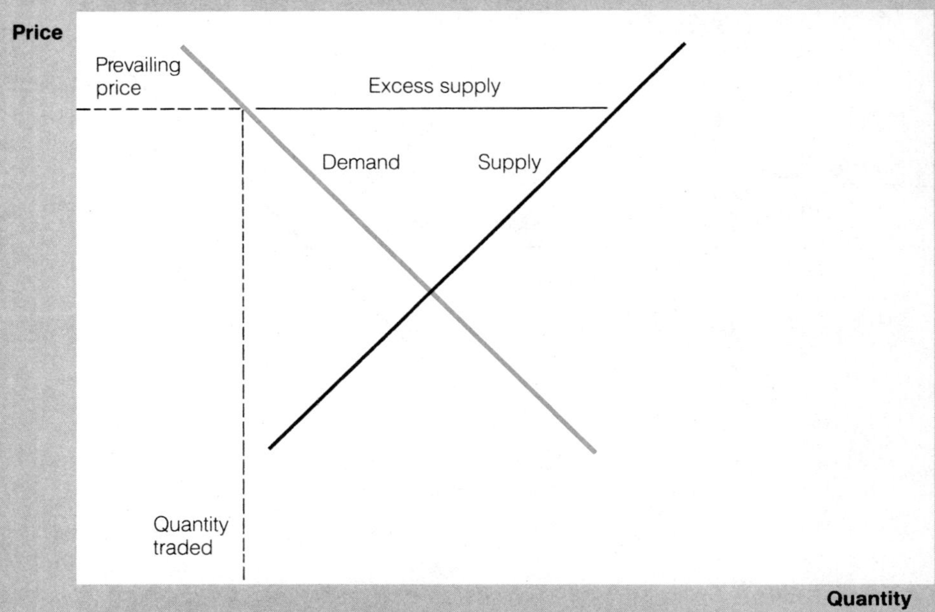

FIGURE 3.2 **DEMAND AND SUPPLY CURVES SHOWING AN EXCESS SUPPLY. If the prevailing price exceeds the market equilibrium price, then the supply at that price exceeds demand. As drawn, transactions are demand-determined and some suppliers are disappointed.**

In the real world, prices are set in decentralized markets rather than by a grand universal allocation. In addition, few individual markets are as pure as the Walrasian ideal.* Some financial and raw-commodity markets approach it, but for most manufacturing, utility, service, and labor markets, prices are described more accurately as "administered" than as "auction." Nobel laureate John Hicks labeled this distinction between administered and auction markets as *fixprice* rather than *flexprice.*

In fixprice markets, there is frequent *disequilibrium,* since prices do not freely adjust to reconcile demand and supply. Instead, quantities adjust, with some agents disappointed in their efforts to make trades at prevailing prices. For example, when auto demand is weak, auto prices and auto worker wages do not freely fall so as to maintain production and employment. Instead, production slumps and auto workers are laid off. The auto firms and workers are frustrated in their efforts to sell at prevailing prices and wages. And when demand is strong, auto prices do not immediately rise to stifle it. Instead, more workers are hired, longer hours are worked, and buyers are put on waiting lists. Now it is buyers who are frustrated.

Figure 3.2 shows a market in which the price has been set so high that sup-

* Recontracting does occur in the London gold market. Academic economists sometimes use Walrasian procedures to bet on presidential elections and to allocate offices.

ply exceeds demand. Where people will not buy more than they demand, transactions are demand-determined; the amount sold is less than the amount supplied. Figure 3.3 shows a market in which the price has been set so low that demand exceeds supply. Where people will not sell more than they supply, transactions are supply-determined; the amount purchased is less than the amount demanded.

These situations arise because there is no omniscient auctioneer who knows every demand and supply and who has the power to simultaneously set every price to clear every market. Without such an all-knowing, all-powerful auctioneer, it would be surprising were prices ever at the razor's edge of demand and supply. Classical economists assumed that market forces keep disequilibria small and temporary. They argued that market pressures would soon pull the price down (in the situation depicted in Figure 3.2) and push the price up for that in Figure 3.3. Were this so, then economists could limit their analysis to market equilibria and be confident that they have a close approximation to the real world. Keynes was more skeptical. For him, the Great Depression was the final proof that market failures need not be small or temporary. He argued that economists had to start thinking about situations in which an excess demand or

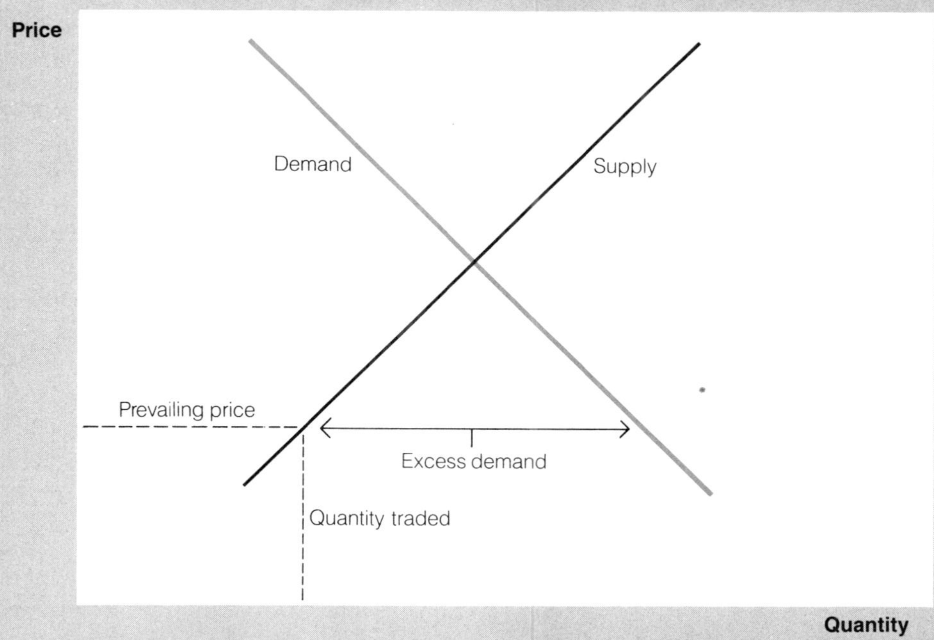

FIGURE 3.3 **DEMAND AND SUPPLY CURVES SHOWING AN EXCESS DEMAND. If the prevailing price is below the market equilibrium price, then the demand at that price exceeds supply. As drawn, transactions are supply-determined and some demand is not satisfied.**

THE GREAT DEPRESSION

The two World Wars and the Great Depression were the three most devastating events in the first half of the twentieth century. Each threatened to tear apart western civilization and each caused fundamental political, economic, and social changes. The story of the Great Depression can be summarized by a variety of depressing economic statistics. Between 1929 and 1933, U.S. GNP fell from $104 billion to $56 billion, while the unemployment rate rose from 3% to 25%. Stock prices fell by 80% and more than a third of the nation's banks failed. Household net worth fell by30%.

Behind these aggregate numbers were millions of private tragedies: One hundred thousand businesses failed. Twelve million people lost their jobs and, with them, their income and, in many cases, self-respect. Many also lost their life savings in the tidal wave of bank failures. Without income or savings, people could not buy food, clothing, or proper medical care. Those who could not pay their rents lost their shelter; those who couldn't meet their mortgage payments lost their homes. Farm income fell by more than two-thirds and many farms were lost to foreclosure. Desperate people moved into shanty settlements (called "Hoovervilles"); slept under newspapers ("Hoover blankets"); and scavenged for food where they could. Edmund Wilson, in the February 1933 issue of the *New Republic*, reported:

> There is not a garbage-dump in Chicago which is not haunted by the hungry. Last summer in the hot weather when the smell was sickening and the flies were thick, there were a hundred people a day coming to one of the dumps. . . . [A] widow who used to do housework and laundry, but now had no work at all, fed herself and her fourteen-year-old son on garbage. Before she picked up the meat, she would always take off her glasses so that she couldn't see the maggots.

Despite Keynes' repeated pleas, government efforts to end the Great Depression were modest at best. As the economy collapsed, federal tax revenues dropped from $3.8 billion in 1929 to $1.7 billion in 1932. Most business and financial leaders argued for lower government spending and higher taxes, because they believed that the government should balance its budget. One of the most respected, Bernard Baruch, advised: "Stop spending money we haven't got. Sacrifice for frugality and revenue. Cut government spending—cut it as rations are cut in a siege. Tax—tax everybody for everything." President Hoover's well-intentioned efforts to ease the suffering were constricted by a desire to balance the federal budget. Hoover increased government spending from $2.6 billion in 1929 to $3.2 billion in 1933, hardly enough to stem the $46 billion drop in GNP. The Federal Reserve's monetary policy was equally cautious. The supply of Federal Reserve notes was increased slightly, from $6.8 billion in 1929 to $7.4 billion in 1933. But this slight effort was swamped by the collapse of the private banking system. The total money supply, M1, fell by nearly a fourth—from $26.6 billion in 1929 to $21.1 billion in 1932.

In the 1932 election, Franklin Roosevelt called Hoover's federal budget "the most reckless and extravagant that I have been able to discover in the statistical record of any peacetime Government anywhere, any time." Roosevelt promised to balance the budget by a 25% reduction in government spending.

Once elected, Roosevelt's balanced-budget objectives gave way to the obvious need to do something, anything, to relieve the economic suffering. But, still, government expenditures increased only gradually, from $3.2 billion in 1932 to $9 billion in 1939. The unemployment rate averaged 19% during the 1930s and never fell below 14%. In 1939, real GNP was still 20% below its potential. The Great Depression didn't end until the government began spending nearly $100 billion a year during World War II.

excess supply persisted for a considerable period. The model we will look at in this chapter is Keynes' simplest analysis of an excess-supply situation.

Tools for model-making

Some of the variables in models are *predetermined variables*—that is, variables whose values are determined outside of the model. A variable may be predetermined because it is essentially fixed, or at least unaffected by the economy. For instance, if building a model to predict GNP three months from now, we can safely assume that the population, factories, and technology are predetermined, in that they will not be affected in the next three months by any conceivable changes in GNP. Some model variables are predetermined because they are discretionary policy variables, such as government spending and tax rates. We can assume various plausible values for these and, on the basis of them, use the model to solve for correspondingly varied values of output and employment. In this way, we are able to predict the effects of government spending and tax policy on the economy.

THE EQUATIONS

The model's actual equations are of three general types:

1. *Identities.* These are relationships such as "net national product is equal to gross national product minus depreciation."

2. Those dealing with *market-clearing conditions.* These may be equilibrium conditions stating how prices adjust to equate *ex ante* demand and supply, or disequlibrium conditions stating how quantities adjust to clear markets. (For example, how purchases may be constrained by available supply when there is excess demand.)

3. Those dealing with *behavioral relations.* These describe the relationship of certain factors to economic decisions—for example, how commodity demand may depend on income.

Behavioral equations are frequently assumed to be linear (straight lines), as illustrated in Figure 3.4. Here the variable e measures expenditures, while the variable y measures national income. As shown, expenditures are positively related to income in that expenditures increase as income increases. The true relationship, however, is inconveniently nonlinear; nonetheless, we might, for convenience, use the linear approximation

$$e = e_0 + e_y y \tag{3.1}$$

(as shown in Figure 3.4), in which e_0 is the intercept of this straight-line approximation, and e_y is the slope. The slope e_y measures the marginal effect on expenditures of a change in income:

$$e_y = \frac{\Delta e}{\Delta y} \tag{3.2}$$

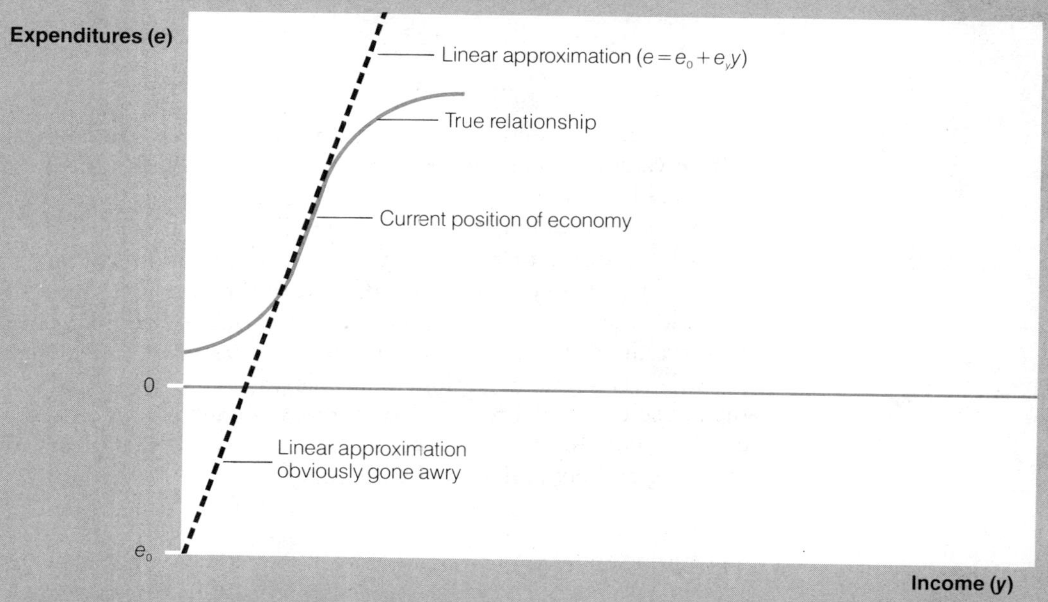

FIGURE 3.4 **LINEAR APPROXIMATIONS are adequate for depicting small changes. Whatever the current position of the economy, a straight line can be drawn that provides a close approximation to the true relationship, at least for small changes. This linear approximation may be very inaccurate for large changes.**

where Δy is the change in income and Δe is the induced change in spending. This parameter, e_y, is called the *marginal propensity to spend.* If e_y is 0.6, then a dollar increase in income causes a 60-cent increase in expenditures.

The intercept, e_0, is sometimes called *autonomous* spending, to show that it is the part of spending that does not depend on income. If expenditures do not depend on income at all, then $e_y = 0$ and $e = e_0$ so that spending itself is autonomous, or predetermined.

Figure 3.4 shows that a linear approximation of a continuous function is satisfactory, as long as we confine our attention to small changes (the region that coincides with the "true relationship"). But when large changes are analyzed, we really should think carefully about possible bumps and wiggles in behavior. The precise functional form of the equation (quadratic? cubic? logarithmic?) is seldom obvious. But it is often clear that we cannot mechanically assume a straight line. For example in Figure 3.4 our linear approximation clearly goes awry when it predicts negative spending at very low income levels. Similarly, we should be cautious in using linear extrapolations to predict such things as the demand for money were the government overthrown, the income of grade-school dropouts were they to go on to earn Ph.D.s, or the productivity of labor 200 years from now.

THE SIMPLE INCOME-EXPENDITURE MODEL

A bare-bones income-expenditure model will now be used to illustrate macroeconomic reasoning and a little modeling technique as well. The fundamental economic moral is the simultaneous interdependence of income and expenditures. Income influences how much people spend, and spending, in the aggregate, influences how much income people earn. If people decide to spend less, others will earn less and consequently spend less, too. This fundamental income-expenditure interdependence explains how recessions can persist and grow like a snowball rolling downhill.

Income depends on spending/spending depends on income

Equation 2.1 $(y = e)$, the national income equation discussed in Chapter 2, states that all expenditures (e) on goods and services provide income (y) to someone. Both income and expenditures are real flows, normally measured at annual rates.

Equation 2.1 can be used to describe a market that is either in equilibrium or disequilibrium. The equation must hold *ex post:* Every dollar that is spent on goods and services is income for someone—wages, profits, interest, or rent. In a market-equilibrium model, Equation 2.1 would also hold *ex ante* in that y would also be the amount of income that workers and producers want to earn. Here we will follow Keynes in using a disequilibrium interpretation, in which unemployed workers and the owners of idled factories are frustrated in their efforts to earn income. With this disequilibrium interpretation, Equation 2.1 states that, in the aggregate, how much people earn is determined by how much people want to spend. Later in this chapter we will see that the analysis is quite different if there is instead a classical full-employment equilibrium.

The second half of this income-expenditure model is the belief that expenditures are influenced by income:

$$e = e_0 + e_y y \qquad 0 < e_y < 1 \tag{3.3}$$

where e_0 is the intercept of this linear approximation and e_y is the aggregate marginal propensity to spend out of income. This equation states that an increase in income tends to increase spending, though not by a full dollar-for-dollar amount.

That aggregate expenditures are often separated, as in Chapter 2, into private consumption, private investment, and government spending $(e = c + i + g)$ is not mandatory. It is a split inspired by Keynes' belief that consumption is predictable, while investment spending is volatile and government spending is controllable. We could instead separate expenditures into those by workers and by capitalists, by easterners and westerners, city slickers and country bumpkins, or whatever.

For our present purposes, there is no real need to divide spending into separate categories. All that currently matters is our assumption that, in the aggregate, an increase in income increases spending. The source might be consumers who routinely spend a certain fraction of their incomes, businesses whose investment plans are stimulated by a strong economy, or a government whose expenditures rise to exhaust available tax revenue (and then some). The important point is that, overall, more income induces more spending.

Given the values of the predetermined parameters e_0 and e_y, the model

$$y = e \tag{2.1}$$

$$e = e_0 + e_y y \tag{3.1}$$

determines values for income and expenditures. We can substitute Equation 3.1 in Equation 2.1 to obtain

$$y = e_0 + e_y y \tag{3.4}$$

so that

$$y = \frac{e_0}{1 - e_y} \tag{3.5}$$

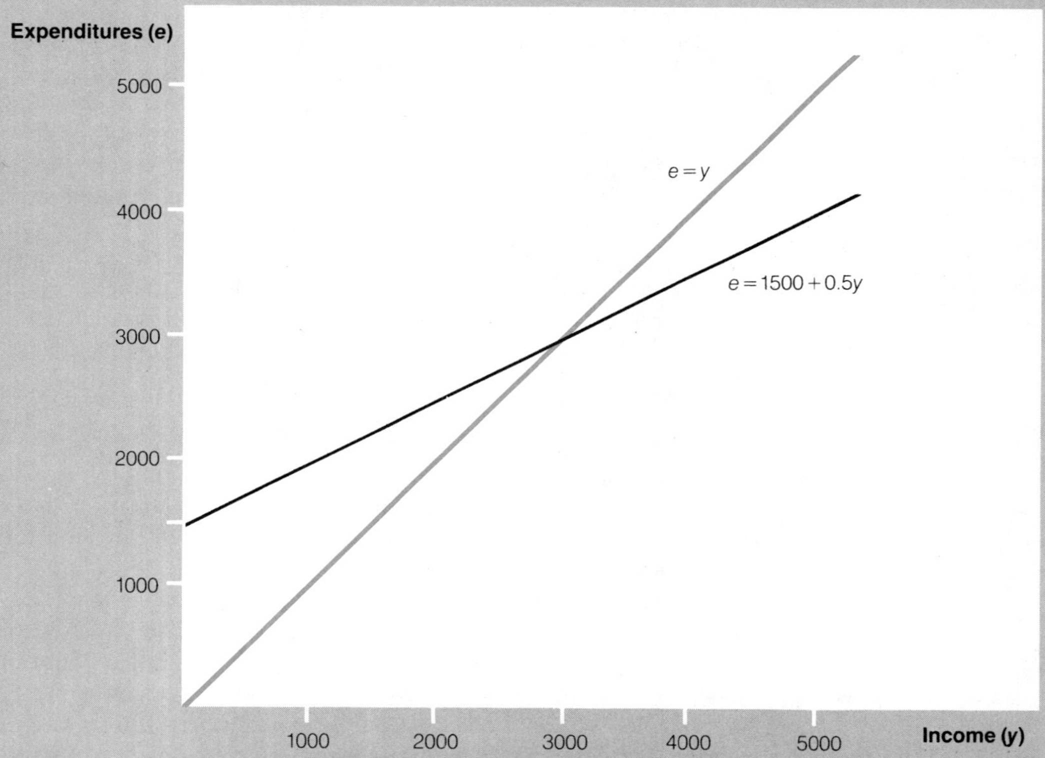

FIGURE 3.5 **A graph of the linear expenditure equation $e = 1500 + 0.5y$ is a straight line with an intercept of 1500 and a slope of 0.5.**

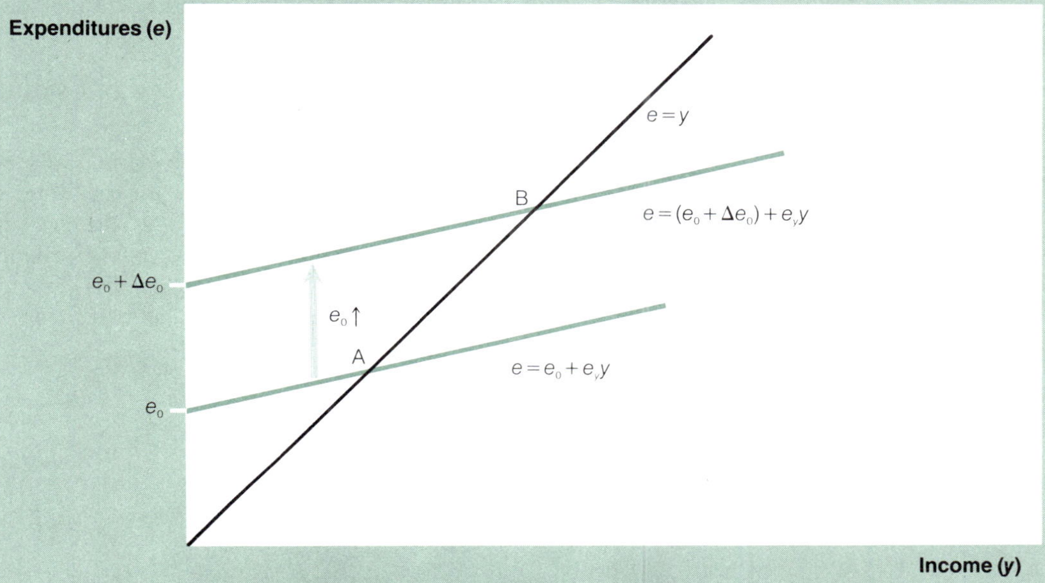

FIGURE 3.6 **GRAPHIC DETERMINATION OF INCOME AND EXPENDITURES. The intersection at Point A of the expenditure equation ($e = e_0 + e_y y$) and the requirement that income equal expenditures ($e = y$) determines both income and expenditures. If spending increases, then income will too.**

And, of course, e is equal to this same value, since $e = y$. Let us assume, for instance, that the marginal propensity to spend is 0.5 and that the intercept of the expenditure equation is 1500. That is, $y = e = 1500 + 0.5y$. The levels of spending for various values of y, graphed in Figure 3.5, are:

y	$e = 1500 + 0.5y$	
1000	2000	$(e > y)$
2000	2500	$(e > y)$
3000	3000	$(e = y)$
4000	3500	$(e < y)$
5000	4000	$(e < y)$

Spending is equal to income at $y = 3000$.

The model is solved generally as shown in Figure 3.6, by the intersection of Equations 2.1 and 3.1. The values of e and y at Point A are the same as for the mathematical solution, Equation 3.5.

Multipliers

Now, what if there were an increase in autonomous spending, Δe_0? Spending would be higher at every level of income:

$$e = (e_0 + \Delta e_0) + e_y y$$

While the increase in spending will directly increase income by Δe_0, there will also be indirect effects since more income causes more spending, which gives even more income. What is the total of these direct and indirect effects?

In Figure 3.6, the expenditure function shifts upward, with the intercept rising by the amount Δe_0, putting the new solution at B. How much e and y increase can be arrived at as follows. Because the old value of income is

$$y = \frac{e_0}{1 - e_y} \tag{3.5}$$

and the new value is

$$y + \Delta y = \frac{e_0 + \Delta e_0}{1 - e_y}$$

the change in income is

$$\Delta y = \frac{\Delta e_0}{1 - e_y}. \tag{3.6}$$

If we divide through by Δe_0, we obtain the change in income per unit change in expenditure:

$$\frac{\Delta y}{\Delta e_0} = \frac{1}{1 - e_y}. \tag{3.7}$$

This Equation (3.7) is an example of a *multiplier*, giving the effects of a change in a predetermined variable on a variable whose value is determined by the model.

It is important to note that the other predetermined parameter (e_y) is held constant while all of the variables determined by the model (e and y) are allowed to move to their new solution values. Thus $\Delta y/\Delta e_0$ includes not only the direct effect that extra spending has on income, but also the fact that any increase in income raises spending and, so, further increases income.

This multiplier, Equation 3.7, shows the crucial role played by the marginal propensity to spend, e_y: If it is large, then the expenditures induced by income changes will magnify the consequences of shocks to the economy. As the following show, the larger the marginal propensity to spend, the greater the multiplier.

Marginal propensity to spend (e_y)	**Multiplier** $\left(\frac{\Delta y}{\Delta e_0} = \frac{1}{1-e_y}\right)$
0.0	1.0
0.1	1.1
0.3	1.4
0.5	2.0
0.7	3.3
0.9	10.0

Keynes reasoned that the "uncontrollable and disobedient psychology of the business world" often causes autonomous drops in expenditures (sudden declines in e_0), which are multiplied through the income-expenditure linkage into sharp recessions.[2] The same linkage will multiply any efforts by the government to soften recessions by increasing its spending. Thus, if the multiplier is 3.3, then a $10-billion increase in government spending will raise national income by $33 billion.

The foregoing has focused on the demand for goods and services (how much people want to buy) and ignored supply (how much producers want to sell). By assuming that people can buy as much as they please we are implicitly assuming there is an excess of goods and services. There *are* idle resources, which firms would employ if only there were sufficient demand for their output. When people do decide to buy more, producers happily expand production and employ more people. The extra wage and profit income further stimulate spending. Conversely, when people decide to spend less, producers cut back production and employ fewer people. Wage and profit income slump, further reducing spending. Thus output and employment vary with the demand for goods and services.

This multiplier analysis is probably the most enduring and influential legacy of Keynes. In analyzing policy or forecasting the future, economists nowadays almost invariably have a multiplier story somewhere in the backs of their heads; the income-expenditure interdependence is built into almost every empirical macroeconomic model used by businesses and government.

Kahn's dynamic interpretation

The income-expenditure equations above seem to give an immediate response of income to an autonomous change in spending. If spending goes up or down, then income changes, too, in accord with Equation 3.5, and that's it. But business cycles seem, in fact, to have a built-in momentum. When spending goes up or down, the effects ripple through the economy, and these ripples take a while to die out.

The actual logic behind the income-expenditure multiplier is that every expenditure gives someone income, of which they will spend part, thereby giving someone else income. Thus any expenditure gives rise to a whole series of expenditures, which, in cumulative total, may be very large. If, for example, the

IN THE NEWS

Pittsburgh's Recession Shows How Layoffs Ripple Through Economy

PITTSBURGH—It's called the ripple-effect theory, and in simple form, it goes like this: A basic industry falters and lays off workers. Suppliers soon succumb and lay off workers too. Next come service firms and more layoffs. Presto, a recession.

The theory works, judging by a visit to the state unemployment claims office in a blue-collar area on this city's South Side. Hundreds of steelworkers who in better times clocked in at Jones & Laughlin Steel Corp.'s big mill just a few blocks away now line up to file for unemployment benefits. J&L, a division of LTV Corp., has laid off about 23% of the mill's 3,200 employes.

And as the slump in steel continues, out-of-work steelworkers are being joined by thousands of other people formerly employed in steel equipment and repair shops, as well as in restaurants, stores and offices that depend on the steel business. "We're seeing unemployment ripple right through the job market," says John Lester, manager of the South Side unemployment claims office. "With so many steelworkers trying to get by on unemployment checks, local merchants aren't selling and have had to lay off people too." . . .

At the unemployment office on the South Side—an old, ethnic, working-class neighborhood two miles south of downtown—the traffic is heavy. Some 5,694 unemployment benefits claims are being processed here each week, a 20% increase over a year ago.

Phillip Slebrich, a steelworker at the J&L mill who has worked on and off for about five months during the last 12 months, reports here on Friday to sign for his unemployment check. . . . His unemployment benefits, he notes, total just $183 a week, less than half the $500 a week he averaged in wages at J&L. And since February, he hasn't received any Supplementary Unemployment Benefits. With so many steelworkers on extended layoffs, the supplemental fund has been depleted and only those with 20 years or more seniority are receiving the benefits; Mr. Slebrich, with only 13 years in the mills, doesn't qualify. . . .

Along with steelworkers, Mr. Slebrich has the company of numerous blue-collar workers from plants that supply the mills. Behind him in line one recent morning were a production worker from a chemical company that manufactures a chemical coating used in steelmaking, several workers from local steel equipment plants and several truck drivers who haul steel.

Most are very aware of the ripple pattern of recession layoffs. "Once the mills shut, the equipment plants shut too, the haulers stop hauling and it's that way down the line," says Regis Lutz Jr., an unemployed machinist . . . . [who] hasn't had any luck finding a new full-time job. "The only openings in the paper are out of town," he says, adding that he doesn't want to leave Pittsburgh or lose the 16 years of seniority he has at Mesta Machine or the equity he has in the house he bought six years ago. "To sell my house in this market and then need a new mortgage at today's high interest rates would mean losing everything I've built up," he says.

For Peggy Finnegan, a photography printer at the Premier Photo Shop, which is near the South Side, it is the first time she has been in an unemployment line in her 21 years of working.

"The last thing people on layoffs are going to spend money on is photos," says Mrs. Finnegan. Since January she has been working just two days a week, instead of full time.

The same sort of work reduction has hit Donna Kissell, a waitress. . . . Mrs. Kissell began noticing the effects of the recession at the restaurant in January: Instead of her usual 80 to 90 customers a day, she suddenly found that she was serving only 35 to 40. In February she was told to report to work just one day a week instead of her customary four days.

Mrs. Kissell, who is supporting herself and her daughter, is earning between $25 and $50 a week and collecting some $37 in partial unemployment benefits. It isn't enough to cover her bills. But, she says, she won't apply for welfare or accept "a $1.35 an hour nonunion waitressing job, which is what Reagan probably thinks I should do. I want a union job that at least offers minimum wage and medical benefits."

Some white-collar professional employes who find themselves at the South Side unemployment office are having a hard time accepting that they are unemployed. "I didn't expect to be laid off, and it's still somewhat of a shock to be here," says 26-year-old Mary Ann Smyth, who until last December was comptroller at a division of Koppers Co. She was one of 60 professional and clerical employes who since November have been laid off at the manufacturing, engineering and construction company. "Obviously they aren't doing well in the recession, and I was one of the youngest and newest," she says. . . . (Carol Hymowitz, *Wall Street Journal*, Mar. 16, 1982) government or private industry decides to buy coal from a depressed coal-mining area, the owners and miners will then buy more and better food, the farmers will then buy new clothes, and the tailors will then start going to the movies again. Not only the coal miners gain; the area's entire economy will prosper.

This logic has a built-in dynamics that will allow us to interpret the income-expenditure multiplier as the ultimate consequence of shocks rippling through an economy. Keynes himself did not describe a dynamic model in his *General Theory.* Indeed, he argued that the multiplier "holds good continuously, without time-lag, at all moments of time."[3] Keynes' argument could be interpreted as a belief that the farmers and tailors will immediately increase their spending in anticipation of the increased coal purchases. Alternatively, the money might pass so quickly from hand to hand that, for all practical purposes, there is no time lag.

Although there is no explicit dynamic model in Keynes' *General Theory,* he acknowledges in it a large intellectual debt to his colleague and former student Richard Kahn, who had introduced dynamic multiplier models several years before *The General Theory* was published.[4] In Kahn's formulation, each person spends a fraction, e_y, of every increase in income. If a dollar is spent on coal, the owners and miners receive a dollar of income. They spend e_y dollars on food, providing e_y dollars of income to the grocer. The grocer then spends a fraction, e_y, of these e_y dollars, which is e_y^2, on clothing. The tailor's income is then up by e_y^2, and he spends $e_y(e_y^2) = e_y^3$ on movies, and so on, round after round. The total amount of increased spending over n rounds is

$$1 + e_y + e_y^2 + \ldots + e_y^n = \frac{1 - e_y^{n+1}}{1 - e_y} \approx \frac{1}{1 - e_y} \tag{3.8}$$

if n is large and $0 \leq e_y < 1$, so that e_y^{n+1} approaches zero.*

The effects, depicted in Figure 3.7, gradually die out with time. The expression $1/(1 - e_y)$ measures the total of these effects initiated by a one-time purchase. In our coal example above, if $e_y = 0.5$, and \$1 is spent on the first round, then 50 cents is spent on the second round, 25 cents on the third, and so on. By the seventh round, spending is only 1.6 cents higher than before the initial \$1 was spent. The ripples have almost died out. Looking back after seven rounds, we would see that the sum of the extra spending was

$$\frac{\$1}{1 - e_y} = \frac{\$1}{1 - 0.5} \text{ or approximately } \$2.$$

However, the usual multiplier, $\Delta y/\Delta e_0$, discussed in the previous section, has a somewhat different interpretation. We want to analyze the effects of a sustained increase in spending rather than a one-time purchase. The government or private industry buys a dollar of coal every round, not just in the first. The area's economy is then permanently stimulated. How large is this permanent increase in income? This answer, too, is $1/(1 - e_y)$.

* The mathematics of Equation 3.8 can be verified by multiplying each side by $1 - e_y$.

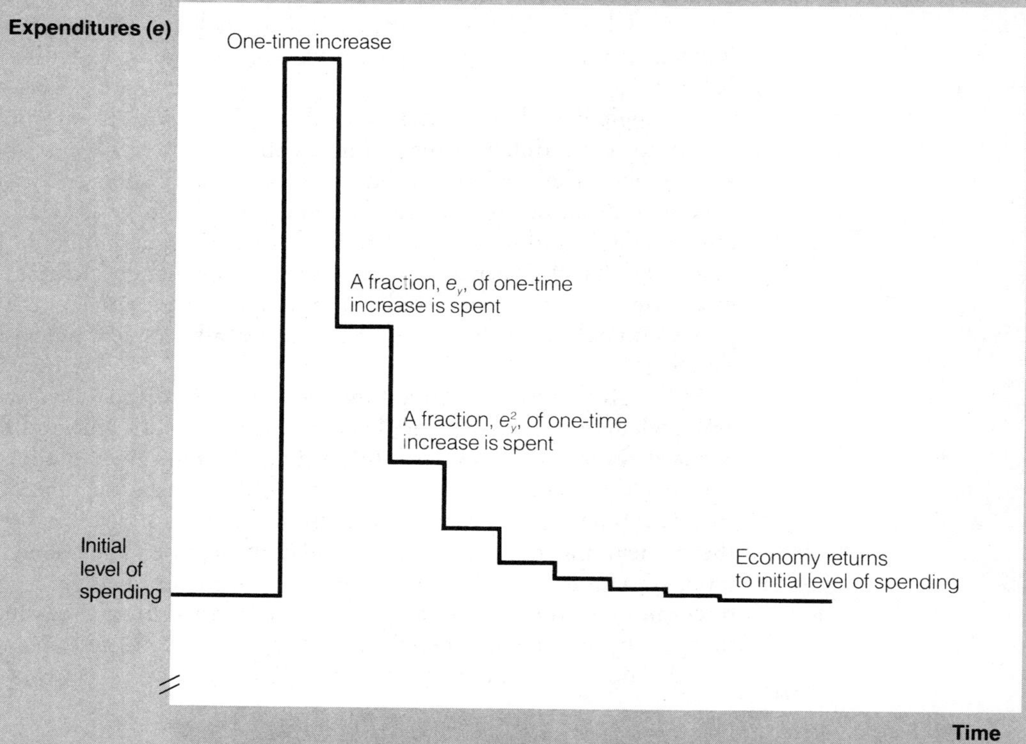

FIGURE 3.7 **ROUND-BY-ROUND EFFECTS OF A ONE-TIME INCREASE IN SPENDING. A one-time increase in spending has continuing effects on the economy as each expenditure provides income and thereby leads to further spending. The magnitude of this further spending gradually diminishes since only a fraction (e_y) of income is spent.**

In the first round, $1 of coal is purchased. In the second round, another $1 is spent on coal plus the miners' fraction, e_y, of the $1 income they received in the first round. So second-round spending is $\$1 + e_y$ higher than initially. In the third round, another $1 is spent on coal plus $\$e_y$ by the miners who received $1 in the second round, plus $\$e_y^2$ by the farmers who received $\$e_y$ in the second round. In sum, third-round spending is $1 + e_y + e_y^2$ higher than initially. And so it goes. Figure 3.8 chronicles the continuing increase in income. During round n, spending is

$$1 + e_y + e_y^2 + \ldots e_y^{n-1} = \frac{1 - e_y^n}{1 - e_y} \approx \frac{1}{1 - e_y}$$

higher than before the coal purchases began. This is the permanently higher level of spending resulting from a \$1 increase in coal purchases. In general, if the new purchases are Δe_0, then the eventual increase in income is

$$\Delta y = \frac{\Delta e_0}{1 - e_y}$$

corresponding to the multiplier in Equations 3.6 and 3.7. Thus one way of interpreting this multiplier is that it represents what Kahn called "the final position of equilibrium when everything has settled down."[5]

Accommodating this interpretation, the income-expenditure model encompasses a period—perhaps a quarter or full year—such that the internal round-by-round dynamics have had sufficient time to work themselves out. The multiplier $\Delta y/\Delta e_0 = 1/(1 - e_y)$ tells us the new sustained level of income that prevails after Kahn's dynamics are largely completed.

It is important to emphasize that this is not a market equilibrium in the sense that demand is equal to supply. If it were, then businesses would already be selling all they want to produce and everyone who wants a job would already have one. If this were a market equilibrium, then additional output would not

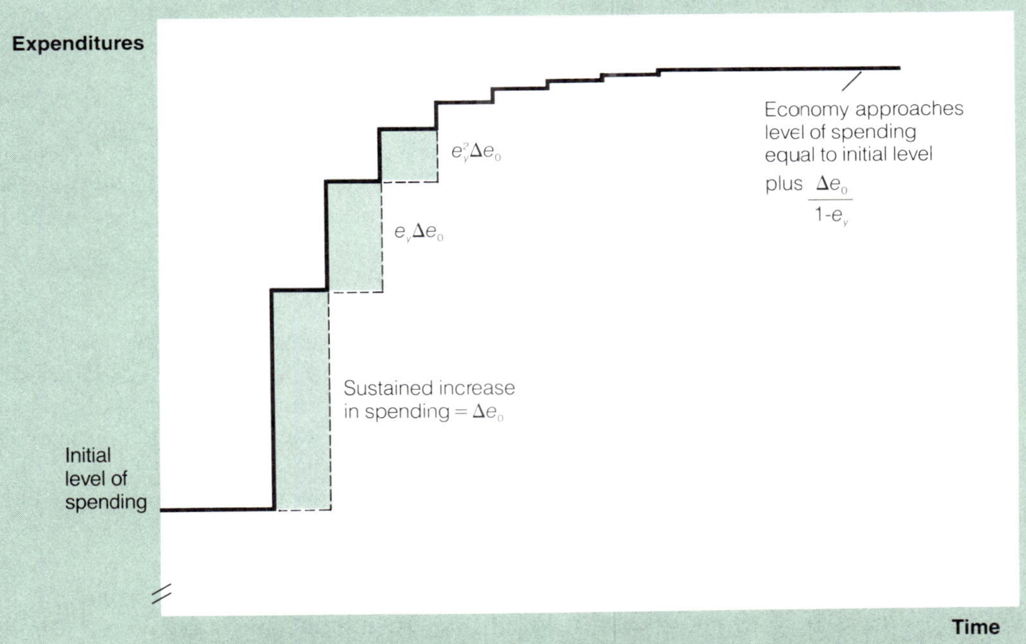

FIGURE 3.8 **ROUND-BY-ROUND EFFECTS OF A SUSTAINED INCREASE IN SPENDING.** **A sustained increase in spending causes a permanent rise in income. The effects gradually build up as each expenditure raises income and then encourages more spending. Eventually, the permanent increase in income reaches $\frac{\Delta e_0}{(1 - e_y)}$.**

be forthcoming as demand increases. The full utilization of factories and the full employment of workers would prevent output from expanding with demand. Instead, this is a market-disequilibrium model in which underutilized factories and unemployed workers are happy to find buyers. Kahn's solution for income, although not a market equilibrium, may be a *dynamic equilibrium* in that, once equilibrium is reached, income has no inherent tendency to continue changing. (An explicit dynamic model embodying Kahn's income-expenditure interaction is described in the appendix to this chapter.) To reinforce this distinction between market equilibrium and dynamic equilibrium, we now discuss another dynamic model.

Inventory dynamics

One possible explanation of an economy's dynamics focuses on the lag between spending and production. As we saw in Chapter 2, the national income accounts are designed to measure production, and unintended inventory accumulation is used to make sales and income equal to these production data. For a moment, think of e as "planned" expenditures, that depend on current income y:

$$e = e_0 + e_y y. \tag{3.9}$$

These planned expenditures encompass households, government, and businesses, and include the planned accumulation of inventories (to use in production, to display to customers, or just to stockpile). In order to make the sales and income data equal to current output, y, unplanned inventory investment, u, is used to take up the slack between output and planned spending:

$$u = y - e. \tag{3.10}$$

For there to be a dynamic equilibrium, there can be no unintended inventory accumulation. If there are undesired fluctuations in inventories, businesses will adjust their production levels accordingly. Production levels can be constant only if firms have the inventories they want. The substitution of $u = 0$ in Equations (3.9) and (3.10) gives the dynamic equilibrium (y^*) at

$$y^* = \frac{e_0}{1 - e_y}$$

No surprise! It is the same value of income that we keep coming back to, differing only in the explanation of the economy's dynamic behavior. The economic logic of these dynamics can be seen in Figure 3.9. When production is at A, planned spending falls short of output, and the difference is unplanned inventory accumulation (unintentional stockpiling of unsold goods). Firms will naturally try to reduce this unwanted accumulation by cutting back production. If, on the other hand, production is at point B, then output falls short of planned spending, which can be met only by an unplanned depletion of inventories, firms selling their demonstration and display goods to meet the robust demand. In this situation, businesses will naturally increase production.

IN THE NEWS

Wherever We Go, Consumers Will Lead Us

This year there have been many comments that we are in the midst of a consumer-led recovery. Of course we are. Consumption accounts for close to two-thirds of the gross national product, and we would have a rough time getting any sort of recovery started without some help from consumers.

Sooner or later, businessmen start helping out as consumer spending, current and prospective, points to a need for larger inventories and increased plant capacity. The consumers, in short, make the whole thing go.

But what makes the consumer go? Albert E. Sindlinger of Media, Pa., who polls consumers continually by telephone, reports that the terrorist bombing in Beirut and the U.S. invasion of Grenada brought a strong surge in consumer confidence. If nothing else, that illustrates the difficulty that businessmen have in deciding just what consumers are up to.

When the nation gets into some kind of serious trouble and its leaders react strongly to the development, the public seems to feel a lot better. For a moment or two, at any rate, Americans get the idea that someone really is minding the store in Washington. The moment usually passes, but for a while it is a nice feeling.

Presumably the U.S. will not go on invading one little Caribbean nation after another to keep consumers happy. Sooner or later the facts of economic life will be more decisive.

Is there enough zip left in the consumer to keep spending growing strongly through 1984? Is there enough zip to encourage businessmen to build up stocks and to put up new factories and offices to undergird the recovery?

Maybe not.

The consensus forecast is still relatively optimistic. The two score analysts polled every month by Blue Chip Economic Indicators, a Sedona, Ariz., newsletter, on the average think that the inflation-adjusted GNP will rise 5.1% next year, substantially better than the 3.3% gain expected for all of 1983. But some suggestion of the major worry is in the forecast that the consumer price index will rise 5% in 1984, compared with 3.4% this year. . . . .

Edward Yardeni, Prudential-Bache Securities economist, notes that during June, July and August consumer credit outstanding rose at an average monthly rate of $4.2 billion, compared with an average monthly increase of $2.2 billion in the first five months of the year. The Survey Research Center reported that in the third quarter, 27% of all families were not reluctant to incur new debt, more than twice the 12% reported a year earlier.

Consumers also are sharply increasing their home-mortgage debt—at high and often at adjustable interest rates.

If a consumer feels good about the economy and himself, he is quite likely to go out and spend. How he feels right now, however, may have nothing at all to do with his spending six months from now.

Over a period of six months, our government is quite capable of converting the economy into a shambles; it has demonstrated such ability in the all-too-recent past. If and when this happens again, the consumers, no matter how bubbly they had seemed six months earlier, are likely to start retrenching.

When they retrench, they can do so with a vengeance. They not only can stop spending current income but they can stop drawing on their savings. They can stop going into debt. The leverage that can speed up a boom can, in reverse, speed up a downturn.

It would be a consumer-led downturn, too. So it behooves us all to pay attention to what those consumers are doing right now. What they say they'll be doing six months from now should be viewed with interest—and skepticism. (Lindley H. Clark, Jr., *The Wall Street Journal,* Nov. 8, 1983)

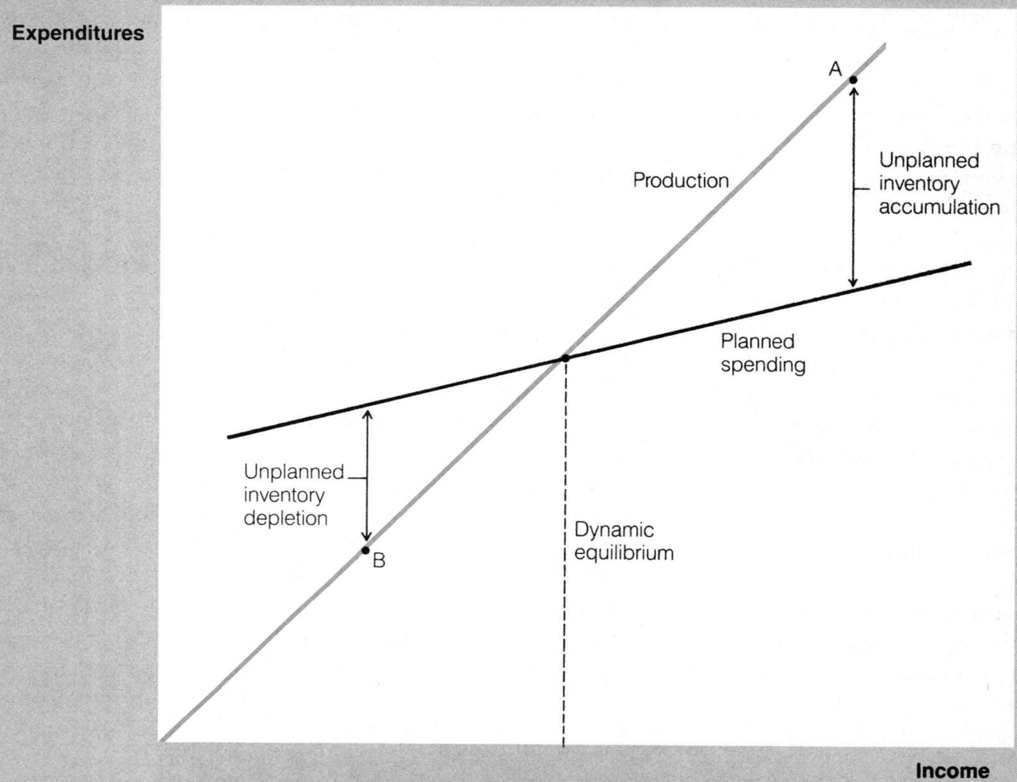

FIGURE 3.9 DYNAMICS WITH UNPLANNED INVENTORIES. **At Point A planned spending falls short of production, and the unsold goods become an unplanned addition to business inventories. At Point B planned spending exceeds production, and businesses must deplete their inventories to satisfy this spending.**

Thus, production will fall if it is at A and rise if it is at B. The dynamic equilibrium indicated in the figure is the only point at which production satisfies expenditures, with no unplanned inventory accumulation or depletion. In this interpretation, **the income-expenditure model describes a dynamic equilibrium. The adjustment of output in response to unplanned inventory fluctuations explains the economy's movement toward dynamic equilibrium.**

Again, it must be emphasized that this dynamic equilibrium need not be a market equilibrium. It is a dynamic equilibrium in the sense that businesses are producing as much as people want to buy. There are, consequently, no unwanted inventory fluctuations. But the output is not necessarily the one that firms would like; they may well wish that spending was at a higher level. They would like to sell more, but they produce only as much as people will buy.

The income-expenditure model assumes that output responds to demand fully. It is implicit that there are unemployed workers and idle factories, which would produce more if only there were demand for their production. The multiplier

$$\frac{\Delta y}{\Delta e_0} = \frac{1}{1 - e_y}$$

tells how, through the income-expenditure interaction, autonomous changes in spending lead to even larger fluctuations in output. As we have said, an increase in spending provides more income and, so, further stimulates spending, while a drop in spending reduces income and, so, further depresses spending. The multiplier shows the magnitudes of these effects, while dynamic models show how these multipliers may take a while to work themselves out. In Kahn's dynamics, it takes time for spending to adapt to income; in the inventory model, it takes time for output to adapt to spending.

TAXATION AND AUTOMATIC STABILIZATION

We will now enrich the income-expenditure model by incorporating government spending *(g)* and net transfer payments *(t)* to the government (taxes minus interest payments, Social Security disbursements, and so on). The expanded model is:

$$y = e \tag{2.1}$$

$$e = c + i_0 + g_0 \tag{3.11}$$

$$c = c_0 + c_y (y - t) \qquad 0 < c_y < 1 \tag{3.12}$$

$$t = t_0 + t_y y \qquad 0 < t_y < 1 \tag{3.13}$$

As before, Equation 2.1 states that income is determined by expenditures. Equation 3.11 separates expenditures into consumption, c, investment, i_0, and government spending, g_0. (Investment and government spending are here assumed to be predetermined, and are consequently given *o* subscripts.) Equation 3.12 states that consumption spending is positively related to disposable income (income minus transfer payments to the government). Equation 3.13 states that these transfer payments are directly related to income, primarily because of taxes on income. I will consequently call parameter t_y the "tax rate," though we should remember that it includes other transfers as well.

Although the model determines values for *y, e, c,* and *t,* we will focus on income *(y).* The solution can be obtained by first substituting Equations 3.12 and 3.13 in 3.11, showing how aggregate spending depends on its components:

$$\begin{aligned} e &= c_0 + c_y(y - t_0 - t_y y) + i_0 + g_0 \\ &= [c_0 + i_0 + g_0 - c_y t_0] + [c_y(1 - t_y)]y. \\ &= e_0 + e_y y \end{aligned} \tag{3.14}$$

The first bracketed expression is the intercept e_0, and the second bracketed expression is the slope e_y of the expenditure equation. The combination of Equation 2.1 with 3.14 yields

$$y = \frac{e_0}{1 - e_y} = \frac{c_0 + i_0 + g_0 - c_y t_0}{1 - c_y(1 - t_y)}. \tag{3.15}$$

Equation 3.15 implies that an autonomous increase in consumption, investment, or government spending has the following multiplier affect on income:

$$\frac{\Delta y}{\Delta c_0} = \frac{\Delta y}{\Delta i_0} = \frac{\Delta y}{\Delta g_0} = \frac{1}{1 - c_y(1 - t_y)}. \tag{3.16}$$

Once we recognize that the marginal propensity to spend is $e_y = c_y(1 - t_y)$, these multipliers can be readily explained by Kahn's logic. In this particular model (Equations 3.11–3.13), both investment spending and government spending are predetermined. Only consumption spending responds to income changes. Out of a dollar of extra income, t_y is allocated to taxes and $1 - t_y$ is left for spending. Consumers spend a fraction, c_y, of this additional $1 - t_y$ in disposable income. Thus a dollar of extra income induces $c_y(1 - t_y)$ of extra spending. If the tax rate is $t_y = 0.3$, and the marginal propensity to spend disposable income is $c_y = 0.7$, then people keep 70 cents of every dollar they earn and spend 70% of this 70 cents, or 49 cents.

This marginal propensity to spend is the key parameter in Kahn's round-by-round scenario. Out of every dollar of income, $c_y\ (1 - t_y)$ is spent and, so, passed on as income to others. As explained in the earlier section, a dollar of additional spending eventually increases income by

$$1 + [c_y\ (1 - t_y)] + [c_y\ (1 - t_y)]^2 + \ldots.$$

which is equal to our new multiplier, Equation 3.16, as long as $c_y\ (1 - t_y)$ is less than 1. This Kahn interpretation explains why the multipliers for increases in consumption, in investment, and in government spending are all the same. It does not really matter who spends the first dollar that gets the ball rolling.

Automatic stabilizers

The Kahn interpretation also explains why multipliers are relatively small when the tax rate, t_y, is large. With a high tax rate, funds are siphoned off to the Treasury, and there is less disposable income to spend and, thereby, to increase the income of others. It can be seen from Equation 3.16 that the multipliers would be larger if t_y were zero. The following numerical examples for some non-zero tax rates show how the multipliers decline as the tax rate rises:

Tax rate t_y	**Multiplier $\Delta y/\Delta c_0 = 1/1 - c_y(1 - t_y)$ for $c_y = 0.7$**
0.0	3.33
0.1	2.70
0.2	2.27
0.3	1.96
0.4	1.72
0.5	1.54

The tax rate, t_y, is an *automatic stabilizer* in that it reduces the income changes caused by autonomous shifts in private or governmental spending. Consider, for instance, a \$10-billion increase in private investment spending. With a 30% tax rate, the people who receive this \$10 billion in additional income will have only \$7 billion left after taxes. Taxes restrain spending and thereby dampen the ripples from economic shocks.

Some of the more important automatic stabilizers are personal income taxes, unemployment compensation, Social Security taxes, corporate income taxes, and excise taxes. All of these tax and transfer rates are higher now than before World War II, and this heavy automatic stabilization is a large part of the reason why business cycles are not as severe as they used to be. In a 1962 study, Wilfred Lewis, Jr., concluded that automatic stabilizers had significantly "limited the duration as well as the severity of postwar contractions."[7] More recently, a macroeconomic model was used to compare multipliers for the two periods 1926–40 and 1951–65. Multipliers before World War II were nearly twice as large as after the war. For example, it was estimated that an autonomous \$1-billion decrease in spending would have reduced real GNP after three months by \$3.23 billion in the prewar period and by \$1.88 billion in the postwar period.[7]

The balanced-budget multiplier

The level of aggregate income is given by Equation 3.15. Note that a dollar of government spending has a larger impact on income than a dollar of government transfers:

$$\frac{\Delta y}{\Delta g_0} = \frac{1}{1 - c_y(1 - t_y)} \tag{3.17}$$

$$\frac{\Delta y}{\Delta t_0} = \frac{-c_y}{1 - c_y(1 - t_y)}. \tag{3.18}$$

If $c_y = 0.7$ and $t_y = 0.3$, then $\Delta y/\Delta g_0 = 1.96$, while $-\Delta y/\Delta t_0 = 1.37$. A dollar more of government spending raises income by \$1.96, while a dollar less in taxes raises income by only \$1.37.

This difference can be explained most easily by using Kahn's interpretation again. A dollar of government spending is, by definition, a dollar of spending that then passes from hand to hand. But a dollar of tax relief is just a transfer payment. There is no additional spending on goods and services until people spend some of their tax rebate. People will spend a fraction c_y, and it is this amount that then begins to be passed from hand to hand. Thus, the multiplier for taxes in Equation (3.18) is only a fraction (c_y) of the multiplier for government spending in Equation (3.17).

An important implication of these unequal multipliers is that a balanced increase in government spending and in taxes is not neutral in its effect on national income. If a dollar of government spending stimulates the economy more than a dollar of additional tax revenue depresses the economy, then the combination of a dollar of spending plus a dollar of taxes is, on balance, expansionary. This net expansionary effect of a balanced increase in government spending and taxes is called the *balanced-budget multiplier.*

To measure the balanced-budget multiplier, we need to combine the government spending and tax multipliers, Equations (3.17) and (3.18). But we must be sure to calculate the change in total tax revenue, $t = t_0 + t_y y$, not just the change in the intercept, t_0. Taxes automatically rise with income, and we need to ensure that government spending and tax revenue do increase equally. If we increase t_0, with t_y constant, then the total change in tax revenue is

$$\Delta t = \Delta t_0 + t_y \, \Delta y. \tag{3.19}$$

For a balanced increase in spending and tax revenue, we must choose Δt_0 and Δg_0 so that $\Delta t = \Delta g_0$. Therefore, we need

$$\Delta t_0 = \Delta g_0 - t_y \, \Delta y. \tag{3.20}$$

This balanced-budget rule, Equation (3.20), states that autonomous taxes, t_0, must be increased by as much as government spending, less any tax revenue generated by a resulting stronger economy. Now, using the spending multiplier (Equation 3.17), the tax multiplier (Equation 3.18), the tax rule (Equation 3.20), and a bit of algebra,* the net balanced-budget effect on the economy turns out to be surprisingly simple:

$$\Delta y = \Delta g_0 \tag{3.21}$$

* The change in income is $\Delta y = \left(\frac{\Delta y}{\Delta g_0}\right) \Delta g_0 + \left(\frac{\Delta y}{\Delta t_0}\right) \Delta t_0 = \left(\frac{1}{1 - c_y(1 - t_y)}\right) \Delta g_0 + \frac{-c_y}{1 - c_y(1 - t_y)} (\Delta g_0 - t_y \Delta y)$. Multiplying by $1 - c_y(1 - t_y)$ gives $(1 - c_y(1 - t_y)) \Delta y = (1 - c_y) \Delta g_0 + c_y t_y \Delta y$, and subtracting $c_y t_y \Delta y$, $(1 - c_y) \Delta y = (1 - c_y) \Delta g_0$. We need only divide this by $(1 - c_y)$ to obtain Equation 3.21: $\Delta y = \Delta g_0$.

This Equation (3.21) is the remarkable balanced-budget multiplier: A dollar increase in government spending, matched by a dollar in additional tax revenue, increases aggregate income by a dollar.* This is explainable as follows. The government collects an extra dollar in taxes and spends that dollar on goods and services. Since income and taxes are both a dollar higher, disposable income is unchanged. Consumption is thus unchanged, while aggregate income has increased by the dollar that government spent. It will, of course, be a hollow increase if the government does not really spend the dollar on useful goods and services, but instead squanders it on an artificial make-work project, such as digging holes and then filling them back up.

The full-employment surplus

A balanced government budget is generally favored by the public—and by many politicians seeking their votes. American presidents from Franklin Roosevelt to Ronald Reagan have promised balanced budgets during their campaigns and then accepted budget deficits during their presidencies. From the outside, the government's budget deficit is an easy target for criticism that predictably brings applause. But from the inside, presidents generally agree with the economics profession that the aesthetic benefits of a balanced budget are not worth what it would often cost in higher unemployment and lost output. Keynes had particularly biting words for those who considered a balanced budget more important than the employment of idle resources. In *The General Theory,* he wrote:

> It is curious how common sense, wriggling for an escape from absurd conclusions, has been apt to reach a preference for *wholly* "wasteful" forms of loan expenditure rather than *partly* wasteful forms, which, because they are not wholly wasteful, tend to be judged on strict "business" principles. For example, . . . the form of digging holes in the ground known as gold-mining, which not only adds nothing whatever to the real wealth of the world but involves the disutility of labour, is the most acceptable of all solutions [to unemployment].
>
> If the Treasury were to fill old bottles with bank-notes, bury them at suitable depths in disused coalmines which are then filled up to the surface with town rubbish, and leave it to private enterprise on well-tried principles of *laissez-faire* to dig up the notes again (the right to do so being obtained, of course, by tendering for leases of the note-bearing territory), there need be no more unemployment and, with the help of the repercussions, the real income of the community, and its capital wealth also, would probably become a good deal greater than it actually is. It would, indeed, be more sensible to build houses and the like; but if there are political and practical difficulties in the way of this, the above would be better than nothing. . . .
>
> Ancient Egypt was doubly fortunate, and doubtless owed to this its fabled wealth, in that it possessed *two* activities, namely, pyramid-building as well as the search for the precious metals, the fruits of which, since they could not serve the needs of man by being consumed, did not stale with abundance. The Middle Ages built cathedrals and sang dirges. Two pyramids, two masses for the dead, are twice as good as one; but not so two railways from London to York. Thus we are so sensible, have schooled

* The same answer is obtained if t_y rather than t_0 is adjusted so as to yield an extra dollar of tax revenue (see Exercise 10). The balanced-budget multiplier is generally less than 1 if, as in later chapters, induced changes in prices and interest rates are taken into account.

ourselves to so close a semblance of prudent financiers, taking careful thought before we add to the "financial" burdens of posterity by building them houses to live in, that we have no such easy escape from the sufferings of unemployment.[8]

Economists, businesspersons, and policy makers nowadays generally accept Keynes' argument that government policies should be judged by their real effects on employment, output, and so on rather than by their financial effects on some accountant's balance sheet.

A somewhat different argument, which we will return to in later chapters, is whether the government should rely entirely on automatic stabilization or should step in with aggressive discretionary policies when these seem necessary. As World War II ended, there was a vigorous debate within universities, businesses, and government about the government's proper role in helping to keep the economy from sliding back into the Depression that had preceded the war. One outcome of this debate was the Employment Act of 1946, which declared that it is the "responsibility of the Federal Government to . . . promote maximum employment, production, and purchasing power." A second important event was that the Committee for Economic Development (CED), a group of prominent business executives, publicly accepted the idea that a continually balanced federal budget is not an overriding policy objective. When the economy slumps, tax revenues will decline and budget deficits will grow. If the government mechanically cuts spending and increases taxes to try to balance the budget, they will only worsen the recession.

While the CED accepted the idea of government economic stabilization, they also believed that automatic stabilization would suffice.[9] They argued that the government should choose its expenditures on the basis of social needs, and then set tax rates so as to yield a budget surplus during economic booms. If there was, instead, a recession, then tax revenue would fall with economic activity and the government's budget would be in deficit. This pattern of budget surpluses (withdrawing funds) during booms and budget deficits (injecting funds) during recessions would automatically cushion the economy. The CED hoped that the surpluses and deficits would roughly balance over the course of many business cycles.

It is true, as we have seen, that substantial, fixed tax rates do stabilize the economy in the sense of automatically reducing the multiplier effects of spending shifts. And fixed tax rates are better than a policy of increasing tax rates during recessions in order to balance the budget. But the many business cycles our economy has been through show that fixed tax rates do not eliminate the possibility of severe booms or busts. In addition, the Committee's proposal gives credence to the naive view that the thrust of government stabilization policy can be gauged simply by the size of the budget surplus or deficit.

A budget deficit is sometimes interpreted as evidence that the government is trying to stimulate the economy by pumping funds into circulation. If that is the case, then a budget surplus signifies the reverse—that the government is trying to cool the economy by drawing funds out of circulation. The problem with this view is that budget surpluses and deficits depend not only on government spending and tax policies but also on the state of the economy. Government budgets do affect the economy, but they are also affected by the economy. A large budget deficit may occur not because the government has shifted to more expansionary policies, but rather because the economy is slumping and tax revenues are automatically falling. This is what Walter Heller called a distinction "between 'deficits of weakness' that arise out of backing into a recession and 'deficits of strength' that arise out of measures to provide fiscal thrust to a lagging economy."[10]

To accurately gauge whether the government has shifted to a more expansionary policy, a less expansionary policy, or has not really changed the thrust of its policy at all, we need to distinguish between the budget effects of policy changes and the budget effects of changes in the economy. This distinction would be simple if policies seldom varied. If government spending went up, we would duly note a more expansionary policy. If tax rates went up, we would record a more contractionary policy. But what if government spending goes up, Social Security payments go down, and tax rates go up—all at the same time? What's the bottom line?

If automatic stabilizers vary with national income, then discretionary and automatic policies can be separated by estimating budget deficits at a constant benchmark level of income. With this in mind, in the early 1960s, the Council of Economic Advisers began estimating the *full-employment surplus*

$$t_0 + t_y y_f - g_0 \tag{3.22}$$

measuring what the budget surplus would be if the economy were producing full-employment output (y_f), which they equated with the realization of potential output.* Over the years, the full-employment surplus has also been called the "high-employment surplus" and the "structural surplus."

Presidents often embrace the full-employment surplus because it defuses vocal advocates of "fiscal responsibility." The President can plausibly argue that the budget would be balanced, or even in surplus, if the economy were only at full employment. The actual deficit is then blamed on the weakness of the economy rather than fiscal sins. For economists, the full-employment surplus is simply a way of gauging the overall thrust of government spending and tax policies. There is no assumption or recommendation that the full-employment surplus should be zero or any particular positive or negative number. The *change* in the full-employment surplus simply tells us whether the government's spending and tax policy is becoming more or less expansionary.

* An even more sophisticated theoretical analysis would take into account our earlier observation that tax cuts and spending increases are not equally expansionary. A dollar of tax relief stimulates the economy by only a fraction, c_y, of the amount that a dollar of government spending does. We should take these unequal effects into account when we construct a gauge of economic stimulus. This logic suggests weighting government dollars by their multipliers. In this spirit, the adjusted full-employment surplus can be stated as $c_y(t_0 + t_y y_f) - g_0$. This particular expression can be more formally justified as follows. Equation 3.17 tells us that, at full employment, autonomous private spending must equal $c_0 + i_0 = y_f - c_y y_f + [c_y(t_0 + t_y y_f) - g_0]$. For every extra dollar of the bracketed expression, autonomous private spending must be a dollar higher to reach full employment. Thus the bracketed expression, which is the adjusted full-employment surplus, correctly measures the overall thrust of government spending and tax policies.

FIGURE 3.10 THE FULL-EMPLOYMENT SURPLUS, 1955–82. **The full-employment surplus is an estimate of the government's budget were the economy at full employment. These data are the Commerce Department's estimates of the federal government's budget surplus at a 4.9% unemployment rate. The full-employment surplus is useful for identifying the extent to which government deficits can be attributed to spending and tax policy, and to a weak economy.**

Figure 3.10 compares the actual surplus with the full-employment surplus. The figure shows that there have been several periods when the observed budget position gave a misleading picture of government stabilization policy. The budget deficits in the late 1950s and early 1960s were interpreted by some people as evidence of fiscal irresponsibility. They opposed any efforts to increase spending or cut taxes to stimulate the economy. The Kennedy Council of Economic Advisers argued that these deficits were due to the weakness of the economy, not to overly aggressive fiscal policies by the Eisenhower administration. The full-employment surpluses were, in fact, very substantial, indicating a rather conservative and, if anything, contractionary policy.

Figure 3.10 also shows how the full-employment surplus recorded a significant shift to expansionary spending and tax policies during the years 1964–66 that would have gone undetected had we looked only at the actual budget surplus. In 1971, 1975–76, and 1980–82, a weak economy again caused a substantial divergence between the actual and full-employment surpluses.

In 1982, President Reagan ran into the now familiar problem of a large budget deficit caused, not by overly expansionary policies, but by a weak economy. For several months, government policy was virtually paralyzed as policymakers argued about the appropriate reaction to large anticipated deficits. (In early 1982, the deficit forecasts ranged from roughly $100 billion to $200 billion.) Many advisers counseled higher taxes and lower government spending to reduce the budget deficit. But the economy was already in a stiff recession in 1982, with an employment rate of about 10%. Higher taxes and lower spending would have pushed the economy in the wrong direction—towards a devastating depression.

The government's budget deficits were not really the problem; they were more a symptom of the problem, which was a terribly weak economy. If the unemployment rate had been, say, 4% lower, then, Okun's Law tells us, real GNP would have been perhaps 10% higher. In 1982, 10% more GNP would have come to about \$300 billion. With, say, a 30% marginal tax rate, \$300 billion in additional output would have generated \$90 billion more in tax revenue. Policymakers, therefore, should have focused their attention on ways to end the recession. A strong economy would have produced hundreds of billions of dollars in extra output and income, enough to take the strain off a great many household, business, and governmental budgets.

INVESTMENT AND SAVINGS

The income-expenditure story can also be told in terms of investment and saving. The requirement that income equal expenditures can be equivalently phrased as a requirement that investment equal saving. The income-equals-expenditures equation, $y = c + i + g$, can be rearranged as

$$i = (y - t - c) + (t - g) = s \tag{3.23}$$

in which the term $y - t - c$ is private saving—income less taxes and consumption spending; the term $t - g$ is government saving—government income (that is, taxes) less expenditures; and s is total saving. Thus, Equation 3.23 states that, if income equals expenditure, investment must equal total private and governmental saving.*

The investment-equals-savings condition, like the income-equals-expenditure condition, can be interpreted as either *ex post* or *ex ante.* Actual investment and actual saving must be equal, and desired investment and desired saving will also be equal if market equilibrium prevails. If there is, instead, disequilibrium, with actual output demand determined, then income is determined by expenditures and saving is determined by investment.

To analyze investment and saving more closely we will use a simple round-number model. Assume that $c_0 = 10$; $c_y = 2/3$; $i_0 = 10$; $g_0 = 20$; $t_0 = -7.5$; and $t_y = 0.25$. Substituting these numbers in Equation 3.16 gives:

$$y = \frac{10 + 10 + 20 - (2/3)(-7.5)}{1 - (2/3)(1 - 0.25)} = \frac{45}{0.5} = 90$$

The multiplier is 2, and income is 90.

This income level can be graphically determined by the income-equals-expenditures or the investment-equals-saving approaches. The former has already

* Equation 3.23 is sometimes rearranged to show that "injections" (investment plus government spending) must be offset by "leakages" (private saving plus taxes): $i + g = s_g + t$. This arrangement can help our understanding of Kahn's dynamic story.

been shown in Figure 3.6, in which the two curves are $e = y$ (expenditures equal income), and $e = e_0 + e_y y$ (expenditures depend on income). Here $e = c + i + g = (c_0 + i_0 + g_0 - c_y t_0) + c_y(1 - t_y)\ y = 45 + 0.5\ y$. Using the specific equations in Figure 3.11 gives $y = 90$. Alternatively, we can equate investment and saving; here, investment is predetermined, while saving depends on income:*

$$i = 10$$
$$s = -35 + 0.5\ y.$$

These two curves are also graphed in Figure 3.11 and again yield $y = 90$; both approaches give the same answer.

Full employment

The investment-equals-saving approach focuses attention on the fact, emphasized by Keynes, that investment and saving decisions are made by different agents and yet, *ex post*, must somehow be reconciled. What mechanism assures that the amount households and government save does turn out to equal the amount businesses invest? Keynes argued that typically it is *income* that adjusts to equate income and expenditure (and to equate investment and saving).

Consider Figure 3.11 again and now assume that full-employment output is equal to 100. The upper graph in Figure 3.11 states that actual income does not equal 100 because, at $y = 100$, people would want to spend only 95. Income cannot equal 100 if people don't spend 100. Keynes believed that income would instead be at 90, where expenditures do equal income. (With a multiplier of 2, a shortfall of 5 in expenditures causes a shortfall of 10 in income.) Thus it is income that adjusts to equate expenditures and income.

The same story, with a different storyteller, is told in the lower graph in Figure 3.11; at full-employment income of 100, saving would exceed investment. Investment demand is insufficient to absorb the saving that would be forthcoming at full employment. So, income is instead below the full-employment level. At lower income levels households and government save less. At $y = 90$, their saving is consistent with the amount businesses wish to invest; thus it is income that adjusts to equate investment and saving.

Keynes' reasoning was a radical departure from classical principles. Classical, preKeynesian, economists believed that investment would always equal saving at the full-employment level of income. This discrepancy between Keynes and the classicists spawned a great deal of rather unproductive debate about whether investment does or does not always equal saving. Economists now realize that the key to this disagreement is the question of whether markets are in equilibrium or in disequilibrium or, equivalently, how it is that saving comes to equal investment. If the commodity market has an excess supply, then agents do not want to buy all of the output that would be produced at full employment, and businesses may well produce only as much as they can sell. Wage and profit income will then be below full-employment levels. Aggregate income will be at that less-than-full-employment level where expenditures do equal income. This is the Keynesian story told in Figure 3.11.

* Equation 3.23 implies that private saving is $(y - t) - (c_0 + c_y(y - t)) = -c_0 + (1 - c_y)(y - t_0 - t_y y) = -7.5 + 0.25y$, and government saving is $t - g = t_0 + t_y y - g_0 = -27.5 + 0.25y$.

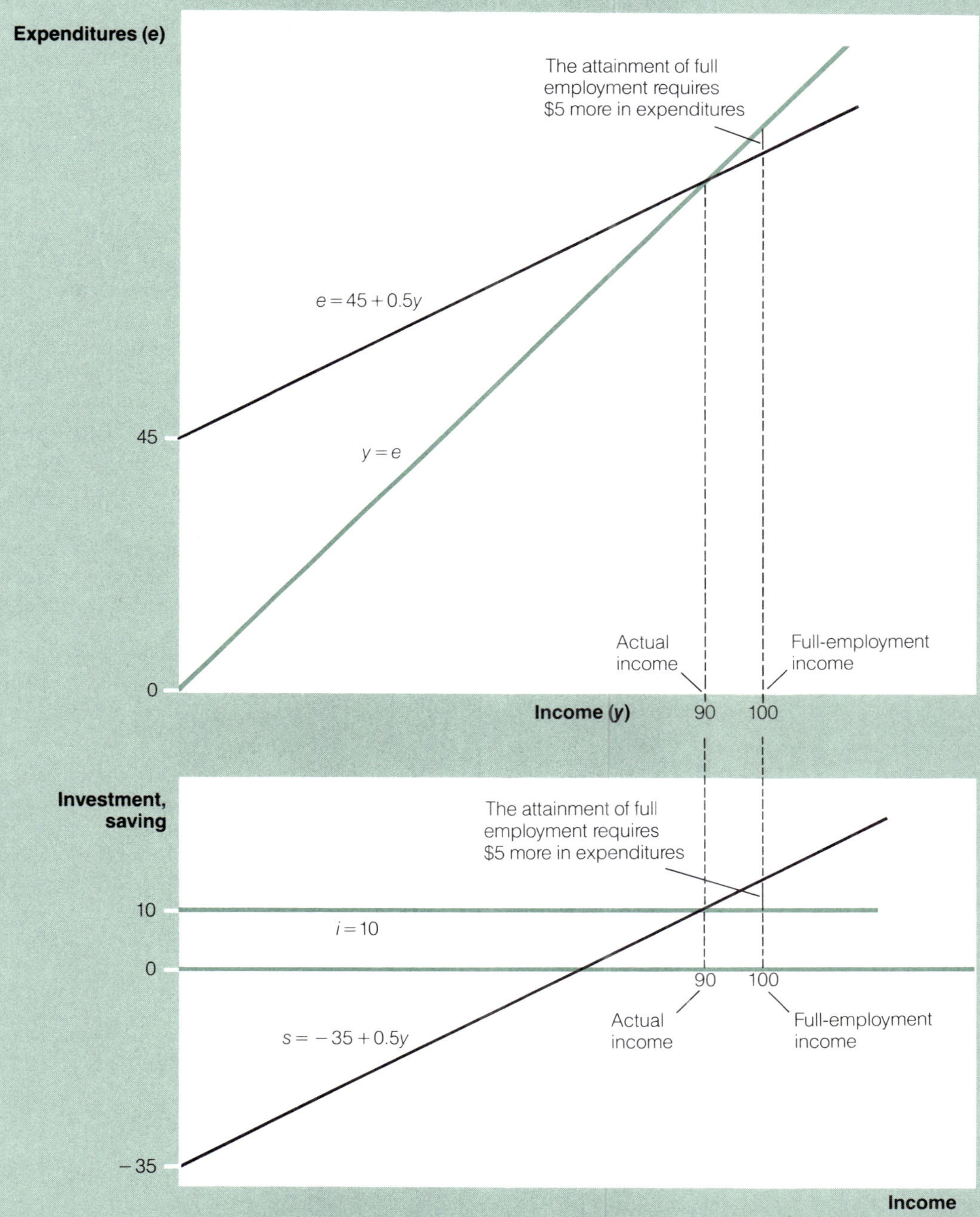

FIGURE 3.11 GRAPHIC DETERMINATION OF INCOME **by income-equals-expenditures or, equivalently, by investment-equals-savings. The requirement that income equal expenditures can be restated as a requirement that investment equal saving. Either approach determines the same level of income, here $y = 90$. And either approach implies that spending must increase by 5 to reach full-employment income, $y = 100$.**

If markets are, instead, always in equilibrium, then wages, prices, and interest rates must all adjust so that *ex ante* demands and supplies are equal. There will be full employment, since the equality of labor demand and supply means that everyone who wants a job has one. Producers will, of course, also be able to sell all of the goods and services that they want to sell. In Figure 3.11, wages, prices, and interest rates must somehow adjust to equate desired expenditures and desired income. It is only at the full-employment level that desired spending and income are equal.

In Keynes' analysis, if there are inadequate expenditures for full-employment income, then income will fall short of the full-employment level. In classical analyses, wages, prices, and interest rates will adjust to keep expenditures at the full-employment level.

If full employment prevails, then output is fundamentally determined by a nation's resources—its land, buildings, equipment, and people. This is why classical economists focused their attention on the amount of resources available to a nation. If, however, demand is inadequate and full employment is not attained, then a significant part of a nation's resources may go unused. Thus Keynes focused his attention on the amount people want to spend, rather than the amount that would be produced at full employment.

The model discussed in this chapter provides a preview of macroeconomics, but it does not formally analyze labor, commodity, or financial markets. In the next chapter, we begin analysis of a richer macroeconomic model, which does include these elements.

APPENDIX: ROBERTSON'S DYNAMIC MODEL

D. H. Robertson proposed a dynamic model that formally combines the income-expenditure multiplier with Kahn's dynamic equilibrium scenario.[11] Robertson, like Kahn, divided time into rounds representing how long, on average, it takes income to pass from hand to hand. These periods are thus chosen so that people receive income in one and spend it in the next. Expenditures in the current period, t, are denoted by $e[t]$, while income in the previous period, $t-1$, is written at $y[t-1]$. So,

$$e[t] = e_0 + e_y\, y[t-1] \tag{1}$$

This expenditure formulation is analogous to Equation 3.1, with the labels t and $t-1$ introduced to keep track of the timing. Current expenditures, $e[t]$, depend on the income $y[t-1]$ received in the previous period.

Each period's income is determined by that period's expenditures:

$$y[t] = e[t]. \tag{2}$$

Thus, people receive income when others spend, but they do not spend out of this income immediately. So, current income is determined by current expenditures, which are influenced by the previous period's income. This dynamic chain, following Kahn's logic, implies that current income is influenced by the previous period's income. The actual relationship can be found by substituting Equation 1 in Equation 2:

$$y[t] = e_0 + e_y y[t-1] \tag{3}$$

In a dynamic equilibrium, the model's variables are constant period after period. It again must be stressed that dynamic and market equilibrium are two very different concepts. Dynamic equilibrium is concerned with the course of the economy, while market equilibrium is the equality of *ex ante* demands and supplies. Market equilibrium and dynamic equilibrium do not automatically imply one another.

In Robertson's model, dynamic equilibrium occurs at a value of income, y^*, such that $y[t] = y[t-1]$, so that income is constant. The substitution of this condition $y[t] = y[t-1]$ in Equation 3 gives $y^* = e_0 + e_y y^*$, so that dynamic equilibrium income is

$$y^* = \frac{e_0}{1 - e_y}. \tag{4}$$

This dynamic equilibrium income is the same as that determined by the income-expenditure model of Equation 3.5. In Robertson's formulation, the solution of the income-expenditure model is interpreted as dynamic equilibrium, while Kahn's model provides the dynamics to this equilibrium.

As an example, assume that $e_0 = 100$ and $e_y = 0.5$. Equation 4 gives the dynamic equilibrium (y^*) at 200. Assume that the economy is, in fact, in this dynamic equilibrium in time period $t = 0$, so that $y[0] = 200$. What if there is an autonomous increase in spending that raises e_0 from 100 to 110? Equation 4 tells us that the new dynamic equilibrium is at

$$y^* = \frac{110}{1 - 0.5} = 220,$$

while Equation 3 traces out the path to this new equilibrium. At the time of the increase in e_0, say at $t = 1$, $y[0]$ is fixed at 200, since the past period is history and cannot be altered. So, substituting in Equation 3 gives $y[1] = 110 + 0.5(200) = 210$. The next period's income, $y[2]$, will be influenced by the previous period's income, $y[1] = 210$. Specifically, $y[2] = 110 + 0.5(210) = 215$. And so it goes, with income gradually approaching the new dynamic equilibrium, $y^* = 220$, as follows.

Time period(t)	**Income** $y[t]$	
0	200	
1	210.0	$= 110 + 0.5(200)$
2	215.0	$= 110 + 0.5(210)$
3	217.5	$= 110 + 0.5(215)$
4	218.75	(and so on, the calculation continuing uniformly)
5	219.30	
6	219.69	
7	219.84	
8	219.92	
9	219.96	
10	219.99	

We can embellish our earlier income-expenditure graph in Figure 3.6 to show this movement between equilibria; the figure in this appendix gives the dynamics. The economy is always on the income-equals-expenditures line, $y[t] = e[t]$, and the expenditure function, $e[t] = e_0 + e_y y[t-1]$, gives current expenditures as a function of the previous period's income. Dynamic equilibrium, with $y[t] = y[t-1]$, is at the intersection of these two lines.

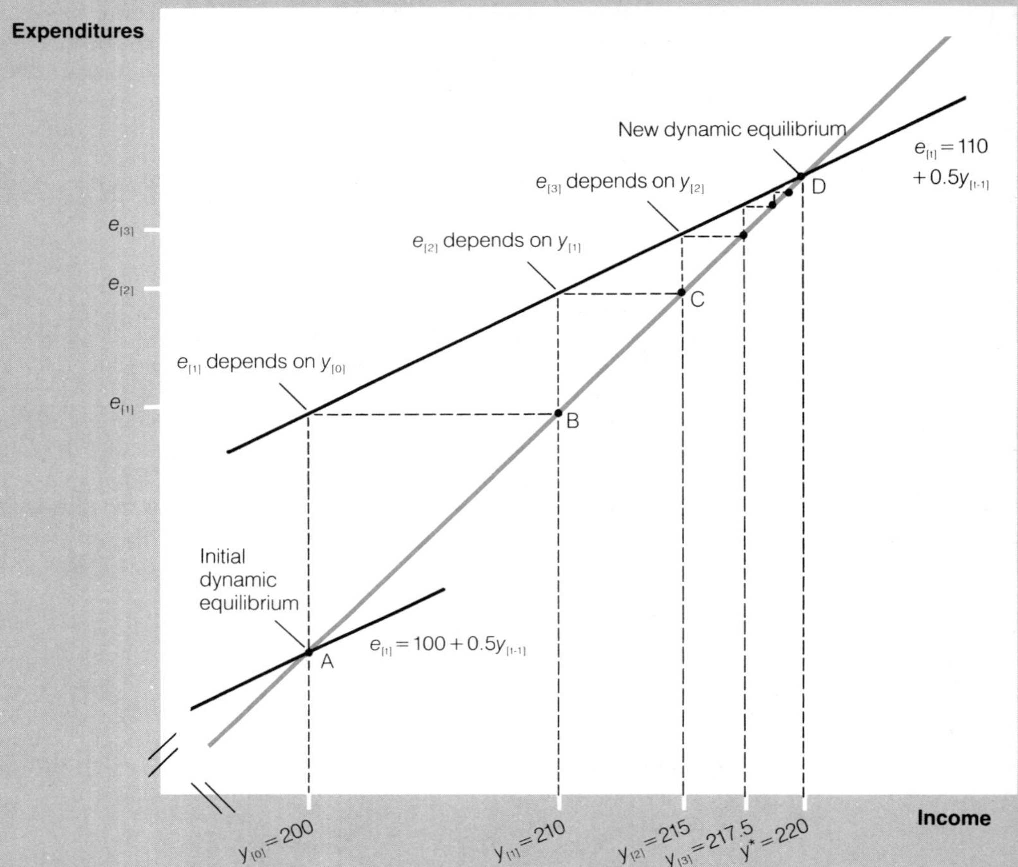

THE TIME PATH BETWEEN DYNAMIC EQUILIBRIA, WITH $e_y = 0.5$ AND e_0 SHIFTING FROM 100 TO 110. The economy initially is in dynamic equilibrium at Point A, with y = 200. An increase in spending by 10 raises income by 10 in the first period, by 5 more in the second period, and by 2.5 in the period after that. The economy moves from A to B to C, and so on. Eventually, the new dynamic equilibrium, (at Point D, with y = 220), is attained.

In the appendix figure the economy is initially in equilibrium at A with $y[0] = 200$. Then autonomous spending, e_0, increases from 100 to 110, shifting the expenditure function upward and giving a new dynamic equilibrium at $y^* = 220$. The economy does not immediately go to this new equilibrium but, instead, gradually approaches it according to the new expenditure function: $e[t] = 110 + 0.5y[t-1]$. At time $t = 1$, we can use $y[0] = 200$ to find $e[1] = 210$. Since $y[1]$ must equal $e[1]$, $y[1]$ will equal 210 at B. Similarly, we can find $e[2]$ on the expenditure function by using $y[1] = 210$. The economy moves from A to B to C, closer and closer to the dynamic equilibrium at (D). Robertson's dynamic model interprets the simple income-expenditure model as describing dynamic equilibria. Robertson uses Kahn's round-by-round explanation to show how the economy might move to a new dynamic equilibrium after an autonomous change in spending. These dynamics are important because they show how business cycles have a momentum that persists for some time.

IMPORTANT TERMS AND CONCEPTS

Autonomous (predetermined) variable	Disposable income
Marginal propensity to consume	Automatic stabilizer
Multiplier	Balanced-budget multiplier
Dynamic equilibrium	Full-employment surplus

Expenditures provide income, and income motivates expenditures. This income-expenditure interrelationship implies that shifts in private or government spending can have a large effect on the economy.

Automatic stabilizers reduce the multiplier effects of shocks to the economy. Income taxes, unemployment compensation, corporate income taxes, Social Security taxes, and excise taxes are all automatic stabilizers. The United States economy has more automatic stabilization now than before World War II.

A dollar of government spending affects income more than a dollar of tax relief, because people do not spend all of the latter. This logic underlies the balanced-budget multiplier, in which a dollar of additional government spending, matched by a dollar of additional taxes, raises aggregate demand by a dollar.

Discretionary policy can be separated from automatic stabilization by using a benchmark income level, as is done in calculations of the full-employment surplus. There have been many times when budget deficits arising from economic weakness were misinterpreted as evidence of expansionary government policies.

"Income equals expenditure" implies that investment equals saving. In classical full-employment analyses, these equalities are *ex ante* equilibrium conditions. In disequilibrium, with employment and output demand determined, these equalities are *ex post* conditions that state that income is determined by expenditures and that saving is determined by investment.

EXERCISES

1. The "paradox of thrift" states that attempts by households to consume less and save more will actually reduce aggregate saving. How is this possible?

2. Consider an income-expenditure model with exports, x, and imports, z, as per Equation 2.2 in chapter 2:

$$y = c + i_0 + g_0 + x_0 - z$$

$$c = c_0 + c_y(y - t)$$

$$t = t_0 + t_y y$$

$$z = z_0 + z_y y$$

With imports assumed to be positively related to income, find the multiplier, $\Delta y/\Delta g_0$, and explain any divergence from the multiplier given in Equation 3.15 in this chapter.

3. Consider the following model in which expenditures depend on the division of income between wages, y_1 and profits, y_2:

$$y = e$$

$$e = e_o + e_1 y_1 + e_2 y_2$$

Assume that wages are a fraction, λ, of aggregate income and that profits are a fraction, $1 - \lambda$, so that $y_1 = \lambda y$ and $y_2 = (1 - \lambda)\ y$. Find the multiplier, $\Delta y/\Delta e_0$. Calculate the values of y and $\Delta y/\Delta e_0$ for $e_0 = 600$, $\lambda = 2/3$, $e_1 = 1$, $e_2 = 0$ ("workers spend all, capitalists save all"). How would y and $\Delta y/\Delta e_0$ be affected by an increase in λ to 3/4? What is the economic logic? Why would your answers be qualitatively different if $e_1 = e_2$?

4. What is the multiplier $\Delta y/\Delta e_0$ if $e_y > 1$ in the income-expenditure model? Explain why this does or does not make sense. What would $\Delta y/\Delta e_0$ be in Kahn's model if $e_y > 1$? Use Robertson's model to reconcile these answers.

5. In 1983 and 1984, President Reagan argued for a balanced reduction in government spending and taxation. According to the income-expenditure model, would this policy have stimulated or depressed the economy?

6. In the income-expenditure model

$$y = e$$

$$e = e_0 + e_y y$$

what is the multiplier $\Delta y/\Delta e_0$ in the special case $e_y = 1$? What are the solution values of e and y? Interpret your results.

7. Some government expenditures are a good substitute for private expenditures. For example, government trash pickup services may replace private collection services dollar for dollar. To take this substitution into account, we modify our consumption function so that a fraction, γ, of government expenditures replaces private spending:

$$y = c + i_0 + g_0$$

$$c = c_0 + c_y(y - t) - \gamma g$$

$$t = t_0 + t_y y$$

Compare $\Delta y/\Delta g_o$ with $\Delta y/\Delta i_0$. What is $\Delta y/\Delta g_0$ when $\gamma = 1$? Explain the economic logic.

8. What did Abba Lerner mean when he argued that "The purpose of taxation is never to raise money but to leave less in the hands of the taxpayer." (*The Economics of Control,* 1944, p. 307)

9. The following model was recently devised:

$$y = c + i_0 + g \qquad c = c_0 + c_y(y - t)$$

$$t = t_0 + t_y y \qquad g = t$$

The fixed parameters are i_0, c_0, c_y, t_0, and t_y. How should we interpret the novel assumption $g = t$? How does this assumption affect the multiplier, $\Delta y/\Delta i_0$, in comparison with the usual assumption $g = g_0$? What is the economic explanation?

10. Calculate the balanced-budget multiplier when t_0 is held constant and t_y is instead adjusted so as to hold the government surplus, $t - g$, constant as g_0 increases.

11. During the Great Depression, some people raised the possibility of pump-priming: A few drops of government spending would stimulate the economy so much that the additional tax revenue flowing into the government would exceed the initial expenditure, thereby actually reducing the government deficit. The same picture was painted in the debates preceding the 1964 tax cut and the 1981 Economic Recovery Act.

Use the income-expenditure model described by Equations 2.1 and 3.13–3.15 to evaluate this possibility. Determine the parametric assumptions needed if an increase in government spending is to reduce the government deficit, $g_0 - t$. (Assume that $\Delta y/\Delta g_0$ is positive.)

12. It has been proposed that government spending be a fixed fraction, α, of national income. The following modified Robertson model

$$y_t = c_t + i_0 + g_t$$

$$c = c_0 + c_y y_{t-1}$$

$$g_t = \alpha y_t, \; 0 < \alpha < 1.$$

can be used to analyze the dynamic implications of such a policy. What is the current period effect on y of an increase in i_0? Is this short-run multiplier larger or smaller if α is increased? What is the long-run dynamic equilibrium effect on y of an increase in i_0? Is this long-run multiplier larger or smaller if α is increased? Does the model always go to its dynamic equilibrium? Is stability more or less likely if α is large? Give an intuitive explanation of these effects of α on the multipliers and stability.

REFERENCES

1. J. M. Keynes, *The General Theory of Employment, Interest, and Money,* New York: Macmillan, 1936.

2. Keynes, p. 317.

3. Keynes, p. 122.

4. R. F. Kahn, "The Relation of Home Investment to Unemployment," *Economic Journal,* (June 1931), 175–95.

5. Kahn, p. 183, N.2

6. Wilfred Lewis, Jr., *Federal Fiscal Policy in the Postwar Recessions,* Washington, D.C.: Brookings, 1962, p. 15.

7. Bert G. Hickman and Robert M. Coen, *An Annual Growth Model of the U.S. Economy,* Amsterdam: North-Holland, 1976, p. 194.

8. Keynes, pp. 129, 131.

9. Committee for Economic Development, Research and Policy Committee, *Taxes and the Budget,* New York, 1947.

10. Walter W. Heller, *New Dimensions of Political Economy,* New York: Norton, 1967, p. 40.

11. D. H. Robertson, *Essays in Monetary Theory,* London, P. S. King & Son, 1940.

SUGGESTIONS FOR FURTHER READING

A classic exposition of multiplier models is Thomas Schelling, *National Income Behavior,* New York: McGraw-Hill, 1951. E. Cary Brown first used the full-employment surplus in an effort to gauge government stabilization efforts during the 1930s in "Fiscal Policy in the Thirties: A Reappraisal," *American Economic Review,* 46 (December 1956), pp. 857–79. For some details on estimating the full-employment surplus see Frank de Leeuw et al, "The High-Employment Budget: New Estimates, 1955–80," *Survey of Current Business,* November 1980, pp. 15–21, 31–43; and Frank de Leeuw and Thomas M. Holloway, "The High-Employment Budget: Revised Estimates and Automation, Inflation Effects," *Survey of Current Business,* April 1982, pp. 21–33.

CHAPTER FOUR

THE *IS-LM* MODEL

Please keep in mind that we are dealing with a drastically simplified story, a "parable," which my dictionary defines as "a fictitious narrative or allegory (usually something that might naturally occur) by which moral or spiritual relations are typically set forth." If moral or spiritual, why not economic? You ask of a parable not if it is literally true but if it is well told.

ROBERT SOLOW[1]

This chapter introduces IS and LM curves to explain the interaction of interest rates, prices, and spending. These curves provide a framework for analyzing the economic implications of changes in private or government spending and in money supply and money demand. Also considered is the question of whether price adjustments automatically stabilize an economy.

THE income-expenditure model is fine as far as it goes, but it doesn't go nearly far enough. In particular, there are no interest rates or prices in the model. To remedy this deficiency, we will now construct a slightly more elaborate macroeconomic model of the economy—one that can explain interest rates and prices as well as output.

It is useful to distinguish at the outset between the demand and supply sides of the economy. The *demand side* consists of those factors that determine spending at various price levels. One of these factors is the income-expenditure interrelationship just analyzed in Chapter 3. Financial markets also affect expenditures, and we will take these effects into account in this chapter. The *supply side* of the economy consists of those factors that determine the production of goods and services at various price levels. These factors include the labor market and the production decisions of firms.

We will look at the demand side of the economy in this chapter and the supply side in the next one. The end result will be a simple graphical apparatus that describes the effects of various economic actions on output, interest rates, and prices. Later chapters will use this model for just those ends.

FINANCIAL MARKETS

In our simple macro model, we are going to assume that there are just two financial assets: "money" and "bonds"—money consisting of cash and checking accounts (what the Federal Reserve calls M1), and bonds consisting of financial securities issued by individuals, businesses, and governments. We also assume for now that all bonds pay the same interest rate, and that money is a means of payment, used for buying goods and services, that earns little or no interest. Later we will look at a variety of money definitions and take note of the multiplicity of interest rates.

Interest rates

Interest rates are reported in the daily newspapers and discussed in somber tones by bankers, politicians, and economists. They have been called "the price of money," "the price of liquidity," and even "the price of bonds." What are they really?

One of the most basic and important concepts in economics is that "time is money"—that time is a limited resource and so has value. If you had a choice, would you rather receive something useful (such as a piece of land, a house, or $1000) today or a year from now? If you had some profitable use for the land, the house, or the money, you would naturally prefer to receive them today so as to gain some profit during the ensuing year.

Thus you will be willing to pay more for a piece of land if you can use it immediately than if you must wait a year before having use of it. The difference, the implicit price of renting the land for a year, is determined by the land's usefulness during the coming year. The same is true of money. One thousand dollars delivered today and delivered a year from now have different values and will have different prices. This difference, the implicit price for renting $1000 for a year, is determined by the anticipated usefulness of that money during the coming year.

A handful of raw commodities (including soybeans, orange juice, and pork bellies) are sold in futures markets for delivery up to two years after purchase. However, the vast majority of commodities are purchased for delivery immediately or, at least, in the very near future. With money, the situation is very different. *A bond is a futures contract for money.* A borrower (seller of the bond) promises to pay stated amounts of money on specified future dates. The lender acquires this futures contract by giving the borrower money now; when he wishes, the lender may sell the bond to someone else. Well-organized bond markets regularly handle securities providing for the delivery of money five, ten, twenty, thirty, and even (in rare cases) hundreds of years hence.

Thus, while one cannot buy steak and beer for delivery ten years from now, bonds can be bought that will deliver money ten years from now. And that money can then be used to buy steak and beer (at the then prevailing prices). Thus money and bonds are stores of value, bridges between the present and the future.

Present value and yield

As we have said, the difference between the price for delivery of an item today and the price for delivery in the future is implicitly the cost of renting the item. The *interest rate (R),* then, is the cost, calculated in percentage terms, of renting money:

$$R = \frac{\text{dollars paid back} - \text{dollars received}}{\text{dollars received}}.$$

If $\$P_B$ is the price paid now for $\$X$ received a year from now, then the annual interest rate is

$$R = \frac{X - P_B}{P_B}. \tag{4.1}$$

Equation 4.1 expresses the return on the bond in terms of its price—the price paid now, commonly called the *present value,* in terms of the interest rate:

$$P_B = \frac{X}{1 + R}. \tag{4.2}$$

Another way of describing present value is as the amount of money, $\$P_B$, that, invested now at a rate of return R, will grow to $\$X$ in one year:

$$\text{principal} + \text{interest} = P_B + RP_B = (1 + R)P_B = (1 + R)\left(\frac{X}{1 + R}\right) = X.$$

Thus, given the terms of the bond, there is a simple relationship between the interest rate and the present value. Given the present value, the interest rate can be determined by Equation 4.1; and, given the interest rate, the present value can be determined by Equation 4.2. This is an inverse relationship; the higher the price of the bond, the lower the rate of return *(R),* and vice versa. For example, say that you loan me \$90.91 and, in return, I promise to pay you \$100 one year later. This \$100 promise, put into writing and duly legalized, is the bond. I issued it, and you, for some reason, bought it. From my standpoint, it is a loan; from yours it is a risky investment. The \$90.91 you gave me for my IOU is its initial price, or present value. Your anticipated rate of return, R, and my cost of renting \$90.91 is

$$\frac{\$100 - \$90.91}{\$90.91} = 0.10, \text{ or } 10\%.$$

The terms of the IOU are legally fixed, but its price and yield may change. Perhaps, right after lending me \$90.91, you find that you need some cash. A bit hastily, you sell my IOU to a friend for \$80. Now your friend has paid \$80 for a bond that will pay \$100 a year hence. Her rate of return will be

$$\frac{\$100 - \$80}{\$80} = 0.25, \text{ or } 25\%.$$

As always happens, when the price of the bond fell, its yield increased. Figure 4.1 shows this inherent inverse relationship.

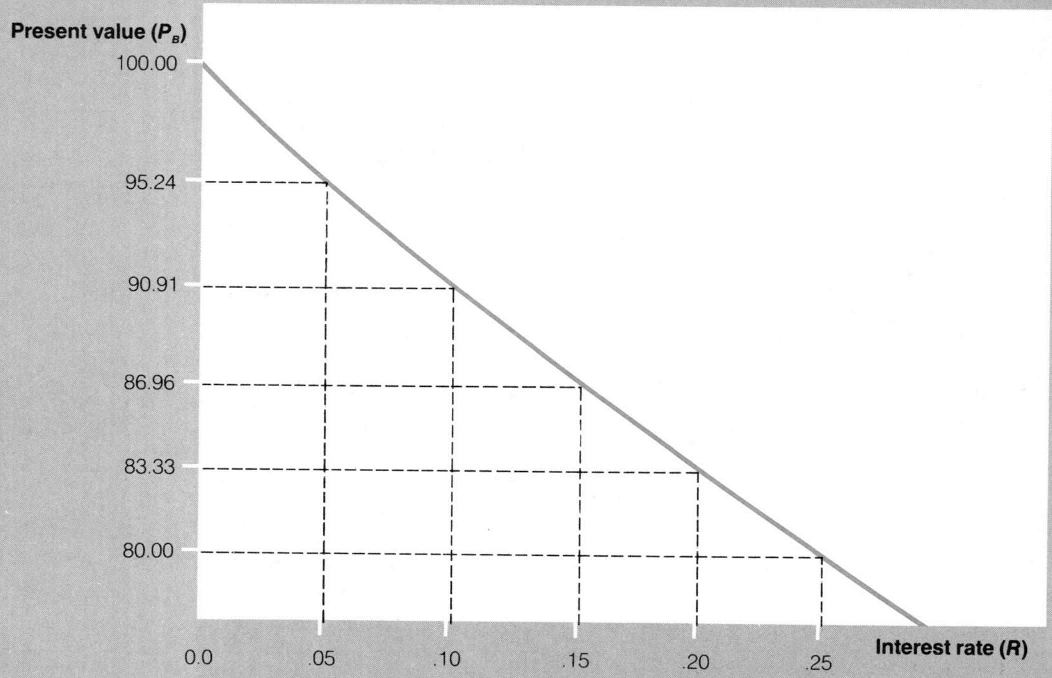

FIGURE 4.1 THE INVERSE RELATIONSHIP OF INTEREST RATE AND PRESENT VALUE. For a $100 one-year debt, the relationship between the interest rate and present value is given by $P = \frac{\$100}{1+R}$. As the interest rises from 5% to 15% to 25%, the present value falls from $95.24 to $86.96 to $80.

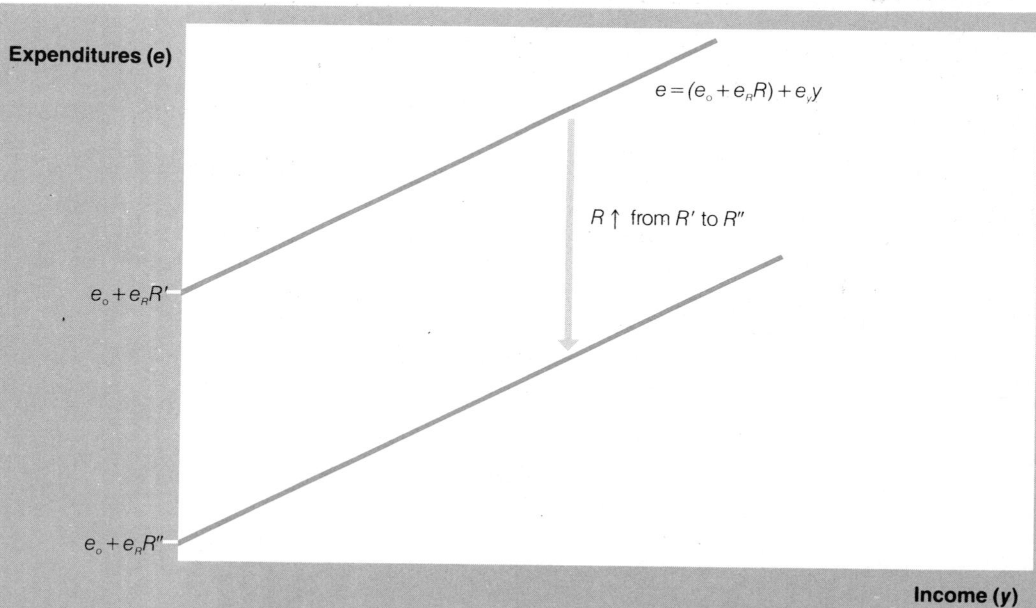

FIGURE 4.2 SPENDING IS RELATED DIRECTLY TO INCOME AND INVERSELY TO THE INTEREST RATE. For a given interest rate, R', the positively sloped expenditure line shows the relationship between income and expenditures. An increase in the interest to R'' shifts this expenditure line downward.

THE *IS* CURVE

In Chapter 3, we analyzed the interrelationship between income *(y)* and expenditures *(e)*. The two fundamental relations are that expenditures determine income, $y = e$ (2.1), and income influences spending, $e = e_0 + e_y y$, $0 < e_y < 1$ (3.1)

Increased output means more income for households and more profits for firms. The former encourages consumption and the latter encourage investment. When households earn additional income, they tend to spend some of it. When firms produce additional output, their profit calculations are enhanced and their expansion plans are bullish. Together, consumption and investment increase. As in Chapter 3, it is usually assumed that the increase in expenditures is less than the increase in income itself (that is, $e_y < 1$).

The most glaring inadequacy of this explanation of spending is that it takes no account of financial markets and the influence of interest rates on spending. For households or firms that must finance some of their purchases by borrowing, high interest rates obviously discourage spending. For households and firms with cash on hand, high interest rates make bonds a more attractive acquisition and commodities (particularly long-lived investment goods) less so. Investment expenditures hinge on a comparison of the rates of return on financial assets with the rates of return on houses, offices, factories, equipment, and inventories. When financial securities offer relatively high yields, there will be fewer expenditures on investment goods.

We can take into account this negative effect of high interest rates on spending by expanding Equation 3.1 to include interest rates:

$$e = e_0 + e_y y + e_R R \qquad 0 < e_y < 1,\ e_R < 0. \tag{4.3}$$

The parameter e_R measures the effect on spending, *e*, of a change in the interest rate, *R*, for a given level of income. The parameter e_R is negative since high interest rates depress spending.* A depiction of the dependence of expenditures on both income and the interest rate would require a three-dimensional graph. Because deciphering such a graph would be as frustrating as attempting to draw one, we will use a two-dimensional graph (Figure 4.2) showing how expenditure depends on income, but for a given interest rate. (A change in the interest rate shifts the spending function.)

For a given interest rate R′, the expenditure equation (4.3) can be rearranged as

$$e = (e_0 + e_R R') + e_y y, \tag{4.4}$$

with $(e_0 + e_R R')$ the intercept and e_y the slope. This is the expenditure function graphed in Figure 4.2. Since e_R is negative, a higher interest rate, R″, reduces spending at every level of income, lowering the intercept and the expenditure function.

* Although interest-rate calculations should take taxes into consideration, tax laws are so complex that, for now, we will simply assume that *R* is an after-tax rate, without specifying the necessary computations .

Finding the *IS* curve

Now we add the requirement that income must equal expenditures (since every expenditure provides income). Figure 4.3 shows the expenditure function, Equation 4.4, together with the 45-degree line representing income equal to expenditures (Equation 2.1). Their intersection at Point 1 gives the value of income *(y′)* such that expenditures equal income when the interest rate is *R′*. With the interest rate at a higher value, say R″, spending will be lower, so the expenditure function shifts downward. If income didn't change, the economy would be at Point 2 in the figure, with income *(y′)* greater than expenditures. Since that cannot occur (income must equal expenditures), income must be lower—at the value *y″* given by the new intersection at Point 3. Thus, if the interest rate rises from *R′* to *R″*, spending slumps and income must fall from *y′* to *y″* in order to maintain the equality of income and expenditures. Points 1 and 3 exemplify the inverse relationship between the interest rate and income that is described by the *IS curve,* which shows those combinations of income *(y)* and interest rate *(R)* at which expenditures are equal to income. The letters *IS* refer to the equality of investment *(I)* and saving *(S),* since (as noted in Chapter 3) the requirement that income equal expenditures implies that investment equals saving.*

Figure 4.4 shows this *IS* curve, with Points 1, 2, and 3 corresponding to those in Figure 4.3. For the interest rate, *R′*, income will equal expenditures at Point 1, with income equal to *y′*. Since income equals expenditures, this is a point on the *IS* curve. If the interest rate is higher, at *R″*, then spending will be below *y′*. Point 2 is therefore off the *IS* curve. To restore the equality of income and expenditures, income must fall to *y″* (Point 3), where income does equal expenditures, and so is on the *IS* curve. **The *IS* curve, then, states that, if nothing else changes, an increase in the interest rate reduces spending and, therefore, must be accompanied by a decline in income to maintain the equality of income and expenditures.**

Designed by J.R. Hicks,[2] the *IS* curve is an ingenious graphical device that makes three-demensional figures unnecessary. It is unlike most graphs in that it shows neither a historical record nor a causal relationship. The *IS* curve does not say that income determines the interest rate or that the interest rate determines income. Instead, income and the interest rate are simultaneously determined (in a way we discuss below). What the *IS* curve does tell us is which values of income and the interest rate can coexist. The combinations of *R* and *y* that constitute the *IS* curve are feasible values, in that they are combinations for which income does equal expenditures. All points off the *IS* curve represent situations in which expenditures do not equal income. Those above the *IS* curve are cases where *R* is too high and expenditures too low *(e < y)* and those below, where *R* is too low and expenditures too high *(e > y)*.

* Remember that the equality of expenditures and income *does not* require commodity market equilibrium. Even if there is a market disequilibrium, *ex post* spending and income will still be equal, since every expenditure provides income. In a market equilibrium, desired spending is equal to desired income. But in a market disequilibrium, actual income can be less than desired income, leaving factories idle and people unemployed.

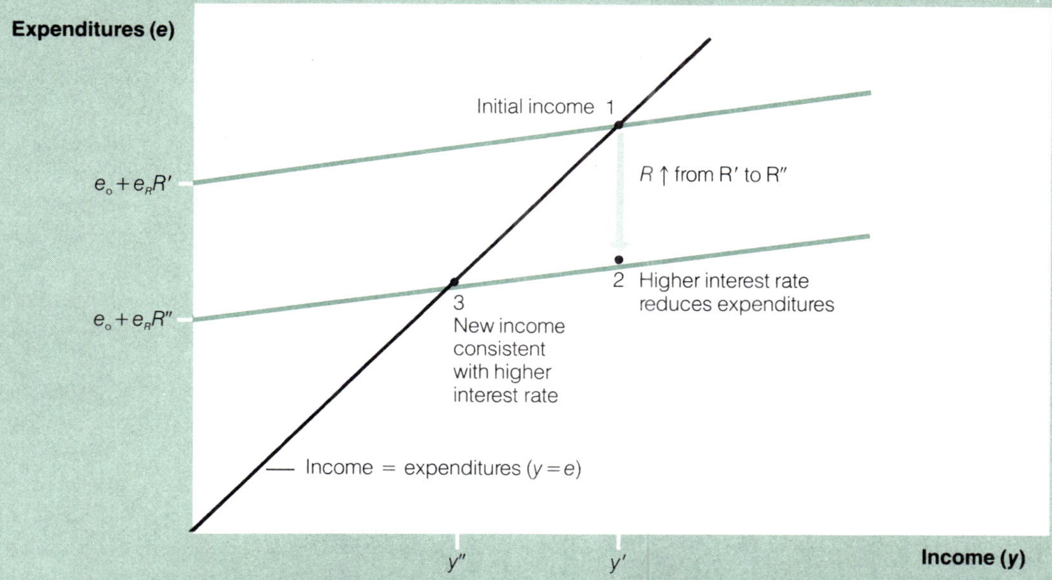

FIGURE 4.3 **A HIGHER INTEREST RATE REQUIRES LOWER INCOME TO MAINTAIN INCOME EQUAL TO EXPENDITURES.** For the interest rate, R', expenditures are equal to income at the income level y'. An increase in the interest rate to R'' shifts the expenditure line downward and reduces income to y''.

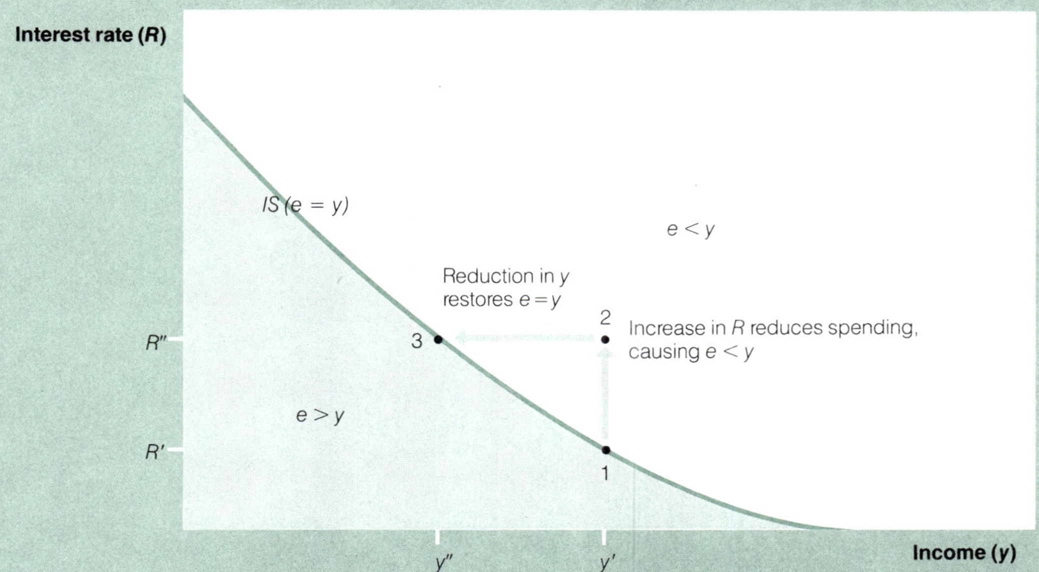

FIGURE 4.4 **THE *IS* CURVE** shows those combinations of income and the interest rate for which spending is equal to income. As Figure 4.3 demonstrated, an increase in the interest rate from R' to R'' reduces spending and, so, reduces income from y' to y''.

Shifts in the *IS* curve

If demand factors other than income and the interest rate alter expenditures, the *IS* curve will shift. **In general, any event (other than a change in y and R) that increases expenditures will shift the *IS* curve rightward.** For instance, an increase in government spending directly raises aggregate expenditures. At any given interest rate, income must increase to maintain the equality of income and expenditures. Thus, as shown in Figure 4.5, with such increases in spending the *IS* curve shifts rightward. This shift in an expansionary, rightward direction can also be produced by an autonomous increase in private spending, due, say, to a tax cut or to more optimistic expectations about the economy. Conversely, an autonomous decline in government or private spending shifts the *IS* curve in a contractionary, leftward direction.

The magnitudes of these *IS* shifts are given by the simple multipliers analyzed in Chapter 3. Moving horizontally, as in Figure 4.5, reflects a change in income for a given interest rate. Since the interest rate is being held constant we can use the Chapter 3 calculations, which omitted interest rate changes. When the interest rate is held constant, the result is as if it were absent from the model. If some economic event, such as a tax cut or government spending increase, causes autonomous spending to increase by Δe_0, and if the e_y is the ag-

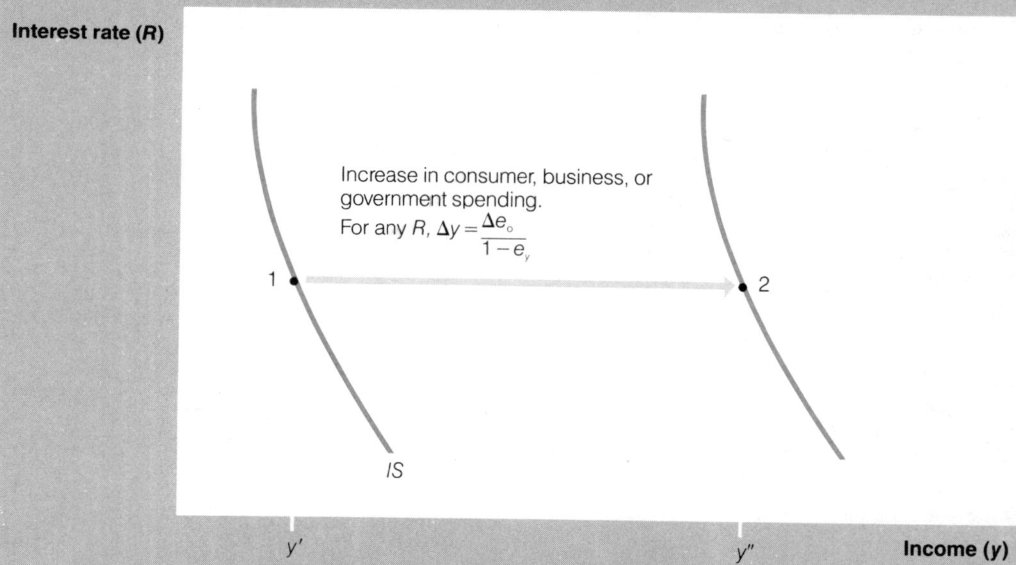

FIGURE 4.5 **A change in any variable other than R or y may shift the *IS* curve. Factors that increase spending will, as shown, shift the *IS* curve rightward. The magnitude of this horizontal shift is given by the Chapter 3 multiplier.**

gregate marginal propensity to spend out of income, then the change in income, Δy, from y' to y'' in Figure 4.5, is given by

$$\Delta y = \frac{\Delta e_0}{1 - e_y}$$

as in Equation 3.6. The horizontal shift from y' to y'' was as far as we could go in Chapter 3. We are soon going to be able to take into account the effects of induced changes in interest rates. The new level of income may turn out to be larger or smaller than y''. To find out which is the case, we need to look at financial markets to determine what happens to the interest rate.

THE *LM* CURVE

Financial markets present a choice between money, which pays little or no interest, and bonds, which pay interest at a rate, R. We can take this choice into account either by equating money demand and supply or by equating bond demand and supply. The first approach is the usual one, and we will follow it here.

We have defined money as cash and checking accounts. In practice, the creation of checking accounts by the banking system depends on the uncertain behavior of the private sector. In later chapters, we will look at some of the important implications of this uncertainty. But for now, we will assume that the nominal money supply, M, can be controlled perfectly by the Federal Reserve (commonly called "the Fed"). The Fed increases M by using Federal Reserve notes to purchase Treasury securities from the private sector (individuals and banks), and decreases M by selling some of its security holdings and retiring the cash it receives.* With M the nominal money supply, the real money supply is M/P, where P is the price level.

We will make two assumptions about money demand:

1. It is positively related to income. (As output and income expand, people will want to hold more money to carry out the increased volume of transactions.)

2. It is inversely related to the rate of return, R, on bonds. (Money is convenient for making transactions, but it does not earn the interest paid on bonds. An increase in the rate of return on bonds makes bonds more attractive and money less attractive.)

We can summarize these assumptions by writing the real demand for money, l, as

$$l = l_0 + l_y y + l_R R \qquad l_y > 0,\ l_R < 0. \tag{4.5}$$

* The Fed does not actually use cash for its transactions. Instead, like you or I, it gives the dealer from whom it buys the securities a check. The bank in which the dealer deposits the check has some of its reserves on deposit with the Fed. When the check is presented for payment the Fed simply credits the bank with having additional reserves equal to the amount of the check. These reserves are as good as cash since the banks can convert them into Federal Reserve notes. Other ways in which changes can occur in the quantity of Federal Reserve notes available to the private sector include borrowing by banks from the Fed and delivery delays that cause reserves to be simultaneously credited to two banks. In theory, the Fed can buy or sell government securities as needed to offset these fluctuations.

Parameter l_y gauges the effect of an increase in income on the demand for money, and is positive. Parameter l_R gives the effect of an increase in the interest rate on the demand for money, and is negative. The intercept l_0 encompasses autonomous changes in money demand (changes due to factors other than y and R).

To show the money demand function in a two-dimensional graph, we again initially set the interest rate at R', so that $l = (l_0 + l_R R') + l_y y$. Figure 4.6 shows a graph of this money demand equation. When the interest rate is at a R'', a higher value than R', money demand is diminished at every level of income, and the money demand line shifts downward. Since the real money supply M/P,

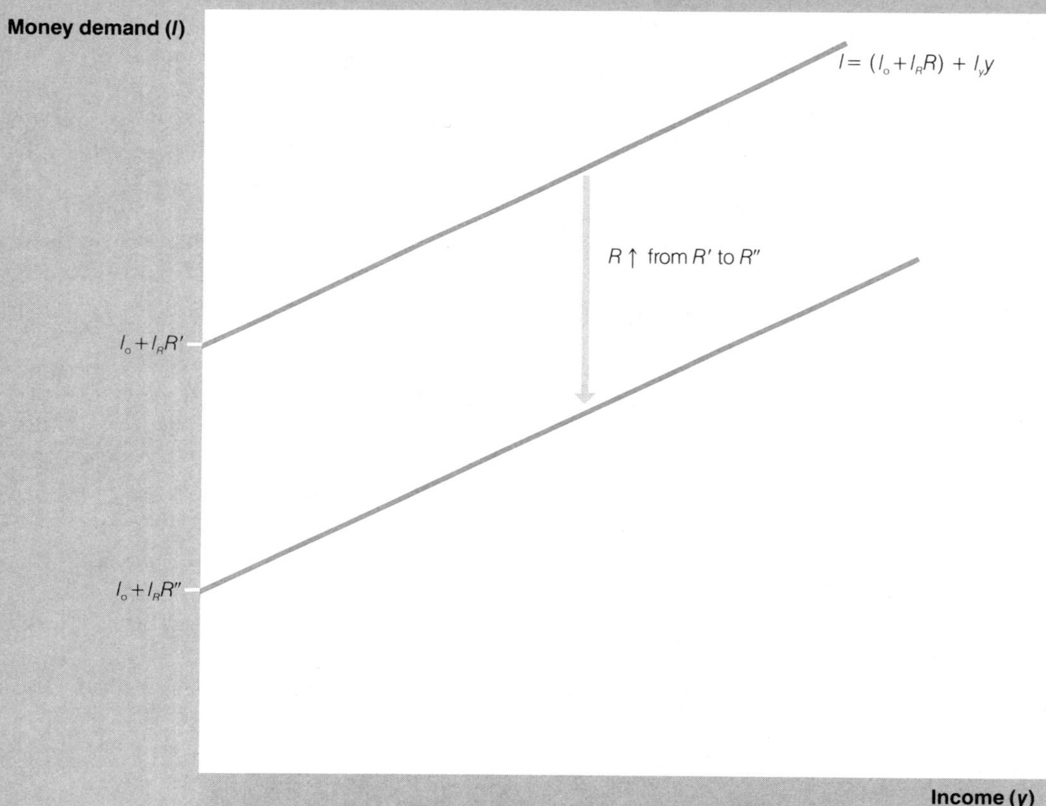

FIGURE 4.6 **MONEY DEMAND is related directly to income and inversely to the interest rate. For a given interest rate, R', the positively sloped money demand line shows the relationship between income and money demand. An increase in the interest rate to R'' shifts the money demand line downward.**

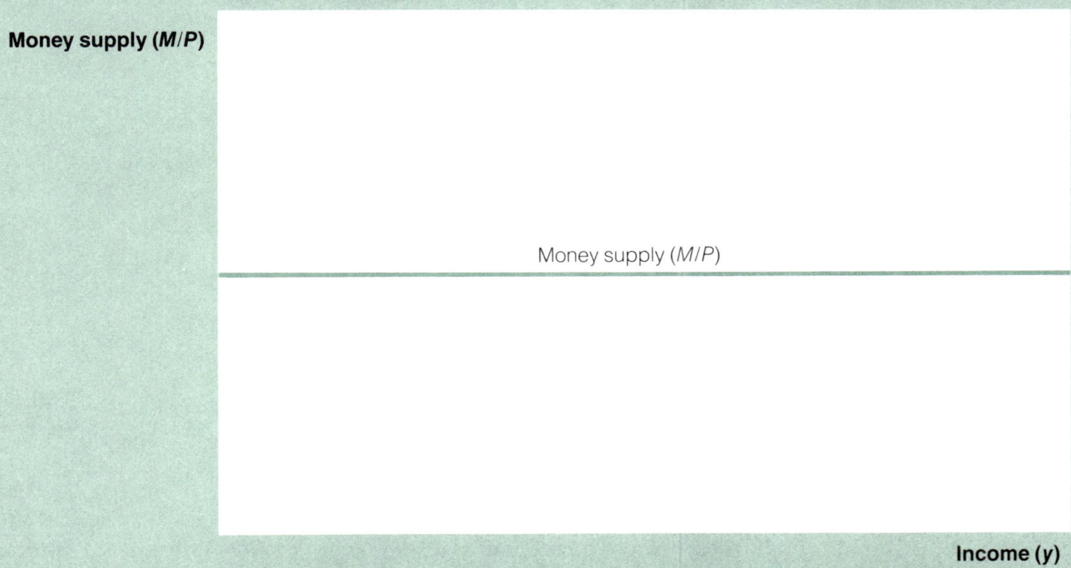

FIGURE 4.7 THE MONEY SUPPLY LINE **is horizontal, since it does not depend on income.**

does not depend on income, the supply curve is a horizontal line, as Figure 4.7 shows.

Finding the *LM* curve

Figure 4.8, which merges the money demand and money supply lines, shows that rises in interest rates reduce money demand, so that the quantity of money demanded is less than the quantity supplied (Point 2). A rise in income restores the equality between money demand and supply (Point 3). Points 1 and 3, then, are examples of the positive relationship between the interest rate and income that is described by the *LM* curve, **which shows those combinations of income *(y)* and interest rate *(R)* at which money demand is equal to money supply.** The letters *LM* denote money demand *(L)* and money supply (M).

Figure 4.9 shows this positively sloped *LM* curve, with Points 1, 2, and 3 corresponding to those in Figure 4.8. Point 1 is on the *LM* curve since the quantities of money demanded and supplied are equal at the interest rate R' and income y'. With a higher interest rate, R'', we are at Point 2, off the *LM* curve, since money demand falls below supply. For money demand and money supply to be in equilibrium, income must rise to y'' (Point 3). **The *LM* curve then states that, if nothing else changes, a higher interest rate requires a higher level of income to keep the amount of money demanded equal to the supply.**

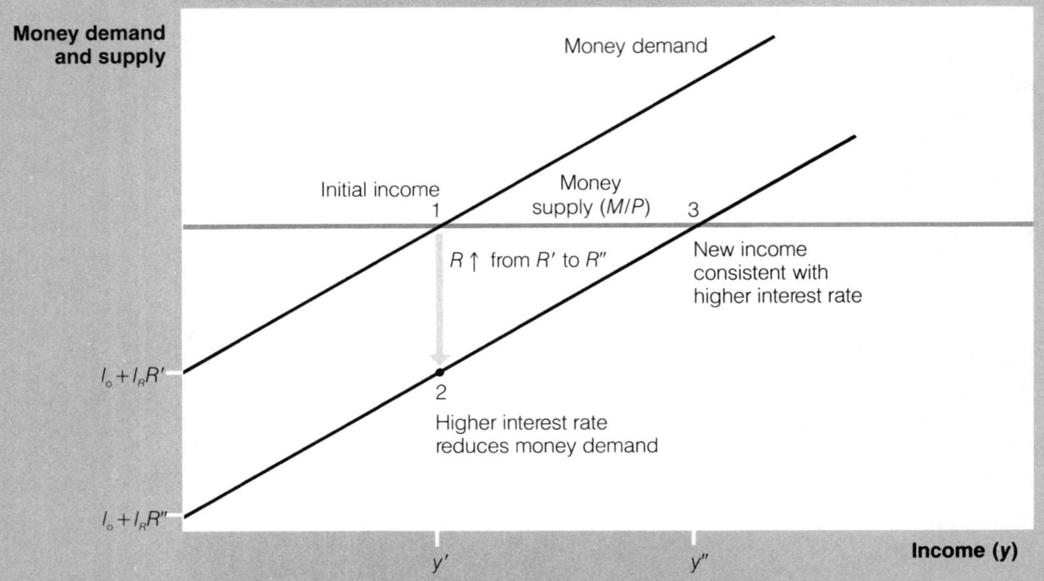

FIGURE 4.8 **For the interest rate, R', money demand is equal to supply at the income level y'. An increase in the interest rate to R'' reduces money demand and increases to y'' the income level needed for equilibrium.**

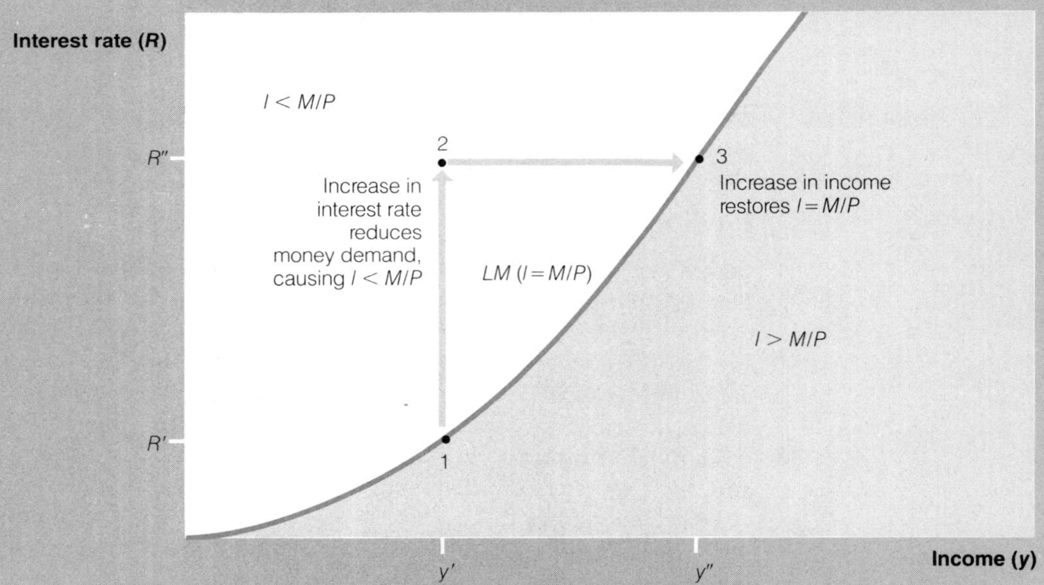

FIGURE 4.9 **The *LM* curve shows those combinations of income and the interest rate for which money demand is equal to supply. As Figure 4.8 demonstrated, an increase in the interest rate from R' to R'' reduces money demand and, so, increases equilibrium income from Y' to Y''.**

Shifts in the *LM* curve

If factors other than income and the interest rate alter money demand or supply, the *LM* curve will shift. Figure 4.10 shows how, at a given interest rate, an increase in the real money supply requires an income increase (increasing demand for money) from y' at Point 1 to y'' at Point 2 if money demand and supply are to remain equal. Thus the *LM* curve shifts rightward, as shown in Figure 4.11.

Note that the real money supply, M/P, can be increased through an increase in the nominal money supply, M, or through a decline in the price level, P. A halving of the price level, to take an extreme example, would double M/P as surely as if the Fed had doubled the number of Federal Reserve notes in circulation. Thus an increase in M *or* a decrease in P shifts the *LM* curve rightward. A decrease in M/P—whether due to a decline in M or an increase in P—shifts the *LM* curve leftward.)

Autonomous changes in money demand are captured by changes in l_0. The economic logic is straightforward. Any event (other than a change in y or R) that reduces money demand has the same qualitative effects as an increase in the money supply. Figure 4.12 confirms this basic conclusion. At any interest rate, a decline in money demand, like an increase in the money supply, requires

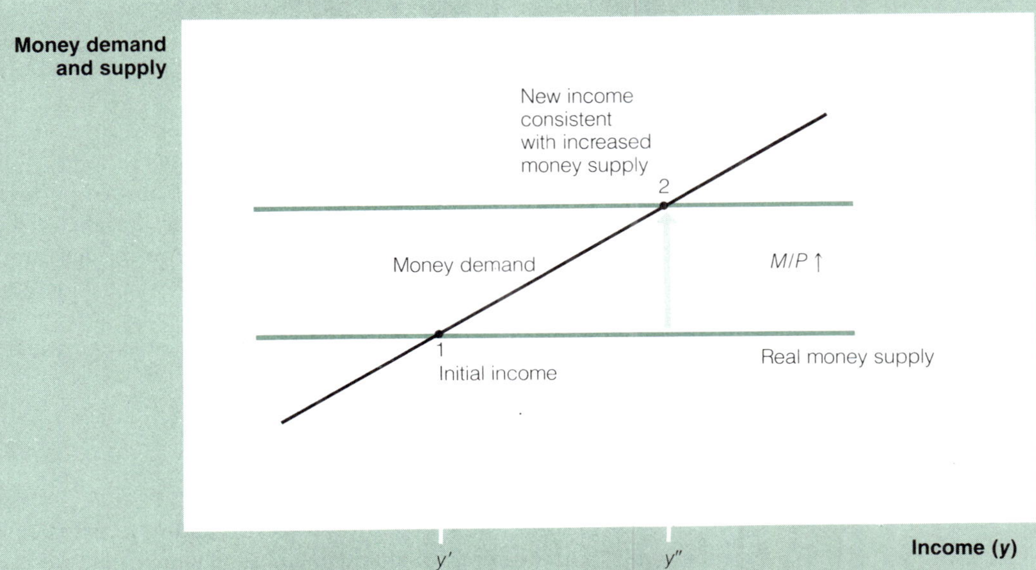

FIGURE 4.10 **At any given interest rate, an increase in the money supply raises the level of income needed for money equilibrium. This increase in income expands money demand to match the additional supply.**

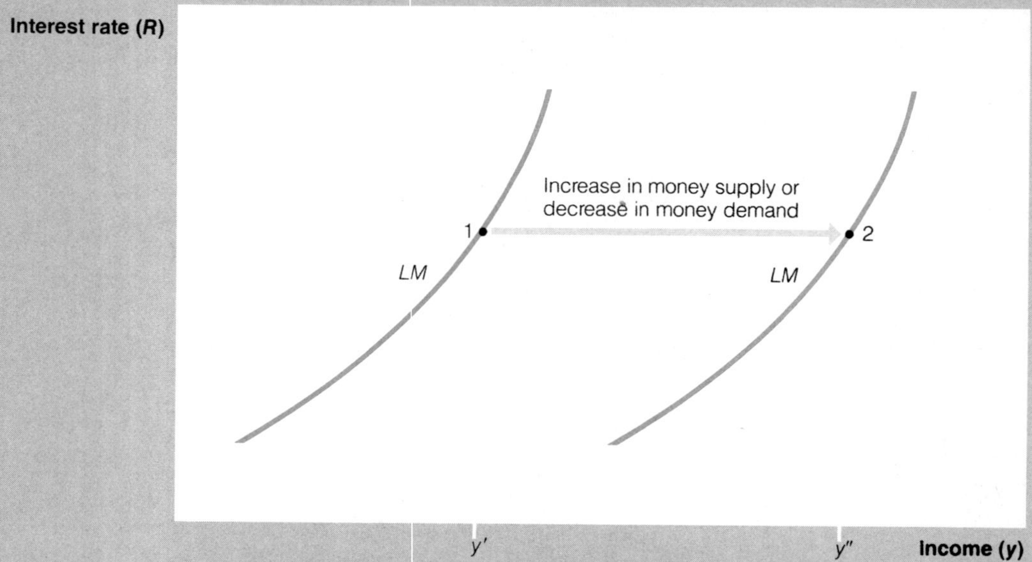

FIGURE 4.11 **A change in any variable other than *R* or *y* may shift the *LM* curve. Factors that increase money supply or that reduce money demand will, as shown, shift the *LM* curve rightward.**

an increase in income to pull money demand back up to the level of supply. Thus a decrease in money demand shifts the *LM* curve rightward. Conversely, an increase in money demand will, like a decrease in money supply, shift the *LM* curve leftward. We can summarize these shifts by concluding that any event (other than a change in *y* or *R*) that increases the real money supply or reduces real money demand shifts the *LM* curve in an expansionary, rightward direction.

IS AND *LM* CURVES TOGETHER

As Figure 4.13 shows, the intersection of the *IS* and *LM* curves determines that combination of the interest rate and income at which income is equal to expenditures and money demand is equal to money supply. With *R* and *y* the axes, the *IS* curve is negatively sloped and the *LM* curve positively sloped. Economic events that increase expenditures shift one *IS* curve in an expansionary, rightward direction; events that increase the real supply of money or reduce money demand shift the *LM* curve in an expansionary, rightward direction. Contractionary events shift the curves leftward. The *IS* and *LM* curves are the keys to understanding the demand side of the economy.

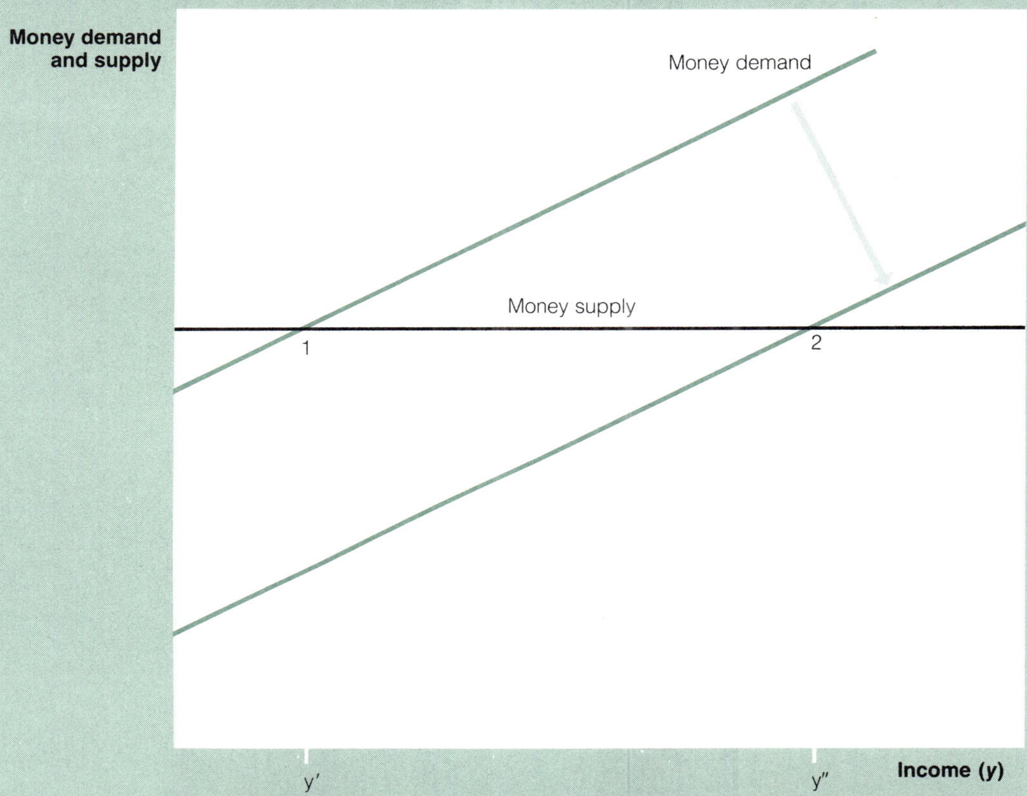

FIGURE 4.12 **At any given interest rate, a decrease in money demand raises the income level needed for money equilibrium. This increase in income expands money demand to offset the initial contraction and keeps demand equal to the fixed supply.**

DEMAND-SIDE CROWDING OUT

To illustrate application of these curves, we extend our Chapter 3 analysis to take into account induced interest rate changes. In Chapter 3, we saw that, neglecting interest rates, an increase in government spending by Δe_0 increases income by

$$\Delta y = \frac{\Delta e_0}{1 - e_y}$$

where e_y is the marginal propensity to spend. In Figure 4.14 we depict this increase in y as a rightward shift in the *IS* curve. As the figure shows, the interest

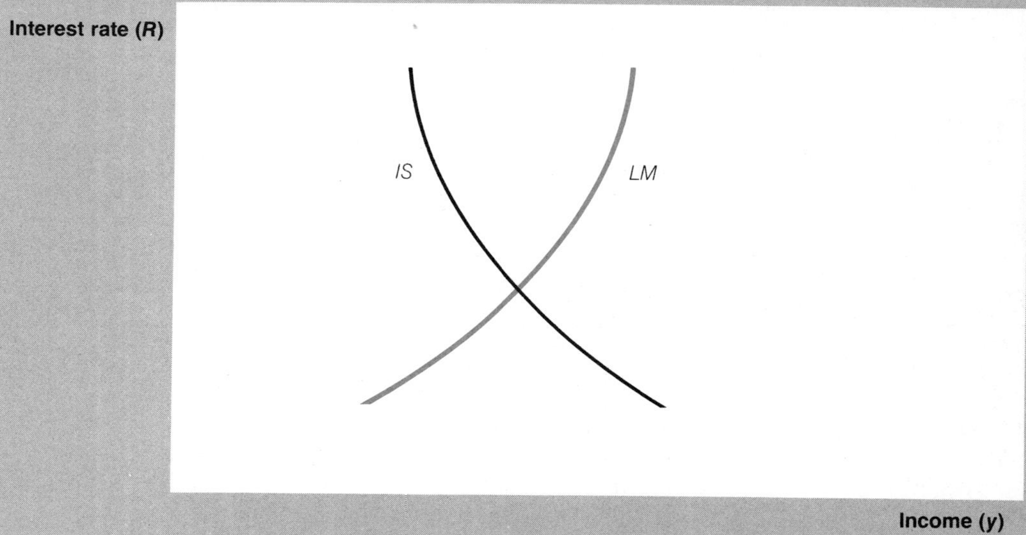

FIGURE 4.13 **Together, the *IS* and *LM* curves determine the levels of *R* and *y* such that income is equal to expenditures and money demand is equal to supply.**

rate will not, in fact, be unaffected by the increase in government spending. Instead, it will rise along the upward-sloping *LM* curve. As a result, the increase in *y* will be less than that given by the Chapter 3 multiplier. The economic explanation is as follows. The increase in government spending directly raises aggregate expenditures and, further, has the multiplier effects attributable to the interaction of spending and income: The increased government spending raises income, stimulating private spending, and so raising other incomes. The increased level of income and transactions also increase the demand for money; yet, there is no change in the money supply: no new money has been put into circulation. (To focus on the effects of government spending, we hold the money supply constant.* Otherwise, the *LM* curve would be shifting along with the *IS* curve.) This money tightness pushes interest rates upward, or, put somewhat differently, the induced increase in interest rates persuades people to economize on their money holdings. The increase in *y* increases money demand, and this is offset by an increase in *R*, which reduces money demand. That is what the *LM* curve is all about: If the money supply is constant, then a higher level of income requires a higher interest rate.

Higher interest rates diminish not only money demand, but also private expenditures, particularly on investment goods. When interest rates go up, households and businesses are less inclined to take out loans and more inclined to

*The Treasury can finance its expenditures by selling bonds to the private sector. Thus it raises funds and promptly spends them, with no net effect on the money supply.

buy high-yielding bonds instead of houses, factories, and equipment. The tightened money market and its accompanying higher interest rates discourage private spending, partly offsetting the initial increase in government spending. Hence, the *IS-LM* intersection is to the left of the Chapter 3 multiplier in Figure 4.14. Income increases, but not by as much as we thought when we neglected interest rate changes in Chapter 3. **This upward pressure exerted on interest rates by increased government spending is the *demand-side crowding out* discussed in the financial press. When the government sells bonds to finance its spending, private borrowers are "crowded out" of financial markets as interest rates soar and private spending crashes.**

Actually, we cannot be sure whether private spending goes up or down from Figure 4.14. Expenditures are discouraged by the higher interest rates but encouraged by the higher level of income. An increase in national income means more employment, increased output, and higher profits. And these positive developments are a stimulating tonic for household and business spending. On balance, we cannot be sure whether the negative effects of higher interest rates will be weaker or stronger than the positive effects of higher income.

One useful way of phrasing the accounting is to recall the income-expenditure equation of Chapter 3, in which expenditures are separated: $y = c + i + g$.

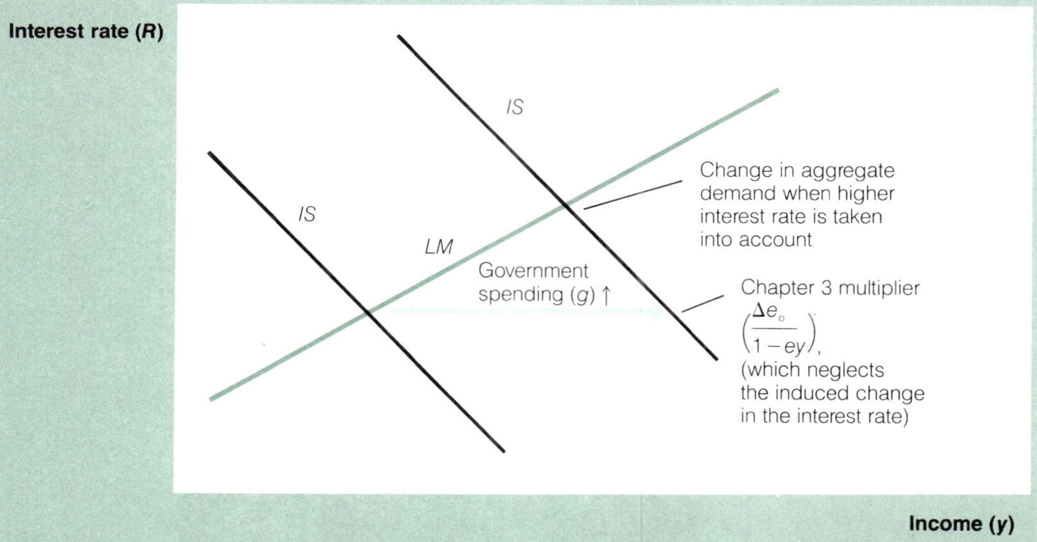

FIGURE 4.14 **An increase in government spending, like any increase in expenditures, shifts the *IS* curve rightward. The size of the horizontal shift is given by the Chapter 3 multiplier. The *LM* curve tells us that the interest rate must rise with income to maintain money demand equal to the fixed money supply. The higher interest rate dampens private spending and reduces the size of the increase in aggregate income.**

IN THE NEWS
Why Deficits Matter . . .

WASHINGTON—The great deficit debate continues. In last week's round, Treasury Department officials complained that the president's annual economic report, which is being prepared by chief White House economist Martin Feldstein, attaches too much importance to the federal budget deficit. While the theoretical arguments fly back and forth, it's worth asking a few practical business executives whether they think looming deficits might harm their companies in the future. Many answer that deficits are causing some problems already.

Everyone agrees that so far the effects of the deficit have been mostly beneficial: The red ink has helped stimulate a rapid recovery. And most forecasters believe that the recovery isn't about to collapse.

But massive deficits contribute to the stubbornly high level of interest rates. Those high rates aren't throttling the economy, but they insidiously erode America's long-term economic fitness. "We constantly ask ourselves—it's a crazy question, I know—but what are we doing in our principal business of producing electronic and electrical parts when the yields are so much better in the money markets?" says David Dibner, chairman of Burndy Corp., a New York Stock Exchange-listed company based in Norwalk, Conn.

Deficits don't boost interest costs all by themselves, economists agree, and deficits don't always coincide with high interest rates. But today, the Federal Reserve Board, fearful that deficit spending will rekindle inflation, is in effect refusing to "print money" to accommodate the federal budget gap.

The figures involved are unprecedented: Mostly because the government had to borrow to finance a $200 billion deficit, the pool of domestic funds available for new private investment shrank to 1.8% of gross national product last year. That compares with about 7% of GNP that was available for new investment during the 1950s, 7.5% during the 1960s, and 6.3% during the 1970s.

The grim supply-and-demand outlook for money, combined with widespread concern that renewed inflation might cause a new financial crunch, is keeping long-term interest rates two to three points higher than they would otherwise be, by some economists' reckoning. (Deregulation of interest payments on bank deposits has also buoyed rates somewhat.)

High rates, in turn, are contributing to the depressed level of investment in "long-lived" assets, such as factories and heavy equipment, even as spending on computers, office machinery and other shorter-lived assets is strong. "We were going to put a new (glass fiber) plant in the Southwest, but we've decided to hold back on it until we see which way the ball bounces," says Ernest J. Nagy, chairman of Riblet Products Corp., a $120 million (sales) manufacturer of parts for the recreational vehicle and mobile homes industries. "I can't afford to go ahead with increased production facilities, because my ultimate customer is being restrained by high interest rates."

Many analysts, however, believe that it's too early to tell whether plant spending has been permanently hobbled: Much existing capacity remains underutilized, and there are some signs of a turnaround in business construction. But high long-term interest rates unquestionably discourage long-range expansion plans.

"Over the past few years, we've changed the kind of expected return that a new plant has to achieve in order to get built," says Dow Chemical Co.'s president, Paul F. Oreffice. "That's directly because of the change in interest rates."
(Paul Blustein, *The Wall Street Journal,* Jan. 30, 1984)

The question of whether private spending, $c + i$, goes up or down is really a question of whether income, y, goes up by more or less than government spending. If the multiplier $\Delta y/\Delta g$, taking into account interest rate effects, is greater than 1.0, then private spending must, on balance, increase with government spending. In most empirical models, $\Delta y/\Delta g$ is, in fact, greater than 1.0. These models, then, predict that government spending actually encourages ("crowds in") private spending.

The quantity theory

If can be seen from Figure 4.14 that the effect of government spending on income will be smaller the steeper the *LM* curve. There will be *no* effect in the special case where the *LM* curve is vertical. This special case arises in an old, and now discredited, theory briefly explained here. (A more detailed discussion is given in Chapter 14.)

People use money to make transactions, to buy and sell things. Classical economists emphasized money's role as a medium of exchange and believed that there is a close relationship between a nation's money stock and the dollar volume of a nation's economic transactions. Indeed, this was thought to be a causal relationship in that any change in the quantity of money would cause a proportionate change in the dollar volume of transactions. This belief, known as the simple *quantity theory,* can be expressed mathematically as

$$Mv = Py \tag{4.6}$$

where M is the money supply, P is the price level, y is national income, and v is *velocity,* the average number of times that money is exchanged during a given accounting period. From Equation 4.6 we obtain

$$v = \frac{Py}{M}.$$

If nominal national income, Py, is \$3,000 billion per year and the money supply, M, is \$500 billion, then

$$v = \frac{\$3{,}000 \text{ billion}}{\$500 \text{ billion}} = 6$$

which says that, on average, there had to be six transactions in a year in order for \$500 billion to make \$3,000 billion worth of expenditures—that is, that money is held, on average, two months between transactions.*

Classical economists assumed that velocity is predetermined by institutional details governing society's bill-paying habits (how often people are paid and

*Actually, many transactions do not involve money and most transactions are not the expenditures on new goods and services that are included in national income. This is why the calculated velocity seems so low. It is this kind of technical deficiency in the quantity theory that is discussed in more detail in Chapter 14.

how frequently they shop) and does not fluctuate with the economy. One way of interpreting this assumption is to rewrite Equation 4.6 as

$$M/P = (1/v)\,y \tag{4.7}$$

and then think of this as an equality between money supply and money demand. The left side of Equation 4.7 is the real money supply. The right side, money demand, depends only on income and velocity (which is predetermined). What is missing? No account is taken of the effects of interest rates on the demand for money. Thus **a useful way of thinking about the simple quantity theory is that it is another way of saying that money supply equals money demand, with money demand influenced by income, but not by interest rates.** Hence, the main inadequacy of the simple quantity theory is that it neglects the effect of interest rates on the demand for money. Sound theoretical arguments and lots of empirical evidence show that money demand does depend on interest rates. When interest rates are high, households and businesses economize on money holdings in order to take advantage of these high interest rates. They keep less money on hand and hold it for shorter periods. When interest rates are high, money demand goes down (and velocity goes up).

If the simple quantity theory were correct, then the *LM* curve would be vertical: Any value of the interest rate is consistent with money demand equals money supply, since neither demand nor supply is affected by it. As Figure 4.15 shows, if the LM curve is vertical, an increase in government spending has no effect on y. When the *IS* curve moves in an expansionary, rightward direction, income rises and, so, the demand for money expands and the interest rate increases. But the quantity theory implies that the higher interest rate does not reduce money demand. According to the quantity theory, $Mv = Py$, so that when M, v, and P are given, there is only one level of y consistent with money equilibrium—the initial level! The interest rate must rise sufficiently to reduce, by itself, private expenditures by as much as government expenditures have increased. It is not necessary for the price level to increase. The higher interest rate alone crowds out private demand. **Thus, the quantity theory implies complete demand-side crowding out, in that aggregate demand is not affected by government spending.** Demand-side crowding out is not absent in our macro model; Figure 4.14 includes an increase in the interest rate that discourages private spending. The difference is that, were the simple quantity theory true, then this crowding out would be complete.

THE AGGREGATE DEMAND CURVE

The *IS* and *LM* curves describe the demand side of the economy. These curves determine the interest rate and output level that are consistent with income equal to expenditures and with money demand equal to money supply. Note, though, that the *LM* curve depends on the price level. If, for instance, the price level is higher, then the real money supply is lower and the *LM* curve is shifted leftward. Thus there are many possible *LM* curves, one for each possible value

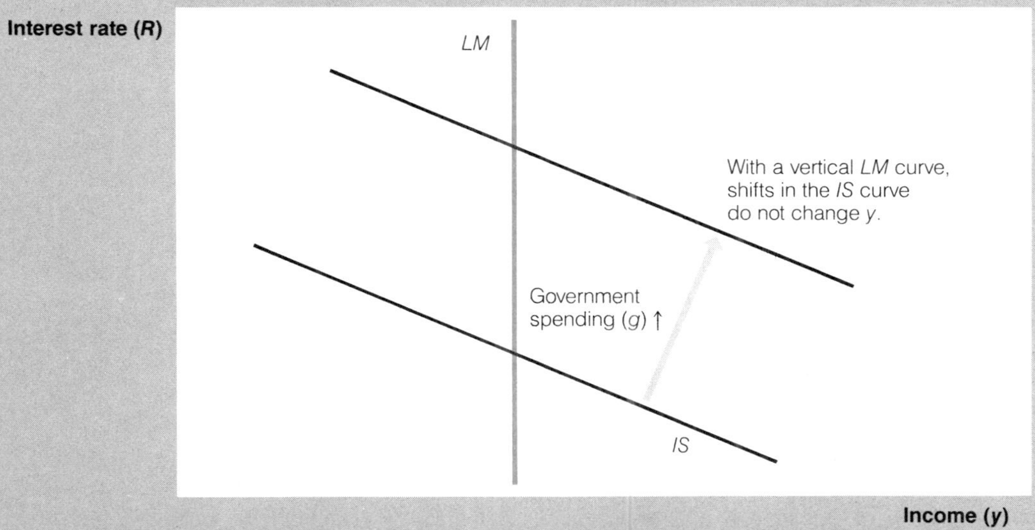

FIGURE 4.15 **In the simple quantity theory, money demand depends on income, but not on the interest rate. Since any interest rate is consistent with money demand equals supply, the *LM* curve is vertical. Further, since money demand depends only on income, if the money supply is constant there is only one income level for which money demand equals supply. Thus increases in spending raise the interest rate but cannot change income.**

of the price level. To know which *LM* curve is appropriate, we have to know the price level. And the price level is, of course, influenced by economic events, such as increases in government spending or in the money supply. So, to describe the full consequences of, say, an increase in government spending, we need somehow to take into account (a) the shift in the *IS* curve, (b) the rise in the interest rate along the *LM* curve, and (c) the shift in the *LM* curve due to an increase in prices. The following section presents the simplest way of doing all this.

We can summarize the demand side of the economy by translating the *IS-LM* interrelationships among r, y, and P into an aggregate-demand relationship between y and P. When this is combined with a supply-side relationship between y and P, we can determine output, prices, and the interest rate. **The aggregate demand curve, then, shows how a change in the price level affects the income level consistent with the demand-side requirements that income equal expenditure and money demand equal supply.** This curve can be derived by noting how a change in the price level affects the *IS-LM* intersection, as shown in Figure 4.16. Here the initial *IS-LM* intersec-

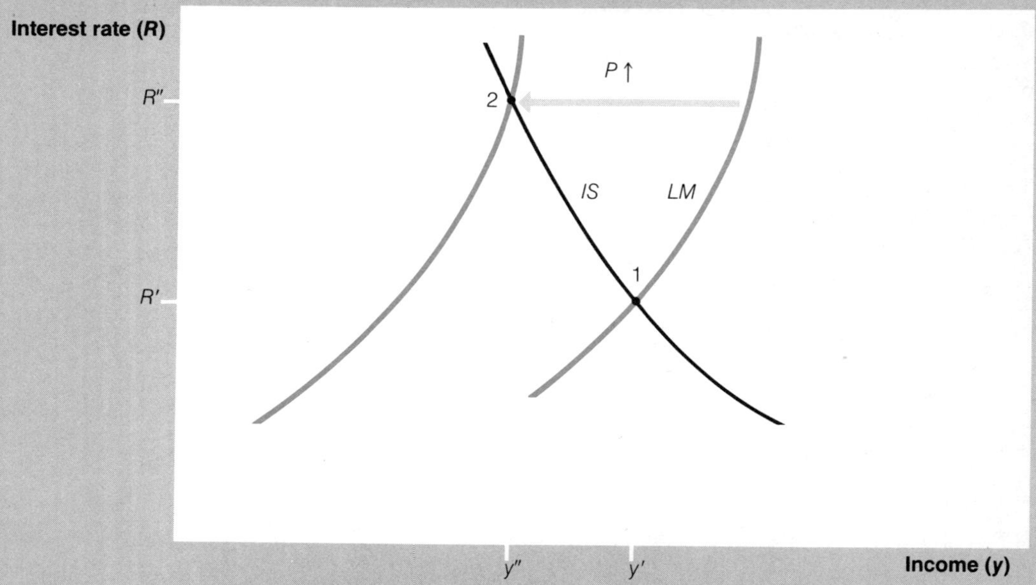

FIGURE 4.16 **Since an increase in the price level diminishes the size of the real money supply, the *LM* curve is shifted leftward. This contraction of the real money supply increases the interest rate to *R″* and, by discouraging private spending, reduces income to *y″*.**

tion is at Point 1 with income y' and interest rate R'. An increase in the price level shifts the *LM* curve leftward since the higher price level reduces the real money supply as surely as if the Federal Reserve had withdrawn money from circulation. The new *IS-LM* intersection is at Point 2, with the lower income y'' and the higher interest rate R''.

Figure 4.17 summarizes this inverse demand-side interrelationship between prices and income. Here, Points 1 and 2 on the aggregate demand curve correspond to those in Figure 4.16. Point 2 shows that the higher price reduces demand-side income to y''.

The interest rate is higher at Point 2 than at Point 1 even though, in Figure 4.17, the aggregate demand curve puts the interest rate adjustments behind the scenes and out of sight. The gain is a cleaner graph, since we are dealing with only two variables instead of three; the cost is that we cannot directly see what is happening to the third variable, the interest rate. The aggregate demand curve, however, does not ignore interest rates; since it is a summary of the *IS-LM* curves, interest rate changes have already been taken into account.

The aggregate demand curve shown in Figure 4.17 is easy to remember because it looks like any standard demand curve—for hot dogs, cottage cheese, or

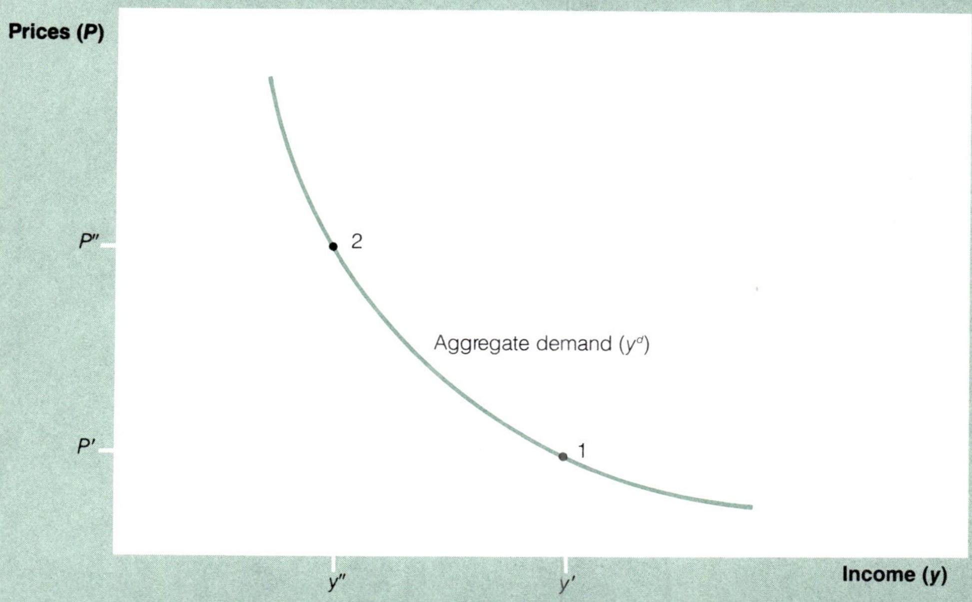

FIGURE 4.17 **The aggregate demand curve shows the inverse relationship between P and y that is demonstrated in Figure 4.16. As the price level rises from P' to P'', the contraction of the real money supply reduces income from y' to y''.**

jogging shoes. The underlying logic, however, is quite different. A micro demand curve involves a change in one price, with all other prices held constant. The resultant change in relative prices twists our spending patterns: When the price of hot dogs goes up, we buy fewer hot dogs and relatively more hamburger, fish, and chicken. The macro aggregate demand curve involves a change in *all* prices. Aggregate expenditures decline, not because we are shifting from hot dogs to hamburgers, but because the real money supply is tightened, pushing interest rates upward.

Shifts in the aggregate demand curve

Any economic event (other than a change in the price level) that shifts the *IS* curve or the *LM* curve will also shift the aggregate demand curve. Figure 4.18 shows a rightward movement in the *LM* curve, due either to an increase in the nominal money supply or to a drop in money demand. At any given price level, income increases from y' to y'', as the *IS-LM* intersection moves from Point 1 to Point 2. Figure 4.19 shows the corresponding shift in the aggregate demand curve. Similarly, *any* event that increases expenditures, shifting the *IS*

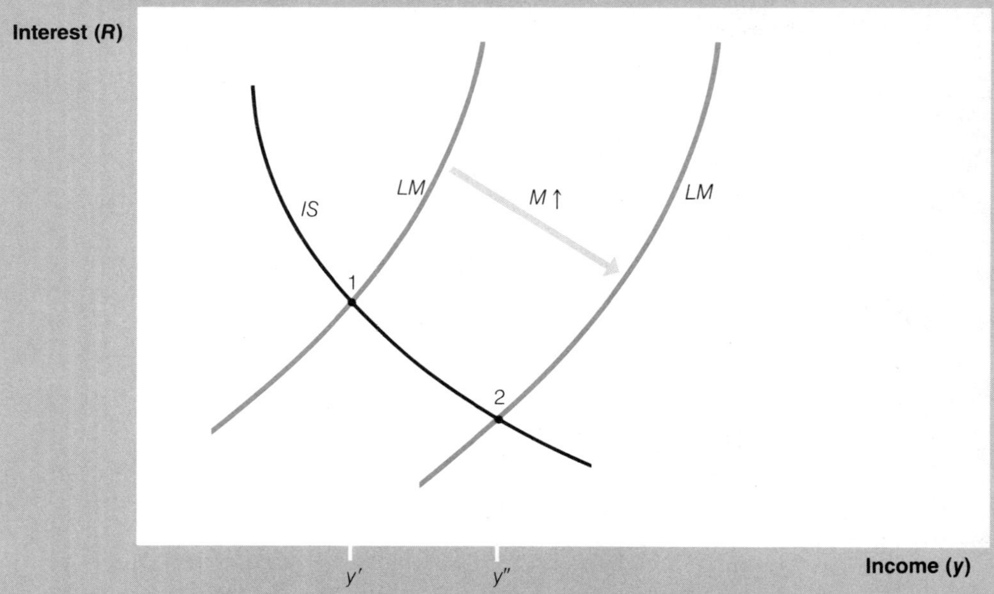

FIGURE 4.18 **An increase in the money supply shifts the *LM* curve rightward. The interest rate falls, and both spending and income increase along the *IS* curve. This drop in the interest rate and rise in income persuade people to hold the additional money supplied.**

curve rightward, will also shift the aggregate demand curve rightward. In general, then, **an expansionary rightward movement of the *IS* curve or the *LM* curve will cause an expansionary rightward movement of the aggregate demand curve. Contractionary, leftward movements of the *IS* and *LM* curves shift the aggregate demand curve leftward, too.**

PRICE ADJUSTMENTS AND STABILITY OF THE ECONOMY

Classical economists did not use *IS* and *LM* curves, taking it for granted that aggregate demand and the price level were inversely related, without really explaining why. They believed that if the economy booms, prices will rise and soon stifle demand. In this way, a booming economy automatically cools itself. If, on the other hand, aggregate demand slumps, threatening a recession, then prices will fall and soon bolster demand, keeping the economy strong. A lower price level is the medicine that an economy takes to cure a recession. Thus an economy automatically stabilizes aggregate demand through price adjustments.

This argument has considerable appeal, but as we have seen, the reasons for a negatively sloped aggregate demand curve are much more subtle than they ap-

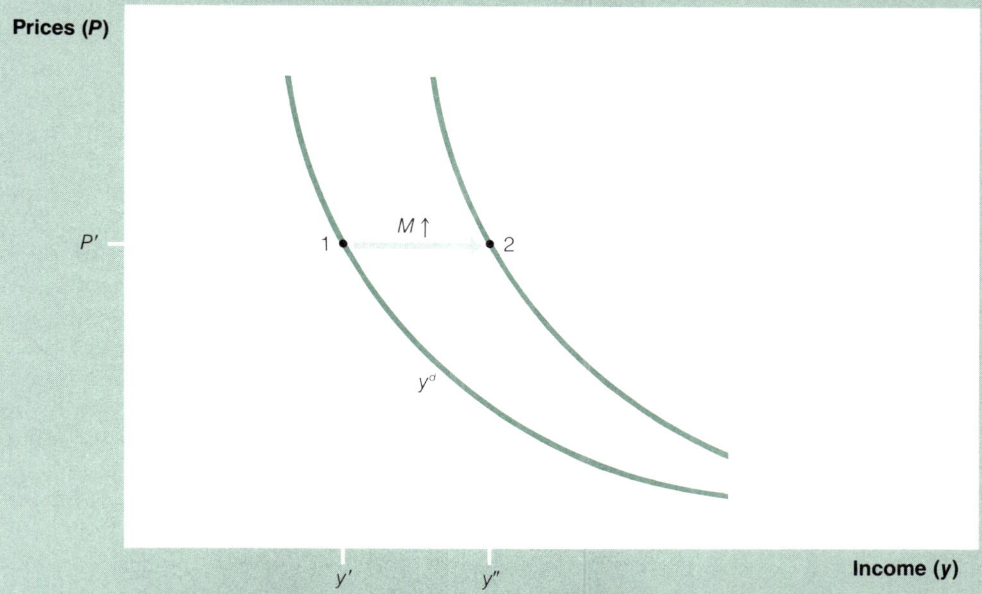

FIGURE 4.19 **Figure 4.18 shows how an expansion of the money supply reduces the interest rate and increases income at any given price level. This increase in income implies a rightward shift, shown here, of the aggregate demand curve.**

pear at first glance. As individual consumers, it is easy to see how we might buy more steak, for example, if its price were lower. But that hypothetical response assumes that other prices are unchanged. One of the reasons we would buy more steak is that it would then be cheaper than hot dogs, chicken, and other alternatives. But in stabilizing aggregate demand, we're talking about a fall in all prices. The proper question is: If all prices fall, will we buy more of everything?

If our dollar incomes were constant while all prices fell, then our real incomes would increase and we probably would spend more. A fall in prices with constant nominal income is like an increase in nominal income with constant prices. Either way, we could afford a higher standard of living and we would probably choose to enjoy one. But, if all prices fell, aggregate nominal income would not be constant. Lower prices do make things cheaper, but they also reduce the income of those who are selling these cheaper things. Sellers are losing what buyers are gaining. And, in the aggregate, we are all both sellers and buyers. If prices drop 10%, then aggregate nominal income will also drop 10%, and aggregate real income will be unchanged. Why, if our real income is unchanged, would we buy more commodities? Wouldn't we buy the same quantity of commodities, so that real spending, like real income, is constant?

The Keynes effect

Keynes pondered this question and concluded that the classical faith was indeed misplaced. Instead, he reasoned that any stimulus to aggregate demand will be indirect and, surprisingly, work through financial markets. Lower prices will increase the real value of the money supply, shifting the *LM* curve to the right just as if the monetary authorities had printed more money. When prices decline 10%, the existing money supply becomes larger relative to people's needs for money to carry out transactions. Not needing so much money, people buy securities, pushing bond prices up and interest rates down. These lower interest rates provide a stimulus to expenditures on goods and services. Put graphically, a lower price level slides the *LM* curve rightward. The interest rate declines, and expenditures increase along the stationary *IS* curve. This price-induced shift in the *LM* curve is now called the *Keynes effect.*

After identifying how lower prices might logically raise aggregate demand, Keynes went on to argue that this was a slim reed on which to hang a faith that recessions would quickly cure themselves. Keynes saw at least three reasons why recessions might persist for an uncomfortably long period. First, prices and wages might not fall quickly. In 1933, the unemployment rate was 25% and GNP was less than half the size of potential GNP. It is hard to imagine a more depressed economy. Yet, still, prices and wages did not freely fall to replenish aggregate demand. Wages fell by about 1% in 1933, while prices dropped by 2%, not nearly enough to have a significant effect on the economy. In 1934, the unemployment rate was still 22% and, yet, wages now went up by 18% and prices by 7%! Where was the Walrasian auctioneer when we needed him or her?

Keynes' second argument was that, during the Great Depression, even had prices fallen, there would have been little stimulus to aggregate demand. In theory, a lower price level will increase the real money supply, reducing interest rates and stimulating spending (particularly investment spending). But interest rates were already very low. In 1933, the interest rate on the safest ("prime") business loans was 1.5% and the rate on Treasury bills was 0.5%. Interest rates had very little room left to fall. (They certainly would not turn negative as long as cash offered a safe 0% return.) In 1934, the prime rate was still 1.5%, while the Treasury bill rate dropped to 0.3%, hardly enough to unleash a torrent of investment spending.

Further, Keynes did not think that interest rates could matter very much to such a prostrated economy. Who would be crazy enough to invest in new plant and equipment when so much was already sitting idle? Gross investment was, in fact, only $1.4 billion in 1933, not enough even to offset the depreciation of existing capital. Net investment was − $5.8 billion in 1933. The nation's capital stock had actually shrunk as businesses were allowed to deteriorate. Entrepreneurs did not need a slightly more favorable interest rate; they needed customers.*

* We would formally model Keynes' argument as follows. If interest rates cannot fall much farther, because money would then dominate bonds, then the *LM* curve is horizontal. If interest rates do not affect expenditures, then the *IS* curve is vertical. In either case, a lower price level shifts the *LM* curve to the right but does not budge the level of y at which the *IS* and *LM* curves intersect. The aggregate demand curve is consequently vertical, with lower prices having no effect on it.

Keynes' third explanation as to why falling prices don't quickly end recessions was that deflationary expectations might actually reduce expenditures. People who expect prices to fall may well hoard cash, postpone expenditures, and wait for lower prices. This drop in demand will weaken the economy even further and put additional downward pressure on prices. There could be a self-fulfilling deflationary spiral, with the economy getting progressively worse instead of better. We will look at some of the consequences of inflationary and deflationary expectations in Chapter 8.

The Pigou effect

While Keynes tried to overthrow classical economics, A. C. Pigou* tried to defend it. After reading the *General Theory* and Keynes' explanation of how falling prices might bolster aggregate demand through financial markets, Pigou suggested another possible avenue.

Pigou noted that the real value of money and bonds hinges on the price of commodities. A higher price level reduces the real purchasing power of accumulated financial assets. And when people find their real wealth diminished, they are likely to try to offset this erosion by reducing their expenditures and saving a bit more. Thus, as the price level increases, the *IS* curve should shift leftward. Conversely, a lower price level increases the real value of cash and bonds, and this increase in real wealth encourages spending, shifting the *IS* curve rightward. This price-induced shift in the *IS* curve is called the *Pigou effect.*

It does make sense that people will spend more if they find themselves wealthier. The Pigou effect is often illustrated by extreme cases. Wassily Leontieff put it this way: "If wages are low enough, this dime in my hand will employ everyone in the nation; and my only requirement on them is that they do not show up at my office for work. . . .[3]" If prices fell low enough, you could buy Cleveland for a dime, and you might be tempted to spend a nickel.

But, in practice, if prices do not fall so drastically, is the Pigou effect of any practical importance? Between 1929 and 1933, the Consumer Price Index fell by about 25%. The outstanding stock of cash and government bonds came to about $20 billion, and economists estimate that an extra $1 billion in wealth increases spending by about $0.05 billion. If so, then even a 50% fall in prices would have increased the real value of these financial assets by only $20 billion and increased spending by $1 billion. That would have been a very light brake on the collapse of GNP from $105 billion in 1929 to $56 billion in 1933.

There are also redistributional consequences that may reverse the Pigou effect. Most financial assets are someone else's financial liability. If you buy a corporate bond and the price level declines, then the real value of that bond increases. You will be wealthier, but the corporation's shareholders will be that much poorer. If you take out a mortgage to buy a house and prices then decline, the real value of the mortgage will increase. The lender will be richer and you will be closer to bankruptcy. The richer creditors may spend more, but the

* Pigou, like Keynes, had been a star pupil of Alfred Marshall and then a celebrated professor at Cambridge University.

poorer debtors will probably spend less. There is no guarantee that aggregate expenditures will, on balance, increase as Pigou predicted.

Indeed, one of the greatest American economists, Irving Fisher, believed that the Great Depression was actually exacerbated by lower prices. He argued that debtors were forced to reduce their spending in order to meet their more burdensome debt payments, while creditors were under no similar compulsion to quickly spend their new wealth. Fisher argued that, on balance, lower prices probably reduce spending so that the *IS* curve, contrary to the effect postulated by Pigou for this case, actually shifts leftward.

Pigou, himself, did not have much faith in the healing powers of the Pigou effect. He criticized Keynes for leaving a hole in his theory, but he admitted that it was of little practical importance. Pigou saw that prices did not fall freely and that their decline was not painless. He witnessed many bankruptcies and even a few riots during deflations. He agreed with Keynes that the real money supply, M/P, could be increased more quickly and less painfully by increasing M, rather than by reducing P. Since the Pigou effect is undoubtedly small and may be reversed by redistributional considerations, we will not include it in our model of aggregate demand.

APPENDIX: THE *IS* AND *LM* EQUATIONS

We can derive explicit equations showing the slopes and intercepts of the *IS* and *LM* curves. Remember that the *IS* curve came from the intersection of the expenditure function (Equation 4.3) and the income-equals-expenditures condition (Equation 2.1). The *IS* curve shows values of R and y that are consistent with these two equations. We can find these values by substituting Equation 4.3 into Equation 2.1, giving

$$y = e_0 + e_y y + e_R R, \qquad 0 < e_y < 1,\ e_R < 0$$

Solving for R,

$$R = \frac{e_0}{-e_R} + \frac{(e_y - 1)}{-e_R} y \tag{4.8}$$

This is the equation for the *IS* curve graphed in Figure 4.4. Since e_R is negative, the denominators $(-e_R)$ are positive. The intercept is $e_0/-e_R$. The slope is $(e_y - 1)/e_R$, which is negative since $e_y < 1$. The *IS* curve is relatively flat if e_y is close to 1 or if e_R is a large negative number (indicating that spending is very responsive to interest rates). If spending is not sensitive to interest rates ($e_R = 0$), then the *IS* curve is vertical (its slope, $-\infty$).

The *LM* curve comes from the equality of money demand (Equation 4.5) with money supply, M/P:

$$l_0 + ly + l_R R = M/P \qquad l_y > 0,\ l_R < 0$$

Solving for R,

$$R = \frac{l_0 - M/P}{-l_R} + \frac{l_y}{-l_R} \tag{4.9}$$

This is the equation for the *LM* curve graphed in Figure 4.9. Since l_R is negative, the denominators $(-l_R)$ are positive. The intercept is $(l_0 - M/P)/(-l_R)$. The slope, $l_y/(-l_R)$, is positive. The *LM* curve is vertical if $l_R = 0$, indicating that money demand is not sensitive to interest rates.

IMPORTANT TERMS AND CONCEPTS

demand side
supply side
M1
IS curve
LM curve
quantity theory
velocity
aggregate demand curve
Keynes effect
Pigou effect

The demand side of the economy encompasses expenditures and financial markets, depicted by the *IS* and *LM* curves. With *R* and *y* the axes, the *IS* curve is negatively sloped and the *LM* curve positively sloped. The *IS* curve is shifted rightward by increases in expenditures, the *LM* curve by increases in the real money supply or decreases in money demand.

The aggregate demand curve summarizes the demand side of the economy. With *P* and *y* the axes, it is negatively sloped. Based on the intersection of the *IS* and *LM* curves, the aggregate demand curve states that an increase in the price level reduces the level of income for which income equals expenditures and money demand equals supply. The economic logic is that an increase in the price level reduces the real money supply, pushing interest rates up and discouraging spending. Expansionary shifts in the *IS* or *LM* curves shift the aggregate demand curve in an expansionary rightward direction.

Demand-side crowding out refers to the fact that, while an increase in government spending will increase national income, it will also raise money demand, pushing interest rates up and thereby discouraging private spending, especially private investment spending. When this crowding out is taken into account the stimulus to national income of government spending is not as large as the income-expenditure multiplier calculated in Chapter 3.

The quantity theory assumes that velocity is predetermined, so that money demand does not depend on interest rates. If the quantity theory were true, the *LM* curve would be vertical and there would be complete demand-side crowding out. But theory and empirical evidence both say that money demand (and, hence, velocity) does depend on interest rates.

Pigou pointed out that changes in the price level also affect the real value of people's wealth and, so, may affect their spending and shift the *IS* curve. But these effects are likely to be small. In addition, price changes affect both debtors and creditors, and it is unclear which effects will be stronger. For these reasons, our model omits the Pigou effect.

EXERCISES

1. How would the *IS* and *LM* curves be affected by an increase in
   a. output, *y*
   b. interest rate, *R*
   c. price level, *P*

2. How would the *IS* and *LM* curves be affected by
   a. increase in government spending
   b. a tax cut for consumers
   c. increased business profit expectations
   d. increased money supply
   e. increased demand for money

3. What would the *LM* curve look like if the demand for money was not sensitive to interest rates?

4. How would the *IS* and *LM* curves be affected by increased service charges on credit cards?

5. How would the *IS* and *LM* curves be affected by an increased availability of money market funds, which reduces the demand for cash and bank checking accounts?

6. How will a bond-financed increase in government spending affect output, prices, the interest rate, money supply, money demand, and velocity?

7. If the marginal propensity to spend out of income is 0.7, then a $1 billion increase in government spending will increase real national income by which one of the following: zero, between $0 and $2.5 billion, $2.5 billion, more than $2.5 billion.

8. Explain how each of the events listed in Exercise 1 will affect the aggregate demand curve.

9. Explain how each of the events listed in Exercise 2 will affect the aggregate demand curve.

10. What might Keynes have meant when he wrote: "It is, therefore, on the effect of a falling wage-and price-level on the demand for money that those who believe in the self-adjusting quality of the economic system must rest the weight of the argument."[4]

11. Derive the curves for the following *IS-LM* model of aggregate demand at a given price level:

$e_0 + e_y y + e_R R = y \qquad e_y > 1,\ e_R < 0$

$l_0 + l_y y + l_R R = M/P \qquad l_y > 0,\ l_R < 0.$

   a. What is the economic meaning of the assumption that $e_y > 1$?
   b. What are the implications, if any, of $e_y > 1$ for the *IS* and *LM* curves?
   c. How does an increase in e_o affect the *IS* curve?
   d. How does an increase in *M* affect the *LM* curve?
   e. Does an increase in e_o raise or lower *y*?
   f. Does an increase in *M* raise or lower *y*?
   g. What must be true of the slopes of the *IS* and *LM* curves if the answers to (e) and (f) are to be "raises y"?

REFERENCES

1. R. Solow, *Growth Theory: An Exposition,* Oxford: Oxford University Press, 1970.

2. J. Hicks, "Mr. Keynes and the 'Classics': A Suggested Interpretation," *Econometrica,* 5 (April 1937), pp. 147–59.

3. Quoted in P. Samuelson, "A Brief Survey of Post-Keynesian Developments," in *Keynes' General Theory: Reports of Three Decades,* Robert LeKachman, ed., New York: St. Martin's Press, 1964, p. 333.

4. J. M. Keynes, *The General Theory of Employment, Interest, and Money,* London: Macmillan, 1936, p. 266.

SUGGESTIONS FOR FURTHER READING

The IS-LM model was originally set forth in the Hicks article described in Reference 2. For a detailed construction of a more elaborate model see the very influential textbook, Don Patinkin, *Money, Interest, and Prices,* ed. 2, New York: Harper and Row, 1965.

CHAPTER FIVE

THE SUPPLY SIDE

Now, as I have often pointed out to my students, some of whom have been brought up in sporting circles, highbrow opinion is like a hunted hare; if you stand in the same place . . . it can be relied upon to come round to you in circle.

DENNIS ROBERTSON[1]

This chapter examines labor demand, labor supply, and production decisions. Classical models assume a labor market equilibrium in which unemployment is voluntary. In disequilibrium models, some unemployment is involuntary. This chapter also discusses the new classical market-equilibrium explanation of business cycles.

WE have now seen how to determine the demand-side level of income that is consistent with any given price level. But what will the price level be? To complete the model, we need to look at the supply side of the economy: production and the labor market. What we are looking for is a supply-side relationship between price level and output. Once we have this, we can put an aggregate supply curve together with our aggregate demand curve and determine the levels of output and prices.

Matters are complicated by the fact that there are two very different views of the supply curve. The classical approach is to assume that the labor and commodity markets are in equilibrium, with demand equal to supply. Keynes argued that the supply side is best characterized by market disequilibria. Recent years have seen the reappearance of the hunted hare (above), the emergence of the "new classical macroeconomics." We will examine these competing views, since each has very different implications for macroeconomic policy.

THE CLASSICAL LABOR MARKET

Conducted amidst the massive unemployment of the 1930s, the classical-versus-Keynesian, equilibrium-versus-disequilibrium debate focused on the labor market. Classical economists believed that both labor demand and labor

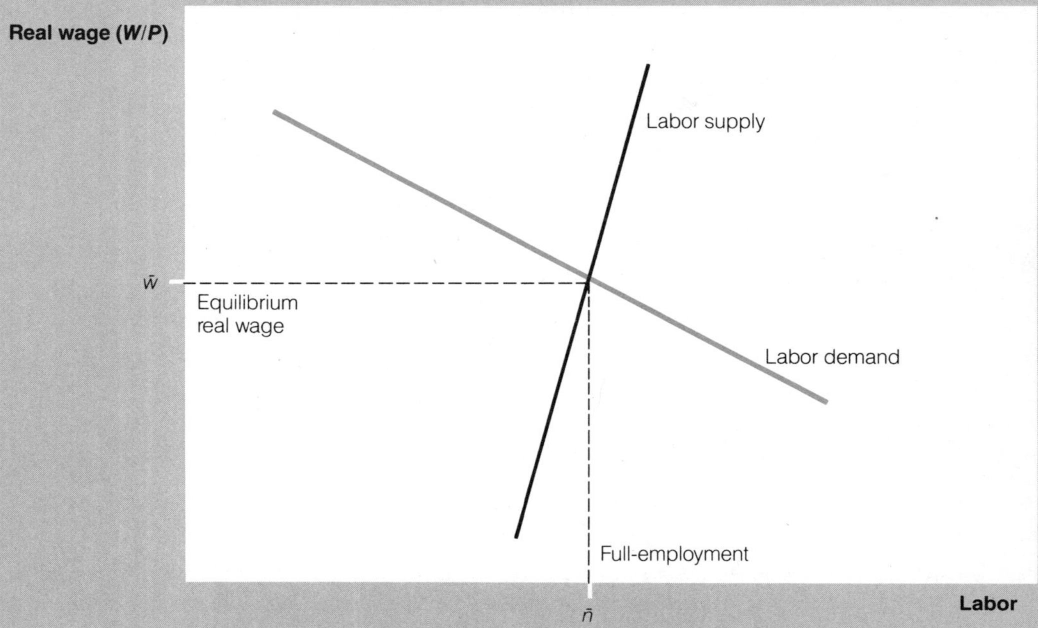

FIGURE 5.1 LABOR MARKET EQUILIBRIUM. **The intersection of the labor demand and supply lines determines the market-equilibrium levels of real wages and employment.**

supply depend mainly on the real wage rate, which measures the price of labor in commodity units:

$$w = W/P \tag{5.1}$$

where W is the nominal wage rate (\$/hour) and P is the price level (\$/commodity).

Firms use labor, plant, and equipment to produce output and make profits. In the short run, plant and equipment are fixed, so that the crucial decision is how much labor to employ in order to produce output. Microeconomics tells us that competitive profit-maximizing firms will hire labor up to the point where the marginal product of labor (measured in commodities per hour) is equal to the real wage rate (also measured in commodities per hour). The marginal product of additional labor declines as employment increases. Thus, the lower the real wage rate, the greater the labor demand. This inverse relationship between labor demand and the real wage rate is graphed in Figure 5.1.

Household labor supply is also assumed to depend upon the real wage rate, since this is the price (in commodity units) received for selling labor. The labor supply decision is a choice between work and leisure. Apart from the effects of the Protestant Ethic, employment is sought because of its wages or, more accurately, the commodities that can be purchased with those wages. People choose between enjoying leisure or enjoying the commodities that can be earned by working. The labor supply curve shown in Figure 5.1 indicates that an increase in the real wage rate increases the supply of labor.

Voluntary unemployment

Classical economists assumed that the labor market is in equilibrium, in that freely adjusting wages keep labor demand equal to labor supply. In Figure 5.1, there is full employment, $\bar{n}$, at the equilibrium real wage, $\bar{w}$. Since demand equals supply, everyone who wants to work at the prevailing wage has a job. Those who do not have jobs are voluntarily unemployed in that they simply do not want to work for the prevailing wages. The unemployed choose to be unemployed, deciding that they have better things to do with their time than working. Thus, if the labor market is in equilibrium, all unemployment is voluntary, with the exception that the unemployed may wish they were smarter or more skilled so as to qualify for jobs that command higher wages. Robert Lucas, a prominent new classical macroeconomist, wrote that

> the unemployed worker at any time can always find *some* job at once, and a firm can always fill a vacancy instantaneously. That neither does so *by choice* is not difficult to understand given the quality of the jobs and the employees which are easiest to find. Thus there is an involuntary element in all unemployment, in the sense that no one chooses bad luck over good; there is also a voluntary element in all unemployment, in the sense that however miserable one's current work options, one can always choose to accept them.[2]

To the classical macroeconomist, then, the statistically unemployed *choose* to be unemployed. The only disappointment suffered is by those who spurn available jobs because they have not yet faced up to the reality of their "bad luck." They are not worth what they would like to be paid, or, as Thomas Malthus wrote long ago, "These are the unhappy persons who in the great lottery of life have drawn a blank."[3]

Employment unaffected by the demand side

Note that in Figure 5.1 the real wage rate, $\bar{w}$, and full employment, $\bar{n}$, are uniquely determined by the intersection of the labor demand and supply curves. The demand for labor depends only on the real wage rate and on the productivity of labor. The supply of labor depends on the real wage rate and on how highly people value leisure relative to the goods and services that can be earned by working. Real wages may vary, but labor productivity and preferences are predetermined, at least in the short run. Productivity depends on intelligence, education, motivation, and training and is not going to be significantly affected by economic fluctuations in prices and interest rates.* Similarly, how highly people value expensive cars relative to dozing at the beach is not going to change overnight with the latest tremor in the CPI or the bond market.

* Interest rates do affect business investment, which does affect worker productivity, but it takes a considerable period to change significantly a nation's stock of factories, offices, and equipment.

Thus, classical economists assumed that the demand side of the economy does not affect labor demand and supply curves and, hence, does not affect the equilibrium (or full) employment, $\bar{n}$, and real wage rate, $\bar{w}$: **In the classical equilibrium model, commodity demand and financial markets do not affect current real wages and employment since they do not affect labor demand or supply.** The demand side of the economy may alter interest rates and the price level, but real wages will stay at the equilibrium level $\bar{w}$. If, for instance, there is an increase in commodity demand that causes commodity prices to rise 20%, then nominal wages will also rise 20% to maintain the equilibrium real wage. If the price level falls 20%, the nominal wage will freely drop 20%. Real wages and employment will be unchanged.

THE CLASSICAL AGGREGATE SUPPLY CURVE

A nation's "production function" specifies how much output will be produced by an efficient utilization of different levels of inputs—plant, equipment, raw materials, and labor. In the short run, we can think of a nation's plant, equipment, raw materials, and technology as predetermined, so that, with these factors held constant, the production function then relates how much output is forthcoming at different levels of employment. This production function is shown in Figure 5.2, along with a classical labor market. The production function is positively sloped because when more labor is employed more output can be produced. It is convex, rather than a straight line, because of the presumed diminishing marginal productivity of labor. With a given stock of plant and equipment, productivity declines as current employees work longer or as new, less qualified employees are hired.

For any given level of employment, n, the production function shows the corresponding level of output, y, **In the classical model, there is full employment, $\bar{n}$, and consequently full-employment output, $\bar{y}$,** as shown in the figure. Using this reasoning, classical economists assumed that output, like real wages and employment, is determined by the supply side of the economy. Thus it is independent of spending and of financial markets, the price level and interest rate being of no consequence to employment and output. All that matters are supply-side factors: labor demand, labor supply, and productivity. Output is thus said to be supply-determined in the classical model. Since employment and output are at their full-employment levels, irrespective of the price level, the relationship between prices and output is vertical, as drawn in Figure 5.3. The price level may rise or fall, but output stays at the full-employment level, $\bar{y}$.

LABOR MARKET DISEQUILIBRIA

The foregoing classical analysis is a simple, tidy theory that Keynes scornfully dismissed as largely irrelevant:

> The classical theorists resemble Euclidean geometers in a non-Euclidean world who, discovering that in experience straight lines apparently parallel often meet, rebuke the lines for not keeping straight—as the only remedy for the unfortunate collisions which

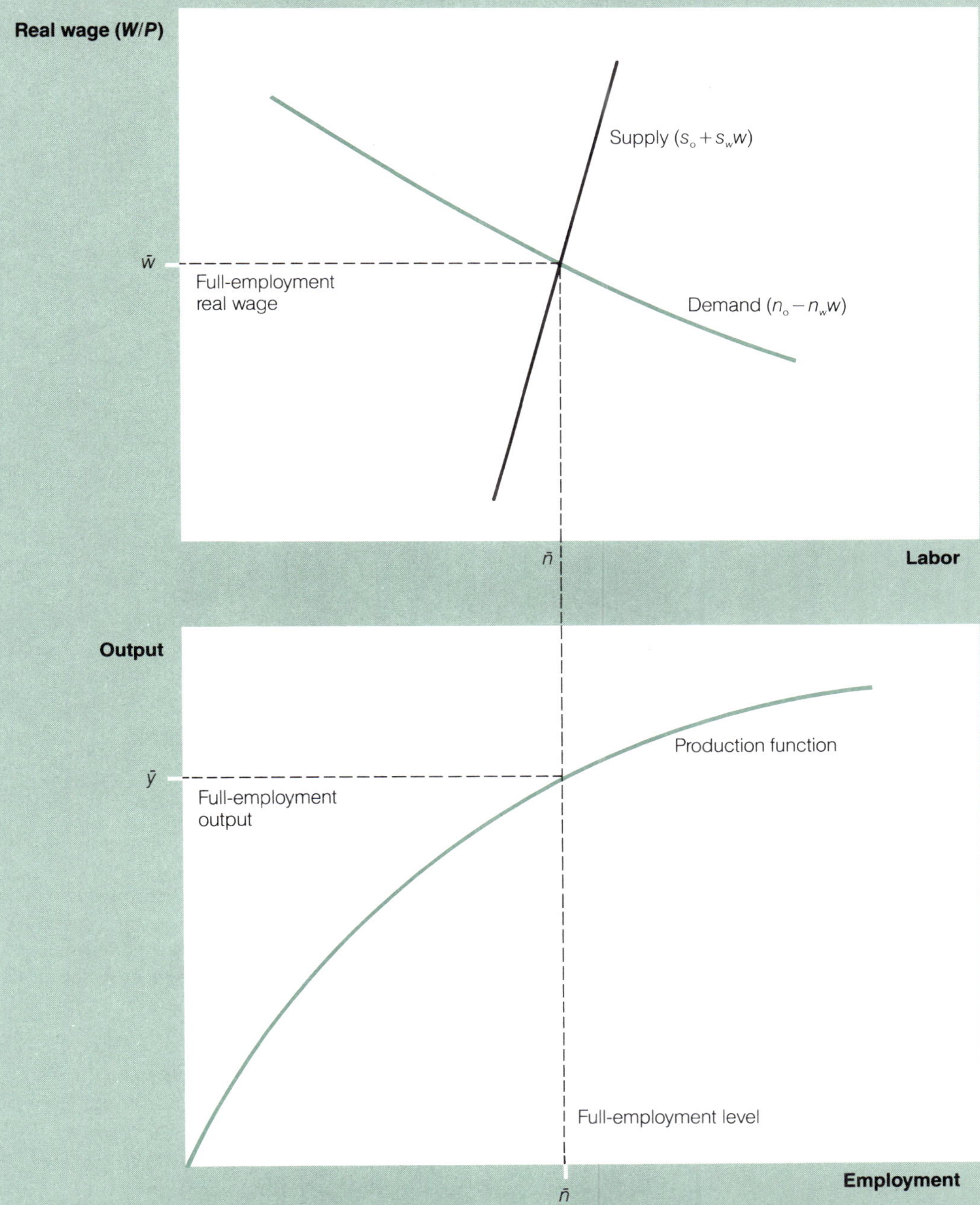

FIGURE 5.2 CLASSICAL EMPLOYMENT AND OUTPUT. In the classical market-equilibrium model, employment is determined by the intersection of labor demand and supply. The production function then tells how much these people will produce. Thus real wages, employment, and output are determined by the supply side of the economy—labor demand, labor supply, and the production function.

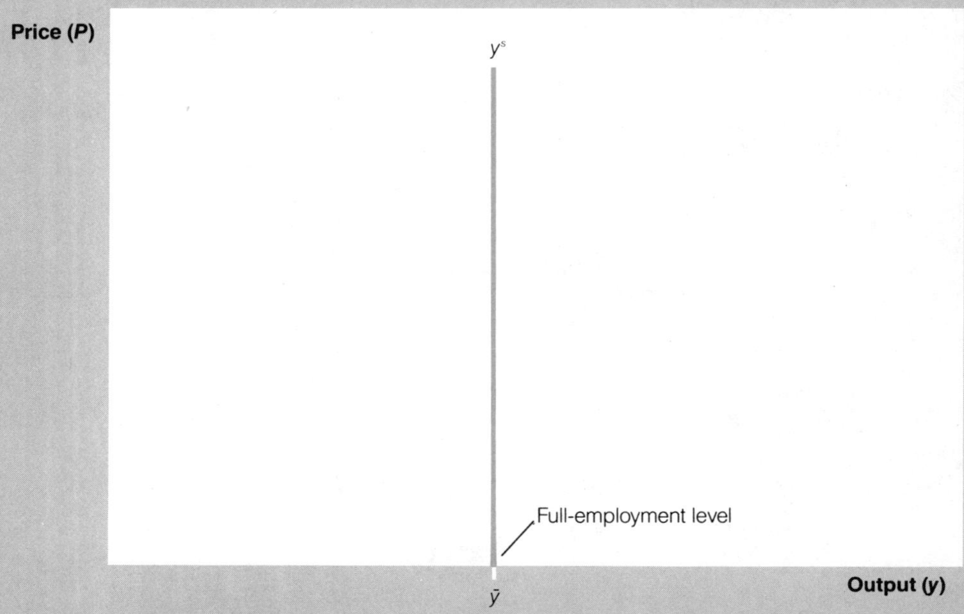

FIGURE 5.3 **In the classical market-equilibrium model, output is unrelated to the price level. Whether prices go up or down, wages adjust to keep real wages constant and to keep employment and output at their full-employment levels. Thus the aggregate supply curve is vertical.**

are occurring. Yet, in truth, there is no remedy except to throw over the axiom of parallels and to work out a non-Euclidean geometry. Something similar is required today in economics. We need to throw over the . . . classical doctrine and to work out the behavior of a system in which involuntary unemployment in the strict sense is possible.[4]

A person is involuntarily unemployed if he or she is qualified for a job and willing to work for the prevailing real wage, but is not offered the job. Consider, for instance, people with PhDs who would like to be French professors. Their unemployment is voluntary if the market for French professors is in equilibrium, so that those people without jobs choose to be unemployed, turning down job offers because, at the prevailing wage, they prefer leisure to work. Their unemployment is *in*voluntary if they are willing to work for the wages paid others with similar skills, but are told, "Sorry, we have no openings now; but we'll keep your application on file." The same test can be applied to unemployed auto workers, carpenters, and financial managers. Involuntary unemployment necessarily involves a market disequilibrium.

Keynes and his major interpreters argued that most labor markets are in perpetual disequilibrium. At any point in time, some labor markets have excess

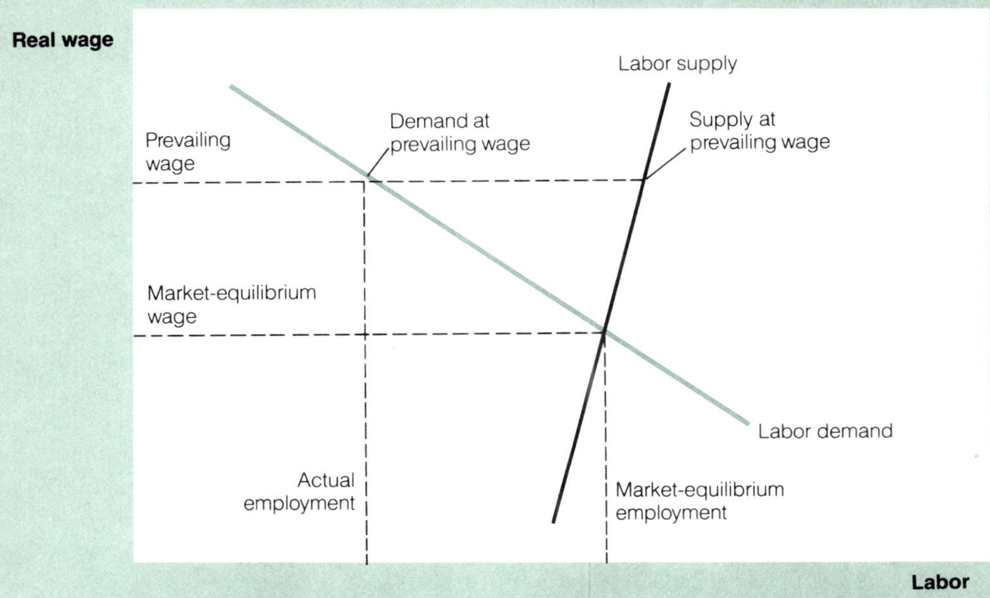

FIGURE 5.4 EXCESS LABOR SUPPLY. **When the prevailing wage is above the equilibrium wage, labor supply exceeds labor demand. If actual employment is demand-determined in this situation, then actual employment will be below the equilibrium level.**

supply (that is, unemployment); some have excess demand (vacancies); and some are close to equilibrium. Everywhere, wages are set for extended periods of time and do not immediately respond to every jiggle in labor demand and supply. In the United States, most nonunion wages are set anually, while union contracts are typically of two- to three-year duration. Wage scales often have a rigid structure (frequently based on seniority) that appears to have little relation to the demands and supplies for different types of labor. Nominal wage cuts are strongly resisted and rarely occur.

Figure 5.4 shows a situation in which wages are sticky and there is an excess supply of labor. Either employment will be greater than demand, with firms hiring more labor than they really want, or employment will be less than supply, with households selling less labor than they would like. If firms employ only as much labor as they want, then actual employment is demand-determined, as drawn in Figure 5.4. With an excess labor supply, then, employment is determined by business' labor demand, rather than the equilibration of demand and supply.

Figure 5.5 shows the reverse situation, where labor demand exceeds labor supply at the prevailing wage. If people will not work more than they want to, then employment is supply-determined. Businesses are constrained in their employment by the availability of willing workers. Thus, with an excess labor demand, employment is determined by the labor supply rather than the equilibration of demand and supply.

Wages in excess-demand labor markets do tend to rise faster than wages in excess-supply markets, and some persons do migrate to unfilled jobs, either from other occupations or geographic areas. But the adjustment is slow and imperfect, and vacancies persist for some time. Similarly, wage increases in excess-supply markets may be smaller than in excess-demand markets, but wages do not decline except in drastic circumstances. Instead of the occurrence of rapid wage cuts to restore equilibrium, unemployment persists for some time.

Employment is a commitment

Minimum wage laws, labor unions, and powerful employers are part of the story. More fundamental is the nature of labor and employment. Buying and selling labor is not like trading soybeans. Decisions to offer and accept employment involve substantial commitments by both sides. An employer invests

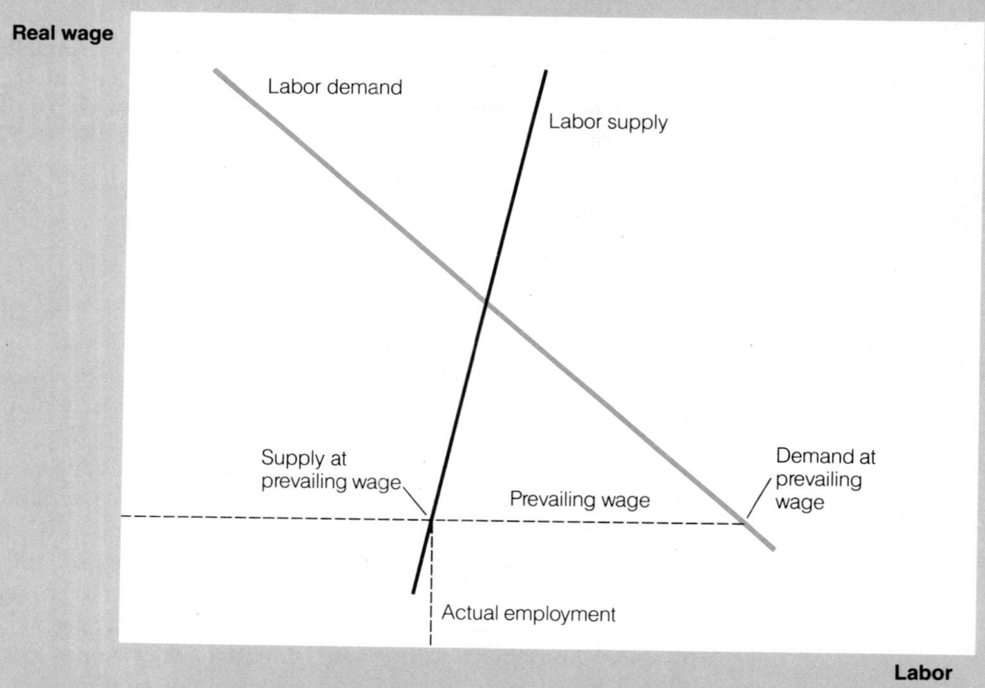

FIGURE 5.5 **EXCESS LABOR DEMAND. When the prevailing wage is below the equilibrium wage, labor demand exceeds labor supply. If employment is supply-determined, then actual employment will be below the equilibrium level.**

considerable resources in selecting, hiring, and training each employee. It is also expensive for an employee to find an attractive job and become proficient at it. There is a substantial bond between employer and employee that neither side is eager to break. An employer does not want to lose experienced and proven employees, particularly those with skills specifically honed to the firm. An employee will want to stay to utilize acquired skills and to avoid the staggering financial and social costs of relocation. In fact, half of all workers are in jobs that last 15 years or more.[5]

In such an environment it is not surprising that businesses do not make impersonal daily hirings and firings in response to fluctuating market conditions. An employer who impulsively slashed wages and fired workers whenever business was slow or when new job applicants were available would find it difficult to attract employees. Workers demand and get stability in wages and employment.

What is full employment?

The classical economists assumed labor market equilibrium, reasoning that, if the labor market was not now in equilibrium, at least it was moving quickly towards it. One difficulty with this view is the treatment of labor as one vast homogeneous market. James Tobin has argued that, "The myth of macroeconomics is that relations among aggregates are enlarged analogies of relations among corresponding variables for individual households, firms, industries, and markets. The myth is a harmless and useful simplification in many contexts, but sometimes it misses the essence of the phenomenon."[6]

In Tobin's view, it is better to think of labor as traded in many partially segmented markets. In such diverse markets,

> intersectoral shocks keep individual labor markets in diverse states of disequilibrium; . . . Aggregate demand may be stable, but beneath its stability is never-ending flux; new products, new processes, new tastes and fashions, new developments of land and natural resources, obsolescent industries and declining areas.[7]

While wages are not very responsive to market conditions, the labor demand and supply curves themselves are continually moving about. Thus there are always excess demands in some markets and excess supplies in others. In such an environment, the level of "full employment" at market-clearing wage rates seldom, if ever, occurs and therefore has little practical relevance. Indeed, the very concept of full employment is ambiguous. An influential British labor economist, William Beveridge, suggested that

> Full employment . . . means always having more vacant jobs than unemployed. . . . It means that the jobs are at fair wages, of such a kind, and so located that the unemployed . . . can reasonably be expected to take them; it means by consequence, that the normal lag between losing one job and finding another will be very short. The proposition . . . means that the labour market should always be a seller's market rather than a buyer's market.[8]

Notice how little resemblance this bears to the classical labor market equilibrium.

While, as Lucas points out, an unemployed French teacher who is told that all such jobs are filled could probably get a job cleaning houses or delivering newspapers, Keynesians view that bleak choice as socially wasteful involuntary unemployment. If markets really worked, the wages of employed French teachers would fall freely, and more jobs teaching French would open up. If there were really full employment, the French teachers without jobs would be those who freely decided that the wages were not high enough to make teaching worth their while, rather than persons without seniority or tenure who are simply told that there are no openings.*

Virtually all economists now agree that most wages are not perfectly flexible in the short run. Explicit and implicit contracts between employers and employees keep wages firm even when there are qualified people available who would work for lower wages. Classical economists were right in arguing that excess labor supplies and demands do exert pressures on wages. But Keynes was right in arguing that wage adjustments are neither perfect nor instantaneous. In a hypothetical long run in which the world stands still while wages adjust, wages should eventually find their equilibrium levels. But in a world that never does stand still, wages often will not be at equilibrium levels.

This labor market disequilibrium does not mean that every person who is counted as unemployed is an involuntary victim of sticky wages and seniority rules. Some of the unemployed are too choosy, asking for jobs and wages for which, realistically, they are not qualified. Such people are really voluntarily unemployed. On the other hand, some of the people who are employed are actually trapped in bad jobs and unable to break into careers for which they are qualified. They have had to settle for less because sticky wages and tenure rules protect the jobs of less qualified people. The reported unemployment rate both overstates and understates the extent to which labor markets are not in equilibrium. In the Appendix we explore further some of the reasons for sticky wages. For now, it suffices to note that labor market disequilibria can cause involuntary unemployment.

Higher prices increase employment

At any one moment, there will be simultaneously unemployment in some labor markets and vacancies in others. This picture of a multitude of shifting labor market disequilibria cannot be painted easily in a model with only one labor market. The essential idea is that nominal wage rates are set sluggishly, so that labor demand does not necessarily equal supply. Wages are not constant, but they are largely predetermined in that they are little affected by current fluctuations in output, prices, and interest rates.

There may be occasions when almost all labor markets are either in equilibrium or have excess demand. If so, then aggregate employment is constrained by the aggregate labor supply.[9] But, since nominal wages rise more easily than they fall, the more normal situation is one in which many labor markets have excess supplies. In these excess-supply labor markets, employment is demand-

* Professional job markets are particularly rigid, due in part to tenure rules and in part to a collegial disdain for aggressive hiring and firing. Academic jobs are a good example. One dean declared that his college would be sued (and would lose) if they ever reduced any professor's salary. In the 1970s, humanities enrollments dropped by 50% while faculty positions in the humanities declined by only 3%. Business enrollments increased by 50% while business faculty positions increased by a mere 1%. It is less stressful for the existing faculties to absorb these dislocations than to slaughter their colleagues as enrollments fluctuate.

INVOLUNTARY UNEMPLOYMENT

The existence of involuntary unemployment has posed a major theoretical problem for economists. Most economics concerns supply and demand. In most markets, it is natural that supply equal demand unless there is some cartel power or legal restriction that prevents market forces from fully operating. In the case of the labor market this could be union power (a cartel) or minimum-wage laws (a legal restriction). But unemployment does not affect only workers whose earning power is close to the minimum wage and workers in unionized occupations or industries. Thus there is the question: Why should demand be equal to supply in the wheat market and in the stock market, but not in the labor market? Why should there be many people, more than 10 percent of the labor force in recent U.S. history, who are unemployed—that is, people who look for work but cannot find it?

To some economists this last question has been so perplexing that they have tried to explain unemployment in models in which supply *equals* demand. According to this view the unemployed can get jobs at the market-clearing wage rate but they are just *searching* for better opportunities. If that is the case, they are searching for a surprisingly long time. In the wheat market and the stock market, contracts are typically sold in hours, if not minutes. In contrast, unemployed workers often look for work for long periods. Since World War II the average person currently unemployed looked for a job for an average of six months. Those unemployed in July 1982 (the height of the recent recession) looked for ten months before they found employment or dropped out of the labor force. This evidence suggests strongly that, indeed, unlike the stock market and the wheat market, not all labor markets clear.

Why do wages, the prices of labor services, not fall so that supply equals demand? A new theory, "the efficiency wage theory of unemployment," explains why firms will not set their wages at market clearing and, therefore, why there will be unemployment in equilibrium. Consider what could happen in many labor markets if firms did not pay workers more than the market-clearing wage. If workers could readily find jobs of the same quality as their current jobs, there would be no incentive to stay in their current ones. Turnover would be very high. Workers would not have much to lose by shirking. If fired, they could easily find another job of the same quality. If workers could readily find jobs of the same quality as their current job, loyalty to their firm would be undermined. Why should good performance be given to an employer who could be replaced easily, as would be the case if the labor market cleared? Because employers wisely ask these questions, they often find it advantageous to pay more than workers' reservation wages. The net result is wages higher than market-clearing and, consequently, involuntary unemployment. This is the efficiency wage argument for unemployment.

This theory may explain involuntary unemployment but, at first glance, it leaves unanswered the question why *changes* in aggregate demand will change the equilibrium *level* of unemployment. Why, for example, should an increase of the money supply, say of five per cent, not result in the same increase in money wages and also of all prices in the economy, with no change in the real wage, so that there is no change in the demand for labor, and, consequently, no change in unemployment? To rephrase this, why should not such an economic system be *neutral*—that is, why should an increase in the money supply not leave all real properties of the economy unchanged, with proportionate increases in prices and in money wages?

With the efficiency wage theory of unemployment there is a simple answer. In the usual model in which wages have no effect on productivity or on the costs of labor turnover, if firms set wages five per cent higher than market-clearing level, loss in profits from such an error is five per cent of wage costs. If wages are lower than market-clearing, firms cannot obtain labor and, therefore, their losses are potentially greater. Therefore, firms have considerable incentive to pay no more or no less than the market-clearing wage.

In contrast, in the efficiency wage model of unemployment, the mistake of having sticky money wages in the presence of increased demand (due to an increase in the money supply, for example) will have very little effect on profits. In this model firms set wages optimally: The loss in profits from higher wage costs with marginally higher wages is just counterbalanced at the margin by the gain in profits from higher productivity due to lower labor turnover, less shirking, and higher morale. In such a world, firms that maintain sticky wages in the presence of shifts in aggregate demand, as is the key assumption of the Keynesian model, do not have much to lose, because the increases in costs due to higher wages is almost offset by the decreases in costs due to higher productivity. Thus firms that keep sticky money wages despite shifts in demand do not lose much. And if firms keep sticky money wages, since there is relatively little to gain by a more closely optimizing policy, changes in aggregate demand will produce changes in employment (and also in unemployment) just as has been taught in this book.

—George A. Akerlof and Janet L. Yellen

determined, as shown in Figure 5.4. The downward stickiness of nominal wages keeps the real wages from collapsing to the equilibrium level.

But if nominal wages are sticky, an increase in the price level will reduce real wages and increase employment! As the price level increases, the economy slides down the labor demand schedule (Figure 5.4).* Real wages decline, employment increases, and unemployment shrinks. **When nominal wages are sticky, an increase in commodity prices reduces real wages, encouraging firms to employ additional labor. Thus an increase in prices increases employment.**

To the classical economist, such behavior reflects irrationality. If more people accept jobs as real wages decline, then workers must not realize that their real wages have fallen. Perhaps they have "money illusion"—paying too much attention to nominal wages and too little to commodity prices. To Keynes, seeing disequilibria rather than equilibria, households are not on their labor supply curves, so that changes in real wages and employment do not reflect voluntary choices.

Relative wages

One consideration not yet mentioned is the all-or-nothing character of most labor supply decisions. When real wages drop, few workers have the option of working one or two fewer hours a week. Instead, the alternatives are to be employed full time or to be unemployed. And though many will complain if real wages decline, few will choose unemployment. A more realistic alternative is to change employers. As noted above, a job switch is far from costless, but it is surely more plausible than choosing unemployment. Notice, though, that a decision to switch jobs depends not on the level of real wages, but rather on wages in one job relative to others. Such reasoning led Keynes to argue that labor is more concerned with relative wages than with the level of real wages.

This explains why nominal wages are stickier than real wages and, specifically, why labor resists nominal wage cuts but accepts a decline in real wages that is caused by higher prices. In Tobin's words,

> Labor markets are decentralized, and there is no way money wages can fall in any one market without impairing the relative wage status of the workers there. A general rise in prices is a neutral and universal method of reducing real wages, the only method in a decentralized and uncontrolled economy. Inflation would not be needed, we may infer, if by government compulsion, economy-wide bargaining, or social compact, all money wage rates could be scaled down together.[10]

Workers with no good alternatives may accept lower real wages caused by a general inflation but will resist individual wage reductions that disturb relative wages. Labor markets are thus more easily cleared by price changes than by wage adjustments. This is one explanation of why higher prices increase employment.

* If wages do not keep up with prices in excess-demand labor markets, then the decline in real wages will reduce employment in these supply-constrained markets. Such reductions are usually swamped by the increases in employment in excess-supply markets because: (a) wages move up more easily than down; (b) there are usually more labor markets with excess supplies than with excess demands; and (c) labor supply curves are probably pretty steep, so that movements along them in excess-demand markets do not change employment much.

The Aggregate Supply Curve

If higher prices increase employment, then they also increase output. For example, in the case shown in Figure 5.6 the real wage rate, W_1/P_1, is too high for labor market equilibrium. Employment is demand-determined, with firms employing n_1 and producing y_1. There is strong resistance to cutting nominal wages to clear the labor market; real wages are more easily eroded through inflation. An increase in the price level, from P_1 to P_2, reduces real wages to W_1/P_2, persuading firms to increase employment to n_2 and production to y_2. Thus a rise in the price level increases both employment and output. The aggregate supply curve is as shown in Figure 5.7, with P_1, P_2, y_1, and y_2 corresponding to those in Figure 5.6.

So far, we have emphasized how an increase in prices can reduce real wages and increase employment. A fall in prices, if nominal wages are sticky (because of formal contracts and informal understandings), increases real wages and reduces the demand for labor. To show this we can use Figure 5.6 again, but this time going in the other direction. A decrease in prices, from P_2 to P_1, raises real wages from W_1/P_2 to W_1/P_1. Employment falls from n_2 to n_1 and production slumps from y_2 to y_1. The economy moves along the aggregate supply curve shown in Figure 5.7, but this time, down the curve instead of up. **The important difference from the classical supply curve shown in Figure 5.2 is that when wages are sticky and employment is demand-determined, output varies with prices.**

It is, of course, not necessary that wages be completely rigid—only that nominal wages be less flexible than prices. When commodity prices change, real wages are altered and so is employment and output. Phrased in this way, it is the changes in commodity prices that cause output to fluctuate. There is an alternative interpretation, described below, in which it is fluctuations in output that cause prices to change, rather than the other way around.

COMMODITY MARKET DISEQUILIBRIUM

So far we have neglected the effects of sales on business employment decisions. It certainly seems that whether a firm decides to expand and hire more people or to cut back and let people go depends on how well its product is selling. Take, for example, the following recently reported newspaper item:

> Osborne Computer Corp., once one of the hottest stars in the personal computer field, laid off nearly all of its non-management workers Friday.
>
> The company, founded 2½ years ago by Adam Osborne, was selling 10,000 briefcase-sized Osborne 1 computers each month at its peak. But competitors have deeply eroded the company's market.[9]

Isn't the demand for a company's product the most important determinant of its labor demand? In the classical equilibrium model, the answer is *no:* If the commodity market is in equilibrium, then every firm can sell all it wants at the prevailing price, and firms are assumed to know this price before they make any employment and production decisions. Firms need only compare worker productivity with the real wage rate and see how many people can be profit-

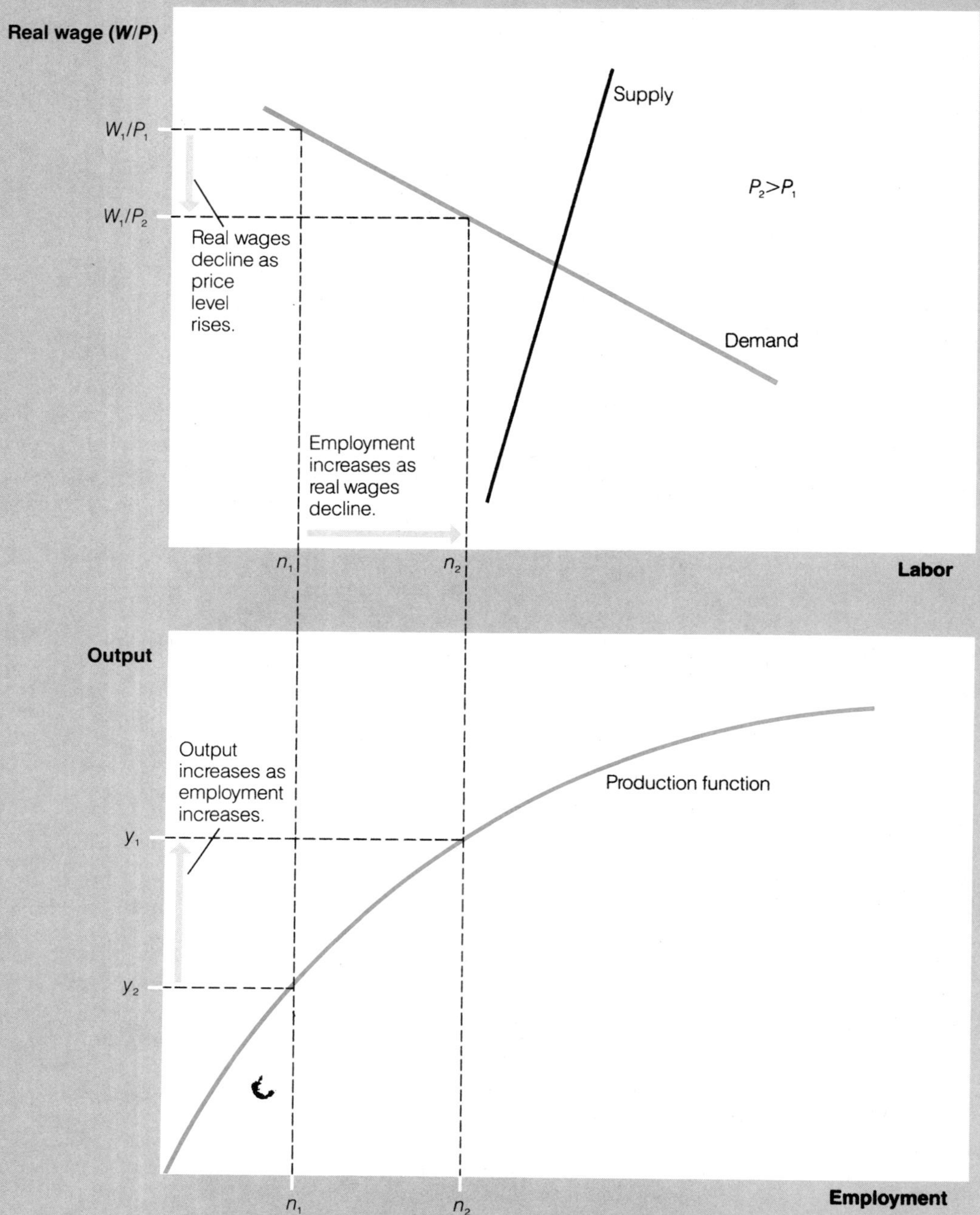

FIGURE 5.6 **EMPLOYMENT AND OUTPUT WITH STICKY WAGES AND EXCESS LABOR SUPPLY. If wages do not rise as fast as prices in an excess-supply labor market, then real wages will fall and firms will be persuaded to hire more workers and increase output.**

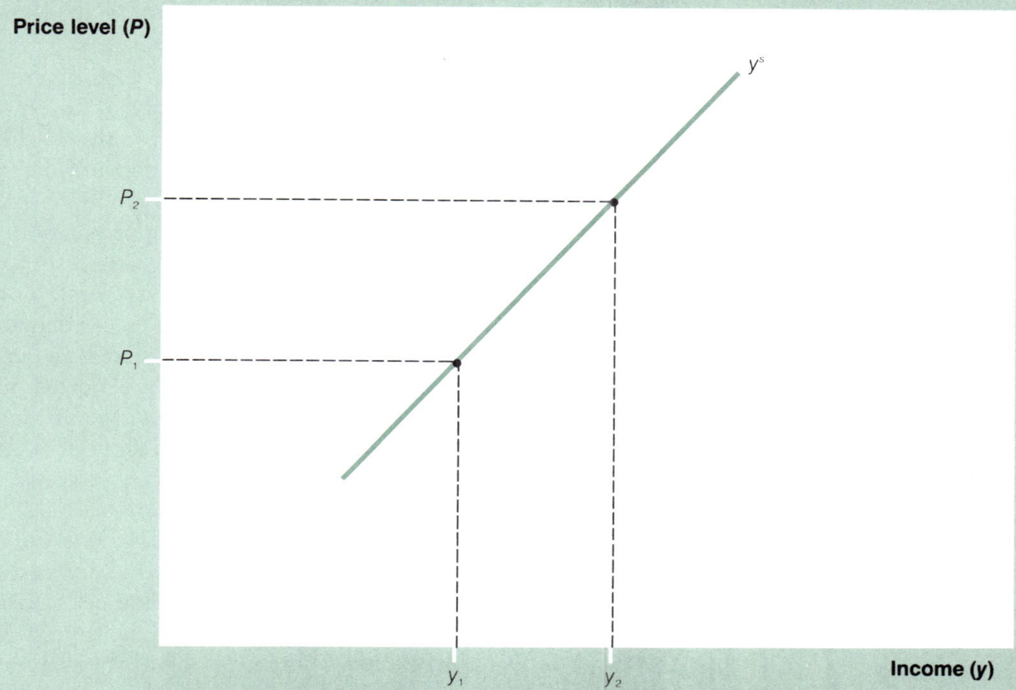

FIGURE 5.7 THE AGGREGATE SUPPLY CURVE WITH STICKY WAGES. **Price and output are directly related because a higher price level erodes real wages in excess-supply labor markets, increasing labor demand, employment, and output.**

ably employed. Firms do not worry about sales because everything they produce gets sold at the quoted price.

The same assumption is made in the first disequilibrium model we looked at. We allowed for sticky wages and labor market disequilibria, but we continued to assume that prices adjust freely to equilibrate the commodity market. So, again, firms do not have to worry about sales, only about whether real wages are low enough to make production profitable.

There is a second disequilibrium approach, which is more popular, though somewhat more complicated. Many commodity markets, as well as labor markets, are "fixprice" rather than "flexprice." Instead of a Walrasian auctioneer, there are imperfect price setters. Most businesses set their prices to cover average costs plus a "normal" profit. This sort of pricing rule is almost inevitable in regulated industries and is widely used by nonregulated businesses as well. Long-run profitability is a large part of the underlying logic. Prices ought to cover costs and provide a "fair" profit, and if the product can not be sold at a profitable price, then it should not be produced. On the other hand, setting the price too high and making "obscene" profits alienates customers, invites government regulation, and encourages entry into the industry by new competitors. Thus many businesses avoid both destructive price wars and price gouging by setting their prices to cover costs and normal profits, while using advertising and product innovations to compete for market shares.

This behavior makes good sense, but it is not a case of the Walrasian auctioneer setting prices to equate demand and supply. If commodity prices are predetermined by costs, then, in the short run at least, there is likely to be commodity market disequilibrium, with sales either demand-determined or supply-determined. Most businesses have built in enough extra production capacity so that they can set prices to cover their production costs and then adapt production to demand. For example, electric utilities set rates, then supply whatever electricity users demand. Similarly, General Motors announces car prices and subsequently adjusts its production to car demand. When a car maker does reduce prices, this is called a special "rebate," an occurrence so rare that it warrants a major advertising campaign and is reported on network television news programs. This same price stickiness is true of most services, too: barbershops, law firms, hospitals, schools, financial services, and on and on. These are all fixprice markets, not because the prices are constant, but because they are not perfectly responsive to competitive market forces.

At times, demand does exceed supply in fixprice markets and there are shortages of electrical power, automobiles, or hospitals. In such cases, higher prices are not used to auction off electricity, cars, or hospital beds. Instead, rationing, waiting lists, and other devices are used to allocate the supply. When this happens, sales are supply constrained. Shortages such as these are unusual because most firms build in some excess capacity so that they can quickly adjust production to meet demand. In this way, they avoid disappointing their customers (and losing them to their competitors). When demand is strong, firms then increase employment and output, and perhaps raise prices. When demand is weak, there are layoffs and some restraint on prices.

When production adjusts to demand, there are "spillovers" from the commodity market to the labor market. The demand for labor depends not just on real wages, but also on the demand for the commodities that businesses sell. When commodity demand sags, businesses cut back production and reduce their demand for labor. When commodity demand improves, businesses increase output and their demand for labor. An extreme version of this spillover is shown in Figure 5.8. Here it is assumed that firms want to employ just enough labor to produce the output that is demanded.* To satisfy commodity demand, firms must produce y_1. The production function implies that an amount of labor, n_1, is needed to produce y_1. So the demand for labor is n_1, and, if there is a sufficient labor supply, the level of employment is n_1 too. Note that the production function now gives the effective labor demand corresponding to a given commodity demand, rather than the commodity supply for a given employment! Instead of employment determining output, it is output that determines employment: **When both employment and output are demand-determined, it is the demand for goods and services that determines (in this order) output, effective labor demand, and employment.**

* In reality, firms do take into account real wages and also the training and severance costs of hiring and firing workers as commodity demand fluctuates. As explained in Chapter 2, labor hoarding causes output to vary proportionately more than employment.

Wages, Prices, and Employment

Many of the wages and prices in modern industrial economies do not seem to be governed by the textbook laws of supply and demand. In the classical equilibrium model (Figure 5.2), the mythical Walrasian auctioneer sets wages and prices to equilibrate all markets and, in particular, so that the real wage rate equates labor demand and supply. The disequilibrium models in Figures 5.6 and 5.8 are more realistic, but less clearcut. Disequilibrium arises whenever wages and prices are set imperfectly, no matter what the nature of the market imperfection. There are many explanations of market imperfections, but no single, coherent model. It is much easier to write a nice, crisp, hypothetical market equilibrium model than it is to model the messy reasons why markets are not, in fact, in equilibrium.

The absence of an omniscient Walrasian auctioneer is sufficient to explain why markets are not in continual equilibrium, but this does not explain how wages and prices are actually set. Some of the most frequent explanations of nonequilibrium wages and prices include minimum wage laws, multi-year union wage contracts, implicit long-term wage agreements, price floors and ceilings, regulatory agencies, and average-cost pricing rules. The overall implication is that demand and supply imbalances may exert pressures on wages and prices, but that there is considerable inertia. Thus, while wages and prices are affected by the amount of slack in the economy, they are also influenced by prevailing laws, regulations, and explicit or implicit agreements. We have all seen "perverse" cases where prices and wages go up even while there are excess supplies of commodities and labor. There have been periods when auto workers, teachers, and administrators were out of work while the wages of their employed brethren rose sharply. When car makers, colleges, and electrical utilities experience a drop in demand, they seem more likely to respond by increasing prices than by reducing them. We have also seen evidences of market disequilibria where people wait in lines for hours hoping to get a job, to buy an admissions ticket, or to buy gasoline. We have seen qualified and responsible people told that there are no job openings, that no mortgage loans are being made, that no apartments are available. But, still, producers are more hesitant about raising prices when commodity demand is weak; and wage increases tend to be more modest when the unemployment rate is high. When commodity demand is strong and unemployment low, wages and prices tend to increase more rapidly.*

The implications for the aggregate supply curve of sticky wages and sticky prices are qualitatively identical to the case of sticky wages and flexible prices: employment, output, and prices all move in the same direction. The difference is in interpretation. In the sticky-wage model, an increase in commodity demand raises prices, causing real wages to decline, causing employment to expand, causing output to increase. In the sticky-wage and sticky-price model, an increase in commodity demand increases output, causing employment, wages, and prices to rise. In the first case, it is the increase in prices that leads to the increase in output; in the second, it is the increase in output that pushes prices

* The appendix to this chapter sketches a few tentative microeconomic explanations of sticky wages and prices.

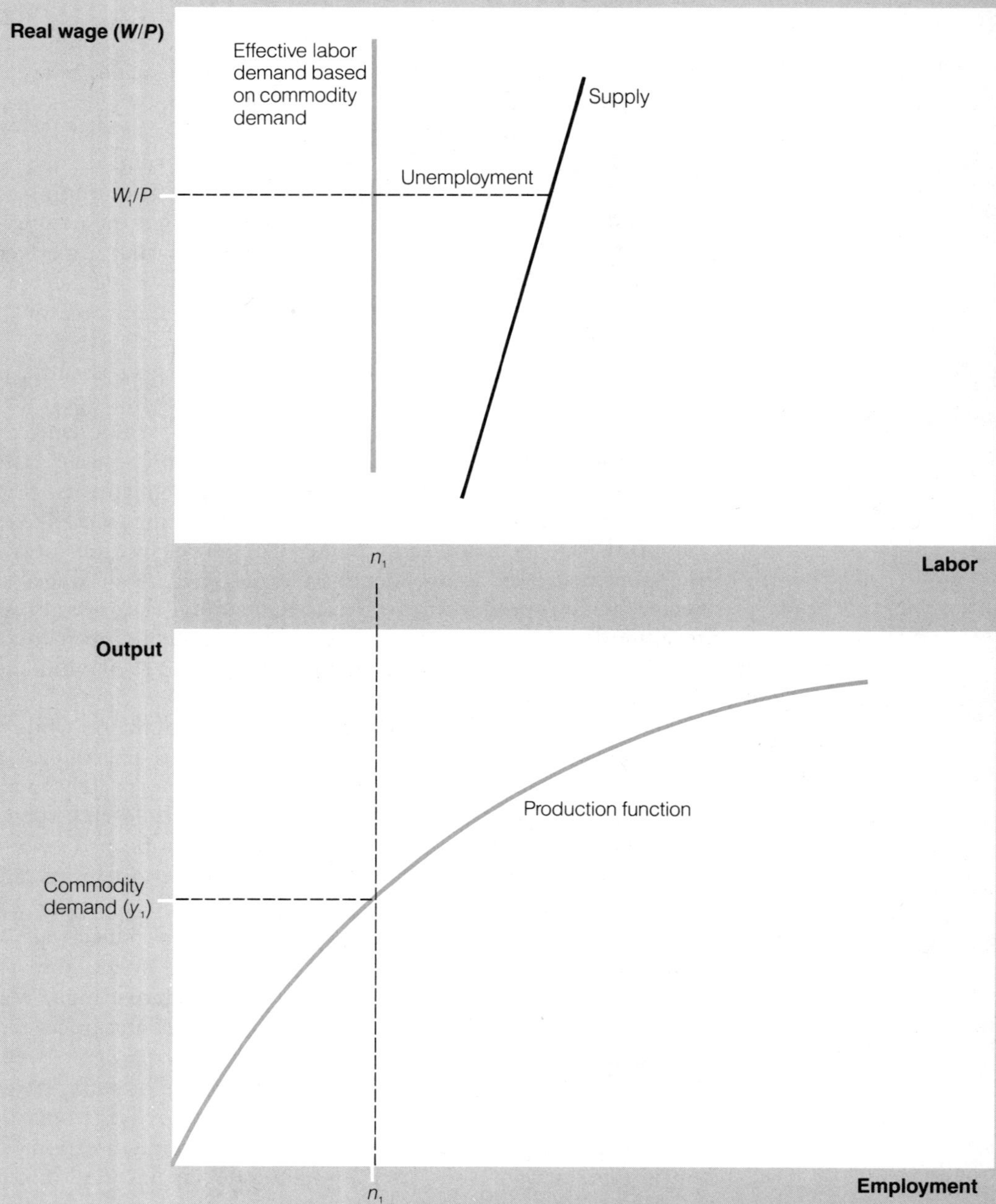

FIGURE 5.8 EMPLOYMENT AND OUTPUT WITH EXCESS LABOR AND COMMODITY SUPPLIES. The production function implies that an amount of labor (n_1) is needed to satisfy the demand for commodities, y_1. The amount of labor demanded by firms is consequently equal to n_1.

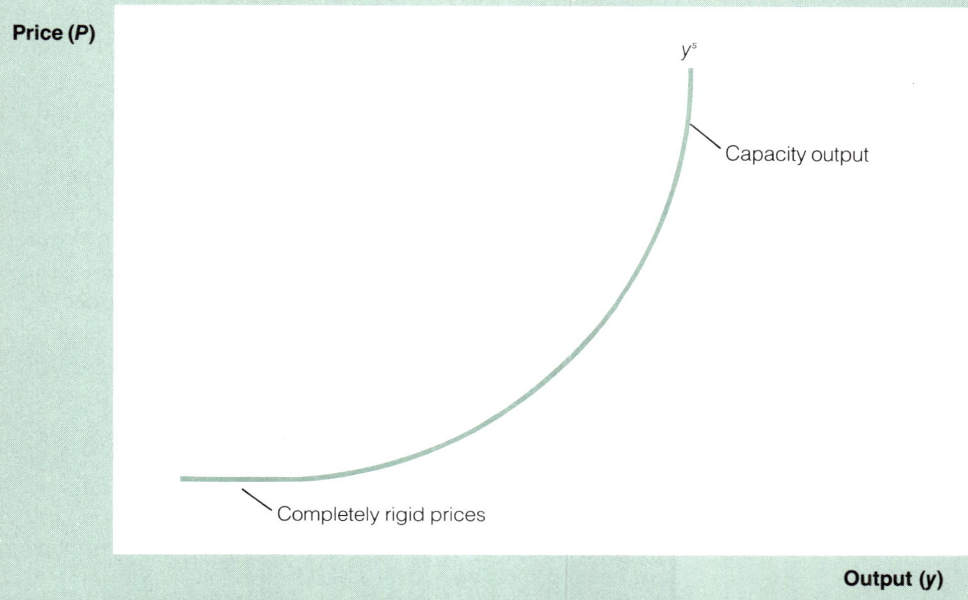

FIGURE 5.9 **The positively sloped aggregate supply curve may be very flat or quite steep. In a deep recession (low *y*), output may fall with little effect on prices (horizontal curve). Near full employment (high *y*), prices may increase greatly and output very little (vertical curve).**

up. Figure 5.9 shows the positive correlation between prices and output that is common to both disequilibrium models.

The supply curve in Figure 5.9 has two extreme regions, one nearly horizontal and the other nearly vertical. Along the horizontal portion, prices are completely predetermined; along the vertical, the economy is operating at full capacity. In the intermediate range both prices and output vary. This supply curve indicates that the relative variations in prices and output depend on the state of the economy. When the economy is severely depressed, output may vary with little or no change in prices. When the economy is extremely strong, however, output cannot easily expand much more; instead, prices will be bid up rapidly as people futilely try to acquire more commodities. Most of the time, the U.S. economy seems to be in the intermediate range, though sometimes closer to one extreme or the other.

The evidence is overwhelming that both labor and commodity markets are predominantly fixprice and that, as a consequence, output and prices are related as shown in Figure 5.9. I will, consequently, treat this as the normal aggregate supply curve. Nonetheless, the vertical supply curve shown in Figure 5.3 does have a long intellectual history and, as you will see, does underlie the policy recommendations of some prominent economists; hence, we will keep track of both views.

NEW CLASSICAL EXPLANATIONS OF BOOMS AND RECESSIONS

The classical model has considerable theoretical appeal. In the classical analysis, demand and supply curves—surely the bread and butter of economics—are brought together, market-clearing prices are determined, and free exchanges executed. It is a clear, consistent, and even elegant theory, loudly proclaiming that the economy is always close to a serene state of full employment. Its only vulnerable feature is its apparent inability to explain business cycles, and, since business cycles are such a pervasive aspect of economic life—breaking up families, bankrupting businesses, and toppling governments—classical macroeconomics has had difficulties recruiting supporters outside of the ivory towers of academe.

The Great Depression of the 1930s was, for many, the final proof of the inadequacy of the classical analysis. A generation of economists turned away and embraced Keynes' alternative analysis.

As adapted by his major interpreters (Hicks, Hansen, Lerner, Modigliani, and Tobin), the Keynesian approach was descriptive and relatively informal, lacking the impersonal, dispassionate, consistent symmetry of classical equilibrium economics. It is hard to build rational, maximizing models of market failures. But an informal disequilibrium explanation of business cycles seemed more realistic than a formal equilibrium approach that ignored business cycles.*

By the 1970s, memories of the Great Depression had faded, dissatisfaction with government policies had grown, and there was a resurgence of interest in classical macroeconomics. The *new classical macroeconomics* offered a market-equilibrium explanation of economic fluctuations.

The old classical macroeconomists acknowledged the possibility of inflexible wages, but gave the impression that these were relatively unimportant aberrations that should be treated with patience, anti-union legislation, or other measures to increase wage flexibility. They also considered the possibility that workers suffering money illusion might look at nominal rather than real wages, but were reluctant to accept the apparent irrationality of such behavior.

The new classical macroeconomists focused on this second possibility. In the 1950s and 1960s, there began a tremendous outpouring of theoretical economic analysis of the rational behavior of individuals with imperfect information about an uncertain future. In the 1970s, the new classical macroeconomics drew upon this economics of uncertainty for a more sophisticated and formal explanation of money illusion. Fully rational people will sometimes base their labor-supply decisions on inaccurate information, since perfect information is

* A pure mathematical economist is one who, when a theory is contradicted by the real world, concludes that it is the world that has erred. Keynes, noting a similar predilection, observed that:

> professional economists, after Malthus, were apparently unmoved by the lack of correspondence between the results of their theory and the facts of observation . . . which has led to economists being looked upon as Candides, who, having left this world for the cultivation of their gardens, teach that all is for the best in the best of all possible worlds provided that we let well enough alone. . . . It may well be that the classical theory represents the way in which we should like our economy to behave. But to assume that it actually does so is to assume our difficulties away.[12]

exorbitantly expensive. They will then voluntarily become employed or unemployed until they realize their miscalculation. In this way, temporary mistakes can cause business cycles.

Rational Mistakes

Classical economists assumed that agents are perfectly informed and certain of the future. But, clearly, a pervasive characteristic of human existence is how little is really known about the future. A second, though less obvious, characteristic is that information is not free. As IBM advertising campaigns point out, it takes substantial resources to gather, process, analyze, and store information. Rational economic agents will, as in other activities, weigh the costs and benefits of acquiring information. Rational agents will choose to be imperfectly informed when they believe that the gains from additional information are less than the expense.

More controversial is the new classical assumption that economic agents are, in practice, better informed about the prices of things they sell than those they buy. Typically, individuals sell few things—mostly their labor—but purchase an enormous variety of goods and services. In addition, many items are purchased weekly, monthly, or even less frequently. It will be very difficult, and expensive, for households to maintain up-to-date information about the prices of these commodities.

For our simple aggregative model, the spirit of this argument can be captured by assuming that labor knows its nominal wage rate, W, but not the commodity price level, P. Instead, it bases its labor-supply decisions upon a possibly incorrect price estimate, P^e, and, hence, a possibly incorrect real wage calculation, W/P^e. Since producers sell relatively few commodities, they are assumed to know these prices as well as their wage rates. Thus it is assumed that firms do not make errors in gauging the real wage rate. For simplicity, we will ignore the effects of price errors on the aggregate demand curve.

This simple and plausible modification of the classical model gives it the flexibility to explain the economic fluctuations that are so much a part of economic life, without abandoning the central classical presumptions that markets are always in equilibrium and that all unemployment is voluntary. The key relationship is that the extent to which labor's estimate of real wages, W/P^e, differs from actual real wages, W/P, depends on the degree to which their price estimate is inaccurate: **If workers underestimate the price level ($P^e < P$), then they overestimate their real wages ($W/P^e > W/P$). When households overestimate the price level ($P^e > P$), they underestimate real wages ($W/P^e < W/P$).**

Surprise unemployment

We'll look at the overestimation of real wages first. For a given real wage, W/P, an underestimate of the price level ($P^e < P$) causes an overestimate of real wages ($W/P^e > W/P$) and a consequent increase in the supply of labor.* This phe-

* A linear approximation to the labor supply curve $s = s_0 + s_w(W/P^e) = s + s_w\ (P/P^e)(W/P)\quad s_w > 0$ shows that, for a given actual real wage, W/P, an increase in P/Pe enlarges the supply of labor.

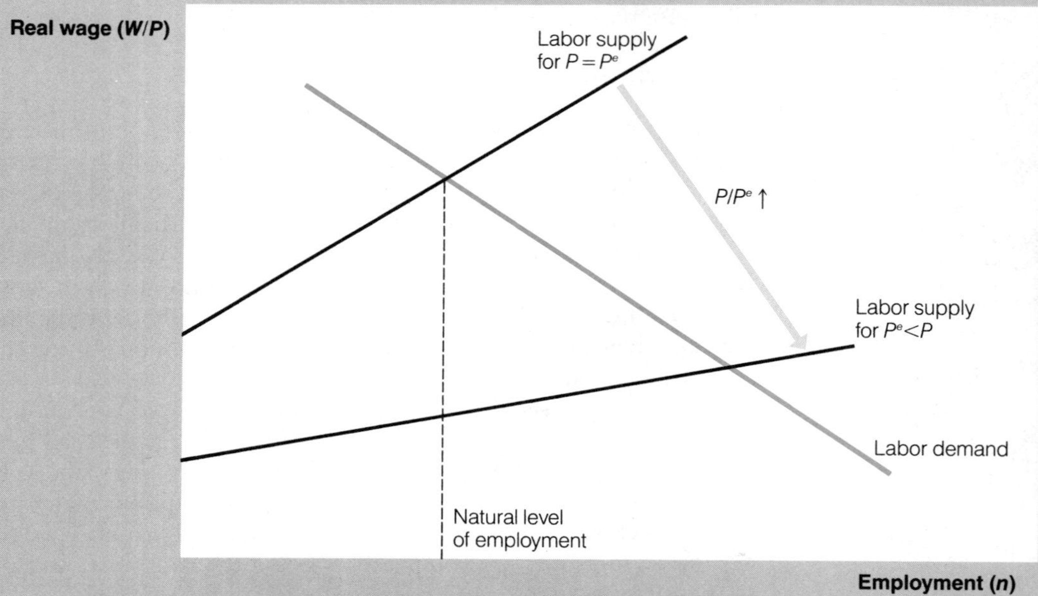

FIGURE 5.10 **When workers underestimate the price level, they overestimate real wages and willingly seek additional work. This expansion of the labor supply reduces market-equilibrium wages and increases employment.**

nomenon is shown in Figure 5.10. With $P^e < P$ the labor supply increases because workers overestimate their real wages.

Since, by assumption, employers are perfectly informed about wages and prices, the labor demand curve does not shift in this fashion. As workers overestimate their real wages and are more willing to sell their labor, the actual real wage is bid down and both employment and output expand. Employers capitalize on employee misperceptions by hiring more labor at lower real wages. The new employees willingly agree to this bargain because their underestimate of prices leads them to believe that real wages have actually increased. This is *surprise employment.* Workers happily collect their high nominal wages, but when they go to the store they are surprised by the high level of commodity prices. To their chagrin, they realize that real wages have not increased but actually fallen. Disappointed and frustrated, they withdraw from the labor force.

The reverse occurs when workers underestimate their real wages, as shown in Figure 5.11, Here households believe the price level to be higher than it actually is. Consequently, because they believe that real wages are low, they voluntarily withdraw from the labor force. As the labor supply schedule shifts leftward, employers must pay higher real wages to keep their reluctant workers. (Perhaps they could better spend their money publicizing the low level of commodity prices.) Real wages rise, though labor believes that real wages have declined, and both employment and output contract. This is voluntary, *surprise unemployment,* called so because labor will be surprised when they realize how low commodity prices are and will return to the jobs they mistakenly left.

This then is the new classical market-equilibrium explanation of business cycles. Booms in economic activity occur when workers underestimate the price level; recessions occur when they overestimate it. These are market equilibria, but not dynamic equilibria. These business cycles are self-correcting because households soon correct any price misperceptions. Some workers may be fooled some of the time, but they will not be fooled all of the time.

The natural state of affairs, or the long-run dynamic equilibrium towards which the economy will automatically gravitate, is with $P^e = P$. The perceived price level will not be permanently higher or lower than the actual price level. When $P^e = P$, then the labor supply is accurate and the *natural level of employment* is attained. This natural level coincides with the old classical notion of full employment with perfect information. The important extension by the new classical economists is that they permit voluntary (though mistaken) departures from the natural level of employment. There is continual labor market equilibrium and, hence, full employment in the sense that everyone who wants a job has one. At the same time, there are booms and recessions as

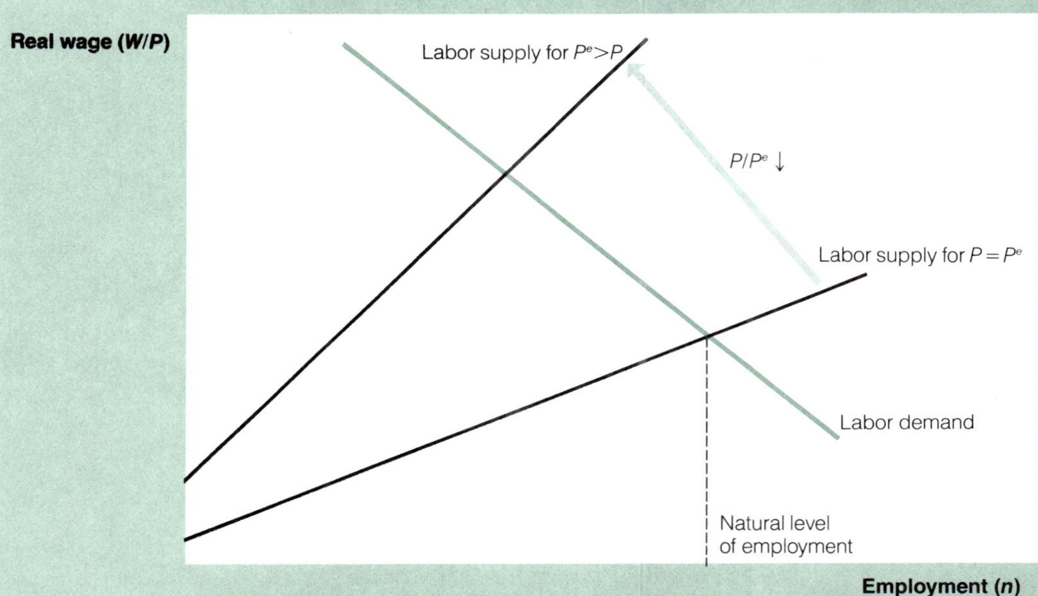

FIGURE 5.11 **When workers overestimate the price level, they underestimate real wages and choose voluntary unemployment. This contraction of the labor supply increases market-equilibrium wages and reduces employment.**

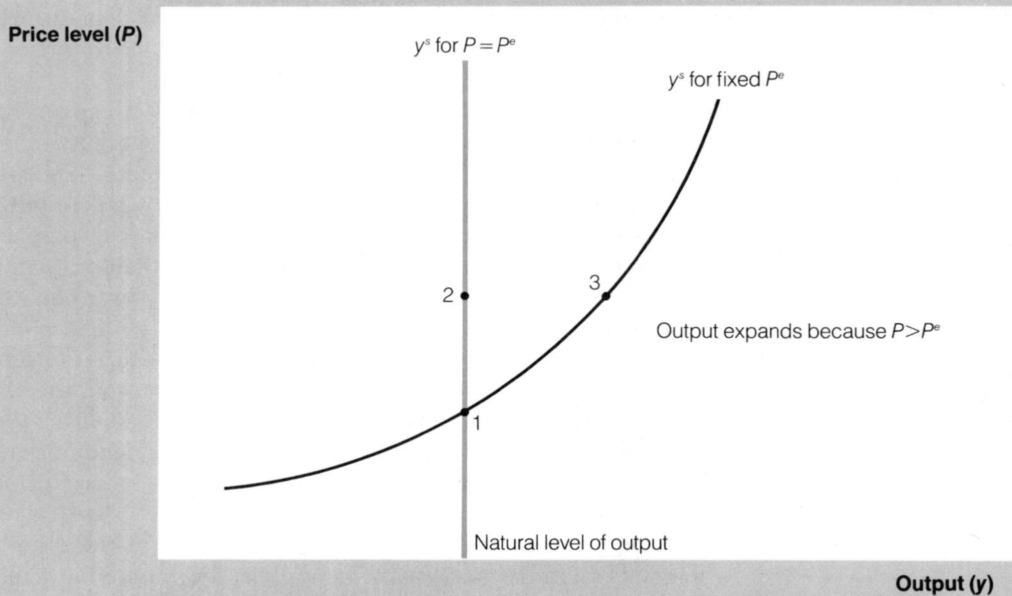

FIGURE 5.12 A correctly perceived increase in prices raises wages proportionately to maintain market-equilibrium real wages, employment, and output. The economy moves up a vertical aggregate supply curve, from Point 1 to Point 2. An unrecognized increase in prices causes workers to underestimate prices, overestimate real wages, and willingly accept additional employment. (The details are shown in Figure 5.10.) The economy moves from Point 1 to Point 3.

real-wage perceptions fluctuate. Since the new classical view assumes that markets are continually in equilibrium, even during booms and busts, this is a market-equilibrium explanation of business cycles, one of the market equilibria being the natural level of employment at which perceptions are accurate.

THE NEW CLASSICAL INTERPRETATION OF THE AGGREGATE SUPPLY CURVE

This new classical model has interesting implications for the aggregate supply curve. Accurately perceived price changes do not cause errors in gauging real wages, and consequently do not alter labor supply, employment, or output. For a correctly perceived price change, output is constant and the aggregate supply curve is vertical. But an imperfectly perceived price change will cause output fluctuations, implying a nonvertical aggregate supply curve. Figure 5.12 shows two aggregate supply curves, one for correct price estimates and one for incorrect.

The economy is initially at Point 1 in Figure 5.12 when the price level increases (because of an increase in aggregate demand). If this price increase is correctly gauged, then nominal wages will increase proportionately and there will be no change in employment or output. The economy will move up the vertical supply curve to Point 2 in the figure. This is the natural level of output corresponding to the natural level of employment in Figures 5.10 and 5.11.

Now, what if the price increase is not fully recognized by households—if, for instance, price expectations are constant and households do not realize that prices have increased? Household-perceived real wages will then be above actual real wages. As explained in the preceding section, labor supply will expand, thereby increasing employment and output. The economy moves up to Point 3 on the nonvertical aggregate supply curve in Figure 5.12. Employment and output are temporarily above their natural levels because of price errors.

Figure 5.13 shows the new classical interpretation of recessions. Here the economy is initially at Point 1 when prices fall (because of a drop in aggregate

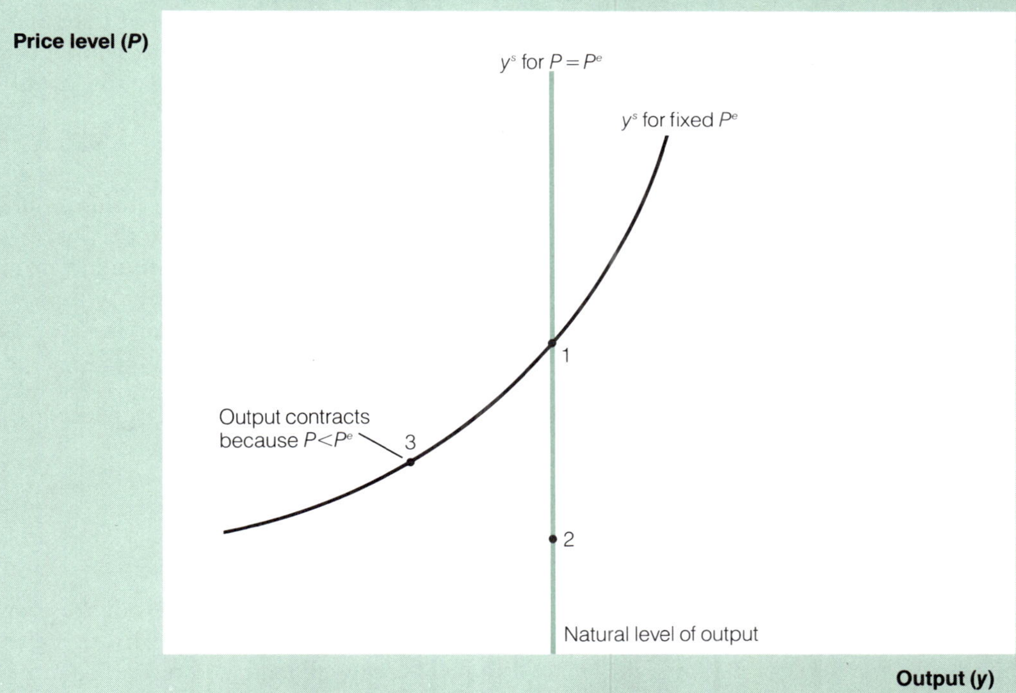

FIGURE 5.13 **A correctly perceived decline in prices reduces wages proportionately to maintain market-equilibrium real wages, employment, and output. The economy moves down a vertical aggregate supply curve, from Point 1 to Point 2. An unrecognized fall in prices causes workers to overestimate prices, underestimate real wages, and become voluntarily unemployed. (The details are in Figure 5.11.) The economy moves from Point 1 to Point 3.**

demand). If this price decline is correctly perceived, then nominal wages will drop proportionately to keep the labor market in equilibrium. Real wages, employment, and output will all be unchanged. The economy moves down the vertical aggregate supply curve to Point 2 in the figure, with output still at the natural level. If, however, households do not realize that prices have fallen, then they will underestimate their real wages and reduce their labor supply. Employment and output will drop below their natural levels. In Figure 5.13, the economy slides down the nonvertical aggregate supply curve to Point 3. Thus, **the new classical economists have a market-equilibrium interpretation of a nonvertical aggregate supply curve.**

It is important to recognize that we have now seen two very different explanations. According to our earlier disequilibrium interpretation, a nonvertical aggregate supply curve is the consequence of imperfectly adjusting wages and prices. Without an omniscient Walrasian auctioneer in control, booms and recessions due to market disequilibria can arise and persist for a considerable period. According to the new classical economists, a nonvertical aggregate supply curve describes an accurate equilibrium adjustment of wages and prices to inaccurate price information. It is price expectations rather than market prices that are sluggish. As soon as people realize the correct price level, the natural levels of employment and output will be restored. The economy will quickly move from Point 3 to Point 2 in Figures 5.12 and 5.13.

Some new classical economists try to merge these equilibrium and disequilibrium models. They recognize that contracts setting wages for years in advance are likely to create market disequilibria at some point, since future demand and supply cannot be foreseen perfectly. So they argue that each contract sets wages equal to estimated future market-equilibrium wages. If there are no surprises, then the natural level of employment will prevail. If there are errors, there will be disequilibrium until the contract is renegotiated. Disequilibrium theorists respond that the recognition of inflexible wage contracts is a step in the right direction, but that the new classical economists should also recognize that wage negotiations are an imperfect substitute for a Walrasian auctioneer.

DEMAND AND SUPPLY TOGETHER

It is now time to bring the demand and supply sides of the economy together to determine r, y, and P. Given government policy, private preferences, and the nation's endowment of people, capital, land, and technology, the economy will have an aggregate demand curve and an aggregate supply curve, as shown in Figure 5.14. The intersection of these curves determines output and the price level. What about the interest rate? It is implicitly determined too, even though it is not in sight. The price level determined in Figure 5.14 tells us the *LM* curve that is appropriate, and its intersection with the *IS* curve gives the interest rate that is implicit in Figure 5.14. If we do not care much about the interest rate, Figure 5.14 suffices; if we do, then we have to go back to the underlying *IS-LM* curves.

The logic underlying the aggregate demand and supply curves is very important. The temptation to view these as ordinary demand and supply curves,

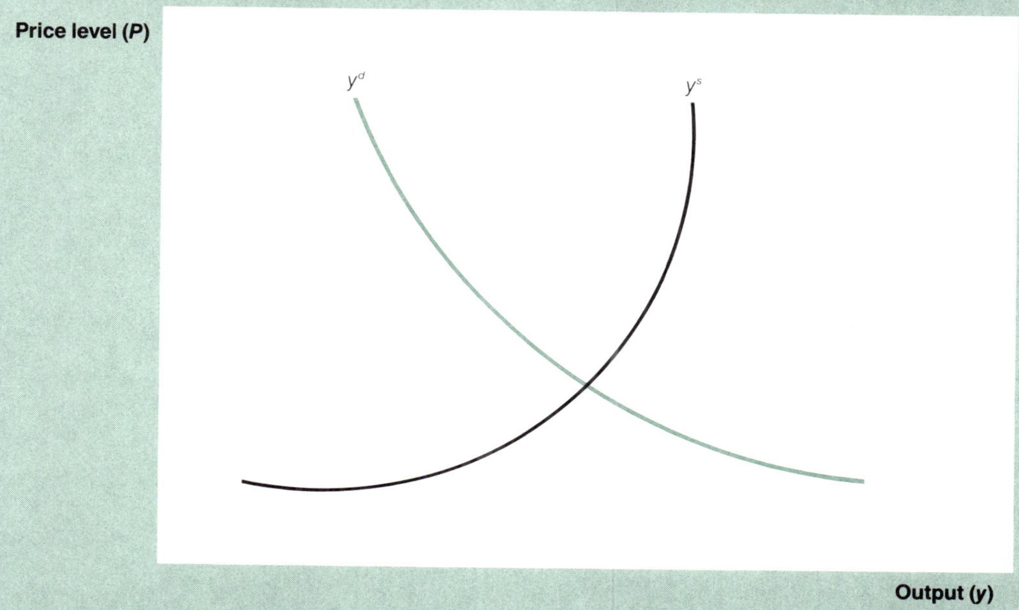

FIGURE 5.14 **Together, the aggregate demand and aggregate supply curves determine the levels of output and prices (and the interest rate, too, though this cannot be seen in Figure 5.14).**

with their intersection giving some sort of macroeconomic market equilibrium, should be resisted. There is a superficial resemblance between aggregate demand and supply curves and the microeconomic demand and supply curves for, say, Idaho potatoes. But these are not ordinary demand and supply curves, and their intersection does not ensure market equilibria.

The aggregate demand and supply curves were invented by macroeconomists to give a simple summary of a number of complex interrelationships. The aggregate demand curve shows, for different price levels, the levels of output such that income is equal to expenditures and money demand is equal to supply. These income levels need not be the desired levels, since workers and factories may be involuntarily idle. The aggregate supply curve shows the price levels at various levels of output. Firms may not be selling all they would like at these price levels, and labor demand need not equal labor supply. The intersection of the aggregate demand and supply curves shows the levels of output and prices that prevail, not necessarily those that simultaneously equilibrate all markets.

Two unrealistic extremes

If there is a classical full-employment market equilibrium, then output is unaffected by price changes and, hence, the aggregate supply curve is vertical. Out-

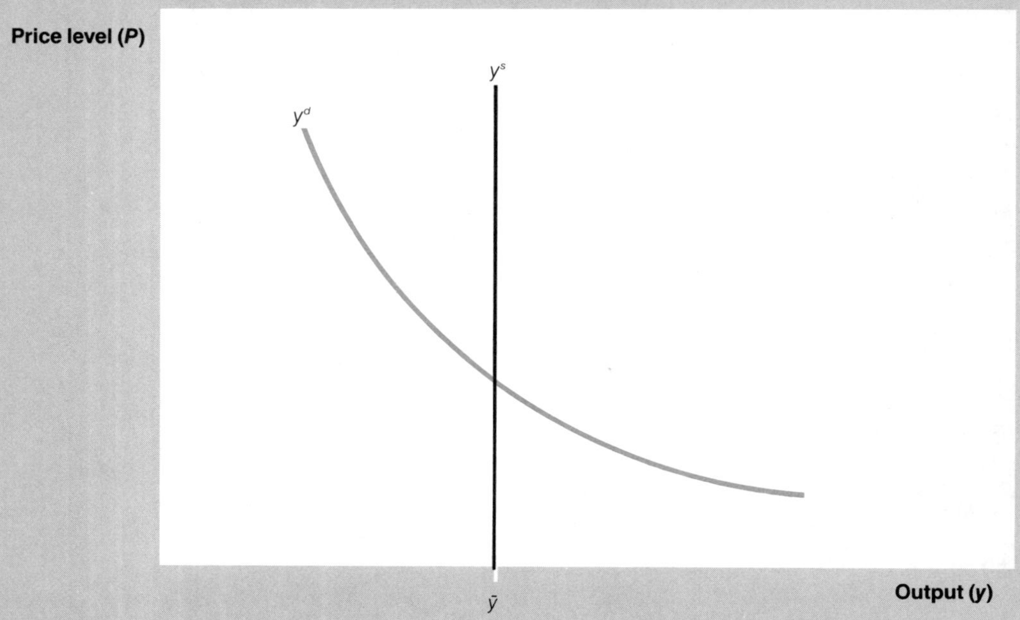

FIGURE 5.15 **In a classical market-equilibrium model, the vertical aggregate supply curve determines the level of output, regardless of the location of the aggregate demand curve. Output is supply-determined and prices adjust to maintain demand for this full-employment output.**

put is always at the full-employment level, as redrawn in Figure 5.15. Aggregate demand has no effect on output and employment, in that no matter where the aggregate demand curve is, prices quickly adjust to the level appropriate for full employment. Nominal wages change proportionately with prices, and both employment and output remain at their full-employment levels. Output is supply-determined and demand adapts to it. This is *Say's law:* supply creates its own demand.* Say's law was a central part of classical economic analysis:

> Until Keynes, Say's Law had ruled in economics for more than a century. And the rule was no casual thing; to a remarkable degree acceptance of Say was the test by which reputable economists were distinguished from the crackpots. Until late in the '30s no candidate for a Ph.D. at a major American university who spoke seriously of a shortage of purchasing power as a cause of depression could be passed. He was a man who saw only the surface of things, was unworthy of the company of scholars. Say's Law stands as the most distinguished example of the stability of economic ideas, including when they are wrong.[13]

*Named after Jean Baptiste Say (1767–1832), credit for Say's law should probably be given instead to James Mill or Adam Smith.

In an extreme Keynesian model, in sharp contrast, output is very sensitive to demand, while prices are largely predetermined (not constant, but preset). In Figure 5.14, the economy is on the horizontal portion of the aggregate supply curve. Thus the aggregate demand curve determines output, but has little or no effect on prices. Now it is commodity demand that creates its own supply. Say's law is turned upside down!

Classical economists studied the supply side of the economy, confident that demand will adapt. Early Keynesians studied the demand side of the economy, believing that this is what determines output. We will pay attention to both demand and supply.

APPENDIX: STICKY WAGES AND PRICES

The following reflect formal attempts at modeling what seem to be important characteristics of observed price-setting behavior. The models themselves are still being improved and extended and have not yet received the mythical Economics Profession's Seal of Approval.

Adjustment costs

Determining a new price involves effort. Models, market tests, memoranda, and meetings all consume time and energy, and there are further costs in posting the new prices and informing employees. Restaurants cannot afford to print revised menus every few minutes; mail-order companies cannot send out new catalogs every day.

Customers also incur adjustment costs—the costs of collecting new price information. Firms like labor contracts because they then know their wage costs in advance. Households like restaurants, markets, and department stores where they know the prices in advance. After some initial careful search, they find out which ones offer the combination of price and quality that best suits their preferences, returning to them again and again, and thus avoiding new search costs.

Risk minimalization

Uncertainty often elicits cautious behavior. Firms uncertain about the effects of price changes on sales can usually reduce their risk by making slow, partial price adjustments,[14] in which case sluggish prices may be the result of rational risk-reducing tactics.

Buyers and sellers can obtain some risk insurance by entering into formal or informal long-term contracts. Buyers can agree to purchase certain quantities at specified prices over a given time, and sellers can agree to supply certain quantities at specified prices and times. Businesses enter into many such agreements among themselves—some formal and written, others implicit in a long-term, buyer-seller relationship in which neither side exploits temporary swings in demand or supply that happen to put one side in a good bargaining position.

For most households, the biggest recurrent transaction is the sale of labor services, and most—at least those in the primary labor market—have explicit or implicit wage contracts that provide insurance against sudden changes in wages and other benefits. Most workers have formal contracts that specify wage or salary over one year, three years, or longer. In addition, there is normally a tacit understanding that each new contract will not be dramatically different from the one before and that wages will be roughly the same as wages paid people with similar skills and experience in and out of the company.

If I sell my house and move my family across the country in order to work for another college, I want some assurance that I will be treated fairly once I get there. I will naturally ask for tenure to ensure my job security. Academic tenure gives professors freedom of speech in the classroom and also protects their jobs from labor demand-supply fluctuations.* But job security is of little value unless it is accompanied by wage security. What good is it to have a guaranteed job if wages can be slashed 50% or 99%? Recognizing this, colleges offer, in addition to formal tenure, informal wage stability. Almost every professor is confident that his or her money wage will not be reduced next year or any year, except in very dire circumstances, and that his or her wage will not diverge greatly from that of others doing the same or similar work. Any college that treats its faculty shabbily will soon acquire a renegade reputation and be forced to pay stiff premiums to attract good staff; the same is true of virtually every firm in the primary labor market. These implicit wage contracts impart a considerable rigidity to wages.[15] Instead of the Invisible Hand, there is what Arthur Okun called the "invisible handshake."

Oligopolistic powers

Price and wage rigidities have frequently been tied to the oligopolistic or monopolistic nature of markets. Such rigidities are certainly true of monopolistic public utilities whose prices are set by regulatory agencies. Auto makers, steel companies, and other large corporations also seem to exercise considerable discretion in setting prices. Powerful unions seem able to negotiate wage increases that have little to do with supply and demand.

In one scenario, oligopolistic firms tacitly agree to set prices that serve their common long-run interests. These prices are not set so high that excess profits will invite entry by new competitors or onerous legislation by government, nor are they set so low as to diminish profits; they are set according to normal mark-up rules that maintain healthy but not excessive profits, at planned operating levels. Costs, rather than demand and supply, are consequently the main determinants of prices. Price increases that are unrelated to cost increases might temporarily swell profits, but these excess profits anger customers, incite employees to demand higher wages, wake lethargic government officials, and encourage the birth of competitors. Price decreases are usually self-defeating. If one firm cuts prices, others quickly follow, and market shares remain unchanged; all that happens is that the industry as a whole has lower prices. Sales in oligopolistic industries are typically not very responsive to prices. So an industry-wide price cut hurts industry profits without increasing anyone's market share. Oligopolistic firms consequently view price wars as mostly self-destructive. Competition for market shares instead focuses on advertising and product improvements.

Businesses are also in a gaming situation with their customers. The firm is in business day after day, and customers seldom have to buy on any particular day. If the firm were to adjust prices based on daily demand fluctuations, customers would exploit this price flexibility by making most of their purchases after the firm posts low prices. Oligopolistic firms do not collect demand commitments and then announce the price that clears the market. Instead, the rules of the game are that, based perhaps on demand estimates, the firm posts a price and stands ready to meet demand at that price. A flexible-price strategy would be ruinous if customers can buy whenever they want; customers, noting that firms reduce prices when demand is weak, would wait for an opportune buying

*Other professions give their members effectively lifetime tenure through bar exams, medical certification, and so on. In addition, doctors and lawyers stabilize wage rates through standard fee schedules and professional codes of ethics that prohibit rate advertising.

time. This waiting would itself reduce demand and lure a myopic firm into cutting prices. Most of the firm's sales would be at low prices. A rational firm will instead maintain stable prices irrespective of daily demand fluctuations and, indeed, announce that prices are firm in order to discourage customer timing strategies.

Monopolistic unions exercise a different tradeoff—that of the jobs of nonmembers for higher union wages. A union can quite rationally decide to negotiate high wages for members even if this means that there will be fewer jobs available. The high wages go to voting members, while the lost jobs mostly come from nonmembers, who have no vote. Similarly, a union could rationally decide to negotiate fixed or even increasing wages in the midst of a recession, when labor demand has fallen below supply. Some members may be laid off, but the majority will keep their jobs and get higher paychecks. This selfish behavior is reinforced by seniority rules that clearly identify who will be laid off. So, unions trade occasional layoffs for a few for wage stability for most. In November 1983, American Airlines and its pilots union agreed to an interesting twist on this double standard—a new two-tiered contract that maintained the jobs and salaries of current pilots, while paying 50% lower salaries to new pilots.

IMPORTANT TERMS AND CONCEPTS

aggregate supply curve
new classical macroeconomics
surprise employment
surprise unemployment
natural level of employment
Say's law

The supply side of the economy encompasses the labor market and output. Labor demand depends on real wages and labor productivity; labor supply depends on real wages and on how highly people value goods and services relative to leisure.

In market-equilibrium, full-employment models real wages, employment, and production are determined by the supply side of the economy. The aggregate supply curve is consequently vertical. Output is not affected by demand fluctuations. This aggregate supply curve will shift gradually as the labor demand curve shifts (because of changes in worker productivity); as the labor supply curve shifts (because of population growth and changes in leisure preferences); and as the production function shifts (because of changes in worker productivity).

If there is labor and/or commodity market disequilibria, then real wages, employment, and output are affected by commodity demand and financial markets. The aggregate supply curve is positively sloped, but not vertical. When there is an excess supply of commodities, output is demand-determined. The production function then tells how much labor is needed to produce the output that is demanded. Thus labor demand depends on commodity demand. If there is an excess labor supply, too, then this labor demand determines employment. The tightness of labor markets affects wages, which, along with other production costs, affect prices. The nonvertical aggregate supply curve says that increased output puts upward pressure on wages and other costs and, hence, upward pressure on prices. This supply curve will be shifted about by changes in the cost of producing a given level of output or by changes in firm profit margins.

The new classical macroeconomists have offered a market-equilibrium explanation of a nonvertical aggregate supply curve. They point out that economic fluctuations can be caused by errors in assessing prices. When workers underestimate prices, they overestimate real wages, causing labor supply, employment, and output to increase. Recessions occur when workers overestimate prices and underestimate real wages. These fluctuations are market equilibria, but not dynamic equilibria. As time passes, workers will correct their mistakes and the natural level of employment will be reestablished.

EXERCISES

1. In the classical model, what do labor demand, labor supply, and employment depend upon?

2. Why are employment and output unaffected by spending plans and financial markets in the classical model?

3. If there is no change in wages, how can a change in prices affect employment?

4. Keynes argued that there could be "unemployment equilibrium." Other economists dismiss such a possibility as a logical contradiction. Summarize and critically evaluate the arguments on both sides of this debate. Be sure to define "unemployment" and "equilibrium" carefully.

5. What is the answer to this question: "Figure 5.4 doesn't make any sense. The supply curve says that people are willing to work for lower wages and the demand curve says that firms are willing to hire more people at lower wages. So, if no one wants the prevailing wage, why does it prevail?"

6. Does Say's law state that "supply creates its own demand" or that "demand creates its own supply"? Explain the economic logic behind the law.

7. Output changes usually precede price changes, and real wages tend to move procyclically (up in booms, down in recessions). Explain why this evidence supports or contradicts the new classical explanation of business cycles.

8. What is the difference between market equilibrium and dynamic equilibrium? Use the income-expenditure model and the new classical price-error model to illustrate your explanation.

9. The text analyzes a model in which prices are flexible, while wages are predetermined. What if wages are perfectly flexible upwards, but are completely rigid downward? Specifically, assume that wages never fall, but that any increase in prices leads to an automatic, proportionate increase in wages and, further, that wages always rise to avoid excess labor demands. What does the aggregate supply curve look like?

10. Consider a situation in which employers, rather than employees, make errors in their price predictions. Here, labor demand, d, is $d_0 + d_w(W/P^e)$, $dw < 0$, and supply, s, is $s_0 + s_w(W/P)$, $s_w > 0$. If the actual price level is higher than anticipated ($P > P^e$), will employment rise or fall? Compare your answer with the new classical analysis given in the text.

11. The classical supply side is insulated from the demand side because labor demand and supply depend upon only a single variable, the real wage rate, and this variable is fixed at its market-clearing level. In theory, labor demand or supply may also be influenced by the interest rate. Say, for instance, that an increase in the interest rate persuades households to trade current leisure for future commodities. Then labor supply, s, can be written $s_0 + s_w(W/P) + s_R R$, $s_w > 0$, $s_R > 0$ and demand, d, as: $d_0 + d_w(W/P)$, $d_w < 0$. What, then, will be the effect of an increase in the interest rate on real wages and employment?

12. Consider the case where there is a "labor-supply Pigou effect" in that an increase in the price level reduces not only the consumption of commodities but also the consumption of leisure. That is, as higher prices erode financial wealth, people work additional hours in order to rebuild their wealth. The labor supply, s, is $s_0 + s_w (W/P) + s_P P$, $s_w > 0$, $s_P > 0$, and labor demand, d, is $d = d_0 + d_w (W/P)$, $d_w < 0$. What is the effect of a higher price level on real wages, employment, and output in a classical equilibrium model?

13. This exercise explores the supply-side effects of relative price changes. Assume that there are separate consumption and investment goods industries with respective prices P_c and P_i. Labor demands in these two sectors depend on wages relative to output prices: $d^c = d^c_0 + d^c_w(W/P_c)$, $d^i = d^i_0 + d^i_w(W/P_i)$, and $d = d^c + d^i$. Assume that labor supply depends on real wages relative to the price of consumption goods, so that $s = s_0 + s_w(W/P_c)$, and that labor market equilibrium prevails: $d = s$. How will a change in relative prices, P_i/P_c, affect real wages and employment? Is there still a classical dichotomy between the demand and supply sides of the economy?

REFERENCES

1. D. H. Robertson, *Economic Commentaries,* London: Staples, 1956, p. 81.

2. R. Lucas, "Unemployment Policy," *American Economic Review,* Papers and Proceedings (May 1978), p. 354.

3. T. R. Malthus, *An Essay on the Principle of Population,* London: J. Murray, 1817.

4. J. M. Keynes, *The General Theory of Employment, Interest, and Money,* London: Macmillan, 1936, pp. 16–7.

5. Robert E. Hall, "Employment Fluctuations and Wage Rigidity," *Brookings Papers on Economic Activity,* 1980:1, p. 99.

6. J. Tobin, "Inflation and Unemployment," *American Economic Review,* Papers and Proceedings, 57 (May 1972), p. 9.

7. Tobin, pp. 9–10.

8. W. Beveridge, *Full Employment in a Free Society,* New York: Norton, p. 18.

9. For an analysis of a variety of disequilibrium scenarios, see G. Smith, "Equilibrium and Disequilibrium Interpretations of the IS–LM Model," *De Economist* (Winter 1980), pp. 497–529.

10. Tobin, p. 3.

11. *Los Angeles Times,* September 9, 1983.

12. Keynes, p. 33.

13. J. K. Galbraith, *Money,* Boston: Houghton Mifflin, 1975, pp. 218–9.

14. The proof is difficult. It follows W. C. Brainard, "Uncertainty and the Effectiveness of Policy," *American Economic Review,* (May 1967), pp. 411–25.

15. C. Azariadis, "Implicit Contracts and Underemployment Equilibrium," *Journal of Political Economy,* 83 (December 1975), pp. 1183–1202.

SUGGESTIONS FOR FURTHER READING

For more on the new classical macroeconomics, see Robert E. Lucas, "Understanding Business Cycles," in *Stabilization of the Domestic and International Economy,* Karl Brunner and Allan Meltzer, eds., Amsterdam: North-Holland, 1977, pp. 7–29; James Tobin, "How Dead is Keynes?", *Economic Inquiry,* October 1977, pp. 459–468; and George Akerlof, "The Case Against Conservative Macroeconomics: An Inaugural Lecture," *Economica,* 46 (August 1979), pp. 219–37. An excellent analysis of sticky wages and prices is Arthur Okun, *Prices and Quantities: A Macroeconomic Analysis,* Washington, D.C.: Brookings, 1981.

CHAPTER SIX

MACROECONOMIC EVENTS

The ideas of economists and philosophers, both when they are right and when they are wrong, are more powerful than is commonly understood. Indeed, the world is ruled by little else. Practical men, who believe themselves to be quite exempt from any intellectual influences, are usually the slaves of some defunct economist. Madmen in authority, who hear voices in the air, are distilling their frenzy from some academic scribbler of a few years back. I am sure that the power of vested interests is vastly exaggerated compared with the gradual encroachment of ideas.

J. M. KEYNES[1]

This chapter describes how monetary policy and fiscal policy, singly and in combination, affect the economy. Also discussed, as illustration of a supply-side event, are the macroeconomic effects of a fuel shortage.

IN this chapter we will use our macroeconomic model to analyze the effects of various demand-side events on output, the price level, and the interest rate. In doing so we will consider mainly the consequences of government monetary and fiscal policies. But it should be remembered that the model can also be applied to past, present, or future changes instigated by the actions of the private sector—changes in the preferences or perceived opportunities of households and businesses. That not all economists agree on all aspects of macroeconomic policy should also be kept in mind. As one wag has said: Ask the same question of 100 economists, and you will get 200 different answers. Actually, most economists do agree on the broad consequences of macroeconomic events, and the model we use reflects this broad consensus. We will also examine the main variant, which is the classical market-equilibrium model.

Government demand-management policies are those whose direct impact is on the demand side of the economy—commodity demand and financial markets. Changes in government spending, taxation, the money supply are all policies of this type. Among such changes, a distinction is usually drawn between monetary and fiscal policies: *Monetary policies* directly affect the *LM* curve, while *fiscal policies* directly affect the *IS* curve. This distinction allows us to follow the useful strategy of looking at *LM* and *IS* curve shifts separately. It also makes good sense because monetary and fiscal policies are conducted by different government authorities.

The President and Congress determine federal expenditures and tax rates. If expenditures exceed tax revenues, then the U.S. Treasury sells securities to make up the difference.* The supply of government money is unaffected; the

* The Treasury also regularly sells new securities to replace old securities that are maturing. When the government budget is balanced, the volume of new securities is just equal to the amount maturing. With a budget deficit, new securities exceed maturing securities, and the stock of outstanding government debt grows. With a budget surplus, maturing securities exceed new securities, and the stock of outstanding government debt declines.

government simply takes in money through securities sales and hands this money back out again in its expenditures.

As we noted in Chapter 4, the money supply is controlled by a separate entity, the "Fed" (the Federal Reserve Board). The Fed can increase the money supply using newly printed money (Federal Reserve notes) to buy Treasury securities from private citizens and banks, and it can reduce the money supply by selling off its security holdings. Thus it is the Fed that ultimately determines the relative proportions of government money and Treasury securities that are in private hands.

The Treasury's budget constraint is: bond sales equals government spending minus tax revenue; the Fed's budget constraint is: bond purchases equal increase in government money supply. Therefore, the net increase in private holdings of Treasury securities (Treasury sales less Fed purchases) is equal to government expenditures minus tax revenue and minus the increase in the government money supply, or, put somewhat differently:

$$\begin{matrix}\text{government} \\ \text{spending}\end{matrix} - \begin{matrix}\text{tax} \\ \text{revenue}\end{matrix} = \begin{matrix}\text{increase in} \\ \text{Treasury securities}\end{matrix} + \begin{matrix}\text{increase in} \\ \text{government} \\ \text{money supply}\end{matrix}$$

This is the consolidated government budget constraint: The excess of government expenditures over tax revenues must implicitly be financed by selling bonds or printing money.

The consolidated government budget constraint is useful because it shows that government spending, taxation, bond supply, and money supply are interrelated. Government spending, for example, must be financed either by higher taxes, bond sales, or money issuance. And we will find that the consequences of an increase in government spending do indeed depend on how the increase is financed.

But the consolidated government budget constraint can also be misleading in that it suggests that government policy is centralized when, in fact, the President, Congress, and Federal Reserve Board each have considerable autonomy. Policy makers do not always agree on policy. It is not uncommon to find them arguing, cajoling, and even trying to offset each other. In view of this we will analyze monetary and fiscal policy separately, then examine various monetary and fiscal combinations.

MONETARY POLICY

A pure monetary policy is an action that affects money equilibrium but does not directly affect spending on goods and services. For this to be the case, government spending and taxation must be held constant. The most common monetary policy is a Federal Reserve *open-market operation.* In an open-market purchase, the Fed buys Treasury securities from the private sector. This transaction increases the supply of money and reduces the supply of bonds. An open-market sale works in the opposite direction: Treasury securities are sold from the Fed inventory, and the money raised is retired from circulation.

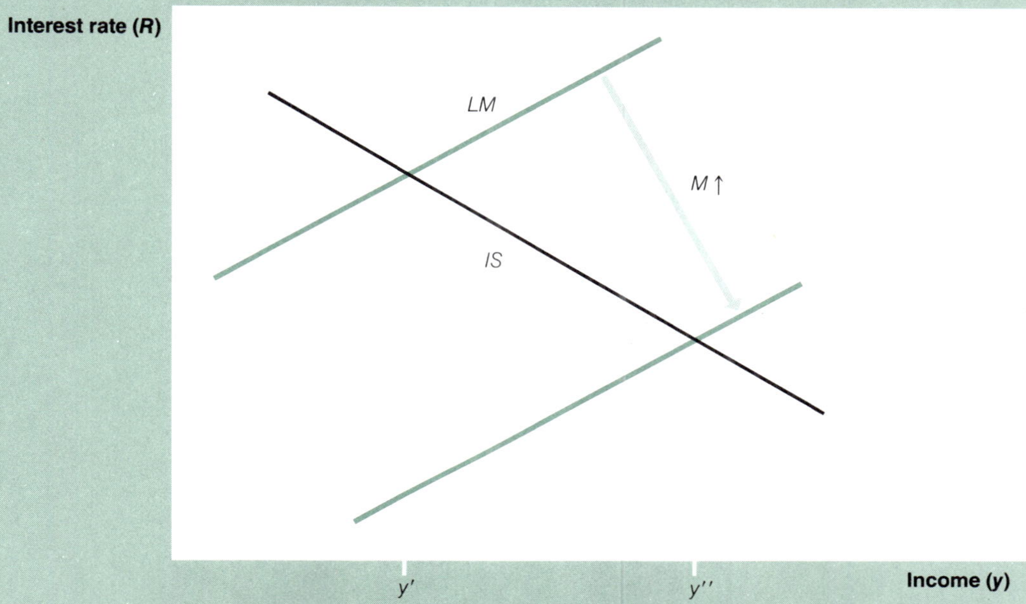

FIGURE 6.1 AN OPEN-MARKET PURCHASE REDUCES INTEREST RATES AND INCREASES AGGREGATE DEMAND. **The increased money supply and reduced bond supply lower interest rates, which encourages spending (particularly for investment goods).**

The model so painstakingly constructed in previous chapters can now be used to deduce the effects of such policies. As shown in Figure 6.1, an open-market purchase shifts the *LM* curve to the right, since the money supply is increased, and there is an increase in the level of income, given by the *IS-LM* intersection. The economic logic is as follows. The Federal Reserve's purchase of bonds drives bond prices up and yields down, bond prices and yields being inversely related. These lower interest rates stimulate household and business expenditures. (The decline in R and increase in y also persuade the private sector to hold the additional money that the Fed has put into circulation.)

To see what happens to output and prices after an open-market purchase, we need to bring in the supply side of the economy, shifting our attention to the aggregate demand and supply curves in Figure 6.2. In Figure 6.1, the *IS-LM* curves told us that, at any given price level, P', an increase in the money supply raises aggregate demand, from y' to y''. Thus the aggregate demand curve in Figure 6.2 is shifted rightward. Output and the price level increase from Point 1 to Point 2 along the y^s curve. Firms hire extra labor and produce more output in order to satisfy the enlarged commodity demand. This tightening of labor and commodity markets puts upward pressure on wages and prices. The new, higher level of output, y''', is less than y'' because the higher price level partly

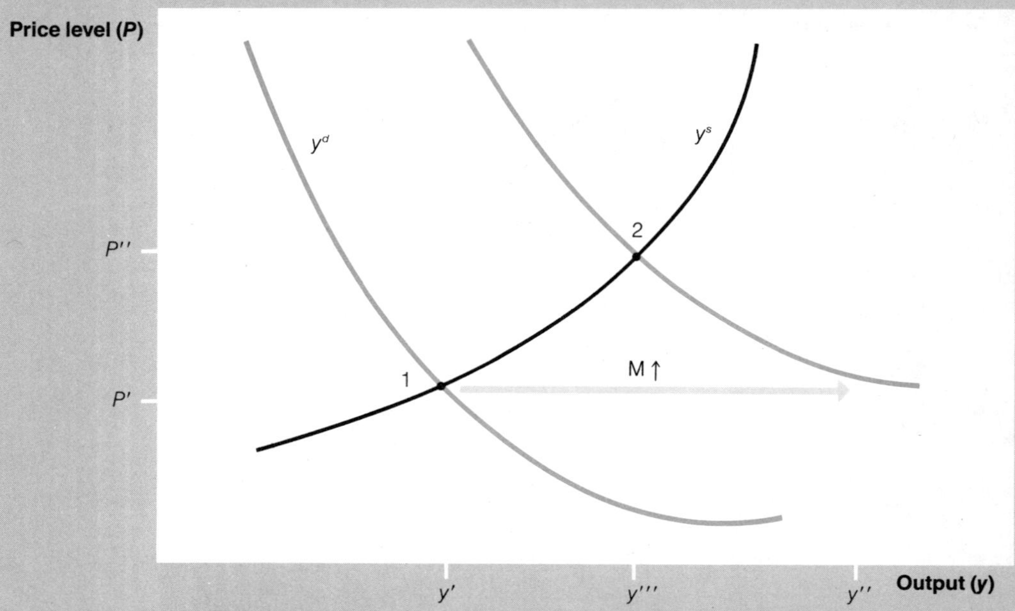

FIGURE 6.2 AN OPEN-MARKET PURCHASE INCREASES OUTPUT AND PRICES. **An open-market purchase increases aggregate demand, which increases both output and prices.**

offsets the increase in the nominal money supply. (The negative slope of the aggregate demand curve states that higher prices restrain aggregate demand through the Keynes effect of a diminished real money supply.)

What is the final change in the interest rate, taking these price and output adjustments into account? Unfortunately, we cannot tell from Figure 6.2, since the interest rate has slipped out of sight. We can keep track of the interest rate by going back to our *IS-LM* curves. The cost is that our graphs begin to get unpleasantly messy.

The details are shown in Figure 6.3, which adds an increase in prices to Figure 6.1. The increase in the money supply shifts the *LM* curve rightward, reducing interest rates and stimulating spending. The price level increases from P' to P'', shifting the *LM* curve back to the left. The higher price level reduces the real money supply somewhat (the Keynes effect) and partly offsets the expansionary monetary policy. The new level of output, y''', is higher than the initial y', but lower than when the deleterious effects of higher prices are neglected (at y''). Overall, **a Federal Reserve securities purchase is expansionary, reducing interest rates and increasing output, employment, and the price level.**

An open-market sale has the opposite effects. When the Fed sells securities, money is taken out of circulation and, as shown in Figure 6.4, the *LM* curve shifts leftward—in a contractionary direction. The bond sales push security prices down and yields up. Higher interest rates discourage spending, particularly investment. The aggregate demand curve shifts leftward in Figure 6.5 and output declines. Commodity prices are imperfectly flexible downwards, so that when commodity demand falls, firms reduce output and employment, as well as prices. The decline in the price level partly offsets the initial contraction of the nominal money supply. This Keynes effect shifts the *LM* curve back to the right. Thus, **a Federal Reserve securities sale is contractionary, increasing interest rates while reducing output, employment, and the price level.**

These analyses also apply to shifts in private preferences between money and securities. For example, an increased availability of credit cards reduces the demand for money and increases the demand for securities. Such a change shifts the *LM* curve rightward just as if a Fed open-market purchase had increased the supply of money and reduced the supply of securities. A reduced demand for money has the same effects on the economy as an increased supply of

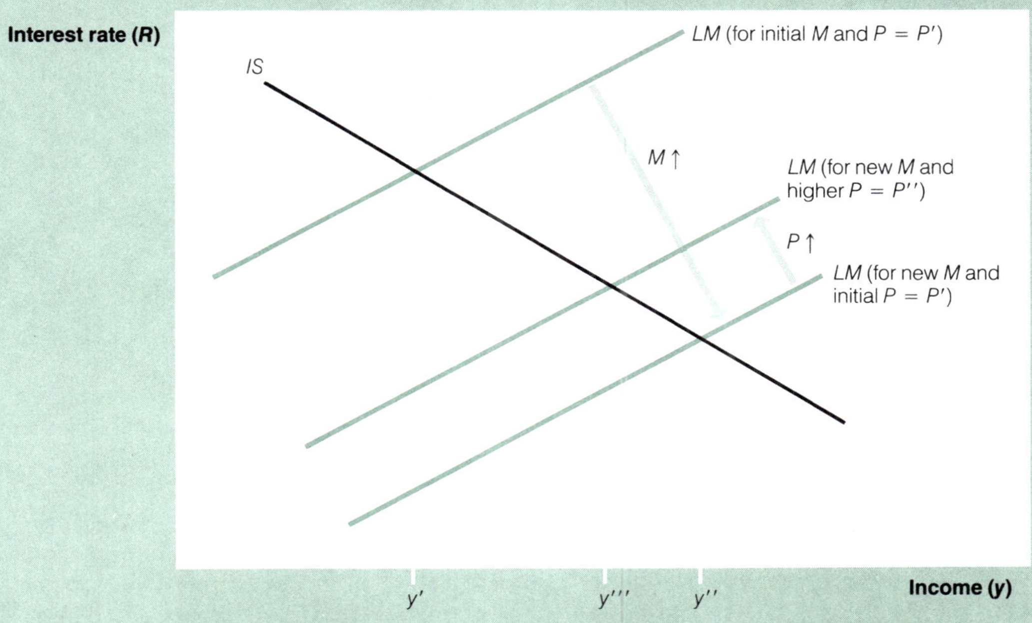

FIGURE 6.3 **AN OPEN-MARKET PURCHASE, WITH A HIGHER PRICE LEVEL. An increase in the money supply lowers interest rates and raises aggregate income. The higher price level that results partly offsets these effects by reducing the real money supply somewhat.**

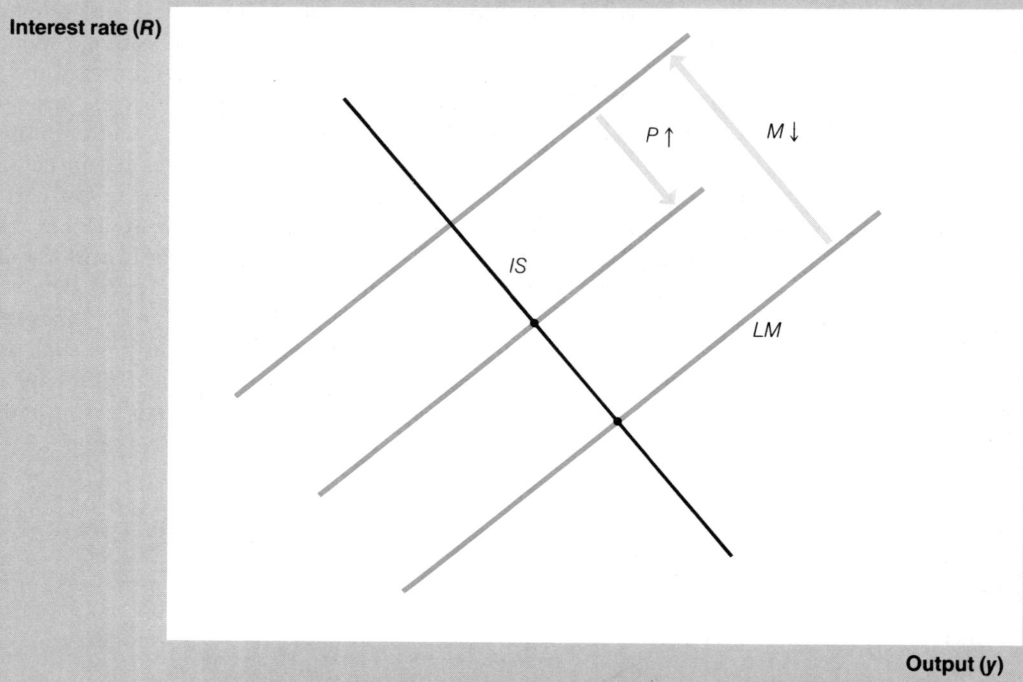

FIGURE 6.4 AN OPEN-MARKET SALE INCREASES INTEREST RATES AND REDUCES OUTPUT AND PRICES. **The reduced money supply and increased bond supply raise interest rates, discouraging spending. The resultant drop in prices partly offsets these effects by increasing the real money supply somewhat.**

money. Thus Figures 6.2 and 6.3 tell us that an increased availability of credit cards is expansionary, reducing interest rates while increasing output and prices.

Similarly, the Fed might increase deposit reserve requirements, forcing banks and other deposit intermediaries to hold more money and fewer securities. How would this policy change affect interest rates, output, and prices? These are two equivalent ways of answering this question: Banks demand more money (to satisfy their increased reserve requirements), and the supply of money created by the banking system contracts. Either way, the *LM* curve shifts to the left. An increased demand for government money and reduced demand for securities has the same macroeconomic effects as a reduced money supply and increased bond supply. Increased reserve requirements are like an open-market sale, which Figures 6.4 and 6.5 show increases interest rates and reduces output and prices.

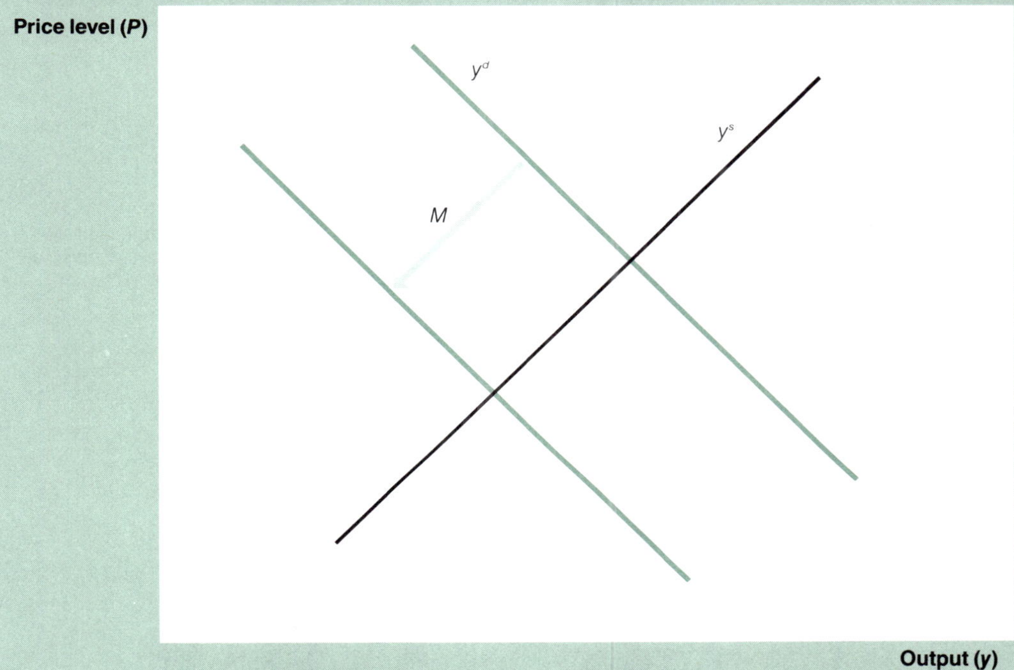

FIGURE 6.5 AN OPEN-MARKET SALE REDUCES OUTPUT AND PRICES.

FISCAL POLICY

A fiscal policy is a government action that alters expenditures but does not directly affect money equilibrium. Changes in government spending and taxation are both fiscal policies. Government spending is a direct component of aggregate expenditures, while taxes alter private spending by changing after-tax income. An increase in government spending or reduction in taxes can be financed by Treasury bond sales, with the Fed holding the money supply constant. A decrease in spending or increase in taxes allows the Treasury to reduce its bond sales.

Our model can be used to deduce the consequences of such policies. Consider a bond-financed increase in government spending, which shifts the *IS* curve to the right, as shown in Figure 6.6. The increase in government spending directly raises aggregate expenditures, with the ensuing multiplier effects discussed in Chapter 3. The horizontal shift in the *IS* curve is equal to the Chapter 3 multiplier. At this higher level of aggregate demand there is an enlarged demand for money, which puts upward pressure on the interest rate. The interest rate increase persuades people to economize on money holdings and reconciles

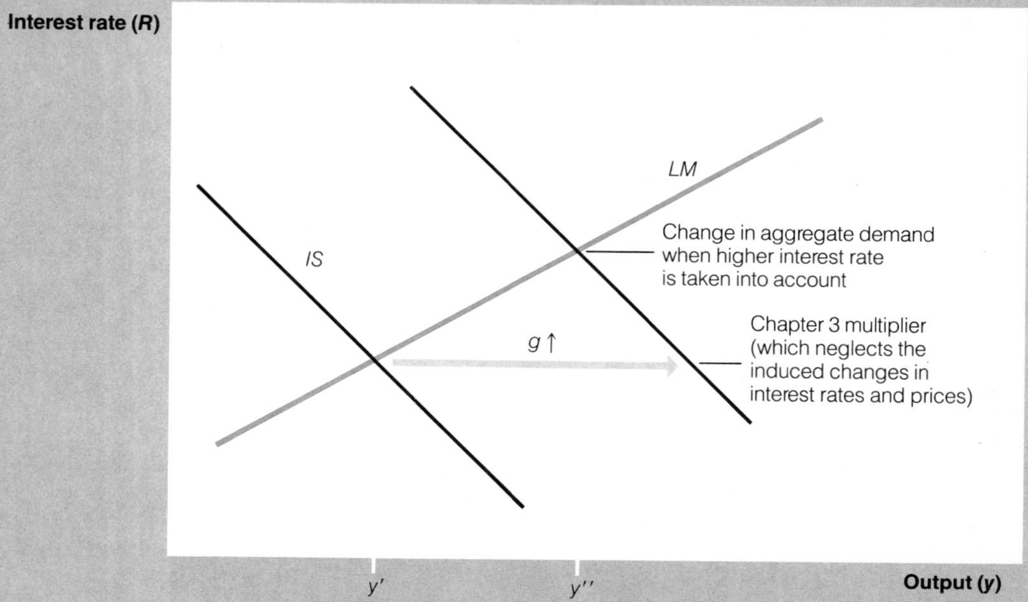

FIGURE 6.6 A BOND-FINANCED INCREASE IN SPENDING INCREASES INTEREST RATES AND AGGREGATE DEMAND. **At a given price level, a higher level of government spending increases aggregate demand from y' to y'', though this increase is dampened somewhat by the accompanying higher interest rate.**

the private sector to a fixed money supply. This is a movement up the *LM* curve.

The higher interest rate up the *LM* curve has a discouraging effect on private spending. Aggregate demand does not increase by as much as it would if the interest rate did not change at all; that is, the *IS-LM* intersection in Figure 6.6 is to the left of the Chapter 3 multiplier. Nonetheless, on balance, aggregate demand does increase.

What happens to output and prices? Again, we need to bring in the supply side. We can do this, as in Figure 6.7, by shifting our attention to the aggregate demand and supply curves. An increase in government spending will, according to Figure 6.6, increase aggregate demand at any given price level. Thus the aggregate demand curve shifts to the right in Figure 6.7 and, as with an expansionary monetary policy, both output and prices increase.

What about interest rates? It is here that expansionary monetary and fiscal policies diverge. To see how government spending affects interest rates, Figure 6.8 takes the price increase, from P' to P'', into account in our *IS* and *LM* curves. The increased aggregate demand puts upward pressure on output and the price level. The higher price level reduces the real money supply, shifting

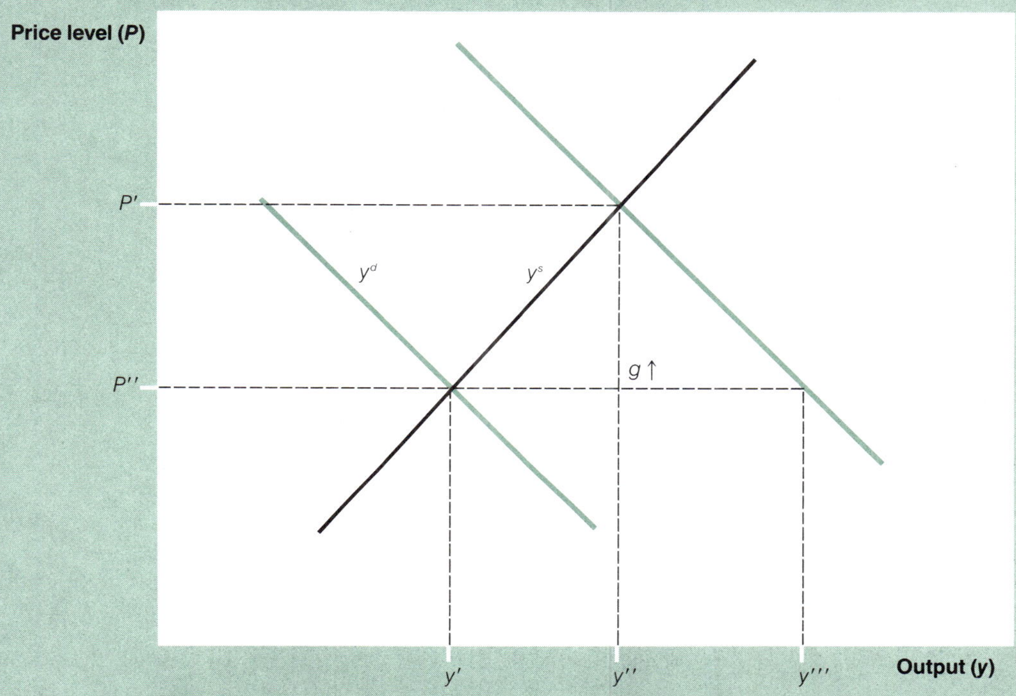

FIGURE 6.7 AN INCREASE IN GOVERNMENT SPENDING RAISES OUTPUT AND PRICES.

the *LM* curve leftward. This reduced real money supply reinforces the upward pressure on interest rates that is exerted by the bond-financed expenditures and partly offsets the stimulus to expenditures. In sum, a bond-financed increase in government spending raises interest rates, output, and prices. As Figure 6.9 shows, a reduction in government spending shifts the *IS* curve leftward, so that interest rates and output decline. The accompanying drop in prices increases the real money supply.

Noteworthy are the similarities and differences between expansionary monetary and fiscal policies. Both expansionary policies shift the aggregate demand curve rightward, increasing output and prices. But monetary policy works through the *LM* curve, while fiscal policy works through the *IS* curve, and the implications for interest rates are quite different. An expansionary monetary policy lowers interest rates, while an expansionary fiscal policy reduces the real money supply and raises interest rates. Since investment spending is sensitive to interest rates, an expansionary monetary policy will stimulate investment more than an equally expansionary fiscal policy will.

The demand effects of tax cuts can now be easily deduced. An income tax decrease gives households more disposable income, encouraging consumption

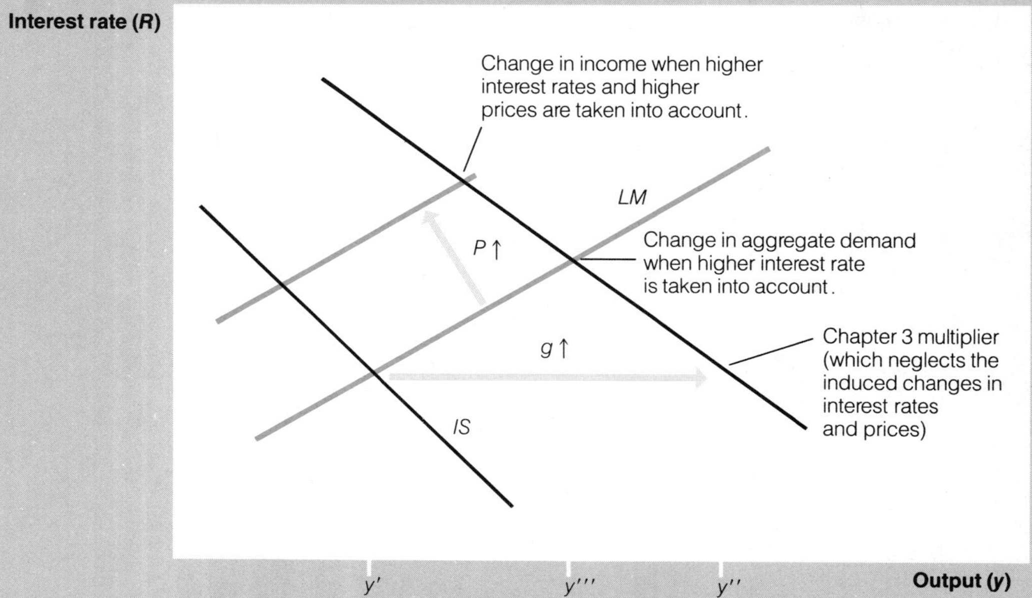

FIGURE 6.8 **A higher level of government spending shifts the *IS* curve rightward. The resultant increase in output is moderated by the higher interest rate (along the *LM* curve) and the higher price level (a shift of the *LM* curve).**

spending. The *IS* curve shifts to the right, with effects similar to an increase in government spending. As in Figures 6.7 and 6.8, output, prices, and interest rates will all increase. The only real difference is in the composition of the spending increase: With a tax cut, it is private spending that initiates the boom.

Changes in private spending for other reasons would have similar effects. If firms decide to sell securities to finance the construction of more plant and equipment, this would have the same macroeconomic effects shown in Figure 6.7 and 6.8: output, prices, and interest rates all rise. The same effects would follow from a decision by households to purchase more commodities and fewer securities. There may be differing long-run effects, though, depending on whether government, businesses, and households purchase consumption or investment goods, since the latter add to the nation's future productive capacity.

MIXED MONETARY AND FISCAL POLICIES

So far, we have looked at the consequences of monetary policy and fiscal policy separately. There is no reason why the government must do only one or the other. It can do both. It can have monetary and fiscal policies both of which are

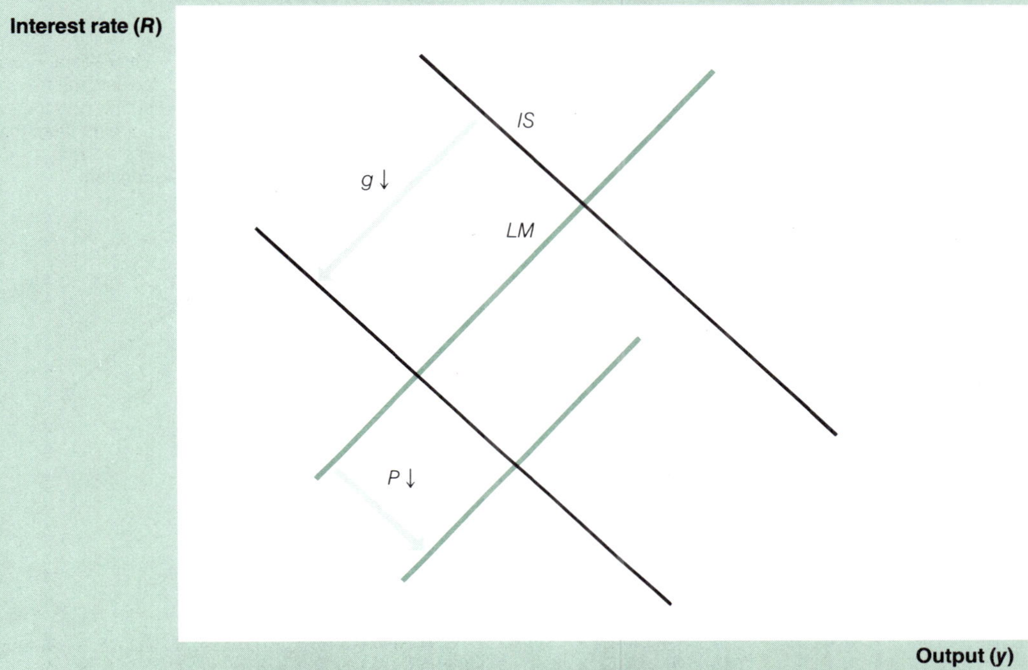

FIGURE 6.9 A DECREASE IN SPENDING REDUCES INTEREST RATES, PRICES, AND OUTPUT. **Reduced government spending, like any drop in expenditures, shifts the *IS* curve leftward, reducing output and interest rates. The ensuing drop in prices offsets this contraction somewhat by increasing the real money supply.**

expansionary, both contractionary, or that work in opposite directions. In this section, we will look at a few selected policy stances; a few more are included in the exercises at the end of this chapter. (And there will probably be another one on the midterm.)

Consider first an increase in government spending accompanied by Fed open-market purchases of Treasury securities—expansionary fiscal and monetary policies together. Both the *IS* and *LM* curves shift to the right, as shown in Figure 6.10. For a given price level, an expansionary fiscal policy alone would raise aggregate demand to Point 1 in the figure, while an expansionary monetary policy alone would raise demand to Point 2. The combination of expansionary fiscal and monetary policies raises demand all the way to Point 3.

The increase in government spending directly raises expenditures on goods and services, and also raises money demand (to carry out the increased transactions), putting upward pressure on the interest rate. But, here, the Fed accommodates the enlarged money demand by increasing the supply of money. This accommodation restrains the interest rate. (Although Figure 6.10 is drawn so

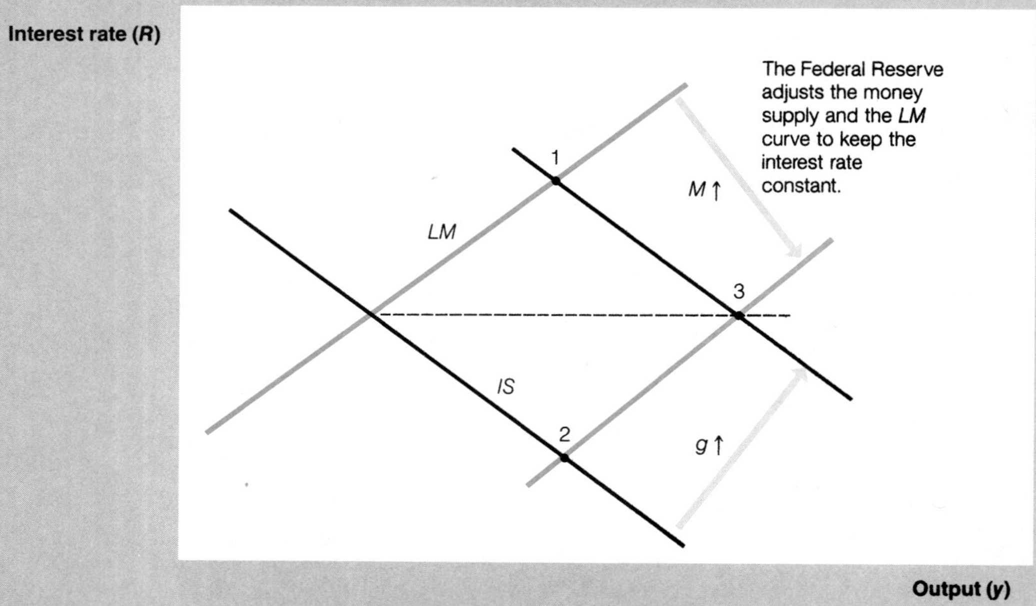

FIGURE 6.10 AN INCREASE IN GOVERNMENT SPENDING, COUPLED WITH OPEN-MARKET PURCHASES HOLDS THE INTEREST RATE CONSTANT.

that the interest rate is held constant, other policy mixes are possible, of course.)

Point 3 in Figure 6.10 is not the end of the story since supply has not been taken into consideration. As output expands, prices will rise, shifting the *LM* curve leftward. This shift is omitted from the figure in the interests of clarity, but the net effects can be easily reasoned through: A bond-financed increase in government spending increases y, P, and R. Fed open-market purchases raise y and P, while reducing R. Thus, **a combination of expansionary monetary and fiscal policies raises output and prices more than either policy alone and has an uncertain effect on interest rates.**

Pegging the interest rate

One special policy, which the Fed followed during the years 1941–51, is use of open-market purchases and sales to hold the interest rate constant. A bond-financed increase in government spending, for instance, would provoke an automatic open-market purchase (to hold the interest rate steady), as shown in Figure 6.10. The increase in government spending shifts the *IS* curve rightward. The *IS* curve moves up the *LM* curve to a higher interest rate. But an appro-

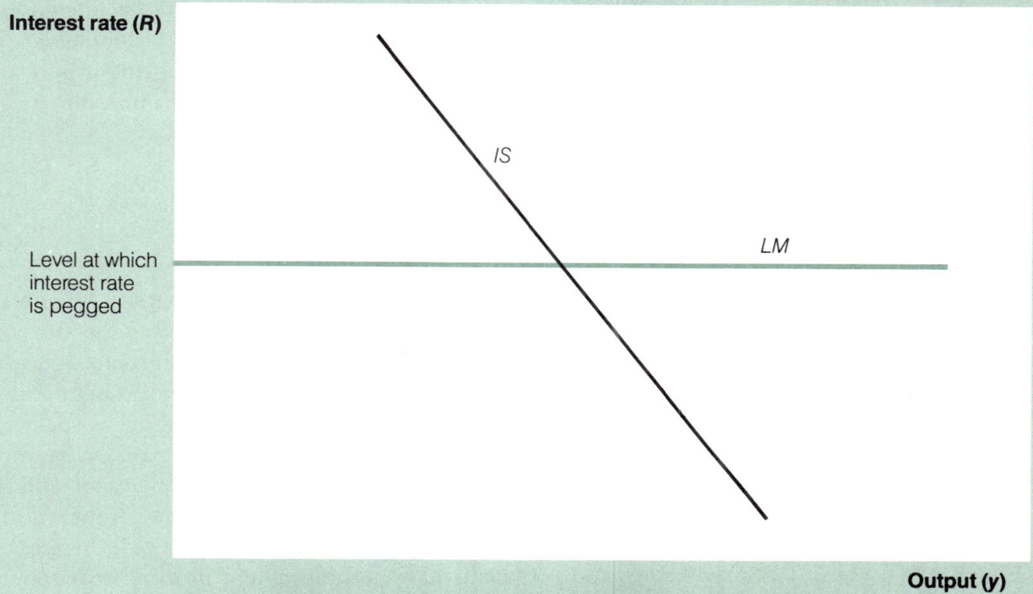

FIGURE 6.11 **If the Fed pegs the interest rate as spending fluctuates, then the *LM* curve is effectively horizontal.**

priate open-market purchase will, as drawn in Figure 6.10, shift the *LM* curve rightward sufficiently to keep the interest rate at its initial level.

The *LM* shift shown in Figure 6.10 is appropriate for the original price level. Further adjustments of the *LM* curve will be required to offset the effects of induced price changes and of other economic events. The nature of these adjustments is such that no matter what occurs, open-market operations will be used to hold the interest rate constant. Any event that puts upward pressure on the interest rate will cause the Fed to make an offsetting open-market purchase; any sign of weakness in the interest rate will provoke an open-market sale. (This point—that an open-market purchase reduces while an open-market sale increases the interest rate—is an important one.)

When the Fed follows this policy of pegging the interest rate, our original, positively sloped *LM* curve is really no longer relevant. Whenever the economy begins to move along this *LM* curve, the Fed shifts the *LM* curve with an open-market operation. Since the Fed freely adjusts the LM curve to peg the interest rate, the effective *LM* curve is horizontal, as drawn in Figure 6.11. (Exercise 16 at the end of this chapter examines such policies further.)

Our focus on the consequences of government policies should not be misread to mean that all would be quiet if only the government would shun monetary and fiscal manipulations. All private demand-side actions feed into the *IS* and *LM* curves and cause changes in the economy very similar to the government policies analyzed here; exercises 5 and 8 at the end of this chapter are examples. On the other hand, it should not be concluded that all will be well when the government does use demand-management policies. In Chapters 10 and 11, we will see how errors and delays can undermine well-intentioned policies.

SOME EXTREMES

There are some extreme assumptions that would modify our analysis of the consequences of demand-side events. These extreme assumptions do not reverse any of our conclusions, but do cause some effects to disappear. For example, although we have seen that an expansionary monetary policy increases both output and the price level, under certain conditions (below), these effects may be very small. But no one claims that an expansionary monetary policy *reduces* output and prices. We will examine a Keynesian unemployment extreme, a classical full-employment extreme, and the combination of the simple quantity theory with full employment. Although all of these extreme cases are interesting and provocative, it should be kept in mind that they are applicable in only very special situations.

Rigid prices and flexible output

In the pre-Keynes, classical full-employment models, output is supply-determined. The aggregate supply curve is vertical, so that demand-side events alter only the price level, with no effects on output or employment. Keynes argued that quantities also will adjust. The aggregate supply curve is not vertical and a decline in aggregate demand not only reduces the price level, but also reduces employment and output. An extreme version is that prices are rigid and only employment and output change: the supply curve is horizontal.

It can be argued that most wages and prices, in the short run at least, are fixed by explicit contracts, informal agreements, and institutional inertia. They are particularly resistant to decline. Changes in labor demand and commodity demand thus affect employment and output, with little immediate effects on wages and prices. When the demand for electricity, cars, or steel increases, more is produced and more people may be employed while wages and prices are hardly affected. The same is true of the demands for medical care, legal advice, education, and most services. When these demands decline, production is slowed and some employees may be let go, while wages and prices remain firm.

The extreme version of this argument is that wages and prices are completely predetermined by past events, decisions, and agreements and, in the short run, unaffected by demand-side events. The aggregate supply curve is horizontal, as in Figure 6.12, so that output is demand-determined. The *IS-LM* intersection determines r and y, while supply passively adapts. The price level is determined elsewhere. Early Keynesian models were usually of this sort. A glance at Figures 6.1–6.9 while assuming the aggregate supply curve to be horizontal will

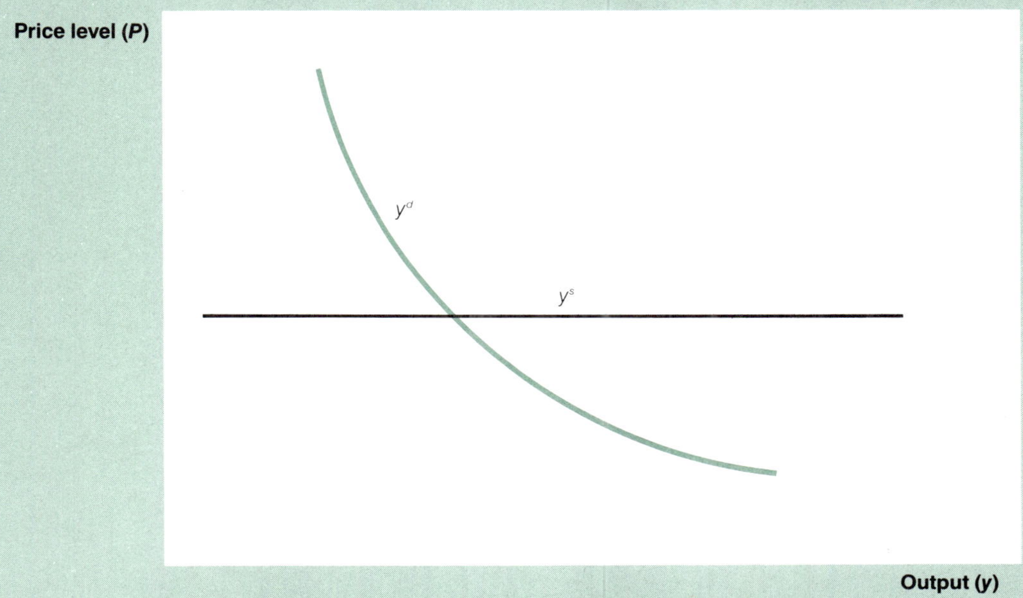

FIGURE 6.12 **Output is demand-determined when the aggregate supply curve is horizontal.**

readily confirm the obvious conclusions: **In an extreme Keynesian model, an expansionary monetary policy increases output and reduces interest rates, while an expansionary fiscal policy increases both output and interest rates. There are no significant immediate effects on prices.**

Classical economists believed that increases in the money supply merely raise prices, with no real effects on economic activity. Keynes, however, argued that an expansionary monetary policy lowers interest rates and encourages spending, particularly investment. But paradoxically, early Keynesian models tended to treat monetary policy as relatively impotent. After identifying how an expansionary monetary policy stimulates the economy (by lowering interest rates and encouraging investment), Keynes went on to argue that these effects were not very reliable in a severe depression. Interest rates were already very low in the 1930s (the prime rate on business loans was 1.5% throughout the period from 1933 to 1947) and profit expectations were so gloomy in the 1930s that marginally lower interest rates would not have made much difference anyway. (Exercises 17 and 18 give the *IS-LM* analytics.) Keynes and his early followers (including Marriner Eccles, the Federal Reserve Board Chairman) were very skeptical of the ability of monetary policy to end the Great Depression. They argued that simply exchanging money for securities does not guarantee more spending. Government public-works projects are more appealing because these insure that jobs will be created. This skepticism of the power of monetary

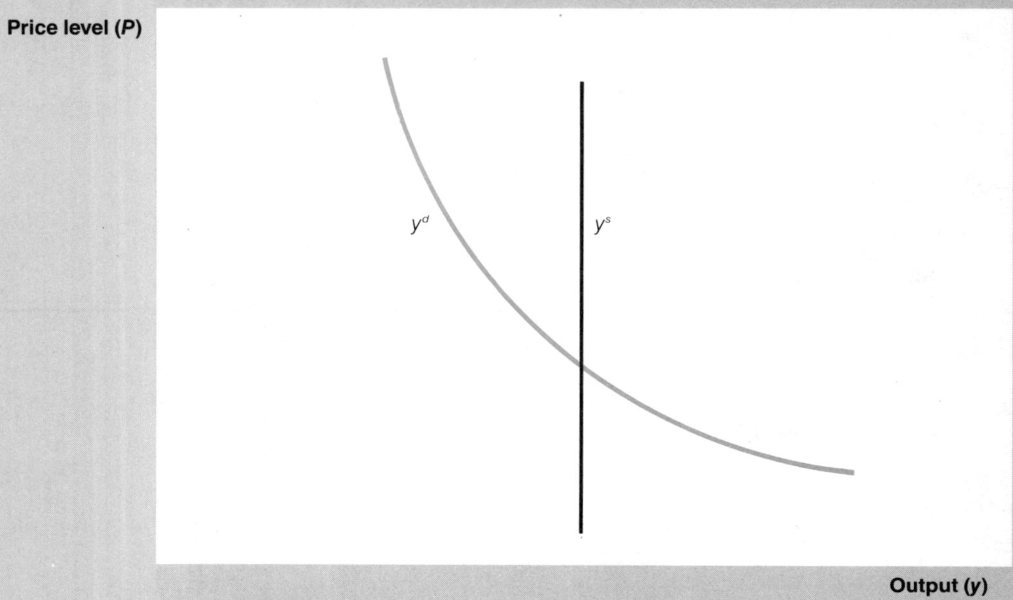

FIGURE 6.13 **Output is supply-determined when the aggregate supply curve is vertical.**

policy persisted well into the 1950s. But, today, almost everyone agrees that, outside of deep depressions at least, monetary policy does have significant effects on the economy. There have been too many credit crunches to argue otherwise.

Rigid output and flexible prices

In a classical full-employment model, it is the price level rather than output that absorbs demand variations. Real wages and employment are determined by labor market equilibrium. Output is determined by this full-employment level and the given production function. All are immune to variations in prices and interest rates. A 10% change in the price level will simply cause a 10% change in nominal wages, without affecting real wages, employment, or output.

This analysis implies that the aggregate supply curve is vertical, as in Figure 6.13. Changes in aggregate demand affect the price level (and, implicitly, the interest rate), but not real wages, employment, or output. In Figures 6.2 and 6.3, for example, when there is full employment, an open-market purchase does not cause output to rise with the price level, since output is already at the full-employment level. Instead, the nominal wage rate increases by the same percentage as the price level; the real wage stays at the market equilibrium level; and full employment is undisturbed. Aggregate demand is reconciled to this fixed full-employment output by a price increase that completely offsets the increase in the money supply. The price increase must shift the *LM* curve back to its initial position in Figure 6.3. Thus, if the nominal money supply goes up 10%, then prices rise 10%, too, in order to hold the real money supply constant. **If there is full employment, then an open-market purchase raises the price level, but has no effect on output, employment, or interest rates.**

Now, reconsider the fiscal policy depicted in Figures 6.7 and 6.8. If output does not budge from its full-employment level, then demand must adapt to this fixed supply. The increase in prices must reduce the real money supply sufficiently to completely offset the expansionary effects of the increase in government spending. Thus, **if there is full employment, then a bond-financed increase in government spending increases the interest rate and price level, but has no effect on output or employment.**

Since government spending, g, is larger while output, y, is unchanged, the equation $c + i + g = y$ implies that private spending $(c + i)$ declines by just as much as government spending increases. This is complete *supply-side crowding out:* Output is a fixed pie, so that if the government takes more, then the private sector has less. Government spending simply reallocates output from private to public uses. This is the basis for the recommendation of Milton Friedman and other classically oriented economists that the burden of government is not its taxes or its budget deficits, but its spending. In their view, it is more important to limit government spending to a certain fraction of national output, than to cut taxes or compel a balanced budget.

If, however, there are idle resources in the economy, then the size of the pie can be expanded so that there may be more output for all sectors of society. There are times when resources are pretty fully utilized, other times when there are obviously idle resources, and yet other times when it is debatable how much slack there is in the economy.

In 1966, the unemployment rate was 3.8%, manufacturing capacity utilization was 91%, and GNP was estimated to be above potential GNP. In this situation, more expansionary monetary and fiscal policies would have mostly increased prices and had little effect on output. Increased Vietnam War spending in 1966 was mostly a bigger slice of a fixed pie, leaving less for nonmilitary uses. Lyndon Johnson was then President and his wishes for "more guns and more butter" could not be realized.

In 1982, in contrast, the unemployment rate was 9.7%, capacity utilization had dropped below 70%, and actual GNP was estimated to be about $300 billion below potential GNP. Supply-side crowding out was not a major concern in 1982. There were lots of idle resources that could have been employed productively. An increased demand by one sector of the economy would not necessarily have reduced the resources available to other sectors.

Full employment and the quantity theory

Very strong consequences would follow if the economy were at full-employment and the simple quantity theory were true. These two assumptions imply

GUNS AND BUTTER IN THE 1960s

The unemployment rate was 3% during the Korea War years (1951–53) and near 4% during the peacetime prosperity of 1955–57. But prosperity faded during the last three years of the Eisenhower administration. The unemployment rate averaged 6.8% in 1958, the highest since the Great Depression, and stayed above 5% during the entire period 1958–60.

John F. Kennedy became president in 1961, determined to use monetary and fiscal policies to "get the country moving again." The cornerstone of his economic program was a substantial reduction in personal and corporate income taxes. But Kennedy couldn't sell his proposed tax cut to a Congress that was fearful of large budget deficits. The economy stayed in the doldrums with a 6.7% unemployment rate in 1961 and a GNP that was 8% below its potential. In 1962, government spending increased by 8% and the unemployment rate fell to 5.6%—encouraging, but still far from the administration's 4% target.

Lyndon Johnson, succeeding to the presidency after Kennedy's assassination in November 1963, managed to coax substantial tax legislation out of a still-reluctant Congress—about a 20% reduction in personal income taxes and a 10% cut in corporate taxes. Government spending for a variety of health, education, and welfare programs increased too as Johnson tried to wage a "war on poverty" and achieve what he called a "Great Society." Together, lower taxes and higher government spending reduced the full-employment surplus (as a percentage of GNP) from 1.2% in 1963 to 0.2% in 1964 and 0.1% in 1965. The Fed followed an accommodating monetary policy, allowing the money supply to increase by 4.0% in 1964 and by 4.3% in 1965. The unemployment rate fell steadily, until it reached 4.1% in the fourth quarter of 1965—almost exactly on target. These two years of economic recovery convinced many skeptics that monetary and fiscal "demand management" policies could end recessions and restore full employment.

The Vietnam War was also heating up in late 1965 and Lyndon Johnson wanted more "guns and butter"—guns to fight a war and butter to achieve a Great Society. As military spending increased, the full-employment surplus fell to a 1.9 % deficit by 1967. The Fed, meanwhile, allowed the money supply to expand faster than prices through 1968, as shown in the table below.
The unemployment rate fell to 3.5%; output ran above potential GNP; and inflationary pressures surfaced. The economy was having trouble delivering more guns and more butter.

Year	Full-employment surplus	Change in M1	Unemployment rate	GNP gap	Change in CPI
1966	− 0.8%	2.7%	3.8%	− 2.2%	3.4%
1967	− 1.9%	6.3%	3.8%	− 1.2%	3.0%
1968	− 1.3%	7.4%	3.6%	− 2.2%	4.7%
1969	0.5%	3.8%	3.5%	− 1.5%	6.1%

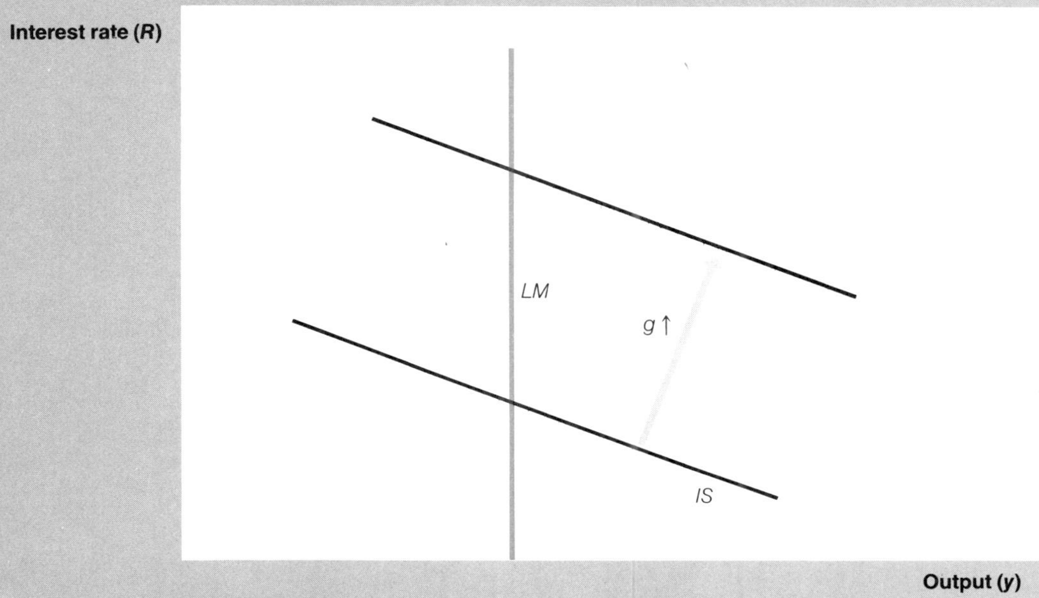

FIGURE 6.14 **If the money supply is constant and money demand does not depend on the interest rate, then there is only one level of income for which money demand equals supply. Thus, with a vertical *LM* curve, shifts in the *IS* curve do not affect aggregate demand or output.**

that both the aggregate supply curve and the *LM* curve are vertical. There would be both complete supply-side and demand-side crowding out, and an interesting segmentation of the model as well. The supply side of the economy would determine real wages, employment, and output. At this output level, the *IS* curve determines the interest rate and the *LM* curve determines the price level. Commodity demand does not affect prices and money equilibrium does not affect interest rates!

Figure 6.14 shows that the quantity theory immobilizes fiscal policy. A bond-financed increase in government spending merely raises the interest rate, with no effect on output or prices. Figure 6.15 shows an open-market purchase. The *LM* curve initially intersects the *IS* curve at the full-employment level $\bar{y}$. At the initial price level, the increased money supply shifts the *LM* curve rightward, reducing the interest rate and raising aggregate demand above the full-employment level. An increase in the price level brings demand back in line with output by shifting the *LM* curve back to its initial position. Thus an increase in the money supply merely raises the price level.

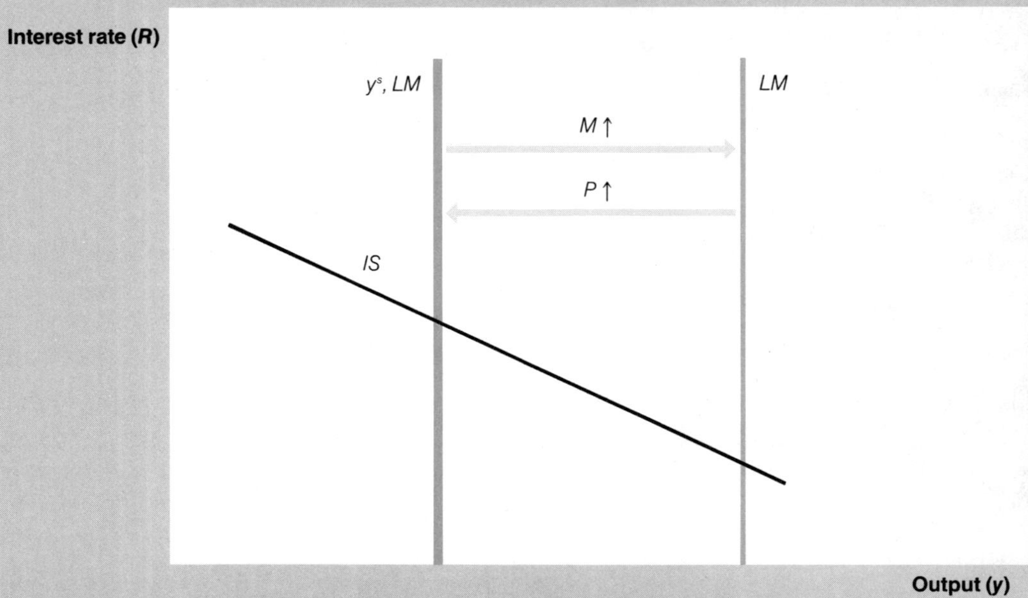

FIGURE 6.15 **In an extreme classical model, an open-market purchase raises prices but does not affect output or interest rates.**

Keynes disputed the two central classical assumptions: that the economy is at full employment (the aggregate supply curve is vertical) and that the simple quantity theory holds (the *LM* curve is vertical). We have seen how the relaxation of these two classical assumptions implies that monetary policies, fiscal policies, and private demand-side actions do affect output, employment, and interest rates.

THE ECONOMIC CONSEQUENCES OF A FUEL SHORTAGE

So far, we have concentrated on the economic consequences of various demand-side events. Now, we examine a supply-side event. The supply side of the economy—labor supply, labor demand, and output—is affected by changes in such things as the size of the population, preferences concerning leisure versus commodities, and labor productivity. Such changes are usually quite glacial—gradual and not very sensitive to prevailing economic conditions—and thus can be safely neglected in short-run analyses. But in the 1970s, the United

IN THE NEWS

The Economic Impact of Cheaper Oil . . .

Ever since the industrial revolution began more than 200 years ago, rapid growth in the world economy has depended on cheap energy. In 1974, when OPEC quadrupled the price of oil, it not only dealt a devastating blow to economic growth but also sent inflation into double digits. The same pattern was repeated with a vengeance after OPEC jacked up prices sharply in 1979.

Now that process is being reversed. With oil prices tumbling, the chances are increasing that the industrial world will see a recovery . . . and experience strong growth and low inflation for the rest of the decade.

Not everyone, of course, will benefit from a sharp drop in oil prices. Heavily indebted oil producers such as Mexico, Venezuela, and Indonesia will see their already squeezed earnings crimped even more. They will import less from the industrialized countries, and they will be even less able to pay their debts. This in turn could put severe pressure on banks throughout the world.

On balance, however, lower oil prices will be a big plus for industrial countries. . . .

The 10 years of OPEC-rigged prices was essentially a huge tax levied on the oil-consuming nations. For 1982 alone that tax amounted to some $200 billion. "What is happening now is like a big tax rebate," says Harvard University economist Richard N. Cooper, who was the first in 1974 to point out that the "tax" on oil-consuming countries would throw the world economy into recession . . .

That savings will be reflected in lower heating costs and gasoline prices. The upshot will be a surge in consumer spending, the sector that everyone has been counting on to lead the U.S. out of recession.

"In the second half of the '70s and early '80s, rising oil prices depressed purchasing power of households and accounted for much of the slowdown in consumer spending," says Sandra Shaber, director of consumer economics at Chase Econometrics. "We should now get the opposite effect. Middle- and lower-income families who must spend a large portion of their budget on energy-related necessities will now have more money to spend on other goods."

Lower oil prices could mean that a revival in capital spending will occur sooner than most observers now believe. For one thing, a strong recovery in consumer spending would allow plant operating rates to return to more normal levels earlier than currently forecast. That would give business the incentive to invest in more plant and equipment. Just as important, because capital equipment requires huge amounts of energy, the fall in oil prices lowers the cost of capital to business.

The break in OPEC-controlled oil prices will also result in lower production costs that translate into lower wholesale prices. From 1973 until the end of 1982, almost 45% of the increase in the producer price index was due to the rise in energy prices. The 1% decline in producer prices in January, the largest drop in the postwar period, was largely accounted for by a decline in energy prices. And at the consumer level, about 22% of the rise in the consumer price index during the last decade is directly attributable to higher heating-fuel and gasoline prices . . .

The favorable impact on inflation could last for years. Most economists do not think a solid economic recovery will trigger another explosion in oil prices. "Even with a broadly based international economic recovery, I would expect oil prices to remain down for several years under continuing pressures from new producers and the cumulative impact of conservation measures," says C. Fred Bergsten, director of the Institute for International Economics. "I don't fear a yo-yo syndrome, because I think that the supply/demand balance will remain on the down side into the late '80s."

If Bergsten is right, at least about the next several years—and most experts agree with him on that—governments in the Western world would be freer to foster growth and fight unemployment rather than be forced to concentrate on battling inflation. For almost a decade these governments have been virtually held hostage by the fear that fast growth would only provoke OPEC to keep raising prices. Federal Reserve Board officials have said that lower oil prices would give the U.S. central bank more room to help stimulate a recovery.

Most European and Japanese officials maintain that a sharp drop in oil prices is not necessarily a blessing for their economies. Almost totally dependent on OPEC oil, they would pass up the benefits of lower prices in exchange for OPEC's guarantees of supply over the long run. "I do not think that OPEC should be allowed to break down, certainly not," says former West Germany Chancellor Helmut Schmidt . . .

Oil-consuming industries both in the U.S. and Europe will be the main beneficiaries of a big drop in oil prices. "For chemicals, airlines, aluminum—anybody for whom energy costs are important—this will reduce costs and help profitability," says Lawrence Chimerine, president of Chase Econometrics.

Cheaper oil will ultimately help almost all industries. It will lead to lower transportation costs, encouraging companies to build plants in low-cost locations, since workers will now be willing to commute longer distances, says L. Clifton Hoch, senior vice-president at Fantus Co., plant location consultants.

Furthermore, the increase in consumers' discretionary income as a result of lower energy prices will encourage sales of consumer products. Consumers will start spending on "impulse items," such as jewelry and toys, says Martin Tolep, a corporate economist for F. W. Woolworth Co. "Apparel will benefit," says Chase's Shaber, "as well as smaller appliances, food, cosmetics, and some services . . ."

For Detroit, however, the drop in oil prices may be a mixed blessing. Lower prices will encourage driving and may lead to higher sales of replacement parts and tires. Higher discretionary income should also boost car sales. But what the consumer may do is shift to big cars again, which would be disruptive for an industry that has spent $50 billion on producing small, fuel-efficient autos.

Some energy suppliers will be hurt by sagging oil prices. Already the decline in deep gas drilling has forced distress sales of rigs, reduced employment, and depressed whole communities in Texas and Oklahoma. And the natural gas industry is fast losing market share as the transition to decontrol in effect forces producers to push prices higher.

But even in the energy industry, there will be winners: electric utilities and, ultimately, their customers. In New England, says DRI's Smith, each $1 decline in a barrel of oil means a reduction of 0.8% in a typical home electric bill. Yet the regulations that make it hard for utilities to raise prices—even through fuel adjustment clauses—now work in reverse: As fuel prices go down, cuts in utility costs will occur only slowly. (Reprinted from Mar. 7, 1983, issue of *Business Week* by special permission.

States was rocked by energy shocks that were too sudden and painful to be ignored: Between 1972 and 1981 the Producer Price Fuel Index rose by a factor of seven—from 106.2 to 694.5. In the following section we will see how this kind of increase in resource costs affects an economy.

Full employment

One pitfall to be avoided is the idea that full-employment output cannot vary. Even macroeconomics textbooks sometimes fall into this trap. One book concludes that unexpected changes in fuel prices may, as in the new classical models, cause voluntary fluctuations in employment and output, but that as soon as the price increase is correctly perceived, the economy will return to the same natural level of output as before. Thus a fuel shortage has no lasting effects on an economy!

Common sense tells us that there must be an error in this logic. The disappearance of cheap fuel surely lowers a nation's standard of living. The error arises because we fall into the habit of looking at the vertical aggregate supply curve and concluding that demand-side events do not affect output in a classical full-employment model. But this vertical supply curve can be shifted about by supply-side events. It does vary in the long run, under the influence of population growth, capital accumulation, technological improvements, and so on. And it can vary in the short run if there are sudden changes in any of these factors.

An increase in the cost of fuel persuades firms to reduce their fuel usage. Labor productivity, in turn, depends on the fuel used to run equipment and heat buildings, so that a drop in fuel usage reduces both the average and marginal productivity of labor. This means that, as shown in Figure 6.16, both the production function and the labor demand schedule shift downward. If the labor market stays in equilibrium, then real wages, employment, and output all fall. There is still full-employment in the sense that everyone who wants a job (at the now lower real wage rate) has one, but there are fewer people employed and they produce less. This supply-side contraction causes the aggregate supply curve to shift leftward (Figure 6.17), putting upward pressure on prices.

There may also be deflationary demand-side effects. A considerable amount of fuel is imported into the United States, so that sharply higher fuel prices have transferred hundreds of billions of dollars abroad. From an aggregate demand standpoint, this unprecedented wealth transfer is like a government tax that is used to finance foreign aid. It diminishes the wealth of U.S. citizens and also reduces their demand for U.S. goods and services. Instead of buying U.S. houses, clothes, and electronic games, they buy foreign oil. Some of these oil dollars do get recycled into the United States as oil-exporting nations buy American wheat, computers, and aircraft. But some oil dollars are spent elsewhere. On balance, the oil price transfer of U.S. dollars abroad reduces the demand for U.S. goods and services, shifting the *IS* curve and, hence, the aggregate demand curve leftward.

Figure 6.17 shows that, when both the supply- and demand-side effects are taken into account, it is uncertain whether the price level will rise or fall. If demand declines more than supply, then the price level will fall. If supply falls

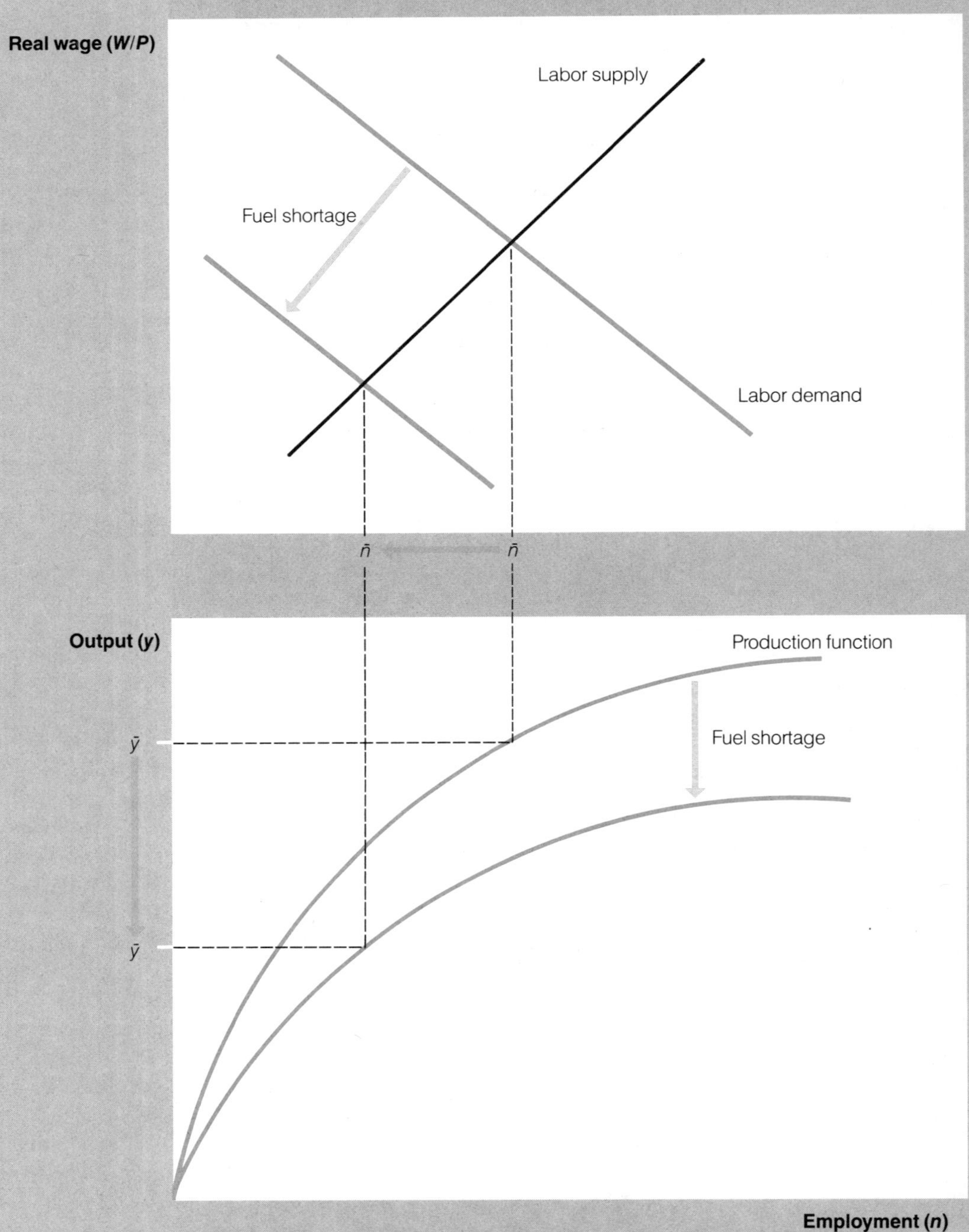

FIGURE 6.16 Mechanism by which a fuel shortage reduces marginal and average productivity of labor, which, in a classical full-employment model, causes real wages, employment, and output to fall.

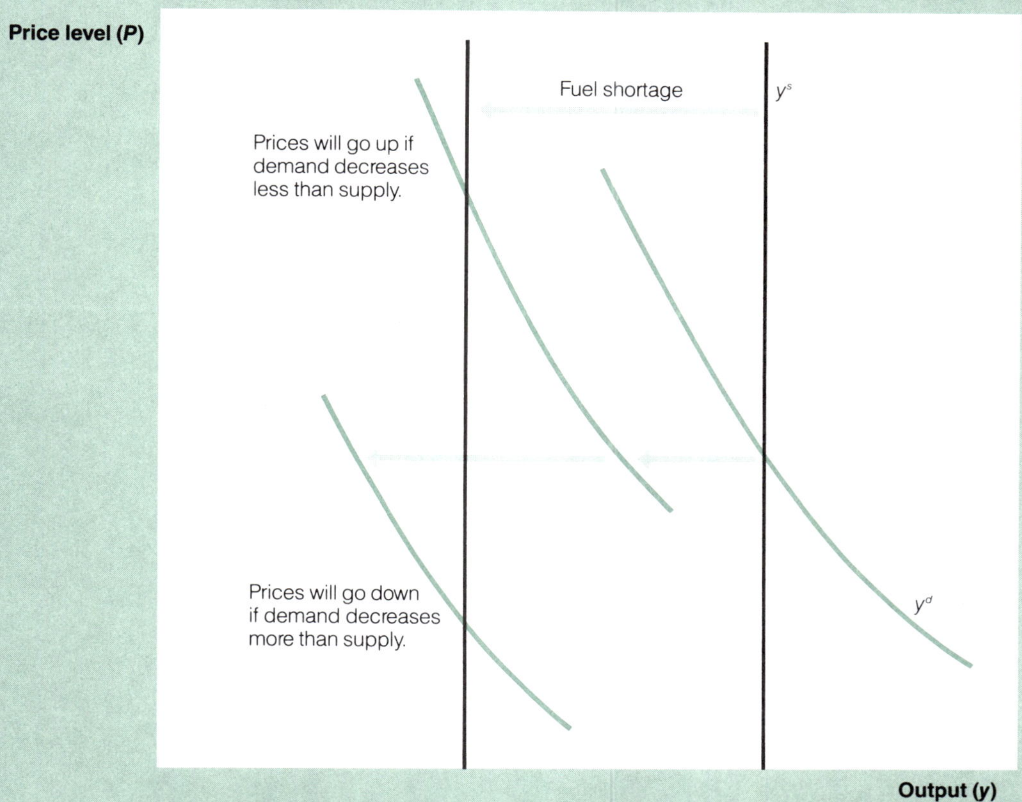

FIGURE 6.17 **Higher cost of fuel imports reduces output and may increase or decrease prices in a classical full-employment model.**

more than demand, then prices will increase. In either case, output falls even though there is still labor market equilibrium and, therefore, full employment.

If the economy is operating at full capacity, and domestic policy makers attempt to use expansionary monetary and fiscal policies to offset the fuel crisis, they will fail. If domestic resources are fully utilized, then output cannot be budged from its reduced level by demand-side policies. Expansionary monetary and fiscal policies only ensure that the decline in real output will be accompanied by higher prices.

Unemployment

If we allow for the fact that wages and prices are not perfectly flexible, then there is more room for demand-management policies. With imperfectly adjusting wages and prices, the fall in aggregate demand may leave slack in the

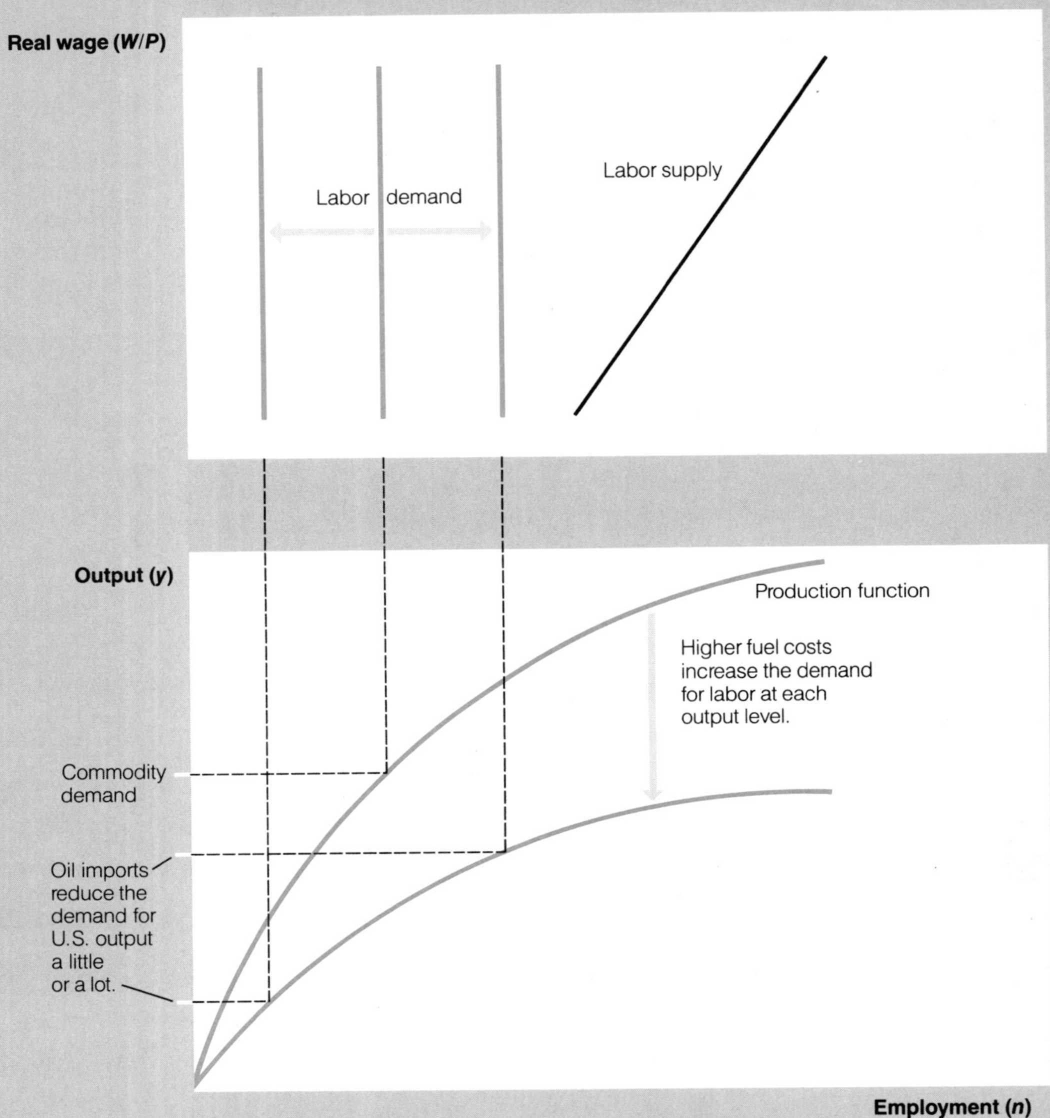

FIGURE 6.18 **More expensive fuel imports may increase or decrease labor demand in a Keynesian disequilibrium model.**

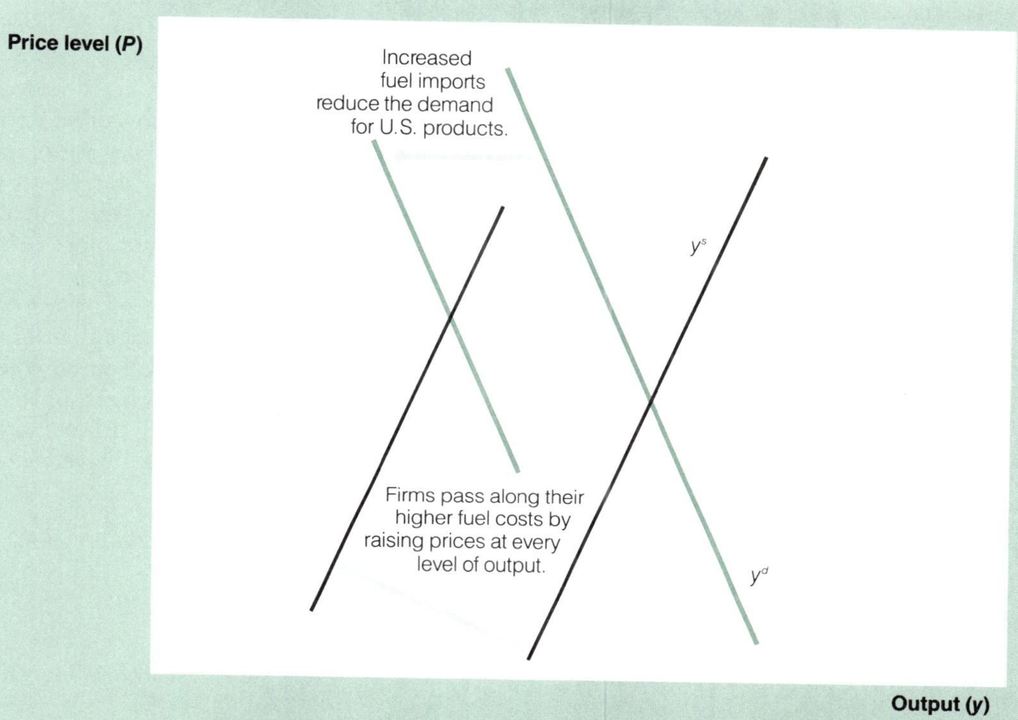

FIGURE 6.19 **If employment and output are demand-determined, then an increase in fuel prices lowers output and may raise prices.**

economy. If wages do not fall sufficiently in the situation depicted in Figure 6.16, then there will be an excess labor supply—that is, involuntary unemployment. In this case, it may be easier to reduce real wages through inflationary monetary and fiscal policies. Such demand-management policies may reduce the unemployment caused by a fuel shortage, but it remains true that the nation is poorer, using less fuel and producing less output at every level of employment and paying much more for this fuel.

If there are excess supplies of labor and commodities, then both employment and output are demand-determined. The causal forces now run from the demand side of the economy to the supply side. The oil dollars leaving the country reduce the demand for U.S. goods and services, and firms respond by reducing production. This drop in output diminishes the demands for both labor and fuel. On the other hand, higher fuel costs encourage firms to substitute labor for expensive fuel in producing this output. As shown in Figure 6.18, the production function shifts downward, now indicating that more labor will be demanded at each level of output. Thus, overall, high fuel costs reduce output and fuel usage and have an uncertain effect on labor demand.

As with the full-employment model, the price level may rise or fall. In Figure 6.19, increased fuel purchases from abroad diminish the demand for U.S.

products, shifting the aggregate demand curve leftward. This drop in demand puts some downward pressure on wages and prices. But firms using "cost plus" or average-cost pricing rules will be tempted to raise prices to pass along the higher fuel costs. The aggregate supply curve then shifts upward, since firms charge more at each level of output. Figure 6.19 shows that output falls, but it is not certain that prices will increase. If policy makers use expansionary monetary and fiscal policies to maintain aggregate demand, then the drop in output will be smaller, but prices will increase. Either way, the United States will be poorer in that output per hour of work declines, and more of this diminished output must be sent abroad to pay for fuel.

In practice, U.S. policy makers, especially the Fed, were more concerned about the inflationary consequences of a fuel shortage than of the unemployment left in its wake. Instead of trying to achieve full employment the government used tight monetary and fiscal policies to fight inflation. Thus they exacerbated the demand shock of oil dollars leaving the country and made the drop in employment and output worse than it would have been otherwise.

IMPORTANT TERMS AND CONCEPTS

monetary policies
fiscal policies
open-market operation
supply-side crowding out

An open-market purchase shifts the *LM* curve rightward and, hence, shifts the aggregate demand curve rightward, too. The interest rate falls, while output, employment, and the price level all increase. Private decreases in money demand have similar effects. Classical economists, assuming that the economy is at full employment, concluded that monetary events only affect prices.

A bond-financed increase in government spending shifts the *IS* curve rightward and, hence, shifts the aggregate demand curve rightward, too. The interest rate, output, employment, and prices all rise. Increases in private spending have similar effects. Classical economists, assuming full employment, concluded that spending cannot affect aggregate employment or output. Full employment implies complete supply-side crowding out in that increased government spending must be fully offset by reduced private spending. Only wages, prices, and interest rates change.

If the simple quantity theory holds, then the *LM* curve is vertical and there will be complete demand-side crowding out: A bond-financed increase in government spending pushes interest rates so high that private spending falls by as much as government spending increases, even without an increase in prices. If there is full employment and the quantity theory is true, then the supply side determines output and employment, the *IS* curve determines the interest rate, and the *LM* curve determines the price level.

The supply side of the economy is affected by changes in the population, worker productivity, leisure preferences, and so on. These things generally change gradually and are not immediately altered by economic fluctuations. The energy shocks in the 1970s did have important supply-side effects. These effects were contractionary in that higher energy costs reduced the average and marginal productivity of workers and thereby diminished the classical full-employment level of output. Even if the aggregate supply curve is not vertical it will still be shifted leftward by these energy shocks, since higher energy prices increase the cost of producing a given output. To cover their increased fuel costs, firms will charge a higher price at every output level, shifting the aggregate supply curve upward (and to the left). Expansionary monetary and fiscal policies can alleviate any resulting involuntary unemployment, but they cannot reverse the negative effect of higher energy costs on America's standard of living.

EXERCISES

1. What are the effects on output, prices, and the interest rate of a Federal Reserve open-market sale of Treasury securities? Explain the economic logic behind these effects.

2. The Federal Reserve wants to use open-market operations to restrain prices. Should they buy or sell securities? Explain your reasoning.

3. The Federal Reserve wants to use open-market operations to fight a recession. Should they buy or sell securities?

4. The Federal Reserve wants to use open-market operations to restrain prices and stimulate output. Will buying or selling securities accomplish these two objectives?

5. Money market mutual funds have made bonds more accessible to small investors. If this development has increased the demand for bonds and reduced the demand for money, how have output, prices, and interest rates been affected?

6. The Federal Reserve wants to stimulate investment spending by lowering interest rates and increasing national output. Should they buy or sell securities? Explain why low interest rates and increased output stimulate investment and why your recommended policy will accomplish these objectives. Why did classical economists doubt that monetary policy could stimulate investment spending?

7. An increase in government spending accompanied by which of the following policies shifts the aggregate demand curve the farthest rightward?
   a. no change in the money supply
   b. a change in the money supply that holds the interest rate constant
   c. a change in the money supply that reduces the interest rate

8. How would output, prices, and interest rates be affected if businesses decide to sell securities and acquire additional plant and equipment?

9. Does increased government spending encourage or discourage private investment spending? Explain your reasoning.

10. The government would like to stimulate investment without encouraging inflation and, so, to reduce the interest rate without affecting the price level. How can monetary and fiscal policies accomplish this?

11. In comparing two full-employment equilibria, the following have been observed. Real wages, the interest rate, and the price level have all declined. Consumption and investment have increased. The government has not taken any policy actions. What could have caused these changes?

12. In a classical full-employment model, what would be the effects of an expansionary monetary policy on y, P, and R? Would your conclusions be any different if you allowed for a Pigou effect, so that a higher price level shifts the *IS* curve to the left? Explain any differences.

13. There has been talk of a capital shortage in the United States. How is the nation's capital stock influenced by government monetary and fiscal policies? Do your answers depend on whether or not there is full employment?

14. How might macroeconomic theory explain the following paragraph from a news story: "Interest rates fell sharply in the money and capital markets as investors were encouraged by government statistics showing a smaller than anticipated rise in the nation's industrial production last month." (Edward P. Foldessy and Peter B. Roche, *Wall Street Journal,* September 17, 1980)

15. Critically evaluate the following paragraph from a newspaper editorial. "The government's expenditures represent its only real claims on the nation's economic resources. It is only a secondary question to what extent these claims are met by taxes (government receipts) or by borrowing (the deficit). In either case the money must come from the private sector, in one instance from its income and in the other from its savings. In either case the real resources come out of the income generated by productive enterprise; someone has to pay for whatever the government spends." (*Wall Street Journal,* March 11, 1980)

16. The Federal Reserve sometimes "leans against the wind" by making open-market purchases when interest rates rise and by selling when interest rates fall. This policy can be modeled by letting the money supply be

$$M/P = M_0/P + M_R R \qquad M_R > 0,$$

where M_0 is the predetermined money supply and M_R gauges the increase in the money supply induced by an increase in the interest rate. Let the real demand for money be

$$l = l_0 + l_y y + l_R R \qquad l_y > 0,\ l_R < 0$$

and find the slope of the *LM* curve. If the Fed leans harder against the wind (larger M_R), does the *LM* curve become flatter or steeper? What if M_R is infinitely large?

17. Early Keynesian models considered the possibility that there might be a "liquidity trap" at a very low interest rate, such that an expansionary monetary policy could not drive the interest rate any lower. In a case where monetary policy cannot affect the interest rate, what does the *LM* curve look like? How powerful will monetary and fiscal policies be?

18. If expenditures did not depend on interest rates, what would the *IS* curve look like? How powerful would monetary and fiscal policies be? Give the economic logic behind your answer.

19. How would output, employment, wages, prices, and interest rates be affected by a decision by the "me generation" to leave the labor force and camp in the desert? Assume a classical, market-equilibrium model.

20. How would output, employment, wages, prices, and interest rates be affected by the discovery of a vast oil field in Wyoming?

21. Milton Friedman once presented the following macroeconomic model:

$$e_0 + e_y y + e_R R = y \qquad 0 < e_y < 1,\ e_R < 0$$
$$l_0 + l_y y + l_R R = M/P \qquad l_y > 0,\ l_R < 0$$
$$R = R_0.$$

The assumption that R is predetermined allows the *IS* and *LM* curves to determine y and P. How are y and P affected in this model by an increase in e_0? How are they affected by an increase in M?

REFERENCES

1. John Maynard Keynes, *The General Theory of Employment, Interest and Money*, London: Macmillan, 1936, p. 383.

SUGGESTIONS FOR FURTHER READING

The most consistently interesting and informative discussions of recent macroeconomic events are in the annual editions of the *Economic Report of the President.*

PART THREE

INFLATION

CHAPTER SEVEN

THE CAUSES OF INFLATION

There is no sight in the world more awful than that of an oldtime economist, foam-flecked at the mouth and hell-bent to cure inflation by monetary discipline. God willing, we shan't soon see his like again.

PAUL SAMUELSON[1]

This chapter defines inflation and examines its causes, especially its relation to booms and recessions.

SO far, our macroeconomic analysis has concerned the determination of employment, output, the interest rate, the wage rate, and the price level. In this chapter, we turn to *inflation,* a sustained elevation of the price level, which should be carefully distinguished from the *rate* of inflation, which is the rate at which the increase in the price level takes place. The price level has the dimensions of a stock, a quantity measured at a point in time, while the rate of inflation is a flow, occurring over time. Thus, on a certain date, the price of a house might be $100,000 and might be increasing at a rate—its rate of inflation—of 20% per year. It is even possible for the price level to increase while the rate of increase (the rate of inflation) is *de*creasing: In our example, if the house price a year later is $110,000, there has been an increase in the price level, but a decrease (to 10% from 20%) in the rate of inflation. That the distinction is insufficiently appreciated, is often seen in surveys in which people are asked their expectations concerning the rate of inflation. Careful questioning often reveals that, in their answers, they are mistakenly referring to the price level.

Inflation is so important and complicated a subject that we will devote two chapters to it. The present chapter discusses some economic explanations of inflation; the next chapter will address the question of how inflation affects citizens' well-being and economic behavior. One of the interesting conclusions we will draw is that people's reactions to a high rate of inflation should be very different from those to a high price level. For example, whether or not you want to buy a house now depends not only on its price, but also on how fast that price is increasing (the rate of inflation). A high price makes the house less appealing, but that house is more attractive if its price is rising rapidly.

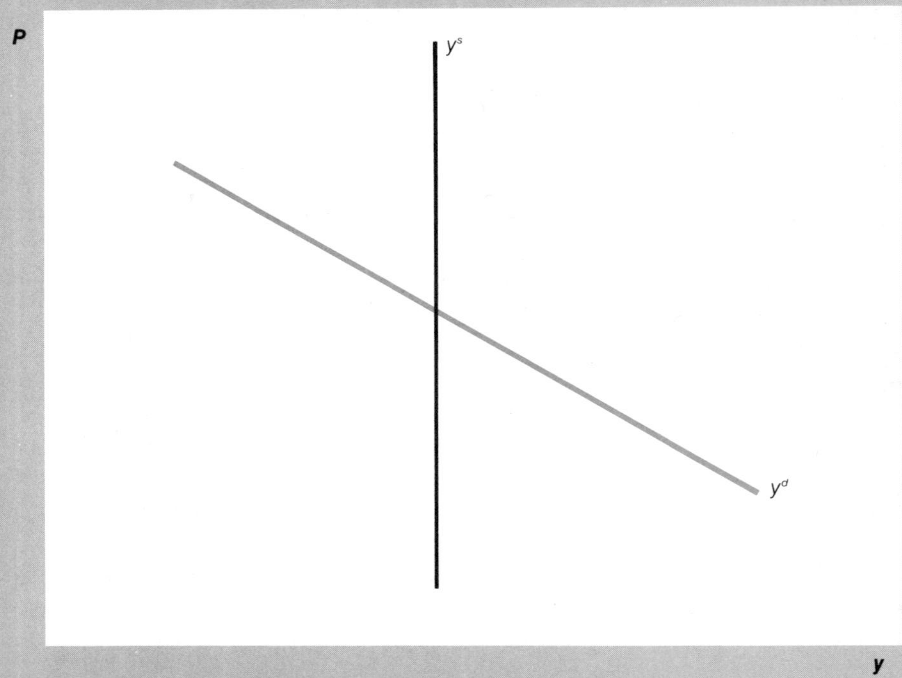

FIGURE 7.1 WITH FULL EMPLOYMENT, PRICES ARE DETERMINED BY DEMAND. **In classical full-employment models, the aggregate supply curve is vertical and, thus, the location of the aggregate demand curve determines only the price level.**

EXPLANATIONS OF INFLATION: IN THE LONG RUN

Inflation is often associated with rapid increases in the money supply. For example, a standard dictionary definition of inflation is "an increase in the volume of money and credit relative to available goods resulting in a substantial and continuing rise in the general price level."[2] This definition presumes that it is increases in money and credit (whatever "credit" is) that cause inflation. Economists, too, have long associated inflation with increases in the money supply. Nobel Laureate Milton Friedman said, plainly enough, "Inflation is always and everywhere a monetary phenomenon."[3]

The economic logic behind the link between money and inflation can be found in the classical analysis. If we assume full employment, then the aggregate supply curve is vertical and fixed in the short run, as in Figure 7.1. Increases in aggregate demand simply raise prices, without affecting output or employment. Conversely, if aggregate demand is stable, then prices are stable. What, then, determines aggregate demand in the classical models? If the simple quantity theory holds, then (as shown in Figure 7.2) aggregate demand is de-

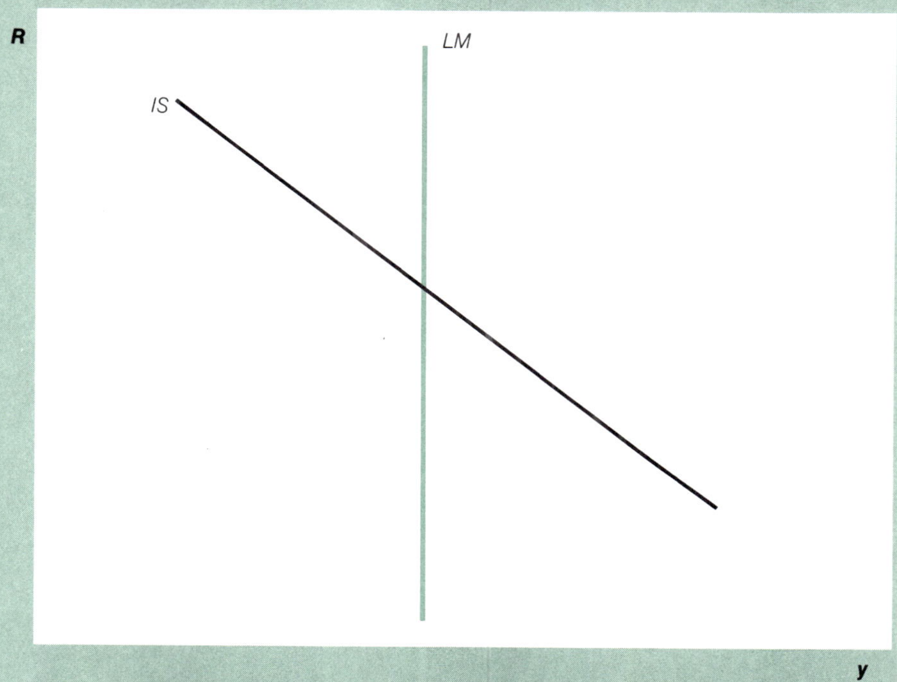

FIGURE 7.2 **THE QUANTITY THEORY. In the simple quantity theory, the *LM* curve is vertical. Thus, the aggregate demand curve is determined by the location of this vertical *LM* curve—that is, by money supply relative to money demand. The *IS* curve determines only the interest rate.**

termined by the location of the *LM* curve—that is, by money supply and money demand. A shift in the *IS* curve does not affect the price level because the vertical *LM* curve causes demand-side crowding out. In contrast, any increase in the money supply does increase aggregate demand and the price level.

We can be even more specific if we write the simple quantity theory equation

$$Mv = Py \tag{7.1}$$

where velocity, v, is assumed to be institutionally determined. This equation can be rearranged as

$$P = Mv/y \tag{7.2}$$

If velocity (v) is predetermined and output (y) is fixed at the full-employment level, then Equation 7.2 says that the price level is proportional to the money supply. A 10% increase in the money supply will simply cause a 10% increase in the price level. The classical economists concluded that money is "neutral," since the money supply determines only the price level and does not affect real economic activity.*

Equation 7.2 also implies that *only* money affects prices. If velocity and output are constant, then P cannot change unless M changes. Government spending, budget deficits, militant unions, and OPEC do not affect prices in the classical model. The price level depends only on the money supply.

So far we have held output constant at the full-employment level, and we have seen how the money supply determines the price level. Any change in the money supply causes an immediate, proportionate change in the price level. What about inflation, which is persistent increase in the price level over time? Continuing changes in prices require continuing shifts of the aggregate supply and demand curves. The aggregate supply curve will gradually move as time passes. Full-employment output grows as a nation's population, factories, machines, and technology increase.

In Figure 7.1, a gradual rightward shift of the aggregate supply curve puts downward pressure on prices. If the aggregate demand curve held steady as time passed, there would be a persistent deflation as the supply curve slides rightward over time. In practice, the aggregate demand curve is not steady, but slides rightward, too, as the Fed continuously increases the nation's money supply. Velocity, too, may change as society's bill-paying habits evolve over time. Whether the nation has inflation or deflation depends on whether the aggregate demand curve slides rightward faster or slower than the aggregate supply curve.

Figure 7.2 reminds us that, in the classical model, the aggregate demand curve is determined solely by the *LM* curve. The rightward slide of the *LM* curve as time passes depends on how fast money supply is growing relative to money demand. Again, the simple quantity theory makes our conclusions very precise. Equation 7.2 implies that

$$\begin{pmatrix}\text{\% change}\\\text{in prices}\end{pmatrix} = \begin{pmatrix}\text{\% change in}\\\text{money supply}\end{pmatrix} + \begin{pmatrix}\text{\% change}\\\text{in velocity}\end{pmatrix} - \begin{pmatrix}\text{\% change}\\\text{in output}\end{pmatrix}$$

If velocity were constant, then whether there is inflation or deflation depends solely on whether the money supply is increasing faster or slower than output. If, for example, output grows at 2% a year, and the money supply grows by 12% a year, then the rate of inflation will be 10%. If improvements in society's bill-paying habits increase velocity by 2% a year, then this is like a 2% increase in the supply of money. Now, 12% money growth plus 2% velocity growth, less 2% output growth implies a 12% inflation. **In classical models, then, with full employment and constant velocity, the level of the money**

* Economists sometimes discuss simple economies in which money is the only nominal asset and where the money supply is increased by mad helicopter pilots bombing the populace with money. A proportionate change in the price level then holds real magnitudes constant, since money is the only nominal asset. In the real world, however, there are many nominally denominated assets that do not change proportionately with the money supply. In a Fed open-market purchase, for instance, the nominal supply of bonds is decreased when the money supply is increased. With the money supply up and the bond supply down, no change in the price level can restore the original real magnitudes of both money and bonds. Thus a simple change in the price level cannot, by itself, fully offset an open-market operation.

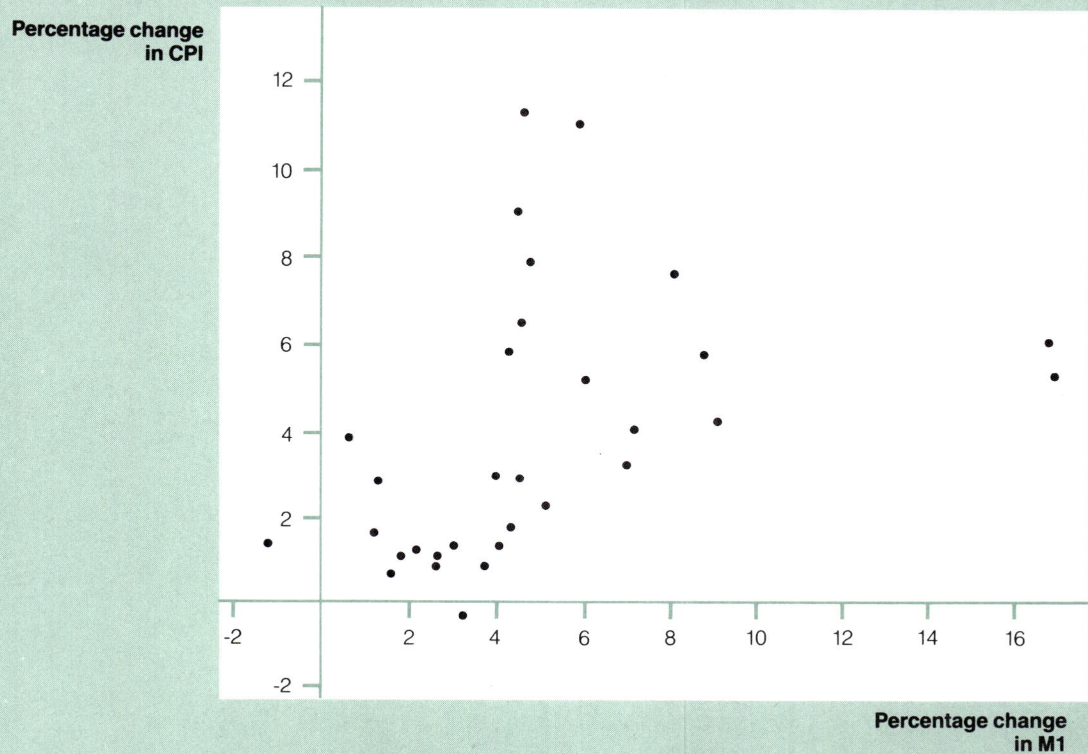

FIGURE 7.3 ANNUAL PERCENTAGE CHANGES IN M1 AND THE CONSUMER PRICE INDEX, 1950–80. **Even with annual data, there is only a very loose relationship between inflation and the rate of growth of M1.**

supply determines the price level, while the rates of the growth of the money supply and of velocity relative to the growth of output determine the rate of inflation.

Figure 7.3 shows some annual data on the rate of inflation and the rate of growth of M1 (currency plus transaction accounts). There is not much correlation between the two. In years when M1 has increased by 4% to 6%, the rate of inflation has been anywhere from 1% to 11%. The rate of inflation depends on more than the money supply.

Remember, too, that even were there a high correlation between the rate of inflation and some monetary aggregate, such as M1, that still would be three or four steps removed from the commonplace refrain that inflation is due to the government's printing presses having run amok. Monetary aggregates include private moneys (such as checking accounts) in addition to government moneys (coins, Federal Reserve notes, and reserves credited to banks). Even were there a perfect correlation between inflation and some monetary aggregate, this

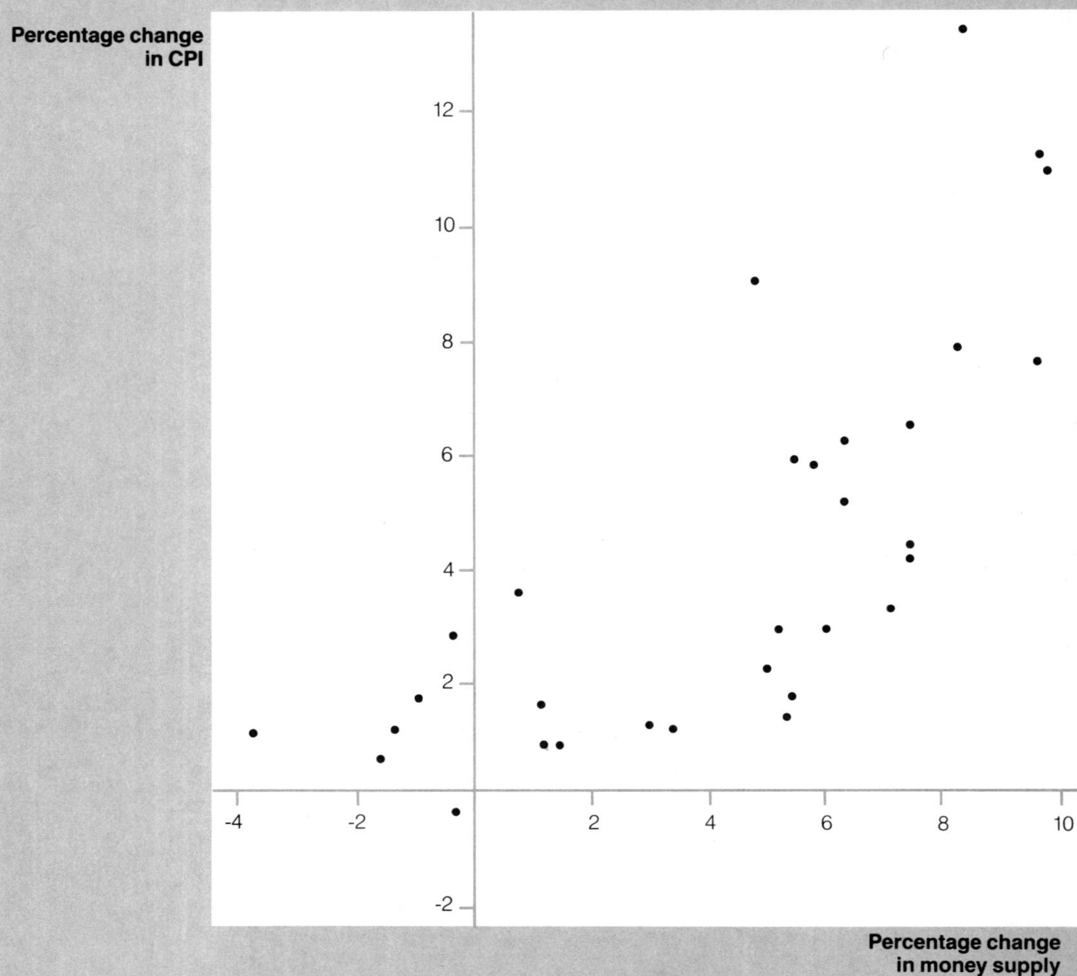

FIGURE 7.4 ANNUAL PERCENTAGE CHANGES IN U.S. GOVERNMENT MONEY SUPPLY AND CONSUMER PRICE INDEX, 1950–81. In years when the Fed increased its money supply by 5%, the rate of inflation has ranged from 1% to 9%. Inflation apparently depends on more than current monetary policy.

would not show that the government's printing presses cause inflation. Figure 7.4 shows some annual data on the rate of inflation and the rate of growth of the government money supply; there is no more than a loose relationship between the two.

The long run

In the classical model, the explanation of inflation is quite simple—too simple, it turns out. The model, as we have noted, says that an increase in the money supply increases prices proportionately. Inflation, continuing increases in prices, depends on the rate of growth of the money supply relative to output (perhaps with some adjustment for gradual changes in velocity). The problem with these proposed classical relationships between money and prices is that, like most classical propositions, they are more appropriate for the long run than for the short.

When Friedman said that inflation is always and everywhere a monetary phenomenon, he did not mean that literally every jog in the CPI is due to a corresponding wiggle in the money supply. Instead, he meant that major inflations, involving rapid and sustained price increases, are generally accompanied by rapid and sustained increases in the money supply. This long-run argument is reasonable. If the money supply grows very rapidly, say at double-digit rates, then (applying the quantity theory equation, $Mv = Py$, again) either output must grow rapidly, velocity must fall rapidly, or prices must increase rapidly. In the short run, some or all of these three things may happen—but not in the long run. Output can increase very rapidly in an economy emerging from a recession. However, the long-run growth of output is limited by a society's resources. It is difficult to imagine real output growing at double-digit rates forever. What about velocity? Velocity does bounce up and down, but there is little reason why it should fall at double-digit rates forever.* That leaves prices: If the money supply grows by 10% a year, year after year after year, it is almost certain that there will be some inflation.

Conversely, if the money supply grows more slowly than output, then a rapid, sustained inflation requires rapid, continuing increases in velocity, so that money circulates progressively faster. Velocity can increase substantially, but there are limits. Velocity alone is unlikely to increase fast enough to sustain permanently a triple- or even double-digit inflation. The higher the rate of inflation and the longer it persists the more certain it is that the money supply is increasing faster than output. **A rapid, sustained increase in the money supply will almost certainly cause inflation, though the inflation need not be constant nor equal to the rate of increase in the money supply. Conversely, a sustained inflation without money growth will be limited by a persistent tendency of money demand to outstrip supply.**

Chapter 18 presents some formal long-run analysis and some limited support for the classical explanation of inflation in the long run. In the remainder of this chapter, we will focus on inflation in the short run.

* Keynes raised the theoretical possibility of a "liquidity trap," in which interest rates have fallen so low that people hoard money because there is no financial advantage in holding other assets. We have not yet witnessed any such sustained "flights to cash."

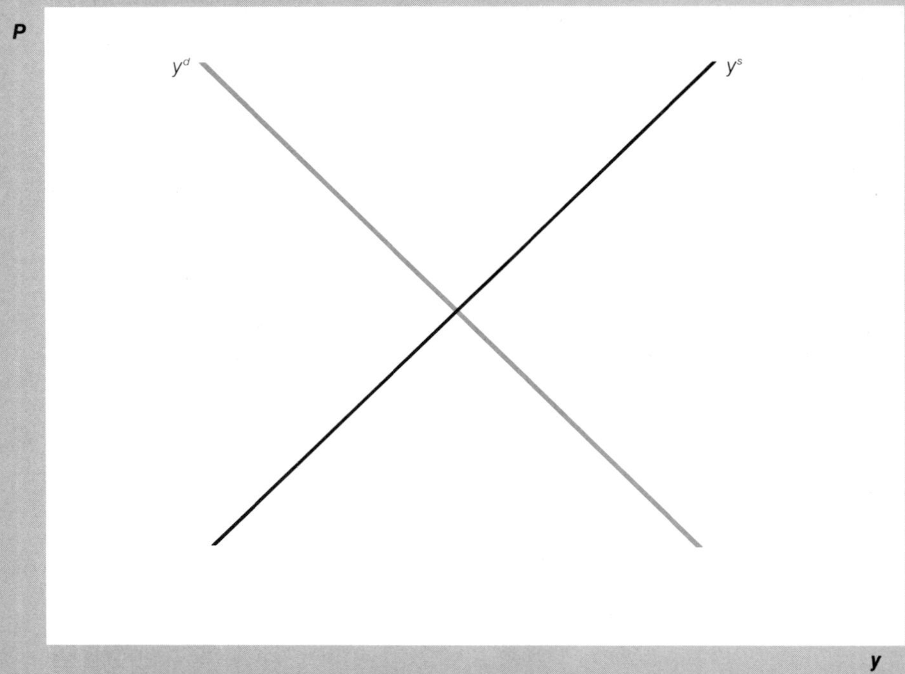

FIGURE 7.5 PRICES ARE DETERMINED BY THE AGGREGATE DEMAND AND SUPPLY CURVES. **The current price level does not depend on a single factor but, instead, on all of the elements that underlie the aggregate demand and supply curves.**

EXPLANATIONS OF INFLATION: IN THE SHORT RUN

In the short run, velocity is not fixed and the economy is not always at full employment. Therefore, as the data in Figure 7.3 show, increases in the money supply are neither necessary nor sufficient for short-run inflation. Not every increase in the money supply raises prices proportionately, and prices *can* rise without a corresponding increase in the money supply.

In our macro model, shown in Figure 7.5, prices are determined by the intersection of the aggregate demand and supply curves. Any shift in either of these curves will affect the price level. The money supply only affects prices to the extent that it changes the location of the aggregate demand curve. Further, it does not matter whether the *IS* or the *LM* curve is "responsible" for the location of the aggregate demand curve. An expansionary monetary policy is no more or less inflationary than an equally expansionary fiscal policy.

Figure 7.6 shows this important point. The *IS* and *LM* curves initially intersect at Point 1, while the aggregate demand and supply curves intersect at Point 4. The output level is y' and the price level is P'. Now, an increase in the money supply changes the *IS-LM* intersection to Point 2, raising the demand-side level

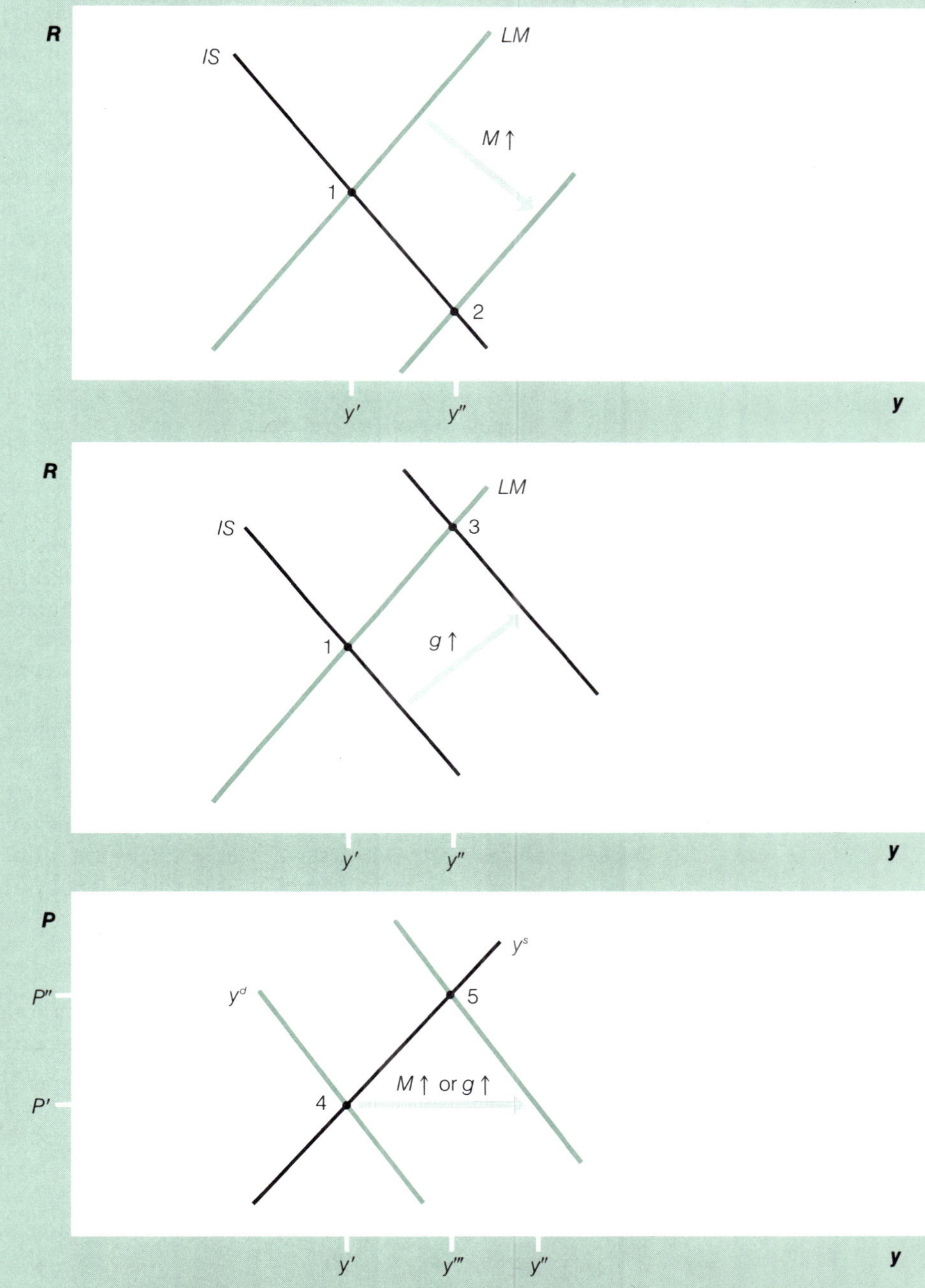

FIGURE 7.6 **EQUALLY EXPANSIONARY MONETARY AND FISCAL POLICIES RAISE PRICES EQUALLY.** **For demand management policies to increase output from y' to y''' (that is, to shift the demand-supply intersection from Point 4 to Point 5), the government needs to shift the *IS-LM* intersection from y' to y''. As shown, this can be accomplished with either monetary or fiscal policies.**

of income from y' to y''. The aggregate demand curve shifts rightward (bottom panel), giving a new intersection at Point 5 and changing output to y''' and prices to P''. An equally expansionary fiscal policy would cause an *IS* curve shift such that the *IS-LM* intersection goes from Point 1 to Point 3. The demand-side level of income still goes from y' to y'' and both the rightward shift of the aggregate demand curve and the resultant increase in prices are the same as with the expansionary monetary policy. **Thus, price changes are due to shifts in the aggregate demand and supply curves, regardless of whether these shifts are caused by monetary policy, fiscal policy, or private actions.**

One big difference between market equilibrium and market disequilibrium models is that the former assume that the price adjustments are completed immediately. In classical models, prices are always at their market-clearing levels. Thus, classical economists assumed that prices change instantly, so that if the nation's money supply were doubled overnight, people would wake in the morning to find prices doubled, too, and economic activity proceeding otherwise undisturbed. Classical inflation, then, which is continuing price changes, requires continuing increases in the money supply, day after day.

In the real world, there is no Walrasian auctioneer to immediately find and set the new prices that simultaneously clear thousands of markets. Instead, prices are set in individual markets by contracts, regulatory authorities, markup formulas, and other procedures that are not very sensitive to demand and supply shifts and are not at all concerned with Walras' general equilibrium. When there are, then, market disequilibria because prices adjust sluggishly and imperfectly, inflation reflects both old and new economic events. We cannot make a clean distinction between the price response to a single change in the money supply and continuing price responses to continuing changes in the money supply. A single change in the money supply will have continuing effects on prices, and, conversely, price changes are influenced not only by current events but also by the gradual playing out of old disequilibria.

Low unemployment and high inflation

Because price adjustments are sluggish, most inflations involve complex responses to disequilibria that may have begun years earlier. To understand inflation it is helpful then to look at how prices are set and at the sensitivity of prices to excess demand and supply; we have to look at the pricing behavior that underlies the nonvertical aggregate supply curve.

In flexprice markets, demand and supply determine prices; in fixprice markets, the effects are slower and often indirect. Interviews with business executives and empirical studies of price data indicate the widespread use of *average-markup* or *target-return* pricing formulas. In these pricing rules of thumb, average costs at normal production levels are calculated. The price is then set at some normal markup over these costs, so as to earn a target profit rate. A simple representation is

$$Py^* = (1 + \gamma)(Wn^* + Cm^*) \tag{7.3}$$

where W is the hourly wage rate; n the number of hours of paid employment; C the price of other, non-labor expenses (such as raw materials and taxes); m

the quantity of these non-labor inputs; and γ the markup that provides profits. (Asterisks affixed to y, n, and m indicate that these are calculated at normal operating levels—87.5% of capacity or whatever it happens to be for this particular firm.) Py^* is total revenue and $Wn^* + Cm^*$ is total cost.

This markup equation can be rewritten on a per-unit basis;

$$P = (1 + \gamma)(Wn^*/y^* + Cm^*/y^*) \tag{7.4}$$

or

$$P = (1 + \gamma)\left(\frac{W}{(y/n)^*} + \frac{C}{(y/m)^*}\right) \tag{7.5}$$

Equation 7.4 says that the price is a markup over unit labor costs (Wn^*/y^*) and other per-unit costs (Cm^*/y^*). Equation 7.5 shows that costs depend on wages relative to labor productivity $(y/n)^*$ and on other costs (C) relative to their productivity $(y/m)^*$ These are, of course, the "normal" profits of a firm producing at its planned operating level and selling all of what it is producing. Actual profits will diverge from normal profits to the extent that actual sales and output differ from normal. (In Chapter 2, we saw that labor hoarding during recessions causes a drop in output per paid employee and in profits, too.)

In the short run, these perceived normal productivities, $(y/n)^*$ and $(y/m)^*$, and normal markups, γ, do not seem very sensitive to demand and and supply conditions. As production fluctuates, companies do not adjust their estimates of normal productivity or their markup percentage. Economic fluctuations instead affect prices mainly through costs W and C. When the demand for a fixprice product increases, production expands and additional resources are utilized. If the costs of such resources increase, then businesses pass these along via a higher price.

Some inputs are raw materials traded in flexprice markets. When industrial demand for such materials expands, their costs increase quickly. In most industries, labor is by far the most important production expense and, normally, the most important source of cost pressures. However, most labor markets are also fixprice, so that higher labor utilization may not immediately translate fully into higher wages. Lower labor utilization seldom brings lower wages.

It is not easy to capture the diversity of markets in a simple model, but a useful, aggregate overview is provided by Figure 7.7, in which the intersection of the aggregate demand and supply curves determine current output and the current price level. At any given moment there are market pressures that have not yet translated into price changes. Some markets have excess supplies and are exerting a downward pull on prices; others have excess demands and are pushing prices upward. We can gauge the overall pressure on prices by comparing actual output with the economy's potential output. When actual output is close to or above potential output, the nation's resources are being fully utilized. There are many excess demands, few excess supplies, and lots of upward pressure on costs and prices. When an economy's actual output is far below its potential, there are few markets with excess demands, many with excess supplies, and relatively less upward pressure on costs and prices.

Figure 7.8 shows how higher input costs translate into higher prices. Output is temporarily above the economy's potential. Factories are operating at greater

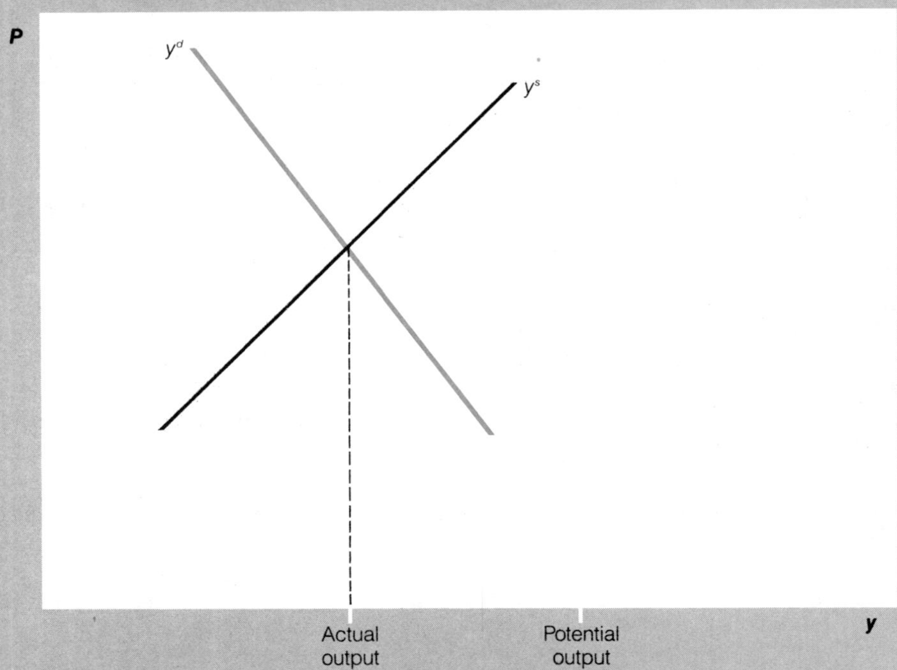

FIGURE 7.7 THE PRESSURE ON PRICES CAN BE GAUGED FROM THE GAP BETWEEN ACTUAL AND POTENTIAL OUTPUT. **The gap is a rough indicator of the number of markets with excess demands (exerting upward pressure on prices) relative to the number with excess supplies (exerting a downward pull on prices).**

than normal capacity, perhaps at levels that could not be sustained without excessive wear and tear on workers and machines. These high production levels require lots of labor, fuel, and other inputs. The strong demands for these inputs pushes their prices upward, though sooner for many raw materials than for labor (which may be bound by long-term contracts). As firms find their input costs increasing, they will cover these costs by raising their prices at every level of production. (Equivalently, they will not be willing to produce as much at the former price level.) The aggregate supply curve shifts upward. The higher prices reduce demand and pull output back towards the potential level. Figure 7.9 shows the opposite picture, when actual output is far below potential.

These examples show why it is important to remember that the intersection of the aggregate demand and supply curves shows not some sort of aggregate market equilibrium, but where the economy is at a given time. From this position, prices may rise or fall, because not all markets are in equilibrium. This inflation or deflation requires not continuing increases in the money supply, but only the playing out of old disequilibria. Of course, in practice, the econ-

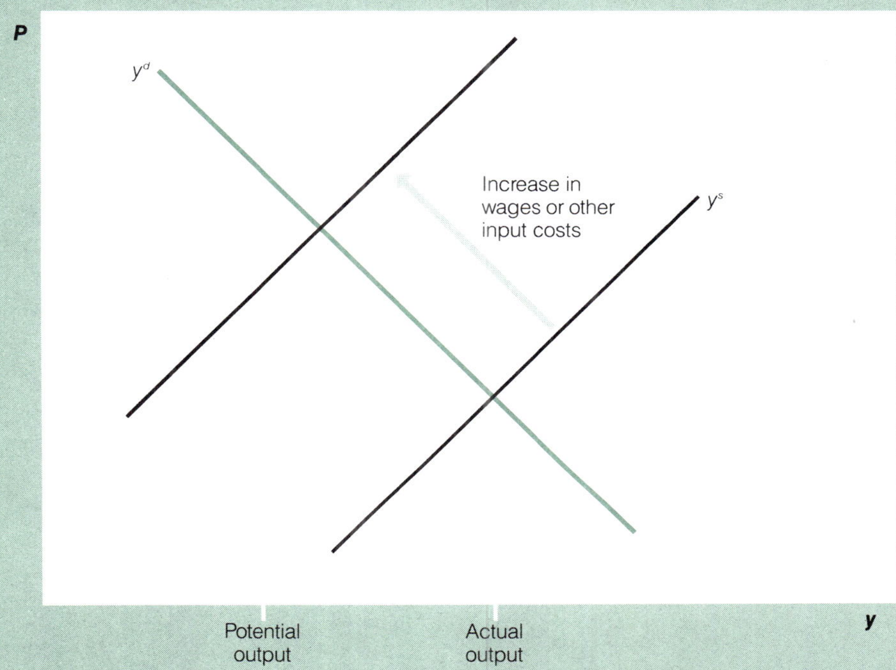

FIGURE 7.8 AN INCREASE IN WAGES OR OTHER INPUT COSTS RAISES PRICES. **When actual exceeds potential output, the widespread excess demand for inputs increases their costs, which firms pass along as higher prices—shifting the aggregate supply curve upward.**

omy will be propelled not only by continuing adjustments to old pressures, but also by new economic events—by labor force growth, capital accumulation, technological improvements, government policies, changes in private preferences, and so on. It can also be seen here why potential output is defined as that level of production at which there are modest pressures on prices.

Wages and Unemployment

We have seen that a simple barometer of inflationary pressures is the gap between actual and potential output. This gap is, of course, closely related to the unemployment rate. When actual output is far below potential, the unemployment rate is high; when output is near or above potential, the unemployment rate is low. In Chapter 2, we saw that Okun's law is an empirical estimate of the magnitude of this relationship—a 1% decline in the unemployment rate tending to be associated with about a 2% to 3% increase in real GNP. Okun's law tells us that we can gauge inflationary pressures either by the gap between actual and potential output or by the unemployment rate.

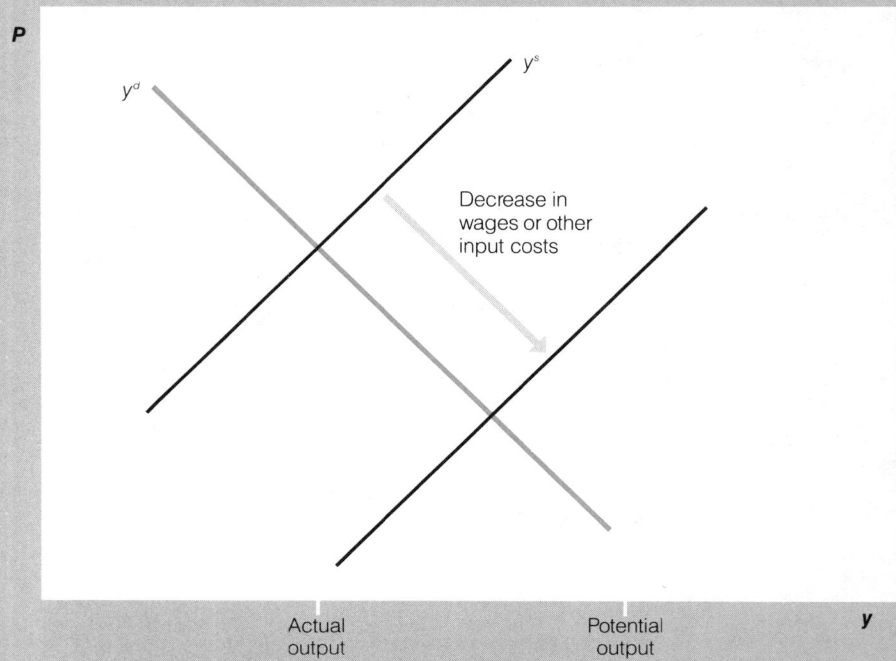

FIGURE 7.9 **A DECREASE IN WAGES OR OTHER INPUT COSTS LOWERS PRICES. When actual output is far below its potential, the aggregate supply curve will be shifted downward to the extent that excess supplies of inputs reduce their cost and firms pass these cost savings along in lower prices.**

The observation that prices depend on costs and that labor is the biggest cost for most employers gives us another reason why the unemployment rate may be a good measure of inflation pressures: The amount of excess supply and demand in labor markets should influence how fast wages increase, and markup pricing passes wage increases along as price increases. The pressure for wage increases will be greatest in those labor markets where demand exceeds supply. In labor markets with substantial excess supply (that is, unemployment), wages will be more restrained and may occasionally even decline. In the aggregate, the average percentage increase in wages, $\Delta W/W$, depends on the overall state of labor markets—how many markets have excess demands and how many have excess supplies. If we use the aggregate unemployment rate u as a crude measure of the overall tightness of labor markets, then

$$\Delta W/W = a + b(1/u) \qquad b > 0 \tag{7.6}$$

This equation is not linear, because the effects of a change in the unemployment rate depend on what the unemployment rate is to begin with: A decline of 1% in the unemployment rate has less effect on wages when the unemployment rate is 11% than when it is 4%.

For example, with parameter values $a = -0.05$, and $b = 0.20$, $\Delta W/W = -0.05 + 0.20(1/u)$, implying the following relationship:

Unemployment rate	Percentage wage increase
10	1.5
9	1.7
8	2.0
7	2.4
6	2.8
5	3.5
4	4.5
3	6.2

These hypothetical data are graphed in Figure 7.10. When labor markets are tight, with little unemployment and many unfilled jobs, the average wage in-

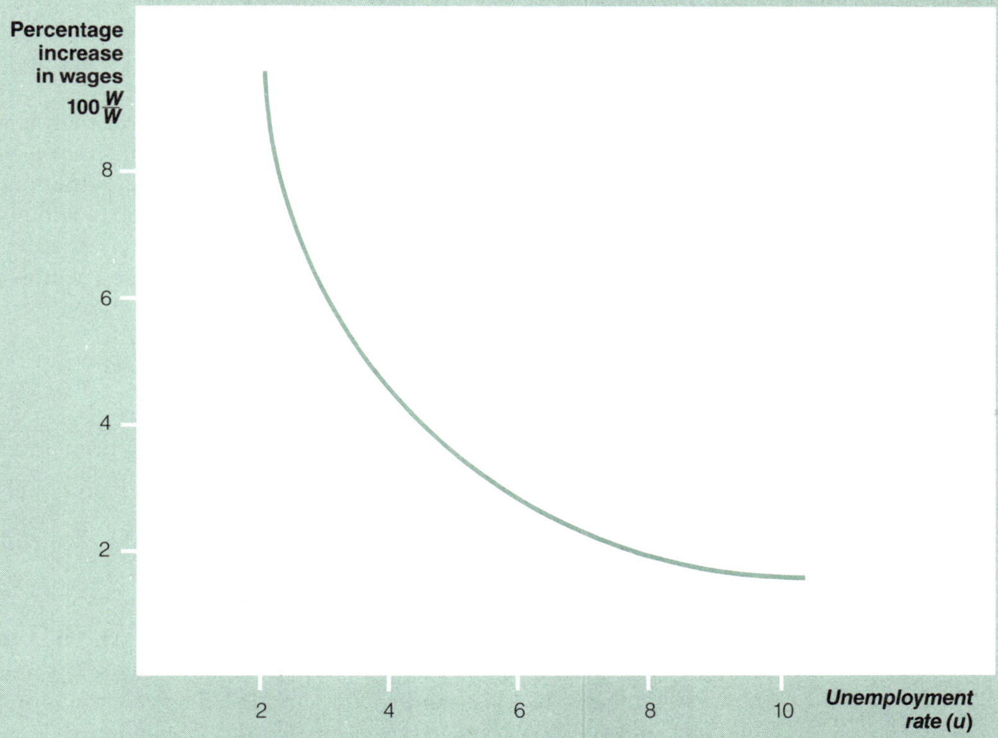

FIGURE 7.10 A HYPOTHETICAL PHILLIPS CURVE.

The equation $\frac{\Delta W}{W} = -0.05 + 0.2(1/u)$ describes a nonlinear relationship between the unemployment rate and the percentage increase in wages. The lower the unemployment rate, the greater the upward pressure on wages.

crease is large. When labor markets are slack, with much unemployment and few vacancies, the average wage increase is more restrained.

Wage declines in the United States are so rare that they are startling news when they do occur. In 1980, several deeply troubled companies (Chrysler, Braniff, and Uniroyal) did persuade their employees to forgo part of previously negotiated pay increases. Even then, wages did not actually fall; they just did not go up as much as previously agreed. At the time, the *Wall Street Journal* wrote that:

> A student of economic theory wouldn't find anything remarkable about such sacrifices. It would be normal to expect pay to rise when companies are prospering and to be scaled back when times are rough. In reality, though, it doesn't usually work that way. Wages, salaries and benefits tend to rise every year in the U.S., through good times and bad. . . . Unless conditions get desperate, managements don't even suggest that employees take pay cuts or give up benefits that have been promised.[4]

The asymmetry in wage changes—that wages rise more easily than fall—means that average wages do not decline unless unemployment is extraordinarily high. In U.S. manufacturing industries, annual average hourly wages have not declined in any year since 1933. In that year, the national unemployment rate was 25% and manufacturing wages declined by about 1%, from 44.4 to 43.7 cents per hour.

In most years, the unemployment rate is far lower than it was in 1933, and wages increase relentlessly. Figure 7.11 shows that, for the years 1952–69 at least, there was a rough inverse relationship between the unemployment rate and the percentage increase in wages, as in Equation 7.6 and in the hypothetical curve of Figure 7.10. This empirical relationship is called the *Phillips curve*, after A. W. Phillips, who first discerned an inverse relationship of this type using British data for the years 1861–1957.[5]

Prices and Labor Costs

With markup pricing rules, wage increases lead to price increases. Equations 7.4 and 7.5 imply that

$$\frac{\Delta P}{P} = \alpha\left(\frac{\Delta W}{W} - \frac{\Delta(y/n)^*}{(y/n)^*}\right) + (1-\alpha)\left(\frac{\Delta C}{C} - \frac{\Delta(y/m)^*}{(y/m)^*}\right) \tag{7.7}$$

where $\alpha = nW/(nW + mC)$, labor's share of total cost. Equation 7.7 states that the rate of inflation depends on how fast unit labor costs and other costs are rising relative to long-run productivity. If labor were the only production cost, then α would be 1 and the rate of inflation would simply equal the difference between the increases in wages and productivity:

$$\frac{\Delta P}{P} = \frac{\Delta W}{W} - \frac{\Delta(y/n)^*}{(y/n)^*} \tag{7.8}$$

Figure 7.12 shows that there is, in fact, a pretty good correlation between the percentage changes in prices and in unit labor costs. One inadequacy of this

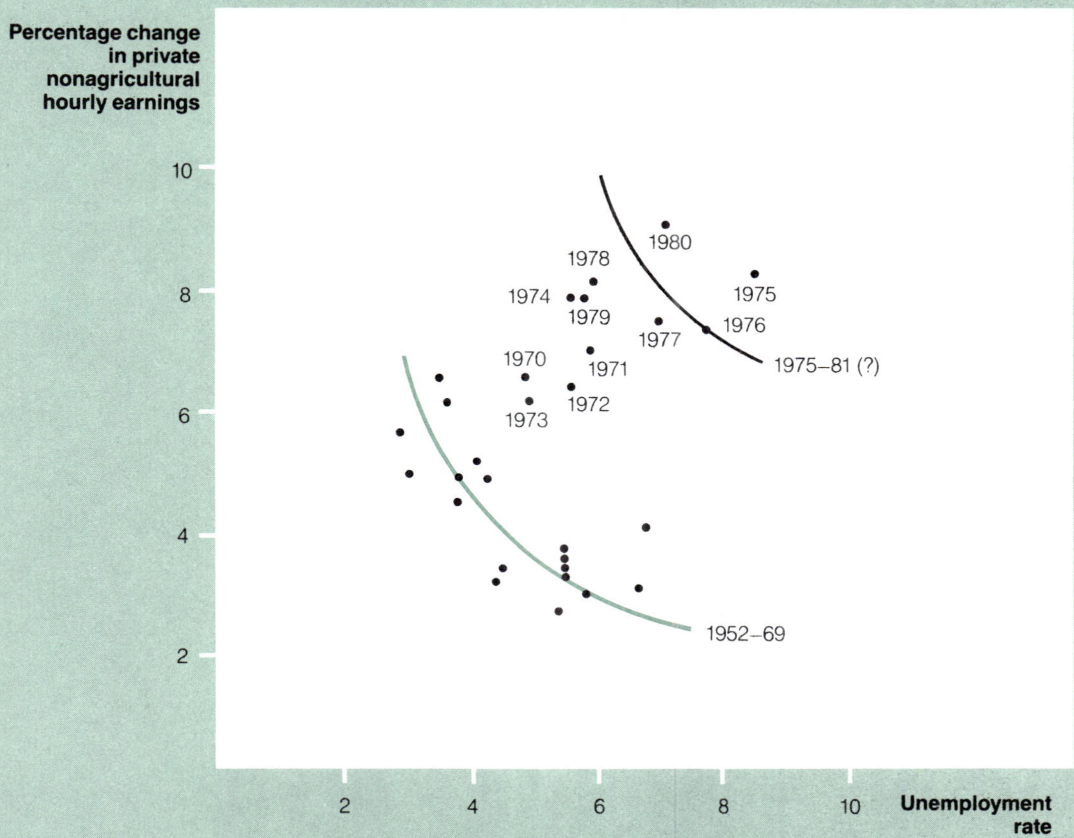

FIGURE 7.11 U.S. PHILLIPS CURVE (NONFARM WAGES), 1952-81. **Unemployment and wage increases were inversely related in the 1950s and 1960s. But, in the 1970s, unemployment and wage increases rose together—stagflation! The Phillips curve for the late 1970s and early 1980s, if there is one, is much higher than for the 1950s and 1960s.**

figure is that it uses data on actual production rather than normal productivity at planned operating levels. Because we do not directly observe normal productivity, and because economists have frequently revised their estimates of long-run productivity growth, we will simply assume that normal productivity has been growing at some constant rate, *g*, since World War II. If so, then Equation 7.8 implies that the difference between price and wage increases will be roughly constant. Figure 7.13 shows that there has been a close relation between the annual percentage changes in wages and in prices. The three historical periods that do not conform to this rule were all times when the cost of nonlabor inputs changed dramatically. In 1952–53, raw materials prices fell at an 8% annual rate; in 1973–75 and 1979–80, raw materials prices rose by 16%

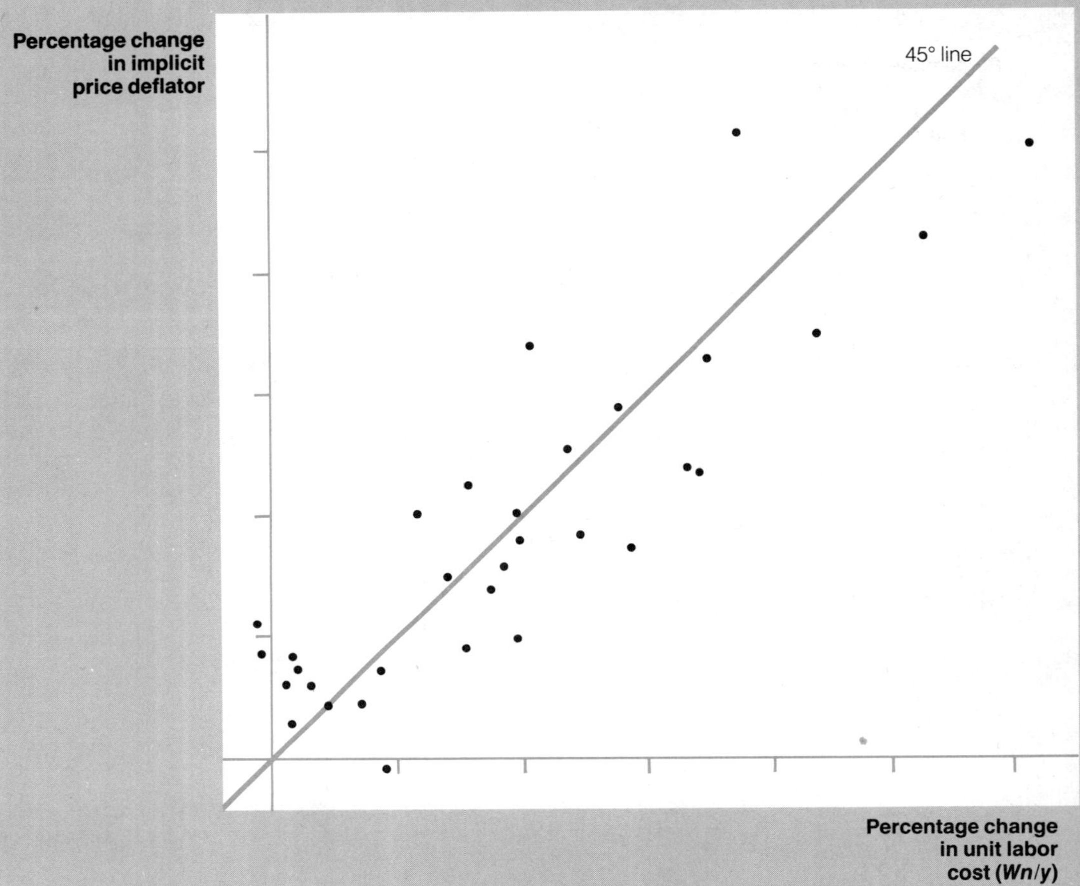

FIGURE 7.12 ANNUAL INFLATION AND UNIT LABOR COSTS FOR THE U.S. NONFARM BUSINESS SECTOR DURING 1948–81. "Cost-plus" pricing rules imply that inflation depends on how fast business costs are rising. This graph shows that there has been a relationship between the rates of increase of labor costs and of prices.

and 15% per year, respectively, mostly because of higher energy prices. Thus we can conclude that **price increases are usually equal to wage increases less normal productivity growth, except when there are unusual changes in the costs of other inputs.**

The tradeoff between unemployment and inflation

If price increases are positively related to wage increases, Equation 7.8, and wage increases are inversely related to unemployment, Equation 7.6, then the percentage price increase, π, is also inversely related to the unemployment rate:

$$\pi = a + b(1/u) - g. \tag{7.9}$$

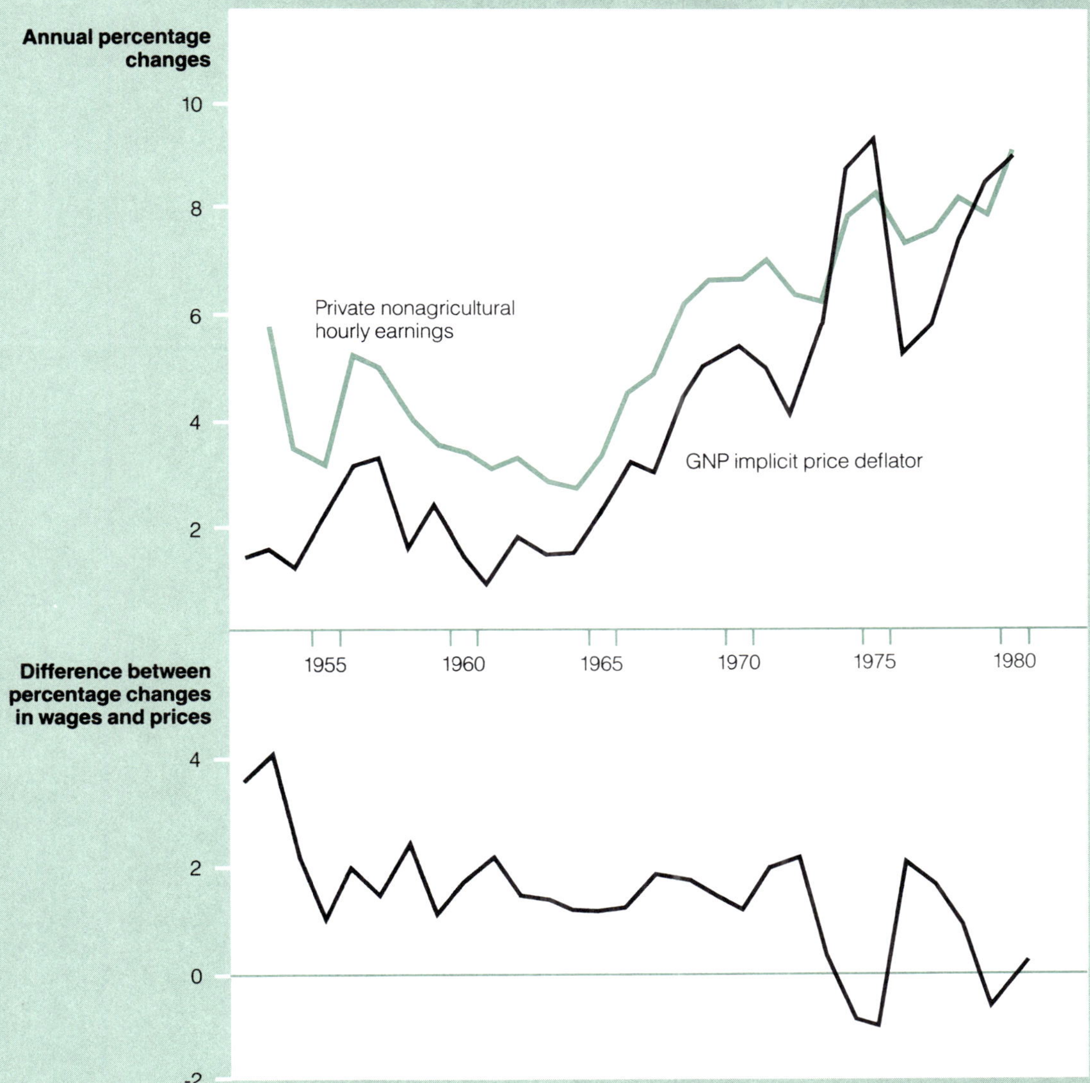

FIGURE 7.13 **PRICES AND WAGES, U.S. ANNUAL DATA, 1952–81.** **Wages and prices have increased together, except for the periods 1952–53, 1973–75, and 1979–80, when the cost of nonlabor inputs changed dramatically. The 8% decline in materials costs in 1952–53 restrained prices, while the 15% and 16% jumps in materials costs in 1973–75 and 1970–80 boosted prices.**

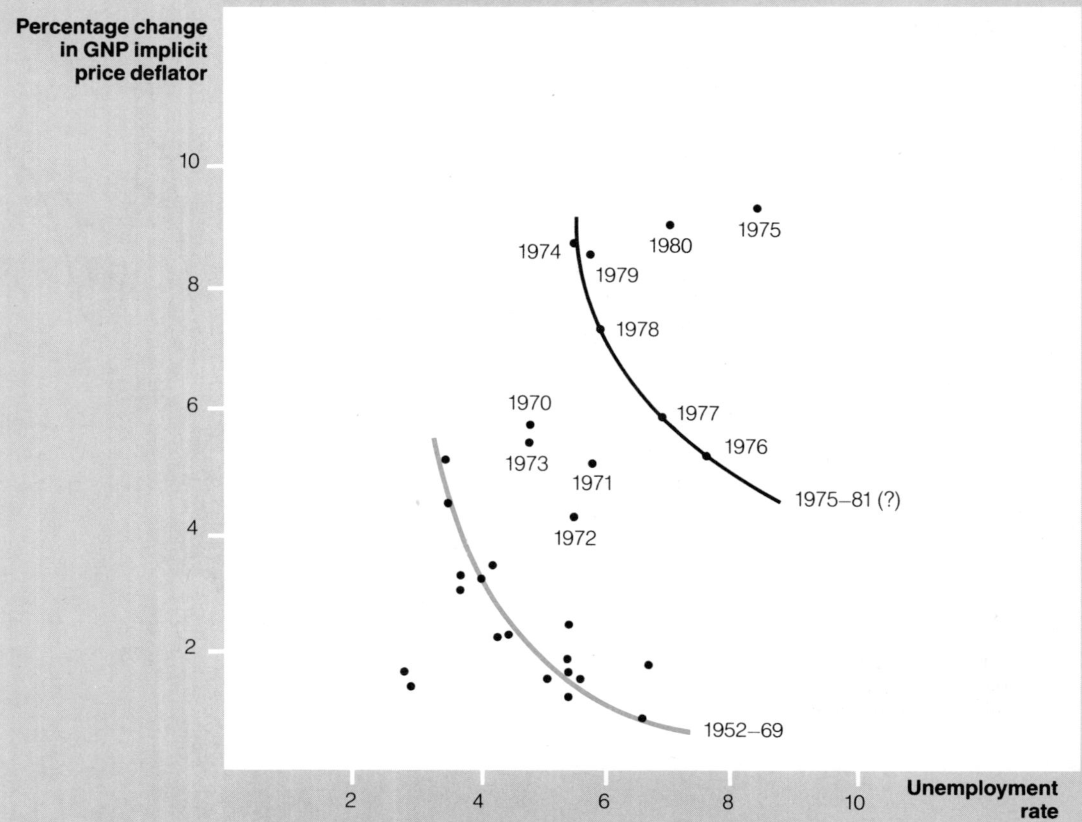

FIGURE 7.14 U.S. PHILLIPS CURVE (GNP DEFLATOR), 1952–81. **Prices, like wages, were inversely related to the unemployment rate during the 1950s and 1960s. If there is a Phillips curve for the late 1970s and early 1980s, it is much higher than the earlier relation.**

As shown in Figure 7.14, there has been a rough Phillips-curve relationship between the unemployment rate and the rate of inflation, at least for the years 1952–69.

The Phillips curve describes a tradeoff between unemployment and inflation: Expansionary monetary and fiscal policies increase output and employment, tightening labor markets as unemployment falls and vacancies grow, thereby causing wages and prices to increase. The hard-nosed cure for inflation is recession, although present company is excepted, of course.* Like a bloodletting,

* It is ironic that some economists with nice government jobs have come up with nothing better than the recommendation that other people should be thrown out of work. Sidney Weintraub wrote: "I have suggested, in all seriousness, that those who advocate unemployment through public policy as a remedy for inflation should be among the first to join the ranks of the unemployed."[6]

IN THE NEWS

Factory Workers View Givebacks Indignantly—and Submissively

MILWAUKEE—Richard A. Blavat, a burly blue-collar worker who has put in 27 years on the factory floor, grows indignant as he talks about companies demanding that union workers take pay cuts.

"How the hell can anybody in their right mind say, 'I'd be willing to take a 10% pay cut'?" he wonders. "If I take a 10% pay cut, I'm cutting my damn throat. I figure if the company is that bad off, I say go to hell, because if I'm going to starve, you might as well starve with me."

But a few minutes later, 50-year-old Mr. Blavat concedes that he would have little choice but to go along if his employer said union workers had to accept a pay cut to save their jobs. "They're in the driver's seat," he says glumly, "whether we like it or not."

Similar ambivalent feelings of defiance and resignation were expressed repeatedly during two discussions last month with 24 rank-and-file union members here. . . . These workers are on the defensive. They know it. And they are bitter—toward management, government, union leaders and even some fellow workers who, they think, don't give an honest day's work for an honest day's pay.

The workers joining in the discussions here—22 men and two women—range in age from 22 to 58. On the job, they brew beer, build motorcycles and automobile frames, make parts for jet engines and earth-moving equipment, and assemble electronic controls for cars. Their views aren't meant to be taken as scientific polling. But they are a blue-collar group in a strong union town; 28% of Milwaukee County's work force is unionized, compared with 21% nationwide.

So far, few of the 24 have themselves been asked to make contract concessions. But more than half expect their employers, citing high labor costs and poor business conditions, to seek such givebacks this year.

That they even have reason to worry about givebacks signals a dramatic change in labor relations in the U.S., experts say. For years, unions won bigger and bigger wage gains at the bargaining table. Now, many union negotiators are having to ask themselves not how much they can get but how much they can hold on to.

Givebacks weren't unknown in the past—to obtain a government bail-out package, Chrysler started winning concessions from workers in 1979—but they were rare. Last year, however, union workers in the rubber, airline, meatpacking and steel industries agreed to givebacks to avoid layoffs or plant closings. And the United Auto Workers is negotiating with Ford to reduce labor costs, although its talks with General Motors broke off without any agreement.

What's more, economists say, givebacks in a few big industries will have wide repercussions. Many smaller unions will be forced to settle new contracts for less than they otherwise would have.

The shift in the balance of power to management is all too evident to the rank-and-file workers gathered for the group discussions here. "The unions are going to have to go along with the company," says Ruben Sillars, a 28-year-old welder laid off by Rexnord Inc., a specialized-machinery maker, "or the company's just going to move right out (of town)."

Indeed, companies frequently use the threat of closing shop and moving South to intimidate union workers, Mr. Blavat says. Corporate executives, he contends, say to themselves, "Let's rattle their cage, let's take them by the throat and shake them and see just how far we can get. If we can back them up against the wall and save enough money, we stay here. If they say, 'No, we can't bend,' the hell with them, we go down there."

Like Mr. Blavat, most of the workers at the group discussions vociferously oppose givebacks. But for many, their anger is outweighed by fear, the fear of possibly losing their jobs if they balk at concessions.

James Hoeppner, a rangy, 37-year-old product inspector, has already made his choice. Along with some 4,800 union workers at A.O. Smith Corp., Mr. Hoeppner last summer gave up his cost-of-living pay increase for a year to help the diversified manufacturer win a contract to make frames for GM cars.

"I figured it's going to save jobs. It was a do-or-die situation," explains Mr. Hoeppner, whose 14 years with A.O. Smith put him fairly high on the seniority list. "If we didn't get that (contract), I'd probably still be working, but two years from now, I probably wouldn't be."

And the job outlook for laid-off blue-collar workers is dismal, most agree. "If you lose the job you've got, chances are pretty slim you ain't going to find another one," says Clarence Fish, 34, a welder at Caterpillar Tractor Co.

James A. Kloss knows that from first-hand experience. . . . he was laid off from his $10.70-an-hour job with Allis-Chalmers Corp. last April. The company sought a wage freeze in October, which Mr. Kloss gladly would have accepted in hopes of being called back. But the UAW leaders rejected the request. "All they said was, 'No.' . . . They never asked us, we never had a chance to vote on it," he says, shaking his head. "It's *my* livelihood, it's all of our livelihoods."

With his unemployment compensation running out now, Mr. Kloss is engaged in a concentrated job hunt. The result: one job offer for $3.35 an hour as a janitor, less than he receives from unemployment benefits. "It's hard to accept that," says Mr. Kloss, and he turned it down. Carol Larson adds, "Right now, what line of work is available? A waitress at Burger King or whatever" that pays around $3 an hour.

Though she is in the minority, Mrs. Larson thinks that some employers are justified in seeking givebacks. "Definitely, the car industry has gone down. I mean, I can see it," says Mrs. Larson, a small, trim 25-year-old UAW member who makes $11.53 an hour as an assembler at GM's Delco Electronics plant in suburban Oak Creek. "For what I'm required to do, I'm overpaid, and I'll be the first to admit it," she says. . . .

But most of the workers clearly harbor a deep distrust of management. They see demands for givebacks as a none-too-subtle ploy to increase profits at the workers' expense.

"How can you trust big business?" asks Donald Ance, a stout 42-year-old who works for Ladish Co., a maker of high-technology forgings and fittings in nearby Cudahy, Wis. "You just can't. You just can't trust them," he says, answering his own question to murmurs of approval. He adds, "We've had Christmas letters given out at Christmas time and the only thing that changes on them is the date, and it's always they're losing money, they're losing money, they're losing money." Then, after "crying wolf" for 25 years, he notes acidly, Ladish was the target of a bidding war last year because, he says, it was so profitable. It was acquired by Armco Inc. last October.

Because of this pervasive distrust, the workers worry that any concessions will encourage management to seek more, whether needed or not. (Lawrence Ingrassia, *The Wall Street Journal,* Feb. 4, 1982) the economy has to be weakened to be made well. In 1980 Paul Volcker, the Chairman of the Federal Reserve Board, was asked if stringent monetary and fiscal policies would cause a recession. "Yes," he replied, "and the sooner the better."[7]

Contractionary monetary and fiscal policies reduce output and employment; with slacker labor and commodity markets, there is less upward pressure on wages and prices. Arthur Okun put it this way:

> When markets are exceedingly weak no businessman will dare raise his prices for fear of losing his markets, and no workers—organized or unorganized—will demand significant wage increases for fear of losing their jobs. The problem of curing inflation is difficult and demanding because we will not take this decapitation cure for the headache of rising prices.[8]

This, then, is the basic short-run explanation of inflation. Factors that influence the aggregate demand and supply curves affect prices and, hence, the calculated rate of inflation. In flexprice markets, demand and supply directly and quickly determine prices. In fixprice markets, demand-versus-supply shifts cause variations in production first and variations in prices later through induced changes in input costs. Since the most important input is labor, the unemployment rate provides a rough gauge of labor market tightness and, hence, of market pressures on wages and prices.

High unemployment and high inflation

In 1961, the unemployment rate was 6.7% and the Consumer Price Index (CPI) increased by 0.7%. On the basis of Phillips curves estimated from 1950s data, the Kennedy-Johnson Councils of Economic Advisers selected 4% unemployment as a target "full employment" goal. At 4% unemployment they anticipated about a 3% inflation rate. (Of particular historical interest was the period 1955–57, during which the unemployment rate had been close to 4%, while the inflation rate did not exceed 3%.) Below a 4% unemployment rate, these advisers feared, the rate of inflation might rise to a politically intolerable level.

As indicated in Table 7.1, in 1965–67 the level of unemployment fell to around 4%, with about 3% inflation. In 1968–69, the rate of unemployment dropped further and the pace of inflation quickened. Concern turned from unemployment to inflation. After Richard Nixon's inauguration in early 1969, he tried the hard-nosed recession cure for inflation for a while and then, with an election approaching, tried wage and price controls. Neither approach eradicated inflation, and from the mid-1970s through the early 1980s (as Table 7.1 and Figures 7.11 and 7.14 show and ordinary households and eminent politicians have been well aware), we had the grim coexistence of high unemployment and high inflation. Where did the Phillips curve tradeoff go? At levels of unemployment where prices were stable in the 1950s there was close to double-digit inflation in the 1970s. Why? Three answers are frequently offered: nonlabor costs, changes in the composition of the labor force, and inflation expectations.*

* An attempt to sort out the relative importance of these factors was conducted via simulations with the DRI model. See Reference 9.

TABLE 7.1

Unemployment and inflation over the period 1952–1983

Year	Unemployment rate	Change in CPI (%)	Change in GNP deflator (%)
1952	3.0	2.2	1.4
1953	2.9	0.8	1.6
1954	5.5	0.5	1.2
1955	4.4	−0.4	2.2
1956	4.1	1.5	3.2
1957	4.3	3.6	3.4
1958	6.8	2.7	1.7
1959	5.5	0.8	2.4
1960	5.5	1.6	1.6
1961	6.7	1.0	0.9
1962	5.5	1.1	1.8
1963	5.9	1.2	1.5
1964	5.2	1.3	1.5
1965	4.5	1.7	2.2
1966	3.8	2.9	3.2
1967	3.8	2.9	3.0
1968	3.6	4.2	4.4
1969	3.5	5.4	5.1
1970	4.9	5.9	5.4
1971	5.9	4.3	5.0
1972	5.6	3.3	4.2
1973	4.9	6.2	5.7
1974	5.6	11.0	8.7
1975	8.5	9.1	9.3
1976	7.7	5.8	5.2
1977	7.0	6.5	5.8
1978	6.0	7.7	7.3
1979	5.8	11.3	8.5
1980	7.1	13.5	9.2
1981	7.6	10.4	9.4
1982	9.7	6.0	6.0
1983	9.5	3.2	4.2

Nonlabor Costs The first of these three lines of reasoning emphasizes that there are production costs other than wages. Dramatic, unprecedented increases in material expenses, especially for fuel (which leaped upward in 1973–74 and again in 1978–81), raise business costs and, hence, prices. If prices were perfectly flexible, a one-time increase in the cost of oil would raise the price level, but not thereafter the rate of inflation. With imperfect markets, though, it may take years for the price adjustments to work themselves out. In addition, the increases in the cost of energy have been repeated, and there have been increases in various other production inputs. Various business taxes have also increased, and firms try to pass these too along in higher prices. Businesses also incurred sizable expenses in the 1970s to meet toughened safety and pollution regulations. These regulations improve our living and working environment, but their costs show up in higher prices. Some business interests have called for relaxed regulations to fight inflation. Presumably, such regulations should be judged by a comparison of their costs and benefits, rather than by their effects on price indexes.

Productivity is another aspect of costs. Improvements in productivity reduce costs and restrain prices, but productivity gains have lagged in recent years. In many circles, this disappointing performance is attributed to inadequate spending on modern plant and equipment. Thus many proposals to stimulate investment spending have been advertised as weapons against inflation. In practice, as Martin Feldstein has observed:

> this effect of productivity on inflation is not likely to be very large and is certainly not very reliable. An increase in productivity doesn't necessarily translate into a slowdown in unit labor costs. Instead, if the rise in productivity pushed wages up by an equal amount there would be no direct change in unit labor costs.[10]

This observation does not mean that increases in productivity are worthless—just that they may have little effect on inflation.*

A Changing Labor Force The second line of reasoning, concerning the phenomenon of low employment with high inflation focuses on the composition of the labor force. In 1970, George Perry noted that over the postwar period there had been a dramatic labor force increase of male teenagers and of females, relative to prime-age males (age 25–64),[11] as shown in Table 7.2. Not only have females and young men increased in the labor force, but they are disproportionately represented among the unemployed. Perry argues that since

* Note that in the case mentioned by Feldstein, wages increase with no effect on prices. Therefore, real wages increase. Greater productivity means that workers will produce more or work less, both of which sound pretty good.

TABLE 7.2

Changes in the structure of labor markets and in unmemployment for the period 1955–79

	% of labor force			Unemployment rate		
	1955	1969	1979	1955	1969	1979
Males (25–64)	55.9	48.9	44.1	2.9	1.7	3.3
Males (16–19)	3.7	4.8	5.0	10.7	11.4	15.8
Females	31.7	37.8	43.2	4.9	4.7	6.8

these females and teenage males tend to be less skilled* and to work fewer hours and for lower wages, measured unemployment understates the tightness of labor markets, for some of the unemployed are not willing or able to take available full-time jobs. Thus, while the overall unemployment rate was very high in the 1970s, the unemployment rate for prime-age males remained closer to the level of the 1950s.

Perry's argument implies that the Phillips curve has shifted outward, so that an aggregate unemployment rate of 6% now means tighter labor markets and more inflation than in the 1950s. Perry uses adjusted unemployment data and an unemployment dispersion index† to explain the outward shift of the Phillips curve from the 1950s to the 1970s. Similar work by Robert Gordon[12] using race, sex, and age and by Charles Schultze[13] using quit and layoff rates has provided additional evidence that the published unemployment rates understate the tightness of labor markets by the standards of the 1950s. A different argument with similar implications is that more generous government assistance programs (including unemployment compensation, food stamps, and Aid to Families with Dependent Children) have swelled the unemployment data with people who are really unwilling or unable to work.[14]

Some economists believe that the employment ratio—the percentage of the population that is employed—is more accurate than the unemployment rate for gauging the tightness of labor markets. The unemployment rate may be misleading because of changes in labor force participation, as mentioned above, and because of errors in the door-to-door surveys that determine whether a person is officially unemployed or just not looking for work. Figures 7.15 and 7.16 show that the employment ratio has been a pretty good indicator of inflationary pressures, even in the tumultuous 1970s. In 1974, for example, when the CPI increased 12.2%, the official unemployment rate of 5.6% seemed to indicate slack labor markets, while the employment ratio was at a record high level, suggesting tight labor markets.

Believers in this structural explanation for inflation counsel that monetary and fiscal policies cannot be used now to reduce unemployment to 4, or even 5 percent. Bottlenecks and rapid inflation would quickly develop. Instead, specific programs are needed that are aimed at those who happen to be in very slack labor markets. Some popular suggestions include training programs, relocation assistance, repeal of minimum wage laws, tax incentives to firms that hire people who have difficulty finding jobs, and programs to aid depressed industries and geographic areas.

* Teenagers have little work experience or other tangible evidence of work skills and, sometimes, only a halfhearted attachment to the labor force. Usually, this attachment comes later, when family responsibilities become persuasive. Many women entered the labor force in the 1960s and 1970s, also ill-prepared for careers and a bit uncertain of their commitment to full-time work. A special Labor Department survey in 1969 found that women who entered the labor force that year had an unemployment rate of 6.9%, while women who had stayed in the labor force continuously since 1967 had an unemployment rate of only 2.9%.

† If these demographic groups are in separate labor markets, then increased dispersion of unemployment will create more wage inflation for a given level of unemployment in the 1970s than in the 1950s. This is because the concentration of unemployment in low-wage occupations (with wages that do not fall) will not offset the rapid escalation of wages in occupations where there are severe bottlenecks.

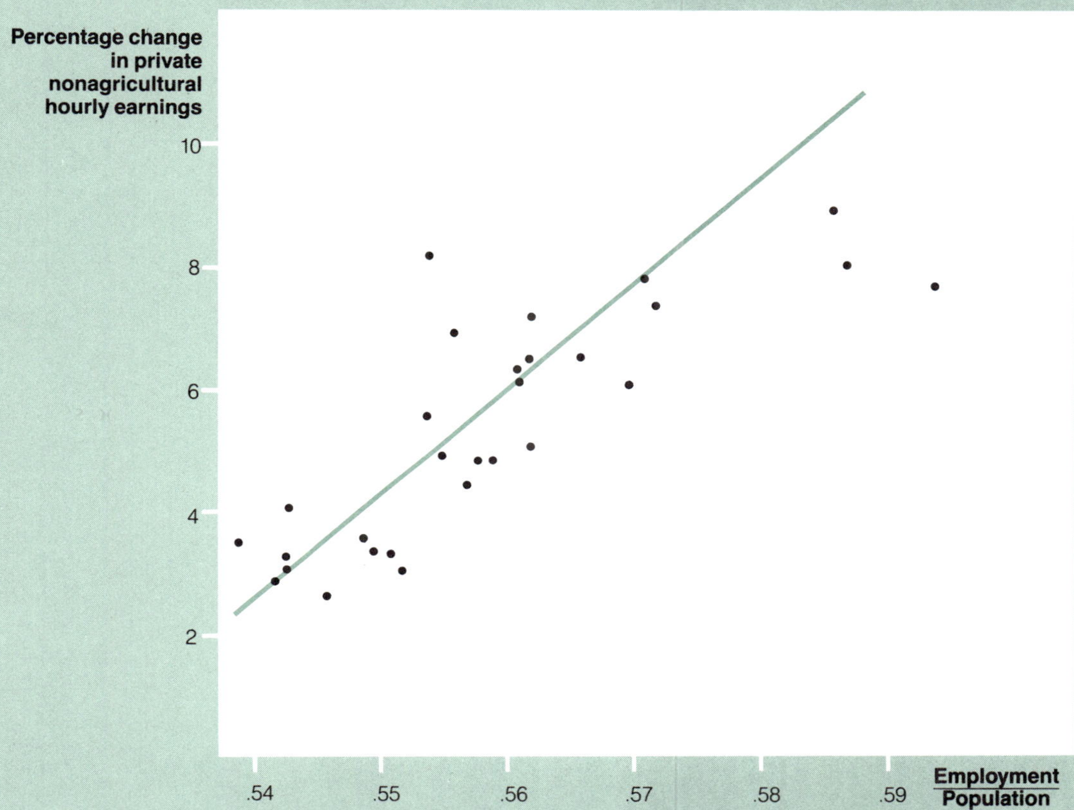

FIGURE 7.15 ANNUAL WAGE INCREASES AND THE EMPLOYMENT RATIO, 1952–81. An alternative to the unemployment rate as a barometer of labor market conditions and wage pressures is the ratio of employment to the total population (not just those currently in the estimated labor force).

Inflation expectations The third explanation of the outward shift in the Phillips curve emphasizes inflation expectations. Consider a labor market that is always in equilibrium. Wages freely adjust so that the real wage is at the market clearing level $\overline{w}$:

$$\frac{W}{P} = \overline{w}. \tag{7.10}$$

If the price level is increasing by 10% per year, then nominal wages will also need to rise by 10% per year to keep real wages from falling. Since future rates of inflation are uncertain, wage contracts set for one, two, three, or even more

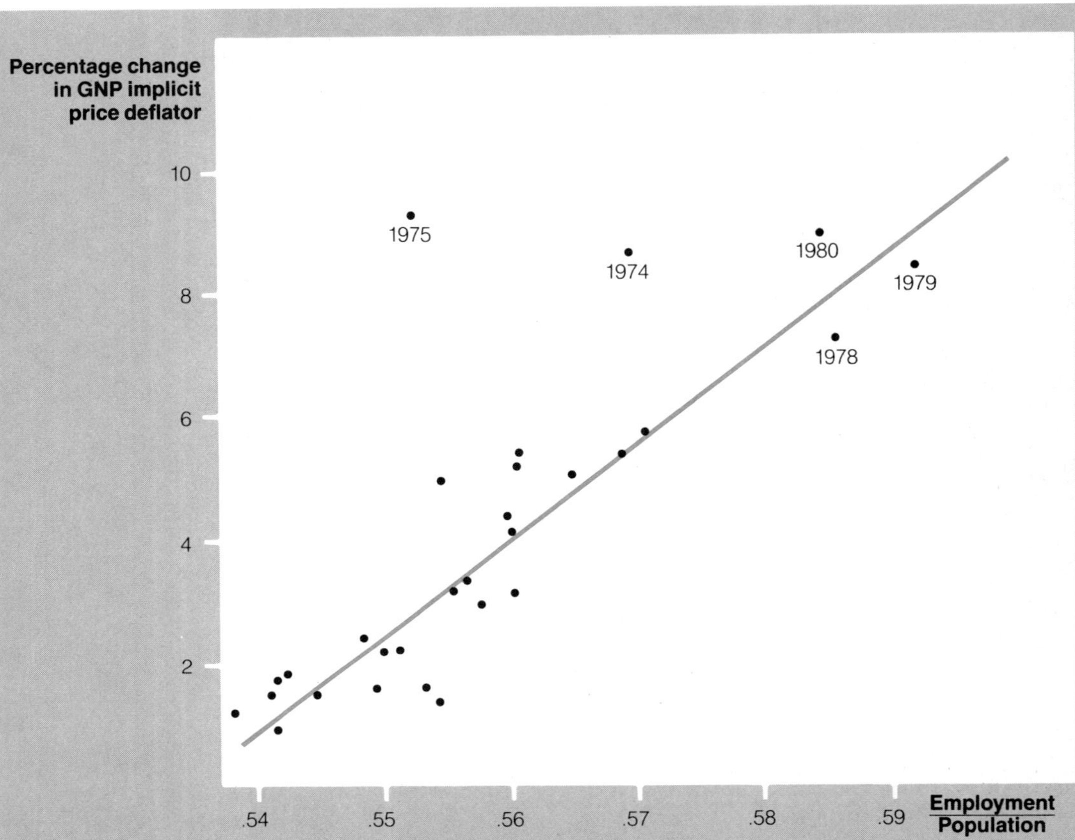

FIGURE 7.16 ANNUAL INFLATION AND THE EMPLOYMENT RATIO, 1952–81. **If the employment ratio is a good barometer of wage pressures, and if wage changes are the primary determinant of price changes, then the employment ratio may be a useful inflation predictor.**

years must be based on the anticipated rate of inflation π^e, over the duration of the contract. If wage adjustments reflect an attempt to maintain market-equilibrium real wages, then workers will want, and employers will grant, wage increases equal to the expected rate of inflation.

A similar, but looser story applies when there is market disequilibrium. To help analyze this case, Figure 7.17 shows two possible market disequilibria. First, consider the case of excess demand (vacancies). With demand greater than supply, there will be upward pressure on wages. In order to reduce vacancies, wages must rise faster than prices, so that real wages increase. If prices rise 10% and wages only 5%, then real wages will decline and the excess demand will be exacerbated. With sluggish and imperfectly adjusting wages, this may well happen. But it is more likely that, if prices are expected to rise 10%,

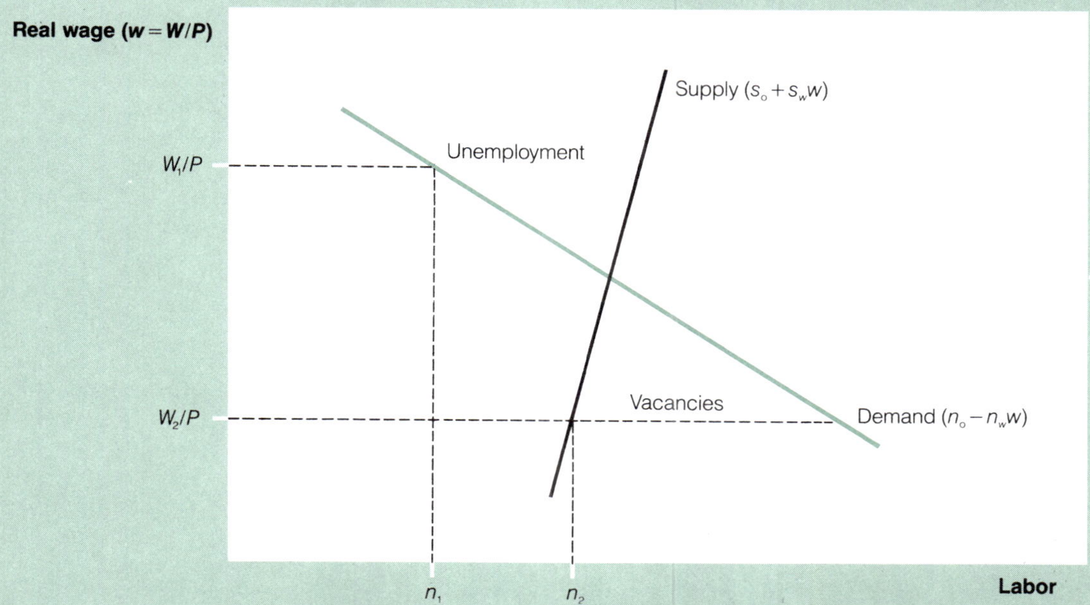

FIGURE 7.17 **LABOR MARKET DISEQUILIBRIA. A labor market might have excess demand (vacanies), with consequent upward pressure on wage W_2, or excess supply (unemployment), with accompanying downward pessure on wage W_1.**

then wages will rise by more than 10% in excess-demand labor markets. The greater the anticipated rate of inflation, the faster wages will rise.

Consider now a situation of excess labor supply (unemployment). Real wages must decline to clear the market, but there is often strong resistance to cutting nominal wages. If the anticipated rate of inflation is zero, nominal wages may be constant. What if the anticipated rate of inflation were 5%: Will wages also rise by 5%? If so, then real wages will be unchanged and the market will be no closer to equilibrium. It is more likely that wages will rise slightly or not at all, so that real wages decline and the excess labor supply is reduced. This is Keynes' conclusion, explained in earlier chapters, based on reasoning and observation. Real wages are reduced and employment increased more easily through price increases than through wage cuts. While nominal wages seldom decline, real wages often sag in excess-supply labor markets during inflations. College French teachers would be in open revolt if their salaries were slashed; but they have accepted wage increases that have not kept up with inflation.

There is, admittedly, some effect of inflation and inflation expectations on wages even in excess-supply labor markets. For example, many union contracts have built-in cost-of-living adjustments. And, at the extreme, if people expected an inflation that threatened to reduce real wages to below the market-equilibrium level, then wages would surely rise. More generally, how much workers ask for and how much firms are willing to give are influenced by how fast people expect prices to rise. However, it is equally true that the effects of inflation on nominal wages is typically weaker in excess-supply labor markets than in equilibrium markets or excess-demand markets.

Putting all three of these market situations together in an uneasy aggregation shows the earlier Phillips-curve equations (7.6 and 7.9) to be incomplete. The aggregate rate of increase of wages depends not only on the overall tightness of labor markets, gauged here by the unemployment rate, but also on the anticipated rate of inflation. Equation 7.6, then, should be expanded to

$$\Delta W/W = a + b(1/u) + \lambda\pi^e \tag{7.11}$$

where λ is a positive parameter. If labor markets are in continual equilibrium or in excess demand, then λ will be very close to 1.0. To the extent that there are excess-supply labor markets that are more easily cleared by inflation than by wage cuts, λ is less than 1.0.

Since wage increases get passed along as price increases, Equation 7.9 should be similarly expanded to

$$\pi = a + b(1/u) - g + \lambda\pi^e. \tag{7.12}$$

For simplicity, the inflation expectations term is simply added to the Phillips curves. More complicated equations are possible, and more plausible, but these simple relations are popular and easier to work with. These expanded equations (7.11 and 7.12) are called "inflation-expectations-augmented Phillips curves," which is a mouthful that misrepresents their rough simplicity.

Representative curves for Equation 7.12 are shown in Figure 7.18. For any given anticipated rate of inflation, there is a short-run tradeoff between unemployment and inflation—represented here by the short-run Phillips curves depicted earlier in Figure 7.14. For any unemployment rate, the higher the anticipated rate of inflation, the higher the actual inflation rate. Thus an increase in inflation expectations shifts the short-run Phillips curve upward.

One explanation of the U.S. data in Figure 7.14 is that, at 6% unemployment, inflation was greater in the 1970s than in the 1950s and 1960s because inflation expectations increased. The economy shifted from a low-inflation-expectations Phillips curve to a high-inflation-expectations Phillips curve. By this interpretation, the rate of inflation is, in part, a self-fulfilling prophecy. If people expect a rapid inflation, they will agree to generous wage contracts and firms will then pass these higher wages along as the higher prices that people expected. If people expect little or no inflation, then wage increases will be modest and firms will restrain prices. In Robert Solow's words, "Perhaps it is simply that we have inflation because we expect inflation, and we expect inflation because we've had it."[15]

The long-run Phillips curve

In a theoretical long-run dynamic equilibrium, those who live to see the long run should have correct inflation expectations: $\pi = \pi^e$. Only if $\pi = \pi^e$ will citi-

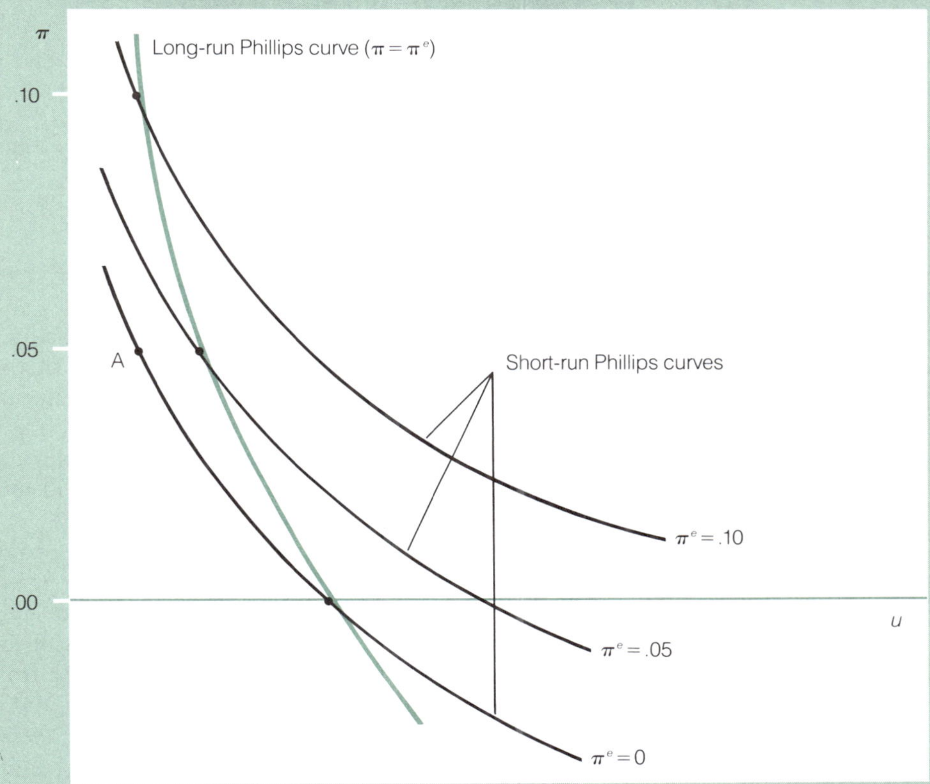

FIGURE 7.18 SHORT-RUN AND LONG-RUN PHILLIPS CURVES ($\lambda < 1$). **There is a family of short-run Phillips curves, each curve reflecting a given anticipated rate of inflation. To the extent inflation expectations are self-fulfilling, the short-run Phillips curve is higher the greater the anticipated inflation rate. The long-run Phillips curve shows the cases in which the actual and anticipated inflation rates coincide. At the employment rate shown at *A*, with $\pi^e = 0$, $\pi = 0.05$ and $\pi^* = 0.10$. We would expect π^e to increase (since $\pi^e < \pi$), shifting the economy to a higher Phillips curve.**

zens not be revising their inflation expectations. For $\pi = 0$ there is only one Phillips curve that is relevant in the long run—the Phillips curve for zero expected inflation. Further, there is only one point on this curve where long-run dynamic equilibrium is possible, the point where $\pi^e = \pi = 0$. Similarly, for a permanent 5% expected inflation, only the $\pi = 0.05$ point on the $\pi^e = 0.05$ Phillips curve is a possible long-run dynamic equilibrium. All such possible long-run equilibria points trace out a long-run Phillips curve such as that shown in color in Figure 7.18.

The equation for the long-run Phillips curve can be obtained by solving Equation 7.12 for the inflation rate π^* such that $\pi = \pi^e$:

$$\pi^* = a - g + b(1/u) + \lambda\pi^e$$
$$(1 - \lambda)\pi^* = a - g + b(1/u).$$

For a given unemployment rate, this long-run, expectations-equilibrium inflation rate π^* is given by

$$\pi^* = \frac{a-g}{1-\lambda} + \frac{b}{1-\lambda}\left(\frac{1}{u}\right) \tag{7.13}$$

As can be seen from Figure 7.18, the economy is below the long-run Phillips curve when inflation expectations are too low. In this situation, inflation expectations should be increasing, moving the economy up to higher short-run Phillips curves and closer to the long-run curve. When the economy is above the long-run Phillips curve, then inflation expectations are too high. Here inflation expectations are falling and the economy will move down towards the long-run Phillips curve.

Note in Equation 7.13 that, at any unemployment rate, u, the slope of the long-run Phillips curve is $1/(1 - \lambda)$ times the slope of a short-run curve. Since $0 < \lambda < 1$, the long-run Phillips curve is steeper than the short-run curves. This means that the long-run inflationary consequences of low unemployment are worse than indicated by the short-run tradeoff. Data from the 1950s gave estimates of a short-run Phillips curve appropriate for low inflation expectations. When the economy was pushed to lower rates of unemployment and higher rates of inflation in the 1960s, it temporarily moved along this short-run, low-inflation-expectations curve. But as inflation expectations increased in line with actual inflation, the economy shifted to higher and higher Phillips curves. There was more inflation as people came to expect that there would be more inflation.

The same mechanism works in reverse. When the economy is thrown into a recession, it moves down a short-run Phillips curve if inflation expectations remain high. For example, the economy might slide down the $\pi^e = 0.10$ curve in Figure 7.18. Large increases in unemployment give relatively small decreases in inflation, but as inflation expectations decline, the economy moves to lower Phillips curves, such as $\pi^e = 0.05$ and $\pi^e = 0$. There is less inflation because people expect less inflation. **In sum, in booms, a given decline in unemployment brings more inflation in the long run than in the short run, as people become accustomed to the inflation and integrate it into their wage agreements. In recessions, a given increase in unemployment reduces inflation more in the long run than in the short run as people revise their inflation expectations downward.**

Reducing inflation expectations

Expectedly, economists who focus on the role of inflation expectations in sustaining a rapid inflation emphasize the need to reduce inflation expectations. For example, in 1980, Martin Feldstein wrote:

> Since the unemployment cost of reducing inflation depends crucially on the credibility of such a policy, it is important that the government and the Fed remain steadfast now in their determination to fight inflation even as the unemployment rate continues to rise. The perception that the government would accept 8% to 9% unemployment. . . for three to four years in order to eliminate inflation would almost certainly bring inflation down so fast that it would be unnecessary to pay such a high cost.[16]

To establish credibility, government leaders stick out their jaws and talk tough, inwardly hoping that public faith will make really tough action unneeded. In practice, this posturing has not been very successful. It took the Reagan administration, including Martin Feldstein as Chairman of the Council of Economic Advisers, three years of 8% to 10% unemployment to bring the inflation rate down to a politically acceptable level.

William Fellner was a particularly vigorous advocate of the view that the war against inflation can be won by destroying inflationary expectations.[17] In his view, labor and businesses keep pushing for higher wages and prices because they are convinced that policymakers do not have the stomach for a prolonged recession. Each new administration says that it is willing to pay the recession cost of stopping inflation, but labor and business know that politicians are timid and that an election is always right around the corner. So citizens ignore the recession threat and press for higher wages and prices, confident that inflationary government policies will soon return. People keep their inflation expectations, thereby helping to maintain the inflation they expect.

A more benign interpretation is that citizens these days have more confidence that, with the government's help, prolonged recessions will not occur. In the old days, when prosperity seemed temporary and major recessions seemed likely, employees and employers were more timid about raising wages and prices. It is economically dangerous, for example, for an employer to agree to an expensive wage contract on the eve of a recession; it is more economical to insist on modest wage increases and to endure a strike if necessary. But it is easier to agree to higher wages and to charge higher prices if there is little danger of economic collapse (or, as the inflation game strategists argue, when the government can be counted on to accommodate inflationary pressures).

Put somewhat differently, modern governments would like to guarantee endless prosperity. An economically secure future encourages business investment spending and helps voters sleep soundly at night. But unions and businesses have little reason for restraint in setting wages and prices if the government guarantees full employment no matter what they charge. For a credible war on inflation, the government must abandon its commitment to full employment and, indeed, insist that any sign of inflation will bring the punishment of recession.

Fellner argued that, as in every war, the government must be resolute and not show the enemy any signs of weakness. Here, as the comic character Pogo said, "We have met the enemy, and they is us." The government must convince us that, this time, they really mean it and that it is we who must surrender by reducing our inflation expectations. Reviewing the credibility record in the 1970s, Tobin said:

> Isn't this what Arthur Burns [the Chairman of the Fed] has done, without spectacular results? Fellner and others would answer, I paraphrase, that the threat has not been

> credible enough precisely because Keynesian economists and politicians undermine it by advocating accommodation. In similar vein, two Presidents have complained that they could win the war in Southeast Asia if only political opposition at home would cease to impair their credibility to the enemy. The analogy underscores the difficulty of the threat approach in a democracy. In any case, I do not see how, in our decentralized system of wage- and price-setting, there is any incentive for a firm or union or individual worker to be the first to de-escalate. I note also that when Dr. Burns disciplines his class for inflationary offenses, the innocent are punished more than the guilty. Even after the punitive recession OPEC is ahead of the game.[18]

This game strategy view of policymaking has had its darker and lighter moments. One unfortunate consequence has been political pressure on administration economists to shade their forecasts—to make unduly optimistic inflation predictions in an attempt to reduce people's inflation expectations: "No one ever sold a used car by admitting that he didn't know if it would work or not." But economists are not salespeople. The false-smile approach to economic policy only undermines the credibility of economists and their political mentors.

Anti-inflation psychology was also behind Gerald Ford's distribution of WIN ("*W*hip *I*nflation *N*ow") buttons. This was a bizarre application of the advertising campaign approach to reducing inflation expectations. These buttons are destined to become collector's items, even though the Gerald R. Ford Library is not stockpiling them. Someone else once proposed using subliminal messages during the Super Bowl to convince people that inflation is slowing.

This emphasis on inflation expectations underlies a number of more concrete, but still gimmicky-sounding, proposals. Some of these involve trying especially hard to hold down the prices of items with heavy weights in the CPI,* since this index is the basis for most household perceptions of inflation. Some economists have even proposed taking the more troublesome items out of the CPI. Suitable redefinitions of the CPI might help reduce inflation expectations. A more extreme proposal is for the government to impose wage and price controls temporarily.

Tax incentives and other measures Intermediate between voluntary and mandatory wage-price restraints is the use of taxes to discourage inflation. Just as high taxes now penalize cigarette and alcohol consumption, so taxes can be used to penalize large wage and/or price increases. Such a system would discourage, but not rigidly control, inflation. For example, the Wallich-Weintraub Tax-based Incomes Policy (TIP) would impose a penalty corporate income tax on any of the roughly 1000 largest U.S. corporations whose average wage increase exceeded some norm, say 5% per year.[19]

Abba Lerner offered an even more flexible proposal. He suggested that the government establish a "market" for price increases. Certificates could be printed that gave the owner the right to raise wages or prices by some specified amount. The government could then auction off these certificates like oil leases. Productive companies that wanted to pay higher wages would be willing

* For example, Arthur Okun proposed subsidies to states that replaced sales taxes with income taxes, since the former are counted in the CPI, but not the latter. With a grin, he called his package of proposals "Okun's gimmicks."

to pay for this privilege, and businesses unwilling to pay for this inflation-licensing fee would not be allowed to raise their wages. In this way, businesses would be given the freedom to pay whatever wages they wanted, but would be forced to pay for their socially undesirable behavior, just as polluters can be required to pay cleanup expenses.

Yet another clever idea is for the government to offer real wage insurance or other social contracts. Workers who settled for modest wage increases (that would be appropriate if inflation were low) would be compensated (via tax refunds) if inflation turned out to be high. Again, the hope is that inflation can be reduced by persuading people to act as if they expect inflation to be reduced.

The natural rate of unemployment Many economists believe that there is no long-run tradeoff between unemployment and inflation. In the long run, all unemployment should be voluntary and unaffected by prices. This is the classical paradigm in which freely adjusting wages keep labor markets in equilibrium. An increase in the anticipated rate of inflation simply raises the rate of increase of wages, percentage point for percentage point, and has no effect on real wages. If so, then the parameter λ in Equations 7.11 and 7.12 should be 1.0.

As λ approaches 1.0, the slope of the long-run Phillips curve in Equation 7.13 becomes infinite. If $\lambda = 1$, then the long-run Phillips curve in Figure 7.18 should be vertical, as redrawn in Figure 7.19. There is no long-run tradeoff between unemployment and inflation. There is only one level of unemployment —where the long-run Phillips curve intersects the axis—that is consistent with long-run equilibrium. Milton Friedman called this unique unemployment rate the *natural rate of unemployment:*

> The "natural rate of unemployment," in other words, is the level that would be ground out by the Walrasian system of general equilibrium equations, provided there is imbedded in them the actual structural characteristics of labor and commodity markets, including market imperfections, stochastic variability in demands and supplies, the cost of gathering information about job vacancies and labor availabilities, the cost of mobility, and so on.[20]

In part, this disagreement about the inflation-expectations coefficient λ is really just the dynamic analogue of the classical-Keynes, market-equilibrium-versus-disequilibrium debate discussed in earlier chapters. Or, as Robert Solow put it, "Twenty-five years and one derivative later . . ."[21] Remember that in the classical models unemployment is voluntary and immune to price changes and other consequences of demand-management policies. In the new classical models there may be some temporary effect on employment if prices go up more or less than workers anticipate.

The very same logic extends to the Phillips curve if $\lambda = 1$. There is a natural rate of unemployment when price expectations are correct ($\pi^e = \pi$). Government monetary and fiscal policies can reduce unemployment below the natural rate temporarily by creating an unanticipated inflation. When $\pi^e < \pi$, workers will not realize that real wages are being eroded by inflation, the labor supply will expand, real wages will fall, and astute firms will expand employment. But when these new employees realize how much prices have increased and how low their real wages have fallen, they will leave their jobs and again be volun-

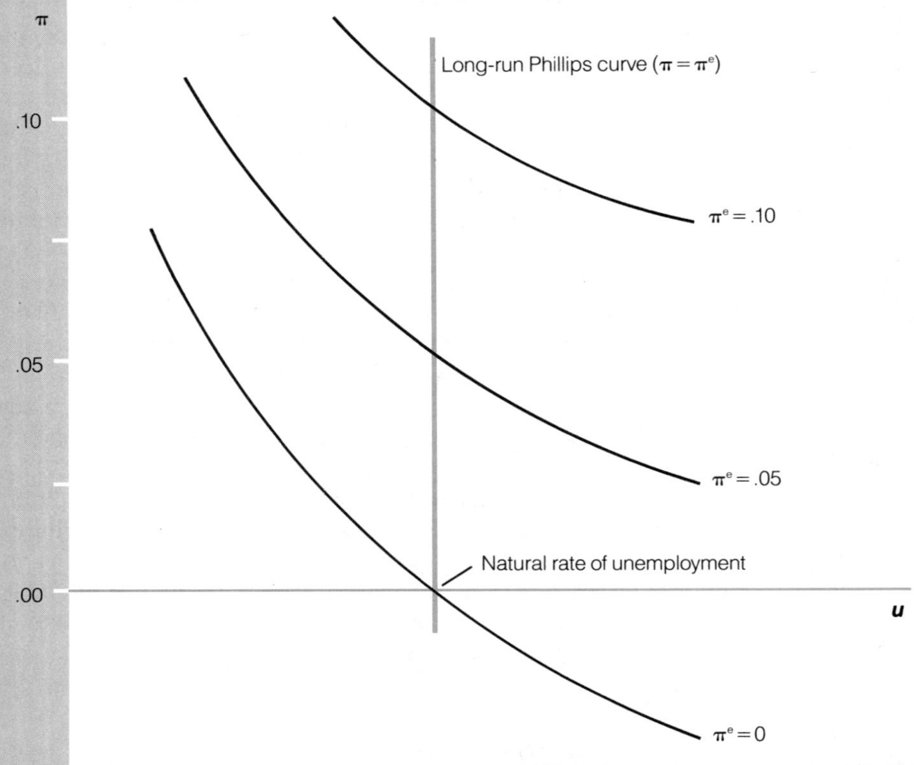

FIGURE 7.19 **SHORT-RUN AND LONG-RUN PHILLIPS CURVES** ($\lambda = 1$). If increased inflation expectations translate fully into higher actual inflation ($\lambda = 1$), then the long-run Phillips curve is vertical, indicating that there is only one unemployment rate—the "natural" rate—at which the actual and anticipated "inflation" rates coincide.

tarily unemployed. Employment and unemployment will return to their natural levels. Thus, **by the new classical interpretation, variations in unemployment about the natural rate are the voluntary consequences of misestimates of inflation.**

Keynesian economists, in contrast, argue that market disequilibria cause a great deal of involuntary unemployment. In their view, fluctuations in employment and unemployment are not just voluntary responses to price misperceptions. It is not unexpected changes in inflation that cause unemployment to go up and down. To the contrary, it is fluctuations in unemployment that cause inflation to go up and down. The long-run Phillips curve is steeper than the short-run curves because the effect of unemployment changes on inflation are greater to the extent that the inflation is anticipated and, consequently, greater in the long run than in the short run.

These are two quite different interpretations of the Phillips curve. **In the first, it is unanticipated inflation that causes voluntary fluctuations in unemployment; in the second, it is changes in involuntary unemployment that cause fluctuations in inflation.**

One way of distinguishing between these two interpretations is to ask whether unemployment would be affected by a change in demand whose inflationary consequences are anticipated correctly. The new classical answer is "no." The Keynesian answer is "yes." Even if the inflation is perfectly anticipated, monetary and fiscal policies still affect unemployment; there is no inevitable natural rate of unemployment to which the economy is inexorably pulled.

Part of this disagreement concerns what is meant by the "long run" Phillips curve. There is no real-world counterpart to the long run. It is a scenario invented by economists to help them analyze the course of the economy as time passes. Since it is fictional, it is not surprising that at least three different interpretations are possible. One possible meaning is, as Friedman suggests, the general equilibrium that would be found eventually by a Walrasian auctioneer. For the classically oriented economist, the economy is never far from general equilibrium and is always being drawn towards it. But the Friedman definition includes market imperfections, and it is difficult to know what a general equilibrium with market imperfections even means. A market can be either in equilibrium or in disequilibrium: It cannot be in equilibrium and disequilibrium at the same time.

The Friedman view also allows for variabilities in demands and supplies. But if demands and supplies are constantly shifting about as tastes, skills, and so on change, then there is no single, unique equilibrium. A more promising path is to imagine a dynamic equilibrium in which some things are held constant while other things are allowed to work themselves out. For example, we might commit the government to certain monetary and fiscal policies and assume that population, capital, skills, and tastes are all fixed. With these things constant, we could allow wages, prices, and interest rates to adjust until a unique Walrasian market-equilibrium is found. Then we could assume different monetary and fiscal policies and again hold everything constant but wages, prices, and interest rates—which are allowed to find the new Walrasian equilibrium. It is certainly plausible that these general equilibrium levels of employment, unemployment, and output do not depend on the price level or the inflation rate.*

Yet a third possibility is an expectational equilibrium with $P = P^e$ and $\pi = \pi^e$. We can ask the question: Given that the world we live in has imperfect markets and continuing changes in population, capital, skills, and tastes, will monetary and fiscal policies whose effects on prices are completely anticipated have any effect on the unemployment rate? The answer is undoubtedly *yes.*

Because markets are imperfect, even a perfectly anticipated contraction of aggregate demand increases unemployment. This cyclical unemployment is not

* Even temporary increases in employment do yield more output and may have permanent effects on employment as well. The temporarily employed acquire job experience and work records, which make them more attractive to employers. Some of the additional output may be physical capital that permanently increases labor demand. In Chapter 18 we will see how long-run full employment changes when we allow the capital stock to vary.

IN THE NEWS

Predictions about Inflation . . . Full of Contradictions

Recently the *New York Times* reported that the "consensus prediction" for inflation was for a "modest acceleration of prices." In the same article, the *Times* also stated that "a significant minority (of economists) rejects such optimism."

This minority includes Milton Friedman, who says that inflation will accelerate during the next year in sizable proportions. He also insists that nothing can be done to stop it.

It seems that there are many economists who spend a great deal of their time searching for ways to obtain foreknowledge of economic events.

For instance, the *Times* also reports a new "leading index of inflation" developed by Geoffrey H. Moore of the Columbia Business School's Center for International Business Cycle Research. His leading indicator of inflation points to double-digit levels by mid-1985.

What do these two pessimistic views have in common that is different from the more optimistic views?

We are going to look at two different ways of obtaining predictions of the future course of economic events. We think it is important to know the different methods in order to make an independent evaluation of the contradictory opinions.

It is true that if the consensus is correct, the pessimists must be wrong. Or, if the pessimistic minority is accurate, then the consensus must be in error.

If any of us decide to put our funds into "inflation hedges" instead of some other investment, we risk losing some income if prices do not go back to double-digit increases.

If the pessimists are right, we would lose by not putting funds into inflation-sensitive assets. It is important to know how likely each of these predictions will turn into reality.

Prof. Friedman bases his prediction on a correlation between the rate of growth in the money supply and the rate of change in price levels. Prof. Moore uses three other economic events that have been correlated with the rate of inflation in past years.

Other economists are basing their predictions on economic circumstances that can be shown to cause an acceleration in price level increases. These economists tend toward the position that no event (such as a "surge" in money growth) makes another event (price level acceleration) unavoidable.

In this view, the rate of inflation is managed (or not) by policies that coincide with the inflationary experience.

They may, for instance, assess the degree to which the Federal Reserve is willing to restrain monetary growth over the next 18 months. If their assessment is that the Fed is resolute on restrictive measures, they will predict a modest rate of inflation. What happened eight to 10 months ago is irrelevant to what will happen 10 to 18 months from now.

In one sense at least, those who rely on past correlation of essentially unrelated events are assuming that people will make the same mistakes in managing their affairs every time they encouner a certain set of economic circumstances.

If a certain change in an indicator of inflation precedes an actual rise in inflation rates in five of the last six recovery phases, this means that there is one chance in six that it will *not* happen this time.

Furthermore, the laws of chance in such correlations are fickle enough to produce five occurrences in six trys when the probability is no more than 50-50. It could be that chance produced five successes in a row that will be followed by five failures.

For many years, economists were convinced by both theory and experience that inflation was tied to the employment rate as well as to monetary growth. Monetary growth would produce inflation only if the employment rate was very high.

Experience over the past 25 years has caused us to question this relationship. Sometimes monetary growth will accelerate inflation, and sometimes it will not, regardless of the employment rate.

Much effort is being spent in an attempt to isolate the causes of inflation. It is fairly clear that this effort has not produced reliable results yet. (Richard Waits and Edward M. McNertney, *Fort Worth Star-Telegram*, Dec. 6, 1983) cured simply by workers discovering the correct price level or rate of inflation. It would evaporate if the world stood still while the Walrasian auctioner came in and found the general equilibrium. By the same token, a recession can be ended by an expansion of aggregate demand, even if that expansion and its effects on prices are known perfectly.

During recessions, when there are lots of excess-supply labor markets, λ is less than 1, since price increases do not raise wages proportionately. If, instead, labor markets are predominantly in equilibrium or excess demand, then price increases may raise wages almost proportionately, and λ is probably close to 1. Thus this expectations-equilibrium, long-run Phillips curve is relatively flat at high rates of unemployment and very steep at low unemployment rates. When there are no excess-supply labor markets left there is no room for increases in demand to reduce unemployment and increase output.

So different interpretations can be attached to the notion of a long-run Phillips curve. If we mean that the world stands still while all markets get cleared, then the long-run Phillips curve is probably vertical. If we mean that the world keeps changing while price expectations catch up with reality, then the long-run Phillips curve is probably not vertical.

Most economists frankly admit that they do not know very much about hypothetical long-run Phillips curves, but repeat Keynes' observation that it is the short run that matters to mortals. Robert Solow put it this way: "There is a tradeoff between the speed of price increase and the real state of the economy. It is less favorable in the long run than it is at first. It may not be 'permanent'; but it lasts long enough for me."[21]

SUMMARY: INFLATION CURES

Inflation is a continuing increase in the price level. In a classical model (with full employment and the simple quantity theory), the rate of inflation is equal to the difference between the rate of growth of the money supply (plus the rate of growth velocity) and the rate of growth of full-employment output. To cure inflation, the monetary authorities need only keep the rate of growth of the money supply in line with output growth. The cure is relatively painless, since output stays at the full-employment level.

When employment and velocity fluctuate with the economy, inflation is more difficult to explain and more painful to cure. Price changes are influenced by demand-versus-supply imbalances. But many prices adjust slowly and imperfectly, so that a demand or supply shift can affect prices for a considerable period. For instance, the large increase in oil prices in 1973–74 reduced the demand for cars, particularly large cars. There were ripple effects on steel, rubber, auto workers, Detroit housing, and many other markets. There were also direct effects on the markets for coal, oil drilling equipment, insulation, and sun belt housing, and innumerable others. No Walrasian auctioneer stepped in and announced the new prices that simultaneously cleared thousands of markets. Instead, prices were set in separate markets by contracts, regulatory authorities, mark-up formulas, and other procedures that were not very sensitive to demand and supply and not at all concerned with Walras' general equilibrium. It took years for the effects of higher oil prices to work themselves out.

In many markets, prices are set by regulatory authorities or according to rules of thumb based on production costs. Each price is set so as to yield a "fair" profit at normal production levels. Costs consequently give a preview of prices. Some costs, particularly for raw materials, are pretty sensitive to demand and supply. Inflation forecasters consequently keep an eye on things that can affect both, noting weather reports, changes in tastes and technology, and political upheaval. Other costs, particularly wages, do not immediately respond to demand and supply. Here, inflation forecasters watch collective-bargaining agreements, keeping track of which years important contracts are renegotiated and watching for pattern-setting agreements. Although rough and approximate, the unemployment rate can be used to gauge the overall tightness of labor markets. Wages hardly ever fall, even if there is lots of unemployment, but wage increases do tend to be smaller when the unemployment rate is high.

This inverse relationship between unemployment and wage increases is known as the Phillips curve. Since wage increases cause mark-up-pricing firms to raise prices, there will also be a Phillips-curve relationship between unemployment and price increases. According to this logic, inflation can be cured by contractionary monetary and fiscal policies. A stiff recession will reduce prices in flexprice markets and restrain prices (by restraining wages) in fixprice markets.

After 1974 there were many years of economic slack that made little in the way of a dent in inflation. One explanation for this focuses on such cost factors as high energy prices, high taxes, and diminished productivity improvements. By this reasoning, an anti-inflation medicine should include enlarged energy supplies, lower taxes, and increased productivity incentives. A second explanation focuses on the increased numbers of inexperienced women and teenagers in the labor force, so that an anti-inflation medicine should include training programs, hiring incentives, and other policies to make these new workers more appealing to employers. A third explanation focuses on the self-fulfilling nature of inflation expectations. When people expect rapid inflation, they set wages and prices to keep up with their expectations and, so, fulfill their prophecy. An anti-inflation medicine should include sufficient promises, threats, or bribes to convince people that rapid inflation will soon end.

IMPORTANT TERMS AND CONCEPTS

inflation
average-mark-up pricing
target-return pricing
Phillips curve
natural rate of unemployment

In a classical model prices are affected by government monetary policy, but not by fiscal policies. The level of the money supply determines the price level and the rate of growth of the money supply determines the rate of inflation.

Inflation in the long run is a largely monetary phenomenon in that a sustained monetary growth that causes aggregate demand to grow faster than potential output will cause a sustained inflation. Conversely, long-run inflation without money growth will be limited by a persistent tendency of money demand to outstrip supply.

When employment and velocity vary, the price level is determined by the aggregate demand and supply curves. It is not important how much of this aggregate demand is attributable to government monetary policy, fiscal policy, or various facets of private behavior. Short-term inflation reflects both current events and the working out of old disequilibria.

There is a short-run tradeoff between unemployment and inflation. Some Keynesian economists believe that there is also a long-run tradeoff but that it is not as favorable as in the short run. Expansionary monetary and fiscal policies increase output and reduce unemployment, putting upward pressures on wages and prices. These inflationary pressures are greatest when wage agreements take the rate of inflation into account. But even if the inflation is perfectly anticipated, expansionary monetary and fiscal policies still increase output and reduce unemployment as long as there are involuntary idle businesses and workers.

Classically oriented economists believe that the short-run tradeoff is due to inflation errors. People who are voluntarily unemployed become voluntarily employed when they underestimate inflation and overestimate their real wages. Since these errors are soon corrected there is no long-run tradeoff between unemployment and inflation. In the long run there is a unique natural rate of unemployment, which is independent of the rate of inflation. This new classical argument makes the most sense if the "long run" comparison is between two Walrasian full-employment equilibria. The Keynesian argument makes the most sense if the "long run" comparison is between the present situation and a situation in which more expansionary monetary and fiscal policies have caused a fully anticipated inflation.

EXERCISES

1. Explain how the price level can increase even while the rate of inflation is decreasing.

2. Is there any logical justification for the conclusion that "inflation is always and everywhere a monetary phenomenon"?

3. Show how a contractionary supply-side event (such as an oil embargo) will increase prices.

4. Using aggregate demand and supply curves, show what happens to an economy initially at its potential output level, in which an expansionary monetary policy increases aggregate demand, output rises about the potential level (as people work overtime and harder), and prices also rise, a little at first and then more as wage contracts are renegotiated.

5. Using aggregate demand and supply curves, show what happens to an economy initially at its potential output level, in which sharply higher energy prices cause firms to raise prices, reduce output, and lay off workers, who, as time passes, agree to work for lower wages.

6. An economy's Phillips curve is $\pi = -0.05 + 0.3(1/u)$. Calculate the rate of inflation, π, for several unemployment rates u (say, from $u = 3$ to $u = 10$). Graph this Phillips curve.

7. An economy's Phillips curve is $\pi = -0.05 + 0.3(1/u) + 0.8\pi^e$. Graph the short-run Phillips curve for $\pi^e = 0$ and the long-run Phillips curve (with $\pi = \pi^e$) How would these short- and long-run curves be changed were the coefficient of π^e 1.0 instead of 0.8?

8. Answer the following question: "I've read somewhere that there is a tradeoff between unemployment and inflation. Does this mean that less unemployment causes more inflation or that more inflation causes less unemployment?"

9. If there is a tradeoff between unemployment and inflation, how can the economy have had double-digit inflation and close to double-digit unemployment at the same time?

10. What is the rationale for the hypothesis that there is a natural rate of unemployment—one that does not depend on the rate of inflation? How does this theory explain the occurence of unemployment rates other than the natural level? In particular, how would it account for the historical data for 1960–66 and 1980–83 shown in table 7.1?

11. Ann Hack has specified the following Phillips curve model to explain inflation.

$$\pi_t = a + b(1/u_t) + \lambda\pi_t^e$$

$$\pi_{t+1}^e - \pi_t^e = \beta(\pi_t - \pi_t^e)$$

The first equation says that, in any year, t, the inflation rate depends on the unemployment rate and the expected inflation rate. The second says that the revision in inflation expectations from year t to $t+1$ depends on the inflation error in year t. Hack estimates $a = -0.125$, $b = 0.01$, $\lambda = 0.5$, and $\beta = 1$. Assume the monetary and fiscal authorities decide to peg the unemployment rate at 5% ($u = 0.05$). Initially (at $t = 0$), the expected rate of inflation is equal to zero—that is $\pi_0^e = 0$.

a. Determine the patch of actual and expected inflation for $t = 0$, 1, and 2.
b. What are the actual and expected inflation rates in the long run? ($t \rightarrow \infty$)
c. What would the long-run inflation rate be if the monetary and fiscal authorities instead pegged the unemployment rate at 10%?
d. Which unemployment rate is consistent with zero inflation in the long run?
e. Using the answers to the questions above sketch the long-run Phillips curve and show the time path the economy follows in Question a.
f. How would the answers to the questions above be affected if Hack assumed $\lambda = 1$, instead of 0.5?

REFERENCES

1. *Newsweek,* June 1969.

2. *Webster's New Collegiate Dictionary,* Springfield, Mass.: G & C Merriam, 1981, p. 586.

3. Milton Friedman, "What Price Guideposts?," in *Guidelines, Informal Controls, and the Marketplace,* G. Schultz and R. Aliber, editors, Chicago: University of Chicago, 1969.

4. *Wall Street Journal,* October 22, 1980.

5. A. W. Phillips, "The Relation Between Unemployment and the Rate of Change of Money Wages in the United Kingdom, 1961–1957," *Economica* (November 1958), pp. 283–99. Phillips' "law" was actually discovered by Irving Fisher, "A Statistical Relation Between Unemployment and Price Changes," *International Labour Review* (June 1926), pp. 785–92.

6. Sidney Weintraub, *Keynes and the Monetarists,* New Brunswick, N.J.: Rutgers, 1973.

7. Arthur Schlesinger, Jr., "Inflation Symbolism vs. Reality," *Wall Street Journal,* April 9, 1980.

8. *New York Times,* February 22, 1970.

9. Otto Eckstein, *The Great Recession: With a Postscript on Stagflation,* Amsterdam: North-Holland, 1978.

10. *Wall Street Journal,* May 20, 1980.

11. George Perry, "Changing Labor Markets and Inflation," *Brookings Papers on Economic Activity* (1970), pp. 411–41.

12. Robert J. Gordon, "Inflation in Recession and Recovery," *Brookings Papers on Economic Activity* (1971), pp. 105–158.

13. Charles Schultze, "Has the Phillips Curve Shifted? Some Additional Evidence," *Brookings Papers on Economic Activity* (1971), pp. 452–67.

14. See Ronald Ehrenberg and Ronald Oaxaca, "Do Benefits Cause Unemployed to Hold Out for Better Jobs?" and Martin Feldstein, "Unemployment Compensation: Its Effects on Unemployment," both in the *Monthly Labor Review* (March 1976).

15. Robert Solow, *Technology Review,* December/January 1979, p. 31.

16. *Wall Street Journal,* May 20, 1980.

17. W. Fellner, "The Valid Core of Rationality Hypotheses in the Theory of Expectations," *Journal of Money, Credit, and Banking* (November 1980), pp. 763–87.

18. J. Tobin, "How Dead is Keynes?," *Economic Inquiry,* 15 (October 1977), pp. 459–68.

19. See S. Weintraub, *Capitalism's Inflation and Unemployment Crisis,* Reading: Mass.: Addison-Wesley, 1978.

20. M. Friedman, "The Role of Monetary Policy," *American Economic Review,* 58 (March 1968), pp. 1–17.

21. R. Solow, "Down the Phillips Curve with Gun and Camera," in D. Belsley, ed., *Inflation, Trade, and Taxes,* Columbus, Ohio State University Press, 1976.

22. R. Solow, *Price Expectations and the Behavior of the Price Level,* Manchester, England: Manchester University Press, 1969, p. 17.

SUGGESTIONS FOR FURTHER READING

Robert Solow has written two excellent expository papers: "The Intelligent Citizen's Guide to Inflation." *The Public Interest* (1975), pp. 30–66, and "Down the Phillips Curve with Gun and Camera," in David Belsley, ed., *Inflation, Trade, and Taxes,* Columbus: Ohio State University Press, 1976.

Useful for a deeper examination of the classical-Keynesian debate, are two American Economic Association Presidential addresses: Milton Friedman, "The Role of Monetary Policy," *American Economic Review,* 58 (March 1968), pp. 1–17, and James Tobin, "Inflation and Unemployment," *American Economic Review,* 62 (March 1972), pp. 1–18. Friedman argues that the long-run Phillips curve may have a positive slope in his "Nobel Lecture: Inflation and Unemployment," *Journal of Political Economy,* June 1977, pp. 451–72.

CHAPTER EIGHT

THE CONSEQUENCES OF INFLATION

Lenin is said to have declared that the best way to destroy the capitalist system was to debauch the currency.

JOHN MAYNARD KEYNES[1]

This chapter examines how inflation affects individual living standards and overall macroeconomic behavior. Two specific questions addressed are whether inflation makes everyone poorer and whether an increase in the money supply may actually raise interest rates.

INFLATION has long been viewed as a disease, causing the decay of a society and exposing the weakness of its government. One writer recently gave inflation enormous historical importance, declaring that it "helped bring down the Roman Empire, almost sabotaged the American Revolution, opened the door for Napoleon in France and gave the Germans an excuse to listen to Hitler."[2]

In 1812, Madame de Staël wrote of how inflation in Austria during Napoleon's rule had quickly corrupted the Austrians:

> I no longer found the same honesty in the people that had struck me four years earlier; paper money stimulates the imagination with hopes of rapid and easy gain, and the hazards of chance upset the steady, even flow of existence, the basis for honesty in the common people. During my stay in Austria a man was hanged for forging counterfeit money just after the old notes had been replaced; on his way to the gallows he cried out that it was not he who had stolen but the state.[3]

In recent years, Americans have repeatedly been told that inflation is "public enemy number one," "the cruelest tax of all," that it arbitrarily and capriciously robs us while we sleep. How exactly does inflation carry out this silent theft, and what can we do to protect ouselves? This chapter examines these questions.

In the 1980 election campaign, Ronald Reagan repeatedly asked voters, "Are you better off now than you were four years ago?" Most people apparently answered with a resounding "No!"; otherwise he wouldn't have kept asking. Yet

TABLE 8.1
Percentage growth in real per capita measures of economic well-being

	GNP	After-tax income	Consumption
1950–59	15.1	12.7	11.3
1960–69	31.5	31.6	29.7
1970–79	26.9	25.0	28.6

the statistics indicate that, in economic terms at least, most people really were better off. During Jimmy Carter's four years as President, real per capita GNP increased 10%; real per capita after-tax income increased 8%; and real per capita consumption increased 9%.

More generally, the 1970s are widely believed to have been near-disastrous economically, with rampant inflation steadily reducing everyone's standard of living. Yet, while the 1970s were not uninterrupted prosperity by any means—recessions repeatedly dropped output below potential—neither were they one long downhill slide. Even when inflation and population growth are taken into account, we still find that real per capita output, income, and consumption all increased in the 1970s—in fact, almost as much as in the 1960s and much more than in the good old, low-inflation 1950s.* Table 8.1 shows some relevant comparisons. The fraction of the population below the poverty level fell from 12.6% in 1970 to 11.7% in 1979. For the elderly, thought to be especially vulnerable to inflation, the poverty rate fell from 24.6% in 1970 to 15.2% in 1979. No matter how we look at it, inflation did not impoverish us. What accounts for this substantial gap between perceptions and experience? One plausible explanation is the asymmetrical interpretation of income and of price increases. An increase in income is usually perceived as a just reward for hard labor and meritorious accomplishment; an increase in prices, on the other hand, is usually perceived as unfair and reprehensible. If income and prices increase proportionately, there is no change in real income, but people in this situation often feel that they have lost something, that the increase in prices has taken away what is rightfully theirs.

When income and prices go up together, people may feel that they are having to struggle to keep their income rising as fast as prices—that they must earn more income to offset the higher prices, wearing themselves out trying to swim upstream. In fact, it may be the higher prices that enable them to earn higher income; or, put somewhat differently, it may be their higher wages that are causing the higher prices. Money illusion, in which people concentrate on their nominal incomes and ignore prices, seems to have given way to "inflation illusion," in which people watch prices and do not pay enough attention to their incomes.

INFLATION'S WINNERS AND LOSERS

There is a widely held belief that an increase in prices automatically reduces everyone's standard of living. This is not true; a price increase does raise the

* As in the 1950s, the real economic problem of the 1970s was that there were several recessions, which reduced output in each recessionary year. Total output for the decade was consequently far below its potential. But, contrary to popular belief, real output, income, and consumption were much higher at the end of the 1970s than at the beginning.

cost to buyers, but it also increases the income of sellers. Thus, one person's higher price is another's higher income. A price increase does not mysteriously obliterate a nation's resources; it merely transfers more dollars from buyers to sellers. And we are all both buyers and sellers. Most of us buy commodities and sell our labor to firms which, in turn, pay us wages out of the revenue they receive from selling commodities. Were all wages and prices increased by the same amount—say 10%—real incomes would be unchanged.

In practice, wages and prices do not all change equally. Thus some real incomes go down, while others go up. In addition, there are many contracts whose dollar value is fixed. As a result, some people do gain while others lose.

Prices seldom, if ever rise uniformly.[4] Within every inflation some prices increase much more than others. For example, in 1973, the CPI rose 8.8% while farm income increased 31%. This relative increase in farm prices transferred income to farmers from the rest of the nation. The tremendous increase in oil prices has similarly transferred hundreds of billions of dollars out of the United States to oil-exporting nations. In 1981, the United States imported almost $100 billion of oil, about $1500 per household. Many of the complaints about inflation in the 1970s were misdirected. The pain many felt was not due to inflation, per se, but rather to relative price shifts in favor of farmers and oil owners.

A uniform inflation does, however, reduce the real value of dollar-denominated assets, such as dollar bills. In fact, most financial assets have their terms specified in dollar amounts. George borrows $100 from Mary, and agrees to pay back $105 a year later. As prices rise, that $105 is worth less and less to Mary (worth *less,* not worthless). Say she was planning to spend the $105 on wine now selling for $5 a bottle. The real value of George's IOU is thus 21 bottles of wine. If the price of wine rises 5%, to $5.25 a bottle, then the $105 IOU is worth only 20 bottles. The price increase has reduced Mary's wealth by one bottle of wine.

Where did that bottle go? It didn't disappear. There was simply a transfer of wealth from Mary to George. Mary's loss was George's gain. He had a debt of $105, which was the equivalent of 21 bottles of wine. When prices increased 5%, his real debt dropped by 5%. The real burden of his debt decreased by just as much as Mary's wealth decreased.

This is what always happens. Increases in prices hurt creditors and help debtors. (Is this why Republicans are usually more worried about inflation than are Democrats?) Conversely, deflations help creditors and hurt debtors. In 1810, David Ricardo wrote:

> The depreciation of the circulating medium has been more injurious to moneyed men. . . . It may be laid down as a principle of universal application, that every man is injured or benefited by the variation of the value of the circulating medium in proportion as his property consists of money, or as the fixed demands on him in money exceed those fixed demands which he may have on others. . . . [The farmer] more than any other class of the community is benefited by the depreciation of money, and injured by the increase in its value.[5]

Ricardo's moneyed men, with sizable financial assets, are hurt by inflation and resist it. Farmers, with large debts and lands that appreciate with inflation, traditionally favor inflationary government policies.

When William Jennings Bryan campaigned against the gold standard in 1896, he was appealing for inflationary policies that would make it easier for farmers to pay off their mortgages. In the 1930s, Franklin Roosevelt promised inflation for similar reasons. In an October 22, 1933, radio speech that was printed on the front page of the *New York Times* the next day, he said:

> Finally, I repeat what I have said on many occasions, that ever since last March the definite policy of the government has been to restore commodity price-levels. . . . The object has been to make possible the payment of public and private debts more nearly at the price-level at which they were incurred.

Here was a shrewd and successful politician promising inflation!

For the conservatively moneyed families who owned safe bonds, the Great Depression was only a rumor. The deflation of the 1930s just made them richer. Many wisely used their cash to buy depressed land, especially property with foreclosed mortgages. In the 1970s the reverse was true. Homeowners who had borrowed at single-digit interest rates to buy houses appreciating at double-digit rates profited handsomely from inflation. This time, it was the people with their money conservatively invested in bonds who were the losers. As with wages and prices, there is often an asymmetrical interpretation of this transfer. Those who profit from an inflation (or deflation) credit themselves as financially expert; those who lose, blame the inflation. In most cases, it would be more accurate to say that some were lucky, and others unlucky.

Real rates of return

These sorts of inflationary gains and losses can be measured by computing the real rate of return from an investment. We have already distinguished between the nominal and real magnitudes of wages, income, and wealth. There is an important analogous distinction between nominal and real interest rates. The nominal rate of return, $\tilde{R}$, is the quoted interest rate, measuring the net yield in dollars gained per dollar invested. For a one-year investment,

$$\tilde{R} = \frac{\text{\$ received next year} - \text{\$ invested now}}{\text{\$ invested now}} \tag{8.1}$$

If a \$100 investment yields \$110 a year from now, then the nominal rate of return is 10%; $\tilde{R} = \$10/\$100 = 0.10$. The real rate of return, $\tilde{r}$, measures the net yield in terms of commodities gained by commodity invested:

$$\tilde{r} = \frac{\text{commodities next year} - \text{commodities now}}{\text{commodities invested now}} \tag{8.2}$$

Normally, we don't actually invest or receive commodities; instead, we invest and receive dollars. The logic of a real-yield calculation is that it takes into account the purchasing power of those dollars invested and received. If a typical commodity bundle costs \$50, then investing \$100 is equivalent to giving up two of those bundles. When we are paid \$110 a year hence, we deflate the \$110 by the prices that then prevail. If the price of the bundle of commodities has gone up 10% to \$55, then \$110 can buy two bundles. We have given up two bundles now for two bundles later, and the real rate of return is zero. We have run fast but stayed in the same place.

In general, the real rate of return is approximately* equal to the nominal rate of return minus the rate of inflation, π:

$$\tilde{r} = \tilde{R} - \pi. \tag{8.3}$$

If, as in the example, we earn a 10% nominal return while prices increase by 10%, then the real return is zero. If prices increase by only 3%, then the real return is 7%. If prices increase by 20%, the real return is negative, a disappointing −10%. We have given up two bundles now for 1.8 bundles a year hence.

There is, of course, a difference between the *ex ante* return and the *ex post* return actually obtained. Many financial assets have guaranteed nominal returns—cash (zero), savings accounts, and Treasury bills for instance. In these cases, the *ex ante* and *ex post* nominal returns coincide. The real returns, however, are not known in advance and *ex post* may diverge considerably from *ex ante.* For other assets—such as stocks, land, and gold—both the nominal and real returns are uncertain. A bond that is indexed to the price level would have a known real return and an uncertain nominal return. In practice, there are many different nominal rates of return: on cash, checking accounts, Treasury bills, AT&T bonds, IBM stock, gold, land, and on and on. And for each nominal rate of return, there are many different real rates of return, corresponding to the various official and unofficial price indexes that can be taken into account.

Inflation expectations and nominal interest rates

In the earlier example, Mary agreed to a 5% nominal rate, which a 5% inflation reduced to a 0% real return (measured in bottles of wine). What if the inflation rate is instead 10%? If wine prices increase 10%, her real return is −5%: She lends $100 (which could have been used to purchase 20 bottles of wine) and gets back $105 (which can buy only 19 bottles).

If Mary anticipates a 10% inflation, she won't be enthusiastic about lending money at a 5% nominal interest rate. Instead, she could just buy 20 bottles of wine and keep them for a year, for a 0% real return. That's not much, but it's better than lending money at 5% while wine prices go up 10%. If George wants to borrow money from Mary, he will have to offer her at least a 0% real return. Otherwise, she will stockpile wine instead of lending him money. If a 10% inflation is anticipated, George will have to offer Mary at least a 10% nominal in-

* The exact formula is:

$$\tilde{r} = \frac{\text{commodities gained}}{\text{commodities invested}} = \frac{(1+\tilde{R})/P_1 - 1/P_0}{1/P_0} =$$

$$\frac{1+\tilde{R}}{P_1/P_0} - 1 = \frac{1+\tilde{R}}{1+\pi} - 1 = \tilde{R} - \pi - \frac{\pi(\tilde{R}-\pi)}{1+\pi}$$

where P_0 is the current price level, P_1 is the price level one year hence, and the rate of inflation is $\pi = (P_1 - P_0)/P_0$. If π and $(\tilde{R} - \pi)$ are both small, then their product is very small and can be ignored.

terest rate. If a 20% inflation is anticipated, he will have to offer at least a 20% interest rate. And with prices rising so rapidly, he may well be willing to pay such high interest rates.

In general, the nominal interest rates that are agreed to will take into account the expected inflation rate, with a higher expected rate of inflation tending to increase nominal interest rates. There is not, however, a simple, fixed relationship between the expected inflation rate and nominal interest rates. An increase in the expected inflation rate does not, for example, automatically raise nominal interest rates by an equal amount, leaving real interest rates constant. Real interest rates depend on demand, supply, and institutional rigidities. Later in this chapter, we will use our macro model to explain real interest rates and to see how they are affected by inflation expectations.

It is not true that real interest rates are invariably positive. Throughout the 1970s, many people kept funds in savings accounts paying about 5% interest while consumer prices relentlessly increased by more than 5% a year. They accepted a negative real interest rate because it was the best of their alternatives. Stocks, bonds, and other assets that might have earned higher yields were too risky or had brokerage fees or minimum investment requirements too high for small investors. It took $10,000 to buy a Treasury bill; it takes millions to buy a shopping center. Nor is it possible to ensure a zero real rate of return by investing in the CPI: Some people may have stocked up on wine and soup, but it is difficult to stockpile gasoline, perishable food, fashionable clothing, new computers, medical services, haircuts, sales taxes, and other components of the CPI.

It is, of course, the actual rate of inflation that determines the real wealth of creditors and the real burden on debtors. Once a loan has been agreed to, both sides have their own view of the expected real rate of return. Errors in inflation predictions allow the actual real interest rate to diverge from the expected rate. A higher-than-anticipated inflation causes the real return to be less than expected. A lower-than-anticipated inflation makes the real return higher than expected. Once the loan has been signed, a higher rate of inflation reduces the real return on any loan whose terms are set in nominal values. Creditors campaign for deflation, and debtors for inflation.

The effects of taxes on real yields

Real-yield computations should take taxes into account and, when we do that, we find that the rich and the poor are not affected equally. If $\tilde{R}$ is the nominal interest rate and t is the tax rate, then the after-tax nominal return, R, is $(1 - t)\tilde{R}$, and the after-tax real return, r, is $(1 - t)\tilde{R} - \pi$. Note that the after-tax real return is equal to the after-tax nominal return less the rate of inflation, π. Figure 8.1 shows the after-tax historical values of one nominal interest rate (on three-month Treasury bills) and the corresponding *ex post* real interest rate (using the GNP deflator).

During inflations, the gap between before-tax and after-tax real returns widens, because taxes are paid on nominal rather than real returns. Therefore, a one-percentage-point increase in the rate of inflation requires more than a one-percentage-point increase in nominal interest rates for real returns to be constant. (See Exercise 3 at the end of this chapter for a detailed example.) Fig-

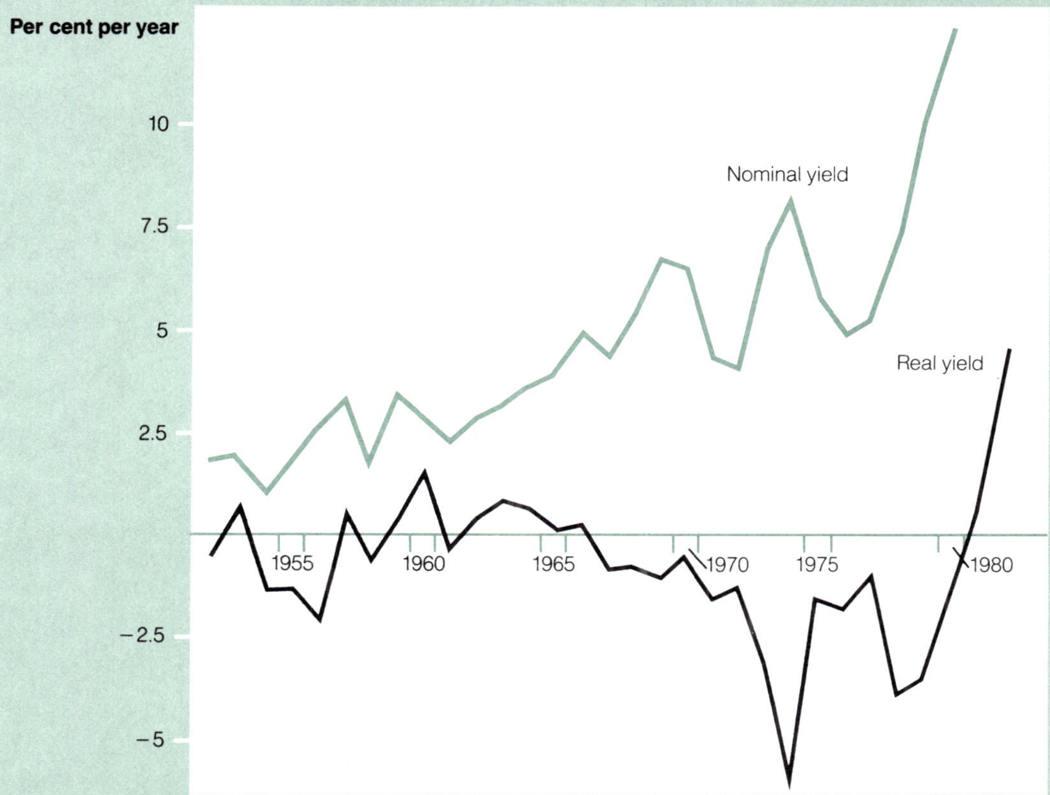

FIGURE 8.1 **REAL AFTER-TAX YIELDS are computed by subtracting inflation from the after-tax nominal yield. The real after-tax interest rate on three-month Treasury bills was negative throughout the 1970s, but turned sharply positive at the beginning of the 1980s.**

ure 8.1 shows that nominal Treasury bill rates did rise during the inflation-ridden 1970s, but not nearly enough to keep after-tax real returns from falling. The real yield on Treasury bills turned positive in 1981 and was very high in 1982. Later in this chapter we will use our macro model to explain why *ex ante* real returns go up and down, and why they often fall during inflations.

The real yields shown in Figure 8.1 would, of course, be lower for people in tax brackets higher than the 30% rate used in calculating these yields. A tax naturally reduces after-tax rates of return; a less obvious principle is that, during inflations, real yields fall relatively more for people in high tax brackets, since taxes are paid on nominal rather than real rates of return. During rapid inflations, increases in nominal yields are least able to offset inflation for people in high tax brackets.

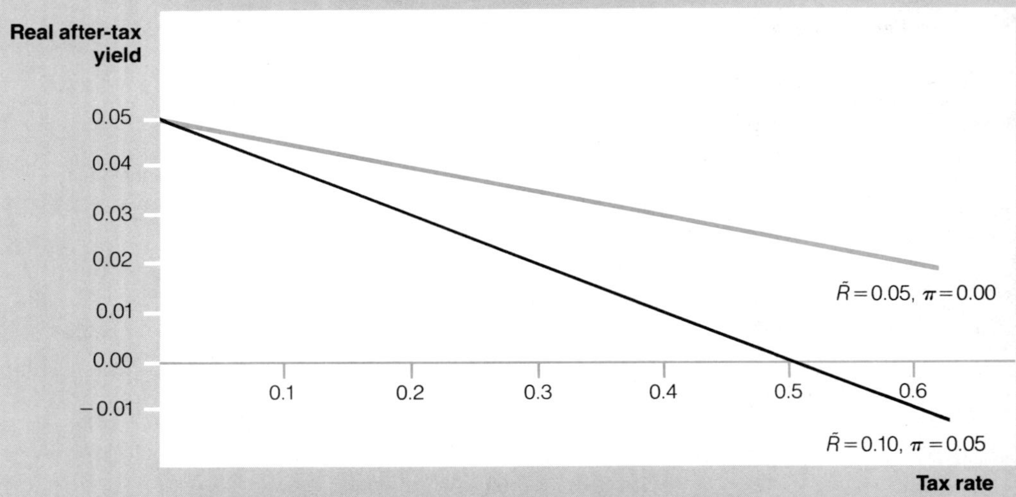

FIGURE 8.2 **Comparison of two cases, showing differential effect of taxes on real yields, during inflations, depending on tax bracket. Were taxes paid on real returns, real after-tax yields for $\tilde{R} = 0.10$ would be the same as for $\tilde{R} = 0.05$, $\pi = 0.00$ (upper curve).**

Figure 8.2 compares two hypothetical cases. In one there is no inflation, and the nominal yield is 5%; in the other there is 5% inflation, and the nominal yield is 10%. In a zero tax bracket, real yields are 5% in each case. But in higher tax brackets, real yields are reduced by inflation. Since taxes are paid on nominal returns, real yields are greatly diminished for those in high tax brackets.

The comparison in Figure 8.2 is between two scenarios with the same before-tax real return. Our conclusions also apply to other scenarios. Figure 8.3 compares two situations, both with the same after-tax real return for someone in a 30% tax bracket. In the first situation, the inflation rate is 3% and the nominal yield is 10%. In the second situation, the inflation rate is 10% and the nominal yield is 20%. In both cases, someone in a 30% tax bracket earns a 4% after-tax real rate of return. The figure shows that those in lower tax brackets do relatively well with the more rapid inflation; while those in higher tax brackets fare better with less inflation. Figures 8.2 and 8.3 also apply to the real after-tax cost of borrowing, and show that debtors in low tax brackets find inflation more burdensome than debtors in high tax brackets.

There are four morals, the first three being that nominal interest rates have to increase by more than the rate of inflation to keep after-tax real returns from falling; that high-income creditors have very sound personal reasons for disliking inflation; and that high-income creditors will avidly seek low-taxed assets during inflations. (Inflation makes it especially advantageous to be in a low tax bracket. High-income taxpayers can reduce their effective tax rates by borrowing money in order to acquire houses, land, gold, art, and other assets whose returns are not taxed or are taxed at low capital-gains rates. The appeal of low-taxed assets is greatest during rapid inflations.) The fourth moral is that inflations transfer wealth from high-income creditors and low-income debtors to low-income creditors, high-income debtors, and the tax collector.

Other inflation transfers

In addition to financial assets, there is a wide variety of contracts and legal constraints that are stated in nominal terms and whose real values and costs are altered by inflation. Among these are taxes, fines, pensions, leases, alimony, and child support payments. In each case, inflation reduces both the burden on the payer and the benefit to the payee.

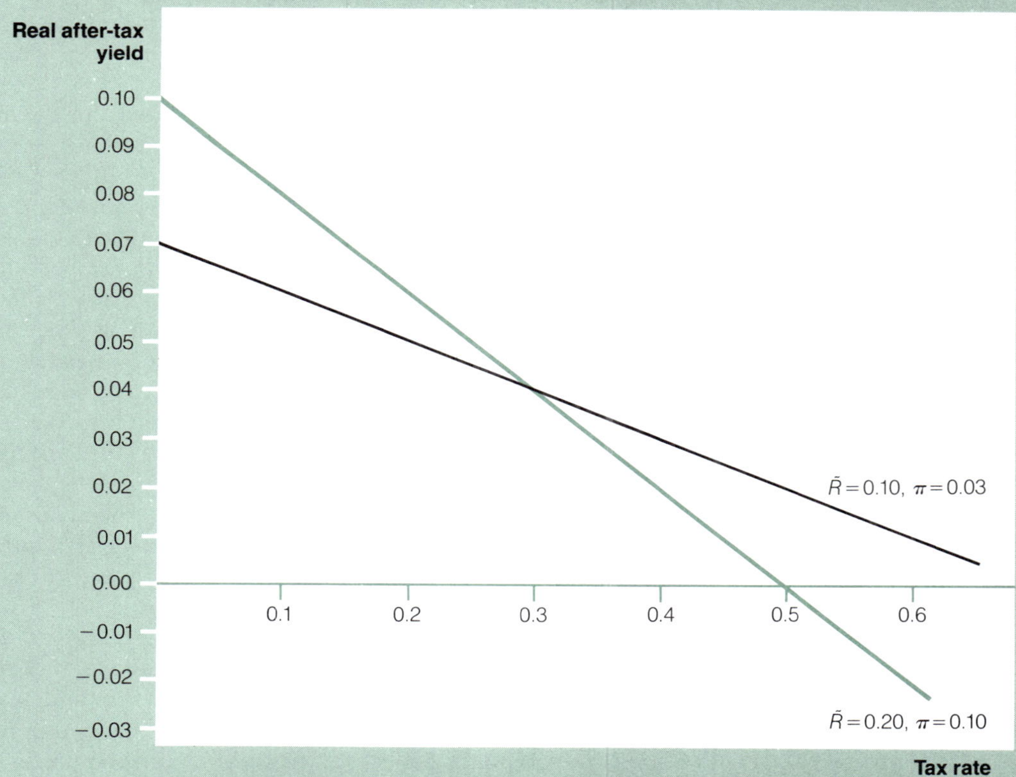

FIGURE 8.3 **People in higher tax brackets fare better with less inflation. In this comparison, people in a 30% tax bracket happen to have the same real after-tax return when the inflation rate is 3% and when it is 10%. Those in higher tax brackets are hurt financially by the inflation, while those in lower tax brackets benefit.**

Taxes are an important example. We have just seen the uneven effects of the fact that taxes are levied on nominal rather than real interest income. A general increase in prices and nominal income also pushes taxpayers into higher tax brackets ("bracket creep"), increasing their real tax burden. In addition, capital gains due to inflation are taxed even though there may have been no change in the real value of the assets. If you buy a piece of land for $100,000 (use your imagination) and all prices double, you will be no better or worse off. But if you sell the land at the doubled price—$200,000—you must pay a tax on the $100,000 nominal capital gain. Inflation transfers wealth from taxpayers to tax collectors (actually from taxpayers to those who benefit from the government programs that spend these tax dollars).

On the other hand, Social Security benefits automatically rise with the CPI, which (until 1983) included housing prices and mortgage interest rates. Social Security recipients who bought houses long ago profited from inflation in that their Social Security benefits went up faster than their expenses. To accurately stabilize their real income, Social Security payments should be linked to a special "Elderly Price Index," which would give relatively large weights to medical expenses and golf balls and small weights to house prices and mortgage rates.

Taxable corporate profits are typically overstated during inflationary periods, because "generally accepted accounting procedures" cause production costs to be understated. In profit calculations the cost of a machine that can be used for ten years is spread over the ten years. This annual depreciation expense is supposed to show how much capital is being used to produce output. In theory the firm should use the current value of its capital—that is, what it would cost to replace the machine. But, in practice, firms calculate their capital expenses each year on the basis of the original cost of plant and equipment, which is like figuring labor costs on the basis of wage rates ten or twenty years ago. The result is that inflation causes capital costs to be understated, profits to be overstated, and businesses with lots of old capital to pay relatively more taxes. To correct this inaccuracy, depreciation (or the cost basis of capital assets) should be indexed for—that is, linked to—price changes. A good index would use the prices of plant and equipment, rather than consumer prices. Accelerated depreciation is often intended to relieve this inflation tax burden, but such relief is rough and inexact since it is not directly tied to the rate of inflation.

Firms also overstate their profits during inflations if they use FIFO (*F*irst *I*n, *F*irst *O*ut) inventory accounting. Businesses keep an inventory of unsold items that, though identical, were produced at different times and at different costs. When one of these items is sold, which cost should be used in figuring profits? With the FIFO accounting method, the cost of the good produced earliest and still in inventory is used. Thus, during inflations, FIFO accounting understates current production costs and overstates profits. The U.S. government estimated that reported corporate profits would have been $50 billion lower in 1979 if all firms had been using LIFO (*L*ast *I*n, *F*irst *O*ut) accounting.

On the other hand, to the extent that firms borrow money, they, along with other high-income debtors, benefit from inflation. A fully indexed tax code would include these gains as income and would also index capital costs. The net effects of an indexed tax system on individual firms would depend on their debt and capital. John Shoven and Jeremy Bulow estimated that, with a full inflation adjustment for depreciation, inventories, and debt, General Motors' 1974 taxable income would have been only $410 million, rather than the reported $950 million. This is because General Motors has little debt. For American Telephone, which has lots of debt, they estimated that taxable income would have increased from $3.2 billion to $8.2 billion. Thus inflation with unindexed taxes hurt General Motors shareholders, but benefited American Telephone shareholders.

There is another factor in the calculation of who wins and who loses from inflation. According to the Phillips curve, rapid inflation is usually associated with low unemployment and high production. During most inflations, the economy as a whole has fewer idle resources and produces more goods and services. Those workers who find employment and those factories that are more fully utilized benefit the most from greater output and income. This increased employment and output are not really a benefit of inflation, *per se,* but they are an important accompaniment of inflation and they are not just a transfer between debtors and creditors.

Some conclusions

Clearly, the net effect of inflation on particular individuals is going to depend on a complex reckoning. Nevertheless, a few venturesome economists have tried to draw some general conclusions. One, Joseph Minarik, found that:

> At the very lowest incomes, households for the most part are better off or unaffected by inflation; . . . Middle income households are still mostly unaffected since the burden of rising income taxes is offset by home appreciation. The results for upper income households are totally different . . . greater real income taxes, lagging corporate retained earnings, and especially the depreciation of the face value of dollar-denominated interest-bearing securities [bonds] combine to make upper income households the big losers from inflation.[6]

Perhaps the most important cost of inflation is that, because it is often unexpected, it does capriciously create winners and losers. It is not that prices increase, but rather that they change (up or down) unexpectedly. Agreements that seemed satisfactory turn into bad deals, with the winners celebrating their foresight while the losers damn the price changes. These haphazard, indiscriminate wealth transfers undermine the social fabric, encouraging the belief that society is unfair. Instead of working and consuming, citizens turn their attention to speculation on the course of prices and to bitterness over bad guesses.

Keynes was well aware of this social cost of fluctuating prices. In the *General Theory,* he argued that the classical equilibrating mechanism of freely adjusting wages and prices was not only unrealistic but also undesirable. In the 1930s, it was deflation that worried Keynes. Years earlier, after World War I, he had warned against inflation for similar reasons:

> The sight of this arbitrary rearrangement of riches strikes not only at security, but at confidence in the equity of the existing distribution of wealth. Those to whom the system brings windfalls, beyond their deserts and even beyond their expectations or desires, become "profiteers," who are the object of the hatred of the bourgeoisie, whom the inflation has impoverished, not less than of the proletariat. As the inflation

proceeds and the real value of the currency fluctuates wildly from month to month, all permanent relations between debtors and creditors, which form the ultimate foundation of capitalism, become so utterly disordered as to be almost meaningless; and the process of wealth-getting degenerates into a gamble and a lottery.

Lenin was certainly right. There is no subtler, no surer means of overturning the existing basis of society than to debauch the currency. The process engages all the hidden forces of economic law on the side of destruction, and does it in a manner which not one man in a million is able to diagnose.[7]

On the other hand, it is sometimes argued that inflation is a socially useful way of lubricating painful adjustments and defusing economic conflicts. Economic dislocations, such as the energy shocks in the 1970s, may call for drastic changes in relative prices and real wages. If some wages and prices are inflexible downward, then these adjustments may be most easily accomplished by raising some prices rather than by reducing others. It could be argued that inflation provides a common scapegoat for absorbing wrath over these painful adjustments. Instead of lynching farmers and burning down oil companies, citizens blame inflation for their real income losses. In a democracy, competing interest groups pressure politicians to promise more than the economy can deliver. Inflation may be the easiest way of relieving these pressures—the least destructive way of disappointing advocates of these competing claims.

EASING INFLATION'S IMPACT

Many of the gains and losses from inflation arise from the fact that the terms of many contracts and laws are stated in dollars, the purchasing power of which varies. One way to offset these variations is to write contracts and laws in real terms or to index them to the rate of inflation. Instead of George owing Mary $105, the IOU could state that he owes her 21 bottles of wine. Alternatively, the agreement could state that he owes her $105, but that every 1% increase in the price of wine raises this debt by 1%, indexing the debt to the price of wine. In either case, she is protected against changes in the price of wine. If she cares for more than wine, men, and song, she could insist that the contract be indexed to the CPI.

Indexing

The persistent inflation in recent years has led to a great deal of indexing. The Congressional Budget Office reported in 1981 that

> almost a third of federal expenditures is directly linked to the CPI or related price measures, and over half of the federal budget is affected if indirectly linked expenditures are added. A one percent increase in the CPI will automatically trigger nearly $2 billion of additional federal expenditures, at 1981 program levels.[8]

These indexed programs range from Social Security benefits to military pay to food stamps to student loans to dairy price supports.

More than 50 million people in the United States have some or all of their income tied to the CPI. Social Security recipients are the most protected. Retired federal civilian and military personnel, postal workers, and several million

UNCONVENTIONAL THOUGHTS ABOUT HIGH REAL INTEREST RATES

At the beginning of 1983, most economists forecast a sub-par recovery because real interest rates were so high. For example, the January 10, 1983 issue of *Blue Chip Economic Indicators* reported that the consensus forecast of 45 top economists for 1983's real GNP growth was 4½%. Instead, real GNP rose 6.0%, only slightly below the 6.4% average gain during the first year of the previous six economic expansions. The economy continued to expand at a higher-than-expected rate during the first half of 1984. The recovery has been better than average, not sub-par.

Most of those economists who expected a weak recovery because of high real interest rates also forecast that real interest rates would trend lower. Some said this would happen as inflation increased. Others anticipated lower nominal interest rates. Instead, interest rates rose while inflation remained under 5% during 1983 and the first half of 1984.

Obviously, economists' forecasts have been wide of the mark lately, perhaps more so than usual. The recovery has been stronger than average; inflation has been lower than expected; and interest rates rose sooner and higher than most projections.

Economists have been confounded by the apparent paradoxes in the economy's behavior. In the past, interest rates and inflation moved very closely together. In the past, a strong business expansion was associated with rising inflationary pressures. Why haven't historically high real interest rates dampened economic growth?

Most economists have been trained to believe that the *nominal* interest rate is equal to the *real* interest rate plus an expected inflation premium. The real rate is largely determined by the productivity of real assets. For example, let's say you buy a widget machine that produces ten widgets a year. Alternatively, in equilibrium you should be able to put your money in a bond paying enough interest to buy ten widgets. To do so, the nominal interest rate on your bond must reflect the real rate of return of the widget machine plus an inflation premium, which reflects the expected price increase in widgets.

Economists frequently assume that real rates are fairly constant—that is, that the widget machine always produces ten widgets a year. So fluctuations in nominal rates should primarily reflect changes in inflationary expectations. Historically, there has been a very high correlation between nominal interest rates and inflation. Recently, the close relationship seems to have broken down. Since 1982, many economists have wondered: Why are interest rates so high when inflation is so low?

The key determinant of bond yields, at least in the short run, is the rates available on money market instruments. Most investors, particularly institutional money managers, don't choose between buying a bond and purchasing a widget machine—in other words, a three-month Treasury bill is a more likely substitute for a 30-year bond than is a widget machine.

Money-market rates are very closely tied to the discount rate set by the Federal Reserve. It follows, therefore, that the discount rate is a key determinant of the bond yield. The ratio of the government bond yield to the Fed's discount rate moves very closely with the Consumer Sentiment Index, which is compiled monthly by the Survey Research Center of the University of Michigan. This relationship suggests that the bond yield is equal to the discount rate—that is, the "underlying" interest rate set by policy, times a risk ratio that depends on the economy's position in the business cycle.

When consumers are optimistic, the economy is expanding, but bond investors, on the other hand, are worrying about rebounding credit demands and resurgent inflation. So bond yields tend to rise relative to the discount rate.

Our model of bond yields suggests that although recent interest rates seem unusually high relative to inflation, they are fairly priced relative to the discount rate at this point of the business cycle. That still leaves an unanswered question: Why is the discount rate so high relative to inflation?

The apparently close historical relationship between interest rates and inflation may be due in part to the fact that in setting the discount rate the Fed is influenced by inflation. Generally, the Fed responds to rising inflation by pushing up the discount rate. Even if the Fed doesn't respond immediately, the market often will anticipate that the Fed at some point down the road will have to respond to rising inflation by tightening monetary policy. Periods of declining inflation are usually coincident with recessions and early recoveries. The Fed typically lowers the discount rate during such times in order to stimulate economic growth.

Prior to 1979, the Fed's response to inflation was reactive rather than preventative. Under the interest rate targeting approach, the Fed tended to raise interest rates after inflation rose to a higher level. As a result, inflation had a definite upward bias because the Fed's response was more often than not too little too late. Of course, once market rates exceeded the maximum rate allowed on bank deposits, the economy would sink into recession, and inflation would abate temporarily as credit became harder to get for consumers, home buyers, and businesses.

Since 1979, the Fed has pursued a more monetarist approach that tries to anticipate inflationary pressures. This switch in policy approach suggests that interest rates could stay high relative to inflation for some time to come. Why are interest rates so high when inflation is so low? The question misses the point: Inflation is so low because interest rates are so high!

With deposit rate ceilings no longer in effect, the economy seems to be able to sustain a recovery at interest rate levels that seem quite high by historical standards. As long as the economy continues to grow and inflation stays down, the Fed can be satisfied that the current level of interest rates isn't too high.

Now let's turn to the issue of why the economy has performed so well in the face of such high real interest rates. Is it possible that the recovery is robust *because* of high real interest rates, rather than in spite of them? Sounds absurd, doesn't it? But let's think it through for a second. Many economists started out 1983 believing that the recovery would be sub-par. They figured that historically high real interest rates would take the bounce out of the rebound in economic activity. Instead, the recovery has been at least par, if not better than average. Did this happen in spite of high real interest rates? Maybe, but we'd like to hypothesize that perhaps the recovery was *boosted* by high real interest costs.

Here's our theory. Actually, it belongs to Irving Fisher (see *The Purchasing Power of Money,* Macmillan, New York, 1981). Fisher started with the simple idea of an accounting identity that whenever a transaction takes place between a buyer and a seller there is an exchange of money. It follows that the quantity of money in circulation (M) times the average number of times that money in circulation turns over per period—that is, the velocity of money (V)—must equal the nominal value of economic activity during the period, which, in turn, equals the price level (P) times real GNP (y): $MV = Py$

That's the heart of Irving Fisher's theory. It follows that, for a given percentage increase in money flow (MV), the lower inflation (the percentage change in P) the higher the real economic growth (the percentage change in y).

In other words, if the Fed increases the money supply by 8%, and velocity increases by 2%, then nominal GNP will increase by 10%. If inflation is 8%, real GNP will increase by 2%. If inflation drops to 5%, real GNP will increase by 5%. Every point decrease in inflation leaves room for a point increase in real GNP growth.

Let's get closer to the punch line. Economists thought that high real rates would depress real economic growth. Instead, it seems that high real rates pushed inflation down much faster and lower than generally expected. High real rates caused the dollar to soar in foreign exchange markets. The strong dollar has been a powerful disinflationary force. High real rates encouraged inventory liquidation, which also is disinflationary. High real rates discouraged inflationary speculation in real assets like land, houses, and commodities. The sharp drop in inflation left a lot of room for real economic growth once the Fed started to pump up the money supply late in 1982 in order to stimulate a recovery.

—Edward A. Yardeni

unionized workers have formal escalator clauses. Some rental agreements and alimony and child support contracts rise automatically with the CPI. In many of these cases, however, the dollar payments rise less than proportionately. For example, a 10% increase in the CPI might raise the dollar payment by 4%.

In Israel, time deposit accounts are fully linked to the Israeli cost-of-living index. If an investor deposits 1000 shekels and the price level doubles, he is credited with having a 2000-shekel account. Taxes are paid only on the interest in the account, not on the doubled principal. The Israeli government has also issued bonds whose value is indexed to the cost-of-living.

In Canada, income taxes have been indexed since 1974. As the Canadian CPI increases, personal exemptions, deductions, and tax brackets all increase proportionately. For example, in 1973 the basic personal exemption was 1600 Canadian dollars. In 1974, the Canadian CPI increased 6.6% and the personal exemption automatically rose 6.6%, to 1706 Canadian dollars. United States income tax tables are scheduled to be indexed beginning in 1985.

In Brazil the minimum wage level, union wages, and government bonds are all indexed, but to different government price schedules. These different indexes reflect a conscious redistribution of income, intended to favor capital accumulation and certain high-priority sectors of the economy.

Shoe leather costs

Even if all contracts in an economy were indexed, there would still be one asset that loses value in an inflation: money. Cash earns no interest, nor did checking accounts from 1933 until 1980. When prices measured in dollars are rising rapidly, the one thing you don't want to be hoarding is dollars. You don't want to keep cash tucked under the mattress, buried in the backyard, or sitting idly in a bank. You, instead, want to hold financial or real assets that are appreciating in value. You can convert these assets back into cash when you want to buy something, and you had best buy it quickly before its price goes up.

In the 1922–23 German hyperinflation, workers were paid several times a day. Their children would bike to the factory gates to collect these wages and then pedal furiously back to town to spend the money as quickly as possible. When the United States experienced double-digit inflation and double-digit interest rates, many people spent many hours trying to minimize the length of time they were caught holding idle cash, either at home, at their businesses, or in their checking accounts. They made daily trips to banks, shuffling funds back and forth. Businesses put billions of dollars into overnight and even hourly loans.

This hectic cash management is one consequence of inflation that is not just a transfer, but a social cost. Citizens devote precious time and energy to economizing on their cash holdings. They rush to buy commodities before prices go up. Any extra funds are invested temporarily in interest-earning assets, and then withdrawn when needed for buying goods and services. This scurrying about consumes time, energy, and shoe leather and, so, is known as a *shoe leather cost* of inflation.

Milton Friedman has tried to estimate the private loss from economizing on money holdings during inflations.[9] In Friedman's classical model, inflation results from the government printing money to finance its expenditures. We should really compare Friedman's inflation cost with the costs (including both collection expenses and distortion losses) of the alternatives—either selling bonds or raising taxes to pay for government spending.[10] In any case, Friedman's estimates are pretty small. This is consistent with the view of most economists that shoe leather costs during moderate inflations can hardly be large enough to merit newspaper headlines and political upheaval. Tobin put it this way:

> According to economic theory, the ultimate social cost of anticipated inflation is the wasteful use of resources to economize holdings of currency and other noninterest-bearing means of payments. I suspect that intelligent laymen would be utterly astounded if they realized that this is the great evil economists are talking about. They have imagined a much more devastating cataclysm, with Vesuvius vengefully punishing the sinners below. Extra trips between savings banks and commercial banks? What an anti-climax![11]

One way of reducing shoe leather costs during inflation is to pay interest on money. Many transactions are, in fact, paid for by check and the payment of interest on transaction accounts (since 1980) has reduced the shoe leather costs of inflation. People no longer have to make extra trips between savings accounts, which pay interest, and checking accounts, which do not. That still leaves cash, though, which pays no interest.

Early moneys sometimes did pay interest—in the form of a small premium when the money was converted to precious metal after a certain date. The same could be done today; dollar bills could be dated and interest paid periodically, perhaps through the Post Office. In the 1930s there was the reverse problem: Money was being hoarded because prices were declining and loans seemed unattractive. To put this idle cash into circulation it was proposed that interest be charged on money. This could be done by requiring the periodic purchase of stamps, which, pasted on the money, would keep it legal tender.

MACROECONOMIC EFFECTS OF INFLATION

There are macro as well as micro consequences of the money avoidance caused by inflation. For any given nominal interest rate, an increase in the expected rate of inflation makes financial assets less attractive and physical assets more so. Increased expenditures on physical assets raise aggregate demand and prices, too. It follows, then, that an increase in inflation expectations can be a self-fulfilling prophecy. Since this macro effect sounds potentially unstable, it is worth a closer look, using our macro model.

Inflation in the *IS-LM* model

The demand for money is inversely related to the nominal, after-tax rate of return, R, on securities. Since the nominal rate of return on money is zero, the after-tax difference between the yield on securities and the yield on money is R. An increase in R makes money less attractive relative to alternative assets.

Expenditures on physical assets depend on the after-tax real interest rate, r, which is the after-tax nominal interest rate less the rate of inflation. Consumers look at after-tax real interest rates since these measure how many future commodities can be gained by consuming less and saving more now. High real interest rates make saving more rewarding, since more future consumption can be obtained for less present consumption.* Investment decisions also hinge on after-tax real interest rates. Firms compare the real rates of return on physical capital with the real yields on securities. For businesses that must borrow to finance expansion, the after-tax real return that must be paid on their loans is of obvious importance. Interest rates are also important to nonborrowers who must choose between acquiring financial or physical assets. When securities offer high yields, financial assets are more attractive and physical assets less so.

Thus we can write our *IS-LM* equations as

$$(IS) \qquad e_0 + e_y y + e_r(R - \pi^e) = y \qquad 0 < e_y < 1,\ e_r < 0$$

$$(LM) \qquad l_0 + l_y y + l_R R = M/P \qquad l_y > 0,\ l_R < 0.$$

The *LM* equation is unchanged. The *IS* equation says that it is the real interest rate that matters to spending decisions.

For any given nominal yield on securities, an increase in the expected rate of inflation, π^e, reduces the real interest rate, increasing expenditures on real assets. Increased expenditures shift the *IS* curve rightward (Figure 8.4). In fact, the vertical shift of the *IS* curve is just equal to the change in inflation expectations. For a given y (for example, comparing Points 1 and 2 in the figure), an increase in π^e that is offset by an equal decrease in R will leave the real interest rate constant and expenditures unchanged. Therefore, the *IS* curve shifts vertically upward by the amount that π^e increases.

This spending stimulus increases aggregate demand (Figure 8.5), putting upward pressure on output and the price level. The higher price level pushes the *LM* curve leftward (Figure 8.4), until it intersects the *IS* curve at a point like Point 3, where P and y are both higher. As long as output goes up, the increase in the nominal interest rate is less than the initial vertical shift of the *LM* curve. Thus the nominal interest rate does not increase by as much as inflation expectations, and the real interest rate declines.† Overall, **an increase in inflation expectations increases nominal interest rates while reducing real interest rates. Lower real interest rates stimulate spending so that output, employment, and prices all increase.**

The classical, full-employment model comes to a different conclusion, as shown in Figure 8.6. If output is fixed at the full-employment level, then an increase in inflation expectations must cause the *LM* curve to shift all the way back to where the *IS* and *LM* curves intersect at the initial level of output. The increase in the nominal interest rate is equal to the vertical shift of the *IS* curve, which is equal to the increase in inflation expectations. Thus the real interest

* Actually, there are both substitution and income effects at work here. High real rates make saving more rewarding, but they also make it unnecessary to save so much. It is theoretically inconclusive whether saving will, on balance, go up or down. We will return to this theoretical ambiguity in Chapter 12.

† These results are for after-tax returns, which, in theory, are what matter to people. Before-tax returns may behave somewhat differently. For example, inflation might increase by 4% while a nominal interest rate increased by 5%. Although in such a case the before-tax interest rate increased by more than inflation, for the average investor in, say, a 30% tax bracket, the after-tax nominal return, R, is up only 3.5% and the after-tax real return, r, is down 0.5%. In practice, both before-tax and after-tax real returns tend to fall during inflations.[12]

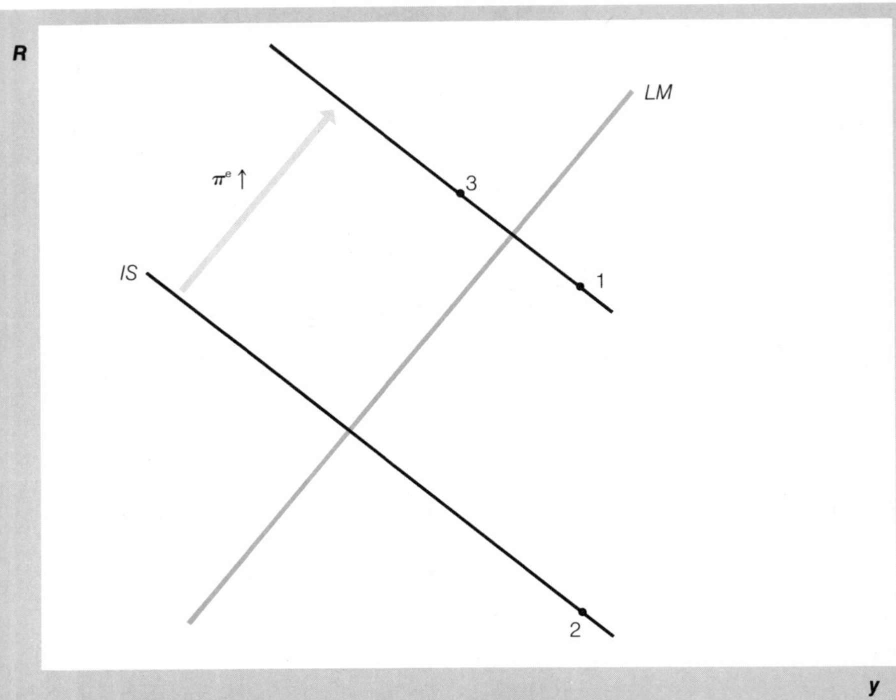

FIGURE 8.4 THE MACRO EFFECTS OF AN INCREASE IN INFLATION EXPECTATIONS. Increased expectations shift the *IS* curve rightward. The distance between Points 1 and 2 is equal to the increase in π^e, since $\Delta R = \Delta \pi^e$ implies that r is constant, and so is spending at any level of income.

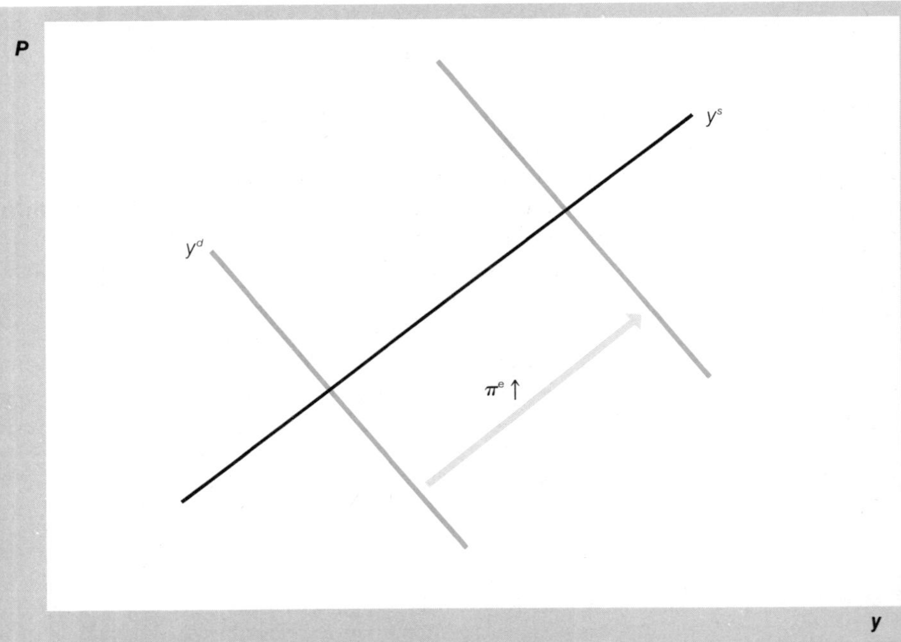

FIGURE 8.5 An increase in inflation expectations shifts the aggregate demand curve rightward.

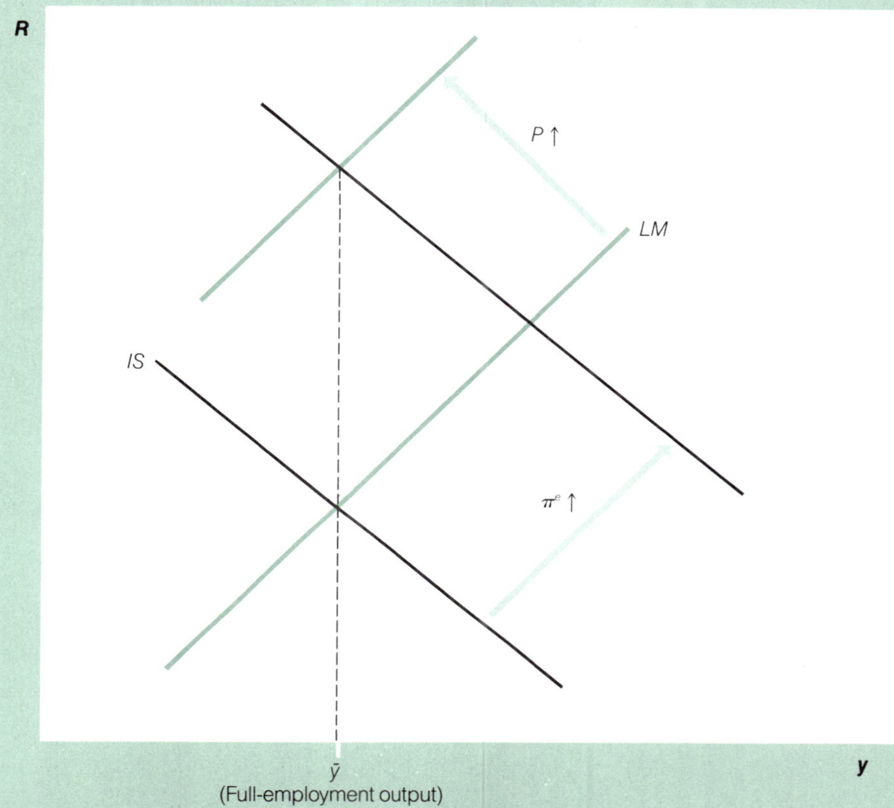

FIGURE 8.6 **In a full-employment model, inflation expectations affect only the price level and nominal interest rates. An increase in inflation expectations shifts the *IS* curve rightward; but the price level must increase sufficiently (shifting *LM* leftward) to bring the *IS-LM* intersection back to the full-employment level of income. Since the increase in the nominal interest rate is equal to the increase in inflation expectations (the vertical shift of the *IS* curve), the real interest rate is constant too.**

rate is unchanged.* **In the classical full-employment model, the nominal rate of interest increases by the amount of the increase in inflation expectations. Inflation expectations do not affect output, employment, or real interest rates.**

Money and interest rates

These results also allow us to distinguish the effects of monetary policy on nominal and real interest rates. In Chapter 5 we saw that an increase in the money supply raises output and prices, while lowering interest rates. Yet, some

* Again these are after-tax returns. For the after-tax nominal interest rate to increase by the inflation rate, the before-tax return must increase by more than inflation.

observers believe that an increase in the money supply actually raises interest rates! Inflation expectations provide an answer to this puzzle.

Figure 8.7 shows the general case. An increase in the money supply shifts the *LM* curve rightward, to an intersection at Point 1. If inflation expectations increase, then the accompanying drop in anticipated real interest rates increases spending, shifting the *IS* curve rightward to an *IS-LM* intersection at Point 2. The increase in inflation expectations reinforces the expansionary monetary policy. If the aggregate supply curve is not vertical, then output and prices both increase. The price increase shifts the *LM* curve back to a place such as Point 3. Output, employment and prices are all higher. The real interest rate has fallen. We cannot be certain whether the nominal interest rate goes up or down. It depends on whether the drop in the real interest rate is smaller or larger than the increase in inflation expectations. Therefore, **if an increase in the money**

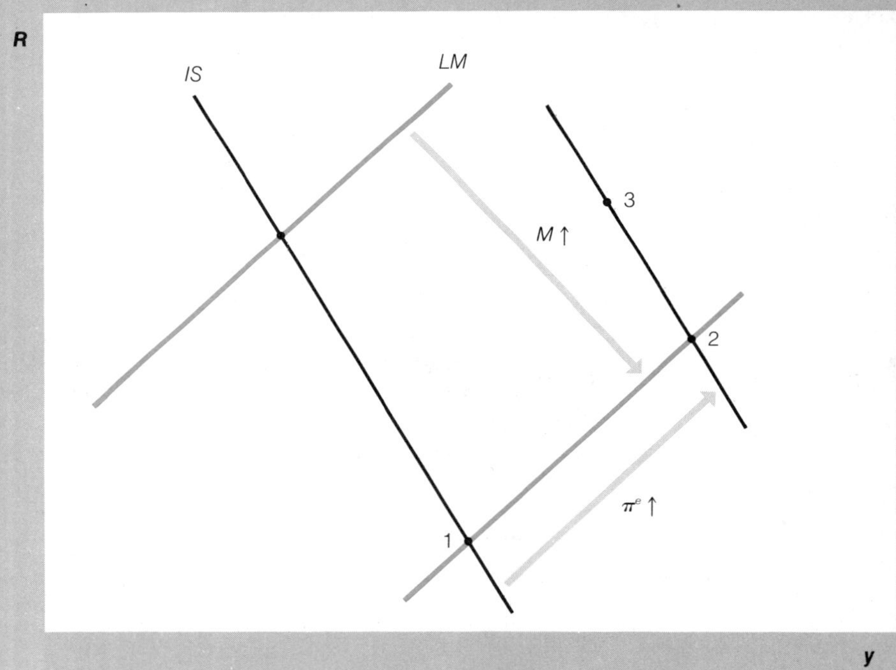

FIGURE 8.7 INFLATION EXPECTATIONS MAKE MONETARY POLICY MORE POWERFUL. **An increase in the money supply shifts the *LM* curve rightward, yielding a lower interest rate and higher income (Point 1). To the extent that inflation expectations increase, the real interest rate falls further still, though the nominal interest rate may actually increase. (Point 2 shows the *IS-LM* intersection when increased inflation expectations are introduced; Point 3 takes into account the resulting increase in actual prices.)**

WHY INTEREST RATES DON'T FOLLOW INFLATION DOWN

Theories die hard in economics. But one widely held view about what determines the level of interest rates appears to have been dealt a death blow. As prices have decelerated over the past year, the true cost of money after adjusting for inflation has been rising steadily and has reached almost 10%, the highest real rate in U.S. history. Interest rates are caught in an inescapable trap. . . . To the dismay of Administration economists—especially the monetarists who are wielding the power these days—all this simply should never have happened. By their system, disinflation should translate almost immediately into lower interest rates.

Back in June, 1981, when rates did not decline much in response to an obvious moderation of inflation, Treasury Under Secretary for Monetary Affairs Beryl W. Sprinkel was steadfastly maintaining that the prime would be 10% to 13% by yearend. His views were echoed by most forecasters and corporate economists. The prime now stands at 16½%, while the drop in inflation has exceeded Sprinkel's wildest dreams—indeed, the dreams of most economists.

The idea that inflation and interest rates are inexorably linked harks back to the theoretical work done at the turn of the century by America's greatest monetary economist, Irving Fisher (1867–1947). With seemingly impeccable logic, Fisher argued that the interest rate consists of two components—a real rate and a premium for expected inflation. The real rate reflects such longer-run factors as the productivity of capital and the saving habits of the public. The more productive the nation's capital stock, the more companies will demand funds to invest and thus bid up the price of money. On the other hand, if people save more of their income, more money will be available for lending, and rates will decline.

These fundamental factors change only slowly, however, so real rates move hardly at all, Fisher argued. What really makes rates bounce, he said, is inflationary expectations. As inflation speeds up, lenders refuse to accept current rates because they expect to be paid back in cheaper dollars. Instead, they automatically add in an inflation premium. As Fisher saw it, a 1% increase in expected inflation would push up rates by an equal 1%, and vice versa.

Monetarists have embraced Fisher with a passion. According to his analysis, the Federal Reserve could not affect the real rate of interest at all and could have only a minuscule, short-run influence on market rates. If the Fed pumped in money in an attempt to lower rates, investors would quickly raise their inflation projections and demand higher rates for their money, thus offsetting the Fed's actions. Like it or not, the monetary authorities could affect only inflation, which would then be translated back into interest rates via the inflation premium. Little wonder that monetarists—Fisher's intellectual descendants—maintain that the Fed should focus only on controlling money and not on interest rates.

As neat as Fisher's ideas sound in theory, though, they do not work in the real world. The critical notion that the public will refrain from lending at current rates if it believes inflation is accelerating assumes that people have attractive alternatives, and that is far from the usual case. Before the rate ceiling was liberalized on some savings accounts in 1978, for example, small investors through most of the last decade were, in effect, forced to accept interest rates of 5%, even though inflation was running at twice that figure. And there are still major restrictions on passbook accounts.

More important, Fisher assumed that stock prices marched arm in arm with inflation because higher prices meant higher company profits. So, in his theory, buying common stock in an inflationary period was another viable alternative to lending money. But, in actuality, inflation can clobber stock prices, as investors have learned to their woe over the past 10 years. These two factors may explain why inflation-adjusted interest rates in the 1970s averaged less than 1%, compared with a 3% adjusted rate in the 1960s.

In fact, the relationship between inflation and interest rates has always been a tenuous one. Lawrence H. Summers of the Massachusetts Institute of Technology, in a new study for the National Bureau of Economic Research, finds that the data from 1860 to 1940 show "no tendency for interest rates to increase with movements in expected inflation." And for most of the postwar period, he demonstrates, the relationship is "statistically insignificant.

Indeed, according to Summers, Fisher himself had doubts about how well his theory worked. In hundreds of the empirical equations that Fisher constructed relating interest rates to inflation, says Summers, the largest effect he found was a 1-to-5 relationship: A five-percentage-point decline in inflation lowered rates by only one percentage point.

Part of the answer to the surge in real rates may be due to a factor to which Fisher justifiably, at least for his day, gave short shrift—fiscal policy. "Just as changes in the productivity of capital add to the demand for funds, an increase in the federal deficit increases the government's demand for funds and raises the real rate of interest," says Thomas J. Sargent of the University of Minnesota, a pioneer in the analysis of how expectations affect economic behavior.

Given the growing government demands for funds, Sargent argues that tight monetary policy is forcing up real interest rates. Although the money supply has increased 5% over the past year, Sargent maintains that because of the changes that have taken place in banking and the growth of money market funds, one should look at what is happening to interest rates in gauging the tightness of monetary policy. "Fisher was wrong. Real interest rates are high because monetary policy is tight," says Neil Wallace, also of the University of Minnesota and a leading thinker on expectations.

If Fisher is wrong—and the evidence certainly points that way—then those who are expecting a quick downturn in rates as inflation continues to unwind will be sadly disappointed. It may well be that the only way for real rates to decline substantially is for the Fed to pump out more money while the Administration brings the deficit under control. (Seymour Zucker, *Business Week,* June 21, 1982 . Reprinted from June 21, 1982 issue of *Business Week* by special permission, © 1982 by McGraw-Hill Inc.)

supply increases inflation expectations (reducing real yields), then the resultant stimulus to spending reinforces the expansionary effects of the increase in the money supply. Prices increase; nominal interest rates may increase; real interest rates decline; and real output increases.

The conclusion is different if there is full employment. In Chapter 5 we saw that, in the classical model, an open-market purchase raises prices with no effect on output or interest rates. In the previous section of this chapter, we noted that, in the classical model, any increase in inflation expectations caused by the open-market purchase raises nominal interest rates but does not change real interest rates or output. Therefore, **in a classical, full-employment model, the monetary authorities can alter the price level, the rate of inflation, and nominal interest rates, but cannot affect real output and real interest rates. Attempts to reduce real interest rates by increasing the money supply are futile: Inflation increases; nominal interest rates increase (instead of decrease); and real interest rates are unchanged.**

Money neutrality and superneutrality

There are really two separate classical propositions here since the price level and the rate of inflation are separate data. The first proposition, *money neutrality,* is that a one-time increase in the money supply will raise the price level proportionately, with no real effects on the economy. The second proposition, *money superneutrality,* is that a continuing increase in the money supply will cause a sustained inflation, with no real effects on economic activity. Neither of these classical propositions holds if there is less than full employment. And it is not certain that they would hold even in a long-run full-employment equilibrium.

One big fly in the long-run neutrality soup is that money is not the only financial asset, and we do not know how or why all nominal assets would increase proportionately to the money supply. If relative asset supplies do change, there are likely to be real effects on interest rates and the economy.

James Tobin has pointed out that money could be neutral in the long run, but not superneutral. His basic argument is that, since cash has a fixed nominal rate (zero), which cannot rise with inflation, any anticipated inflation will encourage people to hold less cash and more of other assets, financial and real, whose nominal returns do increase during inflations. People who are trying to avoid holding cash during inflations will accept reduced real rates of return on alternative assets. Thus the inevitable decline in the real yield on cash during inflations causes a similar decline in the real yields on all substitute assets. Diminished real interest rates have real effects on the economy, encouraging investment spending and capital accumulation. This argument is so closely associated with Tobin that it is called the *Tobin effect.*

We have already seen some evidence of the Tobin effect in the decline of real yields on three-month Treasury bills during the inflationary 1970s (Figure 8.1). Figure 8.8 rearranges these data in a scatter diagram to show that there has been an inverse correlation between inflation and real Treasury bill yields. A study of nearly 200 years of U.S. data on interest rates, during both inflations and deflations, came to the same conclusion.[12] As shown in Figure 8.9, nominal interest rates tend to rise somewhat during inflation (but not as much as infla-

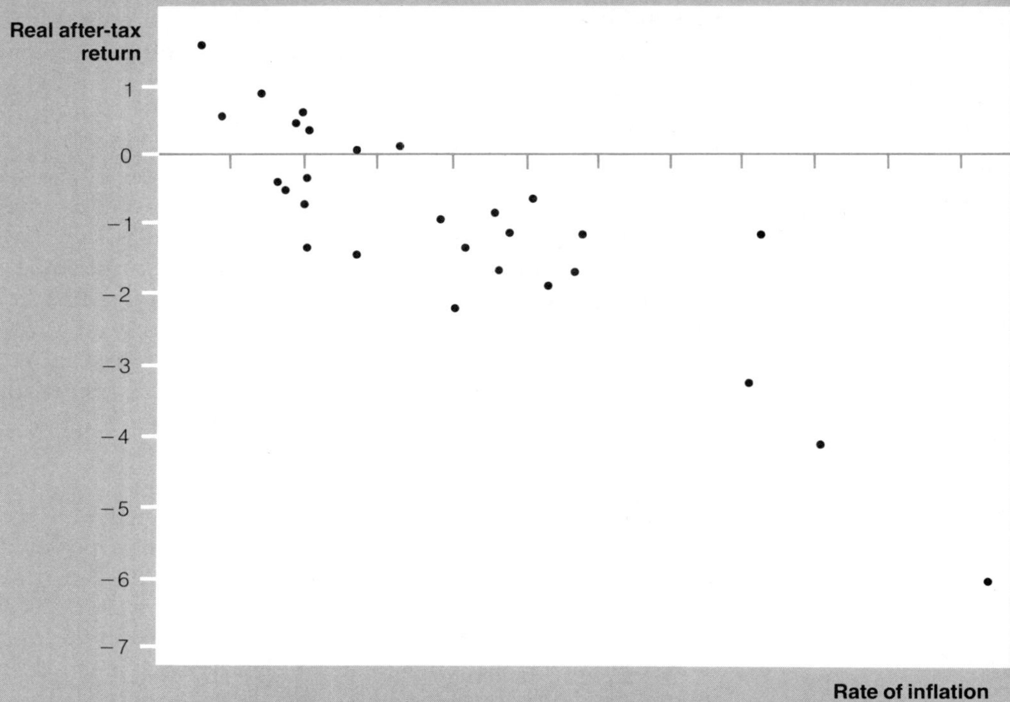

FIGURE 8.8 INFLATION AND REAL TREASURY BILL YIELDS, 1952–81. Although many factors influence real interest rates, there has been a general inverse relationship between real interest rates and inflation: When inflation is high, real interest rates tend to be low.

tion increases) and to rise during deflations, too! Real interest rates fall during inflation (when money is unattractive) and rise during deflations (when money is attractive).

An example of the latter occurred during the Great Depression. Remember that, in the classical cure for a slump, lower prices should raise aggregate demand (via the Keynes effect). On the other hand, an anticipated deflation raises real interest rates, encouraging people to hoard cash and postpone spending. With a 1.5% interest rate for prime business loans, the 2% deflation in 1933, as modest as it was, raised the real interest rate on prime loans to a discouraging 3.5%. No matter what the tax bracket, a 2% deflation gives investors a real after-tax return on cash of 2%. Figure 8.1 shows that a 2% real after-tax return is pretty high by historical standards. A faster deflation in the 1930s would have made real rates even higher and discouraged spending even more. With a 10% deflation, for instance, real interest rates on financial assets must be at least a staggering 10%, since nominal interest rates cannot be negative as long as cash has a zero nominal return.

Hyperinflation

Another interesting moral (implicit in Figures 8.4 and 8.5) is that an increase in inflation expectations raises aggregate demand, the opposite of the effects of an increase in the price level, which reduces aggregate demand by reducing the real money supply (the Keynes effect). This is an example of why it is important to distinguish between the price level and the rate of inflation.

In addition, this inflation-expectations effect suggests that there is the potential for an unstable inflationary spiral. As in Figure 8.5, an increase in infla-

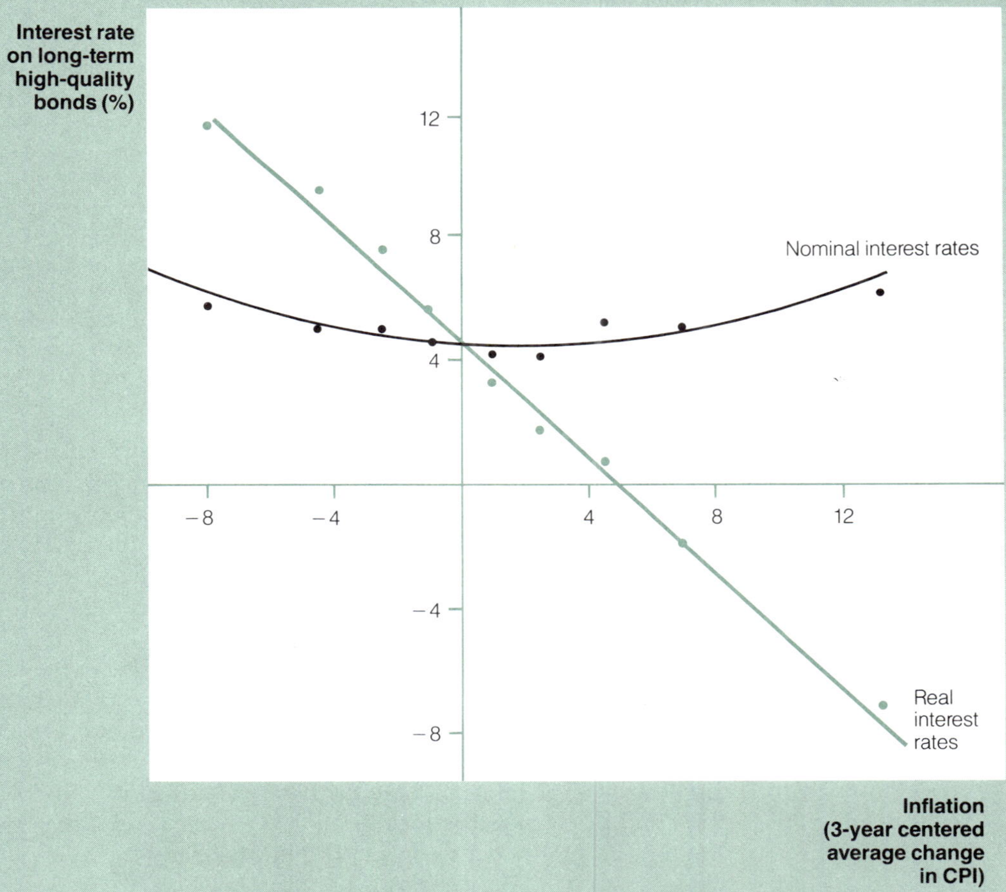

FIGURE 8.9 NOMINAL AND REAL INTEREST RATES, 1791–1979, GROUPED BY RATE OF INFLATION. **Nominal interest rates do not rise and fall, point for point with inflation, so as to keep real interest rates constant; instead real interest rates tend to fall during inflations and rise during deflations. Source: Steven C. Leuthold, "Interest Rates, Inflation, and Deflation,"** ***Financial Analysts Journal,*** **January-February, 1981, 28–41.**

tion expectations puts upward pressure on prices. If prices do increase rapidly, inflation expectations rise further, forcing additional price increases. This chase could degenerate into a vicious self-fulfilling cycle.* Is hyperinflation around the corner? In the past, hyperinflations have been rare but very destructive, destroying confidence in government and wasting the energy (and shoe leather) of citizens trying to avoid holding money. For example, after World War I the victorious Allies demanded stiff reparation payments from Germany. In January 1923, French and Belgian troops, on the claim that Germany was behind in its payments, occupied the Ruhr district. The German government called a general strike and printed hundreds of billions of marks to pay the strikers. Jonas Prager tells what happened:

> Between May and June 1923, consumer prices more than quadrupled; between July and August, they rose more than 15 times; in the next month over 15 times; and between September and October, by ten times the previous month's increase.
>
> The German economy was thoroughly disrupted. Businessmen soon discovered the impossibility of rational economic planning. Profits fell as employees demanded frequent wage adjustments. Workers were often paid daily and sometimes two or three times a day, so that they could buy goods in the morning before the inevitable afternoon price increase. The work ethic suffered; wage earners were both more reluctant to work and less devoted to their jobs. Bankers were on the phone hour after hour, quoting the value of the mark in dollars, as calls continuously came in from merchants who needed the exchange rate to adjust their mark prices.
>
> In an age that preceded the credit card, businessmen traveling around the country found themselves borrowing funds from their customers each stage of the way. The cash they'd allocated for the entire trip barely sufficed to pay the way to the next stop. Speculation began to dominate production.[13]

In late 1923, the hyperinflation was ended with dramatic suddenness. The old currency, reichsmarks, was replaced by rentenmarks. One rentenmark was worth 1,000 billion reichsmarks. The government announced that rentenmarks were sound money, backed by first mortgages on the land and other physical assets of the Reich. This was a meaningless public-relations ploy; what was important was that reparations, strike payments, and business loans ended, and the government printing presses stopped.

To foreign observers, the German hyperinflation was a great source of amusing anecdotes. The *New York Times* told of an American in a Berlin restaurant who asked for all the dinner that a dollar bill would buy. He received a satisfying meal, but, as he was about to leave, the waiter appeared with another soup and entree, explaining, "The dollar has gone up again."[14] Others told of buying beer and receiving more for returning the empty bottle than they had paid for it full. The Associated Press sent out this report:

> "Zero stroke" or "cipher stroke" is the name created by German physicians for a prevalent nervous malady brought about by the present fantastic currency figures. Scores of cases of the "stroke" are reported among men and women of all classes, who have been prostrated by their efforts to figure in thousands of billions. Many of these persons apparently are normal, except for a desire to write endless rows of ciphers.[15]

* The 1922–23 German hyperinflation is the best known, though the 1945–46 Hungarian experience was far worse. Prices increased in Germany at a compounded rate of 322 percent per month, and in Hungary at 19,800 percent per month. At one point Hungary issued a 100,000,000,000,000,000,000-pengo note, which bought less than one U.S. penny.

More seriously, a generation of eminent German and Austrian economists were permanently scarred by these hyperinflations. Even after emigration to America, they retained a lifelong distrust of government and a commitment to sound money.

Hyperinflations are very different from ordinary run-of-the-mill inflations in that they require enormous increases in the money supply. Recall the simple Quantity theory equation, $Mv = Py$. Realistically, if the money supply is steady, output cannot drop nor velocity rise fast enough to support a hyperinflation. In practice, hyperinflations have been fueled by large government deficits that were financed by printing enormous quantities of money.

Reviewing the historical episodes, Tibor and Anne Scitovsky conclude that:

> There is ample information now on many inflations in many countries; and it shows that such flights from cash have occurred and created the self-reinforcing tendencies that render inflation unstable and uncontrollable. This, however, has occurred only in rare cases. . . . The surprising—and comforting—aspect of the empirical evidence is that so many inflations have occurred and continued for a decade or more . . . in countries at varying stages of development and with populations of very different degrees of economic sophistication; and that these inflations, although often proceeding at an average annual rate of 15% or more for over a decade, and occasionally rising to a 60 or even 100% annual price rise for a year or two, should *not* have led to a flight from cash.[16]

IMPORTANT TERMS AND CONCEPTS

bracket creep
indexing
shoe leather costs
money neutrality
superneutrality
Tobin effect

Higher prices reduce the real value of cash and nominally denominated obligations, transferring wealth from creditors to debtors. Anticipated inflation tends to increase nominal interest rates, but not necessarily by the full amount of the inflation. Macroanalysis tells us that nominal after-tax interest rates will generally rise by less than the anticipated rate of inflation.

Inflation expectations reinforce the real effects of monetary policies. Increasing the rate of growth of the money supply increases prices, reduces real interest rates, and increases output. Nominal interest rates may go up or down.

In a classical full-employment model, one-time increases in the money supply just raise the price level proportionately ("money neutrality"). In addition, inflation expectations simply raise nominal interest rates without affecting real rates. Thus an increase in the rate of growth of the money supply increases the rate of inflation and nominal interest rates without affecting real interest rates and output ("superneutrality").

EXERCISES

1. Consider the following scenario. You invest $10,000 in some asset such as gold or vacant land, which yields no income but whose price goes up as fast as consumer prices. Assume that you pay a 20% tax on your capital gains (the price appreciation). What is your after-tax real return if prices go up 10%? If prices go up 20%?

Now assume that consumer prices and the price of your asset go up unequally. If consumer prices increase by 10%, how much does the price of your asset have to increase to give you a zero after-tax real return?

2. A bond sold for $100 promises to pay, after one year, $105 plus $100 times the percentage increase in the CPI. What are the anticipated nominal and real (before-tax) returns on this bond?

3. You are an investor in a 30% tax bracket, so that a 10% before-tax nominal interest rate is a 7% nominal return after taxes. If the before-tax interest rate is 10% and the inflation rate is 2%, what is your real after-tax return? What happens to your real after-tax return if the rate of inflation increases from 2% to 12% while the nominal interest rate increases from 10% to 20%? How much would the nominal interest rate have to increase in order to hold the real after-tax return constant? What tax code change would keep real after-tax returns constant whenever inflation and nominal interest rates increase equally?

4. It is sometimes said that nominal interest rates adjust for inflation so as to hold real rates constant at, say, 3%. If there were a 5% deflation anticipated, what would have to happen to nominal rates to keep real rates at 3%?

5. In 1980, the 3-month Treasury bill rate dropped to 7%, while almost everyone was forecasting about 11% inflation. In 1983, the 3-month Treasury bill rate was 9%, while everyone forecast about 5% inflation. In both cases the inflation forecasts turned out to be accurate. What were the real rates of return in each of these cases? Could the differences in these realized real yields plausibly be explained by unanticipated inflation?

6. Explain Keynes's conclusion:

> . . . this progressive deterioration in the value of money through history is not an accident, and has behind it two great driving forces—the impecuniosity of Governments and the superior political influence of the debtor class. (John Maynard Keynes, *Monetary Reform,* New York: Harcourt, Brace and Company, 1924, p. 12.)

7. Why are nominal interest rates on bonds always positive, no matter what the rate of inflation or deflation?

8. Explain why you agree or disagree with the contention that, "The *ex ante* real interest rate is always positive . . . People will never willingly save, lend, or invest if the expected return is negative." (G. J. Santoni and Courtenay C. Stone, "Navigating Through the Interest Rate Morass: Some Basic Principles," Federal Reserve Bank of St. Louis *Review,* March 1981, p. 18.)

9. Use macro theory to explain the following comment:

> . . . apprehension about inflation nearly wrecked the bond markets earlier this year. (Peter B. Roche and Tom Herman, *Wall Street Journal,* July 18, 1980)

10. It has been argued that most of the dramatic increase in nominal interest rates in the late 1970s reflected an increase in the expected rate of inflation, rather than an increase in real rates of return. How do changes in inflation expectations get translated into changes in interest rates?

11. Between August 1945 and July 1946, the number of Hungarian pengos (their currency) in circulation increased by a factor of 12,000,000,000,000,000,000,000,000, while the price level increased by a factor of 4,000,000,000,000,000,000,000,000,000. Did the real money supply increase or decrease? Why?

12. Increases in the money supply by the Fed will reduce interest rates while raising output, employment, and prices. Would increases in inflation expectations offset or reinforce the Fed's policy action?

13. Give a logical macroeconomic answer to the following:

> The notion is that expanding the money supply would spark a boom by lowering interest rates. This is perhaps the weakest link in the whole Keynesian universe; if expanding money lowers interest rates, how come we have recently experienced both record money growth and record interest rates? *(Wall Street Journal,* September 3, 1974)

14. In 1983, the Fed's tight money policies reduced inflation expectations dramatically. In the *IS-LM* model, spending depends on the real interest rate, r, while money demand depends on the nominal interest rate, R. Holding the price level constant, so that we can examine shifts in the aggregate demand curve, what are the effects on y, r, and R of a decrease in inflation expectations when the monetary authorities:
   a. peg M.
   b. peg r.
   c. peg R.
   d. peg y.

15. Critically evaluate the following quotation:

> The impending huge federal deficit poses a dilemma for the Federal Reserve. If the Fed decides that the deficit must be financed by the public, interest rates will rise and private investment will be crowded out. On the other hand, if the Fed monetizes the deficit by purchasing Treasury securities, it will be fueling the fires of inflation. The only way out of this dilemma is for Congress to recognize the simple lesson that there is no free lunch.

REFERENCES

1. J. M. Keynes, *Economic Consequences of The Peace,* New York: Harcourt, Brace and Howe, 1920, p. 235.

2. D. Markley, "Inflation: Politics or Economics?," *Ink* (1979), p. 143.

3. Madame de Stael, *Ten Years of Exile,* New York: Saturday Review Press, 1972, p. 143.

4. For some formal evidence of how different prices matter to different households, see R. Michael, "Variations Across Households in the Rate of Inflation," *Journal of Money, Credit, and Banking* (February 1979), pp. 32–46; and R. P. Hagemann, *Inflation and Household Characteristics: An Analysis of Group Specific Price Indexes,* U.S. Department of Labor, Bureau of Labor Statistics, Working Paper No. 110 (December 1980).

5. David Ricardo, *The Works and Correspondence of David Ricardo,* Volume III, P. Sraffa, ed., Cambridge: Cambridge University Press, 1951, pp. 136–37.

6. J. Minarik, "Who Wins, Who Loses From Inflation?," *Brookings Bulletin* (Summer 1978), p. 8.

7. J. M, Keynes, *Economic Consequences of the Peace,* New York: Harcourt, Brace and Howe, 1920, pp. 235–36.

8. Congressional Budget Office, *Indexing with the Consumer Price Index: Problems and Alternatives,* Washington, D.C., U.S. Government Printing Office, June 1981.

9. M. Friedman, "The Optimum Quantity of Money," in *The Optimum Quantity of Money and Other Essays,* Chicago: Aldine, 1969.

10. A more fundamental critique is F. H. Hahn, "Professor Friedman's Views on Money," *Economica,* 38 (February 1971).

11. J. Tobin, "Inflation and Unemployment," *American Economic Review* (1972), p. 15. But see M. S. Feldstein, "The Welfare Cost of Permanent Inflation and Optimal Short-Run Economic Policy," *Journal of Political Economy* (1979), pp. 749–68. For a list of inflation costs, see S. Fischer and F. Modigliani, "Towards an Understanding of the Real Effects and Costs of Inflation," *Weltwirtschaftliches Archiv,* 1978, pp. 810–33.

12. S. C. Leuthold, "Interest Rates, Inflation and Deflation," *Financial Analysts Journal,* January-February 1981, pp. 28–41.

13. *Wall Street Journal,* May 12, 1980.

14. *New York Times,* October 30, 1923.

15. *New York Times,* December 7, 1923.

16. In *Inflation, Growth and Unemployment,* Commission on Money and Credit, Prentice-Hall, 1964, pp. 448–49.

SUGGESTIONS FOR FURTHER READING

For a thorough study of the relationship between inflation and interest rates, see Lawrence Summers, "The Non-Adjustment of Nominal Interest Rates: A Study of the Fisher Effect," National Bureau of Economic Research, Conference Paper, 1983.

PART FOUR

MACROECONOMIC POLICY

CHAPTER NINE

POLICY MAKING AND POLICY MAKERS

The science of economics does not provide simple answers to complex social problems. It does not validate the view of the man who thinks the world is going to hell, nor the view of his fellow idiot that ours is the best of all possible tax systems. Quite the contrary, economists would indeed be useless if any sensible man could quickly infer for himself simple answers to the big policy questions of fiscal policy. No need then to feed economists while they make learned studies of the obvious. It is precisely because public policy in the tax and expenditure area is so complex that we find it absolutely indispensable to invest thousands of man-years of scholarly time in scholarly economic research in these areas.

PAUL SAMUELSON[1]

This chapter examines how and by whom monetary and fiscal policies are chosen, the nature of the policies, and their relation to the political process.

HOW should government fiscal and monetary policies respond to the state of the economy? How much money should the government spend, borrow, print and raise through taxes? If there is an economic recession, should the government change its fiscal policy, monetary policy, both, or neither? These are the sorts of interesting but complicated questions that we will wrestle with in the next three chapters. We begin in this chapter by looking at who the policy makers are and some general policy making concerns. Then, in Chapters 10 and 11 we will look at some specific policy issues and examples.

FISCAL POLICY

Congress and the President control fiscal policy while the Federal Reserve controls monetary policy. Fiscal policy encompasses government spending and taxation. Congress has the formal power to authorize expenditures and set tax rates. But ever since Franklin Roosevelt's aggressive leadership, most U.S. Presidents have taken an active role in setting and implementing national economic policies. The President surounds himself with confident economists and formulates economic programs to handle all kinds of real and imagined problems. The President and his most persuasive advisers then try to sell these programs to Congress and the American people.

Foremost on almost everyone's mind is economic stabilization—avoidance of ruinous booms and busts. An economic roller coaster ride inflicts pain on a lot of decent people and on some pretty suspect politicians, too. It's with good reason that each President's spending and tax programs pay careful attention to macroeconomic stabilization. If a recession is feared or at hand, the President will be looking for fiscal policies that stimulate economic activity. During excessive booms, the President looks for ways to gently cool the economy.

Government spending

Early Keynesian analyses emphasized the potency of government spending decisions. Many economists, including Keynes, were skeptical of the ability of monetary authorities to end the Great Depression in the 1930s. Interest rates had sunk to very low levels and it is hard to see how they could have gone much lower, yet even at these extremely low interest rates, there was hardly any investment spending. Households, in fear of losing their jobs, were reluctant to borrow, and borrowing to build factories seemed mad when so many of the nation's factories were already idle. Afraid of the future, households, banks, and businesses all hoarded cash.* If the Fed had pumped more cash into the economy, it probably would have been hoarded, too. Giving people money for their bonds does not ensure that they increase their spending on goods and services: You can lead a horse to water, but you can't make it drink. Government expenditures, on the other hand, definitely are expenditures.

We have seen how government expenditures can have powerful multiplier effects on the economy when there are idle resources looking for some demand for their services. The 1930s had the disease that active fiscal policy is designed to cure. There were lots of idle factories and unemployed people. Interest rates were very low and there was no investment to be crowded out. In these circumstances, large government expenditures undoubtedly could have soon ended the Great Depression, but concerns about government interference and unbalanced budgets kept this fiscal medicine from reaching the sick economy.

It wasn't until World War II that the U.S. Government made the massive expenditures that quickly transformed recession into prosperity. This economic recovery could have been achieved years earlier. There is nothing special about guns, planes, and tanks other than a Congressional willingness to authorize expenditures for them. People and factories could have been employed just as easily ten years earlier producing shoes, trains, and cars.

Boondoggles The usefulness of government expenditures always needs to be taken into account. There is little value in a work program that has teenagers digging holes in the ground and then filling them back up, or in a research project for calculating the average American telephone number. Such make-work projects do keep teenagers and scientists off the streets, but they squander their considerable talents. The government may as well give them money for doing nothing at all; make-work government expenditures are really no better than a helicopter monetary policy (p. 188) or, to avoid unruly mobs, a national-lottery monetary policy.

Government spending programs need to be judged on their intrinsic merits. Do the benefits of highways, missiles, and research outweigh their costs? Policy makers should, of course, take into account the macroeconomic impact of spending, but the government shouldn't build missiles simply because people are unemployed. There are lots of other ways to stimulate the economy—different expenditures, tax cuts, or monetary policy. Similarly, the government should not stop supporting scientific research just to fight inflation.

In practice, government expenditure programs are usually the hybrid product of Congressional study, debate, and logrolling. Some expenditures have broad popular support; some cater to powerful special interest groups; and some are pet projects to please local constituencies. It is not uncommon for members of Congress to trade their votes on important bills for approval of federal construction projects in their districts. Democracy is very susceptible to

* The ratio of currency outside banks to checking accounts doubled, from 1/6 in 1929 to 1/3 in 1933. Member bank excess reserves rose from $48 million in 1929 to $766 million in 1933, to $6.6 billion in 1940. One imaginative proposal to induce lending was to tax money holdings, so as to give cash a negative rate of return. The plan called for small stamps to be purchased and affixed to a dollar for it to remain legal tender.

such horsetrading, especially when there is little direct cost to the President or to Congressional leaders. When the President wants to pass a Constitutional amendment, a tax package, or a budget, a few million dollars for a water treatment plant in a key congressional district seems a small price.

It is sometimes argued that representative government will inherently yield chronic overspending on projects of dubious social benefit. There are innumerable special interest groups in America, and their support can mean the difference between defeat and re-election. This is why successful politicians avoid taking stands on gun control, abortion, and other questions that alienate single-issue voting blocs. By the same logic, a generous expenditure to benefit dairy farmers, truckers, shipbuilders, the elderly, or welfare recipients can gain a crucial bloc of votes. This is why the government uses tax dollars to subsidize tobacco growers and then spends money on cancer research. When certain key voters benefit greatly from expenditures and the costs are diffused over many voters, it can be good politics to spend generously. Of course, the argument could run the other way, too. When the majority has to pay for programs that benefit only a minority, the majority may be very stingy.

These arguments all make sense. But, in practice, U.S. government expenditures are small relative to other Western nations and relative to undemocratic countries (where voters do not need to be stroked). Seventy per cent of government expenditures in the United States is for national defense. Pet projects do get targeted for key congressional districts, but the overall level of defense spending depends mostly on perceived military needs. Since World War II, aggregate federal expenditures have declined relative to national output and employment. Figure 9.1 shows this long slide. Today, federal spending accounts for less than 8% of GNP and less than 3% of total employment. On the other hand, as Figure 9.2 shows, federal transfer payments (especially for Social Security) have increased greatly and have pushed total federal disbursements upward.

Inertia Government expenditures have considerable inertia, which makes them pretty cumbersome as a stabilization tool. It takes a while to get programs going and even longer to stop them. A government program in motion tends to remain in motion.

About a third of the federal budget consists of *entitlement* programs, with legally prescribed disbursements. Their outlays are not determined by the annual Congressional appropriations decision, but are instead set by formulas specifying eligibility and benefit levels. The benefits are typically linked to the CPI. These outlays automatically increase as more people become eligible and as the CPI rises. Social Security is the most important entitlement program; other examples are Civil Service retirement payments, benefits for disabled coal miners, and the school lunch program.

Even for outlays that are not entitlements it is difficult to start and stop spending as needed to bolster or to restrain the economy. What with Congressional hearings, debates, arm twisting, and votes, it can take many months to get spending programs approved and much longer to cancel them. It also takes time to get programs under way once they have been authorized. People have to be hired to supervise the expenditures, and private bids and proposals must be submitted, studied, and approved. Overall, it can take anywhere from a few

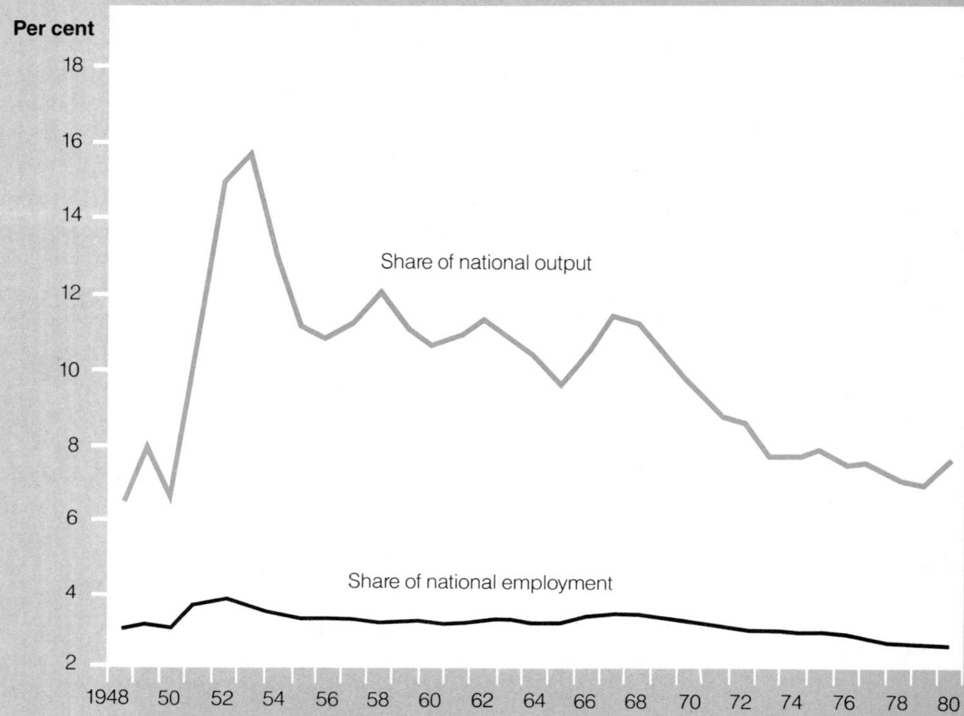

FIGURE 9.1 GOVERNMENT SPENDING AND EMPLOYMENT, 1948–80, **relative to national output and employment. Note the steady decline in share.**

months to several years to put together a spending program, get it approved, and get it going.

In addition, it doesn't make much economic sense to be repeatedly turning government expenditures on and off as the economy fluctuates. It is not very efficient to be starting and stopping the construction of highways, the design of missiles, or scientific research. If the government tries to spend money in a hurry, it will probably get little better than make-work projects; if the government cuts off expenditures in a hurry, some useful work will probably be left half done, and half-done work is seldom worth doing.

Taxation

These sorts of thoughts led to a consensus among economists after World War II that government expenditures should be based solely on merit, with tax policy used to stabilize the economy. Taxes should be levied not to pay for government spending but, rather, to achieve a desired level of private spending. Or as Abba Lerner put it, "The purpose of taxation is never to raise money but to leave less in the hands of the taxpayer."[2] Taxes should be increased when the economy needs cooling and decreased when the economy needs a boost.

Taxes probably are a better stabilization instrument than government spending, but there are still merit issues and inertia problems. Most taxes are not neutral. They redistribute income and they rearrange incentives. Tax reductions or increases need to take into account these redistributive and incentive effects. An increase in Social Security taxes, a cut in capital gains taxes, or an increase in oil depletion allowances should not be judged solely by how many dollars are given to spenders or taken away.

The recognition of these redistribution and incentive effects makes tax legislation about as laborious as expenditure bills. Congress takes its time drafting, debating, and amending tax bills. John F. Kennedy's economic advisers came to Washington in January 1961, eager to cut taxes and stimulate the economy. But

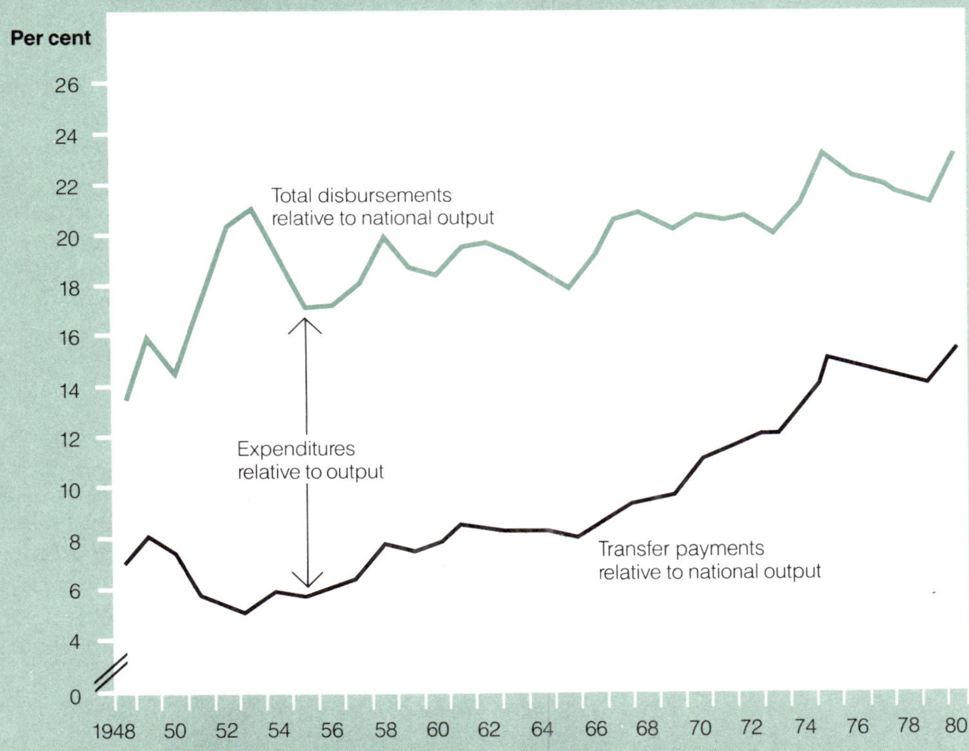

FIGURE 9.2 TOTAL GOVERNMENT DISBURSEMENTS AND TRANSFER PAYMENTS, 1948–80, **relative to national output. While spending on goods and services diminished over the period, transfer payments increased, raising total disbursements.**

it wasn't until March 1964 that Lyndon Johnson finally got Congress to pass the desired legislation. In January 1981, Ronald Reagan came to Washington eager to cut taxes and stimulate the economy. Observers were amazed that it took Reagan only eight months to get his Economic Recovery Act approved. But eight months is still a considerable delay.

Nonetheless, taxes are probably a better stabilization instrument than are government expenditures. Large, sudden changes in government spending are likely to create boondoggles or to cut back socially useful programs. Large, across-the-board tax changes can be made without radically distorting income distribution and resource allocation. In practice, of course, tax legislation seems inevitably to favor certain groups. Politicians do not always follow economists' recommendations. **Government expenditures should be judged mostly by their social value while the level of taxation should be based mostly on stabilization objectives. But the macro effects of government spending and the micro effects of taxes surely do need to be taken into account.**

MONETARY POLICY

In many ways, monetary policy is well suited for stabilization purposes. Open-market operations are a very flexible policy instrument that can be varied almost instantly to cool or stimulate the economy. In addition, major policy decisions are made by a small number of people within the Fed, so that decision making is not nearly as laborious as in Congress. The Fed does not have to worry about choosing between competing projects and winning votes from special-interest groups.

Monetary policies are not neutral, though. Tight-money credit crunches hit some industries—like home building and capital goods construction—much harder than others. Public utilities, municipal governments, and other sectors that do a lot of borrowing are squeezed mightily. These same industries and sectors benefit disproportionately from easy money policies. Monetary policies also redistribute income among individuals. High interest rates are a boon to current savers and the bane of current borrowers. And increased interest rates give substantial capital gains to those who borrowed at the old low interest rates and capital losses to those who invested before interest rates went up.

In the 1930s, economists debated whether monetary policy significantly affected spending. Nowadays there is pretty broad agreement that monetary policy does matter, at least outside of deep depressions. The major debate today instead concerns the wisdom of monetary policy—whether the Fed is capable of using monetary policy to stabilize aggregate demand or whether a passive, hands-off approach would be more successful. In this chapter we will look at how decisions are made, and then, in the next, we'll tackle the question of active versus passive policy.

The Federal Reserve System

The United States has a very diverse and complex governmental structure. Its formal origins are in the American Revolution and the formation of the Union. Fearful of the development of a centralized, authoritarian government, the founders tried to divide power within the federal government, and to reserve substantial powers for the individual state governments. The philosophy behind this complex system of checks and balances, aimed at keeping any single branch of government from becoming excessively powerful, has strongly shaped the development of U.S. financial institutions.

The U.S. Constitution seemingly prohibited the issuance of paper money by either the federal or state governments. Banks were state-chartered, and paper money was issued by individual banks. At the time of the Civil War a new system was established that allowed banks to obtain national charters and issue national bank notes. These national notes were liabilities of the private banks that issued them. The bank notes of state-chartered banks were then taxed out of existence. Private national bank notes were finally prohibited in 1935 and replaced by Federal Reserve Notes. Presently, about two-thirds of all banks have state charters while one third have national charters. Federally-chartered banks are relatively large in that they have more than half of all bank deposits.

Early attempts to establish a central bank in the United States were bitterly opposed and short-lived. The First and Second Banks of the United States each lasted only 20 years (1791–1811) and (1816–36). Nearly a century then passed before the Federal Reserve System was established and operated like a central bank. The Fed itself was originally set up in 1913 as a decentralized organization with due respect paid to state's rights. For example, state-chartered banks are not required to join the system, and 90 percent have chosen not to belong. In addition, power within the system was initially divided among twelve regional Federal Reserve Banks.

After the Great Crash, New Deal legislation centralized considerable authority in the Federal Reserve Board in Washington, D.C. Today this centralization is virtually complete. The district Reserve Banks are now little more than centers for clearing checks and explaining regulations. The *Federal Reserve Board* now has the dominant role in setting monetary policy, and its functions include:

1. The specification of *reserve requirements* for all financial institutions offering transactions accounts (checking accounts, NOW accounts, and the like).*

2. The setting of the *discount rate* charged on temporary loans from the Federal Reserve to financial institutions.

3. *Open-market operations,* the buying and selling of securities.

4. The administration of an alphabet full of bank regulations, including Regulation F (bank security holdings), Regulation T (margin requirements), Regulation Z (truth in lending), and, starting over, Regulation AA (consumer complaints).

The seven Governors of the Fed are appointed by the President of the United States to overlapping 14-year terms, one term ending in January of each even-numbered year. Thus the President will, during four years in office, normally appoint two members to the Fed. Deaths or resignations may create additional openings. In continuing deference to the dispersion of power, no two Board members can be from the same Federal Reserve district. In the past, Governors

* If the reserve requirement is 15%, then the bank can lend 85 cents out of each dollar deposited with it; 15 cents must be kept in reserve, either in the bank's vaults or at the district Federal Reserve Bank.

were often successful private citizens, with backgrounds in business or finance. In recent years, Governors have been predominantly professional economists.

The staff of the board also exercises considerable influence. These staff members are mostly economists who are experts on various aspects of monetary policy. At the request of Board members, they prepare formal or informal staff reports on policy issues. Although Board members normally have well-informed opinions on most issues, the staff studies and discussions help shape some of these opinions. This collaboration between the Board and its staff has been furthered by the recent appointments of staff members to the Board itself.

The Chairman of the Board of Governors, is appointed by the President to a four-year term (not coincident with the President's term), which can be, and often has been, renewed. New Chairmen are normally appointed to the Board and appointed Chairman at the same time. Traditionally, as with the Chief Justice of the Supreme Court, the Chairman is the dominant figure. Thus, as with the "Warren Court" and the "Burger Court," we speak of the "Burns Federal Reserve Board" and now the "Volcker Board."

The Chairmen are purposely chosen for their dynamic leadership and the respect that they command in the financial community. In addition, the chair is given various duties and powers that can be subtly employed to sway the other Governors. (Perhaps Woodward and Armstrong will write a Federal Reserve sequel to *The Brethren,* their peek inside the Supreme Court.) Marriner S. Eccles (Chairman from 1934 to 1948), William McChesney Martin (1951–70), Arthur Burns (1970–78), and Paul Volcker (since 1979) have all been strong, forceful leaders of the Fed.

The Open Market Committee

The Federal Open Market Committee (FOMC) meets every four weeks to discuss and decide policy matters. Its 12 members are: the 7 Board Governors, the President of The New York Federal Reserve Bank, and 4 of the other 11 Reserve Bank Presidents. The permanent seat for the New York Reserve Bank reflects New York's traditional role as the nation's financial capital.* In addition, the FOMC's open-market operations are executed by the New York Reserve Bank. Although the other 4 Reserve Bank voting seats are rotated among 11 banks, all of the Reserve Bank Presidents usually attend the monthly FOMC meetings and participate in the discussion.

The Open Market Committee discusses the state of the economy and financial markets and makes monetary policy decisions. With 7 of 12 votes, the Board of Governors dominates these meetings. In addition, the Board itself has the final say on policy matters. Thus, in essence, the monthly FOMC meetings are where monetary policy is discussed, recommendations are offered by the Reserve Bank Presidents, and decisions are made by the Board of Governors (normally in accordance with the wishes of the Board Chairman).

Open Market Committee meetings are held in secrecy. Before 1967, the FOMC wouldn't announce when they were meeting, let alone what they had

* The New York Reserve Bank is also by far the largest. It holds nearly a quarter of the total assets of the 12 Reserve Banks. The salary of its President is nearly double that of the chairman of the Federal Reserve Board.

decided. With the advent of the 1967 Freedom of Information laws, the FOMC was forced to report its deliberations regularly. Currently, a summary of FOMC discussion and policy actions is released about a month after each meeting and subsequently published in the *Federal Reserve Bulletin.* In addition, since 1975 the Chairman of the Board of Governors has met on a quarterly basis with Congress to discuss the Board's objectives for the coming year. These plans include target rates of growth of key monetary aggregates. The Chairman also meets regularly with White House economists and, presumably, discusses monetary policy.

Open-market operations Most monetary policy actions are direct and precise. For example, the Fed can decide to increase the discount rate that it charges on its loans to banks and other deposit institutions, say from 12% to 14%. A higher discount rate will discourage bank borrowings from the Fed and so tighten financial markets. The Fed can not anticipate the exact repercussions, but at least the policy itself (the two-point increase in the discount rate) is precise.

Similarly the Fed might reduce reserve requirements on checking accounts from 15% to 13%. If a bank has $100 million in checking-account deposits, then its required reserves will fall from $15 million to $13 million. This bank now has an additional $2 million to lend and send circulating through the economy. Thus the Fed can lower reserve requirements when it wants to ease financial markets. Again the Fed will not know the exact effects of its policy, but the policy itself is clear-cut.

Open-market operations, however, are considerably fuzzier. These securities purchases and sales are the primary day-to-day tool for maintaining orderly financial markets, and, with imperfect foresight, the FOMC cannot spell out a precise daily plan for the coming month; instead, they issue a general directive describing their broad objectives.

The Fed's actual open-market operations are carried out by the System's Account Manager, who is a vice-president of the Federal Reserve Bank of New York. The Account Manager trades securities over the counter through electronic links with firms dealing in government securities. These securities are debited and credited to the twelve Federal Reserve Banks, according to the share of total Federal Reserve assets each holds.

The Account Manager's actions are a product of general instructions determined from a decoding of the most recent FOMC directive, a personal interpretation of financial-market conditions, and a daily telephone conference with two members of the FOMC. If, on a given day, financial markets seem tighter than desired, then the Account Manager will make some open-market purchases, easing interest rates and squirting money into the economy. If there seems to be too much ease, then securities will be sold, firming interest rates and sucking money from the economy.

Most open-market operations, perhaps 80 to 90 percent,[3] are defensive, made to offset short-term tremors in financial markets rather than to implement a policy change. With daily fluctuations and aberrations in the economy, the Account Manager will be buying on some days and selling on others. Whether securities were bought or sold on a particular day is consequently not a reliable guide to the overall thrust of monetary policy.

Many of the events that shake financial markets are easily anticipated. Other events surprise even the most knowledgeable market participants. Some events cause only small, almost insignificant jogs in asset demands and supplies. Others threaten to become genuine crises. The public reliably increases its demand for cash before Christmas, Labor Day, July 4, and other holidays. Corporations predictably borrow money at the end of each quarter to pay taxes. The U.S. Treasury, large corporations, and foreign governments buy and sell large blocks of securities at irregular intervals. There are important seasonal variations in the cash needs of different parts of the country. Strikes, accidents, and bad weather create temporary fluctuations in payment schedules and money demand. Rumors, hunches, and tea leaves lead powerful speculators to make staggering transactions. Some markets or agents can be flooded with funds or left high and dry. Through it all, the Fed's Account Manager gamely tries to smooth out the air pockets while keeping financial markets on whatever course the Open Market Committee has charted.

FISCAL VERSUS MONETARY POLICIES

Monetary and fiscal policies do not have identical effects on the economy. Hence, for the achievement of some objectives, monetary policy is appropriate, while for others, fiscal policy is best. Most of the time, a combination of both is needed.

For instance, policy makers may want to stimulate the economy while keeping the real interest rate at the current level (so as to neither discourage nor excessively encourage private investment spending). We have seen that an expansionary monetary policy increases aggregate demand and reduces real interest rates, while an expansionary fiscal policy increases both aggregate demand and interest rates. If the government wants to increase aggregate demand without altering real interest rates, then a combination of expansionary monetary and contractionary fiscal policies is needed.

In practice, this kind of coordination does not always occur, mostly because the monetary and the fiscal authorities do not always have the same objectives and because neither is subservient to the other. For instance, the President and Congress may want to stimulate the economy in order to increase output and reduce unemployment, while the Fed wants to cool off the economy in order to fight inflation. If so, the nation gets expansionary fiscal policy and contractionary monetary policy, which only add up to higher interest rates. As long as neither side gives in, both will be frustrated and the nation will be worse off. If they could agree on a compromise policy—say, leaving aggregate demand where it is—then at least interest rates would not be pushed upward.

Legally, the Fed is a largely independent branch of government, what some have called the "Supreme Court of Finance." It is not quite this, but there are definite similarities. As we have noted, members are appointed by the President for very long terms (14 years), but these are not quite the life appointments given Supreme Court justices. Board members do gather for secret meetings in an ornate building and issue solemn pronouncements. Most have very high opinions of themselves, but few wear robes to their meetings. Congress has little influence on the Fed's day-to-day operations, but it can impose general constraints on it. And finally, though the President and Congress have tried moral persuasion on both, they have had more influence on the Fed.

The Political Business Cycle

The Fed has generally given the President the kind of monetary policy he wanted. In the 1950s the Fed was very cautious and, to avoid inflation, accepted three recessions during Dwight Eisenhower's eight years in office. In January 1961 John Kennedy became President, having pledged to reduce unemployment and get the country moving again. The Fed obligingly swung to easier monetary policies. In 1969, Richard Nixon took office, promising to stop inflation, and the Fed tightened the screws in a painful credit crunch. In 1977, Jimmy Carter became President and his initially expansionary fiscal policies were aided and abetted by expansionary monetary policies. In 1981, Ronald Reagan became President and got the tight monetary policy that he wanted. The Fed apparently has three eyes, one for interest rates, one for the money supply, and one for election returns.

But it hasn't been all romance between the politicians and this three-eyed monster. Fed officials have been repeatedly jawboned by Presidents and called before Congressional committees. Often, the President and Congress are distressed that monetary and fiscal policies seem to be working at cross-purposes. Since 1965 there have been several occasions when expansionary fiscal policies were accompanied by tight-money, contractionary monetary policies.

An only slightly cynical explanation of this periodic conflict is that economic events can have a decisive influence on political elections.[4] People do think of their pocketbooks when they vote. One facet of this preoccupation with the purse is that the incumbent political party is judged by the state of the economy on the eve of an election. Casual observation and formal empirical studies indicate that high output and low unemployment sway votes to the incumbent party.

There are three other, more subtle economics-related political phenomena: First, recent changes in the levels of output and employment may be more important than the levels themselves, for voters seem to respond more favorably to a falling unemployment rate than to a steady, low rate of unemployment. Second, because wages and prices are sticky, changes in inflation tend to lag behind variations in output and employment. Thus, the economy can be stimulated, increasing output and reducing unemployment, with relatively little immediate impact on the rate of inflation. Third, voters seem to care more about unemployment and output than about inflation.

Any one of these three observations explains why an incumbent party might try to stimulate the economy before an election. The first and second observations explain, further, why a government might try to cool off the economy *after* an election. This pre-election stimulus and post-election restraint is called the *political business cycle.* Figure 9.3 shows some crude evidence of this phenomenon. As shown, the unemployment rate seems to decline before presidential elections and to rise afterwards. In 1932, the unemployment rate rose 7.7%, and the incumbent President, Herbert Hoover, was soundly defeated. Since 1932, there has only been one presidential election year in which the unem-

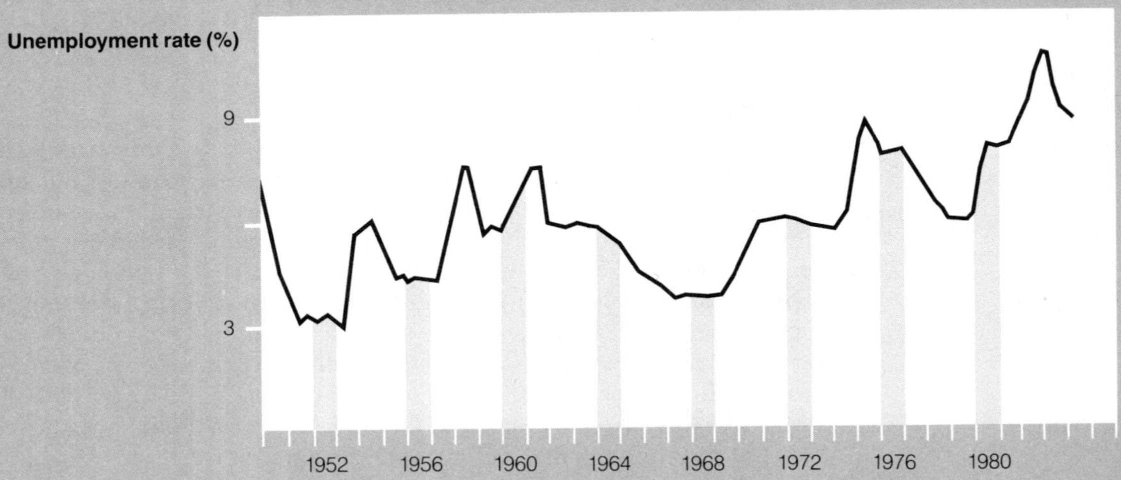

FIGURE 9.3 UNEMPLOYMENT RATE IN RELATION TO RECENT PRESIDENTIAL ELECTIONS. **Policymakers usually manage to reduce the unemployment rate during election years. Jimmy Carter's 1980 reelection bid was the exception in this period.**

ployment rate has risen—1980, with the unemployment rate up 1.3% and the incumbent, Jimmy Carter, beaten decisively.

Since they are not elected officials, members of the Fed are seemingly less tempted to manipulate the economy for personal political gain.* Thus it sometimes seems, particularly before elections, that the Fed is trying to cool off the economy to fight inflation while the President is trying to stimulate the economy to fight unemployment. For example, Jimmy Carter's 1980 loss was preceded by bitter criticism of the Fed.

To some eyes, these conflicts show that the system is working. The political independence of the Fed allows it to follow unpopular but necessary policies. When a president, prime minister, or king has controlled a nation's money supply there has too often been irresponsible and ultimately destructive inflation. Thus it was wise for the United States to resist a central bank and, when forced to establish one, to make it independent of the President and Congress.

In other eyes, including naturally those of the President and Congress, this separation thwarts useful coordination of monetary and fiscal policies. In addition, monetary policy is too important to be trusted to unelected officials, who do not have to answer to the public. There is a long-standing suspicion

* There still may be a temptation to assist favored politicians. Fed Chairman Arthur Burns was accused of pursuing an easy money policy in 1972 to assist Richard Nixon's re-election campaign. He vehemently denied the charge. Another Fed Governor, Sherman Maisel, later recorded the strong, persistent pressure applied by the Nixon administration: "An election was approaching; from their point of view, the faster money grew, the better was monetary policy."[5]

IN THE NEWS

Fed Bracing for Political Criticism...

WASHINGTON—It was 1961, and the new president was leaning on William McChesney Martin Jr., then the Federal Reserve Board chairman, to help rev up the economy.

At the close of a White House meeting, President Kennedy draped an arm around Mr. Martin's shoulder and, according to an observer, turned on the famous charm. "Bill, I know you've got a job to do," he said. "But I like my job, too, and I'd like to stick around here awhile."

This year, Ronald Reagan may be tempted to say the same thing to Paul Volcker, the current Fed boss. Although the president is pleased by the success of the Fed's anti-inflation policies, some aides are worried that the Fed will stay too tough too long and torpedo the recovery—as well as Mr. Reagan's reelection prospects.

With the 1984 presidential election campaign heating up, one Republican strategist says there are "a lot of people hoping that Volcker doesn't put the screws down on the recovery." Fear that he will causes one Treasury official to speculate that Paul Volcker, rather than Democratic front-runner Walter Mondale, "may be our biggest political foe" this year. And a top presidential adviser says he wishes that the Fed would just "drop dead" until after the election.

The White House isn't expressing such views—at least not in public. Presidential spokesman Marlin Fitzwater admits to "some concern" that the Fed may err on the side of monetary restraint this year. But right now, the Fed is following a policy "pretty close to what we want," he says.

However, Rep. Jack Kemp, a conservative New York Republican and an ardent Fed critic, says the Fed should bring interest rates down, and he adds that the current level of rates "certainly won't help the president." In a vague threat to the Fed's independence, he warns, "Volcker and the board are inviting congressional action, and perhaps irresponsible action, if they abort the recovery."

Frederick Schultz, a former vice chairman of the Reserve Board, says conservative-Republican criticism of the Fed may be a new element of the campaign this year. "The liberals always criticize high interest rates, and the Populists always say the East Coast banks dominate the Fed," he says. "But this time, the right will be joining in." Mr. Schultz notes that Mr. Kemp and other promoters of the supply-side tax cuts are angry that the Fed hasn't given the recovery its head. Other conservatives are berating the Fed for not sticking rigidly to a policy of slow, steady monetary growth.

The Fed is used to criticism; it typically goes on the griddle during a presidential campaign. Board member Nancy Teeters predicts that "between the time of the political conventions and the election, the Fed will be constantly accused of doing things for political purposes."

In 1980, when the Fed increased the discount rate six weeks before the election, President Carter blasted its monetary policy as "ill-advised." Rates are lower today than in the fall of 1980 and down sharply from their 1981 peaks, but they remain uncomfortably high. That, coupled with the scars from the long, deep recession, could make the Fed an even more attractive political target than in the past, Mr. Schultz says.

Democrats have begun cranking out campaign papers decrying high interest rates and lecturing the Fed that it is "cruel" to believe high inflation is worse than high unemployment.

So, will Mr. Volcker bow to election-year pressures? Will the central bank pump up the money supply and try to push down rates?

No way, asserts Mr. Schultz. Mr. Volcker, he says, is "absolutely committed" to achieving long-term price stability and "won't back off." Other analysts agree. They see little reason to believe that the Fed boss, after forcing the nation to swallow bitter anti-inflation medicine, would surrender his hard-fought gains for short-term political goals. "Volcker isn't a pinchhitter," one Fed official says. "He's in this for the whole game." Agrees Allen Sinai, the chief economist for Lehman Brothers, Kuhn Loeb Inc.: "Volcker won't cave."

But some economists dismiss such notions as naive. "The Fed always goes along with what the president wants," contends Robert Auerbach, a finance professor at the University of California at Riverside. "Paul Volcker has done exactly what he's been told. But he's very adept at sounding independent."

These charges are "mistaken" and "entirely wrong," says Fed member Henry Wallich. Preston Martin, the board's vice chairman, adds that it is too perilous for the board to play political favorites. "You risk bringing down the wrath of Congress and losing your independence," he says.

With a little luck, Paul Volcker may be able to duck much of the political fire this year. If the economy grows moderately and inflation remains low, the Fed will be able to pursue a steady, middle-of-the road course and avoid becoming a political football, predicts Murray Weidenbaum, the former chairman of President Reagan's Council of Economic Advisers.

That is just what the board wants. "You don't like to make yourself an election issue if you can avoid it," one Fed member says.

But things could go wrong. Economist Milton Friedman gloomily says it is "very likely" that the Fed's restrictive monetary policy will produce a recession in the first half of this year. Other analysts are worried that a worsening U.S. trade deficit could lead to a collapse of the high-flying dollar and a resurgence of inflation. And some economists see a credit clash later this year, as the federal government's huge borrowing needs collide with rising private demand.

In that case, "the Fed will let rates rise, despite administration pressure," predicts Robert Roosa, a partner in Brown Bros. Harriman & Co. and formerly Mr. Volcker's boss at the Treasury and the New York Federal Reserve Bank. One Fed official predicts that if the central bank believes it must raise rates to damp quickening inflation, it will do so, "although with great pain and unhappiness."

In 1980 and 1981, the Fed imposed high interest rates and endured growing political opposition as a consequence of its anti-inflationary policy. In the summer of 1982, congressional outrage over the continuing recession and rising unemployment reached a fever pitch. Proposals for increasing legislative control over the Fed proliferated. Presidential aides James Baker III and Edwin Meese visited the Fed to talk to Volcker.

Then, in an abrupt policy switch, the Fed began pumping money into the economy. Interest rates fell, the stock market took off and congressional muscle-flexing faded. "When Congress rumbled, the Fed responded," one congressional aide says.

But many analysts view the situation differently. They attribute the Fed's switch to economic conditions, including a sharp slowdown in monetary growth and, perhaps most important, the international debt crisis. "The easing resulted in large part because of Volcker's concerns about Mexico," Mr. Weidenbaum contends.

Mr. Volcker's eventual reappointment as Fed chairman last summer—which came despite Mr. Reagan's apparent reluctance and Treasury Secretary Donald Regan's protests—illustrates his talent for political survival. "Volcker was reappointed because the White House became convinced that not reappointing him would create a financial-market crisis," one administration official says.

Trying to predict Fed behavior gets to the tricky question of the central bank's independence. The Fed was created by Congress and could be abolished by Congress. Twice a year, it must report its money-supply targets to the lawmakers (and will do so next week). The president has the authority to appoint the Fed chairman and board members. Beyond that, however, the Fed's relationships with the White House and Congress are vaguely defined and often dictated by the personalities involved.

The Reagan-Volcker relationship has been characterized from the start by a strong dose of mutual mistrust, observers say. Unlike Arthur Burns—a Nixon political crony long before Richard Nixon became president and appointed Mr. Burns

Fed chairman—Mr. Volcker wasn't a member of the Reagan inner circle and didn't try to become one.

For their first meeting, Mr. Reagan offered to come to the Fed for lunch, but Mr. Volcker worried that the gesture would send the wrong signal. So the two settled on somewhat more neutral ground—Secretary Regan's private dining room at the Treasury—"to avoid the appearance that the Fed's independence was being compromised," remembers Martin Anderson, who at the time was the president's chief domestic adviser.

Since that initial meeting, the president and the Fed chief have met infrequently, and neither has disclosed much after the sessions. The secretive Mr. Volcker sometimes doesn't even brief other board members. Whatever he says privately to the president, Mr. Volcker often gives the administration advice in public: Lower the deficit, even if that requires tax increases—hardly what the tax-cutting Mr. Reagan wants to hear.

As for the White House, Jerry Jordan, a former member of President Reagan's Council of Economic Advisers, recalls once being asked to draft a reply to a letter to Mr. Reagan from one of the president's close friends in the "kitchen cabinet." The letter, which blasted the Fed for high interest rates, contained a notation in the corner: "Why do we need a Fed anyway?" It was signed "R.R."

Mr. Volcker, who meets separately each week with Secretary Regan and Martin Feldstein, the chairman of the president's Council of Economic Advisers, has taken his sharpest raps from the Treasury. Mr. Regan and Beryl Sprinkel, the Treasury undersecretary for monetary affairs, have repeatedly criticized the Fed for undershooting or overshooting its money-growth targets.

But the sniping merely brings out Mr. Volcker's obstinate determination to protect the Fed's independence, Mr. Schultz says. Occasionally, the former Fed vice chairman says, Mr. Volcker has postponed an action that was being publicly demanded by the Treasury, to avoid seeming to cave in to administration pressure.

Nevertheless, Fed board members say they view the disputes with the Treasury as "technical differences." In general, "the administration has been very supportive of the Fed's goals," the board's Preston Martin says. Other members agree.

Without the support of the Reagan administration and Congress, "it would have been difficult" for the Fed to engineer abrupt disinflation, one board member says. Adds another Fed official, "You can't conduct a monetary policy that people are up in arms about." And Mr. Volcker recently observed that monetary policy couldn't be pursued "without broad understanding of the objectives and support from the people whose lives are affected."

Past administrations have had repeated—and sometimes nasty—confrontations with the Fed. When the Fed increased the discount rate in 1965 to try to prevent the economy from overheating from the Vietnam war, Lyndon Johnson was "sore as a boil," says Walter Heller, who served as the chairman of the Council of Economic Advisers under Presidents Kennedy and Johnson. President Johnson called Fed Chairman Martin down to the ranch for a Texas-style dressing down, Mr. Heller recalls.

During the Nixon administration, the president became incensed that his old friend Arthur Burns was calling for wage and price guidelines before the White House was ready to consider them. In a hamhanded attempt to discredit Mr. Burns, Charles Colson, a presidential aide, tried to plant in the newspapers a false story that Mr. Burns was privately pushing for a pay raise. But the ploy failed.

A few weeks later, Mr. Nixon embraced sweeping controls. Mr. Colson eventually became a "born again" Christian and apologized to Mr. Burns.

Ironically, many economists contend that, despite Mr. Colson's attempted hatchet job, Mr. Burns did everything he could to reelect Mr. Nixon in 1972. They said Mr. Burns, while making tough, anti-inflation speeches, was pumping up the money supply. But those who worked with Mr. Burns in 1972, including Andrew Brimmer, then a Fed board member, deny that Mr. Burns was trying to juice the economy to help Mr. Nixon. And Mr. Burns himself vigorously denies it.

The Kennedy administration used a subtle approach to influence the Fed. When the Fed wasn't buying enough government securities to keep long-term interest rates down, the president would call a meeting with his top economic advisers and Fed Chairman Martin. Once the meeting was scheduled, the Fed would drive down the rates by the day of the session, and Mr. Martin wouldn't be berated by the president. After the meeting, rates would creep back up, Mr. Heller recalls.

"He concluded," Mr. Heller adds, "that we didn't really need to have a meeting, just to schedule one." (Laurie McGinley, *The Wall Street Journal,* Feb. 1, 1984) that the Fed is run by bankers for the benefit of bankers. This suspicion, together with the notion that bankers like high interest rates, form one popular explanation of why the Fed has so often followed a tight money policy. The late Texas Congressman Wright Patman, who served in the House from 1929 to 1976 and chaired the House Banking Committee for many of these 47 years, was a particularly vocal champion of this view. Off and on, there are calls to weaken the independence of the Fed. Some proposals are for monetary policy to be taken over by Congress or the President. Such plans are usually motivated by a feeling that the Fed's policy is pointed in the wrong direction—that they are being either too expansionary or too contractionary.

We have seen why political leaders and the Fed may have very different objectives. Now, we will look at some reasons why even the best-intentioned policy makers may make mistakes. Then, in the next chapter, we will look at a very different proposal for restraining the Fed: to turn monetary policy over to a dispassionate computer.

OBSTACLES TO EFFECTIVE POLICY

Politicians can be very impatient with economists who admit that they are not omniscient. Harry Truman once exclaimed in frustration, "Give me a one-handed economist! All my economists say 'on the one hand, . . . but on the other' ". If we knew for certain how the economy works and what the future holds it would be easy to make policy decisions. We could just explain *IS* and *LM* curves to the President, Congress, and the Fed and let them negotiate some target values of output, prices, and interest rates. The problem is that we don't really understand the past, canot see all of the present, and have little, if any, idea of what is going to happen in the future. We consequently don't have precise values for the variables and parameters in our macroeconomic models.

One difficulty is that we simply do not have enough accurate, timely data to describe the economy's condition, let alone completely understand why it is the way it is. A policy maker who doesn't even know the state of the economy will almost certainly make some memorable policy errors. In June 1930, for example, with the Great Depression due to continue for years, Herbert Hoover told a group that had come to Washington to urge an expansionary fiscal policy, "Gentlemen, you have come sixty days too late. The depression is over."[6]

One reason he was very wrong was that he didn't have much data on output and employment. The NBER didn't begin its national income accounting until the mid-1930s. There were no regular monthly unemployment data until 1940. Before then, the only unemployment data were collected in the census, once every 10 years. Other economic data were also scarce before world War II and, often, not very reliable.

Today, we have much better information about the current state of the economy. But we still don't have all the data we need, and we probably never will. Some data, like GNP numbers, are only available quarterly. Some data, like real interest rates, are not officially available at all. Some data, like short-run monetary aggregates, are not very reliable. The weekly monetary aggregates data are often substantially revised weeks or even months after issue. A Fed study found that, between 1968 and 1975, in a third of the cases the final estimate of the money growth rate differed from the preliminary estimate by more than 3 percentage points. How can the Fed accurately stabilize real interest rates or monetary aggregates if it barely sees them?

Even worse, the Fed's policies must be aimed at the future, not the present, and forecasts through our economic crystal ball are still pretty cloudy, with a 50% chance of rain. Economists often know which direction the economy is headed, but they seldom know exactly how far. That's why one of the canons of economic forecasting is, "If you give a number, don't give a date." An ideal stabilization policy needs good numbers *and* good dates.

It is not easy to forecast the economic future. Our history is filled with embarassingly inaccurate predictions. Because the Great Depression was so calamitous, it is not surprising that it is also the source of many dramatically incorrect forecasts. In his final message to Congress, Calvin Coolidge boasted on December 4, 1928, that

> No Congress of the United States ever assembled, on surveying the state of the Union, has met with a more pleasing prospect than that which appears at the present time. . . . The country can regard the present with satisfaction and anticipate the future with optimism.

Herbert Hoover took office and, on July 27, 1929, predicted that "The outlook of the world today is for the greatest era of commercial expansion in history." A few months later, the stock market crashed. But Herbert Hoover's optimism persisted. In his December 3, 1929, State of the Union message, he concluded that "The problems with which we are confronted are the problems of growth and progress."

As the economy collapsed, politicians, businessmen, and economists kept predicting a quick return to prosperity. Charles Schwab, chairman of the board of Bethlehem Steel, said, "Never before has American business been as firmly entrenched for prosperity as it is today" (December 10, 1929). Andrew Mellon, Secretary of the Treasury, stated, "I see nothing in the present situation that is either menacing or warrants pessimism" (January 1, 1930). Robert Lamont, Secretary of Commerce, predicted that "Business will be normal in two months" (March 3, 1930). Even Irving Fisher, perhaps the greatest American economist, chimed in: "I expect to see the stock market a good deal higher than it is today within a few months" (October 15, 1929). Fisher lost his family fortune and a good deal of credibility. The politicians and businessmen didn't fare much better.

Unpredictable Behavior

Much of the uncertainty in economic forecasting is due to the fact that economic decisions are not made by robots, but by emotional and fallible humans. Economic forecasting is much better now than in the 1930s, but it is still not perfect and never will be, for we will surely never fully understand human behavior. It would admittedly be a pretty dull world if we could, but at least things would be easier for economic forecasters.

Economic decisions, then, are made by people, and human emotions are not always as predictable as economists might wish. An economist can tell you what is rational, what is reasonable, and what usually happens. But in any situation, fickle humans can turn around and do something entirely different. This is how Keynes explained the mayhem in the stock market and why he wrote that "There is nothing so disastrous as a rational investment policy in an irrational world."[7]

Similarly, in predicting the consequences of government policies, it is necessary to take into account, as best one can, how citizens will interpret these policies and how they will react to them. One benign (and rational) example that has repeatedly occurred in recent years concerns the release of data on monetary aggregates. When the Fed has announced that M1 increased rapidly, stock prices have often fallen. But according to economic theory, an increase in the money supply should raise stock prices. What has gone wrong?

The answer to this puzzle is simple and illustrates the critical role of expectations. Each announcement reported increases that, when they actually occurred, did reduce interest rates and boost both bond and stock prices. By the time the announcement was made, however, the money increase was over and financial markets were looking ahead. What they were anticipating was the fact that, when the Fed discovers that M1 has been growing more rapidly than planned*, it is likely to swing to a tighter monetary policy. Stock prices thus decline, as theory says they should, in anticipation of this tightening of the money supply.

There are other more general examples. Policy makers have long recognized that the public sometimes overreacts to policy announcements. This is why incumbent Presidents often announce potentially popular (but possibly unwise) policies only hours before a primary election or shortly before the Presidential election itself. They are hoping to exploit the initial public enthusiasm before sober reflection sets in. The government follows a different strategy when it does not want to stir things up: With bad news the best timing is long before the election or right after it. Sometimes it is the financial markets that the government does not want to unsettle. Announcements are then made late Friday, after the markets have closed, to give investors the weekend to calm down and digest the news.

Citizens can also react to policies in very unexpected ways. When the government announces an expansionary policy, one possible reaction is: "This will stimulate the economy; a boom is on the way." But another plausible response is: "Things must really be bad for them finally to do something; we must be sliding into a recession." Sometimes citizens react the first way, sometimes the second, and sometimes in other ways.

This fickleness can be very frustrating for government officials. In the Great Depression, President Hoover kept trying to buoy the economy with optimistic pronouncements, such as, "Prosperity is just around the corner." These were embarrassing failures. Simeon Fess, the National Chairman of the Republican Party, complained:

> Persons high in Republican circles are beginning to believe that there is some concerted effort on foot to utilize the stock market as a method of discrediting the administration. Every time an administration official gives out an optimistic statement about business conditions, the market immediately drops.[8]

* In recent years, the Fed has tried to keep the growth of M1 within its target guidelines, but they do not control M1 directly and do not even know how fast M1 has been growing until data are gathered and evaluated.

In the spring of 1970 President Nixon stated that, if he "had any money," he would buy stocks. Stock prices promptly fell by more than 10%. Investors seemed to feel that the economy must be in even worse shape than they had thought if the President had to tout stocks. In 1981, President Ronald Reagan was similarly disappointed by Wall Street's negative reaction to his tax program. We have all seen other government officials surprised by public reaction to their policies and predictions.

Policy Lags

Another reason why policy makers cannot completely stabilize the economy is that there are significant lags between when an economic problem occurs and when policy medicine reaches the economy. These delays are of three kinds:

1. *Recognition delays* We don't have good data on many important economic variables until some time after the fact. For example, GNP data are quarterly and are not available until several weeks after each quarter has ended. Thus GNP data for January through March are not available until mid-April. In addition, economic data are never final, but are always subject to revision. Finally, because the data are inexact and the world is full of little surprises, policy makers like to see confirming data before making decisions. This is the logic behind the traditional rule that a recession is not declared one until real GNP has declined for two consecutive quarters. Recognition delays mean that it may take a while for policy makers to realize that policy changes are needed. A 1963 study concluded that the recognition delay averages around five months.[9]

2. *Action delays* It takes time for policies to be chosen, written up, and approved. Government spending programs are especially slow to set up. These action delays can be shortened somewhat by designing flexible spending programs. For example, the initial legislation can give the President the authority to vary the amount of money to be spent, depending on prevailing economic conditions. Or formula controls can be built into the legislation that automatically adjust spending according to output, unemployment rate, inflation rate, and other economic data.

One big advantage of taxes as a stabilization instrument is that it is relatively easy to reduce timing delays by structuring taxes to vary automatically with the level of economic activity. Most present taxes (on personal income, corporate profits, and capital gains, for example) do have this built-in automatic stabilization. For even more flexibility the President could be given standby authority to change certain broad-based taxes as needed to quickly cool or stimulate the economy.

3. *Transmission delays* Most policies have ripple effects, and it takes some time for these ripples to work themselves out. In Chapter 3, we looked at Kahn's round-by-round explanation of the interaction between income and expenditures. An increase in government spending raises income and increases spending even more. Such ripples never really die out entirely; they (like old soldiers) just fade away. We can speak however, of how long it takes for policies to have the bulk of their effects. Empirical macro models generally find that an increase in government spending has had most of its effects by the end of two quarters.[10]

Monetary policy has a relatively short action delay, in that Fed decision-making can be quite speedy. But monetary policies do have considerable transmission delays between their implementation and their ultimate effects. When the Fed pumps money into the economy, it takes some time for that money to be spent and respent, loaned and reloaned, and to work its way through the economy. Milton Friedman concluded that there is a lag of about 12 to 18 months between changes in the rate of growth of the money supply and economic activity. John Kareken and Robert Solow[11] interpreted the data as indicating substantial stabilizing effects after 6 to 9 months.* Some card-carrying monetarists believe that the lags between money supply changes and output changes are actually very short. Leonall Anderson, a staunch monetarist, turned the Friedman and Kareken-Solow disagreement upside down:

> Monetarist theories and empirical studies point to a relatively quick, but short-lived, response of output to a change in money growth, with a longer time period required for prices to respond fully. Post-Keynesian econometric models, on the other hand, produce an impact of money changes only over a much longer period.[13]

If monetary policies do have quick and short-lived effects, then they are ideal for short-run stabilization.

These three virtually inescapable delays mean that there normally will be a substantial lag between the time when economic stimulus or sedation is first needed and the time when policy changes actually affect the economy. If the recession or boom is brief, then it may be over by the time the counteractive policy is working. Massive expenditures authorized in order to cushion a recession may not stimulate the economy until the middle of the next boom. If so, then stabilization policy may be *de*stabilizing!

Policy makers are usually competent and well-intentioned. But inherent policy lags may require policy makers to be clairvoyant, too. If government officials are mere mortals, who cannot see the future clearly, then the wrong policies may be chosen as often as not. Classically oriented economists argue that business cycles are very short, while monetary and fiscal policies take a long time to take effect. A recession or boom will be over by the time the government has identified it, decided what to do about it, done it, and the stabilization policy has had its effects.

To see how these delays can undermine policies, consider monetary policy during a recession. From data that measure the recent past performance of the economy, the Fed sees some signs of weakness. Is this just a temporary jog or statistical quirk? The Fed decides to gather more data and wait a bit. By the time of the next Open Market Committee meeting, there are some confirming data; but it is still not clear how severe and pronounced the weakness is. Should the Fed make minor open-market purchases or is a major stimulus in order?

Time passes, and the Fed decides that the economy really is in a significant recession and should be given some help. Open-market purchases are used to inject a substantial amount of money into the economy. Interest rates decline and spending begins to rise. With time, this new money is spent, deposited in

* Friedman's 12- to 18-month lag is based on a comparison of the *rate of change* of monetary aggregates with the *level* of economic activity. Karekin and Solow, and others, argue that there are other, more relevant, comparisons, such as those between *changes* in the money supply and *changes* in economic activity, or deviations from long-run trends in the money supply and in economic activity. Friedman himself acknowledges that such comparisons reduce the lag to about five months.[12]

banks, loaned, spent again, redeposited, and loaned yet again. But by the time this monetary tonic is circulating through the economy, the recession has already ended and the economy is growing briskly. Thus, instead of softening the last recession, the monetary elixir exacerbates the next boom. And by the time the Fed realizes this and starts draining money from circulation, the next recession will have already started. The Fed will cool off a cold economy after having heated a hot one; it would have been better had they kept their medicine locked up.

Model with lags Delays, then, may make active stabilization policy infeasible. This can be made more precise by using a simple illustrative model. For concreteness, we will again focus on monetary policy, but the moral we draw applies to fiscal policy as well.

Assume that the economy can be described by the following simple equation:

$$y[t] = 600 + 2M[t] + 4M[t-1], \tag{9.1}$$

where $y[t]$ is national income in period t, $M[t]$ is the money supply in period t, and $M[t-1]$ is the money supply in the preceding period. This equation is intended to be the solution of a macro model. Because government spending, tax rates, and all of the other predetermined variables (except the money supply) are held constant in this analysis, they have been assigned their predetermined values. These values underlie the intercept 600 and the coefficients 2 and 4 in the equation. Thus, the intercept and coefficients implicitly represent the predetermined variables and parameters in a macro model.

This model (Equation 9.1) reflects the key assumption that there are delays in the effects of monetary policy on the economy. This period's income depends on both the current money supply and the previous period's money supply. Equivalently, an increase in the money supply affects the economy now and in the next period as well. Moreover, the lagged effects are larger than the contemporaneous effects. Specifically, a $1 billion increase in the money supply increases output by $2 billion this period and by $4 billion in the next period. The implication of this specification is that it is not feasible to use monetary policy to peg national income!

Consider a case in which the money supply has been $400 billion for some time, and income is consequently $3000 billion. Now there is some shock to the economy—a change in some predetermined variable—and the intercept of Equation 9.1 drops to 590. Income will consequently fall by 10 (to 2990) unless the monetary authorities act. In order to raise income by 10 in the current period, the money supply must be increased by 5 (since every $1 billion increase in $M[t]$ raises $y[t]$ by $2 billion). Hence, for period $t = 0$ (the time of the shock to the economy) $M[t] = 405$.

In the next period ($t = 1$), the $5 billion increase in the money supply will still be affecting the economy. Specifically, income will rise by another $20 billion, to $3020 billion if the money supply is kept at $405 billion. If national income is to be pegged at $3000 billion, then the money supply must now be reduced to offset last period's expansionary policy. By how much? To reduce $y[t]$ by 20, $M[t]$ must decline by 10, to 395. (Thus, $y[1] = 590 + 2(395) + 4(405) = 3000$.)

So far, so good. But in the following period ($t = 2$), the Fed must contend with the lagged effect of the previous period's $10 billion drop in the money supply. If a $40 billion drop in national income is to be avoided, the money supply must now be increased by $20 billion. And, in the next period, this will have to be offset by a $40 billion reduction in the money supply. The whole wild cycle of "stop-and-go" policies aimed at pegging national income at $3000 billion is summarized as follows.

t	$M[t]$
0	405
1	395
2	415
3	375
4	455
5	295
6	615
7	−25(?)

After seven periods, the situation is untenable.

Because the lagged effects are stronger than the contemporaneous effects, the monetary authorities must scramble in each period to offset the effects of last period's policy. The moral is that when there are substantial lags in the effects of policies, active policy may not be able to stabilize the economy completely.

The key parameters in Equation 9.1 are the coefficients of $M[t]$ and $M[t-1]$. Policy is unstable when, as here, the coefficient of $M[t-1]$ is larger than the coefficient of $M[t]$. (Exercise 13 considers the reverse case.) The relevance of these examples depends on our time horizon, which is why I call t a "period," rather than a day, week, month, or year. In the case of days, the lagged effects of monetary and fiscal policies are surely greater than the contemporaneous effects. And, so, the policy makers cannot hope to stabilize national income day-to-day. If the case of months or a year, the answer may be reversed. In terms of years, the lagged effects of most policies probably are smaller than the contemporaneous effects. If so, then the government may be able to stabilize national income year-to-year. In general, fine tuning the economy may be an unrealistic goal; smoothing out the year-to-year performance may be possible.

IMPORTANT TERMS AND CONCEPTS

entitlements
Federal Reserve Board (Fed)
reserve requirements
discount rate
open market operations
Federal Open Market Committee (FOMC)
monetary base
political business cycle
monetary lag
recognition lag

Government spending is a powerful stabilization tool in that it ensures that the money involved gets spent. But make-work projects have no real macroeconomic advantage over tax cuts, national lotteries, or other devices for simply giving people money. In general, government expenditures should be evaluated individually, mostly on the basis of their intrinsic social benefits relative to costs, while the overall level of taxation should be based mostly on macroeconomic stabilization objectives. But the macro effects of government spending and the micro income redistribution and resource allocation effects oftaxes do need to be taken into account.

The Fed is similar to a Supreme Court of finance. It operates largely independently of other government bodies and its actions do not always please the President and Congress. However, broadly speaking, the Fed has given each President pretty much the kind of monetary policy he wanted.

Uncertainties and lags make perfect policies impossible. Policy makers are never sure of the precise state of the economy and do not know the exact effects of their policies. In addition, it takes a while for their policies to get started and to have their effects. Since economics involves emotional and sometimes irrational humans, the future is never known with certainty. Hence, to select perfect policies, government officials would have to be clairvoyant.

EXERCISES

1. With a progressive tax system, inflation can push people into higher tax brackets, reducing their after-tax income. Does this "bracket creep" act as an automatic stabilizer or automatic destabilizer?

2. The government wants to stimulate investment without encouraging inflation and, so, decides to lower interest rates without affecting aggregate spending. What combination of monetary and fiscal policies is appropriate?

3. Congress cuts government spending in order to reduce interest rates and encourage private investment. The Fed doesn't want American dollars going abroad looking for higher yields. So the Account Manager makes open-market sales to keep interest rates from falling. What is the net effect on the economy?

4. In the preceding question, could Congress and the Fed reach a compromise that would be better than their conflicting policies? What for example?

5. An investment journal included this opinion from the association's president:

> The real problem, and the only long-term rational solution, is to address the question once and for all of what percentage of the nation's GNP can be devoted to government spending . . . I don't feel that I have enough information to specify what the government's share of our labors should be . . . Expenditures, however, have not only fluctuated, but have been in an uptrend from 18.5% in 1960 to about 23% today. (James Cloonan, "Deficits: The real issue," *American Association of Individual Investors Journal,* April 1984, p.33)

Write a letter to the editor explaining the confusion in this passage.

6. The *Boston Globe* (July 24, 1982) reported:

> Boston restaurant owners are fuming at the Senate's new tax bill.
>
> One provision of the legislation, passed yesterday, limits the deduction that businesses can take for meal expenses to 50% of their cost, unless those meals are part of an overnight trip. Currently, companies can deduct all such expenses . . .
>
> "It's going to have an adverse impact on our business, a big impact," commented John Sullivan, owner of Joseph's in the Back Bay. "The Senate should stop spending on boondoggles and leave the businessman alone."

Is there any boondoggle difference between a government expenditure on food (for example, school lunches) and a liberal tax deduction for business meals? Should part of these federal tax deductions be counted as a "tax expenditure"?

7. If the Fed increases reserve requirements, will this ease or tighten financial markets? Explain your reasoning.

8. The unemployment rate seems to go up at least as often as it goes down. Yet, the unemployment rate has risen in only one of the thirteen presidential election years from 1936 through 1984. Is this just a coincidence? If not, what is the explanation?

9. Policy makers do not always understand the effects of their policies. In his final State of the Union Address, in December 1932, with the unemployment rate nearing 25%, President Herbert Hoover told the nation that the government could strengthen the economy by "the continued reduction of all government expenditures, whether national, state, or local . . . Embraced in this problem is the unquestioned balancing of the federal budget." Do you agree with this advice? Give your reasons.

10. Explain the following (September 1980) news story:

> The nation's money supply surged upward again in the latest reporting period. Analysts said that while the figures were not a surprise, fears of rising interest rates will grow unless the money supply declines in the next few weeks. "We have to get some down numbers to allay some of the fears in the fixed-income and stock markets," said Edward Yardeni, Assistant Vice President and economist for E.F. Hutton & Co.

11. Two staff writers for the *Los Angeles Times* wrote (November 22, 1982) of government public-works projects to cure unemployment: "Because of . . . , such measures have usually not taken effect until after recovery was well under way." What is the omitted explanation likely to have been? Give a version of the argument that these staff writers probably learned in a macroeconomics class.

12. Consider the following quarterly macro model of the economy:

$y[t] = e[t]$

$e[t] = 1500 + 0.5y[t-1]$

The first equation says that income, y, is equal to expenditures, e, in each 3-month period. The second equation says that spending this quarter depends on income in the previous quarter. The economy is initially (at $t = 0$) in dynamic equilibrium, with both income and expenditures equal to 3000. Then, during quarter $t = 1$, government spending increases by 10, raising the intercept of the expenditure equationfrom 1500 to 1510.

a. What is the new dynamic equilibrium level of income?
b. What is the level of income in the first quarter ($t = 1$)?
c. What is the level of income in the second quarter ($t = 2$)?
d. How long does it take for the increase in government spending to raise income by half of its ultimate increase?
e. How long does it take for income to go up by three-fourths of its ultimate increase?
f. How long does it take for the effects of the increase in government spending to die out completely?

13. Re-analyze the results of trying to peg national income at 3000 when the dynamic model (given by Equation 9.1 in the text) is modified to:

$y[t] = 600 + 4M[t] + 2M[t-1]$.

Explain any differences from the text in your conclusions.

REFERENCES

1. Paul Samuelson, *Economics*, New York: McGraw-Hill, 1961.
2. Abba Lerner, *The Economics of Control*, New York: Macmillan, 1944.

3. J. Wood, "A Model of Federal Reserve Behavior," *Monetary Process and Policy,* G. Horwich, ed., Homewood, Illinois: Irwin, 1967.

4. See W. D. Nordhaus, "The Political Business Cycle," *The Review of Economic Studies* (April 1975), pp. 169–90; and R. D. Fair, "The Effect of Economic Events on Votes for President," *Review of Economics and Statistics* (May 1978), pp. 159–71.

5. S. Maisel, *Managing the Dollar,* New York: Norton, 1975, p. 278.

6. A. M. Schlesinger, Jr., *The Crisis of the Old Order,* Boston; Houghton Mifflin Co., 1957, p. 231.

7. J. M. Keynes, *The General Theory of Employment, Interest, and Money,* London: Macmillan, 1936.

8. *New York World,* October 15, 1930.

9. John Kareken and Robert Solow, "Lags in Monetary Policy," in Commission on Money and Credit, *Stabilization Policies,* Englewood Cliffs, New Jersey: Prentice-Hall, 1963.

10. Gary Fromm and Lawrence Klein, "A Comparison of Eleven Econometric Models on the United States," *American Economic Review,* 63 (May 1973).

11. Kareken and Solow, p. 2.

12. Milton Friedman, "The Lag in the Effect of Monetary Policy," *Journal of Political Economy* (1961), pp. 447–66.

13. L. C. Anderson, "The State of the Monetarist Debate," Federal Reserve Bank of St. Louis *Review,* September 1973, p. 4.

SUGGESTIONS FOR FURTHER READING

For a hard-nosed look at the practice of monetary policy, read Edward J. Kane, "All for the Best: The Federal Reserve Board's 60th Annual Report," *American Economic Review* (December 1974), pp. 835–50. Several economists have constructed formal empirical models to explain Federal Reserve behavior. See, for example, Michael W. Keran and Christopher T. Babb, "An Explanation of Federal Reserve Actions (1933-1968)," Federal Reserve Bank of St. Louis *Review* (1969), pp. 7–20; and Thomas M. Havrilesky, Robert Sapp, and Robert Schweitzer, "Tests of the Federal Reserve's Reactions to the States of the Economy, 1964–74," *Social Science Quarterly* (1975), pp. 635–52.

CHAPTER TEN

DEMAND STABILIZATION POLICIES

We do not know enough to be able to achieve stated objectives by delicate, or even fairly coarse, changes in the mix of monetary and fiscal policy. In this area particularly the best is likely to be the enemy of the good. Experience suggests that the path of wisdom is to use monetary policy explicitly to offset other disturbances only when they offer a "clear and present danger."

MILTON FRIEDMAN[1]

This chapter describes the pros and cons of active and passive economic stabilization policies, examining such questions as whether the Fed should watch the money supply or interest rates, and whether a neutral policy is possible.

AN important part of the Keynesian revolution is the belief that the government should use macroeconomic stabilization policies to smooth out economic air pockets. In recent years, there has been a resurgence of the classical view that stabilization policy is unnecessary and, indeed, may even make matters worse. We'll spend this chapter examining this important debate.

PROBLEMS OF DEMAND-MANAGEMENT POLICIES

We can use our macro model to begin the discussion. *Demand-management policies* are government efforts to move the aggregate demand curve to a desirable location. As represented in Figure 10.1, if the government maintains ongoing policies, output will be y' and the price level will be P'. Perhaps at this level of output, factories will be operating at 80% of their capacity and the unemployment rate will be 10%. Should the government decide that this output is unacceptably and unnecessarily low, an appropriate demand-management policy would be to shift the aggregate demand curve, as shown in the figure, to raise output to some target level such as y''.

To do this, the government could increase spending, cut taxes, or increase the money supply sufficiently to raise demand (at the initial price level) to y'''. This demand increase will bring forth the desired additional output while raising prices to P''. Figure 10.2 shows the details behind the possible fiscal or monetary policies, with the initial *IS-LM* intersection at Point 1. To achieve the target demand y''', the government could *(a)* increase spending or cut taxes so as to shift the *IS* curve to the intersection at Point 2; *(b)* increase the money supply so as to shift the *LM* curve to the intersection at Point 3; or *(c)* employ some combination of *a* and *b.*

The particular combination of monetary and fiscal policies chosen to raise demand to y''' doesn't matter to output or prices, but does affect interest rates and the composition of output. If government spending is increased, then both it and consumption will rise, while investment (which is discouraged by high interest rates) may fall. If, instead, government spending is held constant while income taxes are reduced, then the increased output will be private spending, particularly consumption. If an expansionary monetary policy is used to stimulate the economy, then the increased output will again be private spending, but relatively more investment and less consumption because of the low interest rates.

In theory, demand-management policies can achieve any target level of output permitted by the aggregate supply curve, which describes the tradeoff be-

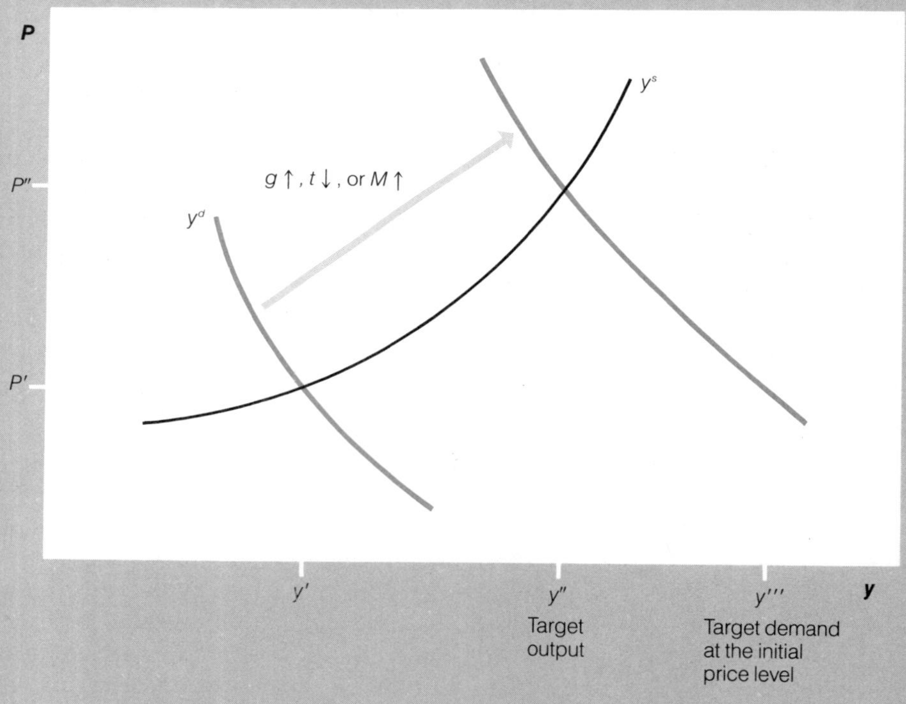

FIGURE 10.1 EXPANSIONARY FISCAL OR MONETARY POLICIES CAN BE USED TO INCREASE OUTPUT AND PRICES. **To raise output to y'', expansionary monetary or fiscal policies can be used to raise aggregate demand at the initial price level to y'''. Target demand must be greater than target output because the accompanying increase in prices chokes off some demand.**

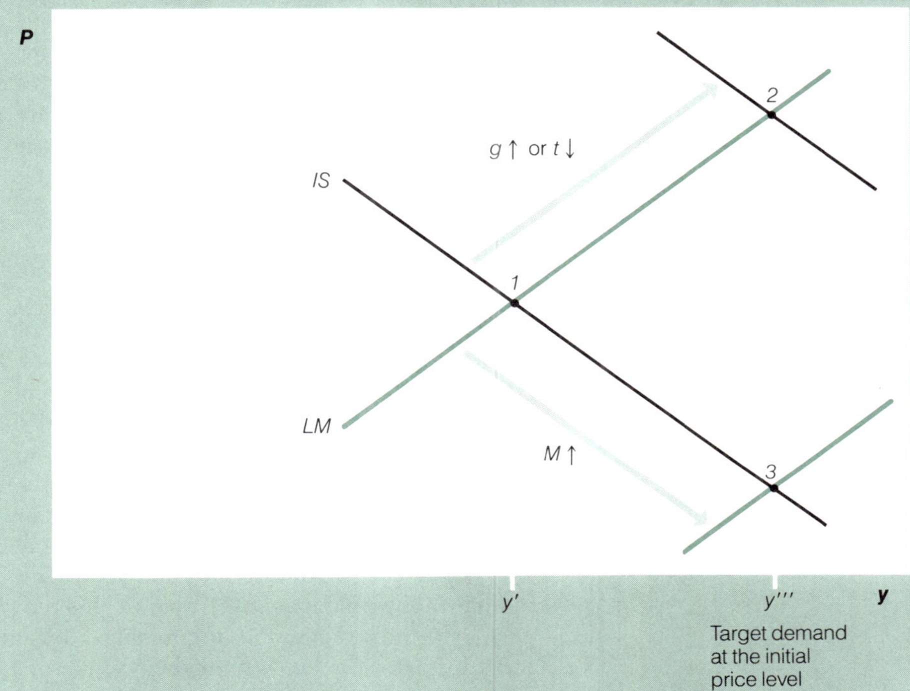

FIGURE 10.2 EITHER FISCAL OR MONETARY POLICIES CAN ACHIEVE TARGET DEMAND. **The target demand *y‴* identified in Figure 10.1 can be attained through higher government spending, lower taxes, or an increased money supply. The primary difference between expansionary fiscal and expansionary monetary policies is in their effect on interest rates and the composition of output.**

tween output and prices that is available to demand-management policies. The "cost" of additional output is an increase in prices; the "cost" of restraining prices is lower output. For any chosen target combination of output and prices, policy makers can also achieve an interest rate target by choosing an appropriate balance between monetary and fiscal policies.

In practice, matters are not so simple. The first complication is that policy makers cannot be certain where the aggregate demand and supply curves are, what their slopes are, and how much the demand curve is shifted by demand-management policies. Policy makers do have empirical estimates of these curves and their slopes and shifts, but like any estimate, they are not exact. As explained in Chapter 9, economic data are imperfect. Some (on real GNP, for example) may be so outdated and imprecise that policy makers cannot tell whether the economy needs to be stimulated or sedated. In addition, policy makers need to know the consequences of their actions, and the economic models necessary to determine this are also imperfect—in part, because we cannot run laboratory experiments with the national economy and in part because we are dealing with unpredictable humans. Finally, as was also discussed in Chapter 9, policy makers can be frustrated by lags, which make fine-tuning impractical.

These lags and uncertainties imply that perfect policy is out of reach. Policy makers may aim for an aggregate demand y''' (Figure 10.2) and an output level y'' (Figure 10.1), but there is no guarantee that they will hit their targets. For a good example of how well-intentioned policies can go awry, we now focus on the policies of the Fed.

An example: Fed stabilization of interest rates

The Fed is interested in the nation's output, unemployment, inflation, and so on, but the Fed does not directly control any of these. If there were no lags and uncertainties, this would make no difference. The link between output and the Fed's open-market operations would be quick and sure. To achieve a level of output y'' (in Figure 10.1), the Fed could use open-market transactions to give an *IS-LM* intersection at y''' (Figure 10.2) and, so, achieve its output objectives. But with lags and uncertainties, the Fed cannot be sure of the effects of its policies, nor can it instantly revise its policies to fine-tune aggregate demand.

What the Fed does control directly is the nation's *monetary base:* the amount of government money outstanding. Some of this money is "currency in circulation," held by individuals and nonfinancial businesses, and some is "reserves," held by banks, either within their vaults or in deposits with the Fed. Federal Reserve notes comprise more than 90% of the U.S. monetary base. A little less than 10% consists of coins issued by the Treasury. There are also $300 million in U.S. Treasury notes (about 0.2% of the monetary base), which trace back to the Greenbacks that financed the Civil War. Treasury notes are fixed by law at $300 million, and coins also require Congressional authorization. So, in practice, the nation's monetary base is controlled by the Fed. **The Fed can increase the monetary base by purchasing securities and paying for them by printing new Federal Reserve notes or by crediting banks with additional reserves. The Fed reduces the monetary base by selling some of its security holdings and retiring Federal Reserve notes or debiting bank reserve accounts.**

Through its daily open-market operations, the Fed can fix either the size of the monetary base or the interest rates on the securities that it is buying and selling. But it cannot peg both the monetary base and interest rates. The Fed can print as much money as it wants and keep the monetary base at whatever level it chooses.* To increase the monetary base, the Fed can buy securities; to reduce it, it can sell securities. But if the Fed is committed to pegging the monetary base, then it cannot act to stabilize interest rates. If interest rates begin to rise, the Fed cannot step in and buy securities to restrain these interest rates, for the monetary base would then rise above its target level.

Similarly, the Fed could announce that it is willing to buy or sell certain securities at given prices. The Fed has then pegged the nominal interest rates on these securities at the levels that correspond to these fixed prices. If there is a

*There are some small technical difficulties. For example, check-clearing delays can cause Fed "float," in which two banks are simultaneously credited with the same reserves.

surge of demand, then the Fed accommodates it by selling as many securities as are demanded. If there are instead sellers, then the Fed buys securities freely. These interest rates are then pegged, as long as the Fed runs out of neither willpower nor securities. But when the Fed pegs an interest rate, it relinquishes control of the monetary base. The monetary base will contract when there is a surge of security buyers, and it will expand when there are sellers. *Thus the Fed can peg the monetary base or interest rates, but not both.*

In practice, the Fed follows neither extreme path. It influences both the monetary base and interest rates, but pegs neither. Through its history, the Fed has sometimes paid more attention to the monetary base, has sometimes concentrated on interest rates, and has sometimes emphasized various monetary aggregates. Following are some of the arguments advanced concerning these competing policies.

Are interest rate targets feasible? The basic argument for interest rate targets is that these are the financial-market variables that influence fundamental economic decisions: whether to spend or save, whether to invest in financial or real assets. If the Fed wants to cool off the economy by discouraging consumption and productive investment, then it should tighten financial markets by increasing real interest rates. It is interest rates that affect saving and borrowing, and that are a barometer of the tightness of financial markets.

One possible criticism of interest rate targets is that the Fed must deal with nominal interest rates, while consumption and investment decisions depend on real interest rates. Some argue that the Fed has no control over real interest rates, that an expansionary monetary policy may simply increase inflation and nominal interest rates equally, leaving real interest rates unchanged. Milton Friedman argues more generally that the Fed cannot control any real economic magnitudes:

> . . . the monetary authority controls nominal quantities—directly, the quantity of its own liabilities. In principle, it can use this control to peg a nominal quantity—an exchange rate, the price level, the nominal level of national income, the quantity of money by one or another definition—or to peg the rate of change in a nominal quantity—the rate of inflation or deflation, the rate of growth or decline in nominal national income, the rate of growth of the quantity of money. It cannot use its control over nominal quantities to peg a real quantity—the real rate of interest, the rate of unemployment, the level of real national income, the real quantity of money, the rate of growth of real national income, or the rate of growth of the real quantity of money.[2]

In earlier chapters, we saw that these sorts of conclusions can be derived from a classical full-employment model. If, however, labor markets are not in equilibrium, then the Fed can cause both short-run and long-run changes in unemployment, real output, and real interest rates.

Sometimes it is argued that all real interest rates must be constant because investors require all yields to equal the fixed real rates of return on physical capital, on the assumption that purchasing bonds, hoarding commodities, and building factories are all equivalent ways of providing for future consumption. Such perfect substitutability would then compel the real rates of return on bonds, commodities, and factories to be the same. And, further, if the real productivity of factories is fixed, then the real rates of return on all of these perfect alternatives must be fixed, too.

Most economists are unconvinced by these arguments. James Tobin has written that, "It is hard to imagine any proposition more divorced from experience."[3] The basic difficulty is that since few of the alternatives are in fact perfect substitutes, few of the yields will move in lock step. Differences among financial assets are small compared with the differences among buying bonds, stockpiling commodities, and becoming an entrepreneur. In addition, there is little theory or evidence that the real rates of return on physical capital are fixed.

It is also sometimes argued that all financial assets must have positive anticipated real rates of return, for, otherwise, investors would shun financial assets and stockpile commodities. Most commodities, however, are perishable or difficult to resell. Storage costs, transactions costs, illiquidity, and indivisibilities all reduce the appeal of investing in commodities. If the CPI is used to measure real rates of return, then it is plainly impractical to stockpile many of its components, such as raspberries, haircuts, medical services, mortgage rates, and taxes. In recent years, many households have, with fully open eyes, kept funds in checking and savings accounts earning negative real returns. They weren't exactly joyful about doing this, but it was the best of their alternatives.

Interest rate targets may be destabilizing A second criticism of interest rate targets is that a Fed policy of stabilizing interest rates may destabilize the economy. We can use our *IS-LM* model to analyze this possibility.[4] The underlying assumption is that the Fed is primarily interested in controlling the aggregate demand for goods and services. Variations in the monetary base and interest rates are just the means to accomplish the end of a certain target level of aggregate demand. The Fed is not always successful in achieving this target demand, because it cannot perfectly anticipate private-sector behavior.

We can formally model this scenario by saying that the Fed has imperfect estimates of the *IS* and *LM* curves. Since we are focusing on aggregate demand, we will omit the y^s curve and price adjustments. Figure 10.3 shows an example of *IS* uncertainty. The Fed's anticipated *IS* curve is labeled $\widehat{IS}$. The actual *IS* curve may turn out to be more expansionary or less expansionary than anticipated. The strong-demand curve is labeled IS^+; the weak-demand curve is IS^-.

Figure 10.4 shows what the *LM* curve looks like under two alternative monetary policy strategies. For now we will continue to assume that the Fed can control the money supply M1. In chapter 4, we saw that the *LM* curve is positively sloped when the money supply is constant. When the Fed instead pegs the interest rate, then the *LM* curve is horizontal at that rate.

In either case, the Fed will choose a money supply or interest rate consistent with its anticipated IS curve so as to yield the target level of aggregate demand $\hat{y}$. These policies are graphed in Figure 10.5. If there were no errors, then both policies would be equally successful; either would hit the target level of aggregate demand.

But what if expenditures turn out to be higher or lower than anticipated? Figure 10.6 shows how the actual *IS* curves, IS^+ and IS^-, cause demand to be above or below the target level. Notice, though, that the size of this demand divergence depends on the Fed's monetary policy. When the money supply is pegged, the LM_M curve applies, and the alternative levels of aggregate demand are as indicated by circled *IS-LM* intersections. When the interest rate is

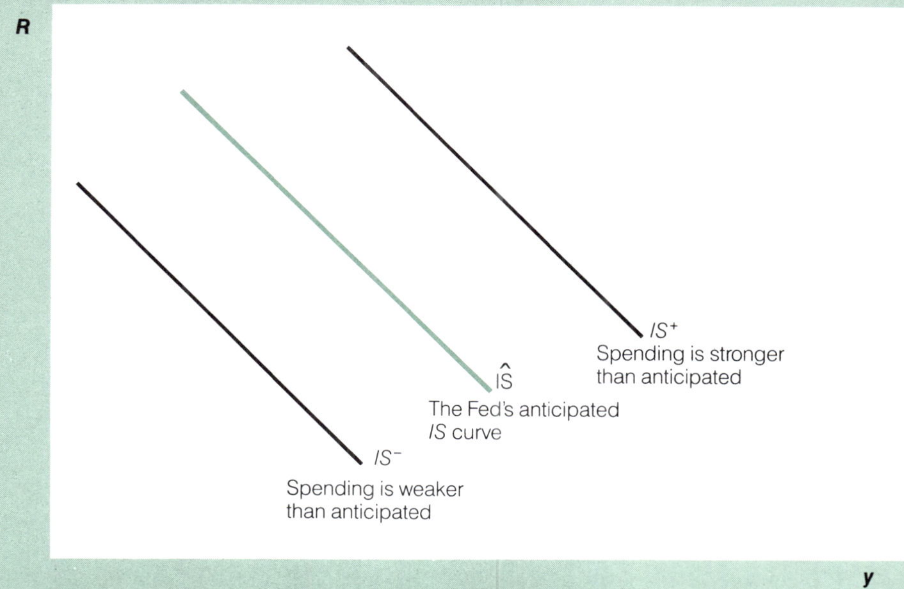

FIGURE 10.3 *IS* UNCERTAINTY. **Policymakers do not know for certain where the *IS* curve will be. Spending may be stronger (IS^+) or weaker (IS^-) than anticipated ($\hat{IS}$).**

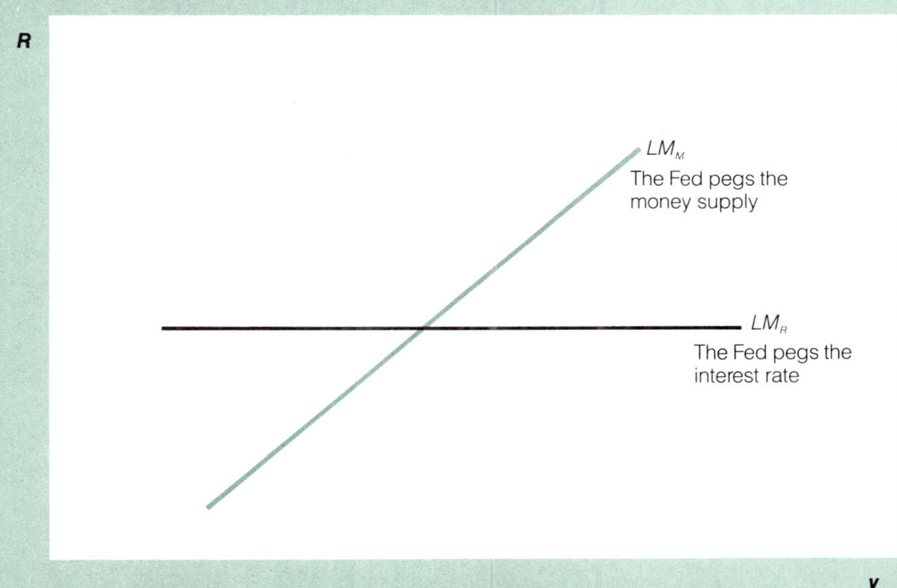

FIGURE 10.4 TWO ALTERNATIVE MONETARY POLICIES. **The usual, positively sloped *LM* curve holds the money supply constant as interest rates fluctuate. An alternative policy, depicted by a horizontal *LM* curve, is to vary the money supply as needed to hold interest rates constant.**

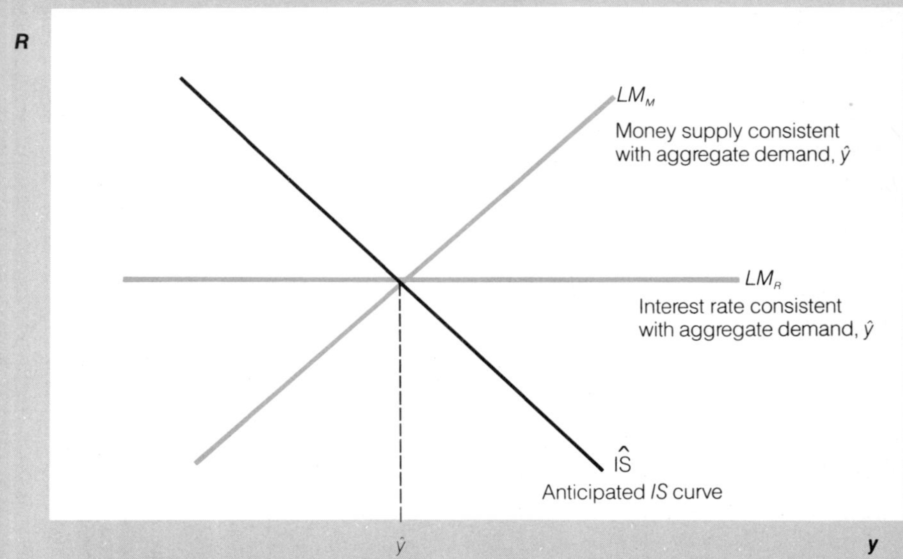

FIGURE 10.5 ON THE BASIS OF THE ANTICIPATED *IS* CURVE THE FED CHOOSES AN *LM* CURVE TO HIT THE AGGREGATE DEMAND TARGET. For any given anticipated *IS* curve, it doesn't matter whether the Fed chooses a money supply or interest rate target. As Figure 10.6 shows, this choice does matter if the actual *IS* curve is different from anticipated.

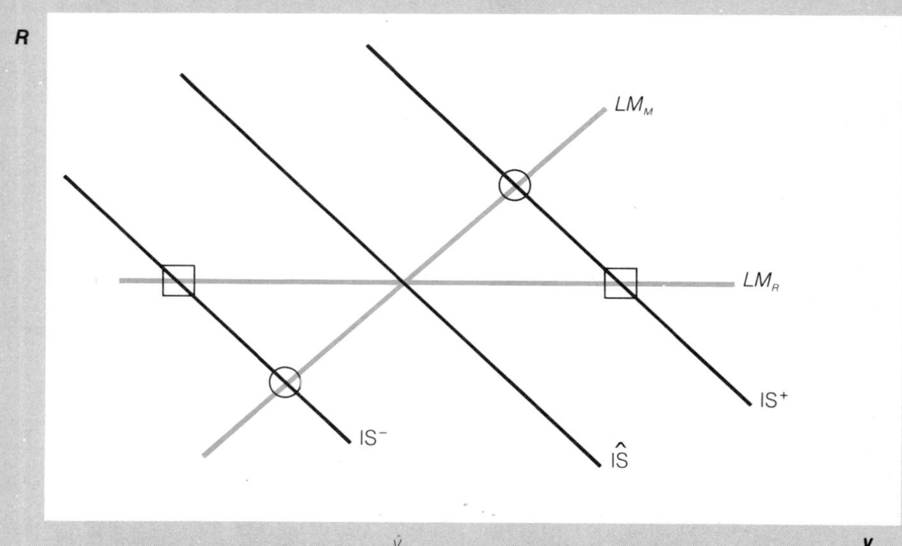

FIGURE 10.6 WHEN THERE IS *IS* UNCERTAINTY, THE FED WILL MISS ITS AGGREGATE DEMAND TARGET GREATLY IF IT PEGS THE INTEREST RATE. Circled intersections show deviations from target demand if the Fed pegs the money supply. Boxed intersections indicate the (even larger) deviations from target demand if, instead, the Fed pegs the interest rate.

pegged, LM_R and the boxed *IS-LM* intersections apply. As shown, there is less variation in y when the money supply is held constant.

The economic logic is as follows. Consider first an expansionary *IS* surprise. Increased transactions enlarge the demand for money, putting upward pressure on interest rates. (If inflation expectations increase, the nominal interest rates will tend to rise by even more than real rates.) If the Fed holds the money supply steady, then the IS^+ curve slides up the LM_M curve, and interest rates are allowed to rise. The increase in the real interest rate stabilizes the economy by discouraging spending and, thereby, dampening the rise in aggregate demand. If the Fed instead uses open-market purchases to restrain interest rates (particularly nominal interest rates), then it will pump more money into an already strong economy, putting gasoline on the fire.

Similarly, the contractionary spending surprise (indicated by IS^-) tends to reduce the real interest rate. (An accompanying decline in inflation expectations will depress the nominal interest rate even more.) If the Fed holds the money supply steady and allows the real interest rate to decline, spending will be encouraged and the fall in demand will be cushioned. If, on the other hand, the Fed makes open-market sales to stabilize interest rates, then they will draw money out of an already weak economy, thereby exacerbating the recession. **Therefore, in the face of *IS* uncertainty, a strategy of stabilizing interest rates tends to destabilize the economy.**

A money supply target may be inferior This is not the end of the analysis. The Fed also makes mistakes in estimating money demand. It consequently does not know exactly where the *LM* curve will be when it pegs the money supply. Figure 10.7 charts some *LM* surprises. The anticipated *LM* curve is $\widehat{LM}_M$. If money demand is smaller than expected, then the expansionary LM_M^+ curve applies; if unexpectedly large, then LM_M^- applies.*

The target level of aggregate demand is $\hat{y}$. If the monetary base is pegged, then money demand surprises will shift the *LM* curve, yielding the circled *IS-LM* intersections in the figure. When the interest rate is pegged, in contrast, variations in money demand are met by offsetting changes in supply. If, for example, money demand is stronger than anticipated, tending to push the *LM* curve back to LM_M^-, then the upward pressure on the interest rate will provoke an open-market purchase. The Fed will increase the money supply to hold R steady, and the *IS-LM* intersection (indicated in Figure 10.7 by the box) remains at the target level. **Therefore, in the face of *LM* uncertainty, a strategy of pegging interest rates stabilizes aggregate demand.**

Interest rates or the money supply? From Figures 10.6 and 10.7 it would seem that pegging the money supply base is a good strategy when there is lots of uncertainty about the *IS* curve, while interest rate stabilization is a good strategy when there is lots of uncertainty about the *LM* curve. However, as is usually the case, matters are more complicated.†

* Remember, an increase in money demand is like a decrease in money supply, and a contraction of money demand like an expansion of supply.

† An additional complexity is the distinction between the monetary base and some monetary aggregate such as M1 (currency outside banks plus deposits in transactions accounts). If, in a boom, market interest rates increase more than ceiling rates on transactions accounts, then funds will flow out of deposit institutions, thereby reducing M1. A policy rule of stabilizing M1 will call for monetary expansion in the midst of a boom—again, gasoline on a fire.

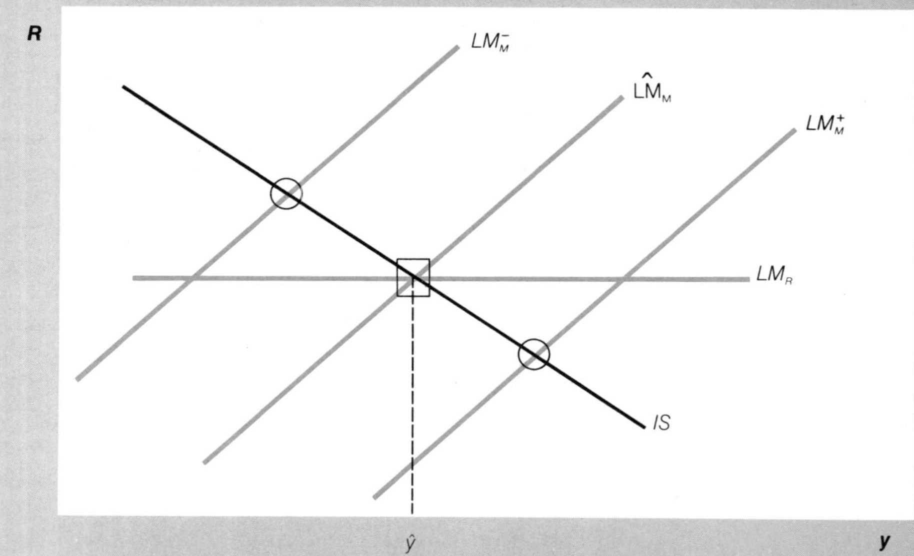

FIGURE 10.7 **WHEN THERE IS *LM* UNCERTAINTY, THE FED WILL MISS ITS AGGREGATE DEMAND TARGET GREATLY IF IT PEGS THE MONEY SUPPLY. Circled intersections show the deviations from target demand if the Fed pegs the money supply. There is no deviation from target demand if, instead, the Fed pegs the interest rate (boxed intersections).**

One inadequacy in this analysis is that it neglects the possibility of using both monetary and fiscal policies to reduce unwanted variations in aggregate demand. Just as investors choose diversified portfolios to reduce their risks, so aggregate-demand risk can be reduced by using several policies to diversify the government's position. Instead of using monetary policy to peg the money supply or an interest rate, it is better to use monetary and fiscal policies together to peg neither but pay attention to both.[5]

Another inadequacy of the analysis in Figures 10.6 and 10.7 is that it considers an unexpected shift in only the *IS* curve or the *LM* curve, but not both. What if there is uncertainty about both? To illustrate, reconsider Figure 10.6, in which there is *IS* uncertainty but no *LM* uncertainty. Any unexpected increase in spending is implicitly financed by a reduced bond demand (or by increased borrowing). What if, instead, any surprise *IS* shift also involves an *LM* shift? That is, any unexpected increase in spending is financed by a diminished money demand.

The analysis, as shown in Figure 10.8, is complicated, but the conclusions are quite interesting. Now, when spending is unexpectedly high (IS^+), money demand is low (LM^+). This accompanying drop in money demand reinforces the expansionary effects of the spending increase. An unanticipated money-financed increase in spending reduces the interest rate to the circled *IS-LM* in-

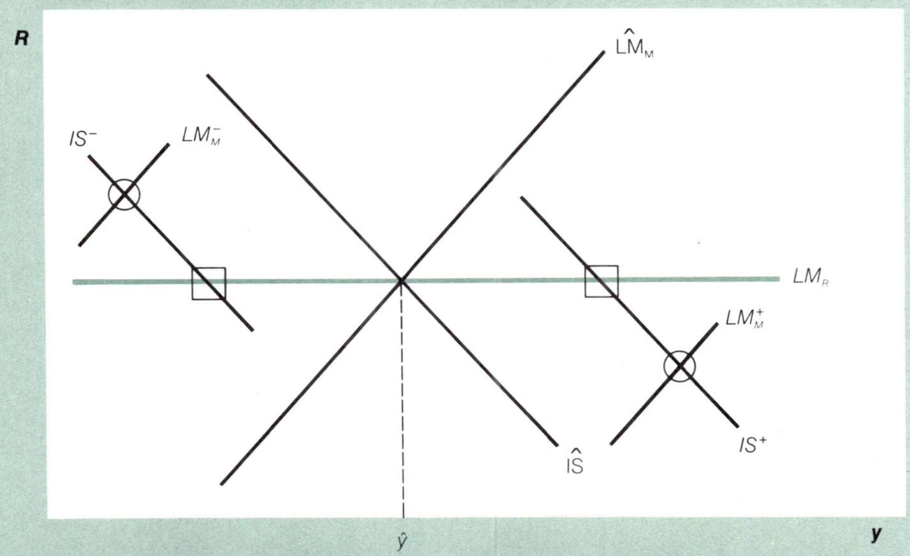

FIGURE 10.8 AN EXAMPLE OF *IS* AND *LM* UNCERTAINTY. **In this case, both the *IS* and *LM* curves are either surprisingly expansionary or surprisingly contractionary. Here, pegging the money supply (circled intersections) gives larger demand errors than does pegging the interest rate (boxed intersections).**

tersection. A policy of pegging *R* now provides monetary restraint, in that the Fed reduces the money supply to offset the drop in money demand. This open-market sale restrains aggregate demand to the boxed *IS-LM* intersection. In contrast to the case of the *IS* surprise shown in Figure 10.6, pegging the interest rate now stabilizes the aggregate demand.

These differing conclusions reflect different interrelationships among the government's errors. Pure theory does not tell us how *LM* uncertainty is correlated with *IS* uncertainty. Figures 10.6 and 10.8 are just two of the many possibilities. An expansionary *IS* surprise could be accompanied by an expansionary or contractionary *LM* surprise, or by no *LM* surprise. Theory does tell us that the optimal government policy in an uncertain world depends on an assessment of such complex and elusive issues.

The foregoing should make it clear that it is no easy matter to determine whether the Fed should peg the money supply or the interest rate. Additional evidence is provided by the observation that reasonably intelligent and well-educated people continue to argue the question. If the issue were really straightforward, the argument would be over by now.

For those who remain unconvinced, we turn to another line of reasoning to deepen the discussion (or the confusion). So far, we have paid little attention to the fact that government tax revenue depends on the level of economic activity.

Many taxes, such as individual and corporate income taxes, increase with output. The government's budget constraint (Equation 4.8) tells us that an increase in tax revenue presents policy makers with three options. The Treasury can spend the additional tax revenue on goods and services or purchase bonds from the private sector. The third option is that tax revenue can be used implicitly to reduce the money supply, in that the Treasury can purchase bonds while the Fed simultaneously sells bonds, so that the bond supply is constant while the money supply declines. Thus, when national income increases, the policy makers' choices are to use the additional tax revenue to increase spending, reduce the bond supply, or reduce the money supply.

If government spending is increased, this will further stimulate the economy. Similarly, purchasing bonds reduces interest rates and thereby encourages private spending. If, however, the money supply is reduced, this cools the expansion. Holding government spending and the bond supply constant, while varying the money supply with tax revenue, commits the government to an automatically counter-cyclical monetary policy.[6] Instead of pegging government spending and either the money supply or interest rates, policy makers might be better off pegging government spending and the bond supply!

The most reasonable conclusion is that there is no simple, perfect policy for all times and all places. Doggedly pegging interest rates, the money supply, or some other pet target will, in some circumstances, be a poor policy. Instead of myopically focusing on one bit of data and ignoring everything else, it is more logical to watch many data. As Paul Samuelson put it, Federal Reserve Governors were given two eyes so that they could watch both interest rates and the money supply.[7] In practice, the Fed is a multi-eyed monster that also watches data on output, employment, inflation, the balance of payments, and election returns. If the economy is in a serious recession, which the Fed wants to soften, then easy money is called for. Rather than single-mindedly pegging interest rates or the money supply as the economy falls apart, the Fed makes substantial open-market purchases, thereby pumping money into the ailing economy, reducing real interest rates, and stimulating spending.

The Fed's Governors keep open minds and look at many facets of the economy before deciding whether monetary ease or restraint is appropriate. Unfortunately, as we saw in the previous chapter, the presence of policy delays may undermine flexible policies that try to achieve too much. This worry has led some observers to recommend that policy makers follow "neutral" policies and let the economy take care of itself. Implicit in this recommendation is the classical belief that the private economy is inherently stable—that booms and recessions are short-lived and self-correcting.

NEUTRAL POLICIES

What government policies should be followed in a very uncertain world? One answer (and another forecasting canon) is "When in doubt, mumble." This approach advises that the government should do nothing, except perhaps get out of the way; the government should pursue *neutral policies,* which do not upset or distort the private economy. Implicit, and sometimes explicit, in this recommendation is the belief that when matters are left to private citizens making decisions in this uncertain world, things will somehow work out for the best.

A fundamental operational difficulty with this advice is that of defining neutral policies. The complete absence of a government might qualify as a neutral policy (though the actual process of shutting down would hardly be neutral). But there are few, if any, responsible advocates of entirely abolishing government. (Would General Motors take over national defense, financed by voluntary contributions?) If we are to have some government, it is very difficult to identify neutral policies. Expenditures on national defense divert bright scientists, skilled workers, and scarce material from other uses and provide more benefits to the young than the old, to the healthy than the ill, to worriers than nonworriers, and to those living in areas most likely to be attacked. More generally, all government expenditures use resources that could be used for other purposes and, thus, convey uneven benefits to the citizenry.

And how are government expenditures to be financed? Tax levies, bond sales, and money printing are not neutral. We could, in theory, levy lump-sum taxes, though these would still distort child-bearing and citizenship decisions. More important, however, is the overwhelming consensus that the well-off should pay more than the poor. This consensus compels tax codes that are not neutral, but rather embody redistribution and incentive effects. What about bond sales? These raise interest rates and crowd out private borrowers. What about money printing? We've seen that it takes some pretty extreme assumptions for money to be neutral. And even if money only affected prices, there would still be redistribution effects between debtors and creditors.

One argument that has received considerable attention over the years is that it is precisely because monetary policy does affect the economy that the government should strive for a neutral monetary policy. But again even the foremost advocates (such as Friedrich von Hayek) have been unable to come up with a satisfactory definition of a "neutral monetary policy." Should the government regulate private money? Should it issue government money? How much? Should it hold this money (or some other monetary aggregate) constant? Or should it allow money to increase at a constant rate? Or should it permit money to rise and fall with the economy? How is the increased money supply to be put into circulation? These are but a sampling of the simple, but apparently unanswerable, niggling questions. And the specific answers chosen do make a difference: If money is not neutral, then no monetary policy can really be neutral.

Fixed rules

A variant on the neutral-money recommendation, one that is more operational, is the belief that it really doesn't very much matter what the government does, as long as it is consistent about it. The seminal statement of this view was made by Henry Simons in 1936:

> In a free enterprise system we obviously need highly definite and stable rules of the game, especially as to money. The monetary rules must be compatible with the reasonably smooth functioning of the system. Once established, however, they should work automatically, with the chips falling where they may. . . . The responsibility for carrying out the monetary rules should be lodged in a federal authority . . . closely controlled in their exercise by a sharply defined policy. . . . Political control in this sphere should be confined exclusively to regulation of the quantity of money and near money.[7]

In Simons' view, monetary authorities should be subservient to monetary rules. In monetary matters, as in other areas, we should be a nation governed by laws rather than by people.

This belief was roughly consistent with the broad anti-government views then espoused by members of what came to be called the *Chicago School,* which strongly extolled the virtues of unfettered markets and sharply criticized government interference. For many years, Milton Friedman was the most visible and effective proponent of the Chicago School; today the leadership has apparently passed to Robert Lucas (again at the University of Chicago) under the banner, "the new classical macroeconomics."

Simons avoided the fundamental difficulties in defining a "neutral monetary policy" by arguing that the most important issue is that discretionary policy be replaced by fixed monetary rules. The actual rules are less important than the private sector's confidence that the rules will not be changed in mid-game. Nonetheless, there remains the practical question of making up the rules.

One of Simons' ideas was to fix the quantity of money,* but this idea foundered on the problems of selecting a money supply to hold constant. In his 1936 essay, Simons expressed his frustration with ". . . the unfortunate character of our financial structure—with the abundance of what we may call "near-moneys"—with the difficulty of defining money in such a manner as to give practical significance to the conception of quantity."[8]

This exasperation with the real world led Simons to recommend seriously the abolition of such near-moneys as bank deposits and short-term securities:

> A liberal program of monetary reform should seek to effect an increasingly sharp differentiation between money and private obligations and, especially, to minimize the opportunities for the creation of effective money substitutes. . . . The abolition of private deposit banking is clearly the appropriate first step in this direction and would bring us in sight of the goal; but such a measure, to be really effective, must be accompanied, or followed closely, by drastic limitation on the formal borrowing powers of all private corporations and especially upon borrowing at short term.[9]

It sometimes seems easier, when a simple model doesn't fit the world, to change the world! The irony here is that a free-market economist, in seeking to reduce government interference with free enterprise, winds up advocating pervasive government regulation of financial markets.

The modern descendants of this Chicago tradition have generally eschewed such radical constraints on financial markets, but they have continued to recommend passive monetary policy via fixed monetary rules. Milton Friedman, for instance, has long advocated that the Fed choose a monetary aggregate, such as M1 or M2, and simply keep this measure of the money supply growing at a constant 3% to 5% per year, regardless of the state of the economy.

Such advocates of passive policy are critics of discretionary demand-management policies. Their central criticism of monetary and fiscal stabilization policies is that policy makers have done a poor job and will continue to do so. Thus Edward Shaw wrote of the Fed:

* His other recommendation was to fix the price level, but he argued that this should be mainly accomplished with government spending and tax policies. One difficulty with this was the selection of an aggregate price index. Simons also seemed to be calling for discretionary fiscal policy in order to make monetary policy less discretionary.

> The antimanagement brief does not deny that monetary policy *could* perform miracles, promoting stable growth and fending off shocks to growth. But our experience contains no miracles. Management skills are not equal to the job of realizing the potentialities of monetary policy.[10]

Uncertainties are one big reason why policy makers make mistakes. The other big obstacle to miraculously successful policies is the delay between shocks to the economy and the effects of policies designed to offset these shocks. If these delays are long and the economy stabilizes itself correctly, then the patient is well before the economic medicine reaches it.

In Chapter 9, We used a simple model to show how delays may undermine well-intentioned efforts to use monetary policy to peg national income. There was nothing special about monetary policy in this example. The mathematical conclusions would have been the same whether we had let the symbol M stand for government spending or for tax policy. The general lesson is that any policy that has important lagged effects may be incapable of fully stabilizing the economy. Since all policies do have delays of some sort (recognition delays, action delays, and transmission delays), it is tempting to conclude that there should be no active policy to stabilize the economy.

But it is not enough to shun active stabilization policy; advocates of a passive policy must define it. Since taxes depend on economic activity, the government cannot literally "do nothing" as the economy fluctuates. When the economy weakens and tax revenues decline, the government budget constraint implies that there must be some response by the government. It can increase tax rates to hold tax revenue steady, cut government spending, print money, or sell bonds. Passive-policy enthusiasts must choose one of these responses or some combination thereof.

Most of the recommended passive policies evade this necessary choice by focusing instead on specific partial rules—such as holding government spending at x% of GNP, balancing the budget, or keeping M2 growing at 4% a year. These partial rules neglect the government's budget constraint. They are also ambiguous and of uncertain merit. A few examples follow.

Fixed government spending

There have been scattered calls for having government spending or disbursements (spending plus transfers) either grow at a constant rate or be a constant fraction of national output. These sorts of rigid spending constraints have serious flaws; for example, a large part of government expenditures are for national defense, and it would be a bit reckless to set these expenditures without regard for changes in national security needs. Similarly, social security payments surely need to take into account changes in the age composition of the population. A more reasonable passive fiscal policy is to base expenditures solely on their intrinsic merit, completely ignoring the state of the economy.

Evasive budget deficits

It is sometimes argued that the government should balance its budget each year. Strict fiscal rules are undermined by difficulties in forecasting and even defining the government's budget. Interest expenses, outlays for entitlement programs, and tax revenues all vary with the economy and may be inaccurately predicted. There are also conceptual ambiguities in filling in the numbers in the government's balance sheets. Some of the troublesome issues are off-budget expenditures (such as the Tennessee Valley Authority), loan subsidies and guarantees, capital gains on government debt, long-lived investments (in such things as highways and research), and future commitments (like Social Security). William Nordhaus estimated that, depending on how these ambiguities are handled, the 1981 federal budget could have shown a \$116 billion surplus or a \$105 billion deficit.[11] No wonder, the annual federal budgets have been called "the most expensive periodic works of fiction ever published.[12]

There are also lots of government laws and regulations that affect the economy but don't show up anywhere in dollars-and-cents ledgers. If, for example, the government cleans up a river, the cost is counted as a federal expenditure. If they, instead, require private industries located near the river to make the cleanup, it's cost won't appear as federal expenditure. Yet, in either case, the government has caused resources to be employed cleaning up the river. A government that is constricted by budgetary rules will use more laws and regulations in place of direct expenditures, but the choice between regulations and expenditures should depend on which does a better job, not which satisfies an arbitrary budget accounting.

Government budgets are also incomplete because they neglect the nonmonetary returns from government expenditures. Just as private houses implicitly yield income to their resident owners, so our nation implicitly derives income from government buildings, parks, missles, and research. Just as we should count the costs of government-mandated river cleanups, so should we count the benefits. Government expenditures and regulations should be judged by a full accounting of their costs and benefits, not by the partial accounting of whether tax revenues cover disbursements.

A monetary deficit in some particular accounting of the government's budget does not automatically mean that the government is spending too much or taxing too little. Nor does a surplus in someone else's accounting mean that the government is spending too little or taxing too much. The first question, regardless of the budget surplus or deficit, is whether the benefits of each expenditure justify its cost. The next question is whether these justified expenditures should be financed by taxation, bond sales, or money issuance.

A further problem with balanced-budget rules is that budget deficits depend in part on the state of the economy. In a recession, tax revenues fall with income, while federal spending for food stamps, unemployment compensation, and so on increases. Overall, every percentage point increase in the unemployment rate raises the federal deficit by about \$25 billion. Because of the progressivity of tax schedules, a 1% increase in the rate of inflation raises tax revenue by 1.5%. A 1% increase in interest rates raises federal interest expense on the national debt by \$3 billion.[13]

President Ronald Reagan took office in 1981, promising to balance the budget quickly. But, in 1982, he was hit with a budgetary triple-whammy: an increase in unemployment, while inflation came down and interest rates stayed up. His projected \$45-billion deficit turned into a \$100-billion deficit. Should he have let this growing deficit dictate his fiscal policy? Should he have cut government spending or increased taxes in the midst of the most severe recession since the Great Depression in the 1930s? Economic theory and common sense say that spending cuts or tax increases would only have weakened the economy further. **Thus, a balanced-budget rule undermines the automatic stabilization provided by our tax system. To continually balance its budget, the government would have to cut spending or raise taxes in the midst of recessions and increase spending or cut taxes in the middle of economic booms.**

While well aware of the political appeal of a balanced budget, Reagan also realized the economic folly of such a policy. So he resisted higher taxes, grumbled about the sins of his predecessors, and proposed legislation requiring future presidents to balance their budgets.

A plethora of monetary targets

There are similar ambiguities and dangers in Friedman's recommendation that the Fed should ignore the economy and keep the money supply growing at a steady annual rate of 3% to 5%. This rule can be rationalized in terms of the classical quantity theory,

$$Mv = Py \tag{10.1}$$

where it is assumed that velocity, v, is stable and that real income, y, is always near full employment, but that both may slowly change in the long run. Empirically, Friedman concluded that real income grows by about 2% to 3% a year while velocity falls by about 1% to 2%. Therefore Friedman recommends that a 3% to 5% growth in the money supply will hold the price level approximately constant.*

The underlying assumptions are that velocity and real output deviate little from their long-run trend paths. Neither of these assumptions is strictly true. We've seen how velocity varies, especially as interest rates change, and that income fluctuates as the economy departs from full employment. But beyond these core issues, there is also the practical matter of deciding which money should grow at 3% to 5%, and how this should be accomplished.

Edward Shaw, an advocate of a constant money growth rule, freely acknowledged the difficulties of selecting a money supply to target:

> If you suspect that growth in money was under tight restraint, you can tailor a definition to your suspicion. If you prefer to think that restraint was mild you can be right again—with a different definition. . .
>
> The "supply of money" that central banks manipulate, that people hold most of the time and spend once in a while, that economists investigage is not, then, a simple concept. It can be a figure so transformed in the statistical beauty parlor as to be hardly recognizable by its closest friends.[14]

Shaw settled for old M1 (currency outside banks plus checking account deposits) as a monetary target. Others simply like the monetary base. Friedman

* For example, say $M = 500$, $v = 3$, $P = 1$, and $y = 1500$. If M increases 4% to 520, while v falls $1\frac{1}{2}$% to 2.955, and y increases by $2\frac{1}{2}$ to 1537.5, then $P = 520\ (2.955)/1537.5 = 1.0$. Many economists to not expect real income to grow this fast in the future, and they expect velocity to continue to increase (rather than decline). Either of these adjustments would reduce Friedman's recommended growth rate for M.

picked old M2 (M1 plus time and savings accounts in commercial banks). After Arthur Burns became Chairman of the Fed, he converted from M1 to M5 (which is M2 plus large negotiable Certificates of Deposit plus deposits in savings and loan associations, mutual savings banks, and credit unions). In Chapter 15, we will look at these competing aggregates more closely and see why there is so much confusion. It suffices here to note that there are several alternative targets and that it does make a difference, because forcing one monetary aggregate to grow at a constant rate does not ensure that others will.

In fact, in dynamic, innovative financial markets, controlling one monetary aggregate almost ensures that new financial assets will develop and expand. When the government tried to restrain bank notes after the Civil War, demand deposits took their place. The explosion of check-like accounts in the 1970s was fueled by the Fed's efforts to restrain traditional bank checking accounts. Financial-market innovations such as these increase the volume of transactions that can be carried out with a given monetary aggregate. For example, the introduction of NOW accounts reduced the appeal of traditional checking accounts and thereby increased old M1 velocity. If M1 velocity is not constant, then a mechanical 5% growth rate for M1 does not imply that nominal income grows by 5%. Charles Goodhart, a senior economist at the Bank of England (which currently watches its M5), offered Goodhart's Law: "Any definition of money which becomes an official target will lose all relationship with events in the real economy within two years."[15]

In 1980, the Fed formally acknowledged the changes that had been occurring in financial markets by completely redefining monetary aggregates. The new aggregates M1A, M1B, M2, M3, and L incorporated a number of new important financial assets: NOW accounts, money market mutual funds, Eurodollars, and repurchase agreements. In addition, several assets were reshuffled. For example, time deposits at savings and loan associations were plucked from M3 and put into M2. A year later, the Fed decided that M1B had to be supplemented by "M1B-shift adjusted."* In 1982, the Fed eliminated M1A and relabeled M1B "M1".

New near-moneys are still sprouting all around us. Attempts to control some are sure to spawn others. Some new moneys and near-moneys, such as electronic payments systems with overdraft privileges, will be exceedingly difficult to monitor. In a rapidly changing world, an up-to-date monetary rule is akin to the economics professor who gives the same exam year after year, but changes the answers each year. In the same spirit, the appropriate monetary rule might be "have the money supply grow at a constant rate year after year, but change the definition of the money supply each year." If so, is that really very different from a discretionary policy?

Economic events seldom affect all financial markets equally. Thus it is often useful to have specific detailed policies directed at particular financial markets or institutions. Before becoming Fed Chairman, Paul Volcker argued that

> There have been a number of occasions in the 1970s when the Federal Reserve had to pay the closest possible attention to particular financial problems and to the potential vulnerability of various credit markets. The recurrent concerns . . . about the capacity of thrift institutions to perform their role as intermediaries between savers and the

* This concoction takes out of M1B an estimate of the money in NOW accounts that is made up of savings rather than transaction deposits.

> mortgage market is one example. The potential disturbances growing out of the Penn Central Railroad and the Franklin and the Herstatt Bank affairs are another class of examples. The strain on the municipal bond markets and the concerns about the rising level of losses commercial banks were taking on loans a year or so ago are other cases in point. Their problems had to be dealt with—actually or potentially—by techniques that cannot be encompassed by any simple monetary rule.[16]

Ironically, Volcker has himself been criticized for paying too much attention to monetary aggregates and too little attention to the availability of credit to specific sectors of the economy. Congressman Henry Reuss noted:

> Because of the Fed's fixation with the overall money supply rather than with the composition of lending, the nation's precious credit pool is being dissipated in a swirl of gambling in commodities, corporate takeovers, conversions of rental housing to condominiums and similar speculative activities that simply bid up the price of existing assets without creating a single new tool of production.[11]

Another basic difficulty with Friedmanesque rules is that it is much easier to recommend a steady monetary growth rate than to achieve it. The Fed controls the monetary base directly and affects monetary aggregates only indirectly. In Chapter 15, we show that there is little if any contemporaneous correlation between changes in the monetary base and changes in the various monetary aggregates. Monetary aggregates are influenced not only by the Fed, but also by the economic decisions of households, businesses, and financial institutions.

In addition, it takes a considerable amount of time for an increase in the government money supply to cycle through the banking system and cause the ultimate changes in monetary aggregates. And there are lots of slippages and external influences, substantial errors and delays, along the way. The very same errors-and-lags argument as to why discretionary policy may not be able to stabilize the economy also implies that monetary policy may not be able to stabilize monetary aggregates.[18]

In December 1981, Anthony Solomon, respected President of the Federal Reserve Bank of New York, speculated that, "We may already be nearing the point where the Federal Reserve can influence the growth of these broad measures only indirectly by first influencing the behavior of the economy itself." A most interesting reversal! Monetarists hoped that the Fed could stabilize the economy by stabilizing the money supply. Thus the Fed is advised to keep the money supply growing at a steady rate. But the Fed responds that, as a practical matter, the only way they can get the money supply to grow at a steady rate is to somehow keep the economy growing at a steady pace. It is apparently at least as difficult to stabilize monetary aggregates as it is to stabilize GNP.

Since 1975, the Fed has been regularly announcing its targets for monetary growth and for the interest rate on federal funds (overnight loans of excess bank reserves). Rather than being pinpointed objectives, these targets have been ranges, such as "keep the rate of growth of M2 between 5% and 8%." The Fed has been relatively successful in hitting its federal funds rate targets. This is because it can directly affect this interest rate and always knows the current rate. With M1 and M2, the situation is quite different. The Fed does not directly observe nor affect these monetary aggregates. Instead, the Fed uses an econometric model to help predict how monetary policies will affect monetary aggregates, and this model has frequently gone awry. This is a large part of the reason why the Fed has missed its monetary targets as often as it hits them.

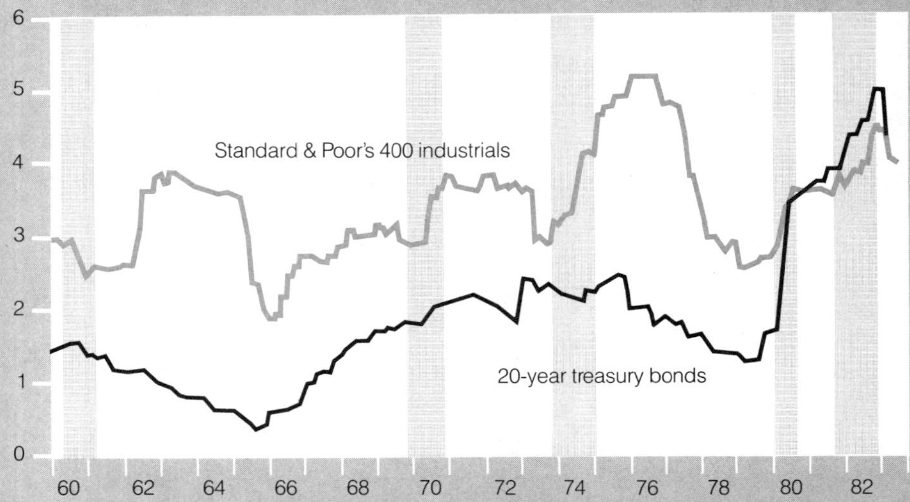

FIGURE 10.9 THIRTY-SIX-MONTH STANDARD DEVIATION OF MONTHLY RETURNS. **After the Fed's October, 1979, decision to stabilize monetary aggregates rather than interest rates, the volatility of interest rates (as measured by their standard deviation) increased dramatically. (Prepared by Michael F. Wilcox of L. F. Rothschild, Unterberg, Towbin. Reprinted by permission.)**

In October 1979, the new Fed Chairman, Paul Volcker announced a determination to stabilize monetary aggregates, even if this caused interest rates to fluctuate greatly. Specifically, whereas the monthly average federal funds rate was previously held within a narrow 0.5% range, the Volcker Fed was now willing to tolerate fluctuations of 5% or more.

Interest rates then went through some truly breathtaking gyrations. In April 1980, the prime lending rate ran up to 20% and then retreated almost as rapidly as it had charged up that uncharted hill. The federal funds rate jumped from less than 13% in mid-February to above 19% in early April, and then fell below 10% in late May. On a single day, August 5, 1980, the federal funds rate swung between 8.75% in the morning and 2% in the afternoon. Apparently the Fed meant what it said about letting interest rates fluctuate.

Such wild interest rate swings caused disarray, even dispair, in financial markets, as both borrowers and lenders came to the historic conclusion that bonds were now riskier than stocks. Figure 10.9, using one measure of risk, the standard deviation of monthly returns, shows the striking increase in the riskiness of bonds after October 1979. The President of the investment house E. F. Hutton said, "This market has made traders queasy, uneasy, and at times shaken. The greatest problem of all is the volatility. Even in government securities, prices have sometimes changed in a single day more than they did in an entire year in the past."[19] The Chairman of Manufacturers Hanover Trust said, "We ask ourselves, where's the roller coaster going in the next 12 months,

IN THE NEWS
Fed Watching Grows in the Markets, Spurring Frenzied, Anxious Trading

Last Friday, 11:37 a.m.: John Spinello's wristwatch alarm starts beeping. He's sitting in the trading room of Merrill Lynch Government Securities Inc. in New York. Like other traders there, he's staring at financial data on his own little video screens. The beeping signals, as it does every weekday, the arrival of what Mr. Spinello calls "Fed time."

Thus do the financial markets enter that crucial, closely watched time: the daily 15-minute period when the Federal Reserve Board tinkers with more than $40 billion of reserve funds in the banking system and traders discover whether they have guessed correctly the market's inevitable reaction.

On this particular Friday, "Fed time" is especially treacherous. Just before the period ends, someone in the trading room shouts "Matched sales!" That means the Fed is draining bank reserves, surprising disappointed bond traders who had hoped the central bank would stay on the sidelines. The market responds quickly: Within minutes, the long-term Treasury bond price plunges almost a full point, or nearly $10 per $1,000 face value.

The action similarly unsettles the Board of Trade and the Mercantile Exchange in Chicago, as traders in financial futures shout and jostle in a mad dash to the trading pits. Most of them seek to unload contracts as their losses mount.

The Federal Reserve Board has long been a market mover. Because the Fed seeks to control the growth of money supply—a process that affects interest rates—and sets the influential discount rate, Fed-watching has become a tradition in the investment community. But in these days of interest-rate preoccupation, the number of Fed-watchers and their anxiety have grown dramatically.

On Oct. 6, for instance, word leaked out that the Fed would temporarily let the basic money supply grow beyond previously set restraints. That was seen as the main reason that the Dow Jones industrial average surged 105 points over four days. But on Oct. 25, a much-anticipated cut in the discount rate—the fee the Fed charges on loans to member banks and savings institutions—didn't materialize. The next trading day, the index plummeted 36.33 points, the largest single-day decline since Oct. 28, 1929.

Fed-watching has gained considerable intensity in recent years following the board's Oct. 6, 1979, decision to combat inflation by controlling money growth rather than focusing on interest rates. Suddenly, interest rates were much more volatile, and misinterpreting Fed actions became more costly.

The fever rose with rapid growth of the highly speculative market in financial futures—16 contracts linked to interest rates have been created since October 1979. . . .

To some, this smacks of mass hysteria. They argue that the Fed influences only interest rates; it's the credit market that sets them. And the central bank's daily tinkerings can easily be misinterpreted, these skeptics insist. The recent rally, says Julian Snyder, who publishes an investment newsletter, was spiked more by the psychology of Fed-watching than by the Fed itself.

But since Fed actions do move interest-rate-sensitive markets—such as bonds and financial futures, and, at times, stocks—Mr. Snyder remains a devoted Fed-watcher. He assigns one member of his staff to collect all Fed-generated statistics and another to record Fed Chairman Paul Volcker's major public utterances for Mr. Snyder's scrupulous study. "Nuances are important," he explains.

Perhaps the market should focus on broader developments, concedes Norman E. Mains, chief economist for the financial-futures division of Drexel Burnham Lambert Inc., but "people want to know about *today;* the atmosphere on the trading floor is so charged that any piece of information can move the market."

Mr. Mains, a former Fed economist, belongs to a growing fraternity of Fed specialists at brokerage houses, economic forecasting outfits, investment advisory services and banks. They try to predict money-supply fluctuations and Fed actions on banking reserves and the discount rate.

They pore over figures on check floats, bank-vault cash, U.S. Treasury balances at Federal Reserve banks and bank borrowings from the Fed. Each Friday afternoon, a gang of Fed-watchers flocks to the Federal Reserve Bank of New York for a weekly fix of statistics, including closely monitored weekly money-supply figures. At 4:05, financial reporters get the numbers at a tenth-floor press conference and start feeding them to their news wires. At 4:10, brokerage house couriers downstairs start leaving to deliver the mountain of data to staff numbers-crunchers.

Still, it's an inexact science, and even the best Fed-watchers aren't right every time. On Friday, for instance, many confidently predicted that the Fed would either do nothing or perhaps add reserves, and that the money supply would decline or rise only slightly. Some expected a cut in the discount rate to 9% from 9.5%. They might have used divining rods, for all the good their calculations did them, and many traders paid a heavy price.

When the day ended, a financial-futures trader observed glumly, "You could see the blood running down the steps." As these glimpses of the trading day illustrate, Fed-watching can be a dangerous business. (Lynn Asinof, John Helyar, Hal Lancaster, and Laurel Sorenson, *Wall Street Journal,* Nov. 8, 1982) but you can't even begin to think that far ahead anymore. You can't even think one month ahead."[20]

For the year 1980 as a whole, the Fed did a pretty good job of controlling M1B (currency outside banks plus transaction accounts), which is the most widely used definition of the money supply. M1B increased by only 6.3% in 1980, as compared to 7.4% in 1979 and 8.2% in 1978. Yet, at the same time that the rate of growth of M1B was slowing, the rate of inflation was accelerating from 7.6% in 1978 to 11.3% in 1979, 13.5% in 1980. This reaffirms our earlier observation that there is not a close positive correlation between the money supply and prices.

There was confirmation in 1980 of two other important points. One is that it makes a difference which aggregate is targeted, since monetary aggregates do not all grow at the same rate. In 1980, the government monetary base increased by 4%, M1A by 3.9%, M1B by 6.3%, M2 by 9.4%, M3 by 10.0%, and L by 9.9%.* By suitably defining the money supply, one can get whatever growth rate is wanted. In 1981, it was more of the same. The Fed's target growth rates and actual monetary growth rates in 1981 were:

	Target %	**Actual %**
M1A	3–5.5	− 6.1
M1B adjusted	3.5–6	2.3
M1B unadjusted	6–8.5	6.3
M2	6–9	10.0
M3	6.5.–9.5	11.4

One out of five ain't bad! The disconcerting problem was that M1A and adjusted M1B were substantially *below* their targets while M2 and M3 were well *above* their targets. What should the Fed do? Some, watching the M1s, argued for monetary ease to avoid a hard recession. Others, watching M2 and M3, argued for more restraint to fight inflation.

The Fed concluded that the low level of M1 in 1981 was misleading because a lot of transaction money had temporarily gone into M2 in search of high interest rates. In 1982, the situation was reversed. M1 grew rapidly and M1 velocity suddenly dropped 5% below its predicted value. The Fed contended that this increase in M1, too, was misleading, because these additional funds were precautionary savings rather than transaction funds. Apparently, monetary aggregates are pretty arbitrary and ambiguous. The *Wall Street Journal* editorialized that "gearing monetary policy to movements in one or another of the Ms is as smooth and steady—and as reasonable—as a Keystone Kops chase."[21] They suggested a new monetary aggregate: M-w for "M-whatever." By the end of 1983, Volcker conceded that the Fed would have to disregard changes in M1 for the foreseeable future. Preston Martin, vice chairman of the Fed, explained succinctly that short-term movements in M1 "are absolutely meaningless."

The second point is that it is as difficult to fine-tune the money supply as it is to fine-tune the economy. Figure 10.10 shows that M1B fluctuated almost as wildly as interest rates in 1980. M1B fell at a record clip in April and soared at a record pace in August. For the rest of the year monetary aggregates seemed to see-saw upwards, though the Fed kept revising its data at a record pace. Those monetarist economists who had welcomed Volcker's demotion of interest rate

* As previously noted, M1A is no longer reported, and M1B is now simply called M1.

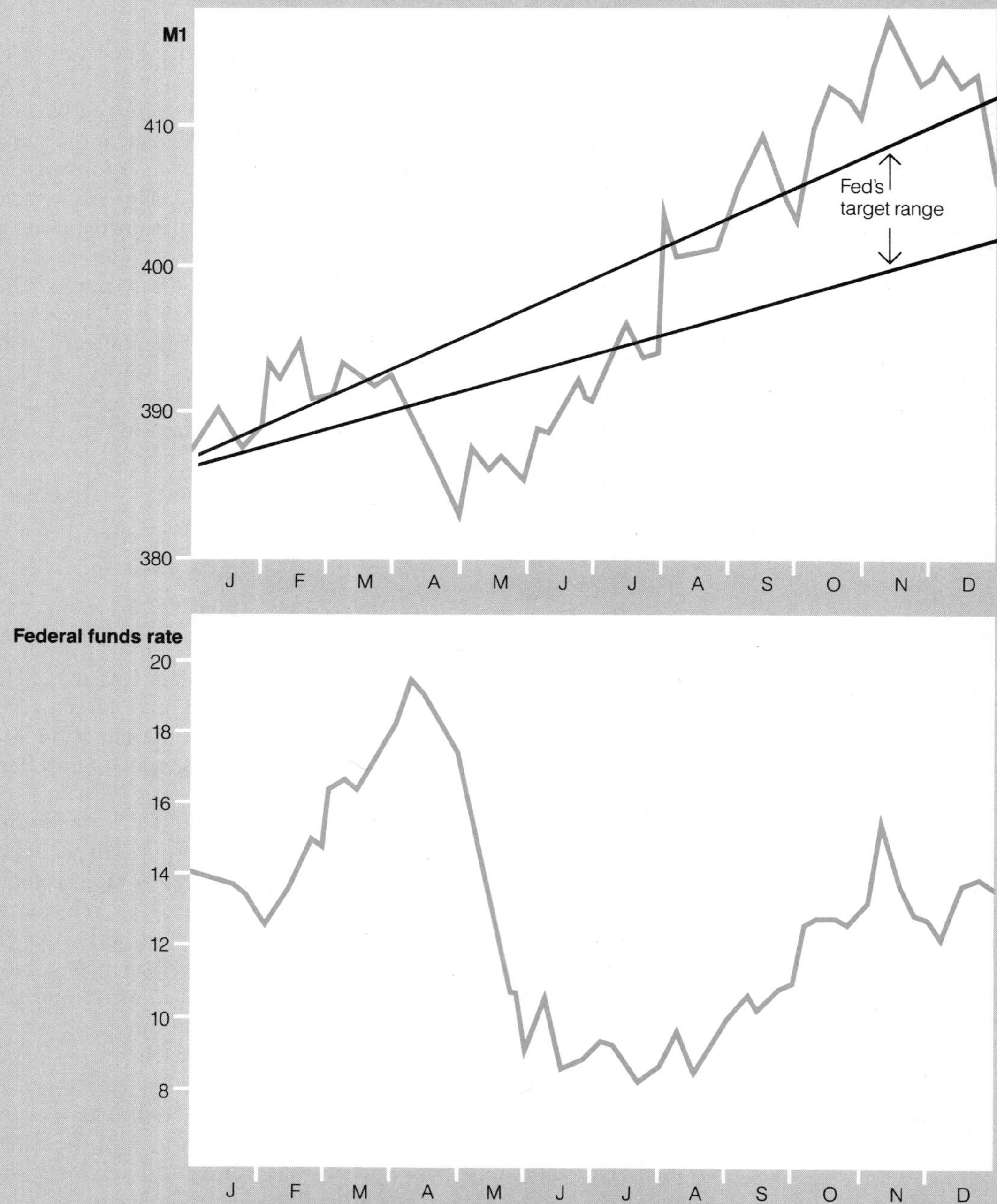

FIGURE 10.10 **MONEY SUPPLY AND INTEREST RATES FLUCTUATED GREATLY IN 1980. M1 ended the year right on target but, during the year, seesawed wildly from above target to below target, then back above target again. In its preoccupation with M1, the Fed had to ignore interest rate fluctuations. The federal funds rate, which banks charge each other, went through unprecedented gyrations.**

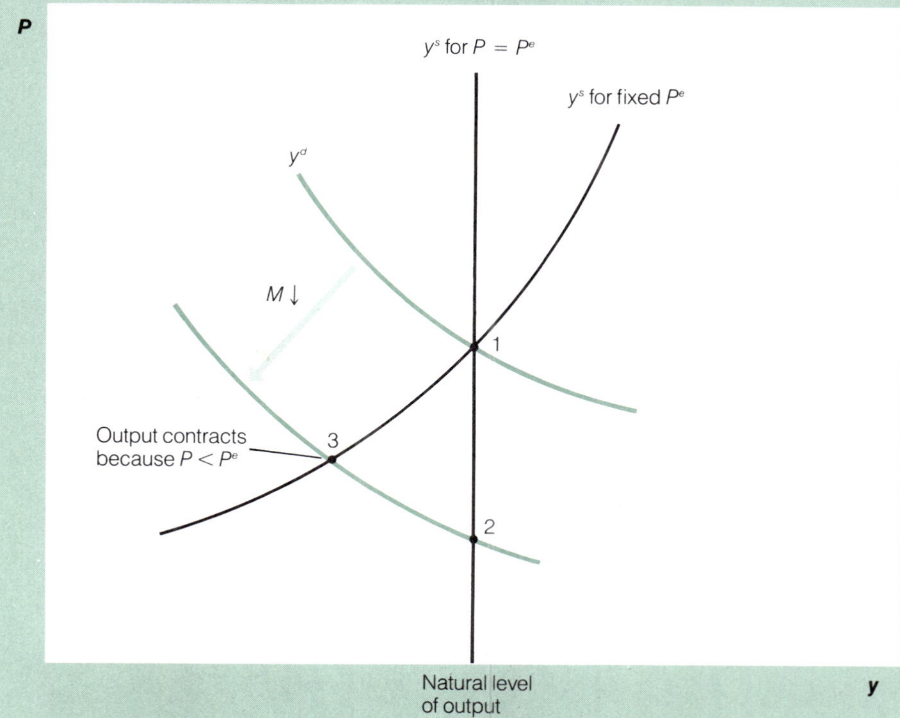

FIGURE 10.11 **NEW CLASSICAL AGGREGATE SUPPLY CURVES DURING A RECESSION. In new classical models, a drop in the money supply drives the economy from Point 1 to Point 3, because workers (not realizing how much prices have fallen) underestimate real wages and voluntarily withdraw from the labor force. When they realize their error and return to their jobs, output reverts to the "natural level" (Point 2).**

stability were, after one year, decrying the instability of monetary aggregates. Volcker responded that the monetary aggregates aren't "something you control from week to week or even month to month. . . . We always knew that, but we learned it in spades this year."[22] After three years of frustration, the Fed discreetly buried its monetarist experiment in October 1982.

RATIONAL EXPECTATIONS

The early classical economists assumed that the economy is always at full employment and that this full-employment output is unaffected by monetary and fiscal policies. They thought economic fluctuations were so brief and unimportant that they simply ignored them. The new classical economists have extended these market-equilibrium models to allow for voluntary fluctuations in employment and output.

Figure 10.11 compares the old and new classical aggregate supply curves. (This figure repeats Figure 5.19; a fuller discussion is given in Chapter 5.) A decrease in the money supply shifts the aggregate demand curve leftward. In the old classical model, wages and prices fall proportionately, and aggregate demand is restored to the full-employment level. The aggregate supply curve is vertical, and the economy moves from Point 1 to Point 2 (in the figure).

In the new classical models, workers sometimes misjudge the price level and consequently miscalculate real wages. Here, for example, workers may not realize how much prices have fallen. If so, then their overestimate of the price level causes them to underestimate the real wages that firms offer. Some workers will decide (mistakenly) that wages are not high enough to make work worth their while. As the labor supply contracts, employment and output both decline. The economy moves from Point 1 to Point 3 in Figure 10.11, along a nonvertical aggregate supply curve. This voluntary, market-equilibrium recession is soon corrected as workers learn that they overestimated prices and underestimated real wages. The economy then moves from Point 3 to Point 2, back to the natural level of output.

Thus, according to the new classical economists, it is unanticipated price fluctuations that cause business cycles. Robert Lucas has drawn the apparent policy conclusion:

> The policy problem of reducing business cycle risk is a very real and important one, and one which I believe monetary and fiscal policies directed at price stability would go a long way toward achieving.[23]

Only surprise policies matter

Why are workers sometimes surprised by the level of prices? If the economy was quiet and unchanging (and a bit boring), there would be little reason for errors. Mistakes occur because of major events that are unforeseen or whose consequences are not accurately perceived. The new classical macroeconomists focus on government-instigated events, in reaction to the persistent Keynesian advocacy of active government stabilization policies. In this way they have carried on the traditional belief of classical economists that government intervention is unneeded and even counterproductive.

The notion of rational mistakes in gauging prices relies on the ideas that economic agents choose to be imperfectly informed because of the high cost of acquiring certain information. Any well-publicized, easily-accessible information will be absorbed by agents. If the government were to announce, and the news services dutifully report, that the money supply will be decreased by 10% on February 8, people will be aware of this contractionary monetary policy. If a 10% decrease in the money supply reliably decreases prices 10%, people will be aware of this, too. They will fully anticipate this price deflation and it will not be a source of error in calculating real wages. These are *rational expectations,* based on the efficient utilization of available information.

With rational expectations, changes in the money supply do not cause mistakes in gauging the price level. With no error-induced change in the labor supply curve, there is no change in employment or output. If a decline in the money supply and its consequences are well-known, then the economy moves from Point 1 to Point 2 (Figure 10.11). A well-anticipated monetary policy has no effects on employment and output!

For output to move from Point 1 to Point 3, the government must engage in a surprise monetary policy, perhaps reducing the money supply after announcing that the money supply was going to be increased. (As a former U.S. Attorney General said, "Watch what we do, not what we say.") But even this trick won't work very many times. A rational public will soon learn to expect the government to do the opposite of what it says. Policy makers will have to tell the truth every once in a while, just to keep the public guessing. In fact, any simple consistent rules for conducting monetary policy will soon be discovered by the public and rendered ineffective. The only monetary policy that can consistently alter employment and output is a random policy, allowing a secret coin flip to determine whether the money supply will be increased or decreased. Of course, by definition, a random policy cannot be used to achieve purposeful objectives.* **In a new classical model with rational expectations, passive policy is best. Active policy only affects the economy to the extent that it surprises people and fools them into making decisions they later regret.**

Expectations and government policy

The foregoing analysis reflects a general classical perception that the government does not do things *for* citizens, but rather *to* citizens. Here the government seemingly is engaged in a precarious guessing game, trying to manipulate the public and fool them into making suboptimal labor supply decisions. In such an environment, apparently the best government policy is a passive policy: Have the money supply grow at a stable well-publicized rate, allowing the private sector to make decisions on the basis of good information.

The government is, in reality, not the only source of surprises. Private demand and supply decisions may surprise people into making regrettable decisions. To maximize information and minimize surprises, it might be most efficient for the government to collect and publicize information. For example, if individual consumers do their own research on the safety and effectiveness of drugs offered for sale, there is wasteful duplication. If only a few consumers carry out the tests and publicize the results, then there is a "free-rider" problem in that there is a large temptation to let others do the testing. Because the private gains to those who conduct the tests are much smaller than the social gains from having tests, not enough tests are conducted. Thus there is a legitimate role for the government: to pool resources and eliminate duplication by conducting national tests and publicizing the results.

Similarly it may be efficient for the government to study and predict shocks to the economy and their consequences. It may also make sense for the government to stabilize prices by promptly offsetting these shocks with demand-management policies. The government is acting on the basis of information that is too expensive for private individuals to gather and analyze. The private sector does not foresee the shocks and would make suboptimal decisions on the basis of erroneous price predictions. By offsetting these shocks, the government stabilizes prices and improves the accuracy of private price forecasts.

* There is a paradox here in trying to explain why, if the rational expectations model is correct, the government bothers to follow systematic, well-publicized policies. Are economists rational when they work in the private sector, but irrational when they work for government?

It might be wondered why the government doesn't simply publicize its predictions of upcoming shocks to the economy and the effects on prices. Instead of using monetary and fiscal policies to offset surprises, the government could simply make its information public. But the government does, in fact, collect and publicize lots of price data. The new classical macroeconomists are right in saying that it would be very expensive for a household to collect and analyze up-to-date price information on its own, but all households need do is listen to a radio, watch television, or glance at newspaper headlines to get the information.

Some households do purchase bundles of goods and services that differ substantially from those included in the CPI, but it does not seem plausible that their price errors are sufficient to cause the large, lengthy swings in unemployment that actually occur. Between 1974 and 1975, unemployment increased by 2.8 million, from 5.6% to 8.5% of the labor force, while the CPI increased by 9.1%. It is hard to believe that this large increase in unemployment was due simply to overestimates of inflation—that is, to people thinking that prices were much higher than they really were. The new classical model is also contradicted by the evidence that output changes usually precede price changes, and that real wages generally move procyclically.

A related problem concerns the structure of information assumed in the new classical model. It turns out that if we modify it so that employees know prices but must estimate wages, or employers know wages but must estimate prices, then unexpected contractionary monetary policies actually increase employment and output! (See Exercise 10 in Chapter 5.) Thus, the new classical explanation of business cycles relies not only on the existence of errors, but also on the predominance of certain types of errors.

The new classical macroeconomics is ingenious and provocative. But even the new classical macroeconomists admit that their models tell only a part of the story—that they contain some interesting insights, but are far from a complete explanation of business cycles. Robert Lucas, prominent new classical macroeconomist, has written that these models

> do succeed in their twin objectives. They provide examples of monetary economies in which money has . . . long-run neutrality . . . , yet retains the capacity to induce short-run disruptions of the sort documented by Friedman and Anna J. Schwartz. . . . Now it does not seem to me a critical or an economic insight to observe that one can detect differences between the world described in this paper and the United States, or that it utilizes "questionable *ad hoc* assumptions," or that it leaves facts unxplained. If ever there was a model rigged, frankly and unapologetically, to fit a limited set of facts it is this one. *Ad hoc?* If you only knew how hard it was.[26]

Lucas and others have shown how price errors can cause voluntary fluctuations in employment. Business cycles may be partly instigated and magnified by such errors. But that is not all there is to it. The Great Depression was not simply a matter of a quarter of the labor force voluntarily deciding to stay home because wages were too low to make work worthwhile. The drop in the unemployment rate to 3.5% in 1969 and the increases to 8.5% in 1975 and to 9.7% in 1982 were not due solely to price errors.

Wages and prices are not always at market-equilibrium levels. Disequilibria do occur and do persist for considerable periods. Both quantities and prices are

IN THE NEWS

Keynes Returns After the Others Fail

During the past decade, the word Keynesian became a pejorative term—as in the phrase, "outmoded Keynesian idea." Advocates of monetarism, new classical economics (also called rational expectations), and supply-side economics claimed that Keynesianism had failed and deserved to be discarded like an old shoe.

Yet Keynesian economics now seems to be staging a comeback. Why this change of heart? Because events of the past decade seem to have discredited the three newer theories and verified many "old fashioned" Keynesian ideas.

Monetarism was the first doctrine to feel the sting of reality, starting in the early 1970's.

Monetarists believe that inflation is *always and everywhere* a monetary phenomenon. But from 1972 to 1974, the rate of inflation rose while the growth rate of M-1 (the most basic measure of the money supply) fell. Then, from 1974 to 1976, the inflation rate fell while the money growth rate rose. Always? Everywhere?

Keynesians do not deny money a paramount role in inflation. But they stress that there are many nonmonetary causes of inflation in the short run. And they have no trouble at all explaining the rise and fall of inflation in 1972–76 by such events as wage-price controls, crop failures and increases in the price of oil.

A central tenet of monetarism is the belief that velocity—the speed of circulation of money—behaves in a regular, predictable manner. But in the 1974–76 period velocity grew much faster than historical patterns suggested—a potentially mortal blow to monetarism. Nonetheless, the relentless advance of monetarism in policy circles continued.

When Chairman Paul Volcker announced in 1979 that the Federal Reserve was converting to monetarism, Keynesians worried out loud that deregulation and financial innovation made velocity hard to predict, and therefore made monetarist policies hazardous. These warnings were prophetic. Velocity fell faster than anyone thought possible, rates soared and the economy crashed.

Yet monetarism succeeded in the political arena because it was seen as a better way to fight inflation than 1960's Keynesianism. So the dramatic fall in inflation between 1980 and 1982 vindicated the monetarists. Right? Wrong. According to monetarist doctrine, you slow inflation by slowing monetary growth. But the growth rate of M-1 was the same in 1981 as in 1980 and then rose during 1982. From a monetarist perspective, this is puzzling. From a Keynesian perspective, it is easy to see what happened: High rates killed the economy.

Events have dealt even more harshly with new classical economics. But to see why, we need to know something about the theory.

According to new classical thinking, people know oodles about economics and statistical inference (that is what is meant by "rational" expectations), but have neither telephones nor newspapers to bring them the important economic data they need. They live in a competitive economy in which prices and wages dance energetically to the drumbeat of supply and demand because all goods, including labor, are sold at auction. There are no unions, no long-term contracts, and all unemployment is voluntary—maybe even optimal.

There's more. According to the theory, tight money leads to recession only if the tightening is unanticipated. Similarly, easy money brings on a boom only if it comes as a surprise. Changes in the money supply that are anticipated cause inflation or disinflation directly, without changing employment. So, in particular, an announced policy of slower monetary growth should bring down inflation without causing a recession.

These ideas are wildly at variance with events of the past decade. Did we lower inflation in 1974–76 and in 1980–82 without recession? Were the high unemployment rates of 1973–76 and 1981–83 really evidence of mass vacations? Were these recession/vacations caused by surprise changes in the money supply? The answer to each is a resounding no. And these are also the Keynesian answers.

Many Keynesians are willing to entertain the notion that expectations are rational. But they doubt that the economy is usefully thought of as an auction. Instead, they emphasize institutional features, such as labor unions and long-term contracts, that tend to insulate prices and wages from fleeting changes in supply and demand. They believe that tight money squeezes the economy whether it is anticipated or not. And they doubt that the rising unemployment that accompanies recessions is optimal, or even voluntary.

These are some of the outmoded ideas that got Keynesian economics branded as the wave of the past. Gradually, however, the force of events is showing that the new classical emperor, though resplendent in theoretical elegance, has no empirical clothes.

Ironically, it was the political success of supply-side economics that exposed its lack of intellectual foundations. We tried it, and it failed. Supply siders claimed that, contrary to outmoded Keynesian (and monetarist) ideas, inflation could be fought from the supply side without recession. In fact, we had the worst recession since the 1930's.

They claimed that sharp reductions in marginal tax rates would get America working, saving and investing again. Instead, working, saving and investing all plunged—just what Keynesians say always happens in recessions.

Supply siders claimed that tax revenues would rise to balance the budget because the gross national product would take off while the tax-avoidance industry withered away. Instead, the deficit ballooned, G.N.P. withered, and the tax loophole industry took off.

In sum, the supply-side experiment restored faith in Keynesian economics in a way that scholarly debate never can.

Does the apparent failure of monetarism, new classicism and supply-side economics mean that we must go back to the Keynesianism of the 1960's? Certainly not.

Each has left its mark on Keynesian economics—as have many other influences. Modern Keynesianism emphasizes the importance of monetary policy without de-emphasizing everything else. It often incorporates rational expectations as a working hypothesis, but rejects most of the rest of new classicism. Keynesians are keenly aware that the supply side of the economy can sometimes be overwhelmingly important. And we all now realize that the job of stabilizing the economy is a lot harder than we thought it was 20 years ago.

But the central tenets of Keynesianism remain much as they were 20 years ago: The private economy is not a giant auction hall, and will not regulate itself smoothly and reliably: recessions are economic maladies, not vacations: the Government has tools that can limit recessions or fight inflation, but it cannot do both at once, and neither constantly growing money supply nor constantly shrinking tax rates will cure all our ills.

It may be premature to declare the Keynesian Restoration is upon us, but someone has to say it first. (Alan S. Blinder, *The New York Times,* Feb. 19, 1984.)

affected by economic events. Monetary and fiscal policies, even when fully anticipated, do have real economic effects.

Keynes emphasized expectations, too; though he stressed the largely inexplicable "mass psychology" and "animal spirits," rather than rational expectations. Expectations were central to his analysis of production decisions, investment plans, money demand, and the stock market. Yet the early Keynesian macro models largely ignored expectations, partly for lack of a theory explaining expectations and partly for a lack of good data measuring them. A major contribution of the rational-expectations literature is to reemphasize the point that expectations are important and are influenced by government policies. Policy makers, in turn, in estimating the effects of their policies, need to take into account private reactions of these policies; government policy does not operate in a vacuum.

The new classical macroeconomists are right that expectation errors can affect the economy, that private expectations are influenced by anticipated government policy, and that expectations should be taken into account in selecting policies. But even with errors and even with rational expectations, well-foreseen government policies do affect the economy when wages and prices are not at their equilibrium levels.

THE ECLECTIC VIEW

The debate between passive and active policy, or rules versus authority, elicits a good deal of passion. The matter at issue is a central philosophical one that covers most of economics and is of deep personal concern to the protagonists as well as to the ordinary citizens whose lives will be affected. In the heat of battle both sides frankly tend to overstate their cases. Both sides have valid arguments and neither is predominant. This is why the debate continues.

One fundamental disagreement is whether or not the private economy is inherently stable. Can the Invisible Hand keep the economy on course, or should the government put a visible hand on the wheel? Classical economists believed that the economy was never far from full-employment equilibrium. After a rough roller coaster ride through booms and busts, culminating in the Great Depression, a lot of citizens with empty stomachs weren't so sure. Keynes legitimatized the view that the private economy is not inherently stable. The government should and could stabilize the economy, smoothing out or even eliminating business cycles. For 30 years, the Keynesian view had the upper hand. But Keynesian economics, too, has not delivered all that it promised, and the pendulum has swung back towards the classical skepticism of government.

The consensus is that there is merit in both beliefs. Because of fundamental, inescapable errors and lags, it is, in fact, very difficult to fine-tune the economy. Very intelligent and well-intentioned experts have tried and have been found wanting. It is also true that in many ways government has become too big and meddlesome. But it is equally true that the good old days were not all that great, the economy on occasion having put itself through some fearsome, stressful times when a lot of decent hard-working people suffered greatly.

Fixed policy rules do mean less uncertainty about government actions, but they may also mean more uncertainty about the economy. A commitment not to let the economy disintegrate may well be more reassuring than a promise to ignore the economy. Big government has helped smooth out the economic bumps since World War II, though much of the credit should go to income taxes, unemployment compensation, and other automatic stabilizers, rather than to discretionary policy. The government may not be able to eliminate business cycles completely, but when things turn sour—really obviously sour—policy makers need to be ready to step in and push the economy hard in the right direction.

It is also evident that many government regulatory agencies, such as the Federal Deposit Insurance Corporation and the Securities Exchange Commission, have been beneficial. The Invisible Hand does not sufficiently help the needy nor does it restrain corruption and banditry.* The fundamental, and perhaps unsolvable, puzzle in economics is when to trust the market and when to trust government.

There are also practical difficulties with implementing both points of view. If policy makers are to have discretionary power, how are they to exercise it? When should they alter government spending and tax rates? When should they tighten financial markets, and when ease them? Should they watch some interest rate, some measure of the money supply, some price index, some output level, some unemployment rate, or what? And when they do decide to act, what action should they take? If they want to tighten financial markets, should they raise the discount rate, raise reserve requirements, make some open-market sales, or what? And how much of whatever they do, should they do?

These are difficult questions, and they apply to passive rules as well as discretionary policy making. If we are going to encode some rules permanently in the lawbooks and a computer, to control fiscal and monetary policies automatically, which rules should they be? Human judgment is fallible, but it must be used whether by exercising discretionary authority or by writing rules. Paul Samuelson has argued similarly that "when men set up a definitive mechanism which is to run forever afterward by itself, that involves a single act of discretion which transcends, in both its arrogance and its capacity for potential harm, any repeated acts of foolish discretion that can be imagined."[26]

It is actually quite paradoxical that the monetarists, like Milton Friedman, who so often argue that economics is an art and not a science and who have been so reluctant to specify an explicit model of the economy, are the ones who argue that we should program a computer to conduct monetary policy. And it is the Keynesians, with literally tons of computer printouts from complex, empirical models of the economy, who advocate discretionary policy. Perhaps each side really does recognize its own limitations.

IMPORTANT TERMS AND CONCEPTS

demand management policies
neutral policies
Chicago school
rational expectations

* Paul Douglas, a maverick at the University of Chicago, later recalled his discomfort with what he saw as the Chicago School's onesidedness: "The doctrine of noninterference with the market meant, in practice, clear the track for big business."[25]

Uncertainties and lags make the conduct of policy difficult. These difficulties lead some observers to recommend that policy makers follow simple mechanical rules instead of trying actively to stabilize the economy. Others argue that these same uncertainties and lags make it exceedingly difficult to select and implement simple rules.

A "neutral" policy is a will-o-the-wisp. All policies affect both individuals and the entire economy, at least in comparison with the consequences of alternative policies. Some "neutral" policies that have been prominently recommended are: keeping government spending at a set fraction of output, balancing the government's budget each year, and having the money supply grow at a constant rate. Each of these recommended policies has conceptual ambiguities and substantial drawbacks.

With information about the economy uncertain, the success of efforts by the monetary authorities to stabilize aggregate demand depends on whether the Fed pegs the money supply or interest rates. Pegging the money supply is more successful when there is *IS* uncertainty; interest rate pegging is more successful with *LM* uncertainty. If there are both kinds of uncertainty or combination policies are considered, then the conclusions quickly become less clear-cut. In practice, the Fed watches various measures of the money supply, interest rates, and other data, but does not myopically peg anything.

The new classical macroeconomists believe that economic fluctuations are due to errors in assessing prices. Employment voluntarily expands when labor temporarily overestimates real wages, and contracts when labor underestimates real wages. With rational expectations, well-anticipated government policies do not cause such mistakes and, consequently, do not affect employment and output in new classical models.

EXERCISES

1. Is it contradictory for Milton Friedman to argue that "money matters" but that we shouldn't use monetary policies to stabilize the economy? Why does he recommend that the money supply grow at 3–5% a year, rather than 0%?

2. In December 1983, Milton Friedman showed a graph for 1980–83 purporting to show a close association between changes in M1 and changes in nominal GNP one quarter later. Explain how this evidence either supports or undermines Friedman's recommendation that the Fed not use monetary policies to stabilize the economy.

3. What could Professor Robert J. Gordon of Northwestern have had in mind when he wrote that "monetarism has been decimated by the collapse of velocity in 1982"?

4. Explain the logic behind the following:

> [Nonmonetarists argue that] whether monetary growth is excessive and inflationary can be judged only in relation to the behavior of many other indicators, such as interest rates and unemployment. To use an analogy, there is generally a fairly predictable relation between the amount of gas the driver feeds to his car and the speed of the car. But it does not follow that the safest way to drive a car is to use a constant pressure on the accelerator. (Franco Modigliani, *New York Times,* Nov. 6, 1977)

5. What did James Tobin mean when he wrote: "Sometimes Friedman and his followers seem to be saying: 'We don't know what money is, but whatever it is, its stock should grow steadily at 3 to 4 percent per year." ("The Monetary Interpretation of History, A Review Article," *American Economic Review,* 1965, pp. 464–485.)

6. Explain and evaluate the logic behind this proposal:

> Perhaps we should abolish the Federal Reserve Board. Its functions could be handled by a new bureau of the Treasury, patterned on the Bureau of Alcohol,

> Tobacco and Firearms. Certainly monetary policy can be as dangerous as booze, butts and guns. . . . [We could] require the Fed to slow money-supply growth steadily until it reached a rate compatible with the economy's ability to grow. If that were the law of the land, all we would need would be a few capable clerks. (Lindley H. Clark, Jr., *Wall Street Journal,* September 30, 1980)

7. In 1980, financial analysts voiced the novel opinion that bonds had become riskier than stocks, as indicated by the following:

> "The long-term markets are in a state of disarray," says Sanford I. Weill, chairman and chief executive officer of Shearson Loeb Rhoades Inc., a large New York investment firm. "We have a lot of clients completely out of the long-term markets, period, because they've been burned so badly."
>
> During the past two weeks alone, bond prices have fallen almost 8%. A decline of the same magnitude in the Dow Jones Industrial Average would represent a drop of 75 points.
>
> "Stocks used to be twice as volatile as bonds," says Leon G. Cooperman, chairman of the investment policy committee at Goldman, Sachs & Co. "Now bonds are more volatile!"

8. Critically evaluate the claim that "Rational expectations is just a thinly veiled reincarnation of Say's law."

9. Throughout history greedy merchants have sold adulterated foods, ranging from milk containing plaster of paris, to sugar with added sand, and molasses with tin chloride. Why does the discipline of the market place not eliminate such practices?

10. In 1981 the Congressional Budget Office reported that over half the federal budget is either directly or indirectly linked to CPI. They estimated that "A one percent increase in the CPI will automatically trigger nearly $2 billion of additional federal expenditures." *(Indexing with the Consumer Price Index: Problems and Alternatives,* Washington, D.C.: U.S. Government Printing Office, 1981) Is this indexing an automatic stabilizer or an automatic destabilizer?

11. What's wrong with the logic of the following: ". . . unless something politically improbable is done about the federal deficit, the deficit will continue to be financed largely with printed money flowing from the government." (Lucien O. Hooper, "Coping with indefiniteness," *Financial World,* April 18–May 1, 1984)

REFERENCES

1. Milton Friedman, "The Role of Monetary Policy," *American Economic Review* (March 1968), p. 14.

2. Friedman, p. 11.

3. James Tobin, "Monetary Policies and the Economy: The Transmission Mechanism," *Southern Economic Journal* (January 1978), p. 426.

4. William Poole, "Optimal Choice of Monetary Policy Instruments in a Simple Stochastic Macro Model," *Quarterly Journal of Economics,* 84 (May 1970), pp. 197–216.

5. An excellent, but complicated, discussion is William C. Brainard, "Uncertainty and the Effectiveness of Policy," *American Economic Review,* 57 (May 1967), pp. 411–425.

6. For a formal analysis see G. Smith, "Monetarism, Bondism, and Inflation," *Journal of Money, Credit, and Banking,* May 1982.

7. Paul Samuelson, "Money, Interest Rates and Economic Activity: Their Interrelationships in a Market Economy," in American Bankers Association, *Proceedings of a Symposium on Money, Interest Rates, and Economic Activity,* 1967, p. 44.

8. Henry C. Simons, "Rules vs. Authorities in Monetary Policy," in *Journal of Political Economy* (February 1936), pp. 13–14, 29–30.

9. Simons, p. 16

10. Simons, p. 30.

11. Edward S. Shaw, "Money Supply and Stable Economic Growth," in H. H. Jacoby, *United States Monetary Policy,* New York: Praeger, 1964, p. 89.

12. William D. Nordhaus, "The Imperfections of the Budget," *New York Times,* March 22, 1981.

13. Richard W. Everett, "Why Budgets Go Wrong," in *The Chase Economic Observer,* July/August 1982, p. 3.

14. These estimates come from Everett.

15. Shaw, pp. 74, 76.

16. Anthony Harris, "Competition vs. Monetarism, Study in Policy Schizophrenia," *Financier,* October 1981, p. 48.

17. Paul Volcker, "A Broader Role for Monetary Targets," Federal Reserve Bank of New York *Quarterly Review,* Spring 1977, p. 27

18. *New York Times,* October 6, 1980.

19. In a number of empirical macro models, attempts to peg monetary aggregates lead to unstable policies. See John H. Ciccolo, "Is Short-Run Monetary Control Feasible?," New York: Federal Reserve Bank of New York, 1974.

20. *Wall Street Journal,* October 30, 1980.

21. *Wall Street Journal,* October 14, 1980.

22. *Wall Street Journal,* August 26, 1981.

23. Quoted in Kenneth Bacon, "Better Economic News Helps Smother Flames of Fed-Carter Dispute," *Wall Street Journal,* October 6, 1980.

24. Robert E. Lucas, Jr., "Unemployment Policy," *American Economic Review,* 68 (May 1978), p. 357.

25. Robert E. Lucas, Jr., "Tobin and Monetarism: A Review Article," *Journal of Economic Literature* (June 1981), pp. 562–63.

26. Paul Douglas, *In the Fullness of Time,* New York, Harcourt Brace Jovanovich, 1972, p. 127.

27. Paul Samuelson, "Reflections on Central Banking," reprinted in *The Collected Scientific Papers of Paul Samuelson,* Volume 2, Joseph Stiglitz, ed., Boston: M.I.T. Press, 1966, p. 1362.

SUGGESTIONS FOR FURTHER READING

For more on rational expectations and the new classical macroeconomics, see Robert E. Lucas, Jr., *Studies in Business-Cycle Theory,* Cambridge, Mass.: MIT Press, 1981, and George Akerlof, "The Case Against Conservative Macroeconomics: An Inaugural Lecture," *Economica* 46 (August 1979), pp. 219–37.

CHAPTER ELEVEN

TAXATION AND INVESTMENT INCENTIVES AS SUPPLY-SIDE POLICIES

Tax reform means don't tax you, don't tax me, tax that fellow behind the tree.

RUSSELL LONG[1]

This chapter introduces a variety of supply-side policies, including the use of tax incentives to encourage work, saving, and investment. It also looks at the underground economy and the supply-side effects of demand stabilization.

CLASSICAL economists assumed that employment and output are determined by the supply side of the economy—by labor supply, labor demand, and the production function. In their view monetary and fiscal policies affect prices and the division of output between private and public uses, but not the total level of production. The new classical macroeconomists allow for some surprise effects of monetary and fiscal policies, but consider these to be only temporary aberrations. Both, old and new, agree that lasting changes in employment and output can be accomplished only by supply-side policies—policies that alter labor demand, labor supply, or the production function.

It is natural to conclude that Keynesians focus on demand-side policies while classically oriented economists concentrate on supply-side policies. However, this dichotomy is far from perfect. The Keynesian councils of economic advisers under Presidents Kennedy and Johnson actively pursued supply-side policies. And the supply-siders who served President Reagan paid a great deal of attention to deficit spending and monetary policy. Most policy makers know that it is unwise to focus on either demand or supply and simply ignore the other.

Many supply-side factors are little affected by government policies, at least in the short run. A population, its productivity, and the value it places on leisure are largely predetermined by a society's historical evolution and cannot be changed quickly by a few new laws. But there are some supply-side factors that can be substantially altered by policy makers. Tax rates, to the extent they affect labor markets and production, are the most notable example. In this chapter, we will look at a variety of ways in which taxes affect economic activity. For a specific example of tax policy, we will scrutinize the Economic Recovery Act of 1981.

TAX INCENTIVES AND DISINCENTIVES

We have so far looked only at the demand effects of tax policy: Taxes affect the amount of disposable income available to households and, so, influence their expenditures on goods and services. Tax policies shift the *IS* curve and, hence, the aggregate demand curve. A tax increase is a contractionary fiscal policy, while a tax cut is an expansionary fiscal policy. Now we want to consider that there may also be supply-side effects of tax changes, in that the amount of taxes we pay depends on how much we engage in taxed activities.

Income taxes depend on how much we earn. Sales taxes depend on how much we buy (and where we live, since sales taxes vary from state to state and city to city). One or the other is true of taxes on capital gains, inheritances, gasoline, alcohol, and cigarettes. The more we engage in taxed activities, the more taxes we pay. Each of these taxes makes some transactions more costly and, therefore, less appealing. **Taxes provide an incentive to avoid taxed activities.** Income taxes discourage income-earning, while sales taxes discourage spending (and also encourage people to move to low-tax areas).

Lawmakers use high taxes to discourage such undesirable activities as the consumption of cigarettes and alcohol, and use low taxes to encourage such desirable activities as home ownership and pension fund contributions. In recent years, it has been argued that high taxes may be significantly discouraging work, production, and investment. If so, then employment, output, and capital formation may be stimulated by appropriate tax cuts. We examine this idea below.

Average and marginal tax rates

It is marginal tax rates that provide incentives and disincentives. The average tax rate is the total number of tax dollars collected divided by some dollar measure of the taxed activity. If, for example, Mitt L. Class earned $30,000 and pays $6000 in income taxes, then his average income tax rate is 20%. The *marginal tax rate* is the additional tax he would pay on an extra dollar of income. Perhaps in Mr. Class's tax bracket, he would have to pay an extra 40 cents in taxes on another dollar of income. If so, then his marginal income tax rate is 40%.

Average tax rates determine the amount of revenue collected and the extent to which taxes diminish the purchasing power of the private sector. Marginal tax rates, in contrast, change the economic incentives to take certain actions. Policy makers often put substantial gaps between average and marginal tax rates. An extreme example would be a fixed "lump-sum" tax of $4000 per year from every adult. Although the average tax might be high for many people, the only ways to avoid it would be to leave the country or die. The marginal tax rate on other actions would be zero. A person would have to pay no extra taxes for earning income or for buying cigarettes. Economic theorists like lump-sum taxes, because these have almost no incentive effects. But, in practice, nations don't use lump-sum taxes, because such taxes are considered unduly burdensome for people with low incomes.

Lump-sum taxes allow the combination of a high average tax rate, together with a low marginal tax rate. Tax laws can also be written so that marginal rates are high while average tax rates are low. One example is a $5-a-gallon tax on gasoline that is rebated in fixed, lump-sum amounts to households. A stiff marginal tax on gasoline usage is a strong incentive to buy less gasoline. Yet, on average, there is no change in the amount of tax revenue collected from the private sector. There would, of course, be some income redistribution from heavy users of gasoline to light users.

More complicated (and difficult to administer) plans can be devised in order to reduce the shock to heavy gasoline users. For example, a $20-a-gallon tax would be imposed on average gasoline consumption in excess of that recorded for some base year. Similarly, households could be given marketable gas-rationing coupons according to the number of cars owned on a certain date. These schemes would reduce the dislocations to heavy gasoline users but still make additional gasoline consumption very expensive. Yet another variation is a stiff gas-guzzler automobile tax, in which the tax is inversely related to the car's fuel efficiency.

This distinction between marginal and average tax rates has influenced many of our tax laws. It affects other economic policies as well—as in the case of price controls that allow different prices on "old" oil (produced before a certain date) and "new" oil. We look now at some specific policies.

INCOME TAXES AND THE LABOR MARKET

Supply-side policies are concerned mainly with work and production incentives. Policy makers may be able to alter such incentives by changing marginal tax rates. A key example is personal income taxes, since these are so substantial and pervasive. As shown in Figure 11.1, statutory income tax rates rise with income,* creating substantial gaps between average and marginal tax rates. In 1982, a married couple with $30,000 in taxable income paid $5607 in federal income taxes, a 19% average tax rate. Their marginal tax rate was 33%, in that they would have paid $33 in taxes on an additional $100 of income. A single person with $20,000 taxable income in 1980 had a 19% average tax rate and 31% marginal tax rate. Taking into account those transfer payments (such as food stamps and unemployment compensation) that decline or stop as income increases, some low-income families face effective marginal tax rates of close to (or even more than) 100%.

The progressivity of federal income taxes is primarily intended to reduce disparities in after-tax income. If the benefits of government apply equally to all income classes, then progressive taxes redistribute economic well-being from high-income groups to low-income groups. Federal taxes are high because the federal government is large and policy makers believe that govern-

* The tax rates shown in Figure 11.1 apply to taxable income, which is often much less than earned income because of legal exclusions and deductions and illegal evasions.

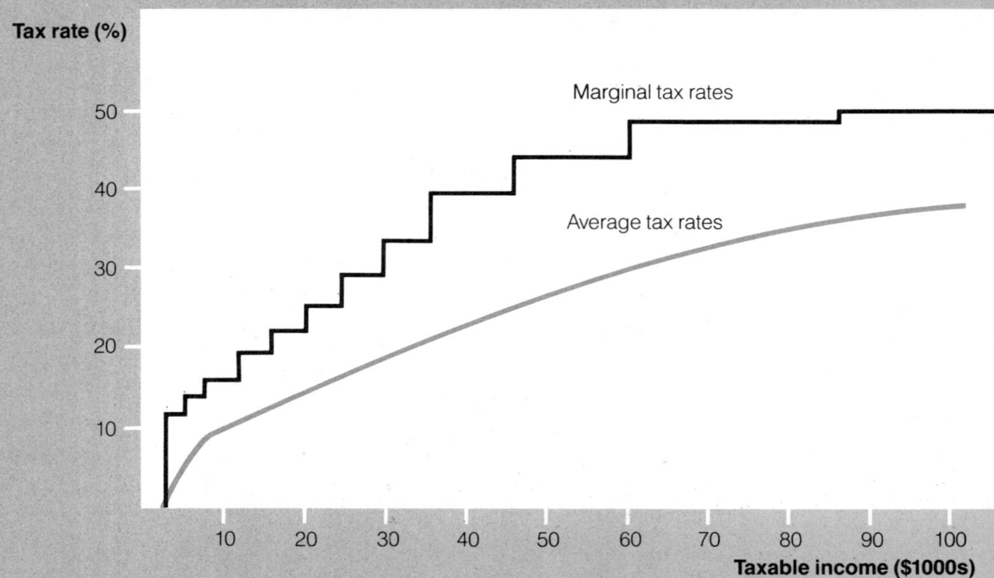

FIGURE 11.1 U.S. FEDERAL MARGINAL AND AVERAGE TAX RATES FOR MARRIED TAXPAYERS, 1982. **Because the income tax is progressive—that is, the marginal tax rate (the tax on an extra dollar of income) goes up as income goes up—marginal tax rates are higher than average tax rates (taxes divided by income).**

ment programs should be financed mostly by taxes, rather than bond sales or money printing.

One consequence of high income tax rates, noted in Chapter 3, is an automatic stabilization of disposable income and aggregate demand. If the marginal tax rate is 30%, then an extra dollar in income is only 70 cents after taxes. High marginal tax rates restrain the ability and willingness of people to spend additional income and, so, help keep economic booms in check. Similarly, in recessions a lost dollar of income is only a 70-cents loss after taxes (where the marginal tax rate is 30%). People will reduce their spending less than if they had lost a full dollar of disposable income. This restraint mitigates the recessionary drop in demand. Unemployment compensation, food stamps, and other transfers also constrain and cushion aggregate demand as needed. These taxes and transfers are known as *automatic stabilizers,* since they stabilize aggregate demand automatically, by transferring money from the private sector to the government during booms and by sending funds the other way during recessions.

Effect on labor supply

Income taxes may also have supply-side incentive effects. One way for a person to increase income is to work more. But with a 30% marginal tax rate, a dollar of additional earnings is only 70 cents of after-tax income. Labor demand depends on the wages firms pay, while labor supply depends on the after-tax wages received. Thus changes in marginal tax rates can shift labor supply relative to labor demand, by narrowing or widening the difference between wages paid and wages after taxes.

A reduction in marginal income tax rates may, in theory, increase the supply of labor. Since people get to keep more of what they earn, they may want to work more—accepting overtime, taking second jobs, coming in most Mondays and Fridays, and even working a few Saturdays and Sundays. Cutting taxes to encourage work is a supply-side policy. If labor supply increases, then, at least in a full-employment classical model, both employment and output will expand. This is shown in Figure 11.2. This rightward shift in the labor supply curve reduces before-tax wages and thus persuades firms to hire more people. Before-tax wages go down while after-tax wages go up. The full-employment levels of employment and output both increase, shifting the aggregate supply curve rightward (Figure 11.3).

An income tax change has demand-side effects, too. A tax cut enlarges after-tax income and thereby increases spending on goods and services, shifting the *IS* curve rightward. This rightward shift of the *IS* curve implies a rightward shift of the aggregate demand curve in Figure 11.3. The relative magnitudes of the shifts of the aggregate demand and supply curves are uncertain. If the demand-side effect is relatively large, then the price level will rise. If the supply side effect is relatively large then the price level will fall. In full-employment models, it is uncertain whether income tax cuts are inflationary or deflationary.

A pure supply-side policy would have to adjust the tax laws so as to change marginal tax rates without changing disposable income. For instance, Congress could simultaneously lower income tax rates and increase cigarette taxes. Working would be encouraged and smoking discouraged. Another possibility is to impose a flat tax of, say 30%, which keeps total tax revenue constant while lowering the marginal tax rate for some income groups. An even more drastic change would be to go to a lump-tax system. If Congress can successfully juggle the tax laws so as to avoid the inflationary demand-side effects, then a reduction in marginal tax rates increases output and reduces prices in this full-employment model.

The fly in the demand-management ointment is that monetary and fiscal policies give a trade-off between unemployment and inflation. Expansionary demand policies bring inflation, while demand policies to cool inflation bring unemployment. The promise of the supply-side elixir is that the economy can have both more output and lower prices! No wonder so many were tempted to try supply-side economics in 1980, after the unemployment-inflation whipsaw of the 1970s.

When Ronald Reagan was elected in 1980, his advisers debated whether income tax cuts have a bigger impact on the demand or supply side of the economy. The more traditional economists emphasized the demand-size effects and cautioned that income-tax cuts are inflationary. In their view, any tax cuts

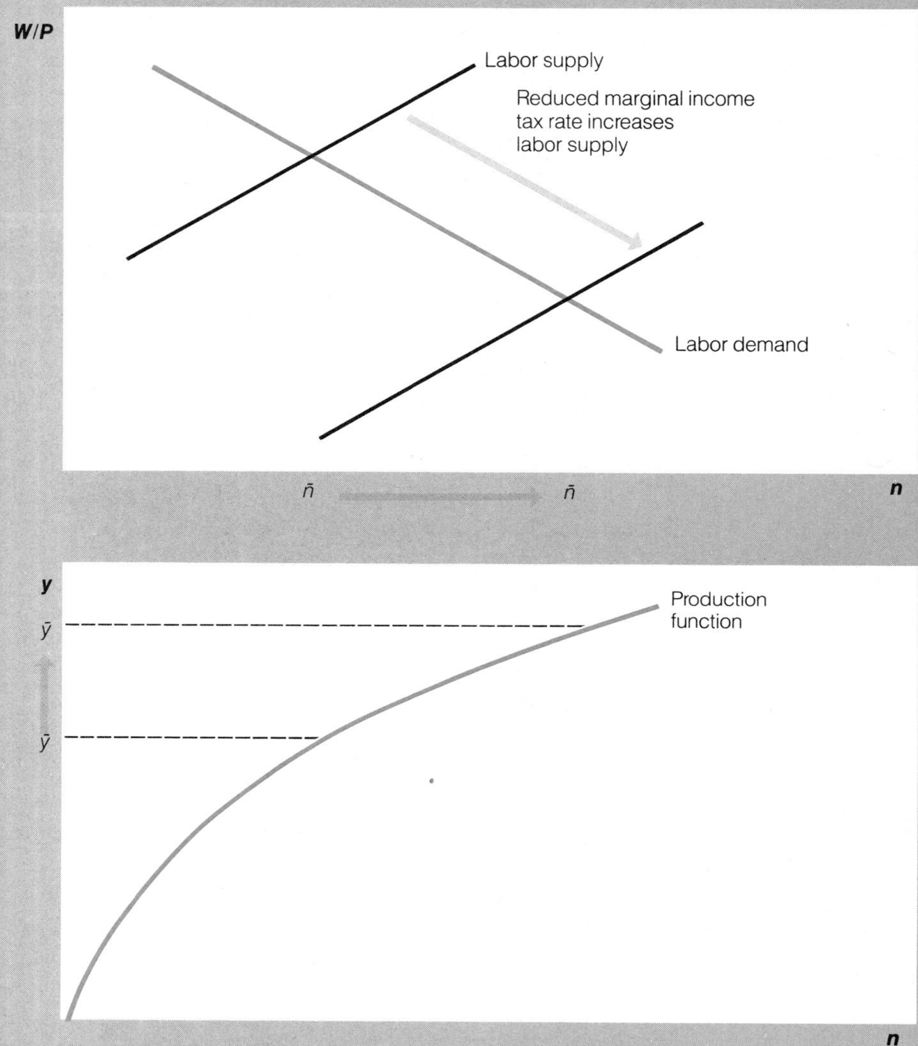

FIGURE 11.2 AN INCOME TAX CUT INCREASES EMPLOYMENT AND OUTPUT IN A FULL-EMPLOYMENT MODEL. **A diminished income tax increases after-tax wages and, so, increases the labor supply, employment, and output in a classical full-employment model.**

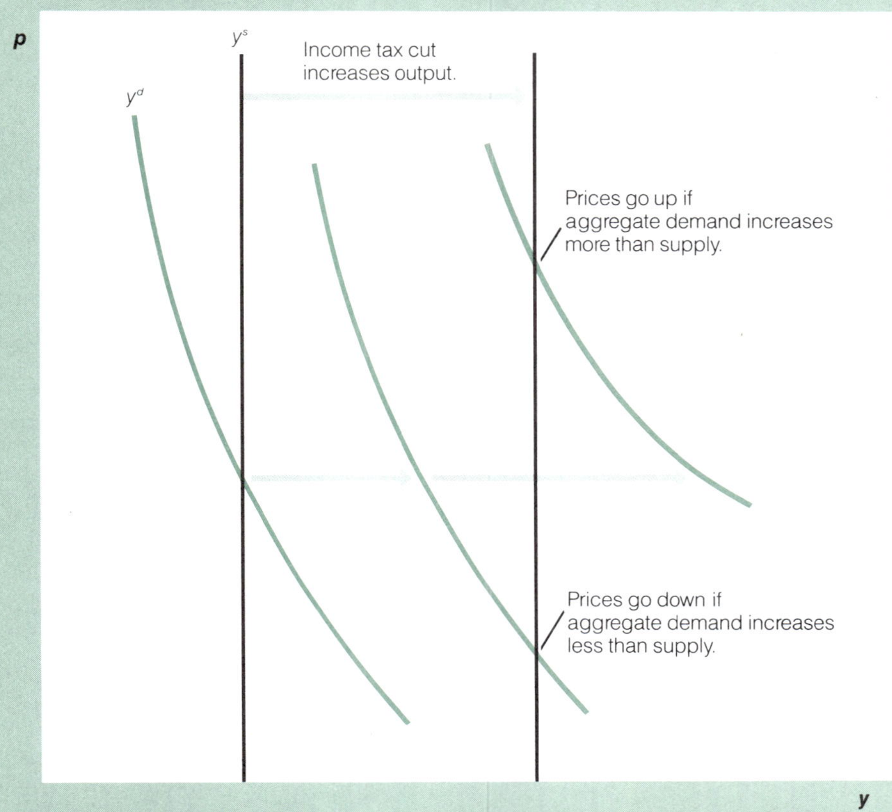

FIGURE 11.3 **AN INCOME TAX CUT MAY INCREASE OR DECREASE PRICES. For the reasons shown in Figure 11.2, a tax cut increases output, thereby shifting the aggregate supply curve rightward. By increasing disposable income, it also stimulates consumer spending, shifting the aggregate demand curve rightward, too. Whether prices go up or down depends on whether the demand- or supply-side effects are stronger.**

should be directed at stimulating business investment. Others, the radical conservative economists, emphasized the stimulative supply-side effects and bemoaned any deflection of their proposed tax cuts from workers to businesses. Irving Kristol lamented that cutting individual income taxes

> is now contemptuously dismissed as being nothing more than a "consumer-oriented" adventure into "demand-side" economics. . . . It is now an unstated article of faith among politicians, businessmen, and liberal and conservative economists alike that corporate executives—no matter how dismal their past performance—can be trusted to respond to economic incentives in a traditional "capitalist" way, but that the American people are so profligate and short-sighted that they will "squander" any additional money they are permitted to earn and keep.[2]

A backward-bending labor supply curve The effect of real wage rates on labor supply is important to many policy questions such as the supply-side-effects of wages, taxes, or subsidies. But theory alone cannot tell us whether an increase in the after-tax real wage rate increases or decreases labor supply. This is because, as is so often the case, there are both substitution and income effects at work. The substitution effect argues for less leisure and more work, to take advantage of the higher wages offered. The income effect notes that all of the hours of work previously planned now provide additional after-tax income. There is consequently no need to work so much.* The income effect argues for working less in order to enjoy both more commodities and more leisure. On balance, labor supply may go up or down, depending on people's preferences.

There is, however, often a presumption in economics that substitution effects dominate income effects. And here, too, it is commonly assumed that the substitution effect dominates, so that labor supply is positively related to the real wage rate. However, the discomforting fact is that many empirical investigations indicate that labor supply curves are "backward bending," in that the labor supply falls as real wages increase.[3]

Figure 11.4 shows a labor supply curve that is slightly backward bending. What is the effect of a tax cut on this labor market equilibrium? At any given before-tax wage rate, a lower tax rate enlarges after-tax wages. Since the income effect is assumed to be dominant here, a tax cut diminishes the labor supply, shifting the labor supply curve leftward. Employment falls, while both before-tax and after-tax wages increase. Contrary to the predictions of supply-side economists, a tax cut may reduce employment and output!

Those who espouse the traditional view that labor supply is positively related to wages can take only small comfort in the fact that these empirical studies are a bit suspect. The most serious problem is that labor markets are often in an excess-supply disequilibrium, with observed employment and wages not reflecting points on labor supply curves. It is difficult to estimate a labor supply curve when the economy is not on it.

A vertical labor supply curve There is another institutional difficulty that may thwart the supply-side tonic of tax cuts. Very few people have the option of earning a little more money by working a few extra minutes every week. Instead, their alternatives are not to work, to work at one job, or else to work at more than one job. People settle into a workstyle and a lifestyle according to their skills and how highly they value leisure and commodities. They become lazy professors, hard-working secretaries, workaholic executives, or whatever. And they are not about to change their work habits just because their real wages go up or down a little bit.

If this view is correct, then the labor supply curve is vertical—at least over a range covering modest changes in real wages—and does not shift about as taxes go up or down. Changes in tax rates alter real after-tax wages, but they don't lure the Great American Novelist into writing another chapter, an auto worker into taking a second job, or an overworked doctor into seeing a few more patients. If the labor supply curve is vertical, then income tax cuts do not have supply-side effects on the labor market.

* This income effect is reinforced to the extent that taxes on nonlabor income are reduced also. An increase in after-tax nonlabor income tends to increase the consumption of both commodities and leisure. More leisure means less work.

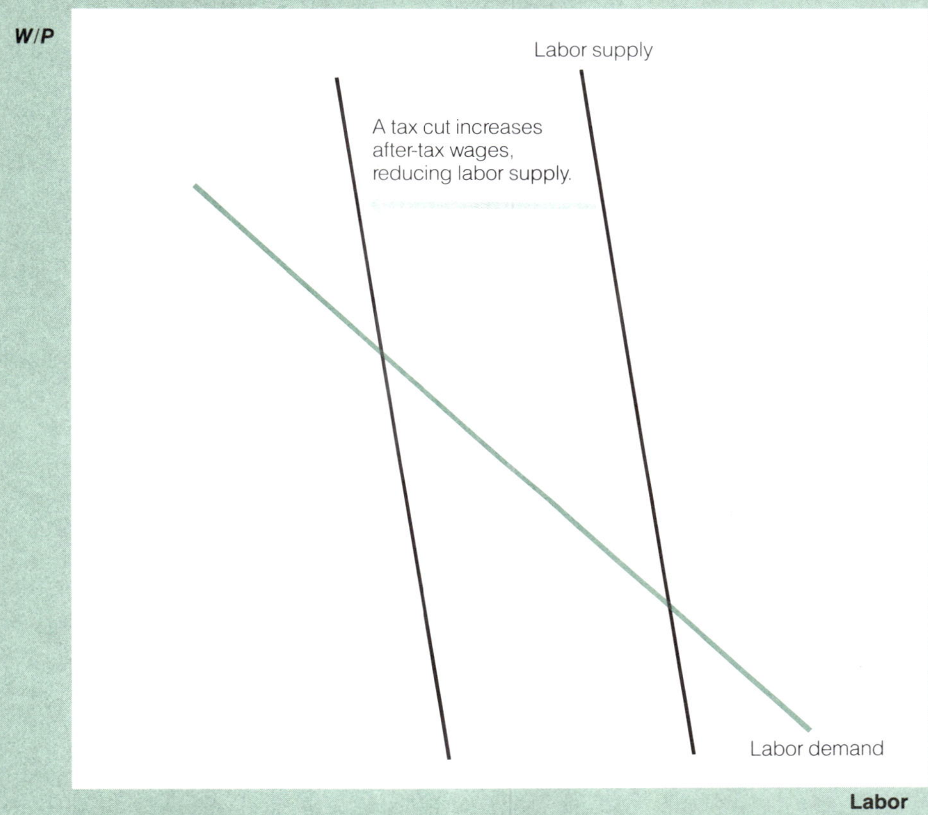

FIGURE 11.4 **WHEN THE LABOR SUPPLY CURVE IS SLIGHTLY NEGATIVELY SLOPED, A TAX CUT REDUCES EQUILIBRIUM EMPLOYMENT. If increased pay persuades people to work less, then the labor supply curve is negatively sloped, and a tax cut reduces the labor supply, employment, and output.**

Sticky wages So, the positive supply-side effects of income tax cuts require a labor supply that is responsive to economic incentives to work more. There is another requirement: Figure 11.2 compared two full-employment, labor market equilibria. If we are to go from one to the other, before-tax wages must fall. It is this decline in wages that persuades firms to hire more people.

In theory, workers should accept such a decline readily, since they do want to work more and their after-tax wages go up at the same time that before-tax wages go down. In practice, though, wages are sticky, especially downward. Unions don't like to negotiate wage decreases. And employers do not like to cut the salaries of executives and other nonunion employees. If wages do not fall, then employment won't increase, since firms will have no reason to hire more people. The increased willingness of some people to work just increases unemployment if workers on the whole do not agree to wage cuts.

Similarly, the supply-side effects of tax cuts are unimportant if there is already an excess supply of labor, with unemployment demand-determined. With an excess-supply disequilibrium, increases in the labor supply affect neither employment nor output. Instead, in this disequilibrium situation, tax cuts work only through the demand side of the economy. Enlarged disposable income increases consumption spending and thereby increases output and employment.

Taxes and labor demand

In the example above, labor demand is not shifted by the tax cut because personal income taxes do not alter the wage costs of employers. However, firms do pay taxes for Social Security and unemployment compensation funds; and reductions in these tax rates may increase labor demand. In addition, there are special employer tax credits that reduce the effective cost of hiring some workers. The "targeted jobs tax credit" reduces the taxes of firms that hire certain disadvantaged workers, and the "work incentive program" gives tax credits to firms that hire recipients of Federal Aid for Dependent Children. In both of these programs, the tax credit is equal to 50% of the first $5000 in wages during the qualified worker's first year of employment, and then 25% of wages during the second year.

In a full-employment model, such wage subsidies increase the demand for labor and, as shown in Figure 11.5, thereby increase before-tax wages, employment, and output. (People work more because their wages increase; firms hire more workers because their after-tax wage costs decline.) This increase in output shifts the aggregate supply curve rightward, reducing prices and thereby creating demand for the additional output.

In a Keynesian sticky-wage model the results are similar. With an excess labor supply and employment demand-determined, wage subsidies that increase labor demand also increase employment and output while reducing prices. If there is an excess supply of commodities as well as labor, then the conclusions are a bit different. Understandably, firms may be reluctant to expand employment if they cannot sell the output that additional workers would produce. If output is demand-determined, then firms may simply substitute subsidized employees for unsubsidized employees, with no change in total employment.*

INVESTMENT AND SAVING

A modern industrial economy produces a tremendous variety of goods and services each year. One important distinction is between those items that are consumed and those that are investments that will produce additional goods and services in the future. Food, toothpaste, gasoline, haircuts, toys, and most clothing are generally consumed within a year of their production. Buildings, vehicles, machinery, hand tools, and education add to a nation's productive capacity. Some investments produce more goods; for example, factories are used to produce cars. Other investments yield implicit services; for example, cars provide transportation, and houses give shelter.

*Firms may also decide to reduce investment in order to substitute subsidized labor for unsubsidized capital.

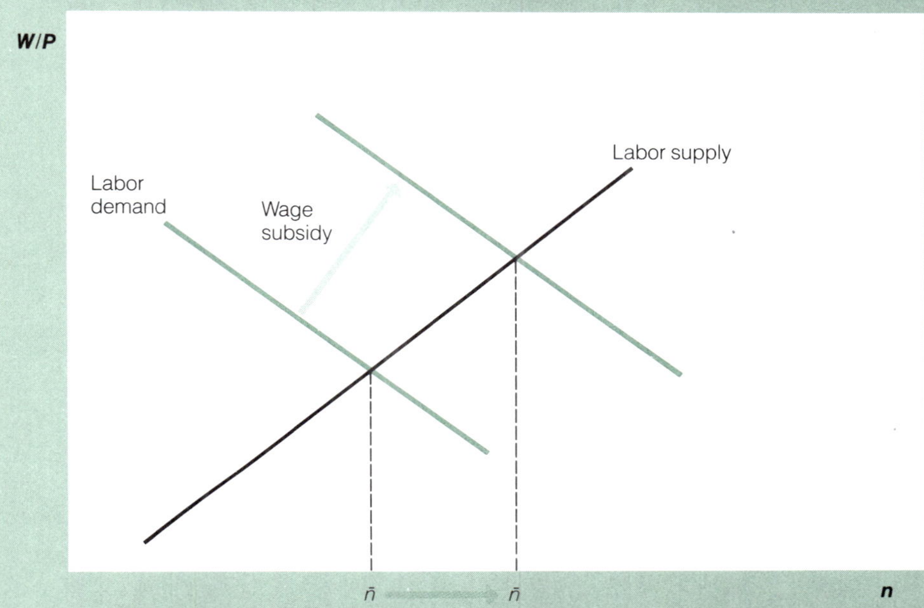

FIGURE 11.5 THE EFFECTS OF AN EMPLOYER WAGE SUBSIDY IN A CLASSICAL MODEL. **A government wage subsidy reduces the effective cost of hiring people and, so, increases labor demand, employment, and output.**

A nation's current investment affects the amount of capital it will have in the future. If current generations produce only strawberries and cream, then future generations will be poor. If current generations devote their energies to structures, equipment, and technology, then future generations will be rich. Undoubtedly, some moderation is best, with each generation enjoying itself but still leaving a fair endowment for the future.

Investment is on the demand side of the economy, since investment is part of the aggregate demand for goods and services. Investment demand can be influenced by special tax incentives and by general demand-management policies as well. The effects of investment on the capital stock will eventually affect the supply side of the economy, too. An enlarged capital stock increases the average productivity of workers, shifting the production function upwards, as shown in Figure 11.6. Output is higher at each level of employment. Additional capital also increases labor's marginal productivity, the amount produced by additional hours of work.* This growth of marginal productivity increases labor demand and employment as long as there is sufficient demand for the additional output that is forthcoming.

* Some capital, such as programmed robots, may reduce labor demand. An extreme example is a switch to an almost completely automated plant. The consensus among economists is that most investment increases both average and marginal labor productivity.

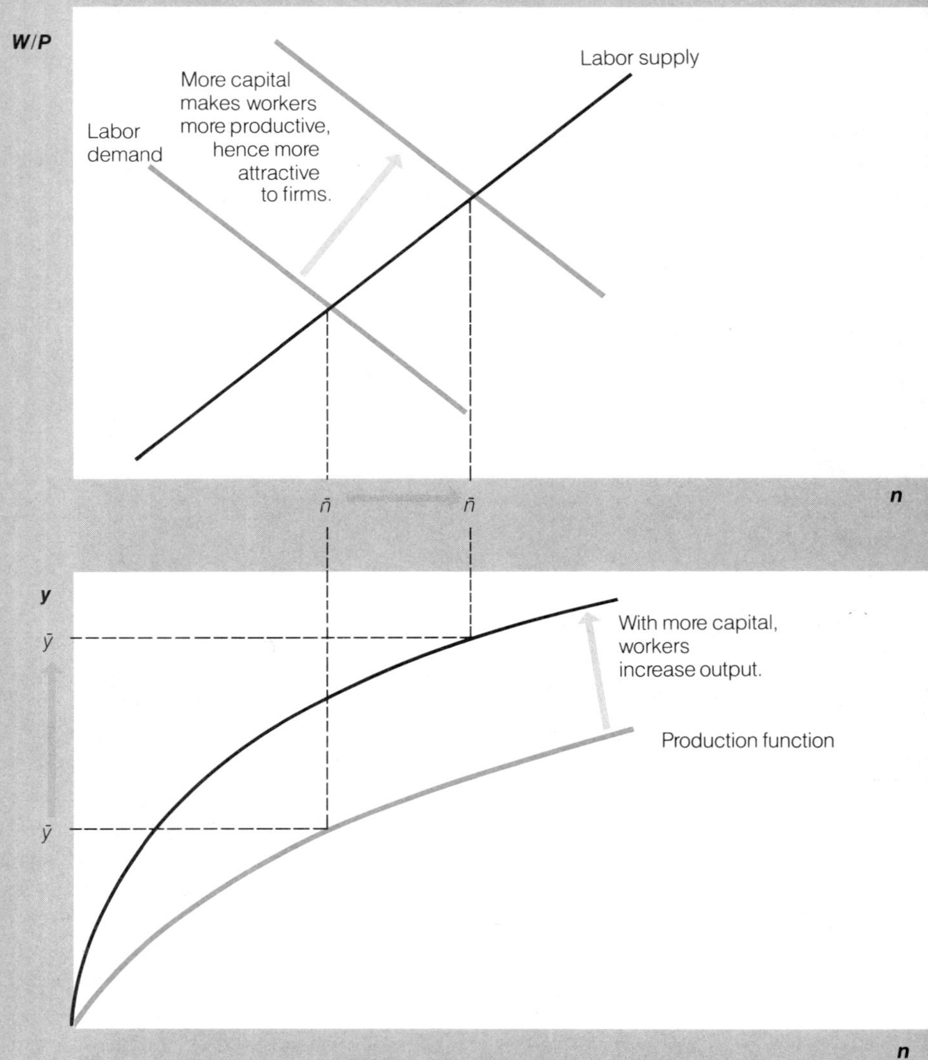

FIGURE 11.6 THE SUPPLY-SIDE EFFECTS OF THE LARGER CAPITAL STOCK THAT FOLLOWS FROM INCREASED INVESTMENT SPENDING. **An increase in the capital stock increases labor demand and also increases output at every level of employment. In a full-employment model, both employment and output expand.**

Demand management and crowding out

Private investment is influenced by output and interest rates. When output is high, business capacity is strained, businesses are making lots of money, and profit expectations are rosy. This is a fertile environment for investment spending. During recessions, the reverse is true. Firms are reluctant to invest when they already have excess capacity, they are losing money, and no customers are on the horizon. In either case, boom or recession, businesses use interest rates to gauge their alternatives. Rates of return on additional capital are compared to the rates of return on securities. High interest rates discourage borrowing and encourage firms to use what cash they have to buy bonds instead of plant and equipment.

The government can enlarge a nation's capital stock directly by purchasing investment goods itself: highways, airports, schools, and even factories. In addition, government support of research may increase the productivity of labor and capital. If, instead, the government purchases butter, tanks, and monuments, then private investment may be crowded out and the nation's future capital stock impaired.

Remember, though, that there are two kinds of *crowding out*—supply side and demand side. Supply-side crowding out emphasizes that, when resources are fully utilized, a fixed pie is divided between the government and the private sector. **When there is full employment, the nation's future capital stock will be enlarged if government investment displaces private consumption, and decreased if government consumption displaces private investment. If, on the other hand, there are unemployed resources in the economy, then government spending may stimulate private consumption and investment, since both increase with output.**

Demand-side crowding out emphasizes a different point—that even if there are idle resources, additional government spending raises real interest rates, which depresses private investment. This suggests the role of monetary policy in influencing investment. There is more investment and less demand-side crowding out if monetary policies keep real interest rates low. Keynes was a persistent advocate of low interest rates, for just this reason. **Monetary policies that alter real interest rates affect the division of a nation's output between consumption and investment. Low interest rates encourage investment at the expense of consumption. To the extent that monetary policies increase aggregate output, they encourage both consumption and investment.**

In a classical full-employment model, there is no role for monetary policy in influencing investment. Output is determined by the supply side, and the real interest rate is determined by the *IS* curve.* Monetary policy affects only prices. Classically oriented economists believe that monetary policies affect investment only to the extent that inflation reduces real after-tax profits because of imperfections in our tax laws. To increase private investment, the government is advised to reduce inflation through monetary restraint; reduce government spending to leave more of the full-employment pie for private

* If the Pigou effect is operative, then the higher price level caused by an increase in the money supply will shift the *IS* curve leftward, lowering the real interest rate. Thus monetary policy does affect the composition of output in a full-employment model, if there is a Pigou effect.

investment; and use special tax incentives to encourage private investment and saving. Keynesian economists are more likely to recommend expansionary monetary and fiscal policies to ensure the high output that stimulates investment and, especially, to use expansionary monetary policies to keep interest rates low. Keynesians agree that special tax incentives can encourage investment but, as we will soon see, are more dubious about the benefits of saving incentives.

Tax incentives for investment

Purchases of plant and equipment are tax-deductible business expenses. However, when a firm buys such capital it does not write off the entire cost in the first year, since the capital will last for many years. Instead, the firm "depreciates" the investment, spreading the cost over many years. To encourage capital acquisition, firms have been allowed to use *accelerated depreciation* for tax purposes, pretending that capital wears out faster than it really does. When firms are able to write off capital expenses very quickly, business taxes are reduced in early years and increased in later years. Firms like this tax shift, because a dollar today is more valuable than a dollar tomorrow.

In 1962, there was a major liberalization of depreciation rules and, in addition, firms were allowed, as an *investment tax credit,* to deduct 7% of their expenditures on new capital directly from the taxes they owed the federal government. This accelerated depreciation and the investment tax credit were designed to encourage firms to acquire more capital. Since then, the depreciation rules and investment tax credits have been revised a number of times.*

Saving incentives

Another possible route for increasing investment is to encourage saving by reducing taxes on the income from savings: dividends, interest, and capital gains.† Saving can also be encouraged by taxing consumption heavily. However, consumption taxes are very burdensome to low-income families, who save very little. Reduced taxes for savers and higher taxes for spenders not only have incentive effects, but also transfer the tax burden from people who save only a small part of their income to those who save a lot. Tax cuts for savers primarily benefit upper-income families, retirees, and the idle rich. But, it is argued, especially by savers, that increased saving means more investment, and that benefits everyone.

For people to save more of their income they must consume less. Thus the immediate impact of increased saving (and diminished consumption) is to shift the *IS* curve to the left, as shown in Figure 11.7, and, hence, to shift the aggre-

* The United Kingdom has had 100% depreciation since 1973, allowing firms to write off all investments in the first year. Yet, British investment has been very sluggish because profit expectations have been so bleak. Tax breaks are fine, but firms need profits first.

† Again, we must distinguish between marginal and average taxes. For example, in 1980 the dividend exclusion was increased from $100 to $200 (from $200 to $400 for couples) and broadened to include interest income. This law was advertised as an inducement to save. Yet, most taxpayers already earned more than $200/$400 in dividend and interest income. For them, this change was a simple tax rebate and contained no tax incentive to save more.

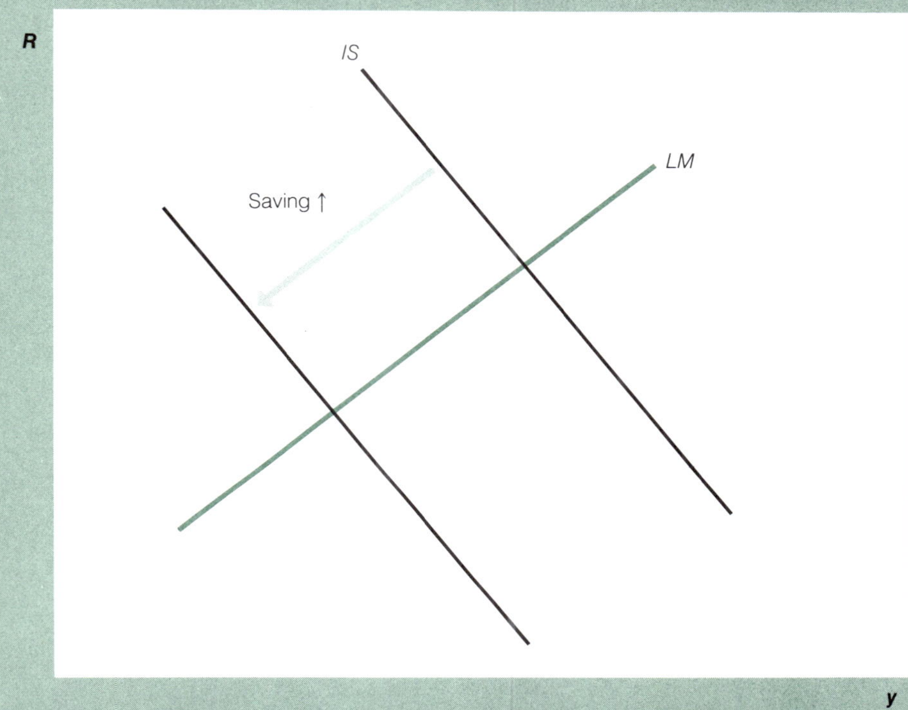

FIGURE 11.7 AN INCREASE IN SAVING REDUCES AGGREGATE DEMAND. **At any level of income, increased saving means reduced consumption, which causes a contractionary leftward shift of the *IS* curve.**

gate demand curve leftward, too, as shown in Figure 11.8. In the full-employment model depicted in Figure 11.8, prices and interest rates fall, keeping aggregate demand at the full-employment level. (Nominal wages must also decline with prices to maintain labor market equilibrium.) Since output is a fixed pie, we can conclude that, if consumption falls and government spending is unchanged, then investment must increase. **In a classical full-employment model, more saving and less consumption ensures more investment.**

Popular discussions often assume that more saving must mean more investment, since people "invest" their savings. But we must distinguish between investment expenditures and the popular usage of "investment" to include bank accounts, IBM stock, and old baseball cards. As Keynes pointed out, people can save without purchasing new investment goods. Indeed, in modern industrial countries, saving decisions and investment decisions are made by different people. Households who decide to consume less and save more may simply hoard cash or acquire old paintings. Extra saving does not directly create purchases of new investment goods. The classical conclusion that more saving creates more investment requires the classical assumption of full employment.

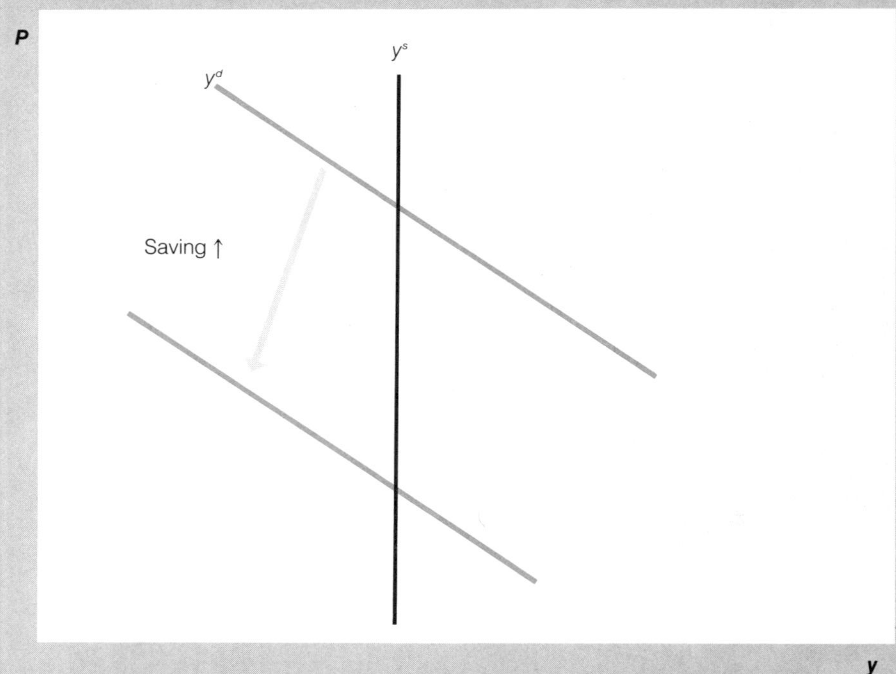

FIGURE 11.8 IN A CLASSICAL FULL-EMPLOYMENT EQUILIBRIUM, INCREASED SAVING REDUCES PRICES WITHOUT AFFECTING OUTPUT. **The leftward shift of the *IS* curve shown in Figure 11.7 shifts the aggregate demand curve leftward, too. In a classical full-employment model, prices fall to restore demand and wages fall equally to keep the labor market in equilibrium.**

Interest rates, wages, and prices must fall in order to persuade households and businesses to buy the output that savers do not want. It is these interest rate, price, and wage adjustments that cause the decline in consumption to be replaced fully by an increase in investment spending, keeping output at the full-employment level. **In disequilibrium demand-driven models, in contrast, an increase in saving and drop in consumption reduces aggregate output.**

Figure 11.9 shows the effects of increased saving and reduced consumption spending when the aggregate supply curve is not vertical. Now both output and prices decline. Since output falls with consumption spending, we cannot say for sure whether investment increases or decreases. Lower interest rates encourage investment, but the drop in aggregate output discourages investment. On balance, investment could go either way. When there are idle resources, and policy makers want to encourage investment, direct investment incentives are more certain to succeed than indirect saving incentives.

Classical economists were certain that increased saving meant more investment, since they assumed output was fixed at the full-employment level. Scat-

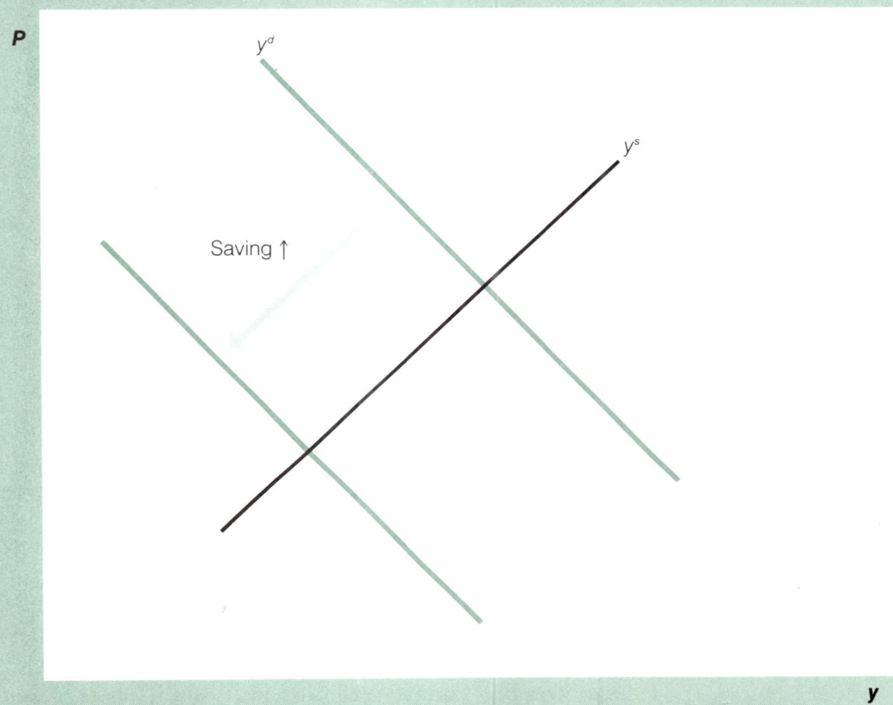

FIGURE 11.9 IN A DISEQUILIBRIUM MODEL, INCREASED SAVING REDUCES OUTPUT AS WELL AS PRICES. **If wages and/or prices do not freely adjust to maintain market equilibria, then the drop in demand that accompanies an increased desire to save reduces output and employment.**

tered disbelievers were ridiculed. In 1723, an English grand jury found Bernard Mandeville's *Fable of the Bees* to be a public nuisance because of its pernicious claim that prosperity was enhanced by spending rather than saving. A century later Malthus argued the same point with Ricardo. Malthus offered the extreme example that

> saving, pushed to excess, would destroy the motive to production. If every person were satisfied with the simplest food, the poorest clothing, and the meanest houses, it is certain that no other sort of food, clothing, and lodging would be in existence.[4]

Ricardo was unpersuaded, and Malthus' concerns about insufficient aggregate demand were ignored for a century, until Keynes argued, this time successfully, against the classical doctrine.

As Chancellor of the Exchequer in the 1920s, Winston Churchill had reiterated the classical view:

> It is the orthodox Treasury dogma, steadfastly held, that . . . very little additional employment and no permanent employment can, in fact and as a general rule, be

created by State borrowing and State expenditure. . . . It will merely substitute employment of State schemes for ordinary employment.[5]

Keynes responded:

The whole of the labor of the unemployed is available to increase the national wealth. It is crazy to believe that we shall ruin ourselves financially by trying to find means for using it and that "Safety First" lies in continuing to maintain men in idleness.

It is precisely *with* our unemployed productive resources that we shall make the new investments.

We are left with a broad, simple, and surely incontestable proposition. Whatever real difficulties there may be in the way of absorbing our unemployed labor, an inevitable diversion of resources from other forms of employment is not one of them.[6]

And the debate goes on, with some economists recently arguing that the United States needs a good dose of saving incentives, while others argue that reduced demand will weaken the economy and so discourage investment.

THE UNDERGROUND ECONOMY

In recent years, the so-called "underground economy" has attracted a great deal of attention. This phenomenon is an extreme and provocative example of incentive effects in action. Taxes can be reduced either by avoiding or not reporting taxed activities. For example, illegal drugs, gambling, and prostitution all yield taxable income which, in practice, often goes unreported and untaxed.* The same is true of many completely legal activities, particularly when payments are made with cash or goods and services. A waitress may not report all of her tips; a plumber may not report all of his fees; a painter may not report all of her sales; and an apartment owner may not report all of his rental income. Stores may keep two sets of "books" or two cash registers, or simply not record some sales. If a typist, mechanic, carpenter, grocer, or doctor asks you to pay in cash, it may be because they don't like to pay credit card fees or because they feel your check may bounce. Or it may be because they don't plan to report the transaction to the IRS. When people barter, trading art for doctor services or trading auto repairs for financial advice, they are supposed to report the transaction to the IRS, but they often don't. When people buy something and resell it later for a profit, they are supposed to report the capital gain to the IRS. Yet many such transactions go unreported, ranging from humble garage sales to high-priced art, jewelry, antique furniture, and stamp collections.

These unreported and untaxed activities make up the *underground economy.* In recent years, many economists have suspected that high marginal tax rates have driven a great deal of economic activity underground and out of sight. A detailed IRS study of selected 1976 tax returns concluded that the underground economy was about 7% of the extimated gross national product. Other estimates range from 11% to 25% of GNP.[8] The Commerce Department, on the

* Jude Wanniski tells the tale of "Mary S., with every intention of trying to get a job at the Metropolitan Opera . . . she learns that the government has just introduced a tax [rate] of 33 percent at the Metropolitan Opera, and it is now more profitable to be a prostitute."[7] There is no telling how many potential opera stars have abandoned their careers in order to reduce their taxes, or how many potential economists have prostituted themselves.

FUNNY MONEY

The Internal Revenue Service figures that there is about $135 billion worth of paper currency in circulation right now, and more than 40% of that is in $100 bills. That works out to about 600 million separate C-notes, or nearly three for every American. But, the IRS estimates, not much more than a third of this money can be accounted for.

Exclude what is in cash-register drawers and bank vaults, take away the holdings of foreign governments and financial institutions, subtract even what is presumed to have been interred in backyard caches by those who have never heard of or don't trust federal deposit insurance, and you still come up short about $40 billion in $100 bills.

Where, as the late W. C. Fields would say, are these elusive simoleons?

The IRS thinks that a lot of them are in the possession of tax evaders, drug dealers, loan sharks, fences, illegal gamblers, crooked politicians and others of that ilk who, for obvious reasons, prefer the liquidity, anonymity and concealability of big bills to more conventional methods of payments and savings. "Nothing but money is sweeter than honey," wrote Benjamin Franklin, whose benign countenance happens to appear on $100 bills, and, for those who depend on illicit wealth, unreported and untaxed money is the sweetest of all.

The $100 bill, in short, has become the common currency of the underground economy—that apparently burgeoning system of off-the-books business transactions, bribery and organized criminality that annually cheats the Treasury out of untold billions in taxes due. How else, the IRS asks, account for the rising demand for $100 bills, whose proportion in the stock of paper money has just about doubled in the last six years? And how else explain the relative invisibility of this currency—known to have been printed in such quantities, only to disappear from sight?

The IRS has a proposal for getting back at the tax cheats. It would call in all $100 bills, setting a deadline after which they would be worthless. Going a step further, the IRS might even propose extending the ban to $50 bills. Would such a combing out of the currency confer instant honesty on drug peddlers, bribers, bribees and those who keep two sets of business books? Not at all. But at least it would help take the portability if not the profitability out of illicit payoffs and tax evasion. At least it could cause some pain.

Consider the possibilities of forcing the cheats and scoundrels to do their corrupt business in lower-denomination bills.

The slim envelope of fat payola that nestles so inconspicuously in a crooked politician's inside pocket would have to be replaced by a telltale wad of mazooma big enough to choke a horse. Or the price of selling favors would have to drop dramatically. The narcotics trade's sleek attache case that readily carries $100,000 in $100 bills would have to give way to a couple of crummy two-suiters, over-weight and bulging with 10s and 20s.

Ah, the hernias that would result, the lower-back problems, the strained shoulders and aching arms. The Treasury isn't too keen on the IRS's proposal right now, and we ourselves are undecided. But the suitcase manufacturers, the chiropracters and the surgeons must love it. (*Los Angeles Times,* Sept. 17, 1982. Copyright, 1982, by *Los Angeles Times.* Reprinted by permission.)

other hand, contends that its GNP data do include the bulk of the underground economy. Their income estimates do not come from tax returns and, therefore, are not really contaminated by underreporting to the IRS. It must, however, be difficult for the Commerce Department to estimate activities that people are trying to hide. In addition, prostitution and other illegal activities are purposely excluded from the GNP, even those they do involve the production of goods and services.

Estimates of unobserved activities must, almost by definition, be very rough "back-of-the-envelope" guesses. For example, some economists emphasize the fact that the ratio of checking account balances to cash outside banks fell in the 1970s. If this ratio reflects reported relative to unreported transactions, then the underground economy has been getting larger. However, there is an alternative explanation for this relative decline in checking account balances: The spread of credit cards, high-interest time and savings accounts, money market funds, and the like have encouraged people to keep their checking account balances small. Thus, people may be keeping relatively little money in their checking accounts because it is so easy to transfer funds as needed from assets that pay high interest rates. Economists don't yet have any convincing evidence for choosing between these two explanations and for estimating subterranean activity accurately.

The underground economy has little if any effect on aggregate economic activity, but it does affect the accuracy of *reported* employment and output. If the underground economy has been growing, then this has important implications for much of our economic data. Actual GNP may be much higher than current estimates. If so, a widespread belief that productivity has slowed may be a myth. Perhaps people are very productive, but their product goes unrecorded. Stagflation may also be a myth. Unemployment rates may be greatly exaggerated if many people (particularly those with welfare or Social Security benefits at stake) do not report their jobs. Inflation may also be exaggerated if low-cost, cash-only transactions go unrecorded. Thus one economist argues that, "The patient is much healthier than we imagine; it is the social thermometer that has gone awry."[9]

INCENTIVE AND DISTRIBUTION EFFECTS OF TAXES

The practical importance of the disincentive effects of high taxes is uncertain. Many people still smoke, drink, and earn income even if they have to pay high taxes to do so. It is certain, though, that taxes can redistribute income greatly. The power to tax can, indeed, be the power to destroy.

Government is sometimes depicted as an alien creature that is on everyone's back with a hand in every pocket. But the government does not dip equally into every pocket, nor does it keep its tax revenue under a federal mattress in Washington, D. C. Instead, the government spends, loans, and gives away its tax revenue and we do not all benefit equally from government expenditures, loans, and gifts. It follows that tax cuts do not benefit all equally. A reduction in cigarette taxes, for instance, benefits smokers more than nonsmokers. We also should take into account what the government would have done with the lost tax revenue. Would hospitals have been built, loans made to Chrysler, taxes cut elsewhere, fewer bonds sold, or fewer new dollar bills printed? Whose ox gets gored and whose gets fed? The incentive and redistributive effects of taxes are fuzzy areas for economists. We don't know very much about the practical importance of the disincentives created by our most important taxes —personal income taxes. And we cannot say very much about whether a certain income distribution is fair, generous, or otherwise attractive. There is just no objective way of assessing whether taking a dollar from Peter to give Paul increases Paul's well-being more than it diminishes Peter's.

Thus tax debates often involve little economic reasoning and lots of greed, shallow philosophizing, and political posturing. The big, unanswerable question is whether tax changes alter a nation's income of just redistribute that income. The proponents of light taxes emphasize the incentive effects, that tax breaks will unleash a healthy flurry of economic activity. Critics rudely suggest that proponents are mostly interested in their own pocketbooks.

Andrew Mellon argued that, "The prosperity of the middle and lower classes depends on the good fortune and light taxes of the rich." This is the "trickle-down" theory of economic growth: encourage the rich to build factories for the commoners to work in. There may well be something to this theory. But Mellon was rather self-centered and unemotional,* and I suspect he was more concerned with his own taxes than with the prosperity of the lower classes.

ECONOMIC RECOVERY TAX ACT OF 1981

The following recent example of supply-side policies, illustrates the political tug-of-war between incentives and income redistribution. Ronald Reagan's presidential election victory in 1980 was partly due to his embracement of supply-side economics—a promise to cut taxes and get America moving again. In the summer of 1981, Congress approved the Economic Recovery Tax Act, a package of tax cuts intended to make good on President Reagan's campaign promises. As usually happens, this historic legislation was an uneasy blend of many tax changes, some designed to achieve macroeconomic objectives and some designed to placate key congressional leaders and powerful special interest groups. Some of the tax code changes created strong incentives to take certain desired actions and other changes were mostly give-aways to favored citizens. David Stockman called the Act a "Christmas tree" bill. He was also quoted as saying, "The hogs were really feeding. The greed level, the level of opportunism, just got out of control."[10] In this section, we will review some of the major provisions of the Economic Recovery Tax Act.

Lower income tax rates The combination of inflation and a progressive tax system written in nominal terms creates *bracket creep*—in which rising prices and wages push people into higher tax brackets even when their real income is unchanged. For example, the above mentioned married couple with $30,000 taxable income in 1982, paying $5607 in federal income taxes, had an 18.7% average tax rate and a 33% marginal tax rate. A 10% across-the-board increase

* Of his marriage proposal, he wrote, "Had I been rejected, I would have left neither sad nor depressed nor greatly disappointed, only annoyed at the loss of time." His economic advice to Herbert Hoover was, "Liquidate labor, liquidate stocks, liquidate the farmer."

IN THE NEWS

Greed, Envy: God-Given Wealth and Poverty, Reagan Style

There will be those trying to appeal to greed and envy—and make no mistake, that is what they are trying to do—who suggest that our tax program favors the rich. This is the same anti-business, anti-success attitude that brought this country to the brink of economic disaster.—President Reagan, Jan. 31

All right, let's talk about greed and envy. Success, too. These are all crucial concepts in the Reagan world view, reflected in the policies of his Administration.

I was surprised to hear Reagan come out against greed. Could this be the handiwork of that nefarious coven of pragmatists we keep reading about—the one the far right claims has taken over the White House? Or is it one of Reagan's famous "gaffes"? No, no, Mr. President, you're *for* greed. Adam Smith demonstrated in "The Wealth of Nations" how the "invisible hand" directs individual greed in ways that produce general prosperity. You're supposed to accuse the Democrats of not understanding this, of killing the goose that lays the golden eggs. Remember?

The claim for supply-side economics is that it can cure a sick economy through the healing power of greed. Indeed, greed is even more central to supply-side economics than to traditional free-market theory. Supply-siders claim to be able to play greed like a fiddle, to ride it like a bronco, to manipulate greed with scientific precision through changes in tax rates. Lower a man's taxes, unleash his greed and stand back.

The plain fact is that Reagan's tax program does favor the rich. The biggest and quickest tax breaks, by far, went to top-bracket investment income and to inherited wealth. Counting Social Security, most wage earners actually have had a tax increase since Reagan took office. True supply-siders make no apology for this. Rewarding successfully applied greed is the whole idea.

Envy is more complicated. This subject brings out the conflict within modern conservatism. Old-fashioned Tory-style conservatism prizes stability and social order. Because social order requires hierarchy, disparities of fortune are healthy. Anyway, they are inevitable. The good society is one in which everyone knows, and is contented with, his or her place.

From this perspective, encouraging people to compare their stations in life with those above them is corrupt and dangerous demagoguery. It creates insatiable appetites and rends the social fabric. That's "envy," and that's bad.

But Reagan and the people around him usually claim to be different and more palatable kinds of conservatives —the kind sometimes self-styled as "classical liberal." This sort of conservative favors maximum individual freedom and an unfettered capitalist economic system where, as Reagan told the unemployed in his recent State of the Union speech, "each of you can reach as high as your God-given talents will take you."

In this world view, invidious comparisons are not corrosive, they're healthy. People are supposed to be constantly reminding themselves of the heights they've not scaled. And Reagan is fond of reminding them by offering success stories in his speeches for audiences to salivate over. Only now it's not "envy." It's "incentive."

What both strains of conservatism agree on is that those who are at the top of our society deserve to be there. And, by implication, those who aren't don't. When Reagan accuses the Democrats of an "anti-success attitude," he apparently detects some skepticism on this score. I wish that I detected more of it. There's nothing wrong with success. In a properly functioning capitalist system successful people really do enrich society as a whole more than they enrich themselves. That kind of success is important to America's prosperity and strength. It should be prized and nurtured. But the smug Republican assumption that success in our economy is the result of applied moral worth, and that it's therefore immoral and ultimately self-defeating to tinker with success and failure as the economy dishes them out, is wrong for at least four reasons.

Most obvious, but least interesting, is the fact that many people at the top got there through blind luck, not through any special effort or talent of their own. They inherited wealth, or happened to own land that became valuable, or oil when OPEC quadrupled its price. Through policies such as virtually eliminating the estate tax and slashing the tax on oil-royalty income, our federal government has made this type of "success" much easier during the Reagan years. (Democrats in Congress, it's only fair to add, share the blame.)

Second, the American economy is not capitalism operating under laboratory conditions, where effort and "God-given talent" are directed by an invisible hand so that they can benefit society as a whole. There's nothing "anti-success" about wondering whether society is getting value-for-money from its highly paid investment bankers and lawyers; from corporate executives who run their companies into the ground, then award themselves big raises and "golden parachutes"; from speculators in various markets.

Reagan, with his tax cuts, has made success in America more successful, but he's done nothing to make it more productive. If anything, opportunities for unproductive success have increased during his tenure.

Third, if individual talent is "God-given," as Reagan says, why is it so obvious that the individual is morally entitled to hoard all the fruits? Thomas Edison said that genius is "1% inspiration and 99% perspiration," but surely that's a better definition of failure than of success. Effort helps, of course, but it's not the key. Most of the elements in financial success are "God-given" in the sense that they are the luck of the draw, and have little to do with innate moral worth.

So even when riches come through individual talent, productively employed, why shouldn't they be spread around a little bit? One answer is practical: If you don't reward effort by talented people disproportionately, they won't put their talent to work. That's a reasonable justification for some disparities of wealth and income. But it's not a moral imperative, and it doesn't necessarily explain or justify the disparities that we have.

Finally, no one's prosperity in America really comes primarily from individual effort. It comes primarily from the efforts of other Americans, past and present. It comes from the economy and the society that all Americans have built together.

Why does a third-generation American barber, say, make four times as much as his grandfather made, and 10 times what a barber makes in some Third World country today? Does he work four times harder? Is he 10 times more talented? Of course not.

The American entrepreneur who makes millions by building a better mousetrap probably learned science at public schools, tapped into generations of mousetrap R&D, produces and markets his mousetrap in the world's most efficient economy, and sells it to the world's most prosperous consumers. Everybody's "success," however great or modest, however augmented by luck or by grit, is largely a product of society. Is it "anti-success" for society to claim a share?

What kind of conservative is Ronald Reagan? Denouncing "greed" and "envy," he sounds less concerned about the state of capitalism and individual liberty (both worthy concerns) and more like that other kind of conservative, who prizes wealth and poverty for their own sake—because they're God-given. (Michael Kinsley, The *Los Angeles Times,* Feb. 21, 1984. Copyright, 1984, *Los Angeles Times.* Reprinted by permission.)

in wages and prices would have raised their nominal income to $33,000 and their taxes to $6597, which is 20% of their income. Thus a 10% increase in prices causes a 17.7% increase in taxes, reducing their real after-tax income.

Congress periodically lowers tax rates to offset bracket creep. In 1981, time for another adjustment, Joseph Pechman estimated that the marginal federal (income plus payroll) tax rate for a typical bread-winner with a spouse and two children had been 18.0% in 1960, 15.9% in 1965, 18.2% in 1970, 18.0% in 1975, and 21.6% in 1980.[11] The 1981 tax cut lowered personal income tax rates so as to offset this bracket creep. In addition, Congress ordered the automatic indexing of the tax table, beginning in 1985, to reduce future bracket creep.

These tax cuts were not a break with the past, but were a radical break from what tax rates would have been had bracket creep been allowed to continue unabated. It is unlikely that these tax cuts will cause people to change their behavior very much, though their behavior might have changed greatly had marginal tax rates been allowed to soar.

All-savers certificates In another provision of the 1981 tax act, thrift institutions were authorized to offer 15-month "All-Savers Certificates" paying 70% of the yield on one-year Treasury bills. These certificates are attractive for people whose marginal tax rate is greater than 30%. For example, such people, buying a taxable Treasury bill paying 15%, would keep 10.5% after taxes—the same as investing in a tax-exempt All-Savers paying 70% of 15%, or 10.5%. These certificates were advertised as way of encouraging saving by people in high tax brackets, but their major effect is actually to pump money into struggling deposit institutions; this is why some observers call them "all-bankers' certificates."

Consider again a 15% Treasury bill yield, but with an average purchaser in a 40% tax bracket and deposit institutions paying 16% on taxable money market certificates. If savers buy money market certificates, they will earn 9.6% after taxes and the Treasury will get the other 6.4% in taxes. If, instead, they buy All-Savers Certificates, they will earn 10.5% and the Treasury will get nothing. The Treasury's lost 6.4% tax revenue is split about 1/7 to savers (who get a extra 0.9% return) and 6/7 to deposit institutions (which save 5.5% in interest payments). The saver's gain is further reduced by the fact that the Economic Recovery Act included a provision reducing the amount of tax-exempt dividend and regular interest income from $200 for individuals and $400 for couples to $100 and $200. All in all, All-Savers Certificates are a multibillion dollar subsidy of deposit institutions.

Liberalized retirement plans Pension fund contributions received favored tax treatment in the Economic Recovery Tax Act. A person putting $1000 of income into the stock market or into a regular money market mutual fund, would first pay taxes on that $1000 income and then taxes on any interest, dividends, and capital gains received. If, however, the $1000 was put into a pension fund, which then invests in stocks and bonds, all these taxes would be deferred until withdrawal of the money. This deferral is doubly beneficial: The taxpayer will probably be in a lower tax bracket when retired, and interest and dividends can be earned year after year on the deferred taxes. Tax deferral is really a loan from the Treasury at very favorable terms.

The 1976 Tax Reform Act extended these benefits to self-employed individuals and others who were not covered by pension plans by allowing the former to set up Keogh plans and the latter Individual Retirement Arrangements (IRA), which give the same tax-deferral advantages as group pension funds. The 1981 tax legislation increased the maximum Keogh contribution from 15% of $50,000 income to 15% of $100,000 income. This will presumably encourage Keogh plan saving by doctors, lawyers, and other high-income self-employed individuals. More saving may mean more investment. To encourage productive saving, self-managed Keogh plans can no longer invest in metals, gems, rugs, stamps, wine, and similar baubles. However, for some reason, Keogh plans managed by trustees can make such investments. The 1981 legislation also allows Keogh participants and those already covered by pension plans to put another $2000 a year into an IRA. The tax-shelter lure of these IRAs is substantial, but it is uncertain whether they encourage additional saving or just shift existing saving out of taxable investments.

The death of estate taxes Estate taxes were virtually eliminated by the 1981 tax legislation, which gives an unlimited deduction on money or property left to the surviving spouse. In addition, there is a $600,000 tax exemption on estates left to people other than one's spouse, and well-designed trusts should be able to avoid taxes on estates valued at more than $600,000.

The effective abolition of estate taxes provides few economic incentives. It is difficult to believe that the rich will significantly alter their ingrained work habits. The new law does virtually eliminate the need for elaborate schemes to avoid estate taxes, thereby freeing lawyers and accountants to do more worthwhile things. And it probably discourages large gifts to nonprofit organizations, thereby negating the President's announced aim to encourage private donations. But, mainly, it just allows family wealth to pass intact from one generation to the next, which most likely encourages the idle rich to remain idle.

The marriage tax For many years, the tax laws were structured so that a married couple paid less in taxes than a single person with the same income, presumably because the couple's needs were greater. One implication was that a single person with high income and a single person with low income would reduce their total taxes if they married; another—the *marriage tax*—was that, with progressive tax rates, two single persons with roughly equal income would pay more in total taxes if they married. So people couldn't rationally get married without carefully calculating the tax implications. The 1981 tax legislation reduced this tension between love and money by allowing tax breaks for working couples, thereby effectively reducing the marriage tax penalty. This change provides a little more incentive for marriage and a little more incentive for both husbands and wives to work. But mostly it must gives working couples a tax break.

Investment incentives Depreciation schedules were simplified and accelerated. Real estate can now be depreciated over 15 rather than 30 or 40 years. Business plant, equipment, and vehicles can now be written off in 10, 5, and 3 years, respectively. More rapid depreciation is valuable because a dollar less in taxes today is more valuable than a dollar less in taxes 20 years from now. Accelerated depreciation encourages investment by increasing the after-tax profitability of investment. The new law also makes it easier and cheaper to switch to LIFO (last in, first out) accounting which, as Chapter 18 explains, raises after-tax profits during inflations. The 1981 law also contains direct investment tax credits: 6% for research equipment and vehicles, 10% for other machinery and equipment. Finally, the windfall profits tax on oil production was reduced, and increased tax deductions were granted to owners of race horses.

All of these changes and numerous little ones as well are designed to stimulate investment directly. In part, the theory is that if businesses are given more money they will invest more. And, in part, the theory is that if you make investments more attractive, businesses will find the money to make investments. The latter theory makes more sense, though the two effects are in practice difficult to separate. This tax legislation, like most tax laws, alters both marginal and average tax rates. There are larger incentives to invest, but there will also be larger profits even if businesses do not invest.

Selling tax credits Depreciation deductions and investment tax credits can be used to reduce taxes on profits. Say that the Minus Company buys some new equipment at a cost of $10 million. Minus gets a 10% tax credit of $1 million that it can deduct from its tax bill, reducing the effective cost of the equipment to $9 million. In addition, it gets to deduct the yearly depreciation of the equipment. To keep it simple, assume a straight-line $2 million-a-year depreciation over five years. Each year, the firm deducts $2 million as an expense, reducing its taxes by $920,000 with a 46% tax. If the firm uses accelerated depreciation, it can deduct even more in the first years of ownership.

But what if Minus doesn't have any profits to take deductions against? What if its revenue is just equal to its expenses for labor, raw materials, and so on? Then it has no tax liability, even without using its tax credit and depreciation deduction. Minus has $1.92 million in first-year tax breaks that it can't use. One possibility that has been proposed from time to time is a negative corporate income tax: If a company makes a $1 million profit, it pays the U.S. Treasury $460,000; if it loses $1 million, then the Treasury pays it $460,000. Presidents Carter and Reagan both considered such arrangements but decided that it was unwise for the Treasury to routinely subsidize unprofitable companies. Money losers should be allowed to go out of business or forced to beg for government loans and other subsidies.

Corporations themselves figured out another way to exploit unused tax breaks. A profitable firm, Company Plus, could acquire Minus and use Minus's tax breaks to offset some of Plus's profits. A number of corporate mergers have, in fact, been primarily intended to acquire unused tax breaks. To avoid both a merger mania and direct Treasury subsidies to unprofitable companies, the 1981 tax law liberalizes leasing restrictions so as to allow companies in effect, to sell tax credits to each other. These are subsidies to unprofitable companies, but they are sufficiently complicated that most voters won't recognize them. Here is how such an arrangement might work. Plus buys Minus's equipment for $10 million by paying Minus $1 million and borrowing another $9 million for five years from Minus. Minus then leases the equipment from Plus, paying a rental fee just equal to the amount Plus is supposed to pay for the $9 million

IN THE NEWS

Double-Dipping in the Hollandaise Sauce

We are on location in New York, shooting background footage for a film. There are 11 of us—cameramen, technicians and production staff. We have been housed, at company expense, in an elegant, once-opulent hotel—the sort with crystal chandeliers, old velvet drapes and mural-covered ceilings.

At breakfast one morning in the hotel dining room, our conversation meanders to the subject of welfare fraud.

"I read in the paper that a woman had her purse snatched. When they got it back they found $68 in cash and $300 in food stamps," one of us says. "Can you imagine that? How does a person get $300 in food stamps?"

Others offer their own tales of public-assistance fraud. A master double-dipper in Chicago. The welfare queen of Los Angeles. Most betray a touch of grudging admiration for ingenuity, as in the case of the entrepreneurial welfare recipient who traveled between states to collect multiple payments. But even in this instance our tone is mainly one of ire and dismay. Around the table, we agree that the public-assistance situation is out of hand.

Understand, this is no Moral Majority revival meeting. Most of us are young (20s and 30s), well-educated and nominally liberal. There is not one person in the lot whom I don't find likable and thoughtful. Yet our conversational targets soon include legitimate welfare recipients, who we assume fatten their welfare checks by producing babies, and then the minimum-wage laws, which we hold responsible for keeping able-bodied poor people on the dole.

Our breakfast bill arrives. It comes to $8 a person. That our poached eggs and asparagus with hollandaise sauce, Canadian bacon and croissants are company tax deductions, and hence paid partly out of taxpayers' pockets, disturbs no one. Neither does the fact that, unlike food stamps and welfare payments, which have ceilings, there is virtually no limit to the cost of our government-supported meals. Indeed, on a subsequent day we will have three-course $15 breakfasts; culinary indulgences even more extravagant would be equally deductible. What distinguishes our meal grants from those of the poor is that our food is prepared for us, served to us on sparkling china and does not require the inconvenience or indignity of federally issued stamps.

The deductions are legal. Whatever the irony in eating a posh breakfast subsidized by Uncle Sam while complaining of government food handouts, the deductions are at least entirely within the realm of the law, and any company or individual will understandably take advantage of them.

But our welfare-wary circle engages in its own version of double-dipping. Since our company deducts from its taxes a fixed amount for each of our meals, we do not have to turn in our breakfast bills. So some of us keep them, stash them away for personal use another time: No reason to let a perfectly good tax-deductible receipt go to waste when it can be used twice.

But the buck, if you will, stops not even here. There are sometimes multiple receipts for the same meal: for example, a credit card slip, a meal tab and a cash-register receipt. In these instances, a single bill can and often does find its way into several persons' tax returns, leaving the government to pick up more than the tab itself. On one occasion, a tip-conscious waiter graciously brought us 11 receipts. The tab came to $240, but with the receipts left blank, as they often are, only imagination limits how much this meal is ultimately going to cost other taxpayers.

And only imagination can estimate the nationwide extent of double-dipping in the upper-income tax brackets, of federal giveaways in the form of Pinot Chardonnay or escargot.

As we get up from the table, I wonder whether we will ever read a news story about a woman found with $300 worth of tax deductions in her wallet. (George Q. Richmond, The *Los Angeles Times,* Apr. 19, 1982. Copyright, 1982, *Los Angeles Times.* Reprinted by permission.)

loan. So the rental fee and the loan charges balance out, and neither company owes the other anything. In addition, Plus agrees to sell the equipment back to Minus after five years for one dollar. In practice, the equipment doesn't go anywhere. It just stays in Minus's plant and is operated as usual. All that has occurred is that Plus has paid Minus $1 million for the right to claim the equipment—and its depreciation allowance—for tax purposes. Minus gets $1 million for the tax credits that it couldn't use, and Plus pays $1 million for tax credits that are worth more than $1 million. Thus, Minus is allowed to sell its unused tax breaks.

Alan Greenspan, the chairman of Gerald Ford's Council of Economic Advisers, called these leases "sort of the equivalent of food stamps for undernourished corporations." There's not much incentive here, except for the lawyers who put together these deals. There is probably a little more incentive for unprofitable and borderline companies to make questionable investments, and a little more incentive to make investments that might turn out to be unprofitable. But, mostly, it's just a subsidy for ailing firms with products people aren't buying.

Winners, losers A simple reckoning of the complex legislation just described and of subsequent laws is difficult, but some suggestive data are available. First, President Reagan did not make good on his pledge to reduce federal spending. In real terms, government purchases of goods and services were 10.8% higher in 1983 than in1980, and total disbursements (including transfers) increased by 8.9%. Relative to GNP, federal spending rose from 6.8% to 8.3%; transfers grew from 16.1% to 16.7%; and total disbursements increased from 22.9% to 25.0%. The President was more successful in his efforts to change the composition of federal outlays (Table 11.1). Military spending increased, while public investment in highways, education, space, and so on decreased. Social Security, Medicare, and the like increased faster than other outlays between 1980 and 1983, but the Reagan administration proposed slowing its growth over the remainder of the decade. Food stamps, unemployment insurance, and other benefits to the poor were restrained, with further restraint proposed. Interest on the national debt grew, swollen by unprecedented federal deficits.

On the tax side, Reagan continued the long-run demise of corporate income taxes. The corporate share of total tax revenue had fallen from above 50% in the 1920s to 26% in 1950 and then 13% in 1980. Under Reagan, the corporate

TABLE 11.1

Percentage Distribution of Government Spending in 1980 and 1983 and that proposed for 1989

	1980	1983	1989
National defense	21.9	24.4	34.6
Public investment	15.7	11.2	7.9
Retirement and disability	38.1	40.4	38.6
Benefits to poor	9.9	9.0	7.6
Interest on debt	8.8	10.5	10.7
Other	5.7	4.5	0.6

TABLE 11.2
Average Tax Rates for 1980 and 1984

Taxable real income (1978 $)	Average tax rates 1980	Average tax rates 1984	% change
7,000	3.8	7.7	102.6
9,000	8.3	9.7	16.9
11,000	10.4	11.3	8.7
13,000	12.1	12.5	3.3
15,000	13.7	14.0	2.2
17,000	15.0	15.0	0.0
19,000	16.1	16.0	−0.6
22,500	17.7	17.8	0.6
27,500	19.1	19.3	1.0
40,000	23.3	22.5	−3.4

share fell even further, to 8% in 1983. Federal tax revenue is now almost entirely individual income and social insurance taxes.[12] With a progressive income tax system, the tax burden falls unequally on different income classes, and the Reagan tax changes have not affected all groups equally. A study published by the Federal Reserve Bank of Philadelphia estimated that tax bracket creep and increased social insurance taxes just about offset legislated income tax rate reductions, leaving marginal tax rates virtually unchanged between 1980 and 1984. Average tax rates, on the other hand, increased for low-income households and decreased for upper-income families (Table 11.2).[13] The gains for upper-income groups are even larger than these figures indicate, since much of their income is from investments that received large tax breaks. Thus "taxable income" is substantially less than actual income.

The Congressional Budget Office made a similar study, taking into account also how much various income classes lost in transfer payments from the federal government. They estimated that in 1984 one-fifth of the nation's families earned less than $10,000 a year and that these people, on average, gained $40 in tax breaks and lost $480 in food stamps and other benefits, for a net loss of $440. Other income classes came out ahead, with the upper-income groups gaining the most:

Household income	Average net gain in 1984 from 1981 and 1982 tax and transfer changes
less than $10,000	−$ 440
$10,000 − 20,000	+$ 60
$20,000 − 40,000	+$1,280
$40,000 − 80,000	+$3,540
more than $80,000	+$8,930

There are, of course, even greater disparities among individual families, who are affected in a variety of ways by specific exemptions and deductions. As with virtually all tax legislation, some gain while others lose. The trick, as Senator Long puts it in this Chapter's epigraph, is somehow to avoid being that heavily taxed person trying to hide "behind the tree."

SUMMARY

The supply side of the economy consists of labor demand, labor supply and production. Changes in population, technology, land, natural resources, and the capital stock are all supply-side events that may alter employment and output. Taxes can also have direct supply-side effects. It is important, though, to distinguish between average and marginal tax rates: Average tax rates affect income redistribution while marginal tax rates affect people's choices between alternative actions—for example, work versus leisure, consumption versus saving, or smoking versus nonsmoking.

Macro stabilization policies involve both average and marginal tax rates. Average tax rates affect how much disposable income people have available for spending. Increased taxes deplete pockets and dampen spending. Marginal tax rates affect the cylical volatility of the economy. High marginal tax rates provide lots of automatic stabilization.

Supply-side policies focus on the disincentive effects of high marginal tax rates. An income tax cut, for example, may increase labor supply and thereby increase employment and output if full employment prevails. Tax breaks and subsidies can also be used to increase labor demand. Accelerated depreciation and investment tax credits are tax policies intended to increase the after-tax return on investment in plant and equipment. Tax breaks can also be used to increase the after-tax returns on various financial assets that are available to households. If households respond by saving more and consuming less, then (in a full-employment model at least) prices and interest rates will adjust to stimulate investment in place of the diminished consumption. Demand-side events also affect investment spending. Low real interest rates and a booming, prosperous economy are wonderful tonics for tired entrepreneurs.

In practice, tax changes inevitably have both incentive and redistributive effects. Tax laws can be written to encourage some activities and to discourage others. Tax laws can also be written to give generous tax breaks to favored groups. These are the two reasons why our tax laws are so detailed and complicated. Changes in the tax laws involve these same two forces: good intentions and self interest.

APPENDIX: LABOR'S CHOICE BETWEEN WORK AND LEISURE

The labor supply choice is between the consumption of leisure and the consumption of the commodities that can be earned by working. This tradeoff can be modeled as follows. An individual derives pleasure or "utility" from both consumption goods, c, and leisure, l. We assume that labor supply decisions are made weekly and that there is no borrowing or saving from week to week; that there is a constant, inherited, nonlabor real income, h; and that there are 168 hours in a week, so that if n hours are spent working, then only 168-n hours are available for leisure activities. If the hourly wage is W, consumption good cost P, and the tax rate is t_y, then consumption is equal to real nonlabor income, h, plus real after-tax labor income $n(1-t_y)W/P$: $c = h + n(1-t_y)W/P$. Leisure is equal to the number of hours spent not working: $l = 168 - n$. Given the real after-tax wage rate, $(1-t_y)w = (1-t_y)W/P$, and the consumption and leisure budget constraints, a person chooses how many hours to work so as to maximize his or her utility. In Figure 1, a graphical depiction, the slope of the opportunity locus is $(1-t_y)w$

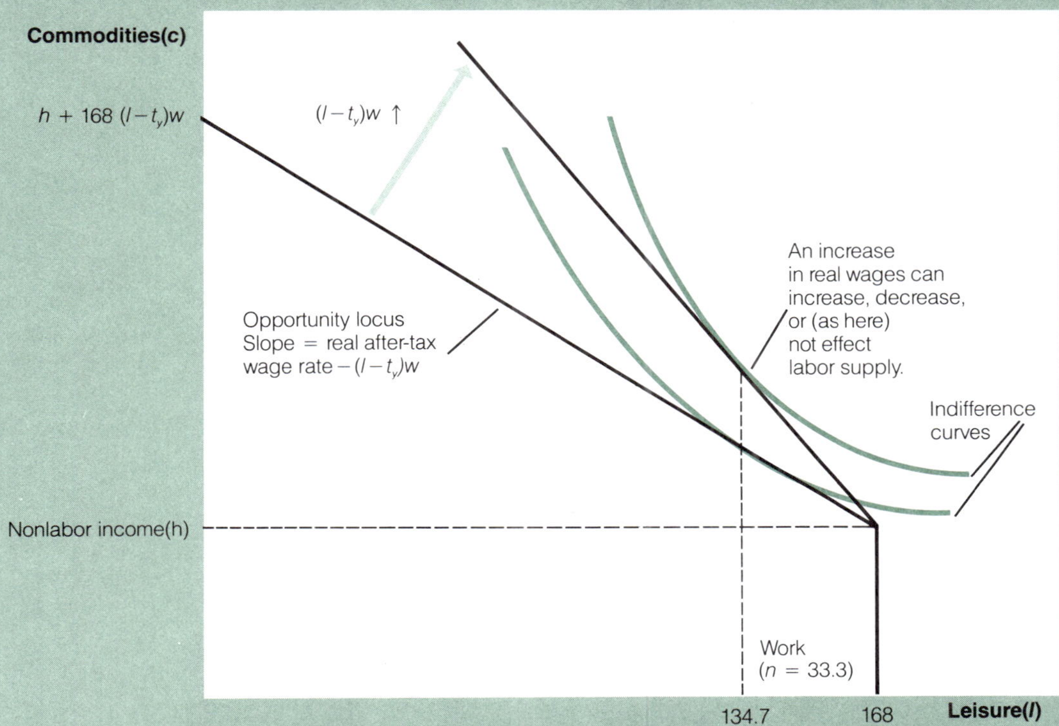

FIGURE 1 THE LABOR SUPPLY DECISION IS A CHOICE BETWEEN THE CONSUMPTION OF COMMODITIES AND LEISURE. **The opportunity locus shows the possible combinations of commodities and leisure offered by nonlabor income and the wage rate. The preferences of the person here hypothesized, summarized by indifference curves, lead to 33.3 hours of work per week. It is theoretically uncertain how this decision would be affected by a higher after-tax wage rate.**

since an extra hour of leisure reduces consumption by an amount equal to the real after-tax hourly wage rate $(l - t_y)w$. A person who does not work at all can consume h commodities and 168 hours of leisure.

The indifference curves depict an individual's willingness to trade leisure for commodities. An indifference curve is negatively sloped because people are willing to sacrifice leisure for commodities. Indifference curves are bowed (convex from below)* because people are reluctant to go to the extremes of consuming either almost no commodities or almost no leisure. (Does a steeper indifference curve indicate that a person values leisure more or less highly, at the margin?)

The individual chooses the number of work hours, n, so as to attain the highest possible indifference curve. In Figure 1 the choice is 33.3 hours of work and 134.7 hours of leisure. Except for the corner solutions of no work ($l = 168$) or no play ($l = 0$), the labor supply choice will be at a tangency of an indifference curve with the opportunity locus.

* An opportunity locus may be bowed (concave from below) if a person's productivity and wage rate decline as the number of hours worked increases.

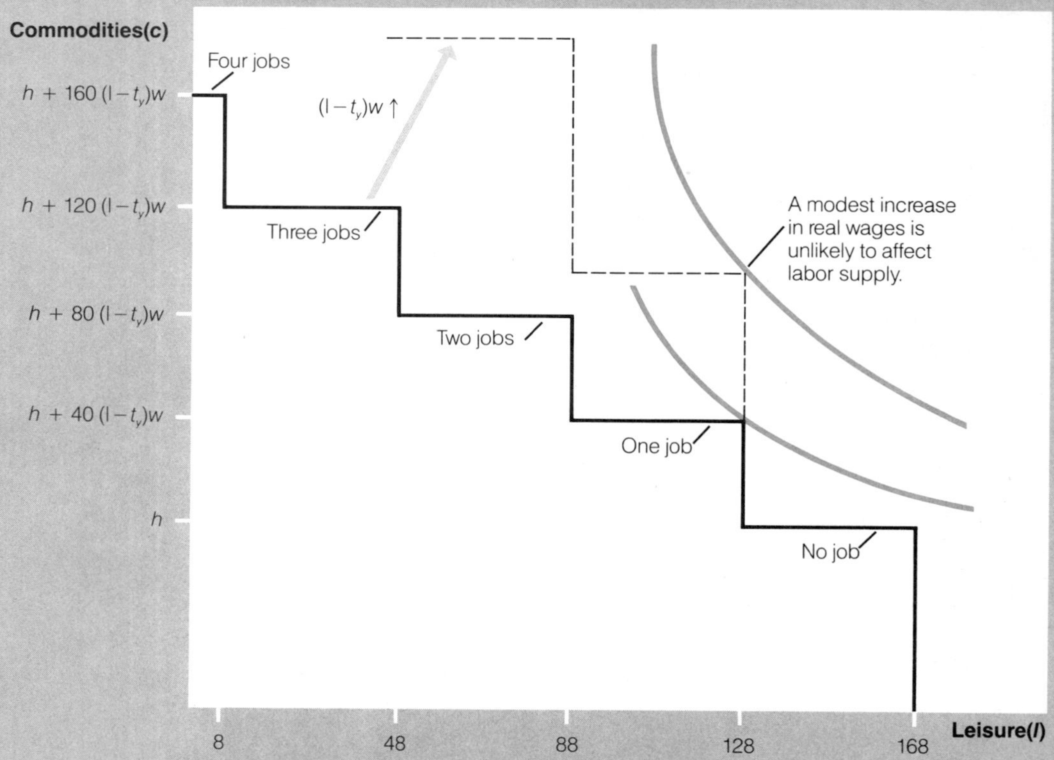

FIGURE 2 THE LABOR SUPPLY DECISION WITH A 40-HOUR WORK WEEK. **The opportunity locus is a series of steps if jobs are a fixed 40 hours per week. The choice is not between a few additional or fewer minutes of work, but between no job, one job, or two jobs.**

At such a tangency, the implicit value of an extra hour of leisure is the real hourly wage rate. It is this sort of reasoning that underlies the calculations that are sometimes made in which wage rates are used to estimate the value of leisure.

Income and substitution effects According to this work-leisure model, labor supply depends on one's preferences for commodities relative to leisure (the indifference curve slopes) and the after-tax real wage rate (the opportunity locus slope). Preferences do not change much week to week, or even year to year. So the after-tax real wage rate is the primary short-run cause of labor supply changes.

The effect of real wage rates on labor supply is important to many policy questions such as the supply-side effects of wage taxes of subsidies. But Figure 1 shows that theory alone cannot tell us whether an increase in the after-tax real wage rate increases or decreases labor supply. The new tangency may be to the left, to the right, or (as shown) right above the old tangency. There is a substitution effect arguing for more work, to take advantage of the higher real wage rate. But there is also an income effect arguing that higher wages make work less necessary. On balance, labor supply may go up or down, depending on the precise slopes of the indifference curves.

Institutional constraints One inadequacy of this model is that it neglects the fact that few people have the option of choosing to work exactly 33.3 hours a week, or whatever they may prefer. Most people have specialized jobs within large firms, and these firms find it most efficient to have people working together over the same standard work week. There is a great need for coordination, both on the assembly lines and in the executive suites. If people wander in and out, working odd hours when they feel up to it, the ability of others to do their jobs is diminished. There are also interactions between firms that argue for standard work weeks. Planning, ordering, and deliveries would all be more difficult if all worked their own strange hours.

Work is consequently organized around a certain standard business timetable—40 hours a week, 9 to 5 Monday through Friday, with regular holidays. There is some flexibility in many jobs about precisely when you work and how much you work. But it is only a very limited flexibility, much less than the variations in individual preferences. You may prefer to work 30 hours a week, 12 to 10 Monday, Tuesday, and Thursday, with three months vacation and a personal celebration of Bastille Day and John Lennon's birthday. But unless you're a writer, painter or college professor, you probably won't have much choice in the matter.

These institutional time constraints mean that most people are locked into a situation where they are unable to work exactly the number of hours they would like. Figure 2 shows a commodity-leisure opportunity locus where the only alternatives are to work in 40-hour-a-week jobs or not at all.* As shown, there are five possibilities, ranging from not working to taking four jobs. The best alternative is no longer a tangency, but is instead at one of the corners of the kinked opportunity locus. This means that the implicit value of leisure (the slope of the indifference curve) is not equal to the real wage rate.

Figure 2 also shows that a change in the after-tax real wage rate is unlikely to affect labor supply. Most people will probably want to work a little more or a little less, but very few will be persuaded to quit a job or take another one. In fact, people with only one job will never quit working because of an increase in real wages (see Exercise 13). The only way to take advantage of the income effect of higher real wages is to reduce the institutionally fixed work week. In modern industrial economies the long-run growth of productivity and real wages has in fact led to periodic reductions in the standard work week. In addition, workers have institutionalized a shorter work year by increasing the number of days allowed for vacations, holidays, sick days, and so on. Whenever the work week or the work year is reduced, the income effect makes its presence felt as higher real wages cause a reduction in labor supply.

Another institutional constraint is that most labor-supply decisions are made jointly by a family, rather than by a single individual. These joint decisions are usually neglected in labor-supply theories because they are difficult to model. A family's utility depends not just on total family leisure, but on how these leisure hours are divided among the family members. Three people working is not the same as one person having three jobs. There may well be interdependencies too, in that one person's enjoyment of leisure hours may well depend on whether or not other family members are busy at work. Child-rearing further complicates family labor supply decisions.

We can, however, easily make the general observation that labor supply changes seldom involve everyone working a few hours more or a few hours less. Instead, labor supply variations are mostly due to a few people taking or quitting jobs. For example,

* A more realistic opportunity locus would allow part-time jobs and reduced wages in second, third, and fourth jobs.

when real wages increase few people have the option of working 40 minutes less each week. And we've just noted that an individual with one job will never quit because real wages are higher. But, in a family, an increase in real wages may well cause some family members to stop working while others continue. Similarly, a decline in real wages will never persuade a single individual who is not working to take a job (see Exercise 13). But, in a family, a decline in real wages may persuade a second or third family member to enter the labor force.

IMPORTANT TERMS AND CONCEPTS

marginal tax rate
automatic stabilizers
crowding out
accelerated depreciation
investment tax credit
underground economy
bracket creep
the marriage tax

High marginal tax rates create an economic incentive to avoid those actions that are heavily taxed; for example high taxes on cigarettes and alcohol discourage their consumption. High marginal tax rates may also influence labor demand and supply, production, investment, and saving. Taxes also redistribute income and wealth.

An income tax cut may increase labor supply and thereby increase full-employment equilibrium levels of employment and output. An income tax cut also stimulates spending, shifting the *IS* curve rightward. It is uncertain whether prices will go up or down. These supply-side effects are undone if the labor supply curve is either vertical or backward bending, or if wages do not freely fall to maintain full employment. If there is an excess supply of labor, then tax-induced changes in labor supply do not directly affect employment or output. Tax cuts instead work through the demand side of the economy, stimulating spending and prices and, so, increasing output and employment.

Demand-side actions that influence capital formation will, with the passage of time, also affect the supply side of the economy. Investment spending is encouraged by low interest rates and by high production and profits. If there are idle resources, then monetary and fiscal policies can increase both consumption and investment. If there is full employment, then output is a fixed pie. The nation's capital stock will be increased if government investment displaces private consumption and will be decreased if government consumption displaces private investment.

If full employment prevails, then more saving means less consumption and more investment. With market disequilibria, more saving and less consumption may reduce output and investment. When there are idle resources, investment is more surely increased by investment incentives than by saving incentives.

EXERCISES

1. What is the economic logic behind the assertion that, "The power to tax is the power to destroy"?

2. Listed below are four policy actions. For each, state whether the immediate direct effect is primarily on the demand or supply side of the economy; and whether the effect on output is positive or negative. Explain your reasoning briefly.

a. The government prints money and buys bonds.
b. Congress imposes a "cancer tax" on tobacco farmers and uses the revenue to support cancer research.
c. Congress reduces tax rates on savings accounts and imposes a nationwide sales tax to maintain its revenue.
d. The government sells bonds and uses the proceeds to repair the nation's railroads.

3. What are the macro effects of an income tax cut if there are excess supplies of labor and commodities?

4. Congress is considering reducing taxes on wage income while simultaneously increasing taxes on cigarettes. Assuming that there is no change in total tax revenue, how would this tax shift affect the economy? Assume a full-employment equilibrium.

5. How would your answer to the previous question be changed if you assume that there is an excess supply of labor?

6. It has been argued that the tax deductibility of interest payments on loans discourages saving and hence diminishes investment. For example, a *Wall Street Journal* staff reporter wrote that "savings become capital that helps finance economic growth and prosperity. . . . By making interest on debt tax-deductible, economists say, the U.S. encourages Americans to borrow rather than save." (Norman Peagam, "Canada's Policies, Tax Laws Help Explain Why Its People Save More Than Americans," *Wall Street Journal,* August 8, 1980.) Explain the arguments for and against this conclusion.

7. A newspaper item reported that consumer spending was fueling the economic recovery that was then (1983) in progress. This was the good news: "Pent-up consumer demand has finally burst loose." But the bad news was that, "Invigorated consumers are apparently opening their pocketbooks at the expense of savings, . . . reduction in the rate of saving is considered bad news because it comes at a time when larger government deficits must be financed. Says Michael Laub, an economist for the American Bankers Association: I wouldn't say that it's a disaster. It's not going to stop the recovery. But its going to make it more difficult.' " "The Consumer Bounces Back," (The *New York Times* July 3, 1983) How can an increase in consumer spending be good news and bad news at the same time?

8. What would be the short-run effects on real wages, employment, and output of an influx of impoverished immigrants? Does your answer depend on whether you assume labor market equilibrium or disequilibrium?

9. Are federal programs to train and retrain workers primarily a demand-side or supply-side policy? Use our textbook macro model to give a graphical analysis of the effects of such programs on employment, output, prices, and interest rates in each of the following cases:

a. Classical full-employment equilibrium.
b. Sticky-wage, flexible-price disequilibrium with an excess labor supply.
c. Sticky-wage, sticky-price disequilibria with excess supplies of labor and commodities.

10. Assume a classical full-employment model with a Pigou effect, so that a higher price level shifts the *IS* curve leftward. Does an expansionary monetary policy stimulate, discourage, or have no effect on investment?

11. Use *IS* and *LM* curves to explain the economic logic behind this quotation:

> Given the Reagan administration's announced goal of stimulating investment and strengthening the nation's industrial base, the combination of policies it has pursued has been questionable from the start. The White House has relied on the

> Federal Reserve Board to fight inflation through a restrictive monetary policy while following a fiscal policy characterized by huge deficits. The unintended result has been a policy that impedes investment and works at cross-purposes with the goal of the Reagan tax cuts. (Kenneth H. Bacon, "The Outlook," *Wall Street Journal,* April 11, 1983)

12. Labor demand, d, and supply, s, are given by the following equations:

$$d = 130 - 2(W/P)$$
$$s = 100 + 1(1 - t)W/P,$$

where W is the nominal wage rate, P is the price level, and t is the tax rate on wage income. The tax rate is 50%; that is, $t = 0.50$. Calculate labor demand and supply for $W/P = 4$, 6, 8, 10, 12, 14, and 16, and then sketch the labor demand and supply curves. What are the labor market equilibrium values of the before-tax and after-tax real wage rates? What is the equilibrium level of employment?

Now, a new president is elected and income taxes are abolished; that is, t is reduced to 0.00. Show the effects on the labor demand and supply curves. What are the labor market equilibrium values of the before-tax and after-tax real wage rates? What is the equilibrium level of employment?

13. Using Figure 2 in the appendix to the chapter, show that an increase in real wages will never persuade a person with one job to quit working, but might persuade a person with two jobs to stop moonlighting. Can you explain this difference? Using Figure 2 again, show that a decline in real wages will never persuade a person who is not working to take a job. Explain the economic logic behind this observation.

14. The hourly wage for part-time jobs is usually less than the hourly wage for full-time jobs. For example, the monthly pay and benefits for a 20-hours-a-week secretarial job are usually less than half that for a 40-hours-a-week secretarial job. Similarly, substitute teachers are paid less per day than regular teachers. What demand and supply factors could account for these pay disparities?

15. Critically evaluate the following:

> It has been usual to think of the accumulated wealth of the world as having been painfully built up out of that voluntary abstinence of individuals from the immediate enjoyment of consumption, which we call Thrift. But it should be obvious that mere abstinence is not enough by itself to build cities or drain fens.
>
> It is Enterprise which builds and improves the world's possessions. . . . If Enterprise is afoot, wealth accumulates whatever may be happening to Thrift; and if Enterprise is asleep, wealth decays whatever Thrift may be doing. (John M. Keynes, *Treatise on Money,* 1930)

REFERENCES

1. Senate debate, 1972.

2. Irving Kristol, "Of Economics and Eco-mania," *Wall Street Journal,* September 19, 1980.

3. See, for example, O. Ashenfelter and J. Heckman, "Estimating Labor-Supply Functions," in G. G. Cain, and H. W. Watts, eds., *Income Maintenance and Labor Supply,* Chicago: Rand McNally, 1973, pp. 265–78; and R. Hall, "Labor Supply and Aggregate Fluctuations," in K. Brunner and A. Meltzer, eds., *On the State of Macro-economics,* Amsterdam: North -Holland, 1980.

4. Thomas Malthus, *Principles of Political Economy,* Boston: Wells & Lilly, 1821 pp. 8–9.

5. Winston Churchill, quoted and paraphrased by J. M. Keynes and H. D. Henderson, *Can Lloyd George Do It?,* 1929.

6. Keynes and Henderson.

7. Jude Wanniski, *The Way the World Works,* New York: Simon and Schuster, 1979, p. 94.

8. Some estimates for 1981 are reported in "The Underground Economy's Hidden Force," *Business Week,* April 5, 1982, pp. 64–70. Some details behinds these sorts of estimates are explained in P. M. Gutmann, "The Subterranean Economy," *Financial Analysts Journal,* November/December 1977; and E. L. Feige, "How big is the Irregular Economy?," *Challenge,* November/December 1979, pp. 5–13.

9. E. L. Feige.

10. William Greider, "The Education of David Stockman," *Atlantic Monthly,* December 1981, pp. 27–54.

11. Cited in James Tobin, "Supply-Side Economics: What is it? Will it Work?" *Economic Outlook ASA,* summer 1981, pp. 51–53.

12. Frank C. Wykoff, "Business Tax Breaks are Causing Budget Deficits," *Los Angeles Times,* December 18, 1983

13. Stephen A. Meyer, "Tax Cuts: Reality or Illusion?," Federal Reserve Bank of Philadelphia, *Business Review* October 1983, pp. 3–16.

SUGGESTIONS FOR FURTHER READING

For some early empirical estimates of the effects of taxes on investment, see Dale W. Jorgenson and Robert E. Hall, "Tax Policy and Investment Behavior," *The American Economic Review,* 57 (1967), pp. 391–414; and Gary Fromm, editor, *Tax Incentives and Capital Spending.* Washington, D.C.: Brookings Institution, 1971.

PART FIVE

MICROFOUNDATIONS

CHAPTER TWELVE

HOUSEHOLD CONSUMPTION AND SAVING

My idea of a full life is to run out of money and breath at the same time.

BOBBY LAYNE*

This chapter investigates the factors that influence households' division of income between spending and saving, and their marginal propensity to consume. It also looks at how these factors relate to the Social Security System and its troubles and examines the significance of these factors to the income-expenditure model treated earlier.

THE income-expenditure model (Chapter 3) emphasizes the interrelationship of income and spending. First, aggregate spending determines aggregate income. Second, income influences spending, particularly household spending. Thus the magnitude of the effect of income on spending (the marginal propensity to spend) is one of the keys to understanding how macroeconomic fluctuations gather momentum.

It makes sense that as people's incomes rise they will buy more goods and services. My marginal propensity to spend is quite high, and it is likely that yours is, too. And, yet, our collective marginal propensity to spend does not total 1.0. We do save some of our income, on average and at the margin. Why is this? What influences our decision as to how much of our income we spend and how much we save?

These are questions we will answer in this chapter. We will see that the consumption-saving decision depends not only on present income, but also on past income and on anticipated income as well. Interest rates, wealth, and demographic variables also matter. We will begin by looking at the simplest Keynesian consumption function, which has proven to be really too simple. Then we will look at some richer alternatives.

*Detroit Lion and Pittsburgh Steeler great.

THE SIMPLE KEYNESIAN CONSUMPTION FUNCTION

Classical economists believed that consumption and saving depended mainly on interest rates. They didn't consider the effects of income fluctuations on spending since they assumed that income did not fluctuate. They assumed that income was fixed at the full-employment level and then asked how much of this fixed income would be spent and how much would be saved. Their answer was that high real interest rates encourage saving and discourage spending, while low real interest rates have the opposite effects.

Keynes argued that employment and income could diverge significantly from full-employment levels, and that when people lose jobs and income they cut back on their spending, thereby reducing output and employment even more. Keynes wrote that the influence of income on consumption is a "fundamental psychological law, upon which we are entitled to depend both a priori from our knowledge of human nature and from the detailed facts of experience."[1]

A simple algebraic representation of Keynes' argument that income (y) influences consumption (c) is

$$c = a + by \qquad 0 < b < 1 \tag{12.1}$$

Where b is the *marginal propensity to consume (MPC)*, representing the effect of an increase in income on consumption. Keynes argued that b is surely positive and most likely less than one (part of an increase in income being saved). This consumption equation played such a key role in early Keynesian income-expenditure models that it is usually called the "Keynesian consumption function."

In the *General Theory*, Keynes actually discussed a number of other factors (such as interest rates and wealth) that influence consumption, but attention focused on his novel argument that income affects consumption which, in turn, affects income. This interdependency seemed to be the cornerstone of his explanation of how economic shocks are magnified into prolonged booms and recessions.

Shortly after Keynes' *General Theory* was published, the National Bureau of Economic Research (NBER) began putting out aggregate data that conformed remarkably to Keynes' postulated consumption function over a wide range of prosperity and recession. Figure 12.1 shows a scatter diagram of aggregate consumption and disposable income. (These are time series data: They show spending and income at different times—here in different years from 1929 to 1940.) A straight line with a slope of $b = 0.79$ fits the data remarkably well. This 0.79 slope indicates that a \$1.0 billion change in disposable income causes a \$.79 billion change in consumption. Two similar, widely read econometric studies published in 1945 estimated the MPC to be 0.80 (using 1929–40 data) and 0.76 (using 1923–40 data).[2]

Family budget surveys were also made at this time, which again strikingly confirmed Keynes' consumption function.[3] Figure 12.2 shows the average consumption of different income classes in 1935–36. There is a remarkable correlation between income and consumption, with some indication that the MPC

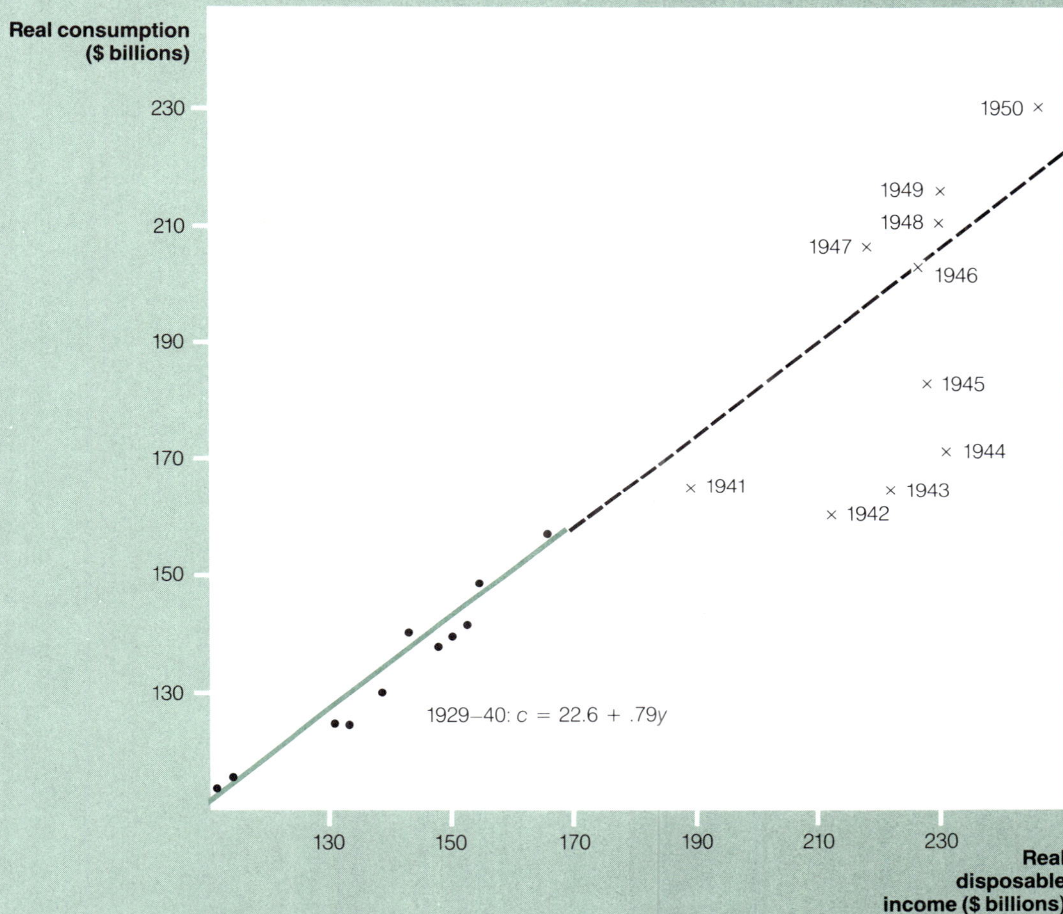

FIGURE 12.1 AGGREGATE CONSUMPTION AND INCOME, **1929–40 and 1941–50. An equation fitted to aggregate consumption and income data for 1929–40 overestimated spending for World War II (when there was rationing) and underestimated spending after the war (when these controls were removed).**

falls at high income levels (something that Keynes had also suggested). All in all, here was a theory followed by data that confirmed the theory.

However, just as the simple Keynesian consumption function was gaining wide acceptance, a major forecasting error forced a reassessment. In the 1940s, economists began extrapolating their estimated macro and micro consumption functions to determine the amount of investment and government spending that would be necessary to achieve peacetime full employment. They estimated that investment and government spending would have to be roughly 25% of

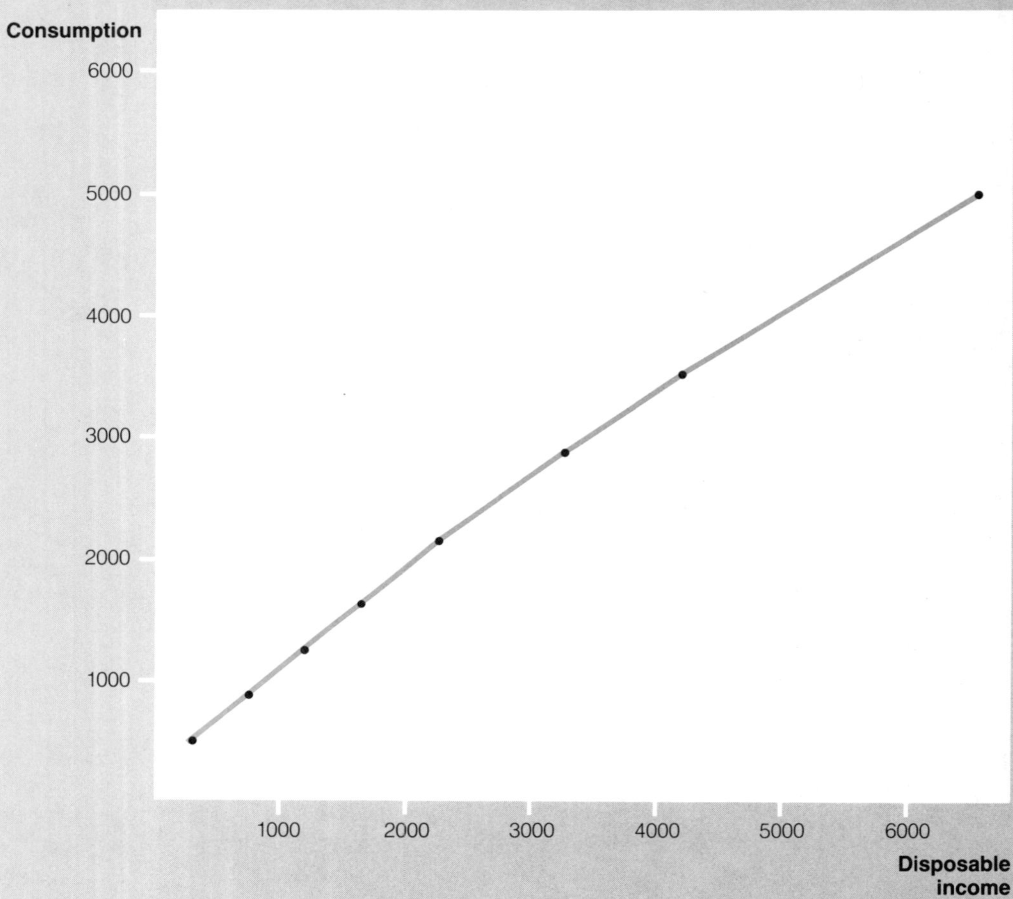

FIGURE 12.2 **HOUSEHOLD CONSUMPTION AND INCOME, 1935–36. High-income households tend to spend more than low-income households. This relationship is roughly linear, except for a slight moderation of spending at the highest income levels.**

GNP, as compared to about 15% of GNP in the prewar years. Since these economists did not foresee so much investment and government spending during peacetime, they glumly (and incorrectly) predicted a post World War II depression.

The culprit is the positive intercept in the consumption function. If $c = a + by$, then the average propensity to consume (APC), $c/y = a/y + b$, falls as y increases (when a is positive). (If the MPC also declines as income grows, this exacerbates the drop in c/y.) Now, if c/y declines as y increases, then y cannot, in fact, increase unless investment and government spending rise as a percentage of national income. If was for just these reasons that Keynes feared a long-run economic stagnation of capitalist nations.

However, to almost everyone's surprise, consumption spurted upward in the late 1940s while disposable income fell somewhat. At first this was thought to be a temporary aberration due to the forced accumulation of liquid assets during the war and a pent-up demand for consumer durables. But then, consumption continued to climb at a sufficiently rapid pace throughout the 1950s and 1960s to hold the APC steady at between .89 and .93. Later estimates of the simple Keynesian consumption function using data for the period 1929–80 give an intercept that is very close to zero and an MPC of around 0.90. Cross-sectional family budget data (data on items from different categories but from the same period) continue to resemble those for 1935–36, with a relatively flat slope (.6 to .8) and an MPC that falls somewhat with income; however, the intercepts have increased over time, shifting the cross-sectional curves upward (Figure 12.3).

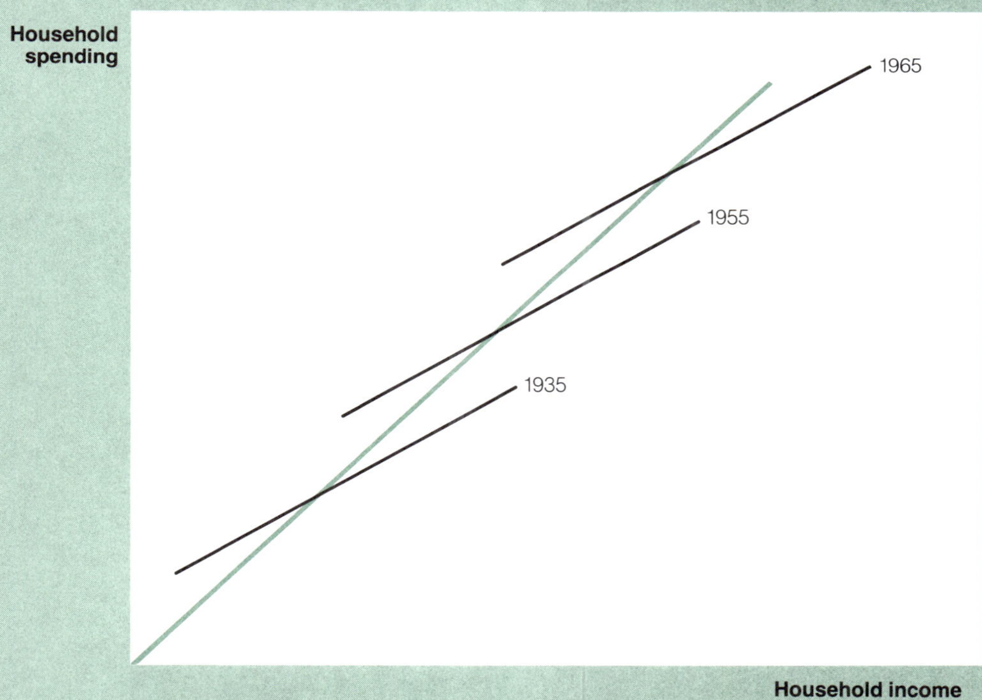

FIGURE 12.3 CROSS-SECTIONAL BUDGET STUDIES yield relatively flat consumption functions, which shift upward as aggregate income increases. The average income and spending in each cross-section lie on a line going through the origin, so that both the MPC and APC are constant.

In addition, economists now realize, in retrospect, that extrapolative backcasts of the original Keynesian consumption functions would also have failed in that they would have forecast dissaving for every year prior to 1908. (If the consumption function has a positive intercept, then consumption must cross the 45° ($c = y$) line at low levels of income.) Clearly, the nineteenth-century industrialization of America was characterized by saving and investment rather than dissaving. Using overlapping decades (to smooth out business cycles and measurement errors), Simon Kuznets found that the division of output between consumption and investment has, in fact, been strikingly stable since the Civil War.[4] For the period 1869–1938, he concluded that the MPC and APC are equal and between .87 and .89. *There is no intercept in the long-run aggregate consumption function.*

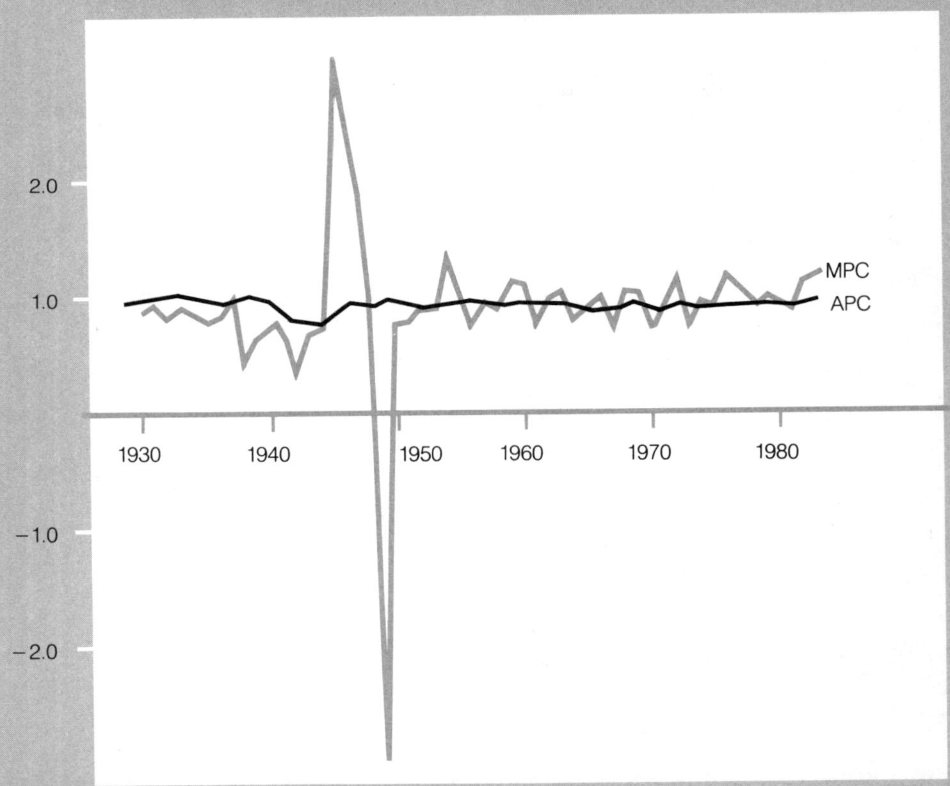

FIGURE 12.4 AGGREGATE AVERAGE PROPENSITY TO CONSUME (APC) AND MARGINAL PROPENSITY TO CONSUME (MPC), 1930–80. **The APC has been very steady, while the MPC varies considerably from year to year. The largest MPC variations were at the end of World War II, when pent-up consumer demand burst loose, despite modest income increases or, in 1949, when there was an income decline.**

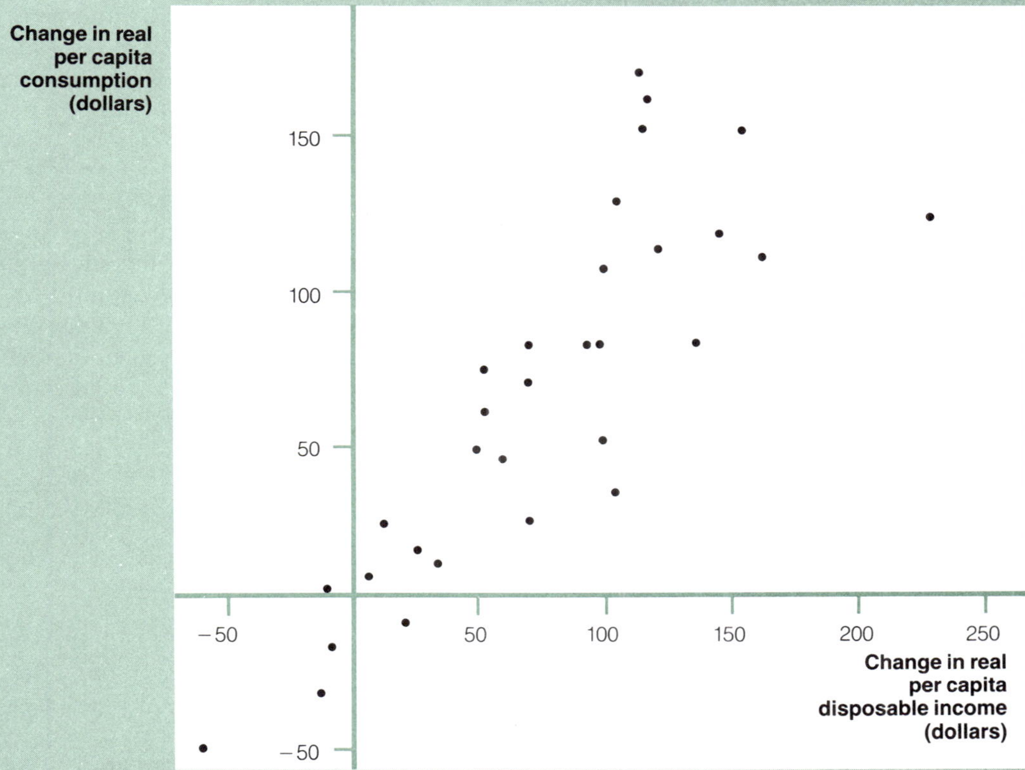

FIGURE 12.5 CHANGES IN AGGREGATE CONSUMPTION AND INCOME, 1950–81. **Annual changes in spending are positively related to changes in income, but the relationship is very rough. Apparently, spending depends on more than just current income.**

The consumption and income data displayed in Figure 12.4 show that the average propensity to consume did rise during the Great Depression and fall during World War II. Since World War II, the APC has been very stable. In contrast, the relationship between the change in consumption and the change in disposable income has been more volatile. A scatter diagram of annual data for the period 1950–81 is given in Figure 12.5. With quarterly data, the volatility is even more pronounced.

Economists have consequently spent a great deal of time and effort trying to modify the simple Keynesian consumption function so as to explain these accepted characteristics of the data:

1. The long-run aggregate APC and MPC have been stable and equal.
2. With time series data, the short-run MPC is volatile.
3. With cross-sectional data, the MPC is less than the APC but the relation shifts upward over time so as to maintain a constant APC and MPC.

THE PERMANENT-INCOME HYPOTHESIS

Analysts of family budget data have long noticed two important characteristics of the data. The first is a regression-towards-the-mean phenomenon: the tendency of those with relatively high income one year to find their relative position deteriorating the next year, while those with low incomes find their relative position improving. This is because a person with relatively high income probably had an unusually good year, while a person with low income is more likely to have had an atypically bad year.

The second characteristic is that family expenditures seem to be related to a smoothed measure of income. Households do not myopically base each moment's consumption on that moment's income. Few splurge on paydays and starve between. Almost everyone tries to plan to the next pay check, and most plan even farther ahead. Households accumulate assets if they anticipate a major expense (for example, education, new car, vacation) or a decline in income (layoff, retirement, change of job). If income is expected to rise, they may borrow in order to spend some of that income now.

Economists early on noted this smoothing of income fluctuations in family budget data. Kuznets observed:

> The composition, absolute and relative, of a family's budget and its other activities are affected by receipts not only in the given year but also in the preceding years and perhaps also by those expected in the immediate future.[5]

Similarly, Margaret Reid wrote:

> It is generally accepted that three months are likely to be unrepresentative of the annual incomes of farm families. So also may be the income of an entire year. The greater the expectation that income will fluctuate—this year up, next year down—the less meaningful is it in an analysis of family expenditures. For example, in the Great Plains where bumper crops, outright failures, and moderately good years can be expected, annual income varies widely. If expenditure curves were available from classifications by what families regard as the permanent component of their income it might be possible to isolate both short and long run effects of income change.[6]

Milton Friedman was persuaded by Reid to formalize this argument that "permanent" income is the crucial variable underlying consumption behavior.[7] Friedman's initial theoretical argument interpreted *permanent income* as that level of consumption that could be maintained indefinitely. If r is the real interest rate and v is the present value of future income, then y_p (permanent income) $= rv$, is the amount that can be consumed each period without reducing wealth, v*. This is an averaging definition of permanent income: it is that constant perpetual level of income that has the same present value as has actual future income.

Friedman argued that household planned or *permanent consumption* will be proportional to permanent income:

$$c_p = ky_p \tag{12.2}$$

*In 1957 Friedman interpreted r as the rate of interest;[7] in 1963 he interpreted it as "a 'subjective' rate (approximately equal to .333) that need bear little or no relation to any market rate of interest."[8] Under the latter interpretation $y_p = rv$ cannot be consumed indefinitely, except in those special cases (such as a consol) where y_p is independent of r.

where k may depend upon interest rates, preferences, and demographic factors. (With durable goods, consumption should be thought of as the enjoyment of the services provided over the life of the asset. The consumption of a car is the annual usage, rather than the initial expenditure.)

The difference between observed and permanent income (or consumption) is defined as transitory income y_t (or consumption)

$$y = y_p + y_t \tag{12.3}$$

$$c = c_p + c_t \tag{12.4}$$

Friedman assumes that permanent and transitory consumption are uncorrelated,* and that transitory income is uncorrelated with both permanent income and transitory consumption. These assumptions imply that transitory income has no effect on consumption. In contrast, a dollar of permanent income increases consumption by k (which Friedman later estimated to be about .9). Thus the effect of an income increase on consumption depends critically on the extent to which this increase is perceived as permanent or as transitory income.

As noted, Friedman's initial theoretical definition is that permanent income is a present value average of anticipated lifetime income, leaving anticipated income variations (such as seasonal fluctuations for farmers) as transitory income. However, when he defines transitory income and consumption, Friedman stresses uncertainty rather than anticipated variations. He describes y_p as "analogous to the expected value of a probability distribution. The transitory component is to be interpreted as reflecting all 'other' factors, factors that are likely to be treated by the unit affected as 'accidental' or 'chance' occurrences." It is reasonable to assume that the realization of anticipated income fluctuations does not affect consumption, but it is not so reasonable to assume that surprise windfalls do not affect consumption at all.

Friedman's definitional ambiguity is intentional as he argues that "it seems neither necessary nor desirable to decide in advance the precise meaning to be attached to 'permanent' . . . The precise line to be drawn between permanent and transitory components is best left to be determined by the data themselves. . ." In order to "bring out more explicitly the wide range of possible interpretations of permanent income," Friedman lists four possibilities for a consumer unit with a head now of age 30 who was 20 when the household was formed: (1) the mean of the probability distribution for measured income in the coming year; (2) the average mean income over the lifetime as estimated at age 20; (3) the average mean income over the lifetime as estimated at age 30; and (4) the average mean income over the remaining lifetime as estimated at age 30. None of these corresponds to the theoretical interpretation of permanent income as the indefinitely sustainable level of consumption; Friedman's empirical work similarly neglects financial wealth and the need to capitalize income by some interest rate.

This vagueness does provide flexibility in explaining the behavior of diverse individuals. The cost is that it is difficult to implement the model and evaluate

*As examples of transitory consumption, Friedman lists expenditures associated with "unusual sickness, a specially favorable opportunity to purchase, . . . an unusually cold spell, a bountiful harvest." Most economists interpret c_t as simply the inevitable error term in empirical models.

its assumptions. Consider, for example, perfectly anticipated annual variations in income. With possibility 1 above, y_p would vary year to year, while y_t would not. For 2 and 3, y_t would vary year to year, while y_p would not. With possibility 4, both y_p and y_t change annually. How are we to decide if the propensity to consume out of transitory income is zero if we can't decide what transitory income is?

Cross-sectional evidence

Despite the conceptual ambiguities, some purely mathematical implications of the model can be derived. It can be shown that observed income will be positively correlated with both permanent and transitory income,* so that above-average values of observed income will be associated with above-average transitory income. Because some of the variation in observed income is transitory rather than permanent, relatively large variations in income will occur together with modest variations in consumption.

Figure 12.6 compares the true relation between consumption and permanent income with the observed data for two households with the same propensity to consume out of permanent income.† The line $c_p = ky_p$ is the true behavioral relation, while the line $c = a + by$ fits the observed data. A household with high observed income, y^2, is most likely to have had an unusually good year and, therefore, to have permanent income, y_p^2, that is somewhat less than observed income. Their consumption, c_p^2, plus or minus random transitory consumption, will be based on permanent income rather than observed income. They consume less than they would if y^2 were their permanent income because their permanent income is less than y^2. Thus the observed consumption and income point is below the $c_p = ky_p$ line. Similarly, low-income households tend to consume more than they would if their observed income were permanent, because their permanent income is actually greater than observed income. Thus the observed data lie on a line, $c = a + by$, that has a positive intercept and a slope less than k. This is a case very similar to the abovementioned regression-towards-the-mean phenomenon first noticed in a study by Sir Francis Galton, who found that unusually tall parents tend to have children shorter than themselves, while unusually short parents tend to have taller children. (This does not imply that the population heights are shrinking towards the mean; instead it represents the fact that the very tall parents are more likely to have been the tall children of more average parents than the short children of extremely tall parents. Thus, their observed height is greater than the average for the generations, or greater than their "permanent" height.)

Similarly, those people who are observed to have relatively high income are more likely to have had a good year than a bad year. They will base their consumption on their more modest permanent income and this will flatten out the consumption function (as in Figure 12.6). This logic directly explains why the slopes in household budget studies are invariably less steep than the group's APC.

*If y_p and y_t are uncorrelated, Equation 12.3 implies that the covariance of y with y_p is equal to the variance of y_p, and that the covariance of y with y_t is equal to the variance of y_t.

†Average transitory income here is zero. (A non-zero value would shift the line $c = a + by$ but not change its slope.)

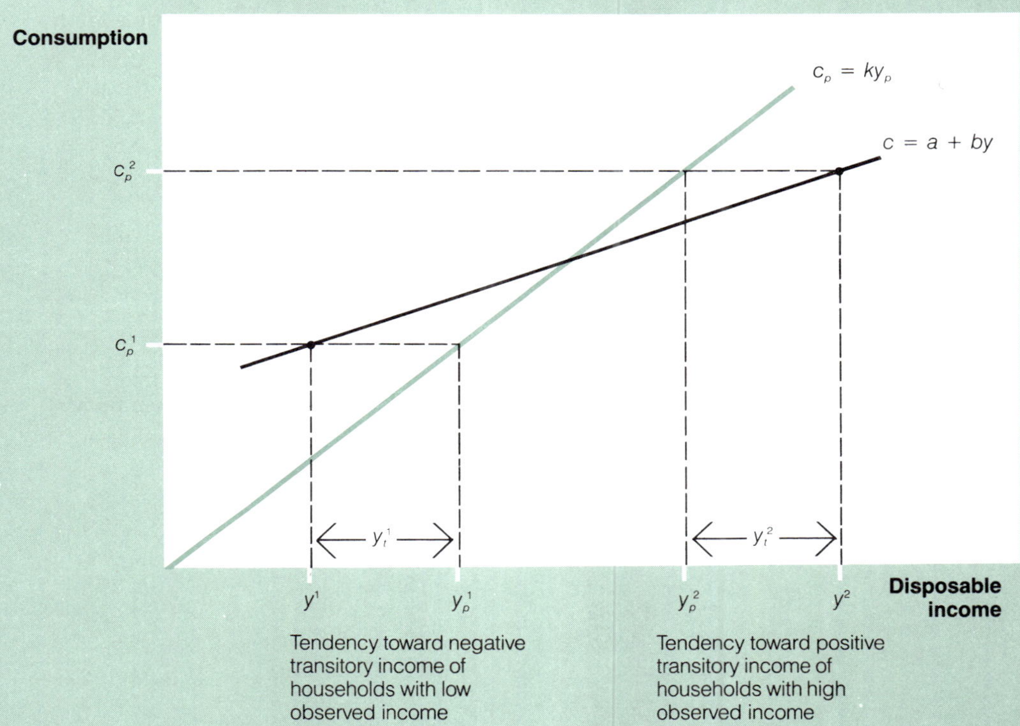

FIGURE 12.6 CONSUMPTION, INCOME, AND PERMANENT INCOME. **A household with relatively high income, such as y^2, is most likely to have a somewhat lower permanent income, such as y_p^2. Since spending is based on permanent rather than current income, a line fitted to the observed data will have a positive intercept and a slope less than k.**

An illustrative cross-sectional test was conducted by Modigliani and Ando using the value of a family's home as a proxy for permanent income.[9] They argue, reasonably enough, that the purchase of a home is a major commitment that will reflect anticipated income over several years. (Few people will choose to move from house to house as their income fluctuates from year to year.) Tables 12.1 and 12.2 show some income and consumption data from the 1950s for non-self-employed homeowners, grouped first by income and then by home value. The APC falls as income rises when households are grouped by income, but is roughly constant when households are grouped by home values. Figure 12.7 shows that these data are consistent with the theoretical Figure 12.6.

Aggregate time series data

If households have identical propensities to spend permanent income or if the distribution of permanent income by APC is stable over time, then there will be a stable proportional relationship between aggregate permanent consump-

TABLE 12.1

Income and consumption for non-self-employed homeowners, grouped according to measured income

Income bracket	Average income	Average consumption	APC
$ 0–999	$ 556	$ 2,760	4.79
1,000–1,999	1,622	1,930	1.19
2,000–2,999	2,664	2,740	1.03
3,000–3,999	3,587	3,515	0.98
4,000–4,999	4,535	4,350	0.96
5,000–5,999	5,538	5,320	0.96
6,000–7,499	6,585	6,250	0.95
7,500–9,999	8,582	7,460	0.87
10,000–above	14,033	11,500	0.82

TABLE 12.2

Income and consumption for non-self-employed homeowners, grouped according to value of home

Value of home	Average income	Average consumption	APC
$ 1–4,999	$ 3,606	$ 3,530	0.98
5,000–7,499	4,274	4,190	0.98
7,500–9,999	4,649	4,600	0.99
10,000–12,499	5,191	5,140	0.99
12,500–14,999	5,729	5,610	0.98
15,000–17,499	5,948	5,949	1.00
17,500–19,999	7,547	7,170	0.95
20,000–24,999	9,607	9,500	0.99
25,000–above	11,267	11,100	0.99

tion and aggregate permanent income. (Aggregate consumption and income are the summation of the corresponding micro variables.) This observation could explain the long-run stability of the aggregate APC if we view the long-run data as an approximation of permanent consumption and permanent income.*

With respect to the short-run MPC and APC, the time series behavior is similar to that of the cross-section model, and we can consequently draw the analogous conclusion. Consider the data in Figure 12.6, this time as aggregate values at different points in time. Fluctuations in aggregate transitory income will cause fluctuations in observed income but not in consumption. The observed aggregate MPC will consequently understate the influence of permanent income on consumption. In boom years, high transitory income pushes up observed income, but not consumption. In recessions, negative transitory income reduces observed income, but not consumption. Thus the observed consumption-income ratio drops in booms and rises in recessions.

Friedman constructed a permanent-income series from aggregate annual data. He assumed that perceived permanent income needs to be adjusted according to the disparity between it and observed income:

$$y_p - y_p[-1] = \theta(y - y_p[-1]) \quad 0 < \theta < 1 \tag{12.5}$$

* Actually, there have been changes in both the distribution of permanent income and in demographic factors that influence household spending propensities. Thus one needs to assume that such changes have offset each other. Friedman argues, for example, that the decline in the fraction of the population on farms (whose k is lower because of a greater income uncertainty) has offset the decline in family size (since k is positively related to family size).

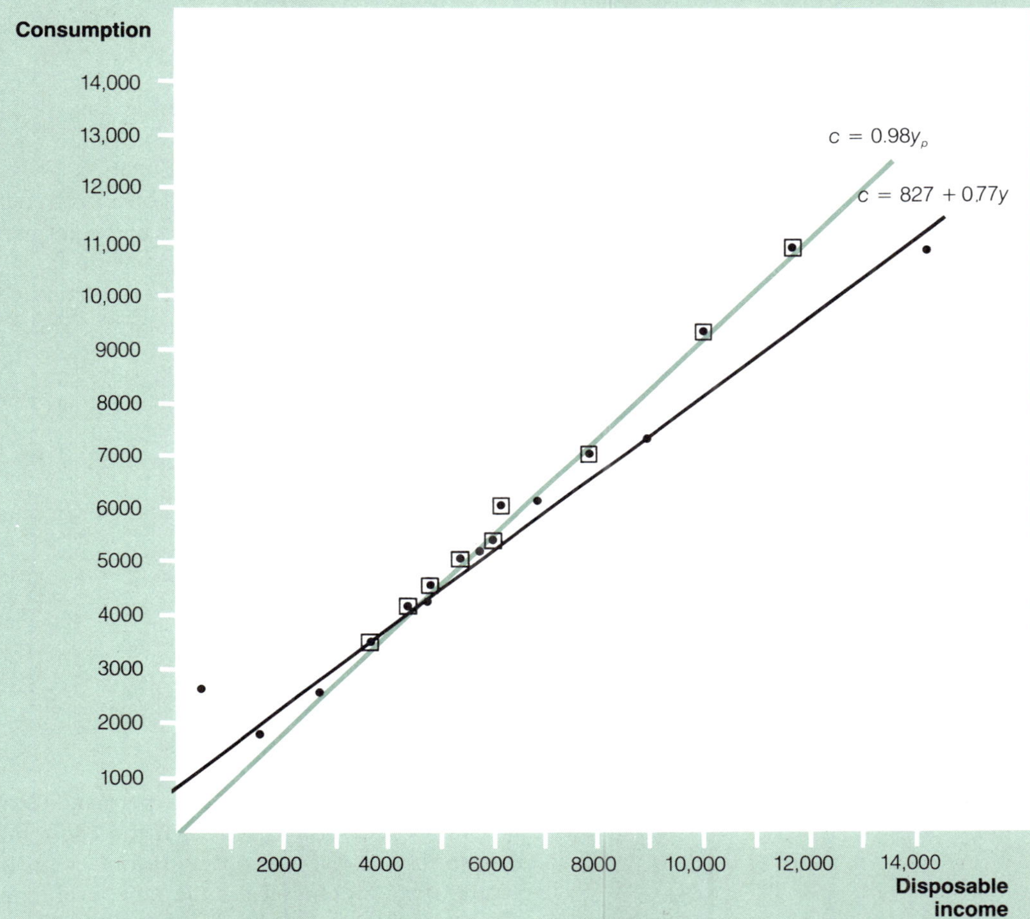

FIGURE 12.7 CONSUMPTION, INCOME, AND THE MODIGLIANI-ANDO ESTIMATE OF PERMANENT INCOME. **When households are grouped by the values of their homes (a proxy for permanent income), the fitted relationship between consumption and income goes through the origin with a 0.98 slope. When households are, instead, grouped by observed income, the fitted line has a positive intercept and a diminished slope. Dot indicates observed income; dot enclosed in square, estimated permanent income.**

where $y_p[-1]$ is the permanent income estimate made in one year and y_p is the new, revised estimate made in the next. Equation 12.5 implies that the current estimate of permanent income is a weighted average of last year's estimate and current income:

$$y_p = \theta y + (1 - \theta)\, y_p[-1] \tag{12.6}$$

Analogous relations apply to $y_p\,[-1]$, $y_p\,[-2]$, and so on. If we repeatedly substitute these equations into Equation 12.6, we obtain

$$y_p = \theta y + \theta(1-\theta)\, y\,[-1] + \theta(1-\theta)^2\, y\,[-2] + \ldots, \tag{12.7}$$

so that estimated permanent income is a weighted average of present and past income.*

The primary virtue of this weighting scheme (Equation 12.7), is that it is extraordinarily simple and yet not wildly implausible. Permanent income is a function of income over many years, but there is only one parameter, θ, that needs to be estimated. The weights progressively decline (by a fraction $1-\theta$) the farther back one looks. This means that recent experience is relatively more important in determining perceived permanent income. The weights also add up to one:

$$\theta + \theta(1-\theta) + \theta(1-\theta)^2 + \ldots = \theta \frac{1}{1-(1-\theta)} = 1, |\theta| < 1,$$

so that, if income is constant for many years, permanent income will equal actual income.

Using annual data for the period 1905–51 (with the war years 1917–18 and 1942–45 excluded) and chopping off the series at $y\,[-16]$, Friedman estimated k to be .88 and θ to be .33: $c_p = .88 y_p$, where

$$y_p = .330y + .221y\,[-1] + .148y\,[-2] + .099y\,[-3]$$
$$+ .067y\,[-4] + .045y\,[-5] + \ldots + .001y\,[-16]. \tag{12.8}$$

A one-dollar increase in current income raises permanent income by \$.33, and so raises consumption by .88 (\$.33) = \$.29. If income remains at its new higher level, consumption will rise again the second year by another .88 (\$.221) = \$.19; if income stays indefinitely at the new level, consumption will continue to rise each year until the new level of income is finally perceived as permanent, and consumption has risen by \$.88. If, on the other hand, income returns the second year to its original level, then consumption will fall to where it is only \$.19 higher than originally. If income now stays at its original level, the initial increase will eventually be interpreted as wholly transitory, and consumption will slowly return to its original level. Figure 12.8 compares the consumption responses to permanent and temporary income changes.

One problem with the permanent income scheme (Equation 12.5) is that y_p can be rewritten as

$$y_p = (1-\theta)\, y_p\,[-1] + \theta(y_p + y_t) = y_p\,[-1] + \frac{\theta}{1-\theta} y_t \tag{12.9}$$

*Equation 12.7 implies that $c = ky_p$ can be alternatively written as $c = k\theta y + (1-\theta)\, c\,[-1]$, which can be interpreted as a habit-persistence model. The specification of spending as a weighted average of current and past income is apparently attributable to Lange.[10]

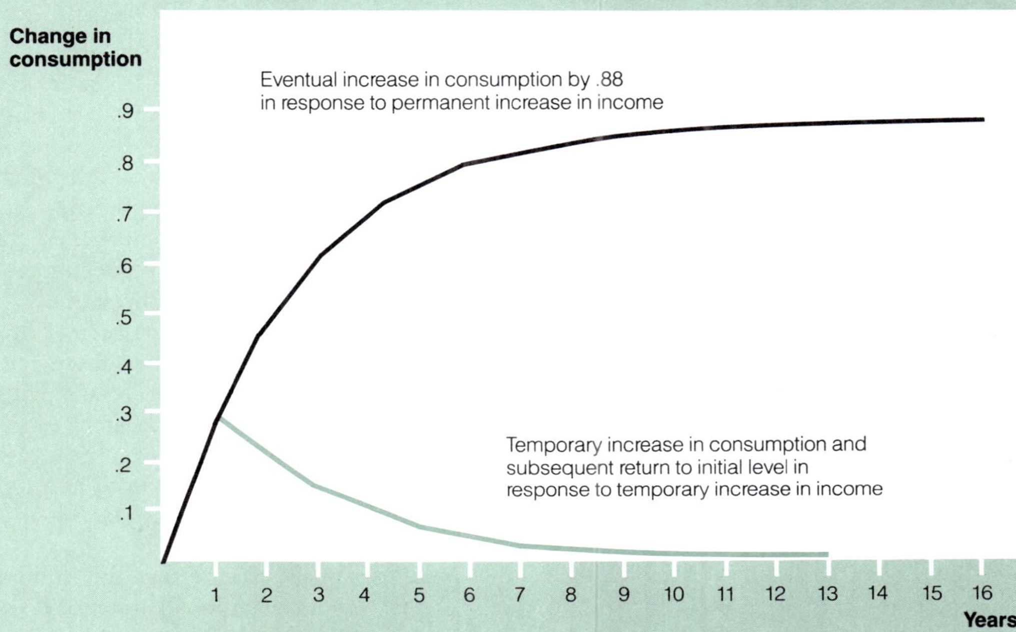

FIGURE 12.8 CONSUMPTION RESPONSES TO PERMANENT AND TEMPORARY INCREASES IN INCOME. **A $1 increase in income raises consumption at first by $0.29. Whether consumption then continues to increase or returns to its initial level depends on whether the $1 increase in income turns out to be permanent or temporary.**

so that the model actually assumes that y_p and y_t are correlated. Using Friedman's data, Holmes found y_p and y_t to be positively correlated, and estimated the propensity to spend out of transitory income to be about 0.3, not zero.[11]

Permanent versus transitory income

Economists have long been confused about the dividing line between Friedman's notion of transitory and permanent income.[12] For example, should a windfall (such as a lottery winning) be considered entirely transitory income or partly permanent income? Most economists interpreted Friedman's original discussion[13] to mean that windfalls are transitory income that have no effect on consumption.[14] Yet Friedman's weighted-average model (Equation 12.8) indicates that any increase in income raises permanent income by 0.33.

In 1963, Friedman responded to the confusion by reviving the concept of permanent income as being proportional to total wealth, $y_p = rv$, arguing, however, that the proportionality factor, r, should not be identified as a market interest rate.* He argued that r (which should also be used to capitalize future income) is roughly .33, so that a windfall increase in wealth raises permanent income by .33 and raises consumption by $kr = .88\ (.33) = .29$.

The exact effect on transitory income depends on the timing of the perceived increase in permanent income and the realized increase in measured income: ". . . all windfalls raise permanent income. Some raise transitory income, some lower it; when they lower transitory income, they may do so for a number of successive accounting periods. It is possible that windfalls introduce a positive correlation between transitory and permanent components of income; it is possible also that they introduce a negative correlation. I see no way to establish a general presumption one way or the other . . . In consequence, I see no reason for revising . . . the tentative assumption of zero correlation".[15]

The practical effect of this elusive distinction between permanent and transitory income is to make it impossible to estimate separate marginal propensities to consume. Since the distinction between permanent and transitory income depends on a subjective and unobserved capitalization rate we cannot hope to distinguish between the consumption out of transitory income and that out of the revision of permanent income. Thus we can never conclusively test what was once thought to be an important assumption—that the MPC out of transitory income is zero.

Friedman himself would presumably argue that the important issue is, in fact, the response by consumers, not our rationalization of how consumers decide upon that response. Specifically, it would be useful to know if the MPC out of windfalls is .29; it really doesn't matter how much of that spending is attributed to revisions of the permanent and of the transitory components of income. Unfortunately, econometric work and policy discussions have often been plagued by metaphysical debates over consumer perceptions of permanent and transitory income.

Summary

Friedman argued that the consumer's horizon is typically longer than is assumed in the simple Keynesian consumption function: Households have memories and plans. Friedman formalized this argument by separating income into permanent and transitory components, with only the permanent component influencing consumption. The general moral is that a perceived long-run change in income will significantly alter resources and hence consumption; a temporary change in income will not. The model is simple and flexible and can usually be interpreted so as to give a quite plausible explanation of events. Its predictive (as contrasted to its explanatory) power is, however, clouded by Friedman's intentional vagueness and flexibility on the distinction between permanent and transitory income. The success of the model seems to depend less upon its inherent virtues than on one's skill in suitably interpreting permanent and transitory income.

In practice, the permanent-income model also suffers from a neglect of the effects of interest rates and financial wealth on consumption. And in neither theory nor practice does the model keep track of the feedback from saving to

* This means that permanent income can no longer be interpreted as the indefinitely sustainable level of consumption.

wealth. Instead, saving is treated as a residual that passively absorbs transitory income and some constant fraction of permanent income. Robert Clower and M. Bruce Johnson are particularly critical: "Friedman's model provides no definite link between income and wealth—an absurdity of the first order of magnitude in a theory that purports to say something about saving behavior .... we regard the permanent income theory as a statistically ingenious but economically irrelevant and misleading description of household behavior."[16] They instead propose a model (at least as consistent with the data as Friedman's model) in which household consumption is related only to current financial wealth. Clower and Johnson do not consider "expected prices and rates of return, expected income, age, occupation, family composition, previous purchases of durable goods, etc. On the contrary, we suppose that the household has a short memory and limited foresight. . ."[17]

There is really no need to ignore these things completely, and no need to stubbornly include wealth but neglect income or to include income but neglect wealth. The remainder of this chapter will show an attractive approach that takes into account all of these factors and in which saving is explicitly directed toward the accumulation of wealth.

LIFE CYCLE MODELS

There may be some numismatists and misers who accumulate financial wealth for the simple pleasures of counting and admiring it. But for most of us, wealth is a means to an end, rather than the end itself. When we save, we are giving up some current consumption in order to enjoy more future consumption. You may be saving to purchase a car, to buy a house, to take a trip, to pay for your children's education, to support your retirement, or to provide your heirs with the pleasures that you denied yourself. In each case, you are saving for future consumption.

Every dollar you save could be spent for current consumption: food, clothing, hi-fi sets. By saving you are giving up some consumption now in exchange for consumption later. *Saving is trading present consumption for future consumption.*

Choosing between alternatives is the foundation of microeconomics: individuals choosing between apples and oranges, firms choosing between the use of labor and of capital, nations choosing between guns and butter. There is a standard, well-developed microeconomic apparatus for handling these decisions, and this apparatus can be applied to the saving decision. The starting point is the distinction between preferences and opportunities.

Preferences

Which do you prefer, consumption now or consumption in the future? Some old-fashioned people admit a slight desire for delayed gratification. Some new-fashioned people profess a slight preference for instant gratification. But almost all prefer a rough balance. Few would choose to swing from famine to feast, or from feast to famine. Instead of consuming some amount one year and four times that amount another year, most people prefer a more balanced lifestyle. If they had to, they would give up much of their feast to avoid famine. This is the general economic assumption about consumption preferences. People will try to smooth out their consumption. When income is unusually low, they will dip into savings or borrow in order to maintain their standard of living. When income is unusually high, they will pay off debts or squirrel away some funds for a rainy day.

Interest rate tradeoffs

Real interest rates measure the terms of a trade between present and future consumption. The annual real interest rate, r_t, on a t-year investment is defined by

$$(1 + r_t)^t = \frac{\text{commodities received in } t \text{ years}}{\text{commodities given up now}}$$

Thus **the gross real interest rate, $1 + r_t$, measures the relative price of future and present consumption.** As usual, there are both substitution and income effects at work. When the real interest rate increases, future consumption is less expensive. The substitution effect arises from the fact that one gets more future consumption in return for forgone present consumption; the income effect from the fact that since savings earn more, one can consume more in every period—and one may decide to do just that, by reducing current saving while still increasing future consumption.* On balance, **an increase in real interest rates will increase future consumption, but it has an ambiguous effect on current consumption and hence on current saving.**

Even though frustratingly ambiguous, this is the central conclusion. Theory alone cannot tell us whether an increase in real interest rates raises or lowers saving. Classical economists generally believed that the substitution effect dominated, so that an increase in real interest rates meant increased saving. In the early Keynesian macroeconomic models, however, financial markets were often neglected and interest rates did not even appear in the consumption-saving equations. In recent years, financial-market turbulence has seemed important, and financial variables have again been included in consumption functions.

For example, household financial wealth is an explanatory variable in the consumption equation of the MPS model, one of the most elaborate and widely respected models.† In this model a decline in real interest rates increases the

* This argument applies to savers, which most of us are. For borrowers, the income effect on current consumption reinforces the substitution effect: An increase in real interest rates increases the interest cost to borrowers, reducing both present and future consumption. The substitution effect still argues for more future consumption and less present consumption. Thus an increase in real interest rates unambiguously reduces the current consumption of borrowers.

† This began life as the Federal Reserve Board—Massachusetts Institute of Technology (FRB-MIT) model, under the direction of Franco Modigliani and Albert Ando. When Ando went to the University of Pennsylvania it became the FRB-MIT-PENN or FMP model. The Social Science Research Council then provided financial support, and the name changed to MIT-PENN-SSRC, or MPS model. The Fed continues to use its own version of the model.

real market value of corporate stock* and stimulates consumption. Every dollar of additional market value raises consumption (and reduces saving) by about 5 cents. This is one of the most important linkages between monetary policy and spending in the MPS model. An open-market purchase of Treasury bills, for example, reduces interest rates (including stock yields), thereby raising stock prices and increasing consumption. **This modern macroeconometric model agrees with the classical presumption that saving is positively related to real interest rates.**

Lifetime wealth constraints

Interest rates are one facet of consumption opportunities. The second facet is budget constraints: We cannot consume all we would like. Our spending is limited by our wealth, our income, and our ability to borrow.

Some people have very short horizons; they plan only a few weeks or months ahead. Others, like the Rockefeller family or Harvard University, plan over an unlimited horizon. In life cycle models it is assumed that the relevant budget constraint for most people is that they die standing pat: that lifetime consumption cannot exceed lifetime income. We cannot, of course, simply add up lifetime consumption and lifetime income, since a dollar of income today is more valuable than a dollar ten years from now. **The requirement that net worth not be negative at death means that the present value of lifetime consumption must not exceed the present value of lifetime income.** The lifetime budget constraint that final wealth not be negative implies† that

$$c[0] + \frac{c[1]}{1+r} + \frac{c[2]}{(1+r)^2} + \ldots + \frac{c[n-1]}{(1+r)^{n-1}} \leq z[0] + y[0]$$

$$+ \frac{y[1]}{1+r} + \frac{y[2]}{(1+r)^2} + \ldots + \frac{y[m-1]}{(1+r)^{m-1}}. \tag{12.10}$$

The left side of Equation 12.10 is the present value of planned consumption over the remainder of a person's life. The right-hand side is current financial wealth plus the present value of anticipated income over the rest of one's life. The right side of the equation comprises one's lifetime wealth constraint. A person must choose annual consumption levels so that their present value does not exceed lifetime wealth. This constraint (Equation 12.10) shows that current consumption is influenced by financial wealth, current income, anticipated future income, and real interest rates. We have already seen that interest rate changes have uncertain effects on consumption; the consequences of income changes are more clear-cut.

* These models do not quite resolve the theoretical debate because they do not distinguish between changes in market value due to interest rates and changes in market value due to dividend expectations. If the historical changes in market value have been primarily due to revised dividend expectations, then we might be mistaken in concluding that the observed positive association between consumption and wealth also holds for changes in market value caused by interest rate changes.

† This equivalence can be formally demonstrated by first multiplying Equation 12.10 by $(1+r)^t$ and then rearranging to show the future value of lifetime saving.

An economic event that increases current or future income will increase lifetime wealth and thereby increase consumption. The general presumption about preferences is that one will smooth out lifetime consumption, choosing not to consume a lot one year and a little the next, or vice versa. This smoothing implies that any increase in lifetime wealth will not all be spent in a single year. There are two corollaries, the first being that *an increase in current income may have little effect on current consumption.* Say, for example, that a person receives a \$100,000 windfall and decides to enlarge consumption equally in every year he has left to live. If the real interest rate is 5% and the person expects to live another 40 years, he can than spend an additional \$5507 each year*—or \$6109 if he expects to live 30 years, and \$5193 if he expects to live 50. (A windfall increases current consumption the most for people who have the fewest years to live.)

The second corollary is that *an increase in future income will have some effect on current consumption.* If a person expects to receive \$110,000 next year, that amount has a present value of \$100,000 at $R = 0.10$, and increases her lifetime wealth by just as much as a \$100,000 windfall this year. If she expects to live 40 more years and to increase consumption each year equally, she will increase current consumption by \$5507, even though current income has not changed. Similarly, anticipated changes in income 5, 10, or 20 years hence will influence current consumption. If she revises downward anticipated Social Security benefits, she will spend less now and save more. Similarly, if tighter energy supplies, or some other bleak predictions, make her more pessimistic about future income then she will cut back on current consumption.

Notice, also, that some event that increases income both now and also in every future year will have a very large impact on current consumption. If I win some super lottery and will receive \$100,000 every year for life, then I can increase my annual consumption by \$100,000.†

The accumulation of wealth

If a person expects real income to be the same in every year of his life, he then has little reason to save, and can spend all his income every year, save nothing, and just break even at the end. Interest rates and a preference for present versus future consumption might tilt this a little, but not much. He might also save a little to bequeath to his children, and save some more to protect himself against future uncertainties. But these factors are not nearly adequate to explain why, as a nation, we have a financial net worth of \$10,000 per capita.

In life cycle consumption models, the primary explanation for wealth accumulation is retirement. I may live for another 40 years, but I will probably work for only 30. If I want to spend these 10 retired years at my accustomed standard of living, then I had better prepare a nest egg. At $r = 0.05$, for every

* One qualification is that he could spend the entire windfall the first year on a house or other durable good, and still consume a relatively constant amount each year. One does not consume a car when one buys it. Instead, one consumes car services as long as the car lasts, which is often more than a year.

† If I want to anticipate inflation and to hold real consumption constant, I would then have to spend somewhat less than \$100,000 in my early years and somewhat more later. (See Exercise 3.)

$1000 a year for 10 years that I want to spend, I will need to have saved $8722 by the time I retire. If I want to spend $25,000 a year, I will need to build a $218,050 nest egg. Social Security benefits will help, but supplementary assets are probably going to be needed. **This provision for retirement may explain why many people accumulate wealth.**

This observation has several demographic implications. An increase in life expectancy will increase saving and wealth accumulation, since a greater nest egg is required to provide for more years of consumption. Similarly, an increase in retirement age will reduce saving and wealth, since there will be fewer retired years to provide for. Also, a person's wealth will tend to increase with age up until retirement, when it declines as it is used, as planned, for consumption. If age is not taken into account, then both income and wealth are misleading measures of economic welfare.*

Liquidity constraints

The pure life cycle model assumes that individuals can freely borrow and lend at the interest rate, r, subject only to the lifetime budget constraint that net worth be positive at death. It is unimportant if income is high in some years and low in others; it does not matter how much an individual borrows in any particular year. All that counts is that the individual at least break even when the books are finally closed.

In practice it is difficult for households to borrow amounts that will make their current net worth negative. There is too much danger that they will declare bankruptcy and default. It is very hard to use intangible human capital—future labor income—as collateral. Usually, individuals can borrow only a fraction of the value of such tangible assets as securities, real estate, jewelry, or consumer durables. To borrow money you must first prove that you don't need it.

Most young adults expect their real incomes to rise throughout their working years. This means that a smooth, level consumption path would require them to be in debt for the first several years. The lumpiness of housing and consumer-durable purchases accentuates this desire for indebtedness. They will want to borrow heavily when young and pay off these debts with the higher incomes they will have when middle-aged. If they are unable to do this or are able to borrow only small amounts at exorbitant interest rates, then they cannot achieve their preferred consumption path. **The illiquidity of their human capital forces them to consume less than they would like to consume in their early years. They are said to be *liquidity-constrained:* They do not have enough liquid assets to reach their preferred consumption level.**

For such households, lifetime wealth is not the binding constraint on their standard of living. They are liquidity-constrained rather than wealth-constrained. In this situation, an increase in future income has little effect on present consumption. It increases the amount that they would like to spend,

* Consider three individuals, 30, 50, and 70 years of age, all with the same constant level of real consumption throughout their lives. Although all three live equally well, we might find that the 30-year-old has high income and low wealth, the 50-year-old has high income and high wealth, and the 70-year-old has low income and high wealth.

but does not affect the amount that they *can* spend. To spend more now, they need more cash. Similarly, changes in retirement age, life expectancy, and Social Security benefits are irrelevant. On the other hand, an increase in current income has a large effect on current consumption because it provides the cash they need.

Liquidity constraints provide another channel by which financial market policies affect consumer spending. "Easy money" policies not only reduce interest rates, but also make it easier for the liquidity-constrained to borrow money. With consumer loans and mortgages, part of the thrust of easy money is that interest rates decline, and part is that more loans are extended to "credit risks." Similarly, part of the impact of tight-money "credit crunches" is that the liquidity-constrained, with only their human capital as collateral, find it more difficult to borrow and are forced to curtail consumption.

Thus there are fundamental differences in the behavior of households constrained by lifetime wealth and the behavior of those constrained by liquidity. **Wealth-constrained households will spend a small fraction of an increase in current income; Liquidity-constrained households will spend all of it.** The spending of wealth-constrained households will be influenced by future income, life expectancy, and other distant factors. These factors will be unimportant to the liquidity-constrained. A decrease in real interest rates will probably increase current consumption of the wealth-constrained because future consumption will be more expensive. A decrease in interest rates will probably increase current consumption by the liquidity-constrained because it will be easier for them to borrow.

Liquidity constraints are theoretically important but difficult to verify empirically. The liquidity-constrained do not walk around with "LC" stamped on their foreheads. Kowalewski and Smith[18] have, however, tried to use some simple rules of thumb to classify some 2000 households in "Dorothy Projector's 1964 Survey of Changes in Family Finances" conducted for the Fed. We classified a household as liquidity-constrained if all of the following criteria were met:

1. The ratio of liquid assets to annual spending was less than ¼.
2. The ratio of net wealth to annual spending was less than 2.
3. The ratio of saving to spending was less than ½.
4. There were no net purchases of bonds and stock.

We found that 65% of the households were liquidity-constrained. These households received 58% of total income but, as Table 12.3 shows, had relatively few assets and lots of debts.

TABLE 12.3.

Percentage Distribution of Total Assets and Liabilities between Liquidity-Constrained and Wealth-Constrained Households

Item	Liquidity-constrained	Wealth-constrained
Checking accounts	27	73
Savings accounts	9	91
Treasury bills	0	100
Bonds	6	94
Stocks	1	99
Home mortgages	67	33
Installment debt	80	20
Net wealth	14	86

The overall aggregate MPC is a weighted average of the MPCs of liquidity-constrained and wealth-constrained households, $MPC = MPC_L(Y_L/Y) + MPC_W (Y_W/Y)$, where the weights Y_L/Y and Y_W/Y are the shares of total income received by liquidity-constrained and wealth-constrained households. If we use our estimate, $Y_L/Y = 0.58$, and assume that the liquidity-constrained have a 1.0 MPC while the wealth-constrained have a 0.2 MPC, then the aggregate MPC is 1.0 (0.58) + 0.2 (0.42) = 0.664.

The Modigliani-Brumberg model

Many of the demographic insights provided by life cycle analysis can be presented in the very simple *Modigliani-Brumberg model.*[19] Consider an individual who begins with only human wealth and who will make no bequests. This person will live for N years and will earn a constant labor income, y, per year for the first $M(<N)$ of these years. It is also assumed that the real interest rate is zero and that the individual desires to consume a constant amount, c, every year. In this case, the budget constraint is $Nc = My$, and a fraction, M/N, of labor income will be consumed during the working years. Wealth will steadily grow until, when beginning retirement, the individual will have accumulated a wealth of $z = M(y - \frac{M}{N}y) = (N - M)\frac{M}{N}y$, which will permit the maintenance of the accustomed standard of living throughout retirement. Money and breath end simultaneously. Figure 12.9 shows the life cycle.

To analyze households after their formation, let m and n be the number of years left until retirement and death, respectively, and let z_0 be current accumulated financial wealth. The relevant budget constraint is $c = (z_0 + my)/n$. If there is a transitory, once-and-for-all increase, A, in wealth or current period income, then consumption will increase by A/n, which is highest for old people. In contrast, a permanent rise in income to $y + A$ will raise lifetime wealth by mA/n, which is highest for young workers. We also see that, for people more than one year away from retirement, the propensity to spend will be much higher for sustained increases in income than for temporary increases. To get some idea of orders of magnitude, consider a life cycle consisting of 40 working years and 10 years of retirement. The APC is 0.8. For a "typical" individual with $m = 15$, $n = 25$, and $z_0 = 5y$, the MPC is 0.04 for a one-year increase in income and 0.60 for a permanent increase.

For a simple aggregate analysis, we can assume a homogeneous population of identical people. The higher the rate of growth of population, the more the age distribution shifts toward younger workers. This shift in the age distribution increases the aggregate saving-income ratio and lowers the aggregate wealth-income ratio. Some illustrative calculations of various aggregate data for $M = 40$, $N = 50$ are:

	Rate of growth of population					
	0.00	0.01	0.02	0.03	0.04	0.05
Aggregate saving / Aggregate income	0.00	0.05	0.08	0.11	0.13	0.15
Aggregate wealth / Aggregate income	5.00	4.50	4.05	3.65	3.29	2.98

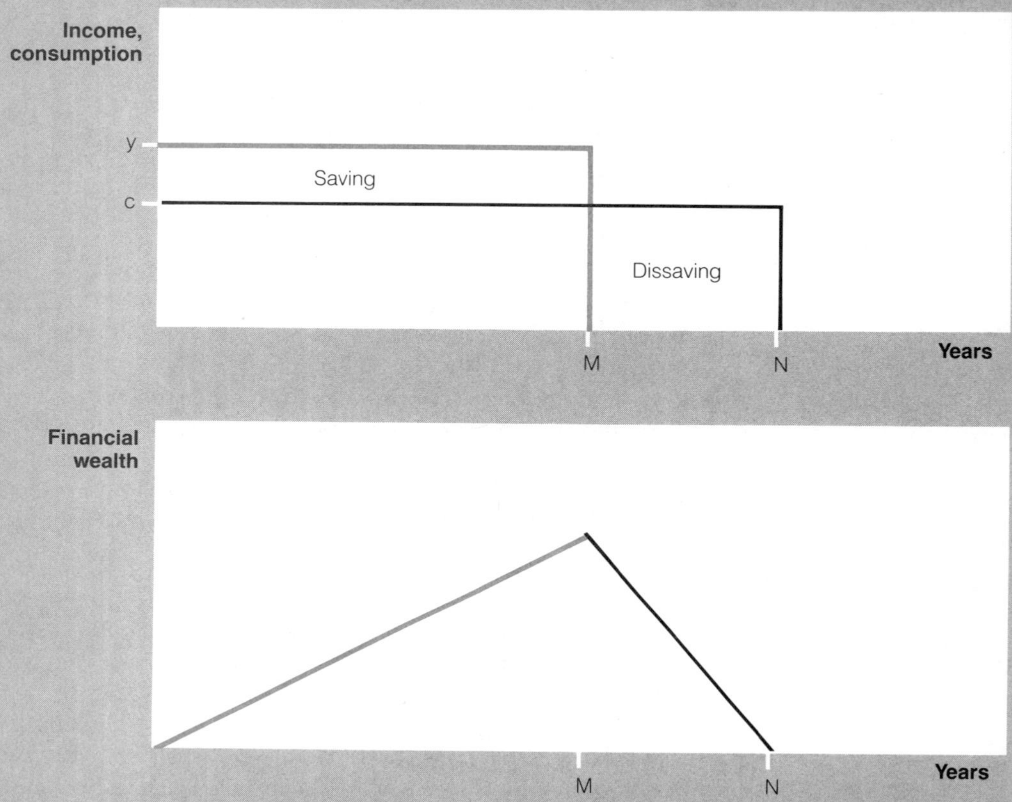

FIGURE 12.9 **MODIGLIANI-BRUMBERG LIFE CYCLE. A person who will work for *M* years and then retire for *N-M* years must save during the working years in order to maintain the accustomed standard of living when retired. Thus wealth accumulates during the working years and is spent during retirement.**

The reasonable ratios that emerge from these calculations indicate that the simplest life cycle model offers the potential of explaining a great deal of actual savings behavior and wealth accumulation.

The stationary state with zero population growth is particularly easy to analyze. When there are p individuals in each age bracket, aggregate income is equal to Mpy, as is aggregate consumption ($N\ pyM/N = Mpy$). The aggregate wealth-income ratio is $(N-M)/2$. Since aggregate consumption and income are identical, there is no aggregate saving. All individuals have the same standard of living. Workers give some of their output to the retired in exchange for financial assets, which they anticipate using to purchase goods when *they* retire. **The nation's financial wealth can consequently be viewed as an imper-**

sonal revolving retirement fund. Each generation purchases its claims in the fund by providing for earlier generations; in return, they expect to be provided for by future generations. Notice that, with our hypothetical values of $M = 40$ and $N = 50$, families must contribute 20% of their output to give the 20% of the population that is not working the same standard of living as that of working households. With a growing population, the burden need not be as great, since there will be more people in each working-age bracket than in each retired-age bracket.

When retirement income is publicly provided, there may be intergenerational strains from such demographic changes as the transition to a stationary population, earlier retirement ages, or longer life expectancies. It is these very demographic changes that are responsible for the current Social Security crisis. The U.S. Social Security worker-to-beneficiary ratio has fallen from 146 in 1940, to 22 in 1947, to 5.8 in 1957, to 3.1 in 1967, to 2.9 in 1972, and is expected to fall below 2 by the year 2025.

A proportionately reduced working population may resist giving up the output necessary to provide nonworkers with a "decent" standard of living. They might express this resistance as political opposition to increased Social Security taxes or through high personal spending levels, which crowd out retirees by reducing the purchasing power of their financial assets. Sluggish productivity growth would presumably create further strains in that members of the working population would not only have to give up a larger share of their income, but would also possibly have to reduce their absolute consumption levels.

Summary

Life cycle models are concerned with the spreading of consumable resources over a lifetime. A substantial merit of such models is that they provide an explanation of the long-run interrelations of consumption, saving, income, and wealth. Aggregate wealth is a weighted sum of the average wealth holdings of different ages, where the weights are the numbers of households of those ages. With a constant age and income distribution of the population, aggregate wealth will grow at the same rate as aggregate income. The wealth-income ratio depends, among other things, on the interest rate, the rate of growth of population, and the rate of growth of per capita income. The model's essential properties would hold even if a bequest motive for saving were introduced, as long as the lifetime accumulation for transfer to the next generation is proportional to lifetime income.

In the short run, income influences consumption in life cycle models by enlarging lifetime wealth or by relaxing liquidity constraints. For wealth-constrained households, a change in income that was fully anticipated (and therefore already incorporated into lifetime consumption plans) will have no effect on current consumption; an unanticipated temporary change will have only a small effect;* and an unanticipated permanent change may have a sub-

* For stabilization purposes, one should distinguish between expenditures and actual consumption. Spending all of a windfall bonus or tax cut on a new car or dishwasher is fully compatible with the life cycle principle of spreading out consumption.

stantial effect. For liquidity-constrained households, on the other hand, any increase in spendable resources is likely to be fully spent. The mirror image of this is that wealth-constrained households will, while liquidity-constrained households will not, alter current consumption in response to changes in illiquid resources—increases in expected future labor income, improvements in prospective retirement benefits, and capital gains on houses and other imperfectly liquid assets.

Life cycle models can also suggest (and simulations can quantify) the way in which consumption is influenced by demographic factors such as life expectancy, family size, and retirement benefits. Life cycle analysis also points out the heavy dependence of current consumption on individual expectations about future income, prices, interest rates, and demographic variables. While these expectational factors can explain short-run variations in consumption, they are unfortunately difficult to take into account empirically since they are largely unobserved.

The life cycle model provides two alternative explanations for the relatively flat cross-sectional relation between consumption and income. One is similar to that of Friedman's: Those with high incomes in any given year are more likely to be experiencing pleasant than unpleasant income surprises; their spreading out of consumption will depress the high-income group's APC. The second explanation is demographic. High-income earners tend to be middle-aged, with a natural life cycle inclination to save for retirement. The young and the elderly have lower incomes and are inclined to save little or to dissave because their income is low relative to life-time wealth.

The primary criticism of life cycle models is that they assume an unrealistic amount of foresight and planning. Households, in practice, use many rules of thumb and sometimes make seemingly irrational decisions. The theory is still useful, however, in pointing out the general logical consequences of certain reasonable objectives.

IMPLICATIONS FOR MACRO MODELS

In the macro model analyzed in Part I, we assumed that household consumption is related positively to real income, negatively to real interest rates, and negatively to the price level. The permanent-income and life cycle models suggest several ways of enriching this consumption function: The effect on consumption of an increase in income will depend on whether this increase a) was anticipated; b) is considered temporary or permanent; c) accrues predominantly to the young or the old; and d) accrues predominantly to the liquidity- or wealth-constrained. Thus, the actual realization of some economic event, such as a tax cut or recession, that had been widely anticipated for some time, should have little effect on the consumption behavior of wealth-constrained households. The 1981 Economic Recovery Act, for example, contained a phased reduction in tax rates over a three-year period. In theory, wealth-constrained households should have increased their consumption in anticipation of lower future taxes as soon as it appeared likely that Congress would approve

SOCIAL SECURITY AND SAVING

The Social Security system is the largest non-defense outlay of the U.S. federal government. For most people, entitlement to future payments from Social Security is their most valuable asset. Also, for most workers, Social Security taxes are larger than personal income taxes. In total, Social Security payroll taxes will amount to about $271 billion in 1985, nearly as large as the total of $328 billion in personal income tax.

Social Security, a massive system important both to individuals and to the economy, is not one program, but five. Included under it are old-age retirement pensions, medical insurance for the elderly, disability insurance, benefits for widows and widowers, and benefits for children with deceased parents. In other words, it is a fairly comprehensive package of insurance programs. The largest part of the system is the retirement pensions, and it is those we address here.

In many ways, Social Security looks like a private pension or saving plan. Workers make "contributions" (or, more accurately, pay taxes) during their working lives and receive a lifetime government pension commencing at retirement. Certainly it makes sense for individuals to treat as an asset that part of their future retirement income to which they have already contributed.

But, Social Security is not just a government-sponsored saving plan. In fact, unlike saving through a regular pension program (or through insurance, bank accounts, or stocks and bonds) Social Security contributions are not used to purchase investments. At present the government takes the contributions of workers and almost immediately and entirely sends the proceeds to the currently retired pension recipients. No "nest egg" is built up. This "pay-as-you-go" method of financing means that there are almost no assets in the system; there is now less than $100 billion on hand to meet future pension obligations. At the current rate of payouts, without continuing contributions these funds would last less than six months. The several trillion! dollars worth of outstanding entitlements for pensions can be met only by future payroll tax collections.

The system must continue simply to honor the obligations already amassed. A normal pension scheme would have assets, such as stocks or bonds (and, indirectly, therefore, have claims on productive assets such as trucks and factories), to match future payout liabilities. The only significant asset of the Social Security system is the power of the government to tax and, therefore, to be able to extract the required resources from future (and in some cases, unborn) generations of workers.

This pay-as-you-go scheme, where workers' taxes are immediately handed over to the current elderly, is a bit like a chain letter. Each generation of workers sends money to the elderly (or, in the chain letter case, to those listed on the letter) in the hope or expectation that later participants will send *them* money. The first generation of elderly, alive at the time the system is started, does extremely well. They receive retirement money even though they contributed little (or zero) taxes. After the first generation, how well you do depends on the relationship between what you contributed and what workers are contributing when you are elderly. Of course, these "contributions" are mandated by the government. If contributions are a fixed fraction of wages, then how well you will do depends on the growth in total labor income relative to the number of retired persons. One reason today's young adults may not do as well as their parents is the slow growth in labor productivity—and, hence, labor income—in the past 15 years, and the anticipated rapid growth in the number of retired people as life expectancies increase and members of the baby boom retire. Today there are 3.2 workers for each retiree; in the early part of the next century this ratio may drop to 1.9. This will definitely decrease the implied rate of return to a pay-as-you-go Social Security program. A second reason today's elderly do better with Social Security than today's young adults are likely to, is that most of today's elderly were part of the above mentioned first generation, which contributed little or nothing to the program.

Because Social Security changes the timing with which you receive income (taking income from you when young and giving you more when you are old), it is likely to change the amount of your life-cycle saving. The government is forcing you to accumulate an "asset," and, therefore, you may save less via other means: Consumption would be increased, and saving decreased. The program is so big that this may affect the total amount of real capital available to the economy. The aggregate consumption function of macro models such as those in this book may be significantly affected by Social Security. The "false wealth" of Social Security may crowd out the real accumulation of wealth for retirement. On the other hand, it is possible that people will not reduce their saving because they recognize that Social Security wealth is "false" in the sense that it is based not on assets, but on future taxes for their children and grandchildren. They may, therefore, transfer or bequest more assets to their younger family members in order to offset this tax burden.

The question of whether Social Security depresses the economy's capital stock ultimately must be examined with data. This is a difficult task. When Martin Feldstein (Chairman of the Council of Economic Advisors under Ronald Reagan from 1982 to 84) looked at the data in 1974, he found that each dollar of "false" Social Security wealth displaced a dollar of real capital. Because of Social Security, personal saving was reduced by half, and the country's capital stock was 38 per cent lower. This reduction in the real capital stock (factories, lathes, etc.) made the country poorer and reduced real wage rates. The chain letter had very serious consequences.

Although scrutiny of Feldstein's analysis showed his early work to contain a serious mistake, his latest calculations still indicate that each dollar of Social Security wealth crowds out a dollar of private savings. Several economists argue that his conclusion is not fully supported by the evidence, but the general consensus today is that Social Security has reduced saving, although perhaps less than dollar for dollar.

Social Security may reduce saving for another reason. It offers an inflation-protected lifetime stream of benefits for retirees. Such assets are largely unavailable from private insurance companies. Economic theorists have, therefore, speculated that Social Security may reduce what could be termed precautionary savings, not only because it produces false wealth, but also because it alleviates inflation risk and life-span risk for the elderly.

All in all, Social Security is a huge government program that affects each person and the entire economy of the United States in major ways. It gives many elderly the financial independence they did not have previously, but it also may reduce savings and our national wealth.

—John B. Shoven

this tax cut. The actual realization of reduced taxes in 1982 and 1983 would then provide no reason for further consumption revisions. Liquidity-constrained households would behave somewhat differently: Since they cannot spend tax cuts until they actually receive them, we would expect to find liquidity-constrained households to be steadily increasing consumption in 1981, 1982, and 1983, paralleling the phased tax reduction for the period. Such households would prefer to spend some of their 1983 tax cut in 1981 but have no practical way of doing so.

The temporary–permanent distinction is important because temporary increases in income have relatively little effect on lifetime resources and, hence, on the current consumption of wealth-constrained households. Part of the force of the 1981 Economic Recovery Act was intended to derive from the fact that it was a long-term reduction in tax rates. People could count on lower taxes for years to come and, so, should significantly change their economic behavior. This permanence, however, was somewhat undermined by continuing debates within the Reagan Administration and Congress about whether the Act had gone too far and should be revised. These sorts of elusive expectations are in theory important, but, in practice, difficult to incorporate empirically. This is why economic forecasting is an art that requires more than the ability to program computers.

The 1968 Revenue and Expenditure Control Act included an explicitly temporary 10% personal income tax surcharge that was retroactive to April 1, 1968, and would expire on June 30, 1969. In theory, this surcharge should have had little effect on the spending of wealth-constrained households since it represented such a small reduction in lifetime income. Equivalently, the wealth-constrained would spread this temporary surcharge out over their lifetimes by reducing their annual consumption only slightly. The liquidity-constrained, of course, would have been forced to curtail consumption by almost the full amount of the tax surcharge. Overall, consumption seems, in fact, to have been little affected by the 1968 tax surcharge, though, as is usually the case, there is a variety of explanations and interpretations of the data.[20] As with the 1981 tax act, we can speculate about consumers' expectations regarding the permanence of the tax change. The "temporary" 1968 surcharge was, in fact, extended for another six months to December 31, 1969, and then extended again, at a reduced 5% rate, for another six months to June 30, 1970.

In theory, consumption also depends on demographics. For example, Figure 12.4 showed an increase in the APC in the late 1970s and a corresponding decline in household saving relative to disposable income. One possible explanation is that the babies of the post World War II baby boom grew up in the 1970s, and young households typically save little, since they want to acquire houses and durable goods and expect higher real incomes in the future. As the baby boom generation ages, saving rates should go back up. An implication is that the effects of a government transfer payment will depend on whether it is directed towards the young, middle-aged, or retired.

The importance for consumption behavior of the distinction between liquidity-constrained and wealth-constrained households has been stated over and over but is difficult to implement empirically. We can at least use it to shade our subjective predictions. For example, a tax cut during a credit crunch will be relatively potent. A transfer payment to college students will always be relatively powerful.

We have also seen that the effect of interest rates on consumption is theoretically ambiguous. Modern macroeconometric models generally show a negative effect running through asset prices, particularly stock prices. Theory implies that all sorts of assets should be embraced in consumption functions, including bonds, stocks, land, houses, and retirement benefits. A collapse of stock prices or retirement benefits should reduce consumption. As in our model, higher commodity prices will diminish consumption to the extent that they reduce the real purchasing power of assets. These factors also suggest two more answers to the question of why consumption was so high and saving was so low in the late 1970s: very low real interest rates and/or high values of assets, particularly housing. Households may have saved so little because real rates of return were so unattractive and/or they may have consumed so much because their houses and other assets were so valuable.

A final issue is the effects of income redistribution on aggregate consumption and saving. In developing countries (including the United States in the nineteenth century), it is frequently argued, a very unequal income distribution aids economic growth. The implicit assumptions are that saving creates investment and that the rich save a greater fraction of their income than do the poor. Therefore, the more income received by the rich, the more saving and investment occur. Other economists, especially after Keynes, have argued that too much saving and too little spending risks recession and economic stagnation. Businesses won't invest and expand if they can't sell their output. It has consequently been argued that the economy will be stimulated by an income redistribution from the rich to the poor, since the poor spend such a large fraction of their income. In the 1970s, there was a revival of the pre-Keynes argument that the economy needs saving to create investment, and that an income redistribution from the poor to the rich will help bring it about. Some supporters of the 1981 Economic Recovery Act argued that an income redistribution to stimulate saving was its major thrust.

Our economic models of consumption and saving provide little support for the view that the MPC varies with income. The permanent-income hypothesis is not explicit on this point, but Friedman and other users have tended to treat the spending parameter, k, as independent of income. They have explicitly argued that observed differences in APCs can be explained by the presence of transitory income rather than underlying behavioral differences. Figure 12.5 shows how observed APCs vary with income even when the true MPCs and APCs do not.

Life cycle models also provide little reason why spending behavior should vary with income, except insofar as income is correlated with age or life expectancy. In the Modigliani-Brumberg model, for example, the MPCs equal $1/n$ or m/n, depending on whether the income increase is temporary or permanent. (Parameter n is the number of years to live and m is the number of years left to work.) A one-time income redistribution from the old to the young should encourage saving. An income redistribution from the poor to the rich will only encourage saving to the extent that the poor are older than the rich.

APPENDIX: THE FISHER DIAGRAM

In standard microeconomic analysis, agents maximize their "utility" by going to the tangency between their indifference surface and opportunity locus. The application of utility maximization principles to life cycle consumption is contained in work by Irving Fisher published early in this century.[21] In recognition of his pioneering work, the indifference curve analysis of intertemporal consumption decisions is called the *Fisher diagram.*

Consider a two-period model with no bequests. (The Fisher diagram is given in Figure 1.) One point on the opportunity locus is with no saving, showing the feasible combinations of present and future consumption, $c_0 = z_0 + y_0$ and $c_1 = y_1$. The slope of the opportunity locus is $-(1+r)$, since every unit of current consumption forgone yields $1 + r$ units of future consumption. The slope of an indifference curve depends upon the agent's relative preference for future or present consumption. The steeper an indifference curve, the more willing the agent is to trade for present consumption. Utility is maximized at the indicated tangency, with consumption $c_0{}^*$ and $c_1{}^*$.

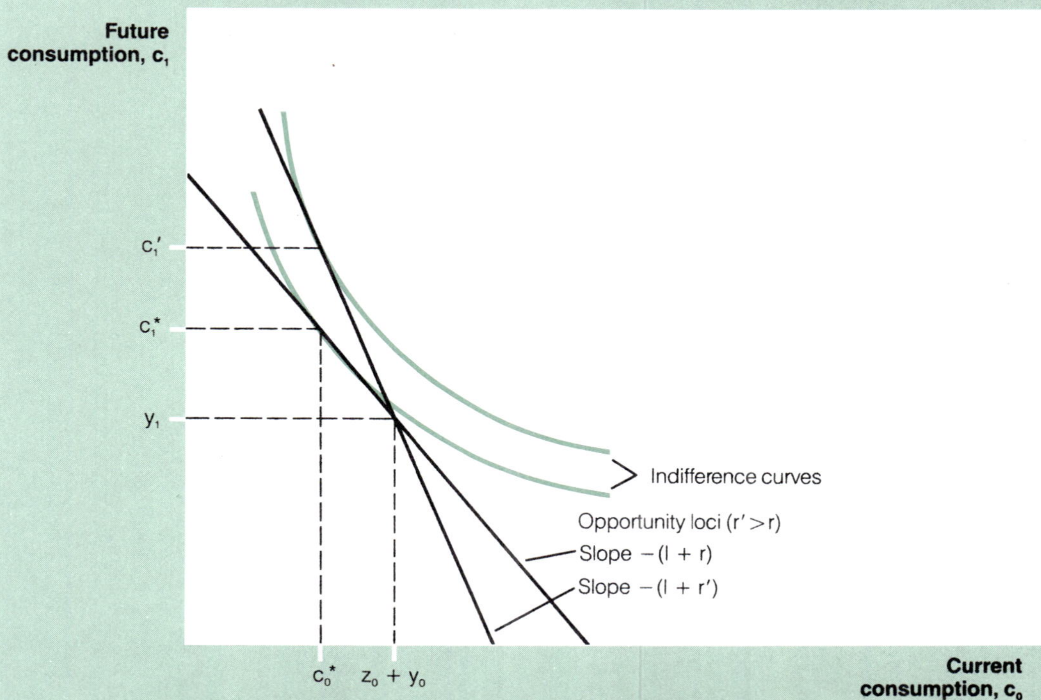

FIGURE 1 **FISHER DIAGRAM WITH TWO INTEREST RATES. An opportunity locus shows the combinations of present and future consumption made available by current assets, z_0, current income, y_0 and future income, y_1. The slope of this opportunity locus is determined by the real interest rate. An increase in this rate steepens the opportunity locus but has an uncertain effect on saving behavior.**

Figure 1 also shows the effect of an increase in the real interest rate from r to r'. The opportunity locus becomes steeper, rotating about the zero saving point. The new tangency is drawn with current-period consumption unchanged to show that saving may increase or decrease, depending on the slopes of the indifference curves.

The Fisher diagram can also be used to depict liquidity constraints. Consider a college student who has meager funds now, but is looking forward to a handsome salary in the future. It would be nice to spend some of that future income now, but banks reject the student's request for a loan for food, clothing, stereo equipment, and a nice apartment. Banks will, however, accept deposits from the student, and will even pay modest interest. Figure 2 shows the kinked opportunity locus for a student with high future income expectations who can save but not borrow. The student is likely to consume at the kink, spending all of the current meager income. It is likely that any increase in current income will be spent. In contrast, an increase in anticipated future income has no effect on current consumption of a liquidity-constrained person, like our student.

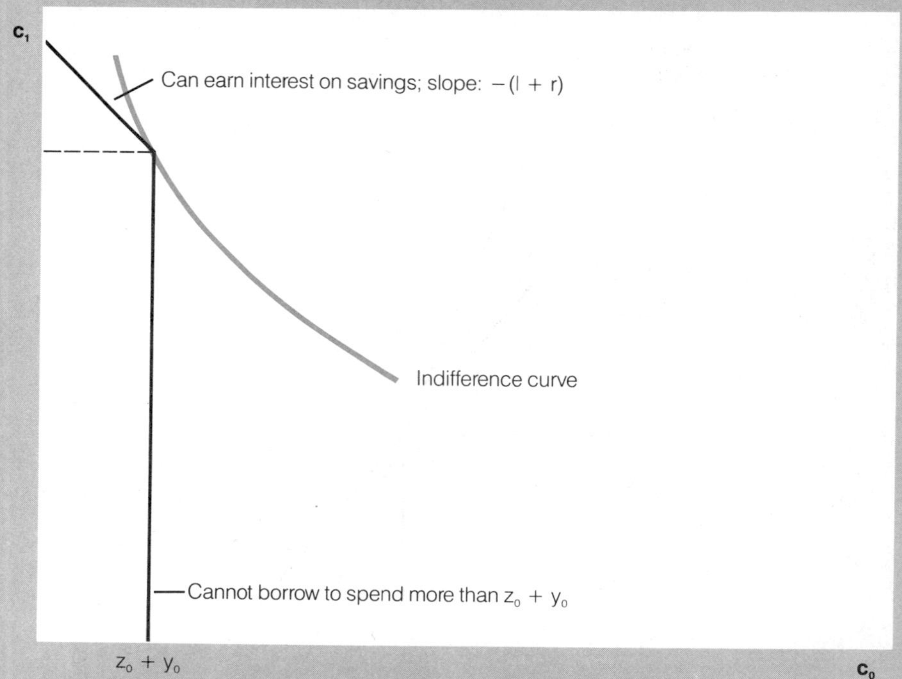

FIGURE 2 **A liquidity-constrained student has a kinked opportunity locus, because loans are not available at the interest rate paid on savings. Because she is unable to borrow against anticipated future income, her spending is constrained by available funds ("liquidity").**

IMPORTANT TERMS AND CONCEPTS

marginal propensity to consume (MPC)
permanent income
permanent consumption
life cycle models
liquidity constraints
Fisher diagram
Modigliani-Brumberg model

The simple Keynesian consumption function relates current consumption to current income. This relationship is a key part of Keynes' explanation of how a decline in income reduces spending, which further reduces income. But the simple Keynesian consumption function is inadequate because it neglects the influence on consumption of interest rates, financial wealth, and anticipated income.

Milton Friedman's permanent-income hypothesis successfully argued that consumption does not simply depend on current income, but rather on some longer-run "average" (or "permanent") income. But Friedman's vagueness in defining permanent income has bogged the model down in still unresolved debates over how to separate income into its permanent and transitory components. In addition, Friedman and other users often neglect interest rates and financial wealth.

Irving Fisher's life cycle model is much more general than the simple Keynesian consumption function and much more specific than Friedman's permanent-income hypothesis. In life cycle models, households plan lifetime consumption subject to a lifetime wealth constraint. The bulk of saving and wealth represent provision for retirement.

Saving is the trade of present consumption for future consumption. The real interest rate is the terms at which this trade can be made. Classical economists and modern macroeconometric models agree that household saving is positively related to real interest rates. Lifetime income also influences consumption in that an increase in present or future income increases current and future consumption.

Liquidity-constrained persons are unable to increase consumption by borrowing against their human capital. The liquidity-constrained will spend almost all of any increase in current income.

Much of a nation's wealth can be viewed as a revolving retirement fund. Each generation purchases its claims in the fund by providing for earlier generations (the young saving, and the old dissaving); in return, each generation expects to be provided for by future generations. There are intergenerational strains when the ratio of workers to retirees changes.

EXERCISES

1. On life cycle grounds, how would the following changes be expected to affect aggregate demand:
   a. The abolition of compulsory retirement rules.
   b. A one-time property tax exemption for elderly home owners financed by higher property taxes for young homeowners.
   c. An increase in the average age at marriage.
   d. A transfer of income from the rich to the poor.
   e. An increase in the real interest rate.
   f. A "pay-as-you-go" increase in social security benefits financed by an increase in social security taxes.

2. It has been observed in cross-sectional data that middle-aged people spend a smaller fraction of their income than do young or elderly people. Can this be explained by the life cycle consumption theory?

3. Assume that I have won a lottery which will pay me \$100,000 a year for life. If the nominal interest rate (R) is .10, the inflation rate (π) is .05, and I am going to live another 40 years, what is the real present value of this bonanza? If I want to consume a constant real amount every year, what fraction of this \$100,000 will I spend each year? Set up and solve this problem if a pocket calculator or present-value table is available.

4. If interest rate ceilings on home mortgages were removed, what effect would this have on home buying?

5. In theory, does an increase in interest rates increase or decrease saving?

6. Some economists argue that the debilitation of the American economy at the end of the 1970s was due to an increase in the APC. What logical basis is there for the assertion than an increased APC weakens an economy? Milton Friedman's permanent-income hypothesis says that the APC should rise *because of* a weak economy. What is the essence of the permanent-income hypothesis and why does it predict an increase in the APC during recessions?

7. In the 1950s, a 65-year-old had a life expectancy of about 14 years. In the 1980s, a 65-year-old had a life expectancy of about 16½ years. According to life cycle models, how would an (unanticipated) increase in life expectancy affect

a. spending by the elderly
b. spending by the young
c. aggregate spending

8. How would an increased life expectancy affect the age distribution of the population and the solvency of the Social Security system?

9. "In 1967 the incidence of poverty among the elderly (29.5 percent) was more than twice that of the entire population (14.2 percent). . . . As a result, social security was expanded to lower the incidence of poverty among the elderly. The poverty gap hasn't quite been eliminated—in 1980 the poverty numbers were 15.7 percent versus 13 percent—but almost. . . . If in-kind benefits, such as medicare, are included, the elderly may have reached parity with the living standards of the rest of the population." (Lester L. Thurow, "Saving Social Security," *Newsweek*, Oct. 26, 1981)

What are some of the pitfalls in using income (as, implicitly, above) to gauge living standards?

10. In a two-period life cycle model, what will be the qualitative effect of an increase in the interest rate on the first period consumption of a borrower (someone with $c0 > z0 + y0$)?

11. Use a two-period Fisher diagram to show the effect on consumption of an increase in second period income ($y2$).

12. Consider the following micro consumption function:

$$c_i = \alpha + \beta y_i + \gamma y_i^2$$

Note that each person has the same consumption function parameters but that the individual MPC will depend upon the level of y_i. Would you expect the MPC to rise or fall with y_i? What restriction does this place on the parameters of this function?

Now consider aggregate per capita consumption:

$$c = \alpha + \beta y + \gamma (\sigma^2 + y^2)$$

where

$c = \frac{\Sigma c_i}{n}$, $y = \frac{\Sigma y_i}{n}$, $\sigma^2 = \frac{\Sigma(y_i - y)^2}{n}$, and $n =$ population.

What would be the effect on c of an income redistribution from the rich to the poor that reduces σ^2 without changing y? Explain why this effect depends upon y.

Income redistribution has been advocated both by those who want to stimulate aggregate demand and by those who want to create the savings that are assumed necessary for economic growth. With this model, which group would argue for a more equal distribution and which for a more unequal distribution? How does this answer depend upon y?

How (qualitatively) does the aggregate MPC ($\delta c/\delta y$) depend upon the effect on σ^2 of changes in y? Explain.

13. In Atlantica, everyone has the same 80-year life cycle: working from ages 20 to 60 for a real income of $30,000 a year, and then spending ages 60–80 in retirement. The real interest rate is zero and there are no inheritances. (They would only weaken the beneficiaries' character.) People consume nothing from ages 0 to 20, and then consume a constant amount from ages 20 to 80.

As shown below, the population has been doubling every 20 years:

	Population (millions) by age group			
Year	0–20	20–40	40–60	60–80
1920	4	2	1	0.5
1940	8	4	2	1

What was the ratio of aggregate consumption to aggregate income in 1920 and 1940?

A special pill is invented that causes couples in Atlantica to have, on average, only two children. The following table shows the transition to zero population growth:

	Population (millions) by age group			
Year	0–20	20–40	40–60	60–80
1960	8	8	4	2
1980	8	8	8	4
2000	8	8	8	8

What are the aggregate consumption-income ratios for 1960, 1980, and 2000? Does zero population growth increase or decrease aggregate demand?

Now consider the case where children consume as much as adults, so that each person consumes a constant amount from ages 0 to 80. Calculate the aggregate consumption-income ratios for 1920 and 2000. Does zero population growth increase or decrease aggregate demand?

REFERENCES

1. J. M. Keynes, *The General Theory of Employment, Interest, and Money,* London: Macmillan, 1936, p. 96.

2. A. Smithies, "Forecasting Postwar Demand I," *Econometrica* (1945), pp. 1–14; and Mosak, "Forecasting Postwar Demand III," *Econometrica* (1945), pp. 25–53.

3. The data in Figure 12.2 are from Dorothy Brady, "Family Saving, 1888 to 1950," in R. W. Goldsmith, D. S. Brady, and H. Menderhausen, eds., *A Study of Saving in the United States,* III, 1956, p. 183.

4. S. Kuznets, editor, *Income and Wealth in the United States,* II, New York: National Bureau of Economic Research, 1952.

5. S. Kuznets, "The Why and How of Distribution of Income by Size," in Conference on Research in Income and Wealth, *Studies in Income and Wealth,* Volume 5, part 1, New York: National Bureau of Economic Research, .943, p. 26.

6. M. Reid, "Effect of Income Concept Upon Expenditure Curves of Farm Families," in *Studies in Income and Wealth,* 15, New York: NBER, 1952, pp. 146–47.

7. M. Friedman, *A Theory of the Consumption Function,* Princeton University Press, 1957.

8. M. Friedman, "Windfalls, the 'Horizon,' and Related Concepts in the Permanent Income Hypothesis," in Carl F. Christ, et al, *Measurement in Economics,* Stanford University Press 1963, pp. 3–28.

9. A. Ando and F. Modigliani, "The 'Permanent Income' and 'Life-Cycle' Hypotheses of Saving Behavior: Comparisons and Tests," in I. Friend and R. Jones, editors, *Consumption and Saving II* (1960), p. 154.

10. O. Lange, "The Theory of the Multiplier," *Econometrica* (1943), pp. 227–45. See also J. Tinbergen, "Does Consumption Lag Behind Income?", *The Review of Economics and Statistics* (February 1942), pp. 1–8; and J. R. Hicks, *A Contribution to the Theory of the Trade Cycle,* Oxford: Clarendon Press, 1950, chapter II and the Appendix, pp. 170–82.

11. James M. Holmes, "A Direct Test of Friedman's Permanent Income Theory," *Journal of the American Statistical Association* (September 1970), pp. 1159–62.

12. See, for example, the comments by Eisner and Houthakker, in the *American Economic Review,* December 1958, pp. 975 and 993.

13. See Friedman, 1957, p. 215.

14. See R. Bodkin, "Windfall Income and Consumption," in I. Friend and R. Jones, editors, *Consumption and Saving,* 1960, pp. 175–87; and R. C. Bird and R. G. Bodkin, "The National Life-Insurance Dividend of 1950 and Consumption: A Further Test of the Strict Permanent-Income Hyporthesis," *Journal of Political Economy* (October 1965), pp. 499–515.

15. Friedman, 1963.

16. R. W. Clower and M. B. Johnson, "Income, Wealth and the Theory of Consumption," in *Value, Capital, and Growth,* J. N. Wolfe, editor, Chicago: Aldine, 1968, p. 84.

17. Clower and Johnson, p. 46.

18. K. Kowalewski and G. Smith, "The Spending Behavior of Wealth- and Liquidity-Constrained Households," Cowles Foundation Discussion Paper No. 536, September 1979.

19. R. Brumberg and F. Modigliani, "Utility Analysis and the Consumption Function: An Interpretation of Cross Section Data," in K. Kurihara, editor, *Post-Keynesian Economics,* New Brunswick: Rutgers University Press, 1954.

20. See Arthur Okun, "The Personal Tax Surcharge and Consumer Demand, 1968–1970," *Brookings Papers,* 1971:1, pp. 167–212; W. L. Springer, "Did the 1968 Surcharge Really Work?," *American Economic Review* (September 1975), pp. 644–59; and the Okun-Springer exchange on pages 166–72 of the March 1977 *American Economic Review.*

21. Irving Fisher, *The Rate of Interest,* New York: Macmillan, 1907 and *Theory of Interest,* New York: Macmillan, 1930.

SUGGESTIONS FOR FURTHER READING

For a very carefully constructed life cycle model, see James Tobin, "Life Cycle Saving and Balanced Growth," in *Ten Economic Studies in the Tradition of Irving Fisher,* W. Fellner, Ed., New York: John Wiley and Sons, Inc., 1967.

CHAPTER THIRTEEN

BUSINESS INVESTMENT

Speculators may do no harm as bubbles on a steady stream of enterprise. But the position is serious when enterprise becomes the bubble on a whirlpool of speculation. When the capital development of a country becomes a by-product of the activities of a casino, the job is likely to be ill done.

JOHN MAYNARD KEYNES[1]

This chapter examines the bases of business investment decisions, evaluating the importance of the stock market in those processes, and the effects of monetary and fiscal policies on business investment.

THE economic output of a nation is critically dependent on its capital stock—its buildings, machines, tools, trucks, roads, telephone wires, and so on. A nation's physical capital allows citizens to be more productive and to enjoy more leisure. If there is inadequate capital, people will work harder and produce less.

Governments bankroll some investment projects such as the construction of highways and airports, but in a largely capitalist nation like the United States most investment decisions are made by private firms. Individual entrepreneurs start businesses, small businesses expand, and giant corporations erect billion-dollar plants. In this chapter we will look at some of the important factors that influence such investment decisions.

ACCELERATOR MODELS

Accelerator models emphasize the dynamic implications of the fact that capital accumulation depends on the state of the economy. In the simplest accelerator model it is assumed that, as output, y, expands and contracts, firms will invest and disinvest so as to keep the capital stock, k, proportional to output:

$$k[t] = \alpha y[t] \tag{13.1}$$

$$i[t] = k[t] - k[t-1] = \alpha(y[t] - y[t-1]) \tag{13.2}$$

Equation 13.1 says that the capital-output ratio is constant. Equation 13.2 states that if the capital-output ratio is constant, then net investment, $i[t]$, which is the change in the capital stock, will be proportional to the change in output. It also implies that the change in investment is proportional to the change in the change in output (that is, the acceleration of output):

$$i[t] - i[t-1] = \alpha((y[t] - y[t-1]) - (y[t-1] - y[t-2])) \tag{13.3}$$

Thus, **according to the accelerator model, level of investment depends on the change in output, and change in investment depends on the acceleration of the growth of output.** There will be no net investment when output is constant. Investment will be constant only if output grows by a constant amount. An increase in investment requires an acceleration of the growth of output. If output increases, but by less than in the previous period, then investment will decline.

In cases where investment demand affects output itself, accelerator models can generate representations of economic cycles. Consider, for example, the implications of putting the accelerator investment function into the income-expenditure model:

$$y[t] = c[t] + i[t] + g[t] \tag{13.4}$$

$$c[t] = a + by[t] \tag{13.5}$$

$$i[t] = \alpha(y[t] - y[t-1]) \tag{13.2}$$

Equation 13.4 is our income-equals-expenditures condition; 13.5 is a consumption function; and the last is the accelerator investment equation (13.2). This is a very simple model with no supply side, no commodity prices, no financial markets, and no interest rates. But it provides an easy vehicle for demonstrating the dynamic implications of accelerator models.

Figure 13.1 shows cyclic behavior according to accelerator theory for two sets of parametric assumptions: $\alpha = 0.2$, $\beta = 0.5$; and $\alpha = 0.3$, $\beta = 0.5$. In both cases, autonomous spending, $a + g[t]$, is initially 500, and the economy is in dynamic equilibrium, with constant output ($y = 1000$). Then, autonomous spending jumps to 550. In both cases, there is initially an investment boom. The increase in output raises the demand for capital, which increases output even more. The investment boom is larger with $\alpha = 0.3$ because capital demand is then more sensitive to output.

In the next period, investment collapses because output does not maintain its rapid growth. (Remember, in accelerator models, constant investment requires a constant growth of output.) The drop in investment demand exacerbates the drop in output. But then, in the following period, output and investment rebound. (Investment would continue at low levels only if output kept falling at a rapid rate; a slowing of a fall in output actually increases investment.) Our accelerator investment cycle is stable with $\alpha = 0.2$ and $\beta = 0.5$, but unstable with $\alpha = 0.3$ and $\beta = 0.5$.

Accelerator models dramatically illustrate a potential source of economic instability. Fluctuations in output encourage similar variations in investment de-

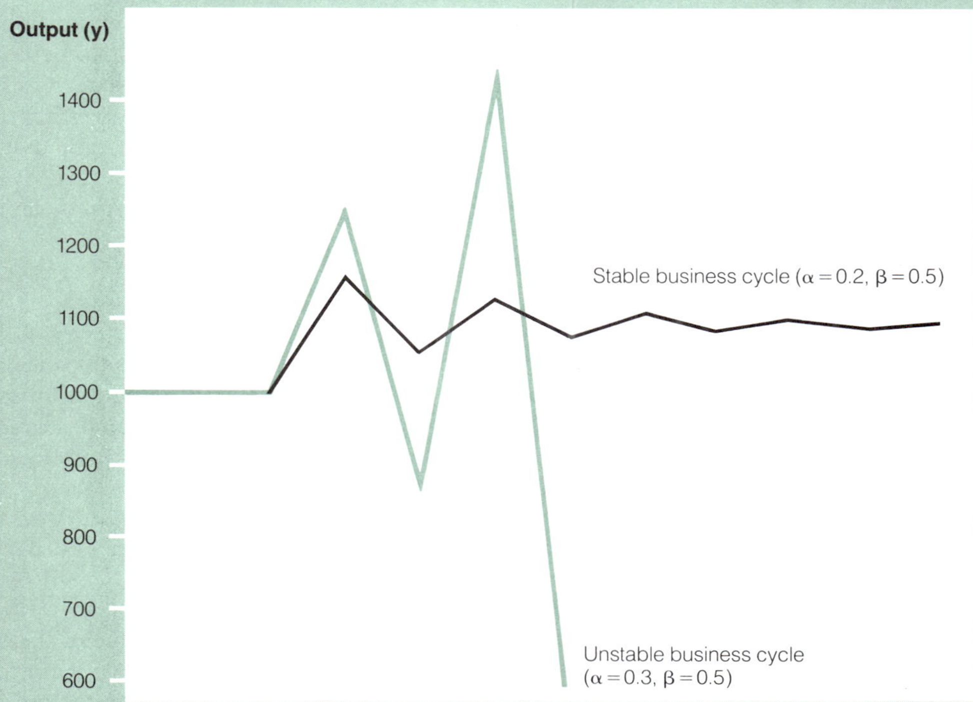

FIGURE 13.1 STABLE AND UNSTABLE ACCELERATOR MODELS. **Accelerator models can generate stable or unstable cycles. Here the model is stable with $\alpha = 0.5$ and $\beta = 0.5$, but unstable with $\alpha = 0.3$ and $\beta = 0.5$.**

mand, which, in turn, amplify the business cycle. Accelerator models are appealing because they provide a plausible story that does correspond with certain aspects of business cycles. Business demand for capital (and household demand for housing and consumer durables) is surely positively related to output. The demand for capital goods typically is more volatile than the demand for consumer goods, and fluctuations in capital goods production usually do precede fluctuations in total output. We have frequently witnessed examples of construction booms and busts: Economic booms in a city or region stimulate construction and, so, further stimulate the local economy. Then, when the economy slows, construction collapses, leaving a surplus of housing and plants.

However, the simple accelerator models we have discussed do not have much of a theoretical underpinning. There is no maximization of profits or anything else in them. The assumption of a fixed capital-output ratio needs some explanation. And the model does not take into account the substitutability of labor and capital inputs and the effects of interest rates on the demand for capital or of supply constraints on the capital stock.

NEOCLASSICAL MODELS

While accelerator models emphasize the dynamic implications of capital accumulation, the *neoclassical investment model* of Dale Jorgenson focuses on the determination of the optimal capital stock.[2] According to this model, firms are assumed to be competitive profit maximizers that can either rent capital from a competitive capital goods industry, or buy and sell capital at production cost. In either case, firms do not have to plan beyond the current production period; in a frictionless world with perfect capital goods markets, capital can always be instantly acquired or returned as needed at a fair price.

Perfect capital markets

Since it is assumed that a firm can always sell its capital at its current cost, there is no need to plan more than one production period at a time. During a production period, the return from buying a unit of capital is equal to the sales revenue from the goods produced by this capital plus any appreciation in the value of the capital itself: \$ gain = sales revenue + capital gains. The sales revenue from this extra capital is equal to its marginal product, $\Delta y/\Delta k$, times the price, P, that this output can be sold for: $P(\Delta y/\Delta k)$. Note that in neoclassical, as in classical, models, the firm does not worry about a lack of buyers for its products. Everything that is produced is sold.

The capital gain is equal to the change in the value of the capital during the production period. This change in value is due to two factors—increases in the cost of producing new capital, and wear and tear on the old capital while it is used in production. Accountants and economists call the wear and tear "depreciation." If a machine lasts ten years and then must be junked, it is natural to assume that the machine loses 10% of its value each year. A car that lasts five years may lose 20% of its value each year. In practice, of course, the wearing out of machines and equipment does not proceed at an even pace. Some things depreciate a great deal the first year. Other things last and last until, all at once, everything breaks down. In addition to that from wear and tear, there is some loss of value through technological obsolescence: New capital may be not only newer, but also better.

For simplicity, let's say that capital loses a fraction, δ, of its value each year. If so, then the net increase in the value of capital is the increase in cost of producing new capital, ΔP_k, less the depreciation δP_k: capital gain $= \Delta P_k - \delta P_k$. Thus the overall gain from buying a piece of capital for a production period is

$$\$\text{ gain} = P\frac{\Delta y}{\Delta k} + \Delta P_k - \delta P_k.$$

To make this calculation a percentage rate of return, we need to divide by the price of the capital. The rate of return on capital is

$$R_k = \frac{\$\text{ gain}}{P_k} = \frac{P}{P_k}\frac{\Delta y}{\Delta k} + \frac{\Delta P_k}{P_k} - \delta. \tag{13.6}$$

That is, the rate of return on capital is equal to its sales revenue, plus capital gains, less depreciation.

Firms compare this rate of return on physical capital with the rate of return, R, on financial assets. High interest rates make it expensive for firms to borrow money to finance expansion. High interest rates also encourage firms with cash on hand to acquire financial rather than physical assets. In theory, firms should acquire capital right up to the point where $R_k = R$. If $R_k > R$, the acquisition of additional capital is attractive. If $R_k < R$, then it's not appealing. If we combine the break-even condition $R_k = R$ with the profit calculation given by Equation 13.6, we obtain the fundamental equation of the neoclassical investment model:

$$\frac{\Delta y}{\Delta k} = \frac{P_k}{P}\left(R + d - \frac{\Delta P_k}{P_k}\right). \tag{13.7}$$

The left side of this equation is the marginal product of capital, something that is determined by a society's skills and technological prowess. The right side takes into account a host of economic factors. Economists have dubbed this right side of Equation 13.7 the *user cost* of capital: To be financially attractive, a piece of capital must be sufficiently productive so that it covers the interest that can be earned on alternative financial investments plus any depreciation in the capital itself, less any increase in its value due to rising production costs.

Firms will acquire capital up until the point where Equation 13.7 holds. The optimal, profit-maximizing capital stock k^* depends positively on the productivity of capital and negatively on the user cost of capital. The user cost can be split into two parts, the price of output relative to the price of capital goods and the real rate of return on capital (calculated using the rate of increase of capital goods prices net of depreciation):

$$k^* = k^*\left[\overset{+}{\frac{\Delta y}{\Delta k}}, \overset{+}{\frac{P}{P_k}}, \overset{-}{R - \left(\frac{\Delta P_k}{P_k} - \delta\right)}\right]. \tag{13.8}$$

Investment with imperfect markets

It is important to note that this is a theory of optimal capital stock, and not yet a theory of investment. One possible assumption is that the actual capital stock, k, is always equal to the optimal stock, k^*. If so, then there will be no net investment unless k^* changes. And since k^* depends on the real interest rate and the price of output relative to capital goods, a continuing nonzero amount of investment requires continuing changes in the real interest rate or in relative prices.

In practice, the capital stock is not always at the optimal level, because of capital-market imperfections that limit how rapidly and cheaply firms can acquire or dispose of capital. One important market imperfection is that used capital cannot be sold for what it would cost to build equivalent new capital. This is because of broker and transportation costs, and because an existing plant usually has expensive custom-built features that are of little interest to buyers. A surplus cotton mill in Massachusetts cannot be cheaply transformed into an oil refinery in Texas or reshaped into an office building in California.

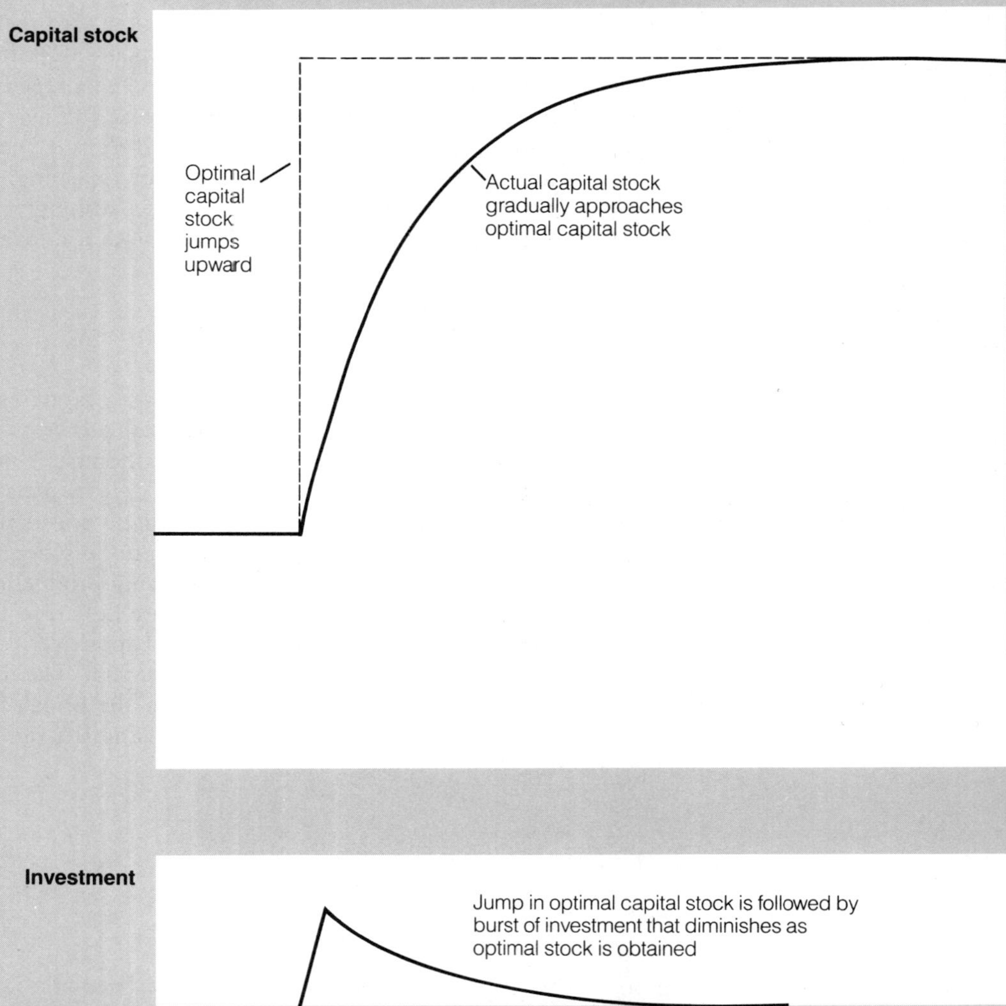

FIGURE 13.2 **CAPITAL ACCUMULATION IN THE STOCK ADJUSTMENT MODEL. In stock adjustment models, investment is intended to attain gradually the optimal capital stock. Thus investment perks up when target capital increases. A jump in the optimal capital stock causes a burst of investment, which then diminishes as the actual capital stock gradually approaches its target.**

In addition, used capital sells at a discount because of buyer anxiety about defects undetectable at the time of sale. Thus we have to distinguish between what it costs a firm to acquire capital and what a firm receives if it disposes of capital. A simple stock adjustment model is commonly used:

$$i = k[t] - k[t-1] = \theta(k^*[t] - k[t-1]) \qquad 0 < \theta < 1 \tag{13.9}$$

The current capital stock is, then, a weighted average of current and past desired capital stocks:

$$k[t] = \theta k^*[t] + \theta(1-\theta)k^*[t-1] + \theta(1-\theta)^2 k^*[t-2] + \ldots$$

This weighting scheme is the same type Friedman used to estimate permanent income from time series data.

The stock adjustment model (Equation 13.9) implies that shocks will take some time to work themselves out. A change in relative prices or real interest rates will not cause a once-and-for-all jump in the capital stock. Instead, as shown in Figure 13.2 for $\theta = 0.2$, investment will persist for some time as firms gradually approach the desired capital stock. This general conclusion is reasonable, but the derivation is dubious.

There is a disconcerting contrast between the careful specification of the optimal capital stock and the simple, almost offhand, adjustment process. It is not really correct to specify the optimal capital stock and the investment path separately. These are joint decisions made simultaneously. A firm's optimal behavior in an uncertain world with imperfect capital markets may bear little relationship to optimal behavior in a certain world with perfect capital markets.

Consider, for example, the case in which there is no rental market for capital goods and no market for disposing of used capital—extreme representations of the commonplace observation that it is difficult to rent a factory or to sell a used one. When capital cannot be rented or easily sold, a firm cannot plan just one period at a time. It will have to plan far ahead and be wary of situations in which the hypothetical optimal capital stock declines.

Figure 13.3 shows a time path for optimal capital stock k^* if capital markets were perfect, and three alternative time paths when capital cannot be sold. A firm cannot follow path k^* (with perfect capital markets) because that calculation unrealistically assumes that capital can be sold at production cost. Instead, the firm could follow a strategy of "never too little capital" and continue to accumulate capital right up until the point where k^* turns downward. As shown, capital does depreciate, but not fast enough. There will be a considerable period when the firm has excess capacity—that is, when funds are tied up in capital that is unprofitable (in that its implicit cost exceeds its marginal revenue product). The firm might instead follow the alternative extreme strategy of "never too much capital." But to do so, the firm will have to endure a period of capital shortage during which it forgoes profits (when capital's marginal product exceeds its implicit cost). In general the firm will follow some intermediate path such as that shown (in color) in Figure 13.3. Because capital cannot be sold at current cost at a moment's notice, it is fully rational for a firm to accept spells of excess capacity at times and insufficient capital at other times.

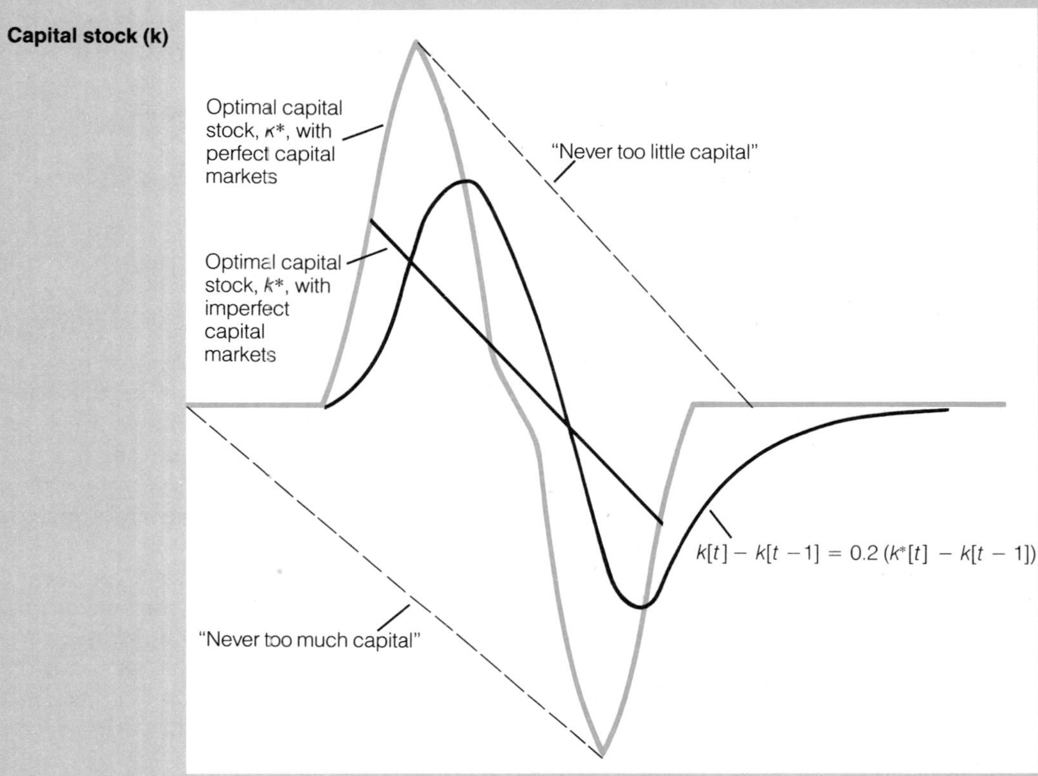

FIGURE 13.3 **CAPITAL PATHS PREDICTED BY FIVE DIFFERENT INVESTMENT MODELS.** **With perfect capital markets, capital, k*, freely rises and falls, because there are no market restrictions on acquiring or dismantling capital. The stock adjustment model—$k[t] - k[t-1] = 0.2(k^*[t] - k[t-1])$—is a crude attempt to depict market imperfections. If used capital cannot be sold, then the aggressive firm will never have too little, the conservative firm will never have too much, and the intelligent firm will choose an optimal capital stock that is sometimes smaller and, other times, larger than k^*, the optimal stock if used capital could be freely sold.**

Figure 13.3 also shows that the simple stock adjustment model (Equation 13.9) does not accurately describe the optimal investment path with imperfect capital markets. The stock adjustment model erroneously predicts that the firm will accumulate more than the optimal capital stock, then reduce its capital faster than physically possible (unless it follows the silly strategy of giving away capital), and finally accumulate capital too slowly when the boom resumes. It would admittedly be difficult, but surely more plausible, to replace the stock adjustment model by explicitly incorporating market imperfections into the profit-maximizing calculations.

A more general model of market imperfections would allow firms to sell capital at distress prices and would also allow the cost of buying capital to rise as the capacity of the capital goods industry becomes strained. Figure 13.4 shows a stylized representation. In this sort of imperfect world, the firm will have to look far ahead if it wants to choose a capital accumulation path that maximizes the present value of profits. Firms will be reluctant to acquire capital that may become unprofitable in the future. On the other hand, if capital goods prices are expected to rise, firms may rush to acquire capital that is unprofitable now but will be profitable later. There will of course be mistakes in which businesses find themselves with a regrettable shortage or a glut of capital. But, even if firms never made mistakes and chose investment plans rationally they would still find themselves with capital shortages at times and excess capacity at other times.

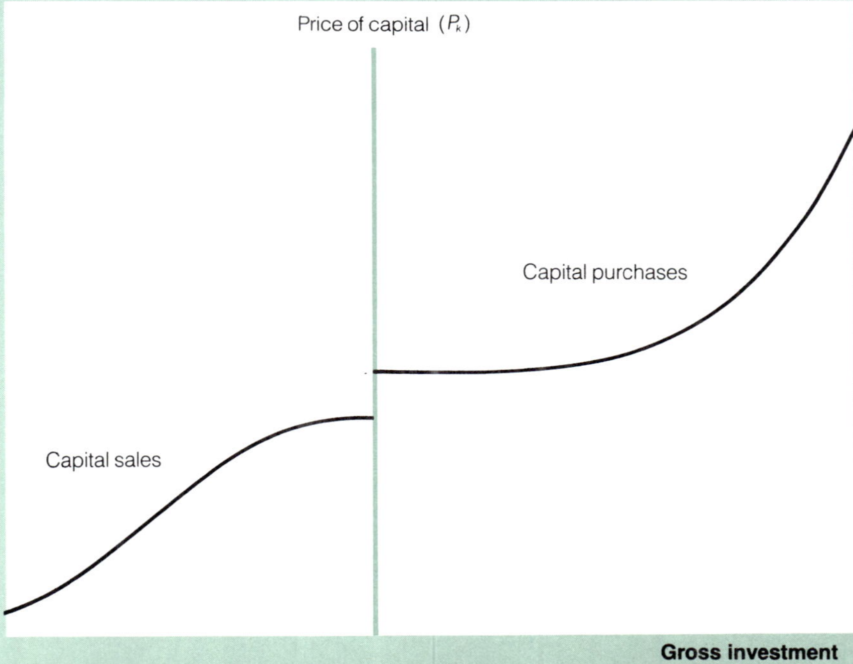

FIGURE 13.4 **THE PRICE OF CAPITAL DEPENDS ON GROSS INVESTMENT. In imperfect capital markets a business must pay more to acquire capital than it would receive from selling what capital it already has. The purchase price rises as high investment spending strains the capacity of the capital goods industry. The amount realized from unloading capital falls as potential buyers are sated.**

NET PRESENT VALUE

Capital market imperfections undermine a strategy of planning one day at a time. Instead, firms must plan on using most plant and equipment until it wears out. But if we look far ahead, then we must take into account that "time is money" by using present-value calculations. The *net present value* (NPV) of a project is the discounted value of the net cash flow of a project:

$$\text{NPV} = Y^0 + \frac{Y[+1]}{1+R} + \frac{Y[+2]}{(1+R)^2} + \ldots \tag{13.10}$$

where $Y[+t]$ is the net cash flow (income minus expenses at time t) and R is the *required rate of return* used to discount this cash flow. There may be some final salvage value or disposal cost that figures into the present-value calculation as a terminal cash flow, but it is not assumed that capital can always be sold at its current cost.

According to the NPV criterion, only projects with positive—or, where there is a choice, the higher—NPV should be undertaken.

The initial cash flow Y^0 is usually negative, since substantial costs are incurred in acquiring plant and equipment. This initial cash flow is often separated out and identified as "the cost": $P_k = -Y^0$. Equation 13.10 can then be rewritten as

$$\text{NPV} = -P_k + \frac{Y[+1]}{(1+R)} + \frac{Y[+2]}{(1+R)^2} + \ldots \tag{13.11}$$

It can be seen that the NPV will be positive if, and only if, the present value of future income is greater than the initial cost:

$$P_k < \frac{Y[+1]}{1-R} + \frac{Y[+2]}{(1+R)^2} + \ldots$$

NPV calculation tells us whether we will come out ahead (1) if we don't invest and instead earn a rate of return, R, on the money, P_k, that we would have spent on the project; or (2) if we do invest and earn rate of return R on all of the cash flow generated by the project. If the NPV is positive, then Option (2) is best.

INVESTMENT AND THE STOCK MARKET

We do not have access to the cash flow estimates or to the NPV calculations made by businesses. How, then, are we to predict investment spending? And how are policymakers to decide if their policies are encouraging or stifling investment? One attractive answer is: Watch the stock market.

Economists traditionally assume that business decisions are intended to maximize the wealth of the owners of the firm. In the United States, businesses are predominantly corporations, which, in theory, are owned by their shareholders. Thus it is argued that a corporation will act so as to maximize the price of its stock.

John Kenneth Galbraith,[3] the most widely-known critic of this view, argues that shareholders have little control over the managers of large corporations. The vast majority of shareholders quietly cash their dividend checks and acquiesce to whatever management does. At annual meetings shareholders are permitted to ratify the board of directors and approve a few general policy decisions. Most shareholders automatically approve management proposals or give management proxies to vote as they please. A handful of proposals from dissident shareholders are usually considered at the annual meetings and overwhelmingly rejected.

In addition, it is argued that, since firms raise few, if any, funds through the sale of new shares, they are not very concerned with the price of their stock. As long as the price does not sag enough to drive lethargic shareholders to mutiny, management is free to do whatever it wishes. It is frequently suggested that the personal objectives of managers center on power and associated prestige. These personal goals can lead managers to sacrifice profits for the sake of growth. They will construct new facilities and acquire other companies, spending whatever funds are available with scant regard for the effects on share prices.

Shareholders know very little about the detailed operations of their company. They have almost no idea what package of policies would maximize the value of their stock. Instead shareholders tend to judge management by simple rules of thumb, which emphasize the avoidance of failure rather than the attainment of some unseen maximum performance. Shareholders are dismayed if there is a decline in a firm's market share, growth rate of earnings, or quarterly dividend. But beyond these minimal criteria, shareholders cannot really gauge management performance. Management is better informed than shareholders, but still uncertain of optimal policies. Even if they do care about shareholders, it is much easier and safer just to focus on the simple rules of thumb that satisfy shareholders. Apart from the need to observe these minimal performance standards, managers can pursue their personal objectives.

These arguments have some merit, but their conclusions are exaggerated. There are good reasons why stock prices should influence management decisions, and there is good evidence that they in fact do. Many top executives have a large part of their wealth invested in company stock. In addition, much of their compensation is in the form of stock options and other incentive schemes whose value depends on the price of the company's stock. Also, a low stock price encourages other firms to buy up enough shares to take control of the company and replace management.* These are all good reasons why even the most selfish executive should keep an eye on the price of the company's stock.

A number of studies[5] affirm that stock prices do influence corporate investment decisions. For example, Charles Bischoff estimated that the drop in stock prices in 1974 reduced real corporate investment by $15 billion.[6] The rest of this chapter will explain the theoretical relationship between stock prices and investment. We begin with an examination of how stock prices are determined.

* Some firms have resisted takeovers mightily, at their shareholders' expense.[4]

Intrinsic value

Why is a share of corporate stock valuable? In theory, because the corporation pays dividends to the owner of that share.

An investor buys

A cow for her milk
A hen for her eggs
and a stock, by heck
For her dividends.

An orchard for fruit
Bees for their honey
and stock, besides
For their dividends.*

The value of a corporate bond is the present value of the coupons and its maturation value (payable by the firm to the bondholder). Similarly, the value of corporate stock derives from the dividends that the firm will pay stockholders. The main differences are that stock has no expiration date, and that there is no legal obligation to pay a set amount of dividends. Nonetheless, in a way analogous to bond pricing, the intrinsic value of a share of stock is the present value of the anticipated dividends:

$$P_E = \frac{d[+1]}{1+r} + \frac{d[+2]}{(1+r)^2} + \ldots \qquad (13.12)$$

where P_E is the price of a share of equity, $d[+t]$ is the real dividend per share anticipated t years hence, and r is the shareholder's real required stock yield.†

Say, for instance, that a large, mature firm is going to pay a dividend of $5 a share forever.‡ If shareholders require a 10% return on their stock, then they are willing to pay $50 a share.

If management were totally unconcerned with shareholders and the value of their stock, the firm would presumably pay no dividends; if management were interested in shareholder well-being, then the effects of investment on stock prices would be taken into account. The intrinsic-value model of stock prices (Equation 13.12) is just a present-value criterion. Firms that choose investment projects to maximize present value will automatically maximize the value of their stock. The important new wrinkle introduced by a consideration of stock prices is that, if firms act on behalf of their shareholders, they will use shareholders' required stock yield to calculate the NPV of prospective investments.

Shareholders' required yield on equity is determined and revealed in financial markets. Shareholders require stock to yield a return competitive with the yields offered on other assets. This is one of the primary mechanisms by which

* Reprinted by permission of John Burr Williams, *The Theory of Investment Value,* Cambridge, Mass.: Harvard University Press, 1938, pp. 57 and 58.

† It doesn't matter whether we discount nominal dividends by the nominal required yield or instead discount real dividends by the real required yield.

‡ This is like a consol bond. The present-value formula (Equation 13.12) simplifies to $P_E = d/r = \$5/0.10 = \$50$.

financial markets affect real economic activity. **When real interest rates fall, required stock yields decline, making it more likely that the real cash flow from prospective investments is sufficient to make these investments attractive.**

Tobin's q

But where do firms (or economic forecasters) find these shareholder-required yields? The stock market is the place to look, but the financial pages don't report the anticipated rates of returns on stocks. An ingenious alternative, suggested by James Tobin, is to look at stock prices. Specifically, Tobin argues that we should look at stock prices relative to the replacement cost of a firm's assets:

$$q = \frac{\text{market value of firm}}{\text{replacement cost of firm}} = \frac{P_E E}{P_k k}. \tag{13.13}$$

where E is the number of shares outstanding.* This ratio, *Tobin's q,* can be calculated readily since stock prices are printed in the daily newspapers and capital construction costs are widely available.

We have seen that an investment project should be judged by the present value of its cash flow relative to its cost. If firms are trying to do well by their shareholders, then they will gauge present value by the market value of their stock. Whether the firm should expand or contract can be judged by the market value of a firm's stock relative to the current cost of its assets. This logic led Tobin to conclude that **A firm should expand (by investing in new plant and equipment) if its q is greater than one.**

A connection between investment and market value relative to cost was pointed out many years ago by Keynes:

> . . . the daily revaluations of the Stock Exchange, though they are primarily made to facilitate transfers of old investments between one individual and another, inevitably exert a decisive influence on the rate of current investment. For there is no sense in building up a new enterprise at a cost greater than that at which a similar existing enterprise can be purchased; whilst there is an inducement to spend on a new project what may seem an extravagant sum, if it can be floated off on the Stock Exchange at an immediate profit. Thus, certain classes of investment are governed by the average expectation of those who deal on the Stock Exchange as revealed in the price of shares. . .[7]

This has a most persuasive logic. Think of the construction of new homes. A builder will compare the cost of constructing a house with its potential market value. It is profitable to build only those homes for which the market value exceeds the construction cost. The same reasoning applies to corporate investment.

A firm should compare the cost of new capital with the value that financial markets will place on that capital. If the market value is greater than the cost

* If a firm has bonds as well as stock outstanding, then these bonds should be added to the market value $P_E E$ or subtracted from the firm's assets $P_k k$.

IN THE NEWS
Business Still Limits Outlay for Expansion

When the economy recovers from a recession, consumer spending usually leads the way upward. After a year or so, however, businessmen become convinced the recovery will last and start spending increasing billions on new plants and equipment.

The 1982-84 recovery is unusual.

Consumers have done their part, all right. Consumption spending rose more than 4% last year, in inflation-adjusted terms, a sharp improvement over the 1.4% rise in 1982. (The recession hit bottom in November 1982.)

But businessmen have come on with unusual speed. "It's notable that we have been able to turn on capital spending this early in the recovery," says Lacy H. Hunt, chief economist of the investment firm of Carroll, McEntee & McGinley. "The rise in business fixed investment in the first three months of the recovery was a record."

Even more notable, however, is that this spending hasn't gone for new factories designed to increase output; the outlay on structures of all kinds actually fell by about 7% in 1983. The gain came mainly from outlays on computers and other machines and devices to make production cheaper.

What's happening, many analysts say, is that businessmen are trying to restructure their output, not increase it. They're trying to become more efficient, in part to meet the import competition that's likely to remain strong for years to come. And they're rearranging production to meet demand.

As a result, there probably won't be anything like the old-fashioned capital spending boom that often has sustained a recovery in its second year. A key problem is the current high level of interest rates, especially rates on the sort of long-term bonds that often are sold to finance new plants.

"There is a reasonable argument that long-term interest rates will have to decline before a full-fledged capital goods boom can get under way," says Morris Cohen, a Hackensack, N.J.-based economic consultant.

Few analysts expect any such rate decline any time soon. The two-score analysts interviewed monthly by Blue Chip Economic Indicators, a Sedona, Ariz., newsletter, on the average expect long-term rates to stay about where they are the rest of 1984.

Computers and similar equipment that promise a quick payoff in increased efficiency can be, and often are, financed by bank and other short-term credit. Such borrowing presumably helps to explain why short-term credit has been rising strongly.

Businessmen spend on capital projects only because they expect a return, a return that must exceed the project's costs. That's a calculation that's relatively easy to make with investments in computers and other equipment. The return on a new factory, however, may be spread over 20 years or more, and in the current atmosphere of uncertainty it's hard to guess what the return will be.

Much of the uncertainty centers on government policy. Jerry L. Jordan, a former member of President Reagan's Council of Economic Advisers, comments, "Reagan campaigned in 1980 to reduce the uncertainty about government policy, but now the uncertainty is greater than ever."

Part of the uncertainty stems from the fact that business is in the midst of rapid technological change. "Besides that," says Edward Guay, chief economist of Cigna Investment Management Co., "there's a change in the mix of goods demanded." Businessmen are reluctant to make long-term outlays on the basis of current technology and demand for fear that further changes may lie directly ahead.

Another deterrent is relatively low capacity utilization rates. As computed by the Federal Reserve Board, such rates have been rising in the recovery but they're still below 80%, lessening the need for additional expansion.

"When anything is surplus," says John Rutledge, chairman of Claremont Economics Institute, "its price is soft. And the fact is that you can buy existing plant space for a great deal less per square foot than you can build a new building."

Some analysts think this situation will change before the end of 1984. "Businessmen already are a lot more confident than they were six to nine months ago," says Norman Robertson, chief economist of Pittsburgh's Mellon Bank. "As they see the recovery continuing, they'll get more confident."

For the present, however, most analysts agree that there isn't much of the business attitude that economist John Maynard Keynes called "animal spirits." At this stage of the recovery businessmen still are very cautious, and the caution is reflected in capital spending policy. (Lindley H. Clark, Jr., *Wall Street Journal,* Feb. 6, 1984)

($q > 1$), shareholders will prefer that the firm acquire the capital rather than distribute its cost as dividends, gladly giving up a dollar of dividends to get a two-dollar increase in the value of their stock. Similarly, the firm should compare the price it can get for selling its existing capital with the value that financial markets place on that capital. If the financial-market value is less than the selling price ($q < 1$), the firm should sell off its capital and distribute the proceeds as dividends. Shareholders prefer two dollars of dividends to one dollar of market value. The firm, then, should contract, because it is "worth more dead than alive."

In recent years, some prominent firms have in fact sold off assets for more than market value. For example, in 1980 Seagram sold \$2.3 billion in energy properties, and the market value of its stock promptly doubled. Similarly, Esmark more than doubled the value of its stock in 1980 by selling 42% of its assets and using the proceeds to buy up 55% of its shares. A low market value relative to replacement cost also frequently motivates takeover bids. An outside group will make a profit by purchasing enough stock to gain control of a company and then liquidate its assets. Indeed, it was a Mobil Oil offer to buy Esmark stock that helped persuade Esmark executives to unload low-valued assets.

Let's do a simple q example. Consider a hamburger chain and assume, for simplicity, that all future earnings are paid out as dividends. Assume also that a new restaurant costs \$1 million to build and will give a constant profit of \$200,000 a year. The rate of return on a new restaurant is then 20%:

$$R_K = \frac{\$200{,}000}{\$1{,}000{,}000} = .20.$$

The value that financial markets will place on the \$200,000 annual profits from this restaurant depends on how highly hamburger earnings are valued. Stock in this restaurant could be priced to give shareholders a 5%, 10%, or 50% return. Perhaps hamburger profits are considered risky because of uncertainty about meat and gasoline prices. If bonds are yielding 5%, then maybe stock in hamburger chains is priced to yield 10%. Since profits are constant, we can use the consol formula (p. 412) to show that the market value of the restaurant will be

$$P_E E = \frac{\$200{,}000}{.10} = \$2{,}000{,}000.$$

Valued at \$2 million, the \$200,000 annual dividend provides the requisite 10% return to stockholders.

With these figures, the market value of the restaurant is twice its cost of construction: $q = 2$. Stockholders would favor this investment, since using \$1 million in potential dividends to build the restaurant provides \$2 million in market value. The reason is that the restaurant's 20% profit rate is greater than the market's 10% required rate. If the market's required rate were instead 25%, then

$$P_E E = \frac{\$200{,}000}{.25} = \$800{,}000.$$

Now $q = .8$, and shareholders would be opposed to the construction of the restaurant.

In recent years, there has been a strongly renewed interest in the influence of stock prices on capital formation. Tobin has argued that q is the channel through which financial market events influence real economic activity. Events that raise market value relative to replacement cost stimulate physical investment. The observed value of q is, then, both a yardstick by which investment should be judged and also a barometer for predicting investment activity. Stock prices are now used in many macroeconometric models to help explain investment and to predict the future course of the economy. Data on q are watched by members of the Fed and of the Council of Economic Advisers.

These policymakers and macroeconometric models use aggregate q data to monitor the overall course of the economy. In principle, there are individual q's for every firm and for every investment project. Firms with high q's should be expanding faster than those with low q's. Investment projects with high q's should be undertaken and those with low q's spurned. An aggregate q index provides a broad measure of the incentives for aggregate investment.

James Tobin and William Brainard[8] estimated individual q's for some 400 corporations over the 15-year period from 1960 to 1974. There is considerable variation in these q's, both among firms and over time. The annual average of these q's is shown in Figure 13.5. This figure also shows the q's calculated from aggregate data for these same years by John Ciccolo and by the Council of Economic Advisers. The Tobin-Brainard q series is considerably higher than the Ciccolo and Council q series. The main computational difference is that the Tobin-Brainard data are a simple average of firms q's, so that large and small firms are weighted equally. In the calculations made by Ciccolo and the Council, large firms have more weight because they are a larger component of the aggregate data. Thus the lower q values in the Ciccolo and Council series indicate that large firms tend to have q's lower than small firms. The Council's q values are less volatile and a bit smaller than Ciccolo's q series. This is because of differences in their treatment of corporate debt.

The general movements in the three q series are very similar. The mid-1960s were very favorable for investment. The years 1973–74 were unfavorable, and particularly so for small firms. Investment did, in fact, plummet in 1975 and 1976. (There is generally a lag of one to two years between q and investment because of the time it takes to plan and implement investment projects.) The Council's q data remained at low levels through the second half of the 1970s.

Some refinements The preceding arguments ignore the taxes that stockholders pay on their dividends and capital gains. These taxes modify the analysis because dividends and capital gains are taxed at different rates. Currently, the effective tax rate on capital gains (t_c) is generally less than the tax rate on dividends (t_y). This difference implies that shareholders prefer a dollar of increased market value to a dollar of dividends.

Say a typical investor pays a 30% tax on dividends on a 10% tax on capital gains. A dollar of dividends puts 70 cents in her purse; a dollar of capital gains puts in 90 cents. This means that shareholders will not be indifferent about projects with a q of one. They will gladly give up a dollar of dividends (which

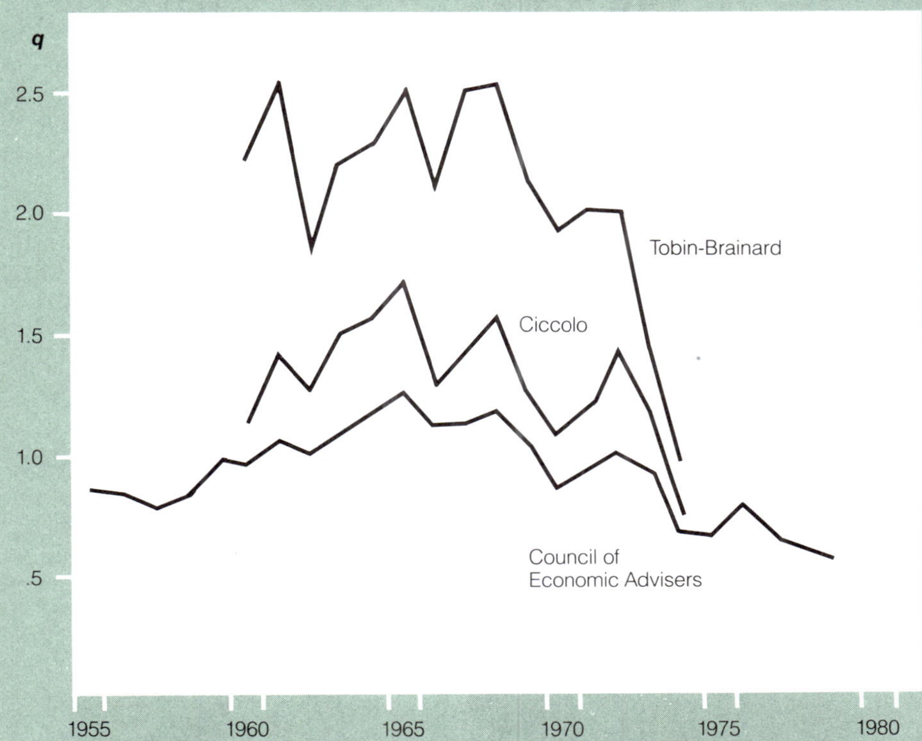

FIGURE 13.5 **THREE INDEPENDENT ESTIMATES OF TOBIN'S q differ in their levels but show similar movements; in particular, high interest rates and a weak economy made investment less appealing in the 1970s than in the 1960s.**

is only 70¢ after taxes) in order to receive a dollar in increased market value (which is 90¢ after taxes). They will benefit from investment projects even when q is less than one.

In general, a dollar of dividends is $1 - t_y$ dollars after taxes. A dollar of increased market vaue is $1 - t_c$ dollars after taxes. Shareholders will profit from firm investments as long as $(1 - t_c)$(market value) > $(1 - t_y)$(cost), or as long as

$$q = \frac{\text{market value}}{\text{cost}} > \frac{(1 - t_y)}{(1 - t_c)}. \tag{13.14}$$

Since t_y is greater than t_c, $(1 - t_y)/(1 - t_c)$ is less than 1.0. If $t_y = 0.3$ and $t_c = 0.1$, $(1 - t_y)/(1 - t_c) = 0.78$. Thus, **shareholders will benefit from firm invest-**

ment as long as q is greater than $(1 - t_y)/(1 - t_c)$, a number less than one. A tax rate that is lower on capital gains than on dividends encourages firms to retain earnings and invest in plant and equipment.

There is a second refinement, which is a good deal messier. The persuasive logic behind q applies to marginal q, the change in market value relative to the cost of the additional investment. But our data measure average q for the firm's current assets. Movements in average q may signal corresponding movements in marginal q, but, then again, they may not. The profitability of prospective ventures may differ from existing capital and may, in investor's eyes, have different characteristics (with respect to risk for example) that command different required yields. This will often be true when new capital is unlike existing capital, perhaps because of technological developments or entrance into new lines of business. Firms may also be imperfectly competitive, so that expansion affects the profitability of existing capital. The proposed expansion may also be sufficiently large to change the yield required if investors are to absorb the company's stock.

Consider, for instance, the likely case in which the firm's profit rate declines as it expands. The average profitability of current capital then overstates the profitability of future investment, and average q is larger than marginal q. The firm's existing capital may have a larger market value than replacement cost, while the market value of additional capital is less than its cost. The firm should invest up to the point where marginal q equals one or, taking taxes into account, $(1 - t_y)/(1 - t_c)$. At the same time, average q will be larger than this marginal q.

Such considerations help explain why the q data in Figure 13.5 are generally greater than 1.0, or $(1 - t_y)/(1 - t_c)$. More significance should be attached to changes in q's than to their absolute levels. If there is a relatively stable relationship between marginal and average q, then changes in observed average q may be a useful indicator of changes in unobserved marginal q. This is an empirical rather than a theoretical issue. So far, the evidence is that average q is a fairly good predictor of investment spending. (Some of this evidence is given in Reference 5.)

Investment by casino

Keynes, an admirably successful investor, was keenly interested in the influence of mass psychology on stock prices. His discussion of the stock market in *The General Theory* contains some of his liveliest and most incisive prose. Keynes argued that the market is dominated, not by farsighted investors, but by speculators trying to guess the direction stock prices are headed:

> For most of these persons are, in fact, largely concerned not with making superior long-term forecasts of the probable yield of an investment over its whole life, but with foreseeing changes in the conventional basis of valuation a short time ahead of the general public. They are concerned, not with what an investment is really worth to a man who buys it "for keeps" but with what the market will value it at, under the influence of mass psychology, three months or a year hence. Moreover, this behavior is not the outcome of a wrong-headed propensity. It is an inevitable result of an investment market organized along the lines described. For it is not sensible to pay 25

for an investment of which you believe the prospective yield to justify a value of 30, if you also believe that the market will value it at 20 three months hence.[9]

The object then is not to estimate intrinsic value, but to anticipate which stocks others will favor. Keynes likened this to

> . . . those newspaper competitions in which the competitors have to pick out the six prettiest faces from a hundred photographs. The prize being awarded to the competitor whose choice most nearly corresponds to the average preference of the competitors as a whole; so that each competitor has to pick, not those faces which he himself finds prettiest, but those which he thinks likeliest to catch the fancy of the other competitors, all of whom are looking at the problem from the same point of view. It is not a case of choosing those which, to the best of one's judgment, are really the prettiest, nor even those which average opinion genuinely thinks the prettiest. We have reached the third degree where we devote our intelligences to anticipating what average opinion expects the average opinion to be. And there are some, I believe, who practice the fourth, fifth and higher degrees.[10]

This is a precarious battle of wits, not much different from ordinary games of chance. The basic reason for this unbridled speculation is that it is exceedingly difficult to estimate future earnings. Keynes put it this way:

> The outstanding fact is the extreme precariousness of the basis of knowledge on which our estimates of prospective yield have to be made. Our knowledge of the factors which will govern the yield of an investment some years hence is usually very slight and often negligible. If we speak frankly, we have to admit that our basis of knowledge for estimating the yield ten years hence of a railway, a copper mine, a textile factory, the goodwill of a patent medicine, an atlantic liner, a building in the city of London amounts to little and sometimes nothing. . .[11]

This lack of solid knowledge about the future allows the emotions of market participants to run free:

> A conventional valuation which is established as the outcome of mass psychology of a large number of ignorant individuals is liable to change violently as the result of a sudden fluctuation of opinion due to factors which do not really make much difference to the prospective yield; since there will be no strong roots of conviction to hold it steady.[12]

Stock prices, then, reflect, not so much a professional evaluation of firms, as the outcome of a precarious battle of wits, as speculators attempt to anticipate "what average opinion expects average opinion to be."

Keynes emphasized the influence of unpredictable mass psychology on stock prices and also argued, as explained earlier in this chapter, that stock prices are an important determinant of corporate investment. If we put these two beliefs together we get Keynes' explanation of why investment spending is so erratic: Precarious stock valuations based on mass psychology cause investment demand to be volatile.

As this chapter's epigraph indicates, Keynes viewed the stock market as a wild casino, with unfortunate consequences for capital formation. This perspective led him to suggest that stock exchanges, like casinos, should "in the public interest be inaccessible and expensive" or investment should be made "permanent and indissoluble, like marriage, except by reason of death or other grave cause."[13] Casinos are no longer inaccessible, nor marriages indissoluble, but Keynes' observed influence of stock prices on investment demand has become fashionable.

In recent years, though, academic economists have generally had a more respectful view of the stock market, telling us repeatedly of the rapid and efficient absorption of information by skilled market analysts,[14] with stocks judged by the cool, bloodless verdict of the marketplace. The stories told by market participants have a somewhat different flavor. These are tales of unrestrained euphoria and unremitting gloom, of sweaty palms and white knuckles. Perhaps mass psychology remains part of the explanation for investment volatility.[15]

INVESTMENT FINANCING

Part of Galbraith's thesis of unfettered corporate managers is the view that modern corporations do not rely on financial markets for funds, that retained earnings are sufficient to finance investment projects. During the 1930s there was in fact so little external funding of corporations that corporate debt was 17% lower in 1939 than in 1929. But this drop in borrowing was due mostly to the perceived lack of profitable investment opportunities. The diversion of industrial capacity towards war materiel made the early 1940s also atypical. Since World War II, financial markets have become a critically important source of funds for businesses. At the end of 1980, the outstanding long-term bonds, loans, and mortgages of businesses totaled about a trillion dollars, nearly as much as the market value of corporate equity.

Because, for tax purposes, firms can write off interest, but not dividends, as an expense, the sale of new stock is only a minor source of funds. Throughout the 1970s, net stock sales averaged about $7 billion a year. For some firms, stock sales were less than repurchases, so that stock was actually a net use rather than a source of funds. Stock sales are generally a last resort, used by small, young firms. Stock sales are also used by companies, often utilities, so heavy with debt that additional debt issuance raises the specter of bankruptcy. Despite the small amount of equity financing, stock prices are still important to investment decisions. Firms interested in shareholder well-being will gauge investments by their effects on stock prices.

Bonds, loans, and mortgages are, as noted, important sources of business funds. Bonds are important mostly for large, well-known corporations. Small- and medium-size firms find it difficult and expensive to issue bonds. Without access to the bond market, they rely on local banks and other financial institutions for loans. Large corporations also borrow from banks. But because they have direct access to financial markets, they are at a considerable advantage, and can demand and get very favorable loan rates. Small- to medium-size firms, without this bargaining power, are the bread and butter of most banks.

Some firms, like households, perceive themselves as liquidity-constrained. Their managers are enthusiastic about the firm's future or willing to take substantial gambles. They would like to borrow heavily, expand greatly, and pay back the loans out of future profits. Because lenders are a bit jaded about enthusiastic profit projections and very wary of the firm's limited liability, the amount that they are willing to lend may fall short of the firm's hopes.

This gap may be widened by a series of loan requests, in which each new loan is junior to the preceding debt. Lenders are understandably nervous about being last in line to be paid. There may even be a suspicion that the new loans are intended to bail out the old loans. Firms may also be constrained in their borrowing by restrictions written into earlier loans. There are also indivisibilities to be considered. It may be very expensive or impossible for small- to medium-size firms to issue bonds or to borrow money from financial institutions outside of their immediate area.

Young, unproven companies, with high hopes and few assets, are the most likely to be liquidity-constrained. For such firms, finding adequately profitable investment projects is not the binding constraint. They view their q's as much higher than one, and their prospective profits much higher than their required return. The relevant constraint is how much capital they can raise. They will eagerly use whatever funds they can get their hands on. Earnings will be plowed back into the firm, available loans will be taken, and despite the comparative disadvantage, new equity will be sold when other sources of funds are exhausted. Liquidity constraints may explain our earlier observation that small firms tend to have higher q's than do large firms.

IMPLICATIONS FOR MACRO MODELS

Neoclassical investment theory assumes that firms try to maximize the present value of profits. If capital markets were perfect, firms would not have to plan very far ahead since there would be no problems in acquiring needed capital or in disposing of unwanted capital. Because capital markets are imperfect, firms make a long-term commitment when they acquire capital. They consequently try to plan far ahead, anticipating future costs, profits, and interest rates. Their NPV calculations are difficult and heavily dependent on distant expectations.

It is not easy, either, for economic forecasters to incorporate these expectations into their macro models, but economists may be able to use stock prices relative to capital goods prices to gauge business investment incentives. Business investment is encouraged when q is high or, alternatively, when real rates of return on physical capital are high relative to real interest rates. Tobin's q is a simple barometer, reflecting the effects of government policies and other events on investment spending.

Changes in q can occur for either of two reasons: changes in the anticipated real returns from capital or changes in the real interest rates used to discount these cash flows. As noted in Chapter 11, the government can use specific tax incentives to raise the after-tax returns on investment projects. But businesses are even more concerned about the overall strength of the economy. When the economy is strong, business people are generally much more optimistic about the profitability of additional capital. Recession and stagnation dampen business hopes and enthusiasm. Low tax rates are little consolation when you have no taxable profits.

Financial markets also affect business expenditures. Increases in real interest rates reduce q, making investment less attractive. In addition, funds simply dry up for smaller, less-established firms. Liquidity-constrained, they must abandon investment projects and even curtail operations. Often they struggle to keep afloat by delaying bill payments, thereby indirectly borrowing through firms that do have access to credit. Some run out of cash and must close.

IMPORTANT TERMS AND CONCEPTS

accelerator models
neoclassical investment model
net present value (NPV)
required rate of return
Tobin's q

Accelerator models emphasize the dynamic consequences of a dependency of investment on change in output. Such a dependency can generate possibly unstable economic cycles.

Neoclassical models emphasize that the optimal profit-maximizing capital stock will be increased by a rise in the price of output relative to the price of capital goods or by a fall in the real interest rate (calculated using the rate of increase of capital goods prices net of depreciation).

With imperfect capital goods markets, firms must plan far ahead and estimate profits over capital's life. They will rationally choose investment plans that cause capital shortages at times and excess capacity at other times.

A firm's investment will increase the market value of its stock if the rate of return on the investment is greater than the shareholders' required rate of return or, equivalently, if the market value of the investment is greater than its cost. Tobin's q is a yardstick by which investment decisions can be judged, and a barometer for predicting investment.

Investment by liquidity-constrained firms is limited by the availability of funds, rather than by the perceived profitability of projects.

Low interest rates and high profit expectations buoy q. Government policies influence business investment through changes in q and through credit availability.

EXERCISES

1. Explain the following: "Firms will rationally choose investment plans that cause capital shortages at times and excess capacity at other times."

2. The traditional "net cost" method of computing life insurance premiums is explained by Consumers Union: "You add up the premiums you will pay over some period (say 20 years). Then you subtract the dividends you expect to receive (if any), and the cash value you can get by turning the policy in at the end of the period (if it's a cash-value type policy)." (*New York Times Magazine,* May 1974.)

Could a policy that is profitable to the company have a negative "net cost"? How would you recommend comparing the costs of life insurance policies?

3. A closed-end mutual fund issues a fixed number of shares to initial subscribers, say a million shares at $10 each. The $10 million that is raised is then used to purchase securities, with the dividends and realized capital gains distributed to the shareholders. Unlike an open-end fund, a closed-end mutual fund does not issue or redeem its shares at net asset value. An investor who wants to buy shares in the fund must buy them from a current shareholder. A shareholder who wants to sell his or her shares must find a buyer. The shares of closed-end funds are traded on stock exchanges and over the counter. These shares may trade at a premium or discount from net asset value. For example, the value of the stock owned by the fund may have risen to $15 million. The net asset value of the shares in the fund is then $15. But these fund shares may trade in the open market at a price of only $12 a share. If so, what is the fund's q? Should it expand or contract? How?

4. Comment on the following argument:

> Equity capital is usually obtained by a process that is wholly independent of the pricing mechanism of the stock market. If the capital comes from corporate saving, this saving goes on without reference to the particular price or course of prices for the company's shares in the open market; managers approve the enlargement of modernization of plant not because their company's stock is selling high or low, but because they believe such a step will increase future earnings.
>
> Untenable, therefore, would seem to be the theory, advanced by some writers, . . . that high prices for shares promote, and low prices retard, the formation of new capital . . . (John Burr Williams, *The Theory of Investment Value,* Harvard University Press, 1938.)

5. Consider a project costing C dollars and returning $Y[+t]$ dollars at time t. The "payout period" of such a project, denoted T, is the time required to accumulate sufficient earnings to cover initial costs—that is, the T such that $C = Y[+1] + Y[+2] + Y[+3] + \ldots + Y[+T]$. For example, a project that costs $5 million and pays $1 million a year for 20 years has a payout period of 5 years. If there are two projects, A and B (with respective costs C_A and C_B and respective returns $Y_A[+t]$ and $Y_B[+t]$), then the payout period criterion directs selection of the project with the shorter payout period—for example, A if $T_A < T_B$.

a. What is the "present-value criterion"? How would it be used to choose between Projects A and B?

b. How would the present-value and payout-period criteria compare in the case of two projects that cost the same amount, ($C_A = C_B$), and that have constant returns $Y_A[+t] = Y_A$ and $Y_B[+t] = Y_B$? Would they always agree on the most desirable project?

c. Explain the strengths and weaknesses of the payout-period criterion. It may be useful to give examples of situations in which it would lead to particularly bad decisions.

6. Define Tobin's q. Describe and evaluate its usefulness. Why might a firm not invest even though its q is greater than one? Why might a firm invest even though its q is less than one?

7. In a recent Ph.D. dissertation, the author, (Trilla Pando, University of Houston, 1981) found that firms that repurchased at least 1% of their shares had relatively low qs. Is this finding consistent with theory?

8. Critically evaluate the following quotation:

> In 1978 the maximum effective federal tax on long-term capital gains was reduced from 49% to 28%. Preliminary results indicate that individual and institutional investors have stepped up investment in corporations that are plowing their capital and earnings into new plant and equipment and research and development.

> Moreover, both big and small corporations have felt the resulting pressure to act like growth companies, and most have increased their capital spending plans and actual capital spending.
>
> In 1979, a period of economic prosperity, dividend increases, extras and resumptions declined from a year earlier while decreases and omissions of dividends increased. Analysts expect the trend to continue through 1980. These are the natural effects of widening the differential between ordinary income tax rates and capital gains tax rates. To the extent that taxes remain the same on dividends and are reduced on capital gains, investors prefer to invest in growth companies and stockholders prefer to see increases in reinvestment of earnings rather than increases in dividends. (Thomas F. Ruhm, "Investment Income Should Be Taxed at Reduced Rates," *Wall Street Journal,* May 30, 1980.)

9. "Good news about the stock market is good news about the economy." Yet the stock market should not affect consumption, since the only way people can realize their paper profits is by selling their stock, which merely shuffles money and stock certificates. And the market should not affect investment, since firms hardly ever sell stock to finance expansion. What, if anything, then, does the stock market have to do with the economy?

REFERENCES

1. J. M. Keynes, *The General Theory of Employment, Interest, and Money,* New York: Macmillan, 1936, p. 159.

2. D. W. Jorgenson, "Capital Theory and Investment Behavior," *American Economic Review* (May 1963), pp. 247–59.

3. J. K. Galbraith, *The New Industrial State,* 2nd ed., Boston: Houghton Mifflin, 1971.

4. *Barron's,* Feb. 5, 1979; May 5, 1980; July 7, 1980; Aug. 24, 1981; and Feb. 15, 1982.

5. For example, J. H. Ciccolo, "Money, Income and Equity Values: Tests for Exogeneity," *Journal of Money, Credit, and Banking* (February 1978), pp. 46–64; and G. M. Furstenberg, "Corporate Investment: Does Market Valuation Matter in the Aggregate?" *Brookings Papers on Economic Activity* (1977), pp. 347–97.

6. *Business Week,* January 27, 1975, p. 89.

7. Keynes, p. 151.

8. J. Tobin and W. C. Brainard, "Asset Markets and the cost of Capital," in *Economic Progress, Private Values and Public Policy,* Amsterdam: North-Holland, 1977, pp. 235–62.

9. Keynes, p. 154.

10. Keynes, p. 156.

11. Keynes, pp. 149–50.

12. Keynes, p. 154.

13. Keynes, pp. 159–60.

14. Burton G. Malkiel, *A Random Walk Down Wall Street,* New York: Norton, 1982.

15. "Adam Smith," *The Money Game,* New York: Random House, 1967.

SUGGESTIONS FOR FURTHER READING

A recent empirical survey of investment models is P. K. Clark, "Investment in the 1970s: Theory, Performance, and Prediction," *Brookings Papers,* 1979:1, pp. 73–124. For a discussion of monetary policies and q, read James Tobin, "Monetary Policies and the Economy," *Southern Economic Journal,* (January 1978), pp. 421–31. The Council of Economic Advisers discusses q in the 1977 *Economic Report of the President,* Washington, D.C.: Government Printing Office, pp. 27–31.

CHAPTER FOURTEEN

MONEY

It is a singular and, indeed, a significant fact that, although money was the first economic subject to attract men's thoughtful attention and has been the focal centre of economic investigation ever since, there is at the present day not even an approximate agreement as to what ought to be designated by the word. The business world makes use of the term in several senses, while among economists there are almost as many different conceptions as there are writers upon money.

A. P. ANDREW[1]

This chapter examines the role of money in a modern economy. It looks at how banks create money and explains how the conduct of monetary policy is complicated by the existence of a variety of moneys and near-moneys.

MONEY is such a familiar and pervasive part of our lives that we seldom stop to think about its nature and importance. As children we quickly learn that dollar bills are not ordinary pieces of paper, to be painted, shredded, eaten, or left out in the mud. Dollar bills are special and valuable bacause dollars are "money." These funny green pieces of paper are special because stores will give food, clothing, and toys in exchange for them. Once we learn that we can use this green paper to buy "real" things, then we too are quite willing to work or to sell things for dollars.

It has not always been this way. For many years, real things were used as money. Tobacco, rice, cattle, sea shells, and whiskey were once legal tender in various parts of the United States. Although they lacked legal sanction, musket balls, peas, hemp, furs, and woodpecker scalps were also used as early American moneys.

In 1792, the federal government began minting gold and silver coins while, up until the Civil War, the only paper money in the United States was issued by private banks. In order to finance the Civil War, the North issued "greenbacks" (using green ink) and the South printed confederate notes. In 1870, the Supreme Court ruled that government paper money was unconstitutional, but a year later decided that greenbacks were constitutional after all. In the 1870s, the U.S. Congress made greenbacks convertible into gold and, in addition, authorized the printing of gold certificates and silver certificates that were redeemable in gold.

In the 1930s, the gold backing for U.S. government money effectively ended and private bank notes were abolished. Today, U.S. legal tender consists almost entirely of Federal Reserve notes, unbacked paper issued by the Federal Reserve banks. The rest is issued by the U.S. Treasury: coins made of inexpensive alloys and some $300 million in Treasury notes (unbacked paper descended from the old greenbacks).

However, most stores will sell you things even if you do not have a pocket full of Federal Reserve notes, gold, tobacco, or woodpecker scalps. You can use a bank check, a traveler's check, a personal check, a credit card, or even (if you are a familiar customer) an informal personal IOU. Which of these, and what else, should be labeled money? More fundamentally, what is money and why does it exist at all? This chapter will explain why societies have found money to be a useful social contrivance, why paper money has value, and how banks still create money even though they no longer print bank notes. We will look at money demand and money supply and how the economy is affected by the existence of a plethora of banks and a gaggle of moneys.

EXCHANGE AND MEDIUMS OF EXCHANGE

Barter Imagine an economy without money of any sort. It would most likely be a primitive one in which little trading takes place. Perhaps the citizens are self-sufficient and a bit isolated or suspicious of one another. When their paths do cross and they make trades, they are simple exchanges of goods—corn for potatoes, wood for leather, knives for arrows. This is *barter,* the trading of goods and services for other goods and services.

When people are largely self-sufficient, barter may be satisfactory for occasional trades. However, a vital element of economic progress has been the replacement of self-sufficiency with specialization. I teach, consult, do research, and write textbooks. With the fruits of this labor I can acquire pizza, beer, computer software, and the other necessities of a good life. Other people specialize in making the pizzas I enjoy. Still others sell the flour for the pizza dough, or turn the wheat into flour, or grow the wheat. Through the division of labor, each of these can become highly skilled at very specialized tasks. In the aggregate, much more will be produced and enjoyed than if all of us are individually self-sufficient, growing our own wheat, making our own flour, concocting our own pizzas, and learning economics on our own.

A necessary accompaniment to such specialization is the ability to easily trade one's specialized product for the products of other specialists. And it is here that barter becomes burdensome. In a barter economy, if there is not what W. S. Jevons called a "double coincidence" of wants,[2] then each person must make a multiplicity of trades before the desired bundle of goods can be obtained. Too much time and energy is spent swapping goods, and too little is spent producing and enjoying them. **Barter is unworkably cumbersome and inefficient when there is an extensive division of labor, private ownership, and voluntary exchange. In modern economies, specialization and the use of money are so tightly linked that, as in the case of the chicken and the egg, it is impossible to say which came first.**

Commodity money In a pure barter economy, trades are made solely for direct consumption. However, trading is easier if everyone maintains an inventory of easily traded goods. In a mixed barter economy, some items are accepted in trade, not for consumption, but for trading later for desired consumables. This process is self-reinforcing. The more a certain item is used for trades, the more confidence people have in accepting it. The more confidence people have in accepting it, the more it will be used for trades. This intermediate item may become so popular for trading, that it becomes a *medium of exchange:* something that is commonly traded, not for consuming but for trading again. A commodity that becomes a medium of exchange is called a *commodity money.*

In practice, over the past 4000 years, the predominant commodity moneys have been precious metals: mostly silver, to a lesser extent gold, and even less frequently, copper. However, in generally small rural communities, the peoples of the world have also used an enormous variety of other commodity moneys, including whale teeth, fish hooks, sugar, silk, rum, and parrot feathers.

Fiat money For thousands of years, commodity moneys were preeminant. But now, modern industrial economies instead use *fiat money,* something that has little value as a commodity but, because of law or tradition, is accepted as a medium of exchange. Currently, all newly minted U. S. coins are inexpensive alloys made of copper, nickel, aluminum, and the like. All U.S. paper currency has no metal backing whatsoever. If you have a $10 bill, the government will not redeem it for gold, silver, or woodpecker scalps. It can be exchanged for two $5 bills, ten $1 bills, or a pocketful of alloy coins. But our government says that these alloy coins and paper money are legal tender, suitable for paying their bills and our taxes. And you and I greedily accept any that are offered, confident that they have value because we can exchange them for useful goods and services. **To each individual, fiat money has value because of laws or simple faith, conditioned by many years of successful exchanges. To a society, fiat money has value because it successfully serves as an inexpensive medium of exchange, avoiding the inefficiencies of barter.**

The price of money

The value of a $10 bill is measured by what can be obtained in exchange. As with all traded items, there is no absolute price, only innumerable relative prices. Say, for instance, that bread trades at $1 a loaf, wine at $5 a bottle, and steak at $5 a pound. What is the value of ten dollars? A $10 bill is worth ten loaves of bread, two bottles of wine, or two pounds of steak. In a monetary economy like that of the United States, prices of goods and services are usually expressed in terms of the medium of exchange, and other relative prices must be calculated implicitly. The price label on a bottle of wine says "$5", not "one pound of steak." The relative values of a dollar are the inverses of these conventional prices: If the price of wine is $5 per bottle, then the price of a dollar, measured in wine, is $1/P = 0.2$ bottles/dollar.

Thus a dollar has many prices, all of which are relative (and all the inverses of the usual price quotations seen in stores). In a market economy, these prices of a dollar (along with all relative prices) are simultaneously influenced by the demands and supplies of all traded items, including wine, steak, gold, bonds, and dollars.

Dollars are supplied by the government and demanded by private citizens as a temporary store of value until they are used as a medium of exchange. An increased demand for dollars will raise their price—that is, reduce conventionally measured prices. Conversely, an increased supply of dollars will reduce the price of dollars—that is, raise conventionally measured prices. If there were an unlimited supply of dollars, they (like clean air in the good old days) would be worthless, by which an economist means "free." If the price of money is zero, then conventionally quoted prices are infinite. In more familiar terminology, an unlimited expansion of the money supply creates hyperinflation. Conversely, **inexpensively produced paper money has value because it is useful as a medium of exchange and is in limited supply.**

We now look briefly at some specific factors that influence the amount of money that people want to hold. Then we will look at the variety of moneys and near-moneys that are available today.

THE DEMAND FOR MONEY

We begin with the original classical explanation of money demand. This approach is an important but incomplete theory. We will then examine Keynes' extension of it and the modern theory of money demand.

The quantity theory

Irving Fisher's classic approach[3] is based on the accounting observation that, in every transaction, a buyer must exchange a quantity of money equal to the price of the purchased item. A given stock of money, M, must be exchanged v_T (velocity) times to pay the T transactions involving items with an average price P_T:

$$Mv_T = P_T T. \tag{14.1}$$

This identity is called the "equation of exchange." If, on average, a dollar is held for a week between transactions, then it is exchanged 52 times a year ($v_T = 52$).

Fisher believed that velocity, the average number of times the money stock is exchanged per year, depends upon the institutional characteristics of transactions, which are predetermined. John Burr Williams argued succinctly:

> Whatever cash most people have in their purses or their checking accounts they are *compelled* to have there in order to pay their bills when the time comes. In consequence it may be said that the velocity of circulation of most cash balances is habitually kept at the maximum figure that the ingenuity of producers and consumers can devise under the existing customs of the country concerning the frequency of pay days, salary days, rent days, and settlements days for charge accounts, and that nothing could substantially increase the velocity of circulation of such cash and deposits as actually do circulate at all in the proper meaning of the term except to make pay days come daily instead of weekly, salary and rent days weekly instead of monthly, and tax days monthly instead of yearly.[4]

If velocity (v_T) is, in fact, predetermined, then Equation 14.1 implies the classical "quantity theory": the nominal volume of transactions is proportional to the quantity of money outstanding.

Later economists replaced transactions (T) with national income (y):

$$Mv = Py \tag{14.2}$$

where P is now a national income price index and v is the ratio of nominal output to the nominal money stock ($v = Py/M$). If v is predetermined, then Equation 14.2 implies that nominal income, Py, depends solely on the money supply, M.

The quantity theory has powerful implications but is not flawless. One fundamental difficulty arises from the imperfect relationship between transactions and production. Transactions are much larger than output and are not linked tightly to production. Some production occurs without transactions, and many transactions occur without production.

For example, GNP includes the imputed services provided by owner-occupied housing, but homeowners do not need money to pay themselves for such services. On the other side, in many transactions the dollars exchanged greatly exceed any production of new output. For intermediate goods, the value added at each step may be much less than the transaction price. For example, the value of a loaf of bread is far less than the total number of dollars that pass between the customer, grocer, baker, miller, and farmer. There are also many pure asset swaps that involve just an ownership transfer and no production whatsoever: old houses, used autos, antique furniture, early paintings, old gold, and all stocks and bonds.

This imperfect mesh between production and transactions weakens the quantity theory. The transactions velocity, v_T, is not really predetermined, since the velocity of asset swaps cannot plausibly be considered institutionally fixed.* And the replacement of transactions, T, with output, y, just shifts the theoretical difficulties by ignoring the need for money to carry out nonproduction exchange and by ignoring the fact that some production does not require exchange. There is no reason to consider output velocity, v, more institutionally predetermined than transactions velocity, v_T.

The Cambridge (England) cash-balances approach developed by Alfred Marshall and his disciple A.C. Pigou ended up with a quantity theory equation, too, but by somewhat different means. Instead of emphasizing the use of money to pay bills, they emphasized money's role as a store of wealth between the sale of items and the purchase of others. When you plan to make purchases, it often makes good sense to hold dollars in anticipation of these transactions. Money is thus a store of value held in anticipation of purchases. People's decisions about how much money to hold will be strongly influenced by their income and expenditures. Marshall and Pigou also briefly noted that the rates of return on other stores of wealth (such as bonds and land) will influence money holdings, but assumed that these rates of return were either constant or else

* Williams admitted that "The price level for stocks and bonds and real estate, however, which are not produced and consumed, and are not bought out of income, and do not require time for passing from one purchaser to the next as goods in process of manufacture do, and which can even be "swapped" back and forth between traders at rising prices without the use of any cash at all . . . does not depend on the quantity of money in circulation."[5]

(conveniently) moved proportionately to income in the short run, so that the nominal demand for money, M^D, is simply proportional to nominal income:

$$M^D = kPy. \tag{14.3}$$

Setting money demand equal to money supply, M, then gives

$$M = kPy \tag{14.4}$$

which, by interpreting $v = 1/k$, is no different from the quantity theory's equation of exchange (Equation 14.2).

But the Cambridge route to this equation was to have profound consequences for economic theory. By emphasizing money as a store of value rather than a means of payment, the Cambridge economists shifted attention away from the technical institutional details constraining the frequency of transactions to an economic analysis of the demand for money. This reinterpretation of the equation of exchange as a money-demand-equals-money-supply condition revolutionized monetary theory by admitting the possibility that velocity is not fixed by society's bill-paying customs.

Keynes' approach

Keynes, a student of Marshall, later joined him on the Cambridge University faculty. Keynes' views on velocity were a revolutionary, and yet, quite logical extension of Marshall's cash-balances theory. Keynes' contribution was to emphasize the decisive influence of rates of return on the decision to hold wealth in the form of money. Whereas classical economists believed that the proximate determinant of the interest rate is the equilibration of investment and saving, Keynes instead emphasized the equilibration of the demand for and supply of money:

> the rate of interest cannot be a return to saving or waiting as such . . . The rate of interest is the reward for parting with liquidity . . . [It] is a measure of the willingness of those who possess money to part with their liquid control over it. The rate of interest is not the "price" which brings into equilibrium the demand for resources to invest with the readiness to abstain from present consumption. It is the "price" which equilibrates the desire to hold wealth in the form of cash with the availability of cash.[6]

This argument directly attacks the quantity theory: If the demand for money depends on interest rates, then velocity depends on interest rates.

The evidence indicates overwhelmingly that money demand does depend on interest rates and that velocity is not constant. Dozens of competent empirical studies have concluded that interest rates do have a significant inverse effect on money demand. (One survey of such studies was reported by David Laidler.[7])

Figures 14.1 and 14.2 give some very crude evidence of the effects of interest rates on money demand and velocity. (The yield on three-month Treasury bills is used as a representative interest rate.) Figure 14.1 looks at money demand relative to nominal GNP, M/Py, while Figure 14.2 looks at velocity. These figures are two ways of saying the same thing. When interest rates have been high, money demand has been low and velocity has been high.

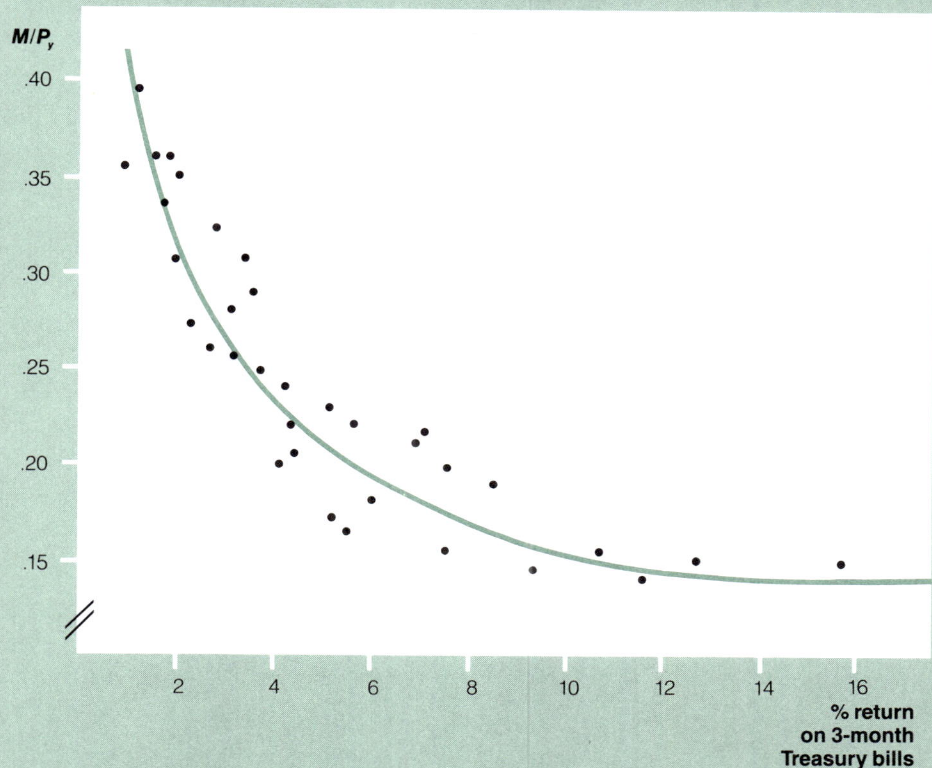

FIGURE 14.1 MONEY DEMAND (RELATIVE TO NOMINAL GNP) AND THE TREASURY BILL RATE, 1950–83. **Money demand has fallen as interest rates have risen. Money, which pays little or no interest, is less attractive when the alternatives offer high interest rates.**

There is also some familiar dramatic evidence. Both physical and financial assets are alternatives to holding money. Like that on a financial asset, the nominal return on a physical asset is the income or services it provides plus its price appreciation, net of taxes and transaction costs. In a rapid inflation, physical assets have very high nominal rates of return. If the demand for money is sensitive to the nominal yields on alternative assets, then during a rapid inflation, money demand should fall sharply and velocity should increase greatly. This is exactly what happens. The essence of a hyperinflation is a flight from currency (an extreme attempt to economize on money balances when prices are rising rapidly)—a flight that pushes prices up even faster. For example, in the Hungarian hyperinflation between August 1945 and July 1946, the velocity of the Hungarian pengo increased by a factor of 300. In more normal times, velocity does not change this drastically, but it is still positively related to interest rates.

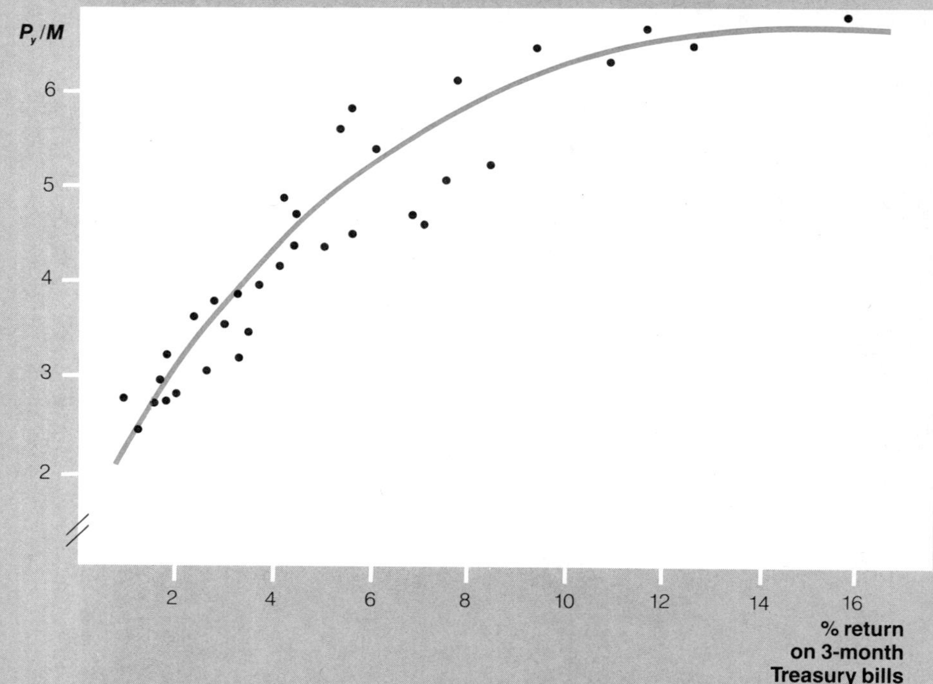

FIGURE 14.2 VELOCITY AND THE TREASURY BILL RATE, 1950–83. Velocity (Py/M) is the inverse of money demand (M/Py). Thus another way to describe the decline in money demand when interest rates increase is to say that velocity increases as people hold money for shorter periods.

While noting that each individual's money is held in a single pool and "need not be sharply divided even in his own mind," Keynes found it helpful to identify three separate motives for holding money: transactions, precautionary, and speculative. The first, the "transactions" motive, was very much in the Cambridge cash-balances tradition:

One reason for holding cash is to bridge the interval between the receipt of income and its disbursement. The strength of this motive . . . will chiefly depend upon the amount of income and the normal length of the interval between its receipt and its disbursement.[8]

Keynes' second (precautionary) motive was:

To provide for contingencies requiring sudden expenditure and for unforeseen opportunities of advantageous purchases . . .

The strength of [this] motive will partly depend on the cheapness and the reliability of methods of obtaining cash, when it is required, by some form of temporary borrowing, in particular by overdraft or its equivalent. For there is no necessity to

> hold idle cash to bridge over intervals if it can be obtained without difficulty at the moment when it is actually required. Their strength will also depend on what we may term the relative cost of holding cash. If the cash can only be retained by foregoing the purchase of a profitable asset, this increases the cost and thus weakens the motive towards holding a given amount of cash.[9]

Early interpreters of Keynes stressed his third motive, the "speculative": When interest rates rise, bond prices fall, giving capital losses to those holding bonds. Money will be held by investors who are sufficiently bearish (pessimistic) on bond prices so that the anticipated capital losses outweigh the interest income. Keynes argued that "what matters is not the ***absolute*** level of r but the degree of its divergence from what is considered a fairly *safe* level of r."[10] When the government buys bonds, this "must raise the price of bonds sufficiently to exceed the expectations of some 'bull' and so influence him to sell his bond for cash and join the 'bear' brigade."[11] Thus an increase in the money supply is absorbed by those speculators who are convinced that the lower interest rates do not provide enough income to offset the risk that rates will rise back to more normal levels. This justification for an interest-sensitive money demand doesn't live up to Keynes' use of the rubric "the general theory," since it only applies when people expect interest rates to rise, and can only be a temporary phenomenon since people will adjust their perceptions of what is normal if low interest rates persist.

James Tobin[12] used the ideas of risk aversion and diversified portfolios to generalize Keynes' argument that investors will hold money even when they are worried about bond prices. In Keynes' approach, speculators switch from bonds to money when an anticipated decline in bond prices reduces the expected return on bonds to less than that on money. Tobin showed that even when bond prices are considered as likely to rise as fall, risk-averse investors will hold both bonds and money to diversify their portfolios.

In the Keynes-Tobin dichotomy between "money" and "bonds," money includes all assets with safe, fixed returns: cash, fixed-interest deposits, and Treasury bills with the same maturity date as the investor's planning horizon. Tobin's portfolio arguments show why investors hold low-yielding fixed-interest assets, and show how that demand is sensitive to interest rates. But they do not explain the distribution of that demand among cash, checking accounts, savings accounts, and Treasury bills. Such an explanation must be based on other considerations such as liquidity, divisibility, and transactions costs. We will look at some of the details of factors determining asset selection in Chapter 15.

Economists today emphasize not Keynes' speculative motive, but his reasoning in explaining the precautionary motive. The fundamental reason money is held is the lack of synchronization between receipts and payments. If all bills were paid at a single location on payday, and expenses never exceeded income, there would be no need to hold a means of payment. But with an imperfect synchronization, funds must be held or readily accessible in order to pay for day-to-day and extraordinary expenses. Because of their convenience, means of payment will be held even if they pay little or no interest.

However, the higher the returns offered on alternative assets, the greater the incentive to hold less means of payment. Individuals will temporarily invest funds in these alternative interest-earning assets and will try to coordinate in-

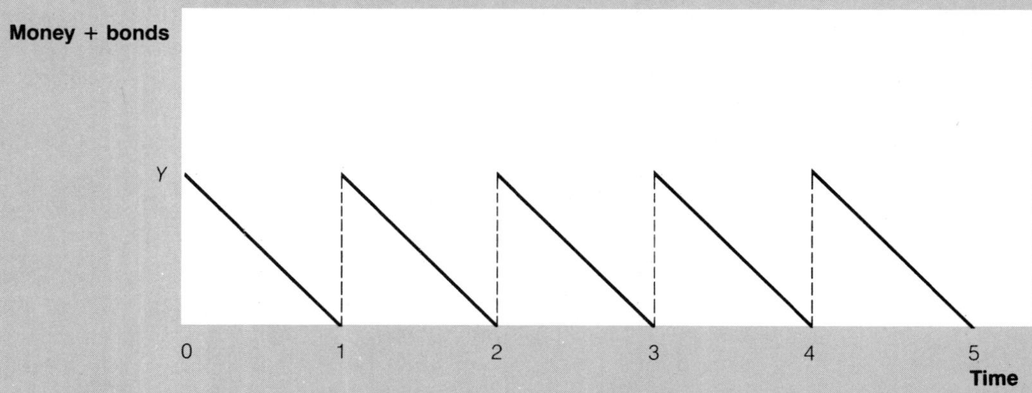

FIGURE 14.3 THE SAWTOOTH WEALTH PROFILE. **Assets are depleted by continual spending and replenished by periodic income.**

come and disbursement. These pressures may incite institutional changes such as more frequent payment or more flexible payment schedules, reduced lags between the payment and receipt of funds, higher yields on means of payment, and less costly transfer between means of payment and other assets. Very high interest rates in recent years have spawned many such changes in the United States. These institutional changes are evidence that money demand really is inversely related to interest rates.

An inventory model

To illustrate the role of imperfect synchronization, Tobin constructed a simple money inventory model,[13] which is sketched below. (For our purposes it is the general principles rather than the specific details of derivation that are important.)

In Tobin's model there are two assets. One is a means of payment—"money" that does not earn interest; the other, a non-means of payment—"bonds" that earn a nominal interest rate, R, but incur a transaction cost, C, whenever they are purchased or sold. Nominal income, Y, is received at evenly spaced intervals, while spending occurs continuously and uniformly throughout each period. There is no net saving in that spending exhausts each period's income. At the beginning of each period, total assets (money plus bonds) equal income that has just been received. As payments are made during the period, total assets steadily decline to zero. This pattern is shown in Figure 14.3.

One asset strategy is to hold only money. This strategy avoids asset transaction costs, but earns no interest. An extreme alternative is to invest all of one's income in bonds at the start of each period, and then sell these bonds continuously to pay expenses. This strategy maximizes interest income, but incurs astronomical transaction costs. A more moderate strategy is to hold some money and temporarily invest some funds in the interest-earning asset.

Consider a two-transaction strategy in which a fraction of income is invested in bonds at the beginning of each period and then withdrawn part way through the period in order to pay the remaining expenses. The portfolio profile is depicted in Figure 14.4. Interest revenue (before transaction costs) is proportional to the shaded areas of these diagrams. A square maximizes this shaded area and therefore maximizes interest revenue. Thus interest revenue is maximized if half of income is invested in bonds for half of the period.

With three transactions, interest revenue is maximized by investing $2Y/3$ initially, withdrawing $Y/3$ after one-third of the period has elapsed, and then withdrawing the remaining $Y/3$ two-thirds of the way through the period. This strategy is shown in Figure 14.5.

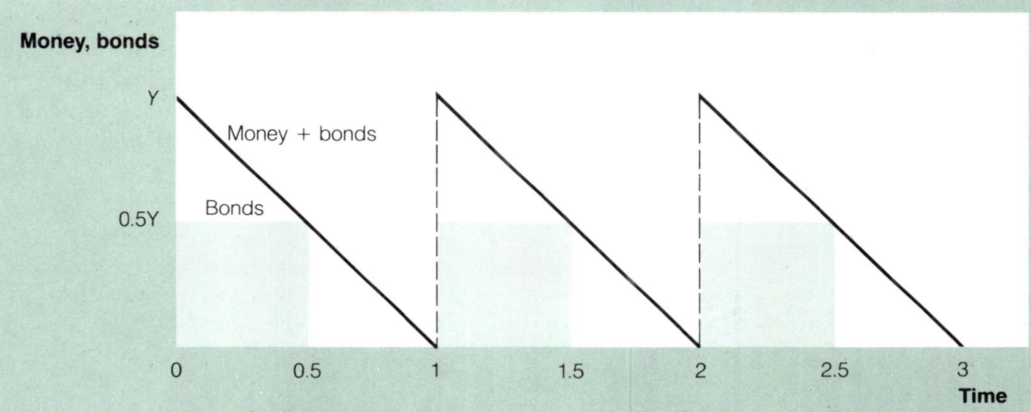

FIGURE 14.4 **THE BEST TWO-TRANSACTION STRATEGY. If two bond transactions are made each period, the most profitable strategy is to use half of income to buy bonds and then sell them half way through the period.**

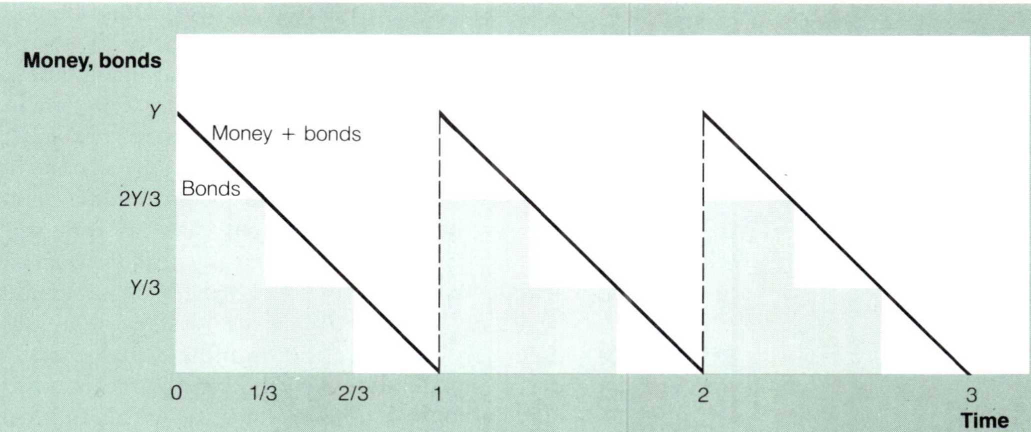

FIGURE 14.5 **THE BEST THREE-TRANSACTION STRATEGY. If three bond transactions are made each period, the most profitable strategy is to use two-thirds of income to buy bonds and then sell these bonds at evenly spaced intervals.**

In general, for n transactions, the optimal strategy is to invest $(n-1)Y/n$ at first and then withdraw Y/n at intervals of $1/n$ of the length of the period between income receipts. Tobin showed that interest revenue net of transaction costs is $(n-1)RY/2n - nC$, and that average money holdings are $Y/2n$. The remaining question is the optimal number of transactions, n. A little calculus yields the answer:*

$$n = (RY/2C)^{1/2}. \tag{14.5}$$

Average money holdings, M, are given by the *square-root rule*:

$$M = Y/2n = (CY/2R)^{1/2}. \tag{14.6}$$

The square-root rule implies that the demand for money is positively related to both income and transaction costs and inversely related to the interest rate. In each case, the absolute value for the elasticity of money demand is ½.

If we let real income be $y = Y/P$ and the real cost of a transaction be $c = C/P$, then the square-root rule (Equation 14.6), can be rewritten as

$$M = (cPyP/2R)^{1/2} = (c/2R)^{1/2}\ Py^{1/2} \tag{14.7}$$

In contrast, the simple quantity theory is $Mv = Py$ (Equation 14.2). According to the square-root rule, velocity (Py/M) is

$$\frac{Py}{(c/2R)^{1/2}\ Py^{1/2}} = \left(\frac{2Ry}{c}\right)^{1/2}$$

The first of two noteworthy points is that each person's velocity is positively related to the nominal interest rate and inversely related to the real cost of making transactions. (People economize on money balances when high interest rates and low transaction costs make it attractive to hold bonds temporarily.) Second of the two points is that each person's velocity rises with income. The demand for money does not rise as fast as nominal income because there are economies of scale in the acquisition of bonds. Interest income is proportional to the size of bond holdings; but transaction costs (trips to the bank, telephone calls, broker fees) do not rise proportionately with the size of the transaction. High-income agents will consequently hold proportionately less money than low-income agents. For the nation as a whole, this reasoning suggests that velocity rises as aggregate real income increases. This conclusion contrasts sharply with the simple quantity theory, in which real money demand is proportional to real income, so that velocity does not depend on income.

However, the inventory model applies to individual agents, and some caution must be exercised in extending it to the aggregate economy. If individual per capita household and business income increase with c and R constant, then aggregate velocity will indeed increase. However, aggregate real income could also increase because of population growth—that is, an increase in the number of households and businesses. If the income distribution is constant, then new

* This result assumes that n can be fractional, but it can not. If we restrict n to be a whole number, then transactions should be increased until the point where $n(n+1) > RY/2C$, which is not much different from Equation 14.5 for large n.

agents will hold the same money-to-income ratios as old agents, and aggregate velocity will be constant. Velocity is also unchanged if an increase in the price level raises nominal income and transaction costs proportionately. Thus **an increase in real per capita income should raise velocity, but an increase in population or the price level may leave velocity unchanged.**

George Akerlof and Ross Milbourne have calculated aggregate income and interest rate elasticities for a variety of assumptions about C and R, using an income distribution based on 1970 U.S. Census data. Their interest elasticities are reasonably large when transaction expenses are moderate, and their aggregate income elasticities are significantly less than one.[14]

However, the Akerlof-Milbourne calculations predict an aggregate demand for money that is only 30% of the size of actual holdings. Households actually have about $1500 each in their checking accounts. There is also about $100 billion in currency outside of banks. It is not known who holds this but if households hold two-thirds of it, that would be almost $1000 per household. It is hard to explain such large money holdings. Probably the most important factor is that transactions are much larger than national income because of intermediate goods, asset swaps, and covert activity. In addition, some money is held out of precautionary motives, and deposits are sometimes held, not for transactions, but as implicit compensation for various services provided by banks.

The basic inventory model can be extended in a variety of directions. One modification is to allow transaction costs to increase (but less than proportionately with the size of transactions). This tends to reduce the optimal number of transactions, increase average money holdings, and increase the interest elasticity of money holdings. A more complex extension is to allow uncertainty about future income and expenses, with some penalty cost of illiquidity if money balances turn out to be inadequate. This modification leads to the holding of extra, precautionary money balances whose magnitude is inversely related to the interest rate, positively related to the penalty for illiquidity, and positively related to the degree of uncertainty about future cash flow.

Such extensions do not upend the basic conclusions of inventory cash-management models:

1. *Money demand is positively related to income.* Because of economies of scale in cash management, low-income households and businesses hold relatively more money than high-income agents. As a nation's real per capita income increases, money demand rises less than proportionately and velocity increases.

2. *Money demand is negatively related to the nominal interest rate on alternative assets.* When interest rates are high, households and businesses reduce money balances, and velocity increases.

3. *Money demand is positively related to the transaction costs incurred in switching back and forth between money and interest-earning assets.* Institutional developments that reduce such transfer costs reduce money demand and increase velocity.

THE SUPPLY OF MONEY

The use of a commodity as money means that less of it is available for use as a commodity, and more time and effort are spent stockpiling it for monetary uses. The story is told of how a Chinese community once used canned sardines as a commodity money. One day, a hungry man opened a can of sardine money and was disappointed to find that the sardines had been used as money for so long that they were now spoilt. "These sardines," he was rebuked, "are for money, not for eating." Yet their use as money meant that there were that many fewer fish available for eating. Similarly, today, the fact that the United States can save tens of millions of dollars a year by making pennies out of aluminum rather than copper accurately reflects the fact that copper can be employed more usefully in things other than pennies. This is why Keynes called the use of gold as money a "barbarous relic" that wasted valuable resources in the digging of holes in the ground (a.k.a. gold mining). Tongue in cheek, he suggested the easier, free-market expedient (for increasing the money supply) of putting paper currency in empty wine bottles, and burying them in easily accessible mine shafts.

But, turning this argument around, a prime virtue of a commodity money such as gold is that its limited availability prevents governments from arbitrarily explosive expansion of the money supply. With hard money, it is exceedingly difficult to create a hyperinflation. Thus hard money is traditionally advocated by those who favor stable prices. Creditors, of course, are first in line. For sound personal reasons, they object to debts being repaid with cheapened currency. Established merchants are also often supporters of hard currency. Trade is easier and less worrisome when you can be confident of what the dollars you accept today will buy tomorrow.

The prices of precious metals, the historically predominant hard moneys, have not been entirely stable. For instance, the extraction of precious metals from the Americas during the sixteenth century quintupled prices in Spain. The California gold discoveries caused inflation in the 1850s, as did increased gold supplies at the turn of the century. The incentives to melt silver coins in the United States in the 1960s rose because sluggish supplies and rapidly increasing commodity demands (for example, for electronic components and photographic film) pushed silver prices sharply higher. Gyrations in gold and silver prices recently made front-page news.

Despite the admitted vagaries in precious-metal prices, hard-money enthusiasts have always argued that hard money is still better than trusting governments to create soft money. In the famous 1811 British debate on the gold standard, David Ricardo conceded that precious metals "are themselves subject to greater variations than it is desirable a standard should be subject to. They are, however, the best with which we are acquainted. . . . [Without a precious-metal standard, money] would be exposed to all the fluctuations to which the ignorance or the interests of the issuers might subject it."[15]

The debate over commodity money versus fiat money reflects a deep philosophical disagreement over whether governments do things *for* citizens or *to* them. On the one side are those who believe that governments greedily exploit the citizenry or stupidly bungle well-meaning attempts at economic stabilization. On the other side are those who believe that educated governments can do things for the common good, here specifically, that governments can intelligently and beneficially manage a nation's money supply. It is then not necessary to divert precious metals from precious uses. Nor is it necessary to abandon a nation's money supply to the vagaries of commercial demand and discovery: Fiat money can be reliably and steadily provided to accommodate commerce and serve dutifully as a medium of exchange.

This debate over hard versus soft money has gone on for many years and has often been heated. But it is increasingly just an academic quarrel that becomes less and less relevant each year. Most of what economists call money is now supplied by banks and other financial institutions. And the future will most likely bring the softest money of all: invisible electronic money.

We will now examine how banks "create" money and then look at several different private moneys.

Bank money

Governments create fiat money simply by printing it and declaring that it is legal tender. Redemptions can be satisfied by printing more of the same, two $5 bills for every $10 bill. As long as nothing more is promised, they need never fear a run on the government with anxious citizens rushing to redeem their currency.* Banks create soft money a bit more mysteriously and a little more dangerously. A run on the bank is a banker's nightmare.

The earliest banks simply stored precious metals for safekeeping, with the depositors paying for this service. When a bank does no more than this, and as long as sufficient armed guards are provided, there is no danger of a bank run and bankruptcy. Each depositor's funds will always be there, collecting dust in some cupboard. If banks operated in this fashion, simply keeping records and guarding a safe full of safe deposit boxes, depositors would be completely protected and banks would not create money. This practice is called "100% reserves."

Banks create money (and risks) when they do not keep all deposits in their safe, but instead loan some of it. As the cynical Mr. Dooley once said, bankers "take care of your money by lending it out to their friends." Keeping only a fraction of deposits on hand is called *fractional reserve banking*. The fractional reserve is the fraction, λ, of deposits that is kept in reserve in the bank vault. The remaining fraction, $1 - \lambda$, is loaned.

Assume that the fraction kept is .1 and that all bank deposits are checking accounts (and, thus, considered to be "money"). If $100 in Federal Reserve notes is deposited in a bank, the bank will keep $10 and lend $90. The person who borrowed the $90 undoubtedly has some worthwhile purpose in mind for the loan. She will soon take the $90 out of the bank and buy something with it. The seller receives $90 and may well decide to deposit it in a bank. If so, he will be credited with a $90 deposit, and this second bank will now have $90 to loan out.

If this bank keeps 10% of this $90 and loans out the remaining $81, then this $81 may be spent and returned to a third bank as yet another deposit. A pattern is definitely appearing. On each round, 90% of the previous deposit is loaned out and then redeposited in a bank. These deposits are $100, $90, $81, . . . If we look far ahead and add up all of these deposits, the sum will be found to be $1000. The sum of the reserves in all of the banks' vaults is $10 + 9 + 8.1 + \ldots = 100$. The banks have converted the initial $100 of government money into $1000 of bank money. Is this magic? No, it's banking.

Except for the possible profits on its lending activities, these banks have not

* There is the danger though of hyperinflation, a flight from currency in which citizens rush to exchange money for goods with other citizens. Such a social crisis might well topple a government.

created any wealth. The banks' assets are the dollars they loaned out and those they held as reserves. Their liabilities are the deposits, their debts to the depositors. The banks' ledgers balance, since every dollar deposited is either loaned out or held as reserves:

	Assets		Liabilities
	$ 10	reserve	$ 100 deposit
	$ 90	loan	
	$ 9	reserve	$ 90 deposit
	$ 81	loan	
	$ 8.1	reserve	$ 81 deposit
	$ 72.9	loan	
TOTALS	$100	reserves	$1000 deposits
	$900	loans	

The banks have a total of $1000 in deposits, $900 in outstanding loans, and $100 in reserves. As for the citizens, depositors have a total of $1000 in assets and borrowers have a total of $900 in debts. For the private economy as a whole, net financial wealth is $100, the initial amount of government money. The banks have not created any financial wealth. What they have done is erect an elaborate structure by means of which some citizens have borrowed $900 from other citizens. In this role as intermediary between borrowers and lenders, banks may well stimulate the economy. To the extent bank deposits serve as money, banks may also facilitate trade.

If there were no banks, and citizens simply loaned money directly to other citizens, borrowers and lenders would have to work out the repayment terms among themselves. In general, borrowers will quickly spend the borrowed money and hope to pay it back in the future. Perhaps they will use the money to open a store, and then use the profits from the store to pay back the loan. Or perhaps they are borrowing money to buy a car, a house, or furniture, and will use their future labor income to pay off the loan. In either case, they probably do not plan to repay the loan for some time, and do not want to repay it until they are good and ready. Borrowers would like a fixed, long-term repayment schedule or, even better, to decide themselves when to pay off their loans.

Lenders have different preferences. They are investing their money by loaning it at interest, but may well prefer to always have the money available if needed. They would like to have the right to call in their loan and demand repayment. With this fundamental conflict, few private loans will be made and those that are will require one or both sides to settle for less than they would like.

The miracle of banking, and its great economic virtue, is that both borrowers and lenders can be accommodated. If you loan money to a friend, you have an illiquid asset. You cannot use the IOU to buy anything and you will have a tough time trying to sell it to raise cash. If instead you deposit your money in a bank and the bank loans this money to your friend, then you have a very liquid asset. **By loaning your money through a bank, you transform an illiquid asset into a liquid asset. The bank monetizes your loan.**

Lenders deposit their money in banks and are permitted to withdraw it whenever they please. The banks loan money to borrowers with fixed repayment schedules that are convenient and consistent with the borrower's planned use of the funds. Both lenders and borrowers are happy, and many more loans are made than would occur in the absence of banks. It is because they fulfill this valuable public service that banks have throughout history been so popular, pervasive, and profitable.

The darker side is that banks succeed only when all depositors do not in fact show up at once to demand their deposits. With a large number of depositors and a reasonable store of reserves, a bank can easily satisfy the occasional depositor who needs funds. As long as depositors believe that their deposits can be claimed at any time, few will actually want to claim them. The danger is that they may lose faith. When depositors think that they may not be able to withdraw their deposits, they will all rush to try. The bank, unable to retrieve immediately the loans it has made with their money, will collapse. This is the fundamental tension in banking that has permitted enormous social benefits and caused unforgettable panics. Fortunately, since the 1930s, modern banks have been pretty successful in handling this tension.

The deposit multiplier So this is the dangerous magic by which banks create money. A simple model can generalize the results. If the fractional reserve ratio is λ, not necessarily .1, then of each \$1 of government money deposited in a bank, λ is held and $1 - \lambda$ is loaned. For each individual bank, reserves are a fraction λ of deposits. The same is true of the banking system as a whole. When the whole business of deposit creation is completed, total bank reserves will be a fraction, λ, of total deposits D. Thus bank reserves $= \lambda D$, and $D = \dfrac{\text{bank reserves}}{\lambda}$. If the supply of government fiat money is H, and if all of this government money ends up as reserves, then the banking system converts every dollar of government money into $1/\lambda$ dollars of deposits:

$$D = H/\lambda \tag{14.9}$$

(Thus, when λ was .1, as before, 100 dollars of government money yielded 100/.1, or 1000 dollars in deposits.)

The smaller λ is, the less banks hold in reserves, the more they loan, and the more deposits are created. If only one penny of every dollar is held as reserves ($\lambda = .01$), then bank deposits will be 100 times the supply of government money ($D = 100H$). What if $\lambda = 0$? Then every dollar deposited is loaned, and no reserves are held. If these loans are redeposited and loaned again and again, then the total deposits that can be created is infinite.

Early banks, which printed their own bank notes, could and did expand deposits astronomically. When you are just printing paper, your loans can be larger than your deposits. You can have one million dollars in deposits, but print two, five, ten, or 100 million dollars in notes to lend to wide-eyed entrepreneurs or a thankful government. As long as these notes just pass from hand to hand, and borrowers never try to redeem them for hard coin, you can remain in the printing business. But you have created a double jeopardy; depositors might try to claim their deposits and borrowers might try to redeem their paper loans. The wildest successes and most spectacular crashes in banking history accompanied such practices.

One complication, so far neglected, is that not all loaned money finds its way back into banks. Citizens hold government money outside of banks for use as a medium of exchange. The amount of this privately held currency will be assumed proportional to deposits: γD. We should also recognize that much of the reserves held by modern banks are there by legal necessity. Federal Reserve Board *reserve requirements* compel banks to hold some fraction of their deposits as reserves. Any reserves voluntarily held beyond those required by the Fed are called *excess reserves.* Excess reserves are held so that banks can satisfy normal deposit withdrawals without falling below required reserves. Bank demand for excess reserves depends on perceived withdrawal risks and the availability of attractive investments. Banks will hold large excess reserves when withdrawal risks are great or when there are few tempting opportunities to invest these funds.

Total bank reserves, required plus excess, also will be assumed proportional to deposits: λD. In practice, banks these days hold very little excess reserves, so that λ is determined mostly by the reserve requirements that are set by the Fed.

We're now ready to put the model together. The stock of government money (H) is called the nation's *monetary base* and is held either as currency outside of banks or as bank reserves; thus $H = (\gamma + \lambda)D$. Solving this for D, the total level of deposits that can be supported by the government monetary base, gives

$$D = \left(\frac{1}{\gamma + \lambda}\right)H \tag{14.10}$$

in which the parenthetical term is the *deposit multiplier,* the ratio of bank deposits to the monetary base. Because the monetary base can support a much larger quantity of bank money, economists often refer to the monetary base as *high-powered money.*

Using some actual figures can illustrate the implications of Equation 14.10. Some round-number estimates for γ and λ in 1980 are:

$$\gamma = \frac{\text{currency outside banks}}{\text{bank deposits}} = \frac{120}{1000} = 0.12$$

$$\lambda = \frac{\text{bank reserves}}{\text{bank deposits}} = \frac{50}{1000} = 0.05$$

The monetary base was \$170 billion. If we plug these data into the equation we obtain the level of deposits:

$$D = \frac{1}{\gamma + \lambda}H = \frac{1}{0.12 + 0.05}\,170 = \frac{170}{0.17} = 1000.$$

Thus, in 1980, the bank deposit multiplier was 1/0.17, or 5.88. Every dollar in government money supported about six dollars in commercial bank deposits.

This multiplier of about 6 would be altered if either of the parameters, γ or λ, were changed.* In particular, an increase in either of these parameters would

* Seemingly small changes in these parameters can have large effects on deposit creation. If γ rose to 0.15, or λ rose to 0.08, the deposit multiplier would fall to 5, and deposits would contract to 850. If γ fell to 0.09, or λ to 0.02, the multiplier would rise to 7, and deposits would expand to 1200.

reduce the multiplier and reduce the amount of deposits supported by government money. If the currency-to-deposit ratio (γ) is higher, then a larger fraction of the money loaned by banks is held by the public rather than redeposited in banks. With less money returning to be reloaned and redeposited, fewer bank deposits are created. Similarly, if the bank reserve-to-deposit ratio (λ) is higher, then a larger fraction of the money deposited in banks is held by banks rather than loaned. With less money escaping to be redeposited and reloaned, fewer bank deposits are created.

What, for example, would be the effect on bank deposits of an increase in the interest rates that banks can earn on their loans? Higher loan yields encourage banks to hold less idle reserves. A decline in λ increases the deposit multiplier, and so increases the amount of deposits supported by a given monetary base. What about higher interest rates on bank deposits themselves? Households would then view currency as less attractive relative to deposits, and the resulting decline in γ would increase the deposit multiplier. So, **higher interest rates in general tend to reduce both γ and λ, thereby increasing bank deposits relative to the monetary base.**

Finally, what if it is a reduction in the monetary base that causes the higher interest rates? We have just seen that the deposit multiplier will expand. Therefore, a contractionary monetary policy that increases interest rates will tend to increase bank deposits. If these bank deposits serve as money, then a change in the quantity of government money tends to induce a partly offsetting change in the quantity of bank money.

These are the standard mechanics for demonstrating and calculating how banks multiply government money into bank deposits. One large pitfall to be avoided is the easy assumption that the various parameters are constants, etched in stone through the ages. Reserve requirements can and have been changed by government. Currency holdings, deposit holdings, and excess reserves are determined by the preferences of citizens and banks, and subject to change without notice. The government may try to influence and estimate these parameters, but they cannot be taken for granted.

In 1980, the bank deposit multiplier was about 6. In that year \$170 billion in government money supported \$1000 billion in bank deposits. This does not mean that a \$10 billion increase in H will necessarily raise D by \$60 billion. It will if the various behavioral parameters are constant. It won't if these parameters change. (In conventional economic jargon, D will expand by \$60 billion only if marginal behavior is equal to average.)

In practice, increases in H are likely to affect the parameters of the bank deposit multiplier. If output and prices rise, people will want to hold more cash and checking account deposits to carry out the increased transactions. If the interest rate and expected rate of inflation increase, people will want to hold less currency and fewer deposits that pay little or no interest. By how much will the parameters and the deposit multipliers change? That will require some careful thought and empirical study. It is not safe to blithely assume that they will be constant.

Two simple general observations can be made. The first is that deposit multipliers, and hence monetary aggregates, can be and have been changed by private-sector behavior. For example, in the Great Depression banking panics, many anxious depositors withdrew what they could from banks. This caused γ, the ratio of currency outside banks to bank deposits, to jump upward. In addition, bank excess reserves swelled enormously, due to fears of bank runs and a perceived absence of attractive loan opportunities. From $48 million in December 1929, excess reserves grew to $6.6 billion in December 1940. These changes, as our model indicates, exerted an enormous contractionary effect on the deposit multiplier. The deposit multiplier fell from over 3 in 1929, to 2 in 1935, and to 1.5 in 1940.

Figure 14.6 shows the historical behavior of two money multipliers—M1 (currency plus checking accounts) and M2 (M1 plus time deposits). Here you can see the monetary collapse in the 1930s and the fact that money multipliers also wiggle around quite a bit in more normal times. Remember, a 10% change in a money multiplier corresponds to a 10% change in the monetary aggregate, which can be the difference between a reckless boom and a stiff recession. Note also that, excepting the banking collapse in the 1930s, the long-run trend in M2/*H* has been strongly upward. This surge reflects the long-run growth of banks. Banks today create many more deposits than they used to. On the other hand, M1/*H* has been relatively stagnant since World War II. This stagnation

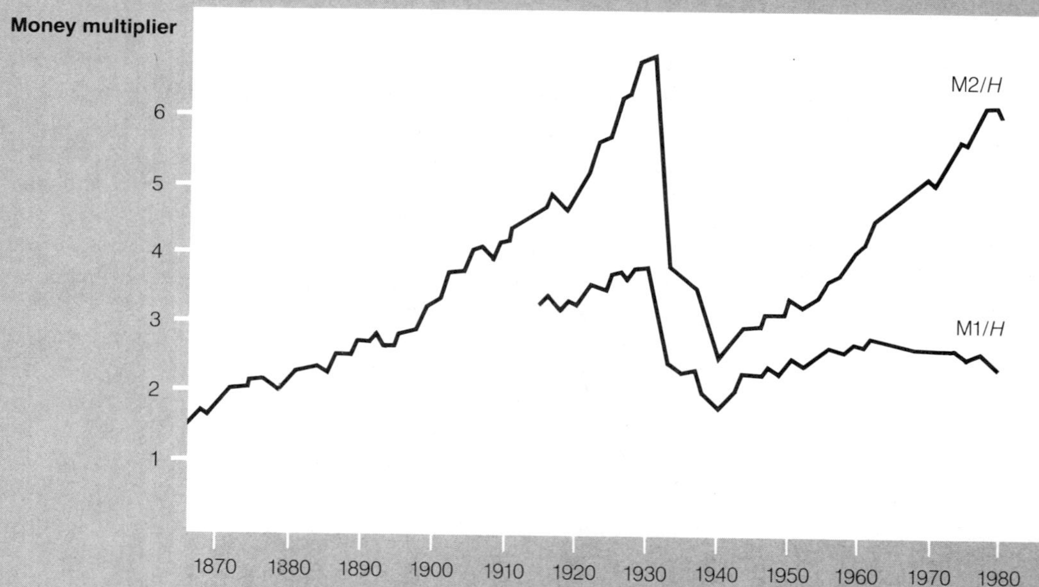

FIGURE 14.6 **THE MONEY MULTIPLIERS increased substantially and then collapsed during the Great Depression. Since World War II the money multiplier for M2 has resumed its upward trend, while that for M1 has been sluggish. Along the way there have been many small ups and downs in both.**

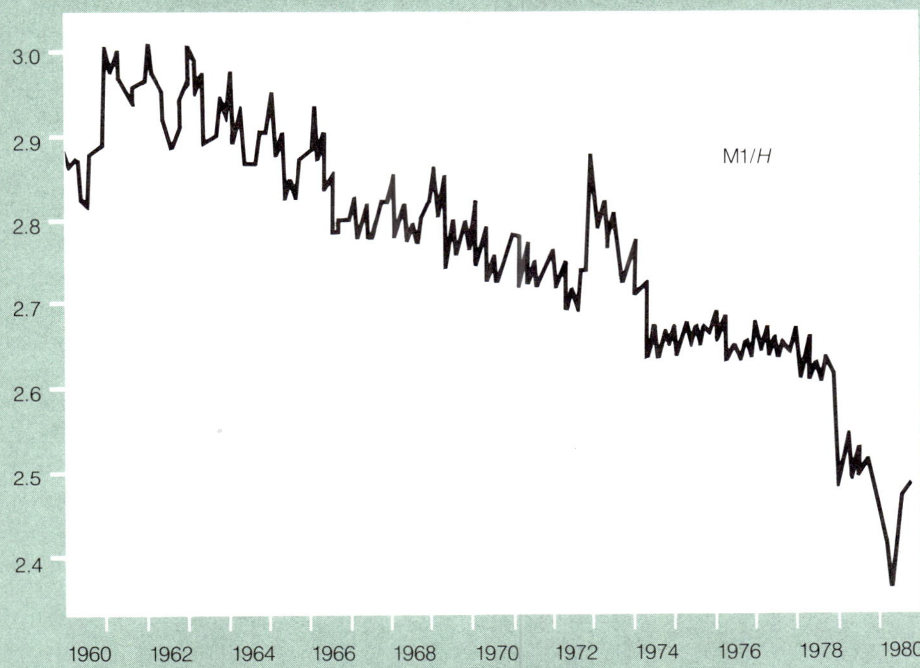

FIGURE 14.7 MONTHLY MONEY MULTIPLIER FOR M1. **Short-term data show considerable variation. For instance, the monthly M1 multiplier is very erratic.**

reflects the rapid growth of credit cards and other attractive alternatives to bank checking accounts.

The data in Figure 14.6 are annual averages that smooth out the day-to-day fluctuations in the money multipliers. Figure 14.7 shows the monthly M1 money multiplier data for 1960–80. With the annual data in Figure 14.6, the 1960–80 period looks pretty sedate. The monthly data in Figure 14.7 give a sharply contrasting picture of erratic fluctuations. Short-term money multipliers are far from constant.

MONEY TODAY

As the epigraph (from 1899!) to this chapter indicates, there has long been disagreement about the proper definition of money. This debate is still unresolved, and data are currently collected on many different monetary aggregates. As financial markets have evolved, new aggregates have been constructed and old aggregates revised. In the 1950s, M1 and M2 were very popular. Then financial market innovations led observers to concoct M3, M4, M5 and on and on; the list grew as the years went by. In some circles double-digit Ms became popular. There were even variations labeled M1+ and M2′.

Then, in 1980, the Fed switched to an almost completely revised set of monetary aggregates: M1A, M1B, M2, M3 and L. Then "M1B-shift adjusted" surfaced in 1981 and M1A sank in 1982. This bewildering plethora of monetary aggregates creates considerable difficulties for harried economics students (and their instructors). As with many popular songs, by the time you learn the words they are no longer popular.

The important moral in all this is that there is no firm, fixed definition of "money." By the time you read these words, the monetary aggregates described here will probably already be out-of-date. In addition, at any moment in time, there is no clear choice as to which, if any, monetary aggregate should be called "money." To those who attach almost mystical significance to money, this is a matter of great importance. If you believe that changes in the money supply explain business fluctuations, inflation, and Super Bowl champions, then you had better figure out what money supply is. Conversely, the fact that true believers cannot agree on a definition of the money supply is pretty good evidence that other factors influence business cycles, inflation, and football games.

A more jaded view is that there is a dynamic ever-changing continuum of financial assets and no real need to single out a specific aggregation of these as all important. For any particular definition of "money," there are other financial assets, "near-moneys," that are not very different from those assets labeled "money." In addition, surprising new-moneys will continue to be introduced. Instead of restricting our attention to some artificially precise definition of money, we should look at many different types of financial assets.

The remainder of this chapter will examine some existing moneys and some that are likely to evolve. We'll pay particular attention to the moneys created by the private sector, for financial institutions have been very innovative in recent years, and financial markets have been quite exciting. The innovations of financial institutions have caused much of our difficulty in precisely defining money. Near-moneys and new-moneys have been aided and abetted by the evolution of near-banks and new-banks. There are now lots of financial intermediaries that do the same sorts of things as traditional banks. And the long list of things that banks do is growing all the time.

Financial intermediaries borrow funds from some economic agents and lend to others. Commercial banks are a well-known example. When you make a deposit, the bank is borrowing from you, but banks do not borrow money only through traditional deposits. Banks also raise funds through large negotiable CDs, federal funds, repurchase agreements, Eurodollars, open-market paper, and corporate bonds. These are all ways of borrowing money for relending. At the end of World War II, 70% of bank funds came from depositor checking accounts. Now, less than 25% does. In part, this change reflects a growth of time and savings accounts—from 20% of bank liabilities in 1945 to 45% in 1980. But there has also been a dramatic increase in direct bank borrowing in the short-term money market—from less than 1% of bank liabilities in 1945 to nearly 20% in 1980. At most large banks, short-term notes are now a more important source of funds than traditional checking accounts. In addition, time and savings accounts have become increasingly similar to short-term notes.

At the same time, other financial intermediaries have been vigorously competing with banks to attract funds for relending. Not too long ago, one would go to a different financial intermediary for a checking account, for a savings account, for insurance, to buy bonds, and to yet another to invest in stocks. Similarly, one might go to one for a business loan, to a second for a car loan, and to a third for a home mortgage. No more! The distinctions among financial intermediaries have been permanently breached and are rapidly fading from view. Specialized financial boutiques are being replaced by high-class financial supermarkets—full-service intermediaries that can handle all financial needs 24 hours a day, at branches all over the nation and the world.

These changes make it increasingly necessary to take a broad view of financial intermediaries. It is not sufficient to focus on commercial bank checking accounts, or on any other specific feature of a selected institution. Instead, we should look at a variety of activities of a variety of institutions.

Checkable deposits

A growing difficulty with the old definition of M1 was its neglect of demand deposits in financial institutions other than commercial banks. For nearly fifty years, from 1933 through 1980, only commercial banks were permitted to offer checking accounts. Mutual savings banks, savings-and-loan associations, and credit unions were considered "thrift institutions," designed for more permanent household savings accounts. These thrift institutions are very large and important, and have long wanted to share in the lucrative checking account business.

Through checking accounts, banks borrow funds inexpensively from their depositors and then lend these funds out at profitable interest rates. Banks do incur expenses in administering checking accounts. Surveys by the Bank Administration Institute in the 1970s indicated that it cost banks an average of 25¢ to 40¢ per check for collection and processing. Nonetheless, with other assets yielding very high interest rates in the 1970s, many thrift institutions wanted to enter the checking account market and many banks wanted to offer interest on checking accounts to attract more depositors.

Starting with a favorable 1972 court decision in Massachusetts, "negotiable order of withdrawal" (NOW) accounts spread through the six New England states, New York, and New Jersey. Terminology aside, these were checking accounts paying 5¼% interest. In 1974, credit unions began offering "share drafts," which are effectively interest-paying checking accounts. In 1978, commercial banks were authorized to offer "automatic transfer system" (ATS) accounts, in which funds are automatically transferred from an individual's savings to checking account as needed. By 1980, the deposits in these various checking-like accounts reached $20 billion, which was almost one-tenth the size of traditional commercial bank checking accounts.

Many of these and other similar developments had uncertain legal status. In 1980, the historic Depository Institutions Deregulation and Monetary Control Act clarified most of these ambiguities by explicitly authorizing this financial revolution. Financial institutions other than commercial banks were permitted to offer checking accounts, and the prohibition of interest payments on checking accounts was removed. On January 1, 1981, commercial banks and thrift institutions throughout the nation began offering NOW accounts paying 5¼% interest. On January 5, 1983, came Super NOW Accounts paying market interest rates.

Other accounts

Much of the savings account funds in depository institutions have long been readily available to pay bills. In recent years, technological developments and the incentives of high interest rates have made access even simpler. Since 1975, banks and savings and loans have provided automatic bill-paying services. Regular bills for utilities, rent, mortgage payments and the like are sent directly to the bank or savings and loan. The appropriate amount is withdrawn from the depositor's savings account and sent on in payment of the bill.* Also, since 1975, Federal Reserve member banks and federally chartered savings and loan associations have been allowed to accept telephone instructions to transfer funds from savings to checking accounts. The depositor can then leave funds in an interest-earning savings account right up until (or even a bit after) funds are needed to purchase something. With both these innovations, savings accounts contain funds that would otherwise be in checking accounts. Since these savings account funds are a good substitute for checking account funds, it is reasonable to argue that they too should be counted as money.

Ready credit and easily liquidated assets Many checking accounts have liberal overdraft provisions, often called "ready credit" or "check credit" plans.† If you have such an account, then you can write a check for more than you have deposited, and the bank will honor the check anyway. The bank uses its own funds to pay your bill, and records this as a small loan to you. You may be able to repay the loan promptly with a slight service charge, or to repay it later with interest. This overdraft privilege means that you have more funds available for spending than are contained in your checking account and are recorded in M1.

Americans are now carrying more than 500 million plastic credit cards. Some 85 million are judged "credit worthy" by the industry, and 90% of these carry one or more credit cards. The average person owns 7½ credit cards and charges $240 per month. As a nation, we have a revolving credit card debt of more than $50 billion.

Credit cards are more widely accepted than checks, and used frequently enough to demand inclusion in a realistic definition of money. But how are we to measure the quantity of credit card money? The average volume of credit card purchases is inappropriate, since that's a flow, and money is a stock. (Checking account money is measured by the amount of money in checking accounts at some point in time, not by the average volume of checks written.)

* It might be objected that the savings account funds that will be used to make mortgage payments cannot be used for discretionary purchases. However, the same is true of checking accounts. Funds kept in a checking account for mortgage payments cannot be used for discretionary purchases.

† Overdraft provisions have been popular in Great Britain for some time. Keynes thought these should be counted as money.[16]

Another possible basis for measurement is the available credit limit specified by the credit card companies. This is the maximum amount that can be charged, just as checking account balances dictate the maximum amount of checks that can be written (neglecting overdrafts). The problem with that approach is that few households could prudently charge the amount of their credit limits on their 7½ credit cards. But this does suggest a more sensible line of reasoning.

For the amount that households can spend via credit cards, the analogue of the checking account balance is the amount households can easily obtain to pay their credit card charges. Therefore, effective credit card money could be reasonably measured by the quantity of readily available funds. These are the assets that could be quickly liquidated to pay credit card bills. Even this yardstick is imperfect since it neglects the frequently used practice of paying credit charges out of future income. But it seems better than completely neglecting credit cards or simply adding up maximum credit limits.

Thus, the reality of credit cards suggests that "money" ought to encompass easily liquidated assets. This provides additional support for the consideration of very broad monetary aggregates.

Series E and H government savings bonds are easily redeemable for stated amounts of money; commercial paper and short-term Treasury bills can be quickly sold for a relatively certain amount of money, and large negotiable CDs (certificates of deposit issued by banks in denominations of $100,000 or more) are traded in the short-term bond market for ready conversion into money. Such traditional instruments have now been supplemented as a result of double-digit interest rates, which spurred the growth of new, very liquid interest-earning assets. One example is Eurodollars, which are U.S. dollars deposited in foreign banks. These Eurodollars can often be quickly withdrawn for spending in the United States. For instance, overnight deposits in Caribbean branches of U.S. banks are available for spending the next business day. Another example is the repurchase agreement (RP), in which an investor buys securities that the seller agrees to repurchase at an agreed-upon price and date, often the next day. For the seller, often a bank, this is a one-day loan; for the buyer, often a corporation, this is a very liquid interest-bearing investment.

For small investors, the major innovation has been money market funds, mutual funds that purchase short-term debt, such as bank CDs and Treasury bills. These money market funds had more than $200 billion in assets by the end of 1982. Shareholders can quickly and easily withdraw their money by giving written or telephone instructions, or by writing checks payable to a specified third party. (However, their service as money is a bit restricted by a typical $500 minimum limit on withdrawals.)

Which combination from this monetary smorgasbord best deserves to be called "money"? The truth, frankly, is that there is no clear answer to that fundamental question. There is a spectrum, and it is difficult to know where to draw the line beyond which an asset is not considered money. This is why the Fed collects and studies data on many monetary aggregates. No single monetary aggregate is decisively more interesting or important than the others.

In recognition of the increasingly obvious ambiguities in its old monetary aggregates, the Fed concocted new M1, M2, M3, and L series, as shown in Table 14.1. The M1 data attempt to measure money as a medium of exchange —funds that can be directly used for transactions. The M2, M3, and L series

TABLE 14.1

Monetary aggregates, seasonally adjusted, for December 1983

Aggregate and component	Amount ($ billions)
M-1	525.3
Currency	148.0
Travelers checks	4.9
Demand deposits	243.7
Other checkable deposits*	128.8
M-2	2196.1
M-1	525.3
Overnight repurchase agreements and Eurodollars	46.8
Money market deposit accounts in depository institutions	379.9
Money market mutual fund shares	138.2
Savings deposits at all depositary institutions	312.8
Small time deposits at all depositary institutions†	793.1
M-3	2706.8
M-2	2196.1
Large time deposits at all depositary institutions	335.8
Term repurchase agreements	134.6
Institutional money market fund shares	40.3
L	3175.5
M-3	2706.8
Commercial paper and bankers acceptances	54.2
Savings bonds	70.7
Liquid Treasury obligations	343.8

* Includes NOW, ATS, and credit union share draft balances and demand deposits at thrift institutions.

† Time deposits issued in denominations of less than $100,000.

(SOURCE: *Federal Reserve Bulletin,* April 1984).

progressively expand to encompass funds that are a store of wealth but can be easily converted into a medium of exchange.* Note that both the new M2 and M3 include RPs, overnight Eurodollars, and money market funds—all of which were completely excluded from earlier monetary aggregates.

MONEY TOMORROW

The plastic revolution is just beginning, and its signs can be seen everywhere. In the 1970s, savings-and-loan associations were allowed to set up electronic remote service units in supermarkets, airports, and other public places. Depositors were given plastic cards that they could insert in a remote terminal, causing funds to be instantly transferred from the buyer's account of the seller's account. Although some courts ruled that there was not yet statutory authority for such terminals, these are a clear glimpse of the future.

* This progression is far from perfect. For example, the small time deposits included in M2 are generally less liquid than the large time deposits included in M3, or the Treasury bills included in L. In 1980, the Fed also began internally monitoring a variety of monetary indexes. These indexes are weighted averages of data on various financial assets. The relative weights are estimates of the relative frequency with which the assets are liquidated. Checking accounts, for instance, are given a heavier weight than savings accounts because funds flow in and out of checking accounts more frequently.

IN THE NEWS

Quest for the Meaning of Money Takes New Direction

What is money?

It sounds like a dumb question but the interpretation of "monetary growth" information depends altogether on what we are measuring. Translating monetary growth into inflation down the road is a risky business at best . . .

Terms like "M1" and "M2" have been used widely in the press over the past 10 years. There has been less discussion of the significance of the difference between these two measures of the money stock. The Federal Reserve banks report regularly on the annualized growth rate of the "monetary aggregates." More information is needed about these aggregates before a great deal can be said about their relationship to the rate of price increases.

It was easy when money meant simply currency and checking account deposits. These were the things we spent when we bought cars, gasoline, chocolate, or bonds. However, many economists began to fret because they could not find a relationship between this money and measures of the total economic output (gross national product). A 10-percent increase in the quantity of money did not necessarily lead to a 10-percent increase in GNP at current prices.

Some of the economists who were frustrated by this imprecision decided that we must be measuring money all wrong. In their minds, people must be using something else for money besides currency and checking accounts. They took it as their job to find out what this something else was.

In their search, they "discovered" that people were keeping part of their transactions balances in savings accounts and other small time deposits rather than in checking accounts. In other words, you might have $500 in your checking account which you plan to use to pay bills next month. This is a transactions balance. Now, suppose you take that $500 and deposit it in credit union shares or in a savings and loan account where it will draw interest.

You have shifted part of your transactions money from the "money stock" to a non-monetary type of asset. However, this money does not disappear. It is now being used by a borrower to purchase something and remains in circulation. The difference is that *you* still regard that $500 as part of your monetary assets while that borrower (or her broker) holds what she considers money.

The net of this is that there is $1,000 out there, now, instead of $500. The measure, M2, captures this effect.

Two things have happened to produce this result. One is that savings accounts now pay interest compounded daily. In the old days one had to leave money on deposit 60 to 90 days before interest was paid. Thus, if you left your $500 for only 20 days, you would have received no dividends. In today's market, you could receive 20 days' interest.

Second is that interest rates have been so high that you are willing to accept some risk of not getting the money when you need it.

Since interest rates tend to be higher in the upswing of the business cycle, the "money supply" increases while GNP is increasing whether or not there is any increase in spendable cash or checking accounts. As interest rates decline during the downswing, the "money supply" shrinks as people pull deposits out of savings and leave them in checking accounts.

One would expect that monetary growth will track current GNP quite well. At least that is true as long as people do not find other places to put transactions balances. Also, it is true until people begin to take money out of stocks and bonds to be deposited in these money-like assets. In this case, M2 exaggerates the measure of monetary growth.

Monetary growth no longer tracks GNP with enough precision to predict increases in demand that might lead to inflation.

There is some evidence that the changes in our saving and spending habits, the new products being marketed by financial institutions, changes in the regulatory environment and high short-term interest rates have caused the growth rate of money stocks to depart from the GNP track. Money no longer gives us a reliable indication of future inflationary pressures. At least, we must wait until there is some history of monetary growth without a redefinition of money. (Richard Waits and Edward McNertny, *Fort Worth Star Telegram,* Mar. 29, 1983)

Within the Federal Reserve System, $200 billion a day is electronically transferred between banks. The New York Clearing House International Payments System transfers a like amount through a computer network linking 80 banking offices. Both these systems are primarily used commercially for large transactions. The federal government uses the Federal Reserve Clearing House to make some 150 million transactions annually, mostly direct deposits for Social Security, salary, and government pension payments. These government payments are electronically transmitted and directly deposited in the beneficiaries' accounts, at their request. This saves time, paper and postage, and eliminates stolen checks. The Treasury estimates that it now saves about 12¢ per transaction.

It is widely believed that these are initial trial stages of a comprehensive electronic funds system in which a nationwide computer network will electronically record transactions, instantly transferring funds from the buyer's account to the seller's account. Government offices and businesses will have computer terminals connected to this network. Wages, dividends, and interest payments will all be directly transferred between accounts. Individuals with plastic (of course) identification cards will pay for most purchases by inserting their cards in terminals located in retail stores. Transactions between individuals can be handled by public terminals or by home terminals. The complete elimination of cash will be resisted by participants in the underground economy, while, for the opposite reasons, governments will try very hard to affect it.

Funds credited within the network of accounts will earn interest. There will be liberal overdraft privileges, with interest charged on debits. Funds held in the system will serve both as a medium of exchange and as savings, a store of value. And with liberal overdrafts, it will not be necessary to have a positive balance in order to make transactions.

In a pure currency system every transaction requires an actual physical transfer of tangible currency. In the accounting system of the future, there need be no physical currency whatsoever. Transactions will require only bookkeeping entries of debits and credits. What then will we call money? And will we call the system a bank? Both terms will be obsolete.

The private advantages of such a system will be improved record-keeping services and the elimination of noninterest-paying checking accounts. The social advantages will be the saving in resources now spent reading and sorting pieces of paper and shuffling them throughout the country. (Processing tens of billions of checks a year at 25¢ to 40¢ a check adds up.) There will also probably be some loss of privacy. There will certainly be some uneasy years for economists trying to measure money, and for public figures urging that we abolish fractional reserve banking and return to the gold standard. Most of us will conclude that the costs are well worth absorbing.

MONETARY AGGREGATES AND MONETARY POLICY

A primary objective of monetary aggregates is to measure the money supply so that policy makers can gauge whether they are following an expansionary or contractionary monetary policy. Which monetary aggregate is the one to watch? The most reasonable conclusion is that there is no single definition of money most deserving of our attention. Financial markets are too complicated and innovative for some single collection of assets to predominate. There are too many assets that are almost, but not quite, the same as others. There is no obvious place to draw a line and say "This is money, but that isn't." Private and governmental analysts of financial markets look at many financial assets, because no single number tells the whole story. In addition, we must adjust our sights as assets and institutions arise, evolve, or disappear. This is why monetary aggregates have been called "*momentary* aggregates." Even President Reagan's monetarist Council of Economic Advisers, who recommended watching M1, admitted that it will have to be "suitably redefined from time to time." This advice is dangerously close to the joke that "anything can be explained by money, appropriately defined."

Some monetary economists, following Milton Friedman, have taken the position that a definition of money should be chosen not for its theoretical coherence, but rather for its practical ability to explain fluctuations in output. The 1980 Federal Reserve monetary aggregate revisions were, in fact, at least partly motivated by a perceived deterioration in the empirical correlations between the old aggregates and output, interest rates, and prices.[17]

Even if there were a close correlation between some monetary concoction and GNP, there would still remain the problem that the monetary authorities control the monetary base, and this may have only a loose influence on monetary aggregates. Consider the quantity theory equation for some monetary aggregate M_w (M-whatever) with velocity V_w:

$$M_w V_w = PY \tag{14.11}$$

It is of little use to construct some broad monetary aggregate, M_w, whose velocity, V_w, is stable, if M_w itself cannot be stabilized.

For example, by putting virtually all assets into M_w, we might find that V_w is little affected by interest rates. High interest rates will cause a shift of funds from the non-interest-paying components of M_w to the interest-paying components, but might not affect the total demand for assets relative to GNP, (that is, V_w would be constant). However, high interest rates will reduce the demand for currency and bank reserves, increasing the money multipliers and M_w. So we would find that higher interest rates raise M_w rather than V_w in Equation 14.11. Nothing is really gained or lost by constructing a fluctuating monetary aggregate that has a stable velocity.

The new monetary aggregates are more logical than the old aggregates, but they are no easier to control. Figures 14.8 and 14.9 show that, even using annual data and a monetary base that has been adjusted by the St. Louis Federal Reserve Bank for changes in reserve requirements, there still isn't much correlation between short-run changes in the monetary base and changes in monetary aggregates, particularly M2.

Summary

The nonstop innovations in financial markets have sent economists scrambling to adjust their definitions of money and have kept them busy arguing over the

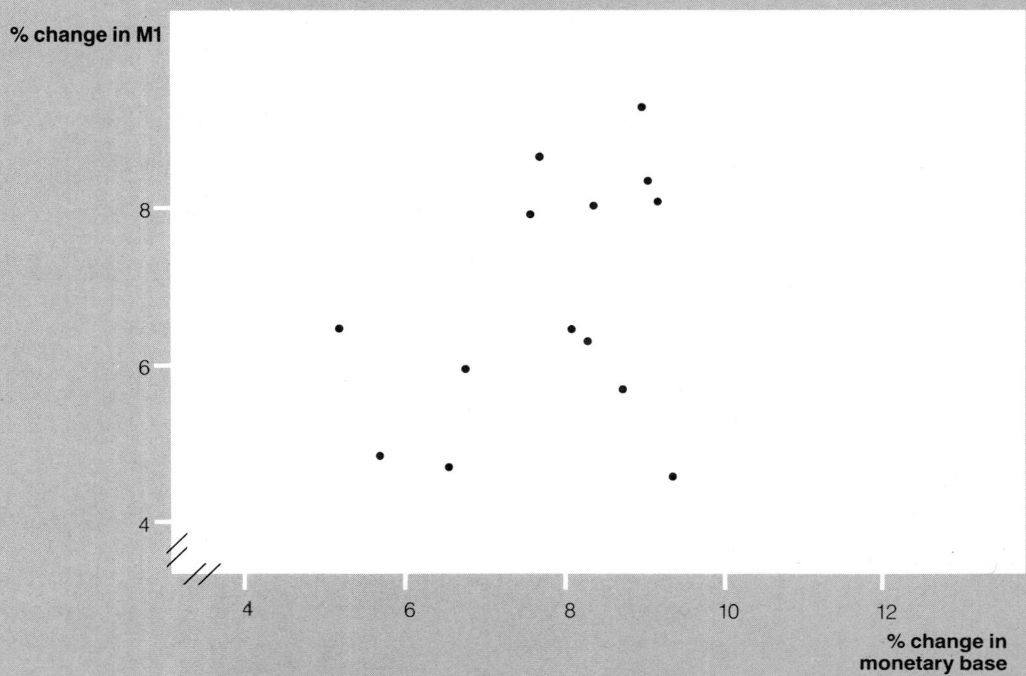

FIGURE 14.8 **ANNUAL PERCENTAGE CHANGES IN ADJUSTED MONETARY BASE AND M1. For any given increase in the monetary base—say 9%—it is not certain how much M1 will increase (anywhere from 4% to 10%).**

best definition. This financial turmoil makes it very difficult for the government to gauge monetary conditions. Since some financial assets grow faster than others, the rates of growth of any particular money measure depend on which assets are included in the measure and which are excluded. In addition, it has become quite difficult to control monetary conditions, since the government has little or no direct control over the size of all these new assets invented by financial institutions. These financial innovations have also undercut any simple quantity theory based on a controllable money supply and a fixed velocity. Neither concept will hold still long enough to provide us with an infallible policy guide. This is why one cynic called monetarism "the undefinable in pursuit of the uncontrollable."[18]

IMPLICATIONS FOR MACRO MODELS

In practice, the Fed watches each monetary aggregate and other, unpublished ones as well. It also watches interest rates, prices, output, unemployment rates, and balance-of-payments data in deciding whether an expansionary or contractionary policy is called for. When the Fed does make open-market transactions, it directly alters the monetary base, H, the supply of government fiat money to the private sector.

While it watches many monetary aggregates, the Fed's primary empirical macro model focuses on the demand for monetary base, *H*, which consists of currency outside banks and bank reserves. The Fed's model predicts that an increase in the supply of monetary base reduces interest rates and stimulates the economy. A decrease in the demand for monetary base has similar effects. (Thus, implicitly, their *LM* curve uses the monetary base, rather than M1, or some other aggregate.) Let's look at some examples of this logic.

The existence of a plethora of moneys and near-moneys implies that it will

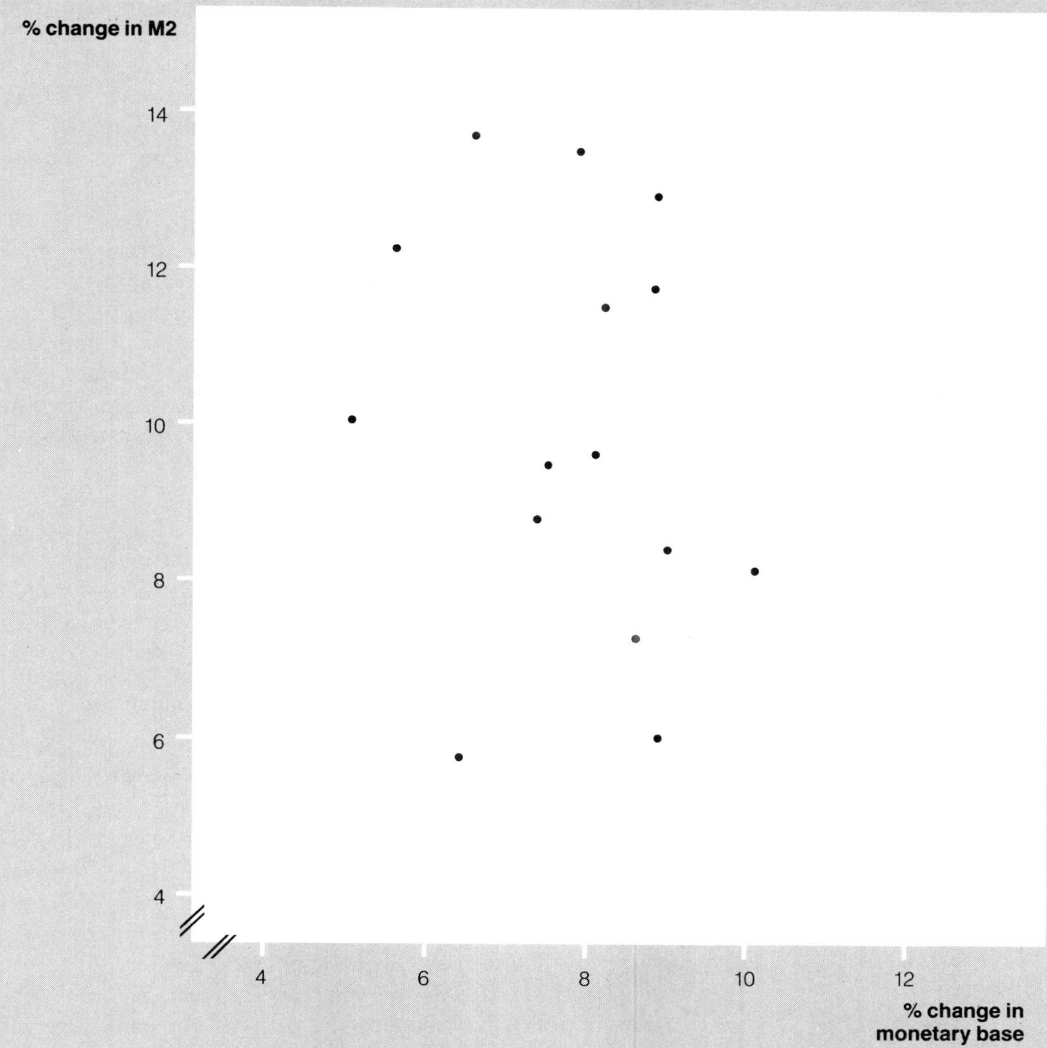

FIGURE 14.9 ANNUAL PERCENTAGE CHANGES IN ADJUSTED MONETARY BASE AND M2, 1970–83. **M2 embraces so varied an assortment of financial assets that it correlates with the monetary base even less than does M1.**

often take a complicated macro model to untangle the consequences of economic events. When there are many financial assets there are many asset demands, supplies, and interest rates. An accurate analysis will often require a model that has many markets and interest rates built into it. Such a model is sketched in the next chapter. We examine here four examples of financial market events whose effects on those markets (easing or tightening) cannot be adequately analyzed by watching a single interest rate or a single monetary aggregate. The moral is that economics is challenging, and simple rules of thumb are sometimes not enough.

Example 1. *An increase in the ceiling rates on time and savings accounts* The induced transfer of funds from currency outside banks and from transaction accounts to time and savings accounts reduces M1 but does not immediately affect M2, M3, or L. The transfer of funds to time and savings accounts from Treasury bills, the stock market, and the like increases M2, M3, and L without affecting M1. Thus we would expect to find M1 down and M2, M3, and L all up. This is a good example of how monetary aggregates do not always move in lock step.

If we look at the demand for monetary base in the Fed's model, the logic is again ambiguous. There is a reduced demand for currency outside banks and also a reduced demand for bank reserves (since transaction accounts have higher reserve requirements than time and savings accounts). The one contrary influence is that the shift of funds from securities to time and savings deposits increases the demand for bank reserves. Backus, et al[19] found that, on balance, the demand for monetary base declined and the increase in ceiling rates was expansionary in that the interest rates on market securities declined. In this case, those who focused on M1 got the wrong answer, while those who watched M2 were right.

Example 2. *The introduction of NOW accounts* NOW accounts represent an increase in the ceiling rate on transaction accounts. The shift of funds from currency outside banks into transaction accounts does not immediately affect monetary aggregates. The shifts into transaction accounts from time and savings accounts, money market funds, Treasury bills, and so on increases M1 and (to a lesser extent) other monetary aggregates. Thus we would expect to find M1 up, and the other monetary aggregates up slightly.

Look now at the demand for monetary base. There is less demand for currency outside banks but more demand for bank reserves because of the shift of funds from outside banks and from time and savings accounts into NOW accounts (since NOW accounts have higher reserve requirements). We cannot say for sure whether financial markets ease or tighten. If the diminished demand for currency is dominant, the M1 gives the right signal. The reverse is true if the increased demand for bank reserves is dominant. In either case, M2, M3, and L fail to show the turmoil in financial markets.

Example 3. *The introduction of money market mutual funds* The loss of deposits to money funds has reduced the demand for bank reserves. There has likely also been a diminished demand for currency outside banks. So the demand for monetary base has declined, which, like an increase in monetary base supply, eases financial markets. (However, M1 is down, M2 up.)

Example 4. *The spread of repurchase agreements* This is similar to the case in the preceding example. The decline in the demands for currency and bank reserves eases financial markets. (Now, M1 and M2 are down, M3 up.) Another variation is that an increased yield on U.S. savings bonds would also ease financial markets (assuming that the government recycles the funds so as to hold the monetary base constant) while increasing L and reducing M1, M2, and M3. Monetary aggregates can and do move in divergent directions.

IMPORTANT TERMS AND CONCEPTS

barter
medium of exchange
commodity money
fiat money
Gresham's Law
fractional reserve banking
reserve requirements
excess reserves
monetary base
deposit multiplier
high-powered money
M1, M2, M3, L
electronic funds transfer system

Barter may be satisfactory in a small, closely knit community of largely self-sufficient people, or in a communal or totalitarian society. Money is very useful in a large community with specialized labor, private property, and voluntary exchange.

When commodities are used as money, valuable resources are tied up in the medium of exchange. Commodity-money inflations usually arise from shifts in the demand or supply for the commodity. The danger with fiat money is that governments will not responsibly manage its supply.

The price of a dollar is what can be bought or sold for a dollar. These are the inverses of conventionally quoted prices. Unbacked paper money has value because it is useful as a medium of exchange and has a limited supply.

Banks create money by holding fractional reserves against deposits. The amount of bank deposits supported by the monetary base is $D = M/(\gamma + \lambda)$, where γ is the ratio of currency outside banks to deposits, and λ is the ratio of bank reserves to deposits. The more currency held outside banks and the more reserves held inside banks, the fewer the deposits created.

Banks serve as intermediaries between lenders and borrowers. Lenders are able to withdraw their deposits on demand, while borrowers are given a fixed repayment schedule for their loans. This bank monetization of illiquid assets channels funds from cautious savers to bold entrepreneurs.

Economists watch many monetary and liquidity aggregates such as M1, M2, M3, and L. As the differences among various assets and various institutions become increasingly blurred, it becomes less and less satisfactory to focus on a specific monetary aggregate. There are just too many near-moneys and new-moneys, and too many near-banks and new-banks, to permit a firm, precise definition of money.

EXERCISES

1. Explain why each of the following would make a poor commodity money: oysters, diamonds, wine, sand, 1959 Thunderbirds.

2. For a hundred years, from 1834 to 1933, the official U.S. price of gold was $20.67 an ounce. If a horse sold for $10, what would have been its price in terms of gold (that is,

ounces/horse)? If gold is $1000 an ounce, how much gold would be needed to buy a 25-cent package of chewing gum?

3. If, while the United States was on the gold standard, the growth of the economy caused the demand for gold to grow faster than its supply, would prices in general tend to rise or fall?

4. In 1834, the price of gold was set at $20.67 an ounce. Overall, consumer prices increased between 1834 and 1980 by a factor of about 8. If the price of gold relative to consumer goods had been the same in 1980 as in 1834, what would have been the 1980 dollar price of gold?

5. When the United States defined a dollar in terms of both gold and silver, the nation was legally on a bimetallic standard. In practice, however, the United States was on either a gold or silver standard since only one of these metals circulated as money. Will a legal two-metal standard always turn into a one-metal standard in practice?

6. A copper U.S. penny contains $\frac{2}{3}$ of a hundredth of a pound of copper. At what copper price (dollars per pound) can a profit be made by melting pennies?

7. If there were no legal reserve requirements, how would the government's ability to control M1 be altered? Would banks bother to keep reserves? Given total government money of $1 billion, what would be the maximum possible level of deposits?

8. "The latest available data show that M1, the basic money supply measure, declined $500 million in the week ended December 19. The broader measure, M2, rose $700 million during the week." *(Wall Street Journal,* 12/29/79)

How could M1 have declined as reported, while M2 rose?

9. The ratio of currency to deposits doubled between 1929 and 1933. What effect did this have on M1?

10. In the 1930s, banks held enormous amounts of excess reserves. What effects, if any, would this have on M1? The government, aiming to eliminate these excess reserves, raised reserve requirements in August 1936, March 1937, and May 1937. However, banks continued to hold large excess reserves. What probably happened to M1?

11. Should $100 bills buried in the backyard be counted as part of M1?

12. According to the square-root rule (Equation 14.6), how would velocity be affected by an income redistribution from the rich to the poor?

13. Use the inventory model of money demand to prove that the square-root rule (Equation 14.6) does maximize net interest revenue.

14. Why have monetary aggregates been called "momentary aggregates"?

15. Consider the following money-multiplier model:

$$C = .12D \text{ (currency relative to deposits)}$$
$$RR = .05D \text{ (required reserves)}$$
$$E = .01(1 - .12)D \text{ (excess reserves)}$$
$$H = C + RR + E \text{ (high-powered money)}$$

Solve for $C + D$ as a function of M. What is the value of $C + D$ if M = 200? By what percentage does $C + D$ change if E increases from .01 to .02? How would your answer change if RR were 10% of deposits ($RR = .10D$)? if they were 100% of deposits ($RR = D$)? What is the policy implication?

REFERENCES

1. A. P. Andrew, "What Ought to be Called Money," *Quarterly Journal of Economics,* 13 (January, 1899), p. 219.

2. W. S. Jevons, "Barter," in *Money and the Mechanism of Exchange,* New York: D. Appleton, 1892, pp. 1–7.

3. For example, Irving Fisher, *The Purchasing Power of Money,* New York: Macmillan, 1911.

4. John Burr Williams, *The Theory of Investment Value,* Cambridge, Mass.: Harvard University Press, 1938, p. 52.

5. Williams, p. 54.

6. John Maynard Keynes, *The General Theory of Employment, Interest, and Money,* New York: Harcourt Brace Jovanovich, 1964, p. 167

7. David Laidler, *The Demand for Money: Theories and Evidence,* 2nd ed., New York: Dun-Donnelly, 1977.

8. Keynes, pp. 195–196.

9. Keynes, p. 196.

10. Keynes, p. 201.

11. Keynes, p. 171.

12. James Tobin, "Liquidity Preference as Behavior Towards Risk," *Review of Economic Studies* (February 1958), pp. 65–86.

13. J. Tobin, "The Interest-Elasticity of Transactions Demand for Cash," *Review of Economics and Statistics* (1956), pp. 241–247; and W. J. Baumol, "The Transactions Demand for Cash: An Inventory Theoretic Approach," *Quarterly Journal of Economics,* (1952), pp. 545–556.

14. G. Akerlof and R. Milbourne, "New Calculations of Income and Interest Elasticities in Tobin's Model of the Transactions Demand for Money," *Review of Economics and Statistics,* (1978), pp. 541–546.

15. D. Ricardo, *The Works and Correspondence of David Ricardo, Vol IV, Pamphlets 1815–1823,* Piero Sraffa, ed., Cambridge: Cambrige University Press, 1951, pp. 59, 62.

16. J. M. Keynes, *A Treatise on Money,* I, London: Macmillan, 1930, pp. 41–43.

17. See, for example, J. Wenninger and C. M. Sivesind, "Defining Money for a Changing Financial System," Federal Reserve Bank of New York *Quarterly Review* (Spring, 1979), pp. 1–8.

18. Sir Ian Gilmore at the 1982 conference of Britain's Conservative Party, quoted in Arthur Schlesinger, Jr., "American Politics on a Darkling Plain," *Wall Street Journal,* March 16, 1982.

19. An interesting empirical study is D. Backus, W. Brainard, G. Smith, and J. Tobin, "A Model of U.S. Financial and Nonfinancial Economic Behavior," *Journal of Money, Credit, and Banking,* 12 (May 1980), pp. 259–93.

SUGGESTIONS FOR FURTHER READING

Carl Menger was an able and influential analyst of barter and monetary economies. See, for example, Chapter 8 of his *Principles of Economics* (Glencoe, Illinois: Free Press, 1950; originally published in 1871). For a study of the Hershey Bar as commodity money, read R. A. Radford, "The Economic Organization of a P.O.W. Camp," *Economic Journal* (November, 1945), pp. 189–201. A classic work on the fundamental nature of financial intermediaries is James Tobin, "Commercial Banks as Creators of Money," in *Banking and Monetary Studies,* Deane Carson, editor (Homewood, Illinois, Irwin, 1963).

CHAPTER FIFTEEN

ASSETS

The greatest of all gifts is the power to estimate things at their true worth.

LA ROCHEFOUCAULD

This chapter discusses how and why assets (and interest rates) differ, examines the term structure of interest rates, describes the construction and importance of multiasset models, and addresses the question of whether it matters what kinds of bonds finance government deficits.

THE macro model that we analyzed in Part I of this book was simple and satisfactory for most purposes. We can use this model to analyze the macro consequences of government spending, open-market operations, tax changes, and a variety of analogous private-sector events. But, in recent years, there have been a great many innovative changes in financial markets that cannot be satisfactorily analyzed with a simple *LM* curve. Changes in interest rate ceilings, the introduction of NOW accounts, the growth of money market funds, and the creation of repurchase agreements are important examples. There are many others and there are sure to be more in the future.

These kinds of financial developments cannot really be adequately handled in a model with only two assets and one interest rate. We need to allow for a variety of assets and a multiplicity of interest rates. The first part of this chapter will explain why all assets are not alike and why all interest rates are not the same. We will formally identify some of the asset differences that investors consider important and see how these lead to different interest rates. Then, in the last part of the chapter, we will explain how one would construct a macro model that allows for a variety of assets and interest rates. In the process we will see how the *LM* curve is replaced by multiple financial-market curves that are solved by means of computers rather than two-dimensional graphs.

Government money, bank money, and other moneys, besides being means of payment, are assets. And, like all assets, they are stores of wealth. They are financial investments that can, at some point, be used to acquire consumable goods and services. There are many other assets that are tempting alternatives to money: government bonds, corporate stock, land, gold, and pistachio nuts. How do investors choose among these diverse alternatives? What makes some assets more attractive than others? Why do you put funds in a savings account, while I buy land and my brother hoards pistachio nuts?

One obviously important consideration is the anticipated rate of return on an investment. Some others are its liquidity, transaction costs, divisibility, taxes, and riskiness. These asset characteristics, discussed below, influence asset demands and supplies. It is through yield adjustments that demands and supplies can be reconciled.

YIELD

There are day-to-day fluctuations in asset demands and supplies. Savers acquire assets and dissavers sell assets. In addition, people rearrange their portfolios, selling some assets in order to acquire others. These demand and supply changes exert pressures on asset prices and yields. Some yields move in lock step, with the structure of relative yields undisturbed. Other yields move independently or even in opposite directions. The flexibility of asset yields depends on the perceived substitutability of assets in investor portfolios.

Many familiar commodities are very close substitutes: brown and white eggs, butter by the pound or quarter-pound, California and Florida orange juice. The prices of such close substitutes are tightly linked. The price of brown eggs cannot double while the price of white eggs is constant; were this to happen, everyone would buy only white eggs. Other commodities are weak substitutes: eggs and geraniums, butter and ketchup, orange juice and beer. The prices of poor substitutes are only weakly related.

The same is true of assets. **Two assets that are equally attractive are called *perfect substitutes*, and are priced to yield the same rate of return.** When two assets are perfect substitutes, their yields move in unison. If the yield on one rises, the yield on the second must rise comparably. Otherwise, no one would want to hold the second asset. With imperfect substitutes, yields generally move in the same direction, but need not move in lock step. An increase in the yield on one asset tempts holders of similar assets to sell them, reducing their prices and raising their yields. The holders of dissimilar assets are not tempted much, and there is little, if any, effect on these yields. **The more two assets are considered substitutes, the more their yields move in unison.**

Now consider a related question: When assets are imperfect substitutes, which have the highest anticipated yields? In general, **those that, yields aside, are the least attractive to purchasers and the most attractive to issuers.** If an asset is otherwise unattractive, people will hold it only if it has a high yield, which compensates for its unattractive features. Investors are not willing to pay much for an unattractive asset, and this low price provides the high yield they require. (Remember, asset prices and yields are inversely related.)

What factors other than yield make certain assets attractive or unattractive? Widely considered important among the hopes, fears, and legal detail embodied in assets are the rather general characteristics identified above (and discussed below): liquidity, transaction costs, divisibility, taxes, cash flow risk, and interest rate risk. In each case, relative attractiveness determines relative yields.

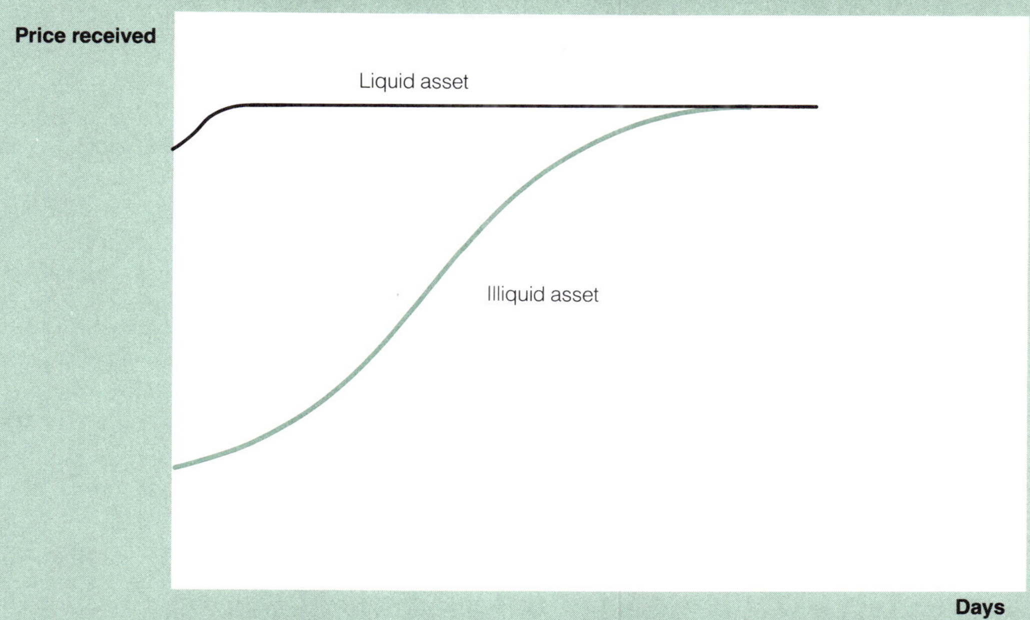

FIGURE 15.1 LIQUIDITY IN RELATION TO PRICE RECEIVED FOR AN ASSET. **A measure of an asset's liquidity is the effort required to realize its fair market value. A liquid asset can be sold quickly for a fair price; an illiquid asset can be sold quickly only at a distress price.**

LIQUIDITY

Liquidity relates to how easily an asset can be converted into a medium of exchange. By definition, cash is the most liquid asset. Some other items are almost as liquid as cash—for example, savings accounts from which funds can be transferred to checking accounts with a telephone call. Other assets are pretty illiquid: It may be very difficult to quickly find a serious buyer for a painting, a car, or a house.

Generally, a buyer can always be found for anything if the price is set low enough. What economists mean by liquidity is that a fair price can be quickly obtained. An illiquid asset is something that can be sold quickly only at a distress price, far less than could be realized by a careful search for buyers.

To quantify liquidity, consider the following hypothetical experiment. What price could I get for a certain asset I decide to sell today? What price could I get had I planned yesterday to sell today? What if I had made up my mind a week ago? A month ago? Figure 15.1 shows the relative prices one could typically expect according to the planning interval. For the liquid asset, full market value can be realized with little planning. After the decision has been made to sell the asset, a fair price can be quickly obtained. With an illiquid asset, in contrast, only a fraction of fair market value can be obtained on short notice. (A graph of this type for cash would be a straight horizontal line.)

Liquidity can be provided via either of two avenues. One is some party, often the issuer, who stands ready to offer fair market value at any time. Banks do this on many types of deposits. The federal government does it with U.S. savings bonds. A second means is an efficient, organized market in which a large volume of trading is always occurring and a fair price can be readily obtained. The New York Stock Exchange and similar exchanges are examples of this. Although relatively little new stock is issued by corporations, vast amounts of existing stock are traded each day on the stock exchanges, which are *secondary markets.* These can involve physical facilities, like the organized exchanges, in which agents meet face to face to buy and sell securities, or a network of electronically linked trading rooms located all over the country (and in some cases outside the country).

Because most asset holders are not certain of when they will want to sell an asset, they prefer liquid assets. Other things being equal, illiquid assets are priced so as to provide higher anticipated yields than liquid assets, the greater yield making up for the sacrifice of liquidity. Issuers, in turn, sometimes guarantee liquidity in order to pay lower rates of interest on their debts, as we have just noted banks do with deposits and the federal government does with savings bonds. (The preference for liquidity also explains why citizens willingly bear the costs of operating secondary markets.)

TRANSACTION COSTS

Transaction costs can be conceptually separated from liquidity. They are those expenses incurred regardless of how far ahead one plans to buy or sell an asset. Examples are brokerage fees on bonds, stocks, and houses. Fees are incurred when one buys and when one sells. Thus transaction costs can be thought of as how much one would lose in buying and immediately selling the asset. Other things being equal, assets with high transaction costs have to offer the promise of high yields to be attractive.

DIVISIBILITY

The cost of buying or selling an asset may depend upon its size. *Divisibility* concerns the ability to purchase or sell a fraction of an asset for a like fraction of the price of the whole. Is the price of 10% of an asset equal to 10% of the price of the whole asset? If so, then the asset is perfectly divisible. Cash and many bank deposits are completely divisible. Some deposits and most bonds have indivisible minimum quantities. Treasury bills have a $10,000 minimum; negotiable bank certificates of deposit have a $100,000 minimum. Real assets—for example, a car, a house, a factory, a diamond, or a painting—are usually even less divisible than financial assets. In fact, financial assets are often created in order to divide indivisible real assets. Corporate stock is the outstanding example of this. To the extent that asset indivisibilities are inconvenient or insurmountable, more easily divisible assets are priced to have lower anticipated yields.

TAXES

One soon learns, from tiring and bewildering personal experience, that tax laws are extensive and complex. Tax liability from holding a particular asset depends upon very specific details concerning both the nature of the asset and one's tax status.

Consider, for example, the fact that some types of income are tax-exempt. Interest income from bonds issued by state and local governments is currently exempt from federal income taxes. Income from U.S. government securities is not subject to state and local taxes. The federal tax exemption is the more important, since federal tax rates are much higher than those of state and local governments. This means that state and local bonds are highly desired by investors in high tax brackets. Such investors accept relatively low before-tax yields on assets that are tax-exempt.

For example, banks pay a corporate income tax rate of 48% on net income above $25,000. A corporate bond paying 10% only yields banks 5.2% after federal taxes. Banks consequently prefer a tax-free municipal bond paying 5.3% to a taxable corporate bond paying 10%. You should, too, if you are in a 48% tax bracket.

The actual yield differential depends on the tax brackets of those who buy the bonds. If there aren't enough banks, doctors, and rock stars to buy all the state and local bonds in existence, then some ordinary folk in lower tax brackets will have to be persuaded. State and local bonds will have to offer relatively higher yields to attract investors in relatively lower tax brackets. In recent years, as shown in Figure 15.2, high-rated state and local bonds have yielded about 2% per year less than similarly rated coporate bonds. This yield spread was smaller in the good old days when tax rates were lower. Note also the similar movements in these two yield series. After adjustment for taxes, these debts are apparently pretty close substitutes.

CASH FLOW RISK

While the cash flow from some assets, such as Treasury securities and insured savings accounts, is known with complete certainty, there is considerable uncertainty about the returns from other assets: stock dividends, housing rents, and insurance benefits. This uncertainty contributes to the riskiness of an asset and, to the extent that investors are risk-averse, makes an asset less attractive. Thus assets with relatively uncertain cash flows are priced to give relatively high anticipated returns, the high hoped-for return offsetting the uncertainty of that return.

Even securities with fixed payment schedules may have cash flow risk, since security issuers are not always able to fulfill their obligations. Individuals may

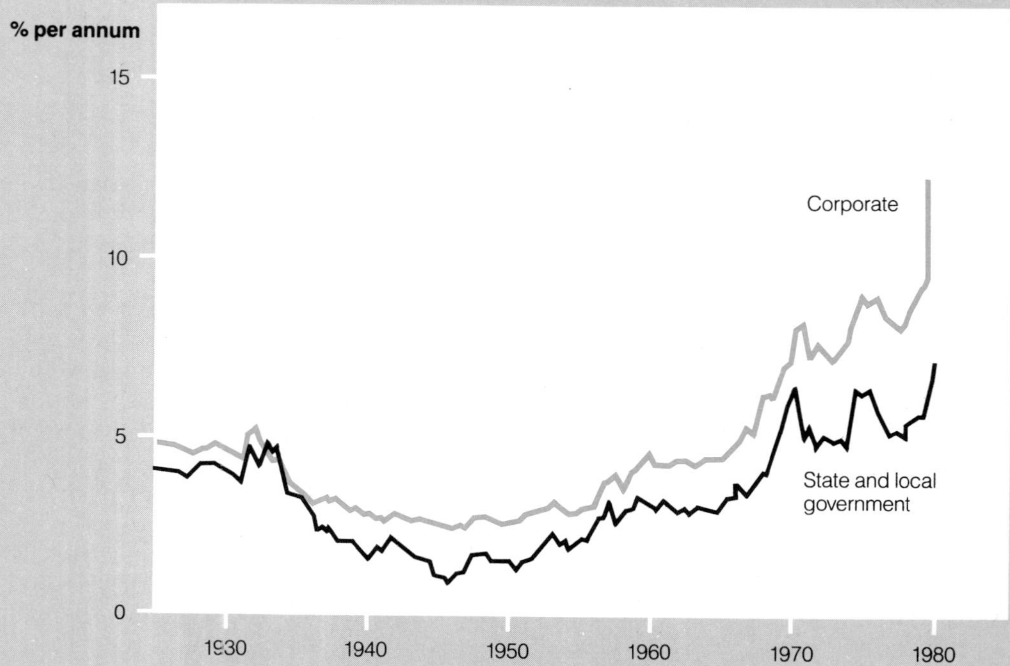

FIGURE 15.2 YIELDS ON HIGHEST QUALITY CORPORATE AND MUNICIPAL BONDS, 1926–80. **Corporate bonds yield more than state and local bonds because their yield is subject to federal income taxes. Yields tend to rise and fall together because, after taxes are taken into account, the assets are good substitutes. (Source: Federal Reserve Board *Historical Chart Book.*)**

lose their jobs, businesses may lose sales, and state and local governments may lose tax revenue. Issuers default when they do not meet the terms of their debts. Holders of defaulted debt may sympathize with the ill-fortune of the issuer, but they feel their own personal loss even more keenly. They may get back nothing or only a few cents out of each dollar they invested.

Figure 15.3 shows the historical differences between the yields on U.S. government, corporate Aaa ("best quality"), and corporate Baa ("lower-medium grade") bonds. In recent years, Baa bonds have been priced to yield about 1% per year more than Aaa bonds. Again notice the striking similar movements in these yield series. Risky bonds are priced to yield more than safe bonds. But this yield spread is usually pretty stable, indicating that the bonds are fairly good substitutes. If risky bonds were to yield a lot more than safe bonds, many investors would be persuaded to switch. If risky bonds yielded only a little more than safe bonds, investors would move in the other direction. Thus yields tend to move up and down together.

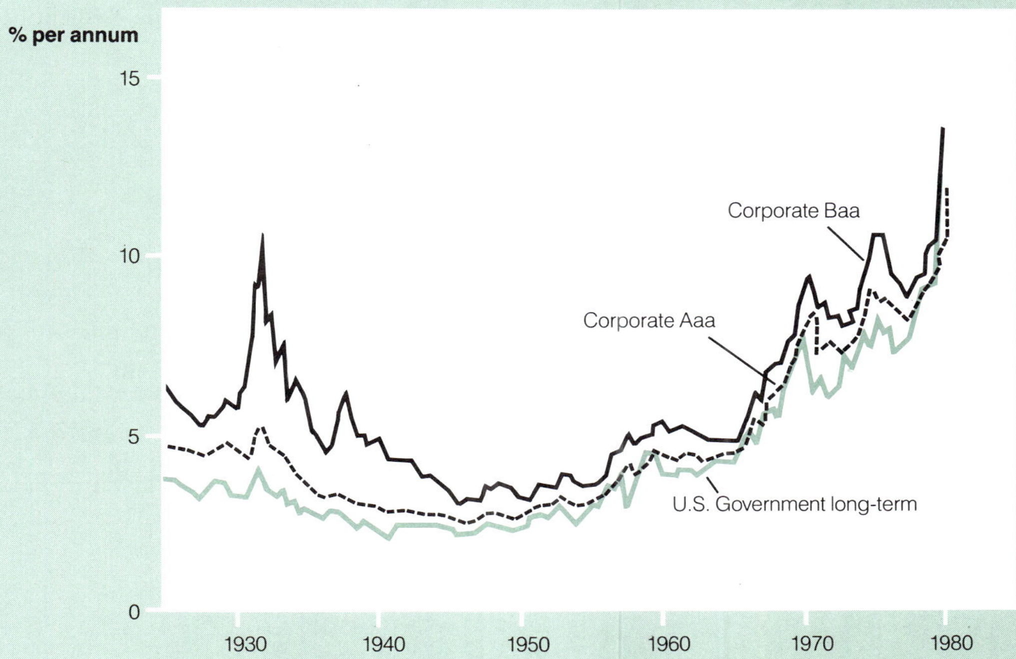

FIGURE 15.3 YIELDS ON MOODY'S Aaa AND Baa CORPORATE BONDS AND ON U.S. GOVERNMENT BONDS, 1926–80. **Lower-rated Baa bonds yield more than Aaa bonds, which, in turn, yield more than U.S. government bonds—the safest of all. The yields tend to move together because the assets are substitutes; investors would switch if risky bonds yielded too large or too small a risk premium. (Source: Federal Reserve Board *Historical Chart Book.*)**

INTEREST RATE RISK

Interest rate risk concerns the effects on investment performance of unforeseen changes in interest rates. This risk is very important to both borrowers and lenders, and has been extensively studied by academics, market professionals, and disreputable scribblers. The resulting analyses are quite broad and often very technical. This section gives a mostly nontechnical distillation of their conclusions. We start with an explanation of the implications of interest rate changes that are perfectly anticipated, and then we look at uncertainty.

The expectations hypothesis

A dollar received now is more valuable than one received a year from now, because the former can be profitably invested for a year. It is similarly true that a dollar received one year from now is more valuable than one received two years hence. If we let $\$P_t$ be the price today for $\$X$ delivered t years hence, the compounded annual rate of return on a t-year asset is the R_t such that

$$P_t (1 + R_t)^t = X. \tag{15.1}$$

Equivalently, the price today is the present value of those $\$X$ delivered in t years,* or

$$P_t = \frac{X}{(1 + R_t)^t} \tag{15.2}$$

Each future delivery date has an associated price and interest rate. This set of interest rates is called the pure *term structure of interest rates.*

A prospective purchaser of a two-year asset will consider the alternative of buying a one-year asset now and then another one-year asset a year from now. Every dollar invested in the two-year asset will grow to $(1 + R_2)^2$. Every dollar invested in the sequence of one-year assets will grow to $(1 + R_1)(1 + R_1^{+1})$, where R_1^{+1} is the anticipated yield one year hence (the +1 superscript) on one-year assets. The *Expectations Hypothesis* holds that these two alternative strategies must do equally well:

$$(1 + R_2)^2 = (1 + R_1)(1 + R_1^{+1}) \tag{15.3}$$

A two-year asset will not be held unless it can be expected to do as well as a sequence of one-year assets. A one-year asset will not be held unless it can be expected to do as well as holding a two-year asset for a year.† Both will be held only if both are equally attractive.

This same logic applied to longer-term assets gives the analogous equation:

$$(1 + R_t)^n = (1 + R_1)(1 + R_1^{+1})(1 + R_1^{+2}) \cdots (1 + R_1^{+n-1}) \tag{15.4}$$

A long-term interest rate is a geometric product of current and future one-year interest rates. Equation 15.4 is the fundamental equation of the Expectations Hypothesis. It is sometimes called the *Hicks' equation* in recognition of Sir John Hicks' important work in this area.

According to the Expectations Hypothesis, the shape of the pure term structure simply reflects the future course of interest rates. If the one-year rate is 10% now and will be 10% next year, then a two-year asset will have to yield 10% a year to be competitive. If the one-year rate is 10% now and will

* If R_t is a personal required return, then P_t in Equation 15.2 is the personal present value and may well differ from the market price. If securities are priced according to present-value principles, then the market price is the "market's intrinsic value," and R_t is the implicit "market's required yield."

† The net rate of return on a two-year asset held for a year is $(P_1^{+1} - P_2)/P_2$. Setting this equal to R_1, and noting that $P_1^{+1} = 1/(1 + R_1^{+1})$, gives Equation 15.3. Try it if you don't believe it!

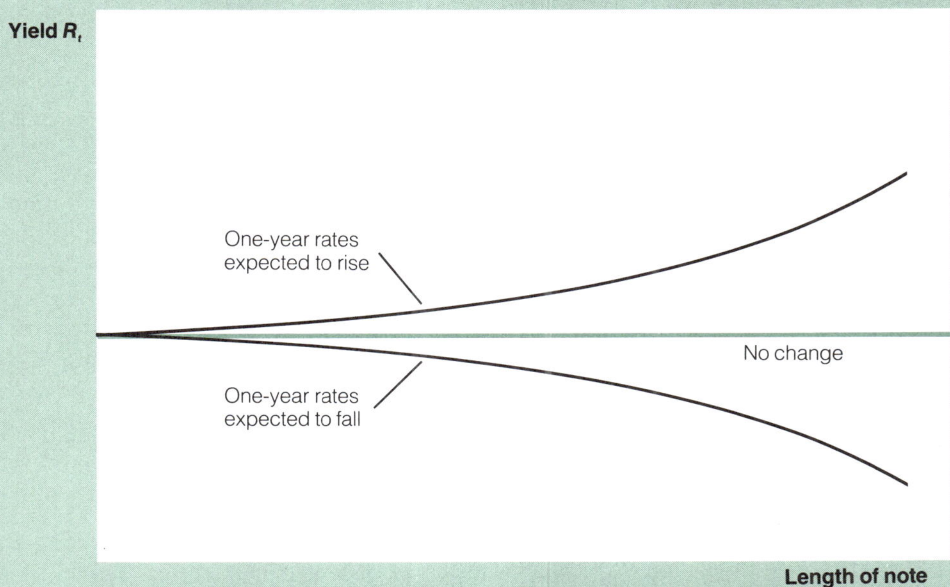

FIGURE 15.4 **PURE TERM STRUCTURES UNDER THE EXPECTATIONS HYPOTHESIS. Long-term bonds yield more or less than short-term bonds according to whether interest rates are expected to rise or fall.**

be 12% next year, then a two-year asset yielding 10% a year is unattractive. The two-year asset will have to yield about 11% a year to be competitive:

$$(1.10)(1.12) = (1.10995)^2.$$

If, on the other hand, the one-year rate is expected to decline from 10% now to 8% next year, then a two-year asset will have to yield about 9% a year to be equally attractive.

The bottom line is short and easy: The two-year rate will be higher or lower than the one-year rate, depending upon whether the one-year rate is expected to rise or fall. This very same logic applies to longer-term assets. If one-year rates are expected to be constant, then assets of differing maturities will be priced to give the same yield. If one-year rates are expected to increase in the future, then longer-term rates will be higher than the current one-year rate. If one-year rates are expected to decline, then longer-term rates will be lower than the current one-year rate. Three term structures are shown in Figure 15.4. With complicated patterns to future interest rates, more complex term structures emerge (Exercise 4, this chapter).

This is a straightforward yet elegant theory. Holding long-term assets and rolling over short-term assets are perfect substitutes in the theory and, so, the yields on long-term and short-term assets are linked. Anticipated interest rate movements determine the relationship between the current interest rates on short-term and long-term notes. Conversely, by examining the current relationship between short- and long-term rates we can detect whether interest rates are expected to go up or down. (A quick test: If long-term rates are below short-term rates, which direction are interest rates expected to be headed?)

Unfortunately, there are a few real-world frictions that undercut the pure theory. The most important assumption is that investors know what interest rates are going to be in the future. However, many of us cannot see the future with complete clarity. When future interest rates are uncertain, the Hicks' equation is jeopardized. Investors with imperfect foresight gamble whenever they invest in assets whose timing does not coincide with future expenses. If I need money one year from now and yet purchase a 30-year asset, then I am gambling on the price of 29-year assets one year hence. If I need money 30 years hence, and roll over 30 one-year assets, then I am gambling on the yields on one-year assets over the next 30 years.

Capital risk

The short-term purchase of long-term debt creates the capital risk of unanticipated interest rate changes causing unforeseen changes in debt prices. In general, the longer the term of an obligation, the more sensitive its price to interest rate fluctuations and the greater its capital risk.*

As Table 15.1 shows, a one-year asset will pay $5000 when it expires in a year, regardless of the interest rates then prevailing. The value of the two-year asset a year from now will depend on what the one-year interest rate turns out to be next year. If, as is currently expected, this interest rate is 10%, then the two-year asset can be sold for $5000 as planned. If, however, the interest rate rises to 20%, then this asset will be worth only $4583.

That would be disappointing, but not nearly as crushing as the potential loss on the purchase of a 30-year asset. At a 10% interest rate, my $4545.45 can purchase a 30-year asset with an eventual delivery of $79,315.46. If interest rates stay at 10%, then this asset can be sold after one year for $5000. If, however, interest rates rise to 20%, the value of my asset will decline sickeningly to $401 and I will have to settle for a good bicycle. Apparently, I should be wary of buying long-term assets.

There is capital risk in any purchase of long-term assets for resale a short while later. With short-term assets, the price cannot stray far from its redemption value. With long-term assets, a large change in price is possible and, in fact, will be necessary (because of compounding) to significantly alter the yield provided by a dollar delivery far in the future. Hicks' "Liquidity Preference" theory hypothesizes that investors do have short horizons and are consequently wary of the capital risk in long-term assets.

* In general, the differentiation of Equation 15.2 shows that the elasticity of price with respect to the gross return is equal to the term of the obligation:

$$\frac{\Delta P_t}{P_t} \Big/ \frac{\Delta(1+R_t)}{(1+R_t)} = -t$$

TABLE 15.1
Price changes for one-, two-, and thirty-year assets

Strategy	Current asset price	Interest rates stay at 10%	Interest rates rise to 20%
Buy a one-year asset	$4545.45 = \frac{5000}{1.10}$	5000	5000
Buy a two-year asset	$4545.45 = \frac{5500}{(1.10)^2}$	$5000 = \frac{5500}{1.10}$	$4583 = \frac{5500}{1.20}$
Buy a 30-year asset	$4545.45 = \frac{79{,}315.46}{(1.10)^{30}}$	$5000 = \frac{79{,}315.46}{(1.10)^{29}}$	$401 = \frac{79{,}315.46}{(1.20)^{29}}$

Investors with short horizons accept relatively low yields on short-term assets in order to avoid capital risk. Long-term assets must offer relatively high yields ("liquidity premiums") to attract investors.

Specifically, for any structure of anticipated one-year interest rates, long-term debt will yield more than would be predicted by the Expectations Hypothesis (Equation 15.4).

Income risk

But there is even more to the story of interest rate uncertainty. What if I have a long-term horizon? Assume that I have just inherited \$100,000 or, stranger still, earned \$100,000 from the sales of this textbook. I decide to invest this money for my retirement 30 years hence. One strategy is to buy a 30-year asset. Let's assume that this asset is priced to yield 10% a year, and thus will pay \$1,744,940 after 30 years:

$$100{,}000 = \frac{1{,}744{,}940}{(1.10)^{30}}$$

Alternatively, I could invest in a 30-year sequence of one-year assets. Each year, I would redeem a one-year asset and buy a new one. If the one-year rates turn out to be 10% each year, which is consistent with a 10% rate on a 30-year asset, then I will do equally well: $100{,}000(1.10)^{30} = 1{,}744{,}940$. But what if one-year rates drop to 5% after a year, and stay there? After thirty years, my nest egg will be a quarter of what it would have been: $100{,}000(1.10)(1.05)^{29} = 452{,}775$. Rolling over short-term assets when I have a long-term horizon entails the *income risk* that I will not earn as much interest as I anticipate. When I want to invest my money for 30 years, the purchase of a 30-year asset locks in the yield and insures the dollar value of the investment 30 years hence. The purchase of a sequence of short-term assets is risky because I don't know for sure how much interest I will earn in the future. If interest rates turn out to be higher than expected, then I will be richer. If they turn out to be significantly lower than expected, then I will be considerably poorer.

Investors with long horizons and a healthy distaste for uncertainty prefer long-term assets and, concerned about income risk, accept relatively low yields on long-term assets.

Capital risks versus income risks

Thus income and capital risks exert opposing pressures on the term structure. Which side wins this tug-of-war on the term structure? Are long-term rates higher or lower than predicted by the Expectations Hypothesis? It depends on whether income or capital risk is the predominant concern. The weight of the evidence is mostly on the side of capital risk, in that uncertainty about future cash needs tends to make short-term investing attractive. Banks are a good institutional example: With future deposit levels and loan demand uncertain, they prefer to invest in short-term assets, which can be liquidated with little danger.

Most borrowers, in contrast, prefer long-term loans. By not having to seek a new loan every year or two, borrowers reduce expenses and can feel more secure in their purchase of long-lived housing, plant, or equipment.* This borrower preference for long-term loans reinforces investor dislike of long-term assets. With lots of sellers and few buyers, long-term rates will be relatively high.

There is another more subtle point. Most investors, like me with my car or retirement, are saving for future expenditures. What matters is not how many dollars are accumulated, but how much can be purchased. Locking in 1.75 million dollars for my retirement does not insure that I will be able to live in the manner that I desire. If prices rise at 20% a year, my 1.75 million dollars will only buy what $7351 will buy today!

In saving for future expenditures, it is the real rate of return, rather than the nominal rate, that matters to investors. Buying a long-term asset with a fixed nominal return gives no protection against unanticipated changes in the inflation rate. A strategy of rolling over short-term assets, on the other hand, does offer the possibility that nominal rates will go up if inflation increases. Thus, investors with long horizons who are interested in real wealth and uncertain about inflation, may well consider short-term assets the safe investment.

This leaves only two categories of investors who prefer long-term assets. The first includes those with long horizons who aren't troubled by inflation uncertainties. Their numbers have probably dwindled in recent years. The second group consists of investors with long horizons who are mainly interested in nominal rather than real returns. Many life insurance companies and pension funds fall into this category. Institutions that are investing funds to provide a fixed nominal insurance or retirement payment 30 years hence are naturally concerned with income risk.† Rolling over short-term assets is risky, and lock-

* In contrast to producers, retailers have traditionally used mostly short-term debt to finance their inventories and consumer credit. But volatile financial markets have been persuading retailers to also use long-term debt. For instance, in 1980, J. C. Penney converted almost all of its debt from short to long term. *The Wall Street Journal* reported that this strategy "reduces the danger of a potential cash shortage, should the nation's financial markets run into a crisis. . . . A company with a large amount of short-term debt must constantly refinance its borrowings as they come due. . . . For some companies, in the worst possible case, failure to refinance their debt could force them into bankruptcy court."[1]

† To the extent that insurance and retirement benefits are linked to the cost of living, these institutions must be concerned with real returns too. For example, many pension plans tie benefits to the employee's highest, and usually last, salary years.

ing up a 30-year nominal return is safe. Insurance and pension funds are, in fact, the largest holders of long-term bonds.

There are many, many investors and issuers with diverse horizons, objectives, and risk preferences. Most investors probably prefer short-term assets; some may prefer to buy long-term assets. Most borrowers prefer to issue long-term securities. All can be persuaded to deal in less desirable assets by the offer of more attractive yields. The term structure implied by the Expectations Hypothesis does not hold exactly, and we cannot say for sure how it is distorted. If, as seems likely, investors predominantly like shorts while issuers prefer longs, then long-term rates will tend to be somewhat higher than predicted by the Expectations Hypothesis.

This means that an observed positively sloped term structure cannot be conclusively interpreted as evidence that interest rates are expected to rise. On the other hand, a flat or negatively sloped term structure is pretty good evidence that interest rates are expected to fall. In addition, horizons, objectives, and risk preferences are not likely to change suddenly. Gradual evolution is possible, such as a change in the relative importance of life insurance companies, but dramatic change is improbable. This means that large, sudden changes in observed term structures mostly reflect changes in interest rate expectations. If the term structure swings from downward- to upward-sloping, then this can usually be interpreted as evidence that expectations about future interest rates have been revised upwards.

Evidence of interest rate expectations Figure 15.5 compares the yields on high-quality corporate 30-year bonds and four- to six-month notes. In the 1930s and 1940s, the short-term rate fell to dramatic lows, but the long-term rate stayed well above the short rate because investors expected short rates to rise back to more normal levels. Note the persistence of this belief. Investors who rolled over commercial paper in the 1930s, waiting patiently for short rates to rise, were not rewarded for their faith; the long rate did not approach the short rate until the 1950s.

For the rest of the period, both earlier and later, the short rate has been sometimes above and sometimes below the long rate. Typically, the short rate gyrates while the long rate moves cautiously in the same direction, suggesting that investors view most short-term interest rate swings as temporary. When the short rate spurts upward, for instance, the long rate usually moves slightly upward. The long rate is then lower than the short rate, indicating that the short rate is expected to decline in the future.

Figure 15.5 compares a very short-term bond with a long-term bond. Other intermediate points on the yield curve are given in Figure 15.6. These breathtaking ski slopes show the diversity of yield curves. Amidst this wide variety of shapes, long-term rates have generally exceeded short rates. The "average" yield curve shows a monotonically increasing spread between one-year and longer bonds that rises to about a half a percentage point for ten-year bonds and is then constant. Burton Malkiel[2] and many others interpret this as evidence that investors are predominantly concerned with capital risk. Similarly, Charles Nelson[3] found that the average realized return from holding an n-period bond has exceeded that for a sequence of n one-year bonds, and that this yield differential rises with maturity.

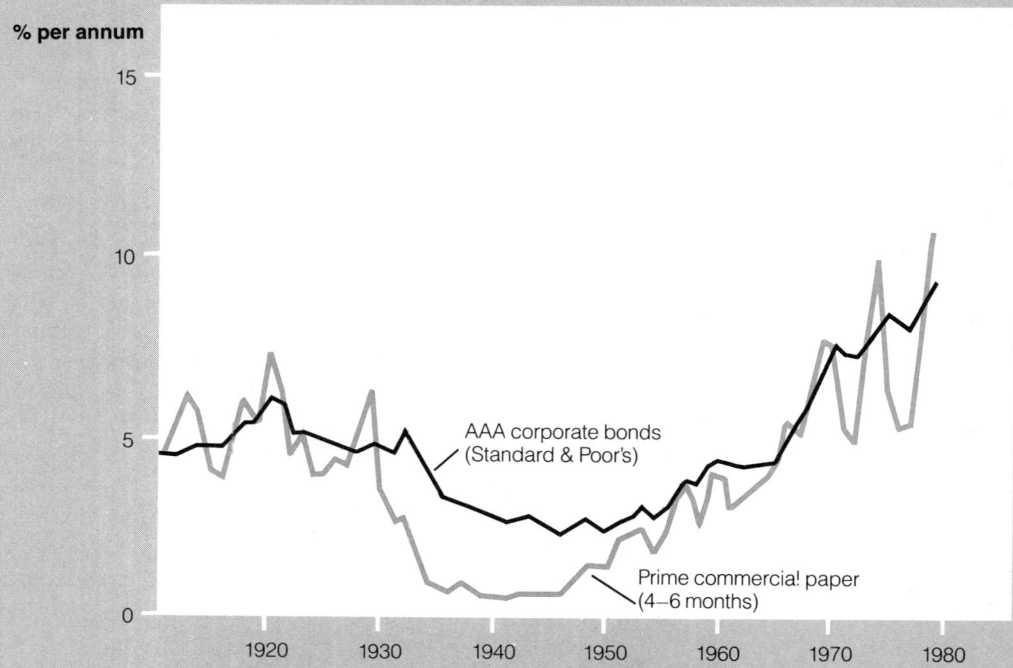

FIGURE 15.5 LONG- AND SHORT-TERM INTEREST RATES, 1911–80. **Historically, short-term bonds usually yield less than long-term, suggesting that their capital risk makes long-term bonds unattractive. (Source: Federal Reserve Board *Historical Chart Book.*)**

HOUSEHOLD PORTFOLIOS

Households have a wide variety of assets from which to choose: cash, checking accounts, bonds, stock, houses, gold, diamonds, paintings, old comic books—and the list goes on and on. In this section, we'll briefly sketch some of the choices made by households. Yields, liquidity, transaction costs, and the other factors that we have discussed all influence the specific portfolios selected. In recent years there have been some interesting and important portfolio shifts.

Physical assets are often neglected in macro models because economists don't have much data on quantities, prices, and yields. Many physical assets differ from financial assets in that they yield a flow of services rather than interest, dividends, or other cash income. For example, the ownership of a home provides services equal to the cost of renting a similar home. Cars, washing machines, and other durable goods provide services too.

Taxes should, of course, be taken into account. Houses, cars, and washing machines all provide "unseen income," which escapes taxation. If you purchase bonds and use the interest income to rent a house and a car and to wash your clothes at the laundromat, you will also have to pay taxes on all of that interest.

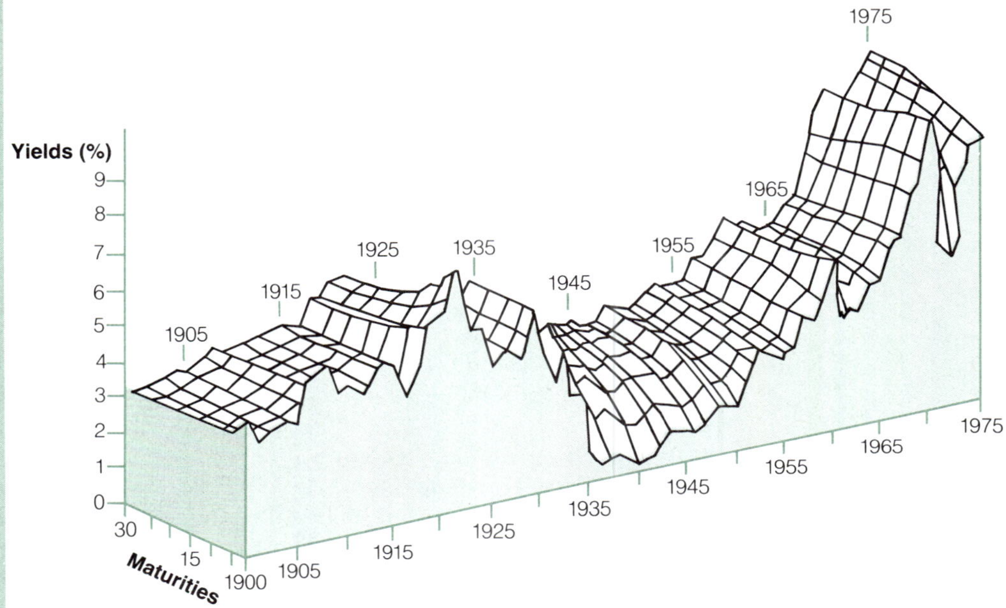

FIGURE 15.6 TERM STRUCTURE OF YIELDS ON U.S. CORPORATE SECURITIES, 1900–75. **Source: Sidney Homer, *A History of Interest Rates,* Rutgers University Press, 1977. Reprinted with permission.**

If you instead invest in a house, a car and a washing machine, then a good deal of your income will be asset services that are unrecorded and untaxed. This tax advantage gives households a strong incentive to purchase a home and consumer durables. That's the main reason, for example, so many rental apartments have been converted to owner-occupied condominiums.

As asset-yield calculation should also incorporate resale value. This is particularly important with a house and, to a lesser extent, with an automobile. Most other durable consumer goods have poor resale markets and are best used until they wear out. One big advantage of a house, as compared to financial assets, is that its capital gains are largely untaxed.

A final point is that the purchase of a physical asset (even one that will wear out and have no resale value) provides some insurance, as long as it lasts, against increases in the price of the asset's services. If you rent a car or a house, your rental cost may rise unexpectedly. If you instead buy a car and a house, you will be largely protected from such painful surprises. Physical assets thus provide consumers with one of the few ways by which they can hedge against inflation. Of course, this insulation has its limits. For example, storage costs, poor resale markets, and uncertainty about relative prices make stockpiling washing machines a poor hedge against increases in the prices of food and medical services.

There are two ways in which financial markets affect consumer investment in physical assets. High yields on alternative financial assets make physical investment less attractive. Consumer investment is also discouraged when financing is expensive and scarce. Usually these yields on financial assets and loans move together, because the assets are substitutes in the eyes of financial institutions and others. When bond and stock yields are high, then, we usually find that mortgage and consumer loan rates are also high.

However, consumer loan rates are often sticky, and loans are often rationed. Thus consumer loans might be drying up even though we see little or no change in consumer loan rates. In addition, the government can pursue selective credit policies that change mortgage and consumer loan rates relative to bond and stock yields. Tax code changes for example, in tax rates on dividends and capital gains—can directly alter relative rates of return. The deductability of mortgage and consumer loan interest payments can also be modified and the tax treatment of interest income can be altered to sway lending institutions toward or away from lending to households.

Figure 15.7 shows the ratio of household physical assets to total assets, financial as well as physical. Apparently, inflation and taxes have lured many investors from financial assets to physical assets: houses, land, and consumer durables. At the conclusion of World War II, the ratio of physical to total assets was depressed by the diversion of production to war materiel. There was a postwar housing and consumer-durables boom, and the physical-asset ratio quickly rose from 0.2 to 0.3. For the next 30 years this ratio continued to increase and it is now 0.4 indicating that, through the 1960s and especially during the 1970s, households increasingly turned from financial to physical assets.

Figure 15.8 shows the division of household financial assets among five aggregate categories: currency and demand deposits, time and savings accounts, short-term notes (such as money market fund shares and Treasury bills), long-term bonds (Treasury, municipal, corporate, and mortgage), and corporate equities. To reduce the clutter, two other aggregates are not graphed: nonmarketable insurance and pension reserves, and miscellaneous assets. The former has gradually risen from about 18% of total assets in the 1950s and 1960s to a little over 20% in the 1980s. The mysterious miscellaneous category has held steady at 1–2%. One other general remark that needs to be made about the ratios in Figure 15.8 is that they wiggle around a bit because the denominator, total assets, fluctuates with the stock market. For example, when the stock market crashed in 1973–74 the equity series nose-dived, and the other four ratios rose somewhat.

But suitably glazed eyes can smooth out these wriggles and recognize the interesting historical changes depicted in Figure 15.8. First is the striking shift away from equities and long-term bonds in household portfolios. (This shift is even stronger than indicated in the figure because these long-term bond data are maturity values rather than market values, and market values have sagged as interest rates have risen.) In part, the shift away from equities may be due to the unfavorable tax treatment of corporate depreciation and household nominal capital gains. More generally, in the face of great inflation and interest-rate uncertainty, there is likely a healthy aversion to the risks inherent in long-term financial assets.

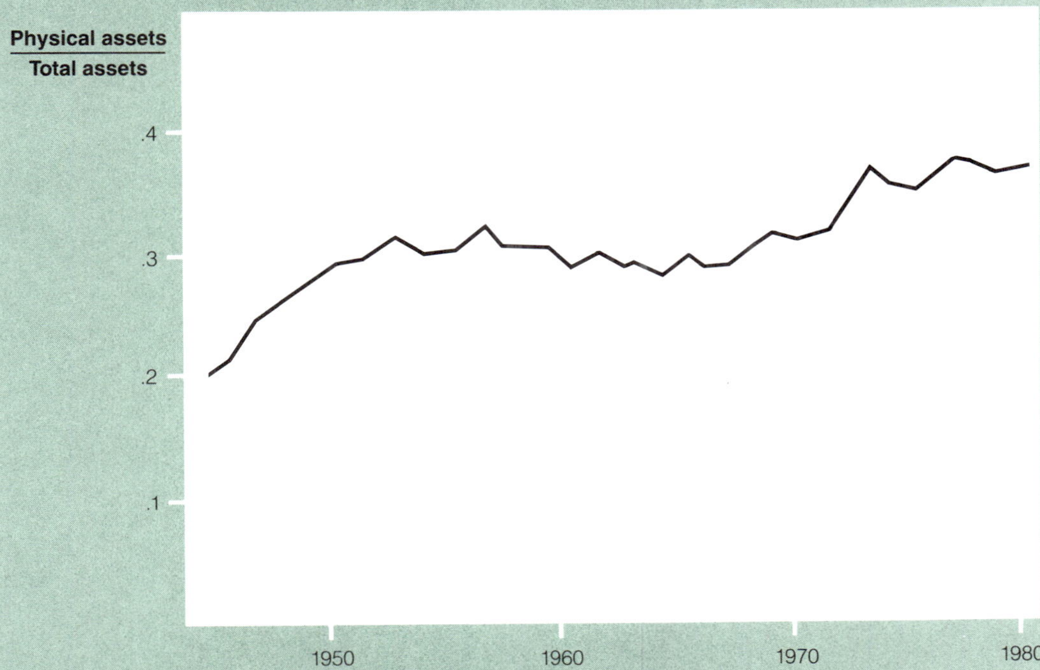

FIGURE 15.7 HOUSEHOLD PHYSICAL ASSETS AS A FRACTION OF TOTAL ASSETS SINCE WORLD WAR II. **Households have gradually increased the fraction of their wealth held as physical assets from 0.2 to 0.4. Taxes and inflation are two good reasons they have done so. (Source: Federal Reserve Board *Flow of Funds Book.*)**

Households have instead turned to short-term interest-paying assets. Figure 15.8 shows a dramatic spurt in short-term note holdings after 1977, predominantly money market funds. The figure also shows an even stronger long-run increase in time and savings accounts. These accounts were less than 15% of household financial wealth at the end of World War II, and they are now more than 30%. Much of this growth represents a shift from long-term government bonds and equity. But it also reflects a striking shift from currency and demand deposits. Cash and checking accounts have sagged badly since World War II, particularly in comparison with other liquid short-term assets. High interest rates on alternative assets have reduced the appeal of currency and demand deposits, which pay little or no interest.

SEPARATE GOVERNMENT AND PRIVATE BONDS

Macro models can be extended to allow for a variety of assets and a multiplicity of yields. But such expanded models must be solved by a computer rather than a two-dimensional graph. There are just two many markets and yields that

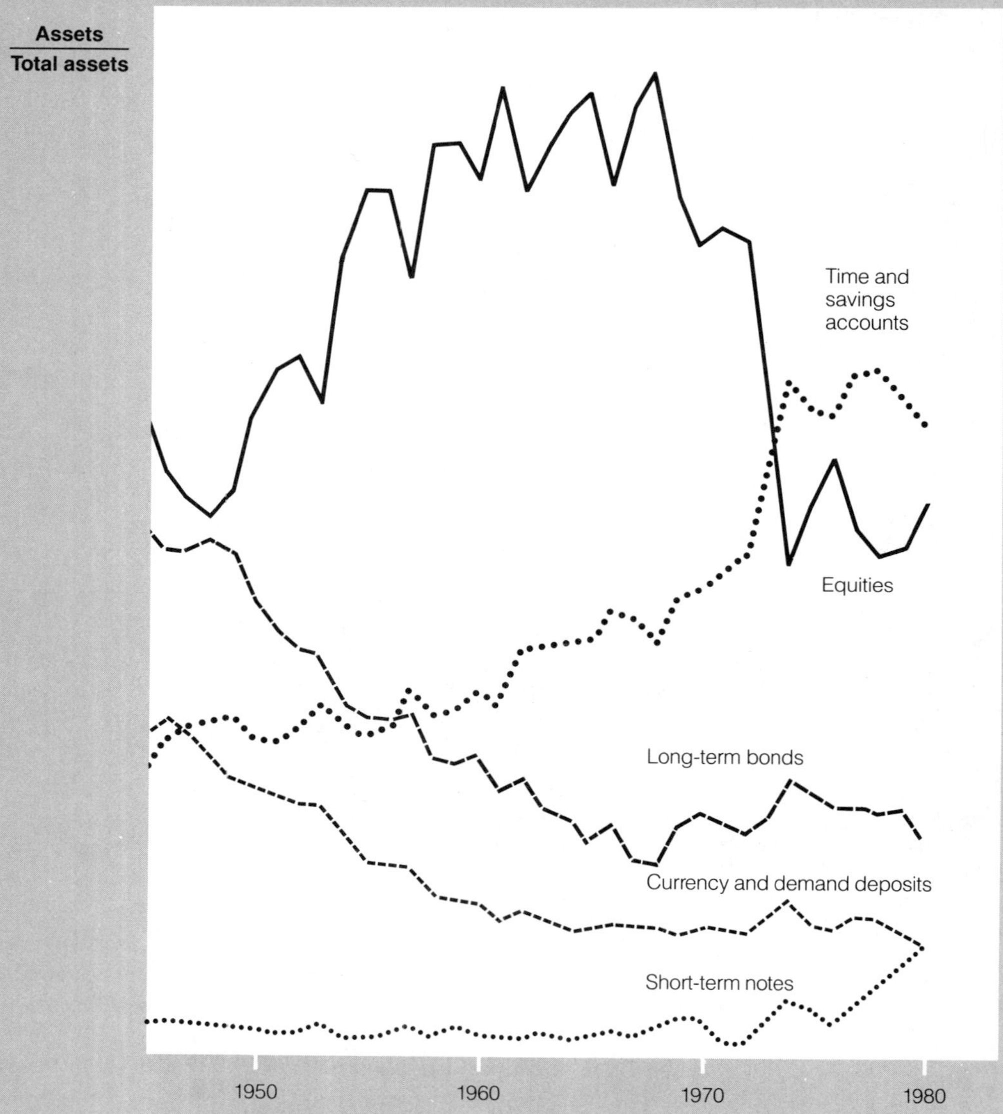

FIGURE 15.8 VARIOUS HOUSEHOLD FINANCIAL ASSETS AS PROPORTIONS OF TOTAL FINANCIAL ASSETS, 1945–80. Over the period shown, investors have tended to switch to time and savings accounts and other short-term investments from cash, checking accounts, and long-term bonds. Cash and low-interest checking accounts are unattractive when other assets offer high interest rates. Long-term bonds have high capital risk and no protection against unexpected inflation.

must be manipulated for us to figure out the answers on the back of an envelope. To see the importance of expanded models, we will first look at the interesting implications of a three-asset model. Then we will see how more complex models can be constructed.

Because of differing risk and other factors, government and business securities are not perfect substitutes. Thus we disaggregate the *IS-LM* model of the demand side of the economy to allow for three assets instead of two:

$$\text{(spending = income)} \quad e[\overset{+}{y}, \overset{-}{R_T}, \overset{-}{R_C}] = y$$

$$\text{(money)} \quad l[\overset{+}{y}, \overset{-}{R_T}, \overset{-}{R_C}] = M/P$$

$$\text{(Treasury securities)} \quad b[\overset{+}{y}, \overset{+}{R_T}, \overset{-}{R_C}] = B/P$$

The *IS* equation says that spending, e, is equal to income, y, and that spending is positively related to income and inversely related to the yields on Treasury and corporate securities, R_T and R_C, respectively. Spending is less attractive when financial securities are more appealing. The *LM* equation says that money demand is equal to money supply and that money demand is positively related to income and negative related to the yields of alternative financial assets. The Treasury securities equation says that supply is again equal to demand and that Treasury and corporate securities are substitutes, though not perfect substitutes. An increase in the rate of return on Treasury securities encourages investors to hold more Treasury securities and to hold less money and fewer corporate securities. An increase in the rate of return on corporate securities shifts demand from money and Treasury securities towards corporate securities.

The imperfect-substitutes assumption implies that **an increased supply of an asset tends to reduce the asset's price and increase its yield relative to other assets, persuading investors to hold the additional supply.** Note that this argument indicates only the implied movement in relative yields, not that in absolute yields. However, government money has a special role in constraining the structure of asset yields, because the nominal yield on money is fixed at zero. For an asset's yield to increase relative to money's zero yield, the nominal yield on that asset must rise. Thus an increased supply of some asset raises that asset's nominal yield both absolutely and relative to the yields on other assets. However, we cannot say for sure whether these other yields will go up or down! We can only be certain that they will not go up by more than the yield on the asset whose supply has increased. When government money is the asset whose supply increases, then the conclusions are much more definite. Since money's yield is fixed at zero, the only way money can yield more relative to other assets is for the nominal yields on the other assets to decline. We will now apply these principles to some fiscal and monetary policies.

The easiest solution procedure is to focus on aggregate demand and simultaneously solve our *IS* condition and the two-asset equilibria for y, R_C, and R_T. Figure 15.9 shows the relevant curves with y and R_C on the axes. The *IS* and *LM* curves are negatively and positively sloped, respectively, for the reasons

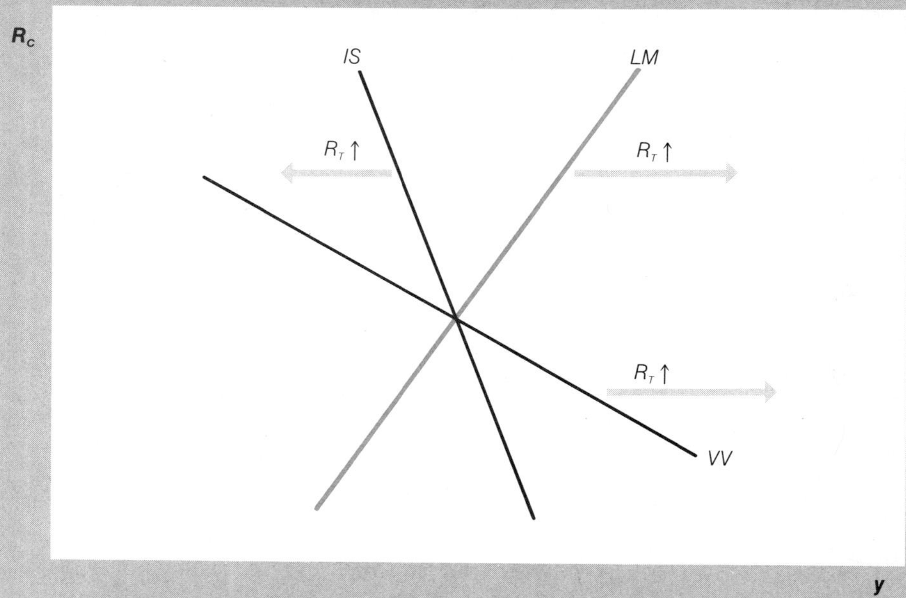

FIGURE 15.9 THE *IS, LM,* AND *VV* CURVES. **The *IS* and *LM* curves have the usual slopes, but are shifted about by the second interest rate (on Treasury securities). The new *VV* curve shows equilibrium in the Treasury securities market.**

given in Part I. The new *VV* curve, describing corporate-securities equilibrium, is negatively sloped: An increase in y raises the net demand for corporate securities, requiring an offsetting decrease in R_C to reduce demand and maintain equilibrium. In addition, we now have a second interest rate, R_T, that has to be determined by the triple intersection of the *IS, LM,* and *VV* curves.* As shown in Figure 15.9, an increase in R_T reduces commodity demand (shifting *IS* leftward), reduces money demand (shifting *LM* rightward), and reduces the demand for corporate securities (shifting *VV* rightward).

Fiscal policy

Consider now the aggregate demand effects of an expansionary fiscal policy, as shown in Figure 15.10. The solution is inside the indicated triangle with y and R_T up, but the change in R_C ambiguous. The increased supply of Treasury securities causes an increase in Treasury rates relative to other yields. The yield on money is fixed and, so, Treasury yields, R_T, must rise in order to increase the attractiveness of Treasury securities relative to money. However, we cannot tie down the direction of change in R_C; we know only that R_T must rise relative to R_C.

One simple way to confirm this ambiguity is to recall the simple *IS-LM* analysis in Part I, where there were only two assets: money and securities. When

* We still have the price level and the supply side, and need a quadruple intersection to solve the model completely. To simplify these analytics, we hold the price level constant here and look just at the demand side of the economy.

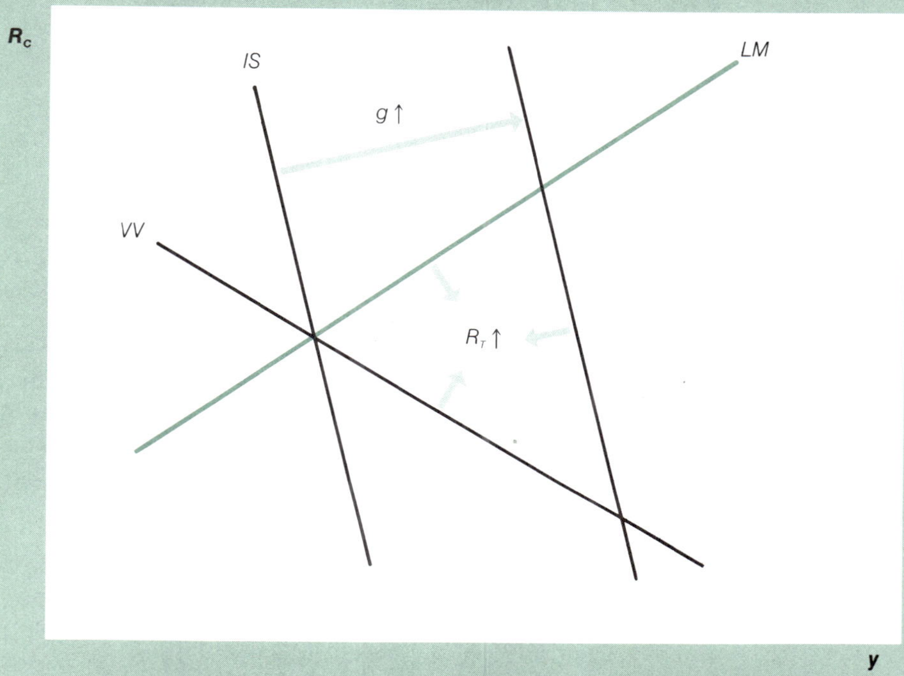

FIGURE 15.10 MECHANISM OF EXPANSIONARY FISCAL POLICY. A tax cut or increased government spending financed by the sale of Treasury securities increases aggregate income and the interest rate on Treasury securities. Interest rates on corporate securities may rise or fall, depending on whether the Treasury securities are closer substitutes for corporate bonds or for money.

the Treasury sold securities to finance government spending, the interest rate went up. But when the Fed offsets such Treasury sales by simultaneously buying securities, interest rates may go down. Thus, an increase in government spending increases the interest rate when it is bond-financed and may reduce the interest rate when it is money-financed. Now, in our present expanded model, the Treasury's securities may be a better substitute for government money than for corporate securities. If so, then Treasury securities, like money financing, may reduce the yields on private securities.*

* Graphically, when Treasury securities are a better substitute for money than for private securities, then a given increase in the Treasury yield, R_T, has more effect on the *LM* curve than on the *VV* curve, so that R_C falls in Figure 15.10. A more formal argument: An increase in government spending increases income and thereby raises the demand for all assets. But only Treasury securities are in larger supply. An increased yield on the Treasury securities expands their demand to match the enlarged supply, and simultaneously reduces the demands for other assets. What further yield adjustments are needed? If Treasury securities are a better substitute for money than for corporate securities, then R_T has little effect on corporate securities demand and the excess demand for corporate securities must be eliminated by a decline in corporate yields.

TABLE 15.2
Average maturity of privately-held marketable U.S. government securities

Year end	Average maturity (months)
1946	124
1950	100
1955	71
1960	58
1965	63
1970	41
1975	29
1980	45

This is important enough and different enough from Part I to bear repeating: **If Treasury securities are a better substitute for money than for corporate securities, then an increase in government spending may reduce corporate yields, crowding private investment in rather than out.** More generally, government spending causes less demand-side crowding out the less that Treasury securities substitute for corporate securities.

In practice, are Treasury securities better substitutes for money or for private securities? It undoubtedly depends on the type of Treasury security sold. At present, the main distinguishing characteristic is maturity, with short-term Treasury bills closer to money and long-term Treasury bonds closer to the private securities used to finance private investment projects. This argument suggests that if the Treasury wants to minimize the crowding out of private investment, it should mostly sell very short-term bills. Table 15.2 shows the actual average maturity of Treasury debt since World War II. The reliance on long-term securities during the war left the average maturity at more than ten years in 1946. This average maturity was then halved during the twenty years 1946–65, and then halved again over the next ten years, 1966–75.

Interestingly, the exceptions to this long-term decline took place during periods when there seemed to be great concern with capital formation. During the early 1960s, spurred by economic comparisons with the Soviet Union, "growthmanship" was in vogue. A variety of government actions were taken to encourage production, productivity, and investment. One of these was "Operation Twist," an effort to buy long-term and sell short-term government bonds in order to twist the term structure of interest rates so that low long-term rates would encourage investment, while high short rates would improve the balance of payments. Little effect on the term structure was noticed. The increase in average maturity of Treasury debt during this period, as shown in Table 15.2, indicates that Operation Twist was so half-hearted that the government actually allowed maturities to go in the wrong direction. In the mid-1970s with the federal government running large budget deficits there were widely expressed fears, particularly from the Secretary of the Treasury, that government debt would crowd out private investment and exacerbate an anticipated capital shortage. Yet, again, the average maturity of the government debt was lengthened.

Monetary policy

A Federal Reserve open-market purchase of Treasury securities increases the supply of money and reduces the supply of Treasury securities. As shown in

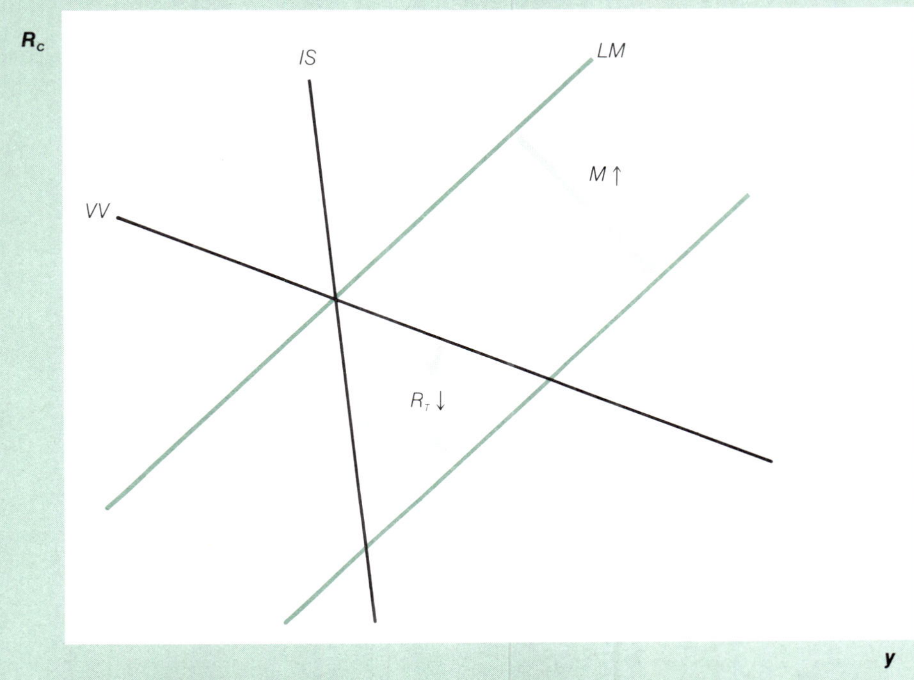

FIGURE 15.11 MECHANISM OF EXPANSIONARY MONETARY POLICY. **A Fed open-market purchase of Treasury securities lowers the interest rates on both Treasury and corporate securities and stimulates the economy.**

Figure 15.11, the interest rates on both Treasury and private securities diminish. The increased money supply argues for a higher yield on money relative to other assets and, since the yield on money is fixed,* the yields on other assets must decline. The diminished supply of Treasury securities argues for a relative reduction in their yield. So, overall, all yields decline, but particularly Treasury yields.

If the Fed is most interested in reducing the yields on, say, corporate bonds so as to encourage investment, then it should purchase securities that are close substitutes for corporate bonds. There can be little effect on the economy when the Fed prints money in order to buy securities that are a close substitute for money. There is a much greater effect on private interest rates, private investment, and aggregate demand when the Fed purchases close substitutes for private securities. One sure way of doing this would be for the Fed to buy private securities: mortgages, corporate bonds, and stock. The Fed is then essentially lending money to finance investment. In practice, this is usually done indirectly when the Treasury (or some other government agency) loans money to the private sector and then sells securities that are eventually purchased by the Fed.

* An increase in inflation expectations would reinforce these effects, driving real interest rates even lower. (See Exercise 8.)

Transactions	Sectors
Labor	Households
Transfers	Commercial banks
Commodity	Thrift institutions
Money	Insurance and pension funds
Demand deposits	Miscellaneous intermediaries
Time deposits at commercial banks	Businesses
Time deposits at thrift institutions	Federal Reserve
Short-term securities	Treasury
Long-term securities	State and local governments
Stocks	Rest of world
Mortgages and loans	
Nonmarketable claims	

IMPLICATIONS FOR MACRO MODELS

The *IS-LM* model of the demand side is infinitely expandable. The number of separate sectors and transactions identified is limited only by our data and interest. The aggregation used in a macro model that I helped construct[4] is as above. The Fed has flow-of-funds data that allow an even more detailed modeling of financial markets than this shows. Researchers choose levels of aggregation based on their assessments of the trade-off between realism and tractability, tempered of course by data availability. The general principles are to lump together agents that behave similarly and assets that are close substitutes. Models are also often shaped by objectives. If you want to analyze the economic activities of certain very specific sectors of the economy, then you are going to need a detailed model. There are professional model builders with very large models who, for a fee, will analyze very specific details, ranging from pizza sales in New Haven to NOW accounts in Fresno.

When we built the model summarized above we were especially interested in capturing some of the turbulence in financial markets. We wanted to see how various government policies affected specific financial markets and institutions. For example, we wanted to predict the consequences of the relaxation of deposit rate ceilings that was mandated by the 1980 Deregulation legislation. At the end of Chapter 14, we noted that the effects are theoretically ambiguous. With the parameter values used in our model, it turns out that an increase in deposit ceiling rates reduces other interest rates.

Earlier in this section, I indicated some of the loose ends in analyzing monetary and fiscal policies in multiple-asset models. The general assumptions in such models are that an increase in income raises the net demand for all assets and that all are substitutes (in that a higher yield on any one will increase the demand for that asset relative to all others). These assumptions imply that:

1. An expansionary fiscal policy will raise commodity demand and the real interest rate on the securities sold by the Treasury. (It is uncertain whether other yields will rise or fall.)

2. An open-market purchase will raise commodity demand and reduce all real interest rates.

3. When the Fed buys one type of security and sells another, the yield on the first will fall and the yield on the second will rise, but the course of other yields is uncertain.

TABLE 15.3
Interest rate effects of asset swaps

Asset purchased	Asset sold	Interest rate changes: Short-term securities	Long-term securities	Mortgages	Stock
Long-term securities	Short-term securities	Up	Down	Down	Down
Mortgages	Long-term securities	Down	Up	Down	Down
Stock	Short-term securities	Up	Down	Down	Down

The first two conclusions have already been analyzed using a model in which Treasury and corporate securities are imperfect substitutes. The third conclusion was not discussed before because it requires three interest rates. The basic argument is that, to persuade investors to hold less of one security and more of another, there must be a relative decline in the first yield and relative increase in the second. With money's yield fixed, we can infer that the first yield must fall and the second yield must rise. But we cannot say, without specific parameter values, whether the absolute values of other yields go up or down.

In our empirical model, we were able to analyze such questions. Table 15.3 shows the effects of three different asset swaps.

As expected, a swap of short-term securities for long-term securities pushes the short rate up and the long rate down. The yields on mortgages and stock also decline. This result confirms my earlier comments about crowding in versus crowding out: If the Treasury sells short-term bills instead of long-term bonds, the yields on private securities will be lower and investment will be stimulated. Low mortgage rates encourage home loans. Low stock yields imply high stock prices, high values of q, and high investment incentives.

A swap of long-term securities for mortgages mimics government agencies (like Freddie Mac) that sell long-term bonds and purchase mortgages. Such transactions lower mortgage rates and increase long rates. According to our simulations they also reduce short rates and stock yields.

A leveraged investment fund might sell short-term securities and use the proceeds to buy stock. The Fed could conceivably make similar transactions. Such trades would increase short-term rates and reduce stock yields (increasing stock prices). In our model, long rates and mortgage rates would also fall.

These are three examples of the sorts of detailed financial market questions that cannot be answered by a simple *IS-LM* model, but can be handled by a more disaggregated model. Corporations, financial institutions, the Fed, and other government agencies all use complicated macroeconometric models to track the economy and to anticipate the detailed consequences of various economic events. You may some day be a consumer or producer of such models.

IMPORTANT TERMS AND CONCEPTS

Perfect substitutes	Term structure of interest rates
Liquidity	Expectations Hypothesis
Secondary market	Hicks' Equation
Transaction costs	Capital risk
Divisibility	Income risk

Investors accept lower yields on assets that are otherwise considered attractive. Issuers pay higher interest rates on debts that they consider otherwise attractive. A liquid asset tends to yield less than an illiquid asset. An asset with low transaction costs tends to have a low yield. An asset with tax advantages tends to have a low before-tax yield. An asset with little cash flow risk tends to have a low yield.

According to the Expectations Hypothesis, the relationship between long-term and short-term interest rates depends only on whether interest rates are expected to rise or fall. Long rates will be above short rates if rates are expected to rise, and below short rates if rates are expected to fall. Capital risk tilts the term structure, causing relatively higher yields on long-term assets. Income risk pushes in the opposite direction, causing relatively higher yields on short-term assets. Capital risk seems predominant.

In recent years, household portfolios have shifted towards physical assets and short-term, interest-earning financial assets and shifted away from currency, demand deposits, and long-term financial assets. These portfolio shifts reflect inflation uncertainties, the tax advantages of physical assets, and the low interest rates on currency and demand deposits.

Multiple-asset models allow us to analyze how changes in the demand or supply of one asset affect the yields on assets that are imperfect substitutes. One of the important lessons is that there is less crowding out when the Treasury finances its deficits by selling short-term securities that are close substitutes for money, rather than long-term securities that are close substitutes for the securities that firms issue to finance their investments.

EXERCISES

1. Comment on the following advice on buying appliances with a new house: "In the very simple arithmetic of interest costs, a mortgage appears to be a very expensive way to finance home furnishings. To illustrate let's assume that the builder is offering a washing machine, clothes dryer and automatic dishwasher. Their total price at an appliance store is \$675. The builder's price is ⅓ less. Let's assume a mortgage of average length, 27 years, at the national interest rate (last December) of 7.75%. Finally, let's compare the mortgage finance charges with those for the same appliances purchased at the store's price and with the store's 2-year, 15% installment contract. Here are the figures:

	cost from store	cost from builder
purchase price	\$675	\$ 450
finance charge	\$110	\$ 625
	\$785	\$1075

At those terms, the appliances would cost \$290 more from the builder than from the store." (Consumer Reports, April 1972).

2. If the tax exempt status of municipal bonds were eliminated, how would this affect interest rates and the level and composition of GNP?

3. If the Hicks' equation (15.4) holds, will it be better to buy a 7-year note followed by a 3-year note, or to buy a 6-year note followed by a 4-year note?

4. Make a rough sketch or use a pocket calculator to answer the following.
   (a) If one-year rates will be $R_1 = .10$, $R_1^{+1} = .15$, $R_1^{+2} = .20$, $R_1^{+3} = .15$, $R_1^{+4} = .10$, according to the Expectations Hypothesis, what will the term structure be?
   (b) If current rates are $R_1 = .10$, $R_2 = .11$, $R_3 = .10$, $R_4 = .09$, what are the implicit future 1-year rates consistent with the Expectations Hypothesis?

5. The text uses an example in which my untimely purchase of a 30-year-bond converted a new car into a bicycle. What would my 30-year bond have been worth after 1 year if the initial 1-year rate jumped to 20%, but all future 1-year rates were expected to remain at 10%? Assume that the Hicks' equation (15.4) holds.

6. In the following assume that the Expectations Hypothesis is correct and the Hicks' equation (15.4) applies.

The yield on 1-year bonds is initially 10% and is expected to remain at 10%. The monetary authorities now sell a large quantity of 1-year bonds, driving the yield up to 12%. However, it is still believed that 1-year yields next year and thereafter will be 10%. What is the yield now on 2-year bonds? On 3-year bonds? Which yield changed the most? If the monetary authorities had bought 2-year bonds instead, do you think that this would have affected expectations about future 1-year rates?

7. In the 1960s the U.S. government wanted to reduce long-term interest rates to stimulate corporate investment while raising short-term interest rates to improve the balance of payments. The Fed tried "Operation Twist," trading in short- and long-term government bonds so as to twist the term structure. Should they have bought shorts and sold longs, or vice versa? What, if any, are the implications of the Expectations Hypothesis for Operation Twist?

8. Use the three-asset model shown in Figure 15.9 to analyze the effects of an increase in inflation expectations.

9. A \$100,000 30-year note with a 10% annual yield pays $\$110{,}000\,(1.10)^{30} = \$1{,}744{,}940$ after 30 years. What will the real value of this payoff be if the annual inflation rate is 0%? 5%? 10%? Alternatively, what would real wealth be after purchase of a sequence of thirty 1-year notes, assuming that 1-year rates adjust to maintain a constant real interest rate of 5%? If interest rates do adjust for inflation, do short-term or long-term bonds offer more protection against unexpected inflation?

REFERENCES

1. Jeffrey H. Birnbaum, "J. C. Penney Switches to Long-term Debt to Fight Burgeoning Interest Expenses," *Wall Street Journal,* October 14, 1980.

2. B. G. Malkiel, *The Term Structure of Interest Rates,* Princeton, New Jersey: Princeton University Press, 1966.

3. C. R. Nelson, *The Term Structure of Interest Rates,* New York: Basic Books, 1972.

4. D. Backus, W. Brainard, G. Smith, and J. Tobin, "A Model of U. S. Financial and Nonfinancial Economic Behavior," *Journal of Money, Credit, and Banking,* 12 (May 1980), pp. 259–93.

SUGGESTIONS FOR FURTHER READING

A useful survey of the term structure is B. G. Malkiel, *The Term Structure of Interest Rates,* Princeton, N. J.: Princeton University Press, 1966. A broader survey of differences among interest rates is J. C. Van Horne, *Financial Market Rates and Flows,* Englewood Cliffs, N. J.: Prentice-Hall, 1978. For a description of a macro model with detailed financial markets, see D. Backus, *et al,* "A Model of U.S. Financial and Nonfinancial Economic Behavior," *Journal of Money, Credit, and Banking,* 12 (May 1980), pp. 259–93.

CHAPTER SIXTEEN

EMPLOYMENT AND PRODUCTION

The chief business of the American people is business. The man who builds a factory builds a temple. . . . The man who works there worships there.

CALVIN COOLIDGE[1]

This chapter reviews labor demand and production decisions and provides additional discussion of labor supply and of unemployment. It explains the job search model of unemployment and the Phillips curve, and also the dual-labor-market hypothesis.

THE basic logic of production decisions and labor demand have been sketched in earlier chapters since these ideas are central to our understanding of economic booms and recessions. That logic will be briefly reiterated here and a few new wrinkles added. We will then look at labor supply in some detail, including theories not presented earlier.

OUTPUT AND LABOR DEMAND

In classical economic theory, both labor demand and output are determined by the profit-maximizing calculations of competitive firms. Given their existing plant and equipment, firms simultaneously decide how much labor to hire and how much to produce by comparing real wage rates with labor's marginal productivity. A firm hires and produces up to the point where marginal productivity is just equal to the real wage. Being competitive wage and price takers, firms do not worry about not being able to find workers or not being able to sell their output.

In the sticky-wage disequilibrium model, the story is pretty much the same as far as labor demand and output go. The novel feature is that there is an excess supply of labor. Firms still base hiring and production decisions on a comparison of real wages and marginal labor productivity. But, because nominal wages are sticky, both real wages and output can vary in the short run.

Matters are more complex in disequilibrium models in which both wages and prices diverge from market-clearing levels. Firms now must worry about some of their output going unsold. How much labor they want to hire and how much output they produce are heavily influenced by anticipated sales. When commodity demand is weak, firms cut back on production and employment; when demand picks up, firms expand.

There is not a simple, fixed relationship between commodity demand, output, and employment. Output and employment cannot be freely turned on and off like a water faucet. Adjustments take time and mistakes are expensive. If a firm produces too much, it has to bear the costs of storing and carrying unsold goods. If the firm produces too few goods, then customers get frustrated and leave, looking for more reliable suppliers. If too many workers are employed, then wages are paid to people who either sit idle or produce commodities that go unsold. If too few are employed, then the firm either cannot satisfy customers or must try to produce more by paying overtime rates, pushing employees harder, or hiring and training new people. Firms try to cope with uncertainty and adjustment costs by maintaining buffer stocks of output, capital, and labor.

Inventories of output accommodate temporary surges and lulls in demand while output is kept on a steady, orderly pace, keeping customers happy without overly disrupting production. It is, of course, expensive to carry an inventory of unsold goods. The money the firm spent on their production—wages, materials, and other costs—could instead have been invested in Treasury bills, apartment housing, or old postage stamps. The higher the rates of return on the alternatives, the less attractive is inventory investment. On the other hand, inventory investments can be very profitable if there is an increase in the commodity's price during the time between its production and its sale. In general, **a firm's desired inventory will depend positively on anticipated sales, positively on the volatility of sales (because of a wish to avoid antagonizing customers), negatively on nominal interest rates, and positively on anticipated price increases.**

Realized inventories bump up and down with sales variations, in that sudden increase in demand reduces inventories, while a drop in demand causes inventories to swell with newly produced goods that the firm had expected to sell. As sales and inventories change, the firm's managers must decide whether these are temporary aberrations or the beginning of a trend. They may use empirical models or informed judgment to separate fundamental demand shifts from random blips. On the basis of these guesstimates, production may either be cautiously increased or reduced in order to rebuild or deplete inventories.

Because it takes a while to acquire plant, equipment, and employees and to get them all working smoothly, firms find it economical to maintain reserves of each—to keep some extra capital and labor that can be unleashed if needed. Similarly, it can be costly to redirect capital and discard labor hastily. It is not all that easy to convert a shoe factory into a racketball club, a gas station into a fast-food restaurant, or a tractor into a tank. There are several costs in firing employees: severance pay, unemployment contributions, and the expenses involved in finding replacements when demand picks up again. The firm may also want to avoid acquiring a reputation for being quick to let people go. All in all, most firms find it cheaper in the long run to hold on to capital and employees when demand slumps and to avoid rushing into new commitments when demand surges. Thus, the buffer stocks of capital and labor swell during recessions and shrink during booms.

SEARCH THEORIES OF UNEMPLOYMENT

Classical economists assumed that labor demand and supply are always equal, so that everyone who wants a job has a job. How then are we to interpret economic data on unemployment, idle capacity, and recessions? A partial answer is given by the equilibrium model of the business cycle used by the new classical macroeconomists: Errors in gauging economic conditions, particularly real wages, cause voluntary fluctuations in employment and output.

But why is there persistently, year after year, even in the best of times, an unemployment rate of four or five per cent? Why is the natural rate of unemployment in the new classical model not zero per cent? To maintain an equilibrium interpretation of labor markets, one needs to explain why the millions of people who are labeled "unemployed" by the Bureau of Labor Statistics are really voluntarily not working. One explanation is provided by *search models* of unemployment: Many of the unemployed have chosen to be unemployed so that they can engage in an efficient search for a good job. These choosy people are only temporarily unemployed, and this unemployed search period is actually beneficial to the unemployed and to society since it helps people find the jobs for which they are best suited.

As we will see, search models do successfully explain why people may voluntarily choose to be temporarily unemployed. They also offer an alternative explanation of unemployment fluctuations and of a temporary Phillips-curve relationship between inflation and the unemployment rate. Yet search models are not a convincing explanation of all unemployment. A great deal of unemployment and the bulk of changes in unemployment seem to represent involuntary disequilibrium rather than voluntary search.

Searching for the best job

Search models blossomed in the 1960s under the green thumbs of George Stigler and Edmund Phelps.[2] Their fundamental departure from the early classical economists was in the treatment of information. Traditional classical analyses assumed that everyone is perfectly informed about the available economic options. Search models instead emphasize how costly it is to collect reliable information. People who must spend much time searching for detailed facts may rationally choose to be imperfectly informed. This sort of analysis might be applied to agents trying to find a good price at which to buy or sell just about anything. Here the application is to workers trying to learn the wages and other characteristics of various jobs.

In the typical search model, workers know the kinds of wages that are available but don't know which specific firm is paying which wage. For example, I might be looking for a summer job and believe that for my skills most firms will pay $10 an hour and that 95% will pay between $8 and $12 an hour. But I don't know which firms pay above average and which pay below average. To find out I have to engage in a costly search—going from firm to firm, filling out questionaires, and submitting to interviews—in order to collect wage offers. After each job offer, I can weigh the benefits from acceptance against the expected benefits from continuing to search for a better offer.

The reservation wage

The minimum wage offer that will persuade me to stop looking and start working is called a *reservation wage.* I will accept a job only if it pays at least my reservation wage. A fixed reservation wage is appropriate when conditions do not change from one wage solicitation to the next. At any point, past search costs are gone, cannot be reclaimed, and therefore should be forgotten. The relevant question is: Should one continue searching? If conditions have not changed, then it makes no difference whether one asks this question after receiving an $11-an-hour offer on the first or on the twentieth try. A calculation of the prospective benefits and costs of continued search will be the same in either case. So, if, on my first job application, I decide to accept $11 (but no less), then I should continue to use this rule: My fixed reservation wage is $11.

In a simple example, suppose there are five equally likely hourly wage rates of $8, $9, $10, $11, and $12. Each has a 0.2 probability of being offered. I am going to work 40 hours a week for 10 weeks, so that an additional dollar in hourly wages is worth $400 to me. And we further assume that the cost of each job solicitation (time, energy, haircut, and so on) is $100. What is my reservation wage?

A $12 offer will, of course, immediately be accepted since it can't be surpassed. If I am offered only $11, should I continue looking for a $12 offer? Each additional search costs $100 and has a 0.2 probability of being successful. Since a $12 offer raises my summer income by $400, my net expected gain is

$$\begin{pmatrix}\text{probability}\\ \text{of \$12 offer}\end{pmatrix}\begin{pmatrix}\text{gain from}\\ \text{\$12 offer}\end{pmatrix}-\begin{pmatrix}\text{cost of}\\ \text{search}\end{pmatrix}$$

or (0.2) ($400) − ($100) = −$20. If I base my decision on the expected gain, then additional search is unattractive; I should accept an $11 offer as soon as I get it.

What if I get a $10 offer before either $11 or $12? An extra job search costs $100 and there is a 0.2 probability of gaining $400 (with an $11 offer) and a 0.2 probability of gaining $800 (with a $12 offer). My expected net gain is 0.2 ($400) + 0.2($800) − $100 = $140. I should reject $10 offers and keep looking. I will, of course, also reject $8 and $9 offers. So my reservation wage is $11: I will not accept a job unless I am offered at least $11. This logic implies that **the voluntarily unemployed will be predominantly people with low search costs or unrealistically high wage expectations.**

These calculations implicitly assume that my initial offers remain open if I decide to go off and try my luck elsewhere. What if I have to accept or reject an offer on the spot, with no turning back? In the simple situation described here it makes no difference. If I turn down a $10 offer and then am offered $9 by the next firm, I will turn that down, too, and continue searching just as if it had been another $10 offer. Since nothing has changed, I have no desire to go back and accept any offers that I have already refused. I have a fixed $11 reservation wage, regardless of how many offers I have refused and irrespective of whether I can recall old offers.

The search model implies that the supply of labor (the number of people willing to accept the wage offers being made) is positively related to search costs and negatively related to the dispersion of wage offers. High search costs clearly encourage people to stop searching and start working. A high dispersion of wage offers has the opposite effect. People will do little searching when everyone pays pretty much the same wage, and will search a great deal when wages vary considerably.

Extensions and implications Further implications can be drawn by extending the search model in several directions. The following summarizes some of the more interesting conclusions.

The discussion so far has not fully taken into account that searching takes time, so that the more one searches the less one can earn. My $100 search cost figure presumably does include the implicit cost of the hours actually spent searching. A day off from work at $10 an hour is $80 lost. However, I did not take into account the fact that I have a finite work horizon that gets shorter every day I search. My benefits calculation incorrectly assumed that I would be able to work 10 weeks this summer, no matter how many days I spend searching. In fact, the longer I search, the less time I will be able to work and so, the smaller the prospective gains from a higher wage rate. This decline in expected gains means that my reservation wage also declines as time passes. By the end of the summer, it won't make much sense to keep searching, and I will consequently accept jobs that I would have rejected at the start of the summer.*

The simple search model considered above assumes that people know the distribution of wages across firms but nothing about which firms pay which wages. In practice, people are neither completely certain about the general wage distribution nor completely ignorant about the wages paid by specific firms. These two types of uncertainties are different and do make a difference to the analytics. For example, I might be firmly convinced that all firms pay the same wage, but uncertain what that wage is. Perhaps I believe that $8, $9, $10, $11, and $12 are equally likely. My reservation wage is now $8 rather than $11, in that I will accept my first offer, no matter what it is, because I am convinced that I cannot do any better. I will also revise my probabilities once I find out what the standard wage is.

We learn two things through job search: information about what specific firms are paying and information about what firms in general are paying.[3] The latter causes careful searchers to revise their beliefs about the distribution of wages across firms and so, to revise their reservation wages. If, in the initial example, I keep getting $8 and $9 job offers, I will become less optimistic about the odds of receiving $11 and $12 offers and more willing to accept lower wages.

There is a bias here that causes reservation wages to decline as search proceeds. If I get a high offer, I will accept it and stop searching. If I instead get disappointingly low offers and keep searching, I will also be continually lower-

* It does make a difference now whether I can keep job offers open, since that option allows me to change my mind. My reservation wage will be lower if I must accept or reject offers on the spot.

ing my sights and my reservation wage. These probability revisions consequently imply that **the supply of labor willing to accept current wage offers is positively related to the duration of unemployment.**

Job search and the Phillips curve

The government's unemployment data count as unemployed those people without jobs who are actively looking for work. The disequilibrium interpretation of these data is that the unemployed are frustrated in their efforts to find suitable jobs. The unemployed look for jobs for which they are trained and qualified, but find that there are no openings. There are individual and social losses from a French teacher or a construction worker who cannot find work, or who must eventually take a job for which they are overqualified. Search models interpret the unemployment data differently. They view the unemployed as voluntarily turning down good jobs in order to find slightly better ones. The unemployed could, at any moment, work if they wanted. But it is to their advantage (and society's, too) that the unemployed carefully select a job from the many alternatives.

In excess-supply models, unemployment changes as labor demand changes. Variations in real wages or commodity demand cause firms to hire more people or let some people go. Thus changes in the number of job openings cause fluctuations in employment and unemployment. In search models, unemployment variations are instead due to revised calculations of the costs and expected benefits from job search. In search models, it is labor supply changes that cause employment and unemployment to fluctuate.

It is not surprising that these two views of unemployment give very different interpretations of the Phillips-curve relationship between unemployment and wage or price inflation. **The market-disequilibrium interpretation of the Phillips curve is that an increase in commodity demand increases labor demand, thereby reducing unemployment and putting upward pressure on wages and prices. The search view of the Phillips curve looks at the relationship from the other way around, asking how increases in wages and prices affect job search and unemployment.**

In most search models,* a perceived uniform shift in the distribution of wages and prices has no effect on search activity. Consider a neutral, across-the-board 50% increase in all wages and prices. In my summer job example, the firms paying $8, $9, $10, $11, and $12 now pay $12, $13.50, $15, $16.50, and $18. My search costs also increase 50%, from $100 per job solicitation to $150 per job. The costs and benefits of job search have simply been rescaled and there is no real change in my behavior. My reservation wage goes up 50% to $16.50 and, as before, I choose to search until I find one of the firms whose pay scales are in the top 40%. There is no change in my odds of finding one of these firms, in the number of wage offers I will solicit before I am successful, and in

* A few scattered search models do imply a long-run relationship between unemployment and inflation. Reuben Gronau has noted that, because of finite work horizons, the unemployed will lower their reservation wages the longer they are unemployed. This can imply that high unemployment is associated with low wage increases. Charles Holt obtains a similar conclusion by emphasizing that the costs of changing jobs will persuade those who are employed to keep working even when they receive smaller wage increases than those who hop from job to job.[4,5]

the amount of time I spend unemployed and searching. The 50% price increase has no effect on unemployment.

An across-the-board increase in wages and prices affects unemployment in search models only when the inflation is misperceived. For example, I may not realize that everything has gone up 50%, and so use my old, outdated $11 reservation wage. On my first try, I get a $12 wage offer and celebrate my good fortune, thinking that I have hit one of the top 20% of firms. Instead, I have, of course, hit one of the bottom 20%. I accept a job and cut short my job search because of my mistake in assessing the current wage distribution. The unemployment rate is now inversely related to wages and prices a la the Phillips curve because labor's knowledge lags behind reality.

This search theory explanation of the Phillips curve is very similar to the new classical explanation given earlier in Chapter 5. In both cases, inflation causes voluntary but short-lived increases in employment. In the earlier explanation, workers make an incorrect work-leisure choice because of errors in calculating real wages. Here workers make an incorrect work-search choice because of errors in calculating the distribution of wages across firms.

In both cases, the changes in employment are of dubious benefit since they are due to poor choices made by misinformed workers. And in both cases the government is advised to avoid disruptive inflations that confuse people's economic calculations. Search theory, in addition, makes explicit one of the subtle costs of inflation—or of any economic events that make current information obsolete. When wages, prices, and other important economic data change unexpectedly, people must pay to gather new information, or make decisions based on out-of-date information.

Search theory limitations

Search theory provides a formal apparatus for understanding the behavior of economic agents who are trying to find good prices for what they are buying and selling. Search models are an important first step in analyzing decentralized markets, in which there is no omniscient, Walrasian auctioneer. When applied to labor markets, search models may help some of us become more rational searchers. But search models are not a complete explanation of why millions of people are unemployed. Most unemployment does not really seem to be voluntary, optimizing search activity. A fundamental inadequacy is the crucial assumption that people choose to be unemployed while they learn about the wages paid by different firms. As an explanation of unemployment, search models must assume that there are very large gains to being unemployed while soliciting job offers. Yet, in practice, most job searching and job changes involve little or no unemployment at all. For example, every year, from roughly November to May, thousands of college professors test the job market while never missing a pay check. In fact, this on-the-job search has an added benefit to the extent that it provides an excuse for missing academic committee meetings. Every summer, professors criss-cross the country in an apparently random reshuffling of jobs. Search theory may help explain which professors solicit offers and which change jobs, but it doesn't explain why some talented people with prestigious PhDs cannot get teaching jobs.

These frustrated academics have chosen fields in which there are surpluses of talented PhDs, and in which tenure rules and wage rigidities keep markets out of equilibrium.* They are not turning down good offers in order to solicit better offers; they *have* no offers! If they do receive an offer, they will gratefully accept and then, while working, continue looking for better offers.

The overwhelming majority of the labor force find it relatively easy to solicit job offers during working hours, before work, or on days off. There is no need to quit a job or remain unemployed in order to learn about job alternatives.† Indeed, it is probably harder to get a job when one is unemployed. Unemployment is a warning signal that starts the worry gears moving in the minds of prospective employers. Most employers will think you either dumb or deceitful if you lamely try to explain that you've voluntarily chosen to be unemployed in order to solicit wage offers.

Search models are also unrealistic in their assumption that the unemployed face a plethora of job opportunities, and need only make up their minds which offers to accept. In reality, a job solicitation usually yields another disappointing rejection rather than another interesting tidbit of wage information. One survey found that only 10% of the unemployed had actually rejected any job offers.[8] There is not much room for layoffs, firings, and rejected job applications in search models.[9] Nor is there any easy explanation of why plant and equipment are idled during recessions, why shifts are discontinued, and why factories are closed. Are the owners of capital also engaged in voluntarily job search, carefully collecting information on rental rates? How could closing a plant possibly assist in such a search?

Search models also have a number of specific implications that are contradicted by experience:

1. If variations in labor supply cause business cycles, then real wages should move countercyclically (falling in booms, rising during recessions), as shown in Figure 16.1. Yet, in practice, real wages typically move procyclically (rising in booms, falling during recessions).

2. Search models similarly imply that job vacancies should move countercyclically, since employment expands and unemployment falls when job searchers decide to accept job offers. Yet job vacancy rates actually move procyclically. The disequilibrium interpretation is that employment is demand-determined, so that when labor demand increases, then employment increases, unemployment falls, and vacancies increase.

3. Search models assume that unemployment is largely due to people voluntarily leaving jobs to look for better ones. Yet voluntary quit rates are actually lowest when unemployment rates are high. A natural excess-supply interpretation is that people are fearful of leaving their jobs when others are having trouble finding work.

4. Search models imply that a searcher's reservation wage declines as search proceeds. Yet the odds of becoming employed are actually the lowest for those who have been unemployed the longest. The discrepancy might be accounted for by a kind of statistical mirage: People have different reservation wages, and those who are

* Remember, market equilibrium and dynamic equilibrium are two separate concepts. A semi-permanent excess supply would be dynamic equilibrium, but not market equilibrium.

† One survey found that people unemployed four weeks or more spent only an average of four hours a week in job search.[6] Another survey of successful job seekers found that only 35% found a job directly applying to firms. Most of the others found jobs through friends, relatives, or want ads.

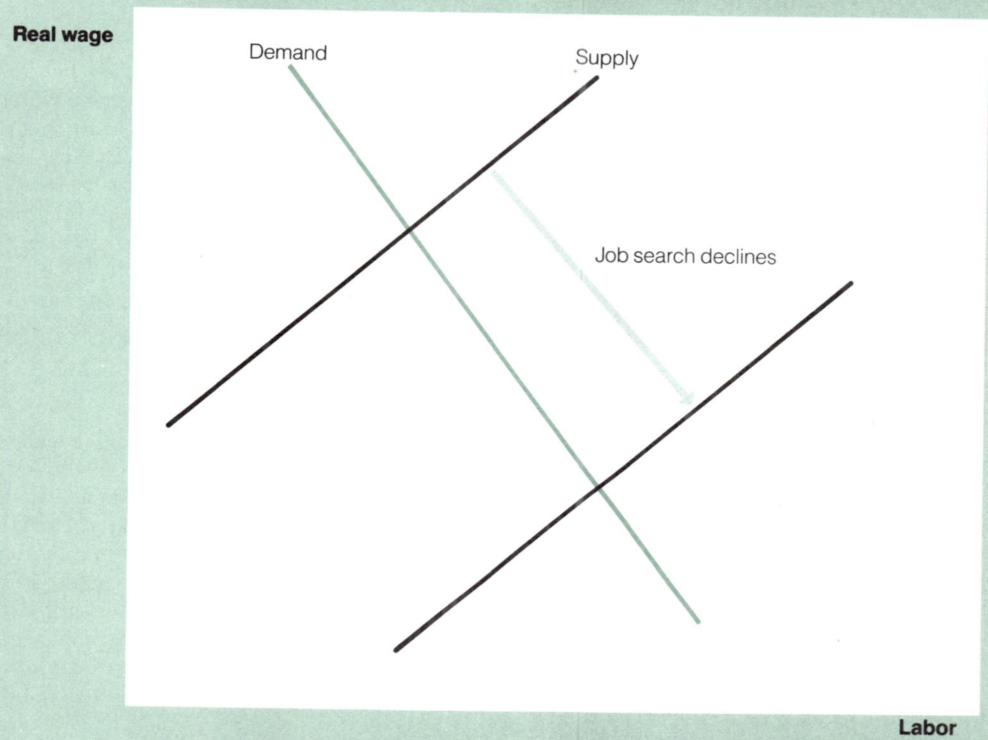

FIGURE 16.1 THE COUNTER-CYCLICAL MOVEMENT OF WAGES IN SEARCH MODELS. **When expected wage gains decline relative to search costs, job search diminishes, thereby increasing labor supply and employment while reducing real wages.**

unemployed the longest are extremely choosy, with high reservation wages that have not yet declined to realistic levels.[10] A more natural explanation is that the long-term unemployed do not have skills that employers are currently interested in and, consequently, have great difficulty finding jobs. In addition, actual and perceived skills deteriorate the longer one is unemployed.

Finally there are problems involving theoretical loose ends. Mostly, these are related to the fact that only one side of the market is analyzed. Here, we have analyzed how people decide whether to work or collect information about the wages offered by different firms. But we haven't justified the assumption that different firms offer an individual very dissimilar wages. How can low-wage firms hire enough people to stay in business? And how can high-wage firms make enough profits to stay afloat?

One explanation is that workers have a wide variety of search costs and perceived wage distributions, and thus have a wide variety of reservation wages.

IN THE NEWS

Recession's Victims Show Lasting Shift in Labor Force

For John Breedlove, there was new life in the old job after all.

When the economy picked up, so did work at the lumber mill in Roseburg, Ore., from which he had been laid off for 13 months. Last year, Mr. Breedlove earned $25,000, his highest income ever. Even so, he's still studying hard to become an airline dispatcher, hoping to leave the industry where he has worked all his life. "I'm still committed to making the change," he says. "I don't want to put my family through layoffs any more than they have been already."

Mr. Breedlove, 34 years old, was one of several victims of the recession profiled last year in a Wall Street Journal Series on switching careers. Revisiting them seven months later, after the rebounding economy in many cases has revitalized their old jobs, it becomes even clearer that the deep shift in the labor force caused by the most recent recession will remain even if the economy recovers fully.

People like Mr. Breedlove and ex-mechanic Bob Mahoney have been forced to take a good look at their old jobs. They are turning to new careers because they know now that their old jobs hold no secure future. Others, like meatpacker turned insurance salesman Clifford Rotert, are doing so well in their new jobs that there's no reason to look back.

At the same time, revisiting people like former industrial machinist Richard Fenner and bankrupt farmer Jerome Zeimet also shows that without determination and job retraining, refugees from the recession have little chance to grab hold of new opportunities in growing industries.

Mr. Mahoney, 34, lost his job when the garage where he worked went out of business. He studied to become a computer repairman, but still couldn't get a job. Then the economy improved, and he was offered three jobs—as a mechanic. "It was difficult to turn down those jobs," he says. "I wasn't sure I could really succeed as a computer technician, but I also had to look at the overall picture. There isn't any future in being a mechanic. There is no advancement possible, just a daily struggle."

Now Mr. Mahoney is a field service representative in Waltham, Mass., for Greyhound Computer Corp. Greyhound says he's doing outstanding work and could become a supervisor. Another company is courting him. And although he's earning only $14,400 a year—$6,000 less than he made in his last full year as a mechanic—Mr. Mahoney says: "I don't miss being a mechanic at all."

Similarly, Frank LaRosa, a steelworker who retrained as a computer programer, is doing well at Development Dimensions International, a Pittsburgh management and personnel consulting company. The transition from blue collar to white wasn't easy. "It was a good three months on the job before I knew I loved it," says Mr. LaRosa, 24. Then he was given a project writing a program to computerize all of the questionnaires his company sends to clients. "It took me two weeks to write it, and I sweated until I got it," he says. "But once I did, I felt great." After that, he says, "I knew I never wanted to go back to the mill and be a laborer ever again"—although jobs in the steel industry, even after wage concessions, still pay far more than his current job.

Mr. LaRosa says he received great support from his mother and fiancee, and the revisits emphasize the way the changes in the work force are affecting whole families. Robert Pillar, a production scheduler at a Midland, Pa., steel plant, was earning $29,000 a year when the plant closed in 1982. He didn't retrain, but he doggedly looked for work, sending out nearly 500 resumes. After the article about him appeared in the Journal, he was hired by New England Data-products Inc., in Wallingford, Conn., as a supervisor in its copying and duplication center and mail room.

But Mr. Pillar, 39, his wife, Jeanne, and their two children had never lived outside of Midland. "The toughest part, the absolute hardest part, was getting in the car, kissing everybody goodbye and pulling away, with the unknown staring you in the face," says Mr. Pillar.

After driving all day from Midland, the Pillars pulled up to their rental duplex in Connecticut at about 10 p.m. "It was across the street from a cemetery," he says. "I'd say we were very depressed."

For the first time in their lives, the family had to start over—new stores, new doctors, new schools. And the new job: "I'd go home and tell my wife, 'I'm overwhelmed.' I was worried that after 13 months out of work, my mind had gone stale." But now Mr. Pillar is comfortable at work. "I used to say I'd give my half-interest in heaven to end up at a company like this one," he says. "It's a company with a future."

He feels the same way about Connecticut. "There's a positive attitude here you didn't have in Midland," he says. "I wouldn't go back there for the world."

Like Mr. Pillar, Mark Lorah was depressed seven months ago after dozens of unsuccessful job applications. Mr. Lorah, 56, lost his job as a slag processing shift supervisor in 1982 after steel cutbacks led to the closing of his plant in Allentown, Pa. Untrained in any new field, he was rejected for jobs ranging from bank guard to building maintenance.

But then Mr. Lorah enrolled in a 15-week floor-covering course organized at a local junior college by Operation JOBSearch, a federally funded program designed to train and find jobs for the large number of unemployed workers in the Lehigh Valley. At the end of his training, Mr. Lorah received four job offers. Now, at the $5-an-hour starting wage, Mr. Lorah won't earn anywhere near the $21,000 he made when the plant was open—but this year, unlike last, he may be able to afford a vacation.

Operation JOBSearch—renamed the Dislocated Workers Program—says that of more than 1,100 clients enrolled so far, about 600 have found jobs. But Richard Fenner's experience shows how important the program's retraining aspect is. Six months ago, Mr. Fenner, 36, was struggling with an electronics course after losing his job as an industrial machinist. He dropped out in July, one of the 11 jobless workers in the course who didn't finish. Of the 17 who finished, all but one have found jobs. But Mr. Fenner is still unemployed.

"It was too much too fast," Mr. Fenner says of the course. Now he is enrolled in a slower-paced electronics class at a vocational school, and he has submitted about 50 job applications—mostly for work as a machinist.

Jerome Zeimet has no intention of retraining. His interest in computers for instance, is limited. "I have a hard time setting those computer watches," he says. "Actually, I let my wife set them."

Mr. Zeimet, 31, lost his farm to bankruptcy last March. For a while, his wife, Madge, worked at a McDonald's while he worked for his cousin harvesting corn at his own former farm. Then, as the farm economy improved, Mr. Zeimet found work with a construction crew putting up hog houses and turkey barns for about $250 a week. Christmas 1983 was happier: He spent $30 to $35 on each of his two kids, compared with $10 to $15 a year before.

But he still cherishes the dream of getting enough money to start fresh in farming. He is encouraged by local banks' ads saying they have money to lend. "You hear them advertising on radio and TV that they have all kinds of money," he says. "I'll hit them up on it."

The chance of getting money from a bank or a federal program, Mr. Zeimet says, is 49–51—"51 on my side." In most cases, though, the likelihood of a bankrupt farmer getting more loans is slim.

Mr. Zeimet has applied for jobs at local meatpacking plants and has placed his name with the state employment service. But he doesn't have any promising leads, and the construction job has ended for the winter. Now, he says, he will "collect unemployment until I find something else." (*The Wall Street Journal,* Jan. 6, 1984)

Low-wage firms are consequently able to hire the people with low reservation wages, while high-wage firms get those people with high reservation wages. The people who accept low wages don't know that higher wages are available, or are extremely averse to job search. This kind of answer helps. But it still doesn't really explain the assumption that some firms pay substantially higher wages than their competitors. It would surely be cheaper to pay only slightly higher wages and buy a little advertising.

More fundamentally, what incentive is there to pay above-average wages? If the high-wage firms reduce their wages, the choosy people will have to reduce their reservation wages and settle for what they can get. And if the firms paying above-average wages keep reducing wages, then the wage distribution collapses to where every firm pays the same wage.

Apparently, we need to allow for some uncertainty on both sides of the market. Firms, as well as workers, may be unsure of the wage distribution. Then we can have an equilibrium with dissimilar wages in which low-wage employees underestimate prevailing wages while high-wage firms overestimate prevailing wages. This kind of model leads off in some interesting directions. If wage information and job interviews are costly for firms, then they should bargain with job applicants instead of passively accepting rejection. Say that my reservation wage is $11 and I happen to apply to a firm that offers me $10. It may well be cheaper for this firm to up its offer to $11 rather than to evaluate additional applicants. Suspecting as much, I may well bluff and try to pretend that my reservation wage is actually $12. The firm may well anticipate my ploy and initially offer me only $9. Search theory can be exceedingly complex when both sides of the market are uncertain about market conditions and participant strategies.

LABOR MARKET DYNAMICS

Search models can give the impression that most unemployment is just a temporary, productive search period between jobs. The unemployed are apparently making a brief transition from employed to unemployed and then back to employment in a better job. In practice, however, unemployment is often punctuated not by employment but rather by withdrawals from the labor force. Table 16.1 shows some relevant data for a year of low unemployment (1969), moderate unemployment (1974), and high unemployment (1975).

Entry 2 in the table shows that the most common cause of unemployment is not voluntary quits but rather the involuntary loss of jobs. During recessionary years like 1975, unemployment swells not because people are increasingly eager to leave their jobs and search for better ones, but rather because jobs are lost as firms reduce employment. In fact, contrary to the search explanation of unemployment, voluntary job departures actually become less important during recessions.

These data also show that many of the unemployed were previously not in the labor force. Some are new, first-time job seekers, but most were previously in the labor force and have returned to again look for work. These re-entrants were counted as unemployed (not working, but looking for work), then as out

TABLE 16.1

Unemployment data for years of low, moderate, and high unemployment

	1969	1974	1975
1. Unemployment rate	3.5	5.6	8.5
2. Percentage of unemployed that were			
Job losers	35.9	43.4	55.4
Job leavers	15.4	14.9	10.4
Re-entrants	34.1	28.4	23.8
New entrants	14.6	13.2	10.4
3. Percentage of unemployment spells ending within one month	79	60	55
4. Average length of unemployment spell (weeks)	6.2	8.4	9.6
5. Percentage of unemployment spells ending in withdrawal from labor force	44	45	46
6. Average weeks unemployed, excluding those who withdraw from labor force	8.8	14.6	18.3
7. Average weeks unemployed this year for those currently unemployed	24.1	25.2	29.3
8. Percentage of unemployment weeks attributable to people who			
Become employed within two months	42	28	23
End unemployment by leaving labor force	46	47	48
Have been unemployed six months	3	19	27

SOURCES: Entries 1 and 2, *Economic Report of the President, 1980;* Entries 3–8, K. B. Clark and L. H. Summers.[11]

of the labor force (not working and not looking for work), and now as unemployed again (still out of work, but looking again).

The remaining data in Table 16.1 show some further evidence of this movement in and out of the labor force. Not surprisingly (except perhaps to search theorists), the average length of unemployment rises during recessions. Search theories can, however, find some support in the fact that the average length of unemployment is fairly short, even during stiff recessions. The majority of people who become unemployed end their unemployment within a month, either by taking jobs or by leaving the labor force. On average, a person who becomes unemployed will remain in the labor force but out of work for six to ten weeks, depending on whether the economy is booming or in recession.

On the other hand, as Entry 5 shows, nearly half of all unemployment spells end with a withdrawal from the labor force rather than a job. The fairly brief average spell of unemployment of six to ten weeks is consequently misleading, since this period of job seeking ends in failure nearly as often as success. Entry 6 is an estimate of how long it would take a typical unemployed person to find a job if those who withdrew from the labor force stayed and experienced the same success as those unemployed who actually do stay and keep looking for jobs. It is clear that the average length of unemployment spells seriously understates the difficulties the unemployed have in finding jobs.

These difficulties are brought out by the calculations shown in Entry 7 of the table. These data answer the question: How many total weeks of unemployment this year can someone who is currently unemployed expect to experience? The answer is, about 24 weeks when the economy is strong, and 29 weeks when the economy is weak. These data show that calculations of the average duration and length of unemployment are misleadingly short. The unemployed typically experience repeated spells of unemployment that are temporarily interrupted by work or by withdrawal from the labor force.

Entry 8 gives yet another way of looking at the unemployment data, this time apportioning unemployment by weeks. In good times and bad, nearly half of the aggregate weeks in unemployment are spent there by persons who will end their unemployment by leaving the labor force. The rest will sooner or later find jobs—sooner during booms, later during recessions.

Labor force entrance and withdrawal are actually even more important than these unemployment data indicate, because most movements into or out of jobs don't involve periods of observed unemployment. Two-thirds of the people leaving jobs also leave the labor force before they can be counted as unemployed. And two-thirds of the people taking jobs come from outside the labor force and so were never counted as looking for work. In an average month, about four million people leave the labor force, while another four million people enter it. If these were repeatedly different individuals, then nearly 50 million people (half of the labor force) would be leaving each year, to be replaced by another 50 million people. This is plainly implausible. Clearly, there are a lot of people who jump about between employment, unemployment, and out of the labor force. Some evidence of this jumpiness comes from the fact that, of those who do withdraw from the labor force, 34% return within a month and 78% return within a year.

The dual labor market and other interpretations

One explanation of temporary labor force withdrawals is the discouraged-worker phenomenon—unemployed people who leave the labor force because their job search has been so unsuccessful. These are people who want jobs but have given up hope of finding them. Job search is abandoned because it is costly and yields no reasonable offers. These discouraged workers return to the labor force (and often employment) when they hear that firms are hiring again. The validity of the discouraged-worker phenomenon is supported by the fact that labor force participation data are strongly procyclical. By this interpretation the discouraged workers who have left the labor force are really hidden unemployed, and they should be included in the unemployment statistics. Government surveys indicate that the number of people outside the labor force who "want a regular job now" is almost as large as the number of people officially counted as unemployed.

A related interpretation of movements in and out of the labor force is that the survey data that separate the unemployed from those out of the labor force are not very reliable. The nonemployed really don't change their behavior that much from month to month. But responses to subjective questions about actively seeking work yield pretty random classifications, sometimes putting people in the unemployed category and, at other times, putting them out of the labor force. Some evidence of these classification errors is provided by the Census Bureau's reinterview surveys, conducted by supervisory personnel. Of those classified as unemployed in the reinterview surveys, 13% were initially labeled outside the force and another 4% were initially labeled employed.

Another interpretation is that there is a *dual labor market* with some people in the mainstream and others on the fringe.[12] Those in the mainstream (or "primary" sector) work for large firms or in strongly unionized occupations. They have steady jobs with nice pay, benefits, and chances for advancement. They have well-defined careers and high hopes. They are disproportionately adult, white males. Other people are left on the outside (in the "secondary" sector), with no real chance of entering the mainstream job market. They don't have the right skills, the right education, the right behavior, the right appearance, or the right friends.* They can get only unpleasant, low-paying, dead-end jobs. They work only because they need money and may soon quit or provoke a firing in order to escape the drudgery of their jobs.

Those on the fringe often have very erratic work records, with intermittent spells of employment, unemployment, and withdrawal from the labor force. They would work much more than they do were good jobs only available. But the longer they are on the fringe, the harder it is to escape. Firms shy away from the costs of finding, hiring, training, and socializing people with poor work records who will probably not fit in and who will only work for the firm for a short while. It is a matter of continuing debate whether fringe people are really bad workers or whether they are potentially good workers trapped in bad jobs.

With a dual labor market, unemployment is very unevenly distributed. Unemployment in this case is not a brief productive job search that everyone engages in once in a while. Instead, the unemployed are a relatively small part of the labor force that chronically drifts in and out of unpleasant, low-paying jobs. These repeatedly unemployed people cannot get good job offers. They spend their unemployment in frustrating, unproductive search and in brief respite from bad jobs.

Primary-worker unemployment is mostly involuntary in that these workers are waiting to get their accustomed jobs back and resume their careers. But primary unemployment is also voluntary in the sense that these unemployed could always lower their sights and accept unpleasant secondary jobs. Secondary-worker unemployment is mostly voluntary, in that it reflects a recurrent temporary reprieve between jobs. But secondary unemployment is also involuntary in the sense that no good jobs are available.

During recessions, those in the secondary labor market soon find themselves unemployed. Workers in the primary sector have some job security and are less likely to be let go. Those primary workers who do lose jobs often have good unemployment benefits. In addition, they may temporarily take jobs in the secondary sector, displacing fringe workers.

During booms, labor shortages can arise in the primary labor market even while there is still considerable fringe unemployment. Firms are reluctant to hire fringe workers and, instead, rapidly bid up wages by trying to lure primary workers away from their competitors. But if the boom is strong enough and

* In this view, most work skills are taught on the job by friendly coworkers. Because of race, sex, or background, fringe workers do not fit in. They have difficulty acquiring mainstream work skills when their potential coworkers are hostile and their potential employers are dubious.

the pay differentials big enough, firms may lower their hiring standards and be tempted to recruit and train fringe workers.

There are several policy interpretations that can be drawn from the dual labor market model. One approach emphasizes the voluntary nature of much unemployment.[13] The fringe unemployed can always find jobs, but often prefer not working to taking another unpleasant job. For those who trust in consumer sovereignty, it is tempting to argue that the unemployed should be treated with benign neglect. A more sophisticated laissez-faire argument is that present laws and institutions distort the alternatives and should be done away with. Minimum-wage laws, licensing requirements, and union membership all limit the jobs available to fringe workers. In addition, unemployment compensation, welfare, food stamps, and other social services all reduce the private cost of unemployment (the lost income) below the social cost of unemployment (the lost output). The elimination of these various laws and institutions would reduce unemployment by broadening the job alternatives and discouraging idleness.

A very different policy view is that more active government intervention is needed to help the absorption of the fringe unemployed into the mainstream.[14] A choice between several unpleasant, low-paying jobs is no choice at all. The unemployed are ready and able to take good, steady jobs but haven't been offered any. Lower minimum wages and reduced unemployment benefits aren't going to open up any good jobs. To break the bad-job cycle, fringe workers need access to good jobs where they can acquire the kinds of skills and experience that mainstream employers want. There are two ways to expand their opportunities. One is a strict enforcement of anti-discrimination laws to surmount any employer reluctance to hire atypical workers. The second is a strong economy, so that there will be enough good jobs to go around and employers will be persuaded to take chances.

IMPLICATIONS FOR MACRO MODELS

There are important differences between equilibrium and disequilibrium models of labor and commodity markets, which yield very different interpretations of unemployment and business cycles.

Equilibrium models emphasize the incentives that influence demand and supply. In the simplest equilibrium model, labor demand, labor supply, and output depend only on real wages and, as a consequence, employment and output are insulated from demand-side events. The new classical macroeconomists emphasize the possibility of errors in gauging wages and prices. They advise that labor demand, labor supply, and output equations should allow for inaccurate expectations. Labor-leisure theory and search models suggest that wealth, search costs, and the dispersion of wage offers may all influence voluntary employment and unemployment decisions. We might also include future expected wages in our models, to allow workers to trade labor tomorrow for leisure today.

In disequilibrium models, wages and prices may be influenced by demand and supply, but they do not continually clear markets. The wage and price equations in most empirical models are Phillips-curve variations including such explanatory variables as the unemployment rate, past wage and price increases, anticipated wage and price increases, and materials costs. The quantities traded in disequilibrium models are determined by the short side of markets. When there is an excess labor supply, employment is demand-determined and attention is consequently focused on labor demand. Labor supply only determines the amount of unemployment and the market pressure on wages. Most empirical macro models assume that both employment and output are predominantly demand-determined. Commodity demand is the proximate determinant of output, and output is the primary determinant of labor demand and employment. Wages and prices do depend on the magnitudes of the disequilibria, and wages and prices do feed back into commodity demand. But these wage and price adjustments are slow and imperfect, so that market disequilibria persist for some time. In the short run, at least, commodity demand has relatively large effects on output and employment and relatively small effects on wages and prices.

IMPORTANT TERMS AND CONCEPTS

Search models
Reservation wage
Dual labor market
Discouraged-worker phenomenon

Search theories of unemployment emphasize the cost of job information. People will solicit job offers as long as the prospective job improvement outweighs search costs. Search models generally imply that the supply of labor is related positively to search costs, negatively to the dispersion of wages, positively to interest rates, and positively to the duration of unemployment. In most search models, inflation has no effect on employment and unemployment unless it causes labor to misassess the distribution of wages across firms. As a theory of unemployment, search models rely on the very tenuous assumption that it is easiest to search for jobs when one is unemployed. These models are also unrealistic in their assumption that the unemployed face a plethora of job opportunities and counterfactual in their implications that real wages move countercyclically, that job vacancy rates move countercyclically, that voluntary quit rates move procyclically, and that employment odds increase the longer one is unemployed. Nor do search theories explain why plant and equipment sit idle during recessions, unless we are to pretend that the owners choose to keep capital unemployed while they search for the highest rental rates.

Most periods of unemployment are brief (six to ten weeks), but unemployment is as likely to end in withdrawal from the labor force as in employment. In addition, two-thirds of the people who leave employment also leave the labor force, without ever being recorded as unemployed. And two-thirds of the people taking jobs come from outside the labor force, without being counted as unemployed. These large movements into and out of the labor force make the interpretation of unemployment data difficult.

Apparently, unemployment does not represent occasional, brief job searches conducted by just about everyone. Instead, the bulk of unemployment is attributable to relatively few people who repeatedly move between employment, unemployment, and out of the labor force. These people are unemployed a great deal of the time, but their unemployment is frequently interrupted by employment or withdrawal from the labor force. One interpretation is that these are discouraged job seekers who withdraw from the labor force when job search becomes too frustrating. A second interpretation is that the dividing line between unemployment and being out of the labor force is pretty arbitrary. At any moment there are, consequently, many people classified as out of the labor force who really are not very different from those classified as unemployed. A third interpretation is that the unemployed are mostly fringe workers, who cannot get good jobs. For them unemployment and labor force withdrawal are a brief respite between unpleasant, low-paying jobs.

EXERCISES

1. Give one reason why reservation wages may decline as search proceeds. If they do so decline, will reservation wages depend on whether job offers can be collected and accepted at a later date? Carefully explain your reasoning.

2. Since searching takes time, the cost of search should include the wages that could have been earned by working rather than searching. Search costs, then, are not really constant, but instead change as wage offers are collected. As search continues, will search costs then go up or down? Will this change in search costs cause reservation wages to rise or fall as search proceeds?

3. Comment on the following: "[The] picture of a hard core of unemployed persons unable to find jobs is an inaccurate description of our economy. . . . A more accurate description is an active labor market in which almost everyone who is out of work can find his usual type of job in a relatively short time." (M. S. Feldstein, *Lowering the Permanent Rate of Unemployment,* a study for the Joint Economic Committee, 93rd Congress, Washington, D.C.: Government Printing Office, p. 11.)

4. List five jobs that you would classify as in the primary labor market and five that you would classify as in the secondary labor market.

5. What, briefly, is the search theory of unemployment? In particular, how does it explain a nonzero unemployment rate?

6. How does the search theory of unemployment explain fluctuations in the unemployment rate? Why would the search theory model be contradicted by evidence that real wages, job vacancy rates, and voluntary quit rates move procyclically (up in booms, down in recessions)?

7. How would the involuntary-disequilibrium model explain procyclical movements in real wages, job vacancy rates, and voluntary quit rates?

8. Do you agree or disagree with the following explanation of the conclusion that a lot of unemployment is voluntary: "Job losers are barely over half of all the unemployed, and are mostly adults. Many others are unemployed because of actions they took more or less voluntarily: they quit their last job, just joined the labor force, or just rejoined it." (*Fortune,* October, 1976)

REFERENCES

1. Calvin Coolidge, quoted by Robert S. McElvaine, "The Coolidge Model: What Better Choice?", *The Boston Globe,* June 27, 1981.

2. Two early influential papers by G. J. Stigler are "The Economics of Information," *Journal of Political Economy,* 69 (June 1961), pp. 312–25 and "Information in the Labor

Market," *Journal of Political Economy,* 70 (October 1962), pp. 94–105. One of Phelps' papers is in the collection of essays mentioned in the Suggestions for Further Reading.

3. The case of an unknown wage distribution across firms is analyzed in M. Rothchild, "Searching for the Lowest Price When the Distribution of Prices is Unknown," *Journal of Political Economy,* (July/August 1974); and M. DeGroot, *Optimal Statistical Decisions,* chapter 13.

4. R. Gronau, "Information and Frictional Unemployment," *American Economic Review,* 61 (June 1971)

5. C. C. Holt. See his paper in the Suggestions for Further Reading.

6. C. Rosenfeld, "Job Search for the Unemployed, May 1976," *Monthly Labor Review,* (November 1977), p. 41.

7. Bureau of Labor Statistics, *Jobseeking Methods Used by American Workers,* Bulletin 1886, Washington, D.C.: General Printing Office, 1975, p. 7.

8. Rosenfeld.

9. A search model in which job applicants may simply be rejected is analyzed by S. C. Salop, "Systematic Job Search and Unemployment," *Review of Economic Studies,* 40 (April 1973), pp. 191–201.

10. See S. W. Salant, "Search Theory and Duration Data: A Theory of Sorts," *Quarterly Journal of Economics,* 91 (February 1977), pp. 44–45.

11. These data and much of the data used in the rest of this section are from K. B. Clark and L. H. Summers, "Labor Market Dynamics and Unemployment: A Reconsideration," *Brookings Papers on Economic Activity,* 1:1979, pp. 13–60.

12. See, for example, R. E. Hall, "Prospects for Shifting the Phillips Curve Through Manpower Policy," *Brookings Papers on Economic Activity,* 3:1971, p. 681.

13. See M. Feldstein, "The Economics of the New Unemployment," *Public Interest,* (Fall 1973), pp. 3–42.

14. See P. B. Doeringer and M. J. Poire, "Unemployment and the 'Dual Labor Market,' " *Public Interest,* (Winter 1975), pp. 67–79.

SUGGESTIONS FOR FURTHER READING

A landmark collection of articles on voluntary unemployment in an uncertain world is E. S. Phelps et al, *Microeconomic Foundations of Employment and Inflation Theory,* New York: Norton, 1970. One of the most well-known and realistic search models is C. C. Holt, "Job Search, Phillips' Wage Relation, and Union Influence: Theory and Evidence," in the Phelps volume.

PART SIX

INTERNATIONAL ASPECTS AND GROWTH

CHAPTER SEVENTEEN

INTERNATIONAL TRANSACTIONS

Most dangerous of all would be democracy. The Bank of England was the instrument of a ruling class. Among the powers the Bank derived from that ruling class was that of inflicting hardship. It could lower prices and wages, increasing unemployment. These were the correctives when gold was being lost; euphoria was excessive. Few or none foresaw that farmers and workers would one day have the power that would make governments unwilling to impose these hardships even in so righteous a cause as defense of the currency.

JOHN KENNETH GALBRAITH[1]

This chapter examines the relationship between domestic prices, foreign prices, and exchange rates, and how economic events in one country affect other countries.

IN 1981 the United States exported $230 billion in merchandise to the rest of the world and imported $206 billion in merchandise. Tens of billions more dollars were exchanged in international transactions for such things as military expenses, travel, gifts, and investment income. Purchases and sales of financial assets likewise hurdle national boundaries. Consortiums of international banks lend tens of billions of dollars to multinational companies and to governments. These same banks finance much of their lending with international certificates of deposit traded in such disparate places as Nassau, Luxembourg, and Hong Kong. Every day billions of dollars worth of foreign currencies are traded worldwide by individuals, businesses, banks, and governments.

The linkage of world markets means that economic events in one nation have worldwide repercussions. For example, when interest rates are high in the United States, U.S. banks will borrow in Europe, raising interest rates there as well. There can also be very specific repercussions. The 1974 downfall of the Franklin National Bank was partly due to capital losses incurred in its foreign-exchange transactions. In 1984, economic difficulties in many debtor nations threatened to topple many U.S. banks.

Our macroeconomic analysis has so far been concerned with a so-called *closed economy,* in which international transactions are unimportant. In this chapter we will look at an *open economy,* like the United States, which affects and is affected by foreign economies. First we will examine the relationship between domestic and foreign prices of currencies, commodities, and financial assets. Then I will briefly sketch the twentieth-century evolution of the international financial system, after which we will use a formal macroeconomic model to analyze the international consequences of economic events in a large open economy.

EXCHANGE RATES AND PURCHASING-POWER PARITY

Every nation has a domestic currency in which prices are generally quoted and internal transactions conducted. There is the U.S. dollar, German mark, Swiss franc, Japanese yen, British pound, and so forth. When transactions cross national boundaries, a currency conversion is usually necessary. For example, Americans have U.S. dollars to spend on wine, but French wine producers want French francs to spend at their local McDonald's. When Americans want to buy French wine, their dollars will at some point be converted into French francs.

This conversion takes place through the exchange of dollars for francs. Currencies, like tomatoes and football tickets, have a price at which they are bought and sold. An *exchange rate* is the price of one currency in terms of another, such as the price of a French franc in U.S. dollars or German marks. In 1984, a French franc could be bought for about 12 cents, a German mark for about 36 cents, and a British pound cost around $1.40. What then was the franc price of marks and pounds? A mark cost 3 francs, and a pound almost 12 francs.

A nation's currency undergoes *devaluation,* or "depreciation," when foreign currency becomes more expensive. A currency "appreciates" as foreign currency becomes less expensive. For example, a British pound cost $4.76 before World War I, but only $1.40 in 1984. Over this period, U.S. dollars have appreciated relative to the pound, and the pound has depreciated relative to the dollar. Figure 17.1 shows some recent exchange rate movements. There have been zigs and zags, but over most of the 1970s the U.S. dollar has appreciated relative to the British pound and Italian lira, and depreciated relative to the German mark and Swiss franc. Between 1980 and 1984 the dollar appreciated relative to virtually all foreign currencies.

Exchange rates are important because they determine the domestic price of foreign goods. Say a certain French wine costs 50 francs. How much is that in real money, U.S. dollars? If a franc costs 12 cents, then the wine implicitly costs $6. In general, the domestic price of a foreign item is equal to the foreign price multiplied by the exchange rate:

$$\text{domestic price} = \text{foreign price}\left(\frac{\text{domestic currency}}{\text{foreign currency}}\right)$$

In our wine example,

$$\begin{aligned}\text{price in dollars} &= \text{price in francs}\left(\frac{\text{dollars}}{\text{franc}}\right)\\ &= 50\text{ francs}\left(0.12\,\frac{\text{dollars}}{\text{franc}}\right)\\ &= 6\text{ dollars}\end{aligned}$$

Now, **purchasing power parity (or "the law of one price") holds that the domestic price of a foreign item will equal the domestic price of a compa-**

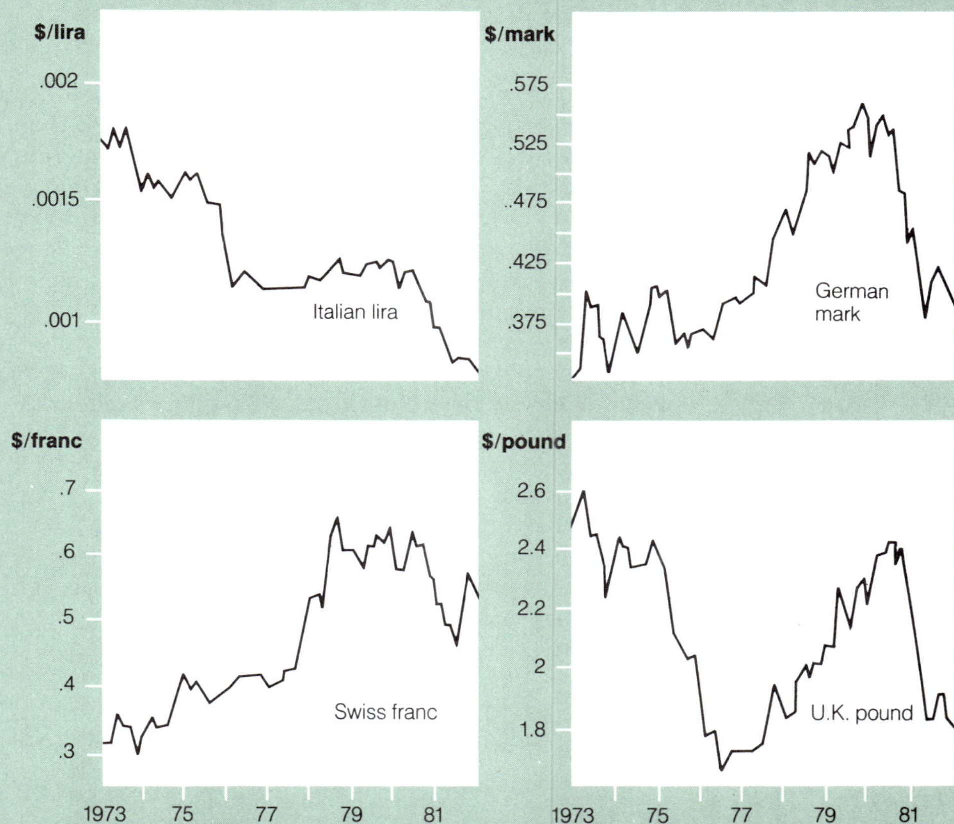

FIGURE 17.1 **EXCHANGE RATES FOR THE LIRA, MARK, FRANC, AND POUND. An increase in the dollar price represents a depreciation of the dollar, since it then requires more dollars to buy the foreign currency. The dollar appreciates when foreign currencies become less expensive.**

rable domestic item. If the U.S. price of French wine is \$6, then purchasing power parity implies that the U.S. price of a comparable U.S. wine must also be \$6. Otherwise, people would buy only the wine that was less expensive. In general,

$$P_d = eP_f \tag{17.1}$$

where P_d is the domestic price of a domestic item, P_f the foreign price of a foreign item, and e the exchange rate—domestic currency/foreign currency. An increase in e is a depreciation of the domestic currency. In our example, $P_d = 6$ dollars, $P_f = 50$ francs, and $e = 0.12$ dollar per franc.

Purchasing-power parity also implies that the rate of inflation in the first country is equal to the rate of inflation in the second country plus the exchange rate appreciation of the second currency:

$$\pi_d = \pi_f + \Delta e/e \tag{17.2}$$

where π_d and π_f are the percentage changes in P_d and P_f, and $\Delta e/e$ is the percentage change in e. **If the exchange rate is fixed, then purchasing-power parity requires the two nations to have the same rate of inflation. If the exchange rate is not fixed, then purchasing-power parity implies that a change in the exchange rate will equal the difference between the two rates of inflation.** Later in this chapter we will see how these two observations help explain the breakdown of fixed exchange rates and of movements of exchange rates in recent years.

Purchasing-power parity applies to all traded items—not only goods and services, but also assets. Before, we compared the prices on similar wines. Now we can compare the yields on assets that have similar risk, liquidity, and other characteristics considered important by investors. Purchasing-power parity holds that comparable domestic and foreign assets will be priced to yield the same percentage rate of return.

Such international rate-of-return calculations are a bit complicated, though, because the possibility of exchange-rate changes must be taken into account. Let R_d be the nominal rate of return on a domestic asset (denominated, say, in U.S. dollars), and let R_f be the nominal rate of return on a foreign asset (denominated here in French francs):

$$1 + R_d = \frac{\text{dollars earned}}{\text{dollars invested}} \qquad 1 + R_f = \frac{\text{francs earned}}{\text{francs invested}}$$

To make these yields comparable, they must be expressed in one currency (either dollars or francs). Let e be the exchange rate (dollars for francs) at the time of the investment, and let $e + \Delta e$ be the exchange rate at the end of the investment period. Then the earnings in dollars divided by the cost in dollars for the French investment is

$$\frac{\text{dollars earned}}{\text{dollars invested}} = \frac{(\text{francs earned}) \quad (e + \Delta e)}{(\text{francs invested}) \quad (e)} = (1 + R_f)\,(1 + \frac{\Delta e}{e})$$

For the rate of return on the French investment to equal the rate of return on the American investment,*

$$(1 + R_d) = (1 + R_f)\,(1 + \frac{\Delta e}{e})$$

or, approximately,

$$R_d = R_f + \frac{\Delta e}{e}. \tag{17.3}$$

* Equation 17.3 can also be derived by equating the two real rates of return, $r_d = R_d - \pi_d$ and $r_f = R_f - \pi_f$, since purchasing power parity implies that $\pi_d = \pi_f + \Delta e/e$.

Thus, purchasing-power parity implies that American interest rates will equal French interest rates (on comparable investments) plus the anticipated percentage appreciation in the French franc relative to the U.S. dollar.

If the exchange rate is expected to be constant when French bonds yield 10%, then comparable American bonds will also be priced to yield 10%. Otherwise, funds will be invested only in the bond with the higher anticipated return. If American bonds have higher yields, then funds will flow out of the French bond market into the U.S. bond market, driving French bond prices down and U.S. bond prices up until parity is restored.

When the U.S. dollar is expected to depreciate against the franc, then U.S. investments are less attractive. If, for example, the dollar-to-franc exchange rate is expected to rise 5% over the next year, then U.S. one-year interest rates will have to be 5% higher than French one-year interest rates for purchasing-power parity to hold. Analogous comparisons can naturally be drawn for interest rates in other countries.

Purchasing-power parity does not, in fact, hold precisely, at least in the short run. For example, as the U.S. dollar depreciated relative to the German mark in 1978, the dollar price of imported Volkswagen Rabbits rose relative to the dollar prices of American cars. According to the theory of purchasing-power parity, this should not have happened. There should have been a massive shift in demand from high-priced Rabbits to low-priced American cars that forced the dollar prices of German and American cars to remain in parity. As the dollars-per-mark exchange rate increased, the dollar price of American cars should have risen or the marks price of German cars should have fallen, so as to maintain purchasing-power parity.

Actually, there was some shift in American demand from Rabbits to American cars, but this demand shift didn't translate into price adjustments. The increased demand for American cars was met by production increases rather than price increases. Similarly, in 1978 American buyers were on waiting lists to buy Rabbits. When the demand for Rabbits fell, the price stayed firm and the waiting lists simply got shorter.

Such price rigidities are the biggest reason why purchasing-power parity doesn't quite hold in the short run. Purchasing-power parity applies to items that are close substitutes, and buyers often perceive unique qualities in what they buy. This uniqueness gives seemingly competitive firms some monopolistic control over prices. This monopolistic competition is true of such commodities as cereals, toothpastes, and automobiles.

This is why people happily buy Mercury Zephyrs costing hundreds of dollars more than Ford Fairmonts, or pay more for a Pontiac LeMans or Buick Century than a Chevrolet Malibu. Similarly, as the dollar price of Rabbits rose relative to American cars, there was no mass exodus because most Rabbit buyers didn't consider American cars to be good substitutes. This perceived uniqueness gives producers a degree of monopolistic power, and one way they have chosen to exercise that power is to stabilize prices.

Another barrier to perfect purchasing-power parity is transaction and transportation costs, including tariffs, fees, quotas, and other trade barriers. For example American workers may be paid considerably more than British workers, as long as commuting from England is infeasible. Similarly, French wine and automobiles can be relatively expensive in France, when the French prohibit or heavily tax foreign alternatives. To the extent that transportation and other transaction costs protect domestic industry, they promote price rigidities and disparities. Thus, the U.S. price of a foreign item is not just the foreign price multiplied by the exchange rate. To this frictionless price must be added all of the transaction and transportation costs. The frictionless price ratio, P_d/eP_f, need not equal one, but instead, can vary over a sometimes wide range within limits set by import and export expenses.*

Thus, because of price rigidities and transactions costs, pure purchasing-power parity is not quite accurate. Nonetheless, Equation (17.1) is a useful aid in remembering the rough relationship between domestic prices, foreign prices, and exchange rates. Later in this chapter, we will repeatedly come back to this equation to inform and confirm our reasoning.

If, for example, an expansionary monetary policy causes prices to increase in the United States, how will this affect foreign prices and exchange rates? According to Equation 17.1, as P_d increases, e or P_f should increase also. Thus an American inflation should cause a foreign inflation or a depreciation of the dollar. Again this makes good sense. As American prices increase, demand will shift to foreign goods and people will exchange dollars for foreign currencies to carry out these transactions. There will be upward pressure on the foreign price of foreign goods, and on the dollar price of foreign currencies.

In practice, purchasing-power parity is probably most applicable to raw commodities and financial assets. Many financial assets are commonly perceived to be close substitutes, with some risk-premium adjustment. Indeed, it is because international financial assets are close substitutes that hectic international financial markets have developed. Changes in U.S. interest rates quickly affect the financial markets of other nations, and vice versa.

For example, the London Interbank Offered Rate (Libor) is a measure of what the big international banks charge each other for large Eurodollar loans (international loans denominated in U.S. dollars). Libor is then commonly used like an international prime rate to fix the minimum interest rate charged on Eurodollar loans by bank syndicates. In April 1980, Libor and the U.S. prime rate were both around 20%. In June 1980, Libor dropped to 9%, but the quoted U.S. prime rate only fell to 12%. The big U.S. corporations then demanded and got loans from U.S. banks based on Libor rather than the reported U.S. prime rate. They were able to do this because of their very real threat to borrow, otherwise, from foreign banks.

BALANCE OF PAYMENTS

International transactions take many different forms. Americans buy French wine, and the Soviet Union buys American grain. Americans visit China, and the English tour America. Americans invest in the Japanese stock market, and

* If transaction and transportation costs raise the U.S. price of a foreign item δ_f percent to $(1 + \delta_f)eP_f$, then the purchasing-power parity argument is that $P_d \leq (1 + \delta_f)eP_f$. Otherwise, only the foreign item would be bought. Similarly, if transaction and transportation costs raise the foreign price of the U.S. item δ_d percent to $(1 + \delta_d)P_d/e$, then $P_f \leq (1 + \delta_d)P_d/e$. Therefore, $1/(1 + \delta_d) \leq P_d/eP_f \leq 1 + \delta_f$ specifies the flabbiness conferred on the theory of purchasing-power parity by transaction and transportation costs.

Saudi Arabians buy American Treasury bills. The U.S. government gives aid to Ecuador, and Japanese firms pay dividends to American stockholders. Americans buy Swiss francs and Israelis buy American dollars.

With a long exhaustive compilation of all such transactions, the totals will balance. Every use of funds is someone else's source of funds. Sources equal uses, assets equal liabilities, and balance sheets always balance. Statisticians, economists, and politicians have, however, traditionally scrutinized selected subsets of a complete accounting. For example, there has long been considerable interest in a nation's *trade balance:* exports of commodities minus imports. This is a rough barometer of the competitiveness of a nation's industries. Long ago, when trade surpluses and deficits were financed by precious metals, the Mercantilists watched trade data because they believed that a nation's wealth was its holdings of gold and silver.

Adam Smith, in his appropriately named *The Wealth of Nations,* argued that this was a rather incomplete accounting. Gold and silver could buy foreign commodities, but the sale of commodities for gold does not increase a nation's wealth. It merely substitutes one item for another. The true wealth of a nation is the size and productivity of its resources: its people, its land, and its capital. Only a miserly nation could be happy perpetually foregoing consumption in order to hoard metal.

By the same logic, spending U.S. dollars on German cars, Japanese televisions, and French wine is not a complete loss. Instead of buying U.S. goods, Americans buy foreign goods. The foreigners who accept these dollars will presumably eventually use them to buy the U.S. goods that Americans spurned. If they don't, then so much the better. Would you rather drive a BMW or count pieces of paper?

The *goods-and-services balance* is similar to the trade balance but includes services as well as goods. These services include interest and dividend payments, tourist expenditures, purchases and sales of military equipment, and expenses of operating U.S. military bases located in foreign countries. This conglomeration is a bit strange. Interest and dividend expenses are normally treated as a factor payment by businesses or as a transfer payment from the government, rather than as a purchase of a service. Also, the domestic purchase of military equipment is normally treated as a good rather than a service. This contrary international treatment is probably intended to preserve the trade balance as a barometer of the relative competitiveness of a nation's industries.

The *current-account balance* adds net transfer payments to the goods-and-services balance. These transfers include foreign aid and private gifts to or from individuals and organizations. Figure 17.2 shows the historical trade and current-account (excluding government grants) balances.

The current-account balance is important because it must be financed by the acquisition of financial assets; that is, an increase or decrease in foreign claims against the United States—either U.S. dollars or assets that can be converted into dollars. Table 17.1 shows some balance sheets for 1981.

There are three other balance-of-payments figures that reflect the composition of these claims. The *basic balance* nets out purchases and sales of long-term securities. This leaves short-term claims against the United States. The *net liquidity balance* nets out illiquid short-term transactions. This leaves short-term liquid claims. The *official settlements balance* nets out private short-term liquid assets, leaving official short-term liquid claims against the government.

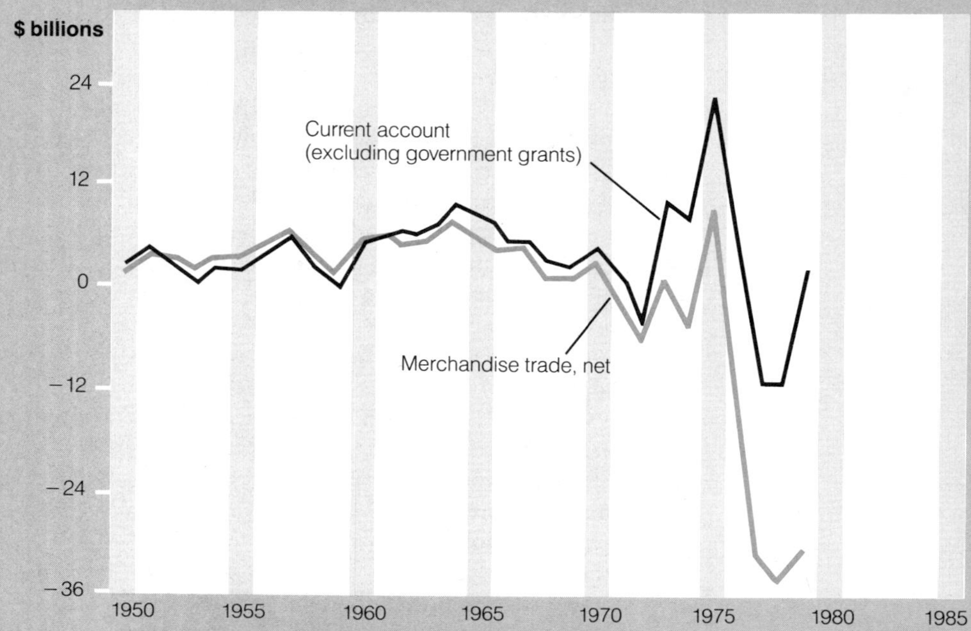

FIGURE 17.2 **U.S. CURRENT-ACCOUNT BALANCES, 1950–79. The trade balance shows U.S. exports of merchandise less imports. The current-account graph includes services as well as goods, plus transfer payments. A current-account deficit must be financed by financial claims against the United States—either U.S. dollars or securities. (Source: Federal Reserve Board *Historical Chart Book.*)**

TABLE 17.1
U.S. international transactions, 1981

	$ Billions Source	$ Billions Use			
Merchandise	236.3	264.1	= −27.8 (trade balance)	= + 11.1 (goods and services balance) (Merchandise + Services)	= + 4.5 (current account) (Merchandise + Services + Net transfers)
Services	136.6	97.7			
Net transfers		6.6			
Net financial assets		4.5			
TOTAL	372.9	372.9			

All of these calculations are just measurements of different facets of U.S. international transactions. While they may seem almost mystical, none has any magical or religious importance. They describe how much Americans are buying and selling, how much they are giving away, and how much they are borrowing and lending.

From World War II until the 1970s, the United States exported more goods, and more goods and services, than it imported. The United States shared some of its output with the rest of the world. Much of this export surplus was financed by gifts to foreign individuals, organizations, and governments. Subtracting these gifts, leaves a current-account balance that has fluctuated between surplus and deficit, roughly balancing over the years. This means that the United States' borrowings from the rest of the world have roughly matched its loans to it.

There has been a compositional difference, however. The United States has acquired mostly long-term investments while supplying gold, dollars, and liquid short-term assets to the rest of the world. Thus if long-term assets and illiquid short-term assets are netted out, the net liquidity balance has been in persistent deficit for three decades. This deficit reflects the fact that the United States has been providing liquid assets, "world money," to carry out international trade. About two-thirds of the world's central-bank reserve assets are U.S. dollars. Central banks in the large industrial countries hold almost entirely dollars, while developing countries have about half of their reserves in dollars.

When newspapers report the "balance of payments deficit," this is often what they mean—that the United States has supplied more gold, U.S. dollars, foreign reserves, and other liquid assets to the rest of the world. This is *not* an ominous sign of the collapse of America. Instead it is, if anything, a healthy sign that the American supply of world money is growing with international commerce. These balance-of-payments deficits occur because the world desires liquid U.S. assets to use as world money. The international accumulation of U.S. dollars reflects the strength, not the weakness, of the dollar.

These data are sometimes misinterpreted because of an understandable confusion about the various balance-of-payments statistics. For example, many people hear of a deficit in the net-liquidity balance or official-settlements balance, and mistakenly interpret that as a deficit in the goods-and-services or current-account balance. Another confusing factor is the unique position of the United States as a supplier of world money. When small countries have deficits, they must use their foreign-currency holdings to pay their bills, because their domestic currencies are of little use to other nations. With the United States, the situation is different. When the United States has a deficit in its liquidity balance, other nations acquire more U.S. dollars, dollar deposits, and other liquid assets. Foreign nations are willing to hold U.S. dollars because, as a world money, these dollars can be used to pay bills.

In a world of fixed exchange rates, balance-of-payments data were studied by governments and speculators for evidence of unrealistic exchange rates. With freely floating exchange rates, there is less reason for this scrutiny, since governments no longer have the responsibility for making exchange rate adjustments and need not put themselves at the mercy of speculators.

As the world moved toward floating exchange rates in the 1970s, the U.S. government adopted the recommendation of a Presidential advisory committee that balance-of-payments data be deemphasized. The data are now called U.S. "international transactions" rather than "balance of payments," and the basic, net-liquidity, and official-settlements balances are no longer even reported. Only the goods-and-services and current-account balances are given, and the perjorative words "deficit" and "surplus" are avoided in press releases.

We now look at the historical transition from fixed to flexible exchange rates.

THE GOLD STANDARD

The United States, along with other Western nations, was on an international gold standard through much of the nineteenth century and into the twentieth century.* The U.S. government stood ready to buy and sell gold at the fixed price of $20.67 per ounce. The U.S. twenty-dollar gold piece contained a little less than an ounce of gold, and the U.S. ten-dollar "golden eagle" contained slightly less than a half-ounce of gold.

The British government bought and sold gold at the fixed price of 4.34 British pound notes per ounce of gold. Implicitly then, if an ounce of gold could be freely traded for 20.67 U.S. dollars or 4.34 British pounds, then 20.67 U.S. dollars had the same value as 4.34 British pounds. Thus, one British pound was worth 20.67/4.34 or 4.76 U.S. dollars. This, then, was the fixed exchange rate at which dollars and pounds were traded. There were similar fixed exchange rates between all of the currencies issued by gold-standard nations.

Importers, exporters, and banks that deal in foreign exchange generally like fixed exchange rates because they eliminate exchange-rate risk, which arises because there are invariably delays between when a deal is struck and final payment is received. An exchange-rate fluctuation during such a delay can turn a good deal into a bad one. Hence, just as it is widely believed that price instability impedes domestic commerce, so it is believed that exchange-rate instability hinders international commerce.

Automatic balance-of-payments equilibrium

Classical economic theorists widely celebrated the way that an international gold standard preserves purchasing-power parity and automatically eliminates balance-of-payments deficits. Recall the purchasing-power parity equation (17.1), $P_d = eP_f$, and let P_d be the U.S. price level and P_f the British price level. The exchange rate e is fixed by the international gold standard. Now suppose that U.S. prices increase, giving $P_d > eP_f$, so that American items are more expensive than their English counterparts. Both the English and Americans will buy more English goods. U.S. dollars will be cashed in at the U.S. Treasury for gold to pay English merchants. As the United States loses gold, its money supply will shrink, since, under a pure gold standard, U.S. money consists solely of gold and notes backed by gold. As the U.S. money supply contracts, U.S. prices

* The United States adopted the gold standard in 1834 and then temporarily dropped it from 1861 to 1879 because of the paper-money financing of the Civil War. The First World War similarly forced most European nations off the gold standard, and the world never quite returned to it.

fall proportionately. The increased gold in England will similarly expand the English money supply, increasing the English price level proportionately. Thus P_d falls and P_f rises until their equality is restored and the balance-of-payments deficit is eliminated. Only when this payments deficit ceases does the flow of gold stop exerting its pressure on relative prices.

A central aspect of this gold-standard enthusiasm was the classical belief that the price adjustments would be painless. In the classical view, the economy was always near full employment, and money was a thin veil. A doubling of the money supply would merely double prices, with no effects on real economic activity. In practice, however, monetary fluctuations have caused booms and recessions, speculative binges and panic.

When, in our example, gold flowed to England, enlarging its money supply, output and employment would expand along with prices. When gold left the United States, employment and output would contract, inflicting real economic hardship.* The international gold standard broke down because money was not neutral, and nations were unwilling to sacrifice domestic stabilization to balance-of-payments equilibrium. As the epigraph to this chapter indicates, some authors see the triumph of democracy over the old order as the fundamental reason why governments could no longer maintain the gold standard.

Abandonment of the gold standard

There were three twentieth-century calamities that broke up the old order. These were the two World Wars and the Great Depression. These catastrophes had their direct as well as indirect effects on international finance. In World War I, heavy European imports of food and munitions from the United States undermined the gold standard. The European economies could not have held up if they had reduced their money supplies by the size of their trade deficits. Instead, they went off the gold standard. European governments called in private gold holdings, prohibited gold exports, and stopped selling gold to private citizens. The United States meanwhile found itself with nearly half of the world's monetary gold. The United States had replaced England as lender to the world, and champion of the gold standard. Indeed the United States was virtually the only nation still on the gold standard. The United States dutifully increased its money supply along with its new gold, and the U.S. economy and price level generally sizzled.

The 1920s were a tumultuous period for international trade. Austria and Germany experienced hyperinflations. Great Britain, under Winston Churchill, tried to induce a deflation in order to return to the prewar gold standard. Exchange rates changed greatly and fluctuated wildly in speculative anticipation of future price changes.† Most European nations longed for a return to a tranquil gold standard. The United States tried to assist this return by inflating domestic prices and resisting further gold inflows.

* The variability of output reinforces the classical adjustment mechanism, since the decline in U.S. output and income reduces its imports, further stemming the gold outflow.

† If British prices are stable while German prices double, what should happen to the exchange rate? According to purchasing-power parity, the exchange rate should be halved, in that a British pound will buy twice as many German reichsmarks. In 1923, German prices actually increased by the billionfold.

By 1927, an international gold standard was close to being reestablished. However, the situation differed from the prewar gold standard in two important ways. The first was that many of the official exchange rates differed from what would have been the free-market rates. Thus many governments were unwilling to redeem their currencies with gold, and many currencies were traded privately at unofficial exchange rates.

The second difference was that many countries were no longer willing to let their economies fluctuate with international gold flows. They would not allow their money supplies to expand and contract automatically with the nation's gold stock. When a nation's gold stock increased, the central bank might withdraw some of the increase from circulation by making open-market sales or, alternatively, the central bank might raise reserve requirements to reduce bank-created money. Similarly, when gold left a country, the central bank could make expansionary open-market purchases or cut reserve requirements to sustain the nation's money supply. Governments also borrowed from one another to maintain their gold monetary bases in the face of balance-of-payment disequilibria. **All of these actions helped stabilize the domestic economies, but in so doing avoided the price adjustments that were needed to eliminate balance-of-payments disequilibria.**

Look again at the purchasing-power parity condition, and assume that, at the prevailing prices and exchange rates, P_d is lower than eP_f. Currency and gold will then flow from the foreign nation to the home country. At the given fixed exchange rate P_d should rise and P_f should fall. In the prewar years the international flow of gold would have altered the two nations' money supplies, inducing these equilibrating price adjustments. But in the late 1920s, the inclination was to undertake offsetting monetary policies. The foreign nation would use expansionary monetary policies to avoid deflation, while the home country used contractionary monetary policies to avoid inflation. As a result, P_d remained below eP_f and the balance-of-payments disequilibria persisted.

As long as nations are unwilling to realign prices, the only way out of this impasse is for the exchange rate to adjust. When governments resist this adjustment, the problem is then exacerbated by private speculators who anticipate a future adjustment. Expecting the value of one currency to decline relative to a second, private speculators will trade it for the second. To maintain the fixed exchange rate, the two governments involved must accommodate these speculative demands, using their holdings of the second currency to buy up the first. The dam will break when the governments decide that the unrealistic exchange rate is no longer worth saving.

During the Great Depression, the international gold standard came crashing down like everything else. Two dozen countries, including England, suspended gold payments in 1930 and 1931. Another dozen followed in the first few months of 1932. The United States held out until Franklin Roosevelt's inauguration in March of 1933. By 1936, virtually all countries had greatly modified or completely abandoned their gold standards.

One reason for this collapse was that international lending dried up in the Great Depression. The banking panic was worldwide and hit central banks as well as private banks. With misaligned exchange rates, many central banks had borrowed heavily to prop up their overvalued currencies. When these loans were not renewed and new funds could not be found, these central banks had no choice but to suspend gold payments at the old prices.

In addition, many nations correctly saw their inflated exchange rates as a restraint on foreign sales. With their economies sinking fast, they tried to boost export demand by leaving the gold standard and devaluing their currency.* As their currency became cheaper, so did their commodities, and this boost in export demand might keep the economy afloat. But this ploy is of little help when all nations are devaluing their currencies at the same time. For example, by the spring of 1933, the British pound had been devalued by 30% against the U.S. dollar. (Its price had been reduced to $3.40.) But most other currencies had also been devalued against the U.S. dollar by 30% or more. Thus the British had gained ground only against the United States in their efforts to stimulate export demand.

Roosevelt's decision in 1933 to devalue the dollar was largely intended to offset these earlier devaluations by other nations. Between 1929 and 1933, U.S. imports had grown and exports shrunk. This imbalance directly hurt the economy, especially farmers. In addition, gold had been flowing back out of the country and, with the bank runs, the nation's monetary aggregates had fallen by a third.†

Roosevelt was given emergency authority to raise the dollar price of gold (devaluing the dollar), and he raised the price to $35 an ounce on January 31, 1934. This offset most of the foreign devaluations, and more than offset some of them. For example, the dollar price of the British pound was raised from $3.40 to slightly over $5, compared to $4.76 under the old gold standard.

The Gold Reserve Act of January 1934 nationalized all U.S. gold, requiring citizens to turn in their gold and gold coins at the government's new price of $35 an ounce. Gold could be held privately only for "legitimate" nonmonetary uses. The U.S. government no longer sold gold to private citizens, but did trade gold at the new price with foreign governments and central banks.

During the remainder of the 1930s, gold poured into the United States. Much of this was due to the export stimulus provided by the devaluation of the dollar. In addition, both people and gold immigrated to the United States, refugees from the political and economic turmoil in Europe. Also, the increase in gold prices relative to other commodities stimulated gold production and encouraged private sales to governments. In all, the U.S. Treasury's gold stock swelled from $4 billion in the beginning of 1934 to $23 billion in 1941.

BRETTON WOODS

In preparation for the resumption of widespread international trade interrupted by World War II, an international monetary conference was held in July, 1944, at the Mount Washington Hotel in Bretton Woods, New Hampshire. More than 700 persons from 44 countries went to this small mountain

* Trying to stimulate an economy by selling goods to foreigners at bargain prices seems strange (it seemed so to OPEC), but exchange-rate competition appeared less painful than deflation and more respectable than deficit spending.

† In the 1920s, the Federal Reserve Banks used contractionary monetary policies to offset the gold flowing into the United States. But from 1929 to 1933, they did not take the symmetrical action of using expansionary monetary policies to offset the gold leaving the country. After 1933, as gold again flowed into the United States, the Fed again undertook partly offsetting monetary policies. This asymmetrical behavior during the 1929–33 disaster has been strongly criticized by most economists.

resort to hammer out a workable international monetary system. As is usually the case in this sort of thing, a few experts quietly drafted the plan, which was largely accepted beforehand by the principal nations. In this case, England and the United States were the most important participants, and the principal architects were John Maynard Keynes and Harry D. White, an Assistant Secretary of the U.S. Treasury.

The Bretton Woods agreement attempted to recapture the tranquility of fixed exchange rates without the domestic disruption caused by the pure gold standard. Fixed exchange rates were again established, and the participating nations agreed to make whatever currency transactions were necessary to keep exchange rates within 1% of this initial fixing. If there was a "fundamental disequilibrium" then a nation would be permitted a one-time devaluation of up to 10%.

A central reserve fund, the *International Monetary Fund (IMF)* was established to loan money to nations that needed to buy up their currency in order to stabilize exchange rates. These loans were intended to give a nation reasonable time to strengthen its currency. A scale of fees on these loans was calibrated to discourage procrastination. It was felt that such an adjustment period was preferable to the deflationary shock inflicted by the pure gold standard.

The central reserve fund, $6.8 billion in gold and U.S. dollars and other strong currencies, was financed by contributions from the members, principally the United States and Britain. The IMF was given a home in Washington, D.C., and a staff to administer the reserve fund. This staff also advises and prods nations with weak currencies. In the smaller countries, these IMF advisory missions were to "acquire a certain reputation for the astringency, even political sadism, of their recommendations."[2]

In 1970, the IMF expanded its reserve base by creating "paper gold," *Special Drawing Rights (SDRs),* which are credited to members and can be used within the IMF to purchase hard currency. The SDR was initially valued at one U.S. dollar. Between 1974 and 1980 the value of an SDR relative to the dollar was determined by a weighted average of the exchange rates of sixteen countries relative to the dollar. Because of the dollar's weakness, the value of the SDR rose to about $1.33 in 1980. In 1981, the number of currencies represented by an SDR was reduced from 16 to 5: The U.S. dollar, German mark, Japanese yen, French franc, and British pound.

These SDRs enlarged the IMF pool of funds that can be loaned to troubled central banks. They are also a tentative step toward an international money, with the IMF as the international central bank. It has been proposed that the IMF raise funds by selling SDR-denominated securities and that SDRs be used by central banks as a multicurrency reserve, in place of U.S. dollars. Several Arab nations, including Saudi Arabia, now value their currencies in SDRs and large private banks also issue international bonds with values indexed to SDRs. These SDR-linked securities are intended to reduce exchange-rate risks for international banks and businesses.

As noted, the intention of the Bretton Woods agreement was to establish the stable exchange rates that everyone seemed to covet, without also accepting the booms and busts that came with the international gold standard. This separation was to be made possible by the central reserve fund, which would make temporary loans to allow a nation time to decide the best way to strengthen its

IN THE NEWS

New Chips for Bankrupt Countries

Dollars will get you drachmas that not one American in a hundred has heard of Special Drawing Rights, the hybrid money irregularly created by the International Monetary Fund. An S.D.R. is money that exists only as an electronic entry in the accounts of government central banks. It is backed only by the agreement of the I.M.F. to accept S.D.R.'s in lieu of other money. Invented in 1970, to supplement gold and dollars, S.D.R.'s helped to grease the wheels of trade.

Now an economist at the Institute for International Economics, John Williamson, ingeniously suggests that S.D.R.'s could also be used to ease the grave debt problem of Third World countries.

A worldwide shortage of internationally recognized money was first felt by the major trading nations about 15 years ago. Banks and businesses lacked enough gold to support the explosive growth in trading. And dollars, the other main unit of account, varied capriciously with changes in U.S. domestic policy.

The I.M.F. therefore created a third currency of account. Issued periodically, S.D.R.'s cannot buy grain or anything else. But if I.M.F. members accept them, they can help settle nation-to-nation obligations. They're like poker chips for players who agree to recognize them.

One S.D.R. is now worth a little more than a dollar, the exact amount being derived from the average value of five designated currencies. That averaging makes an S.D.R. more stable than any single currency. Any central bank that accepts S.D.R.'s from another bank is, in effect, making a loan and earns interest on the amount at market rates.

How then might S.D.R.'s relieve the problem caused by the huge Third World debts to private banks in America, Europe and Japan?

To prevent the collapse of international trade and banking, the overextended nations need at least a decade to work their way out from under the debt burden. But even if the lending nations and their banks could agree how much repayment to forego or delay, they have no way of deciding how much relief to give to any individual debtor.

A fresh draft of S.D.R.'s could provide new credit in proportion to the already established I.M.F. quotas. These S.D.R.'s could still not be used by, say, Brazil to repay a debt to the Banque Nationale de Paris. But Brazil would use the S.D.R.'s as a substitute for the dollars it employs in day-to-day trade accounting, liberating dollars for a debt deal with Paris.

Such an S.D.R. distribution could not magically wipe out debt. Unless the total number issued is carefully limited to the growth in world trade, and recognized as part of a cooperative effort to improve the Third World's liquidity, this approach could misfire and produce worldwide expectations of greater inflation. Mr. Williamson estimates that a prudent limit would be about $34 billion, a mere fraction of the total debt.

But this kind of partial relief would have some clear advantages: No Congressional gauntlets to run; no advertising of any direct "bailout"; no humiliation for debtors. The very obscurity of the mechanism could be an advantage, shielding the rescue from political controversy and giving the fund's technocrats a chance to address a problem now widely described as intractable. (Peter Passell, *New York Times,* May, 1984.

currency. It sounded plausible on paper, but two eventually fatal flaws were soon found.

The first flaw was that speculators stalked weak currencies like vultures circling a wounded animal. When devaluation seemed possible, speculators would rush to sell that currency, thereby forcing a devaluation. From the speculators' viewpoint, it was a one-sided bet. The weak currency was surely not going to be revalued upwards. The worst that could happen then was that the exchange rate wouldn't change, with no loss to the speculator other than interest and transaction costs.* If a devaluation was forced, the speculators would have a large gain on a brief investment.

From the beleaguered nation's viewpoint, it was all a bit immoral. To preserve the exchange rate it had to buy (at a high price) from the very speculators who were causing most of the trouble. When its foreign currency reserves were exhausted, surrender and devaluation gave fat profits to those same delighted speculators. This aggressive international flow of speculative funds meant that a nation did not in fact have much time to take the fundamental economic steps necessary to strengthen its currency.

The second flaw in the Bretton Woods agreement was that nations were too often unwilling to take these necessary steps. Consider again the purchasing-power parity comparison, and assume that the domestic currency is overvalued at the existing exchange rate: $P_d > eP_f$. The domestic country's products are overpriced, and the country will run persistent balance-of-trade deficits. If the existing exchange rate is to be preserved, then at least one of the following must occur:

1. The domestic country must submit to a deflation.
2. The foreign country must accept an inflation.
3. Governments must continue to accumulate the domestic country's overvalued currency.

In practice, governments had little enthusiasm for any of these options. Since stable exchange rates are possible only when nations pursue mutually consistent domestic policies, fixed exchange rates cannot persist. This lesson was painfully learned in the quarter century following the Bretton Woods agreement. We will briefly review some of these instructive crises, and then we will look at the eventual retreat to flexible exchange rates.

The fall of Bretton Woods

Under the Bretton Woods agreement, currency prices were specified in terms of gold, though the United States and other nations would only sell gold to each other (and not to their citizens) at these official prices. These gold prices were used to implicitly set the currency exchange rates. For example, the U.S. gold price was $35 an ounce. The initial English gold price was 8.75 British pounds per ounce, so that the fixed exchange rate was $4.00 per British pound. The specification of all currency prices in terms of gold allowed a nation con-

* It was not necessary to have held the currency to speculate against it. If for example, the British pound was weak, Belgian speculators could borrow pounds from English banks, and then sell these pounds (at the prevailing high price) for other currencies. After the anticipated devaluations, pounds could be purchased at the new low price to repay the loans.

fronted with a "fundamental disequilibrium" to devalue its currency against those of all other currencies simultaneously. For example, in 1949, the English gold price was raised to 12.5 British pounds per ounce, and this reduced the pound's exchange rate with respect to all fixed currencies by 30%. Thus, the U.S.-English exchange rate fell 30% to $2.80 per British pound.

The United States held a crucial role in this arrangement because it had the strongest economy and owned three quarters of the Western world's monetary gold. U.S. dollars served as the world's money. Dollars were used for many transactions and price quotations, and were held as reserves by most central banks. The U.S. dollar took its place alongside gold as an internationally accepted medium of exchange, and as evidence that a central bank had something solid behind its currency. Central banks were correspondingly interested in the soundness of the U.S. dollar.

The Bretton Woods system worked tolerably well until the 1960s. Britain, Italy, and many smaller countries seemed to have chronic difficulties, but at least the system held together. However, in the 1960s people began to wonder aloud if the U.S. dollar was really as good as gold, at least at $35 an ounce.

The United States had been steadily supplying dollars to the world and exchanging gold for some of these dollars. By 1960, the foreign liquid short-term claims against the United States surpassed the value of the U.S. gold stock (at $35 an ounce). Since the United States no longer had enough gold to meet these foreign claims, many expected the U.S. dollar to be devalued against gold.

This logic was incomplete. Internationally, the United States had put itself in the position of world banker. It had made long-term illiquid loans and issued short-term liquid claims. The fact that its liquid liabilities were not backed by precious metal need not have been worrisome. But, like the smallest bank on a Nebraska prairie in the 1930s, the government of the world's strongest nation feared a run on the bank.

On the London and Zurich gold markets, the price of privately traded gold reached $40 an ounce. This was unnerving to many central bankers* and tempting to a few who contemplated buying gold from the United States at $35 an ounce and reselling it privately for $40. To remove this anxiety and temptation to sin the United States and the leading Western European nations formed a "gold pool" syndicate to peg the free-market price of gold at $35 an ounce. They agreed to pool their resources to buy or sell gold at this price. To drive the price down from $40 they had to sell some of their gold.

This was reassuring to some. To others, it was a signal that the dollar really was overpriced. But despite some speculative tests, the gold pool managed to hold the market gold price at $35 an ounce until 1968. This effort was successful because the private gold market was very thin, with light trading, while governments held enormous gold reserves.

In 1968, wholesale and consumer prices in the United States were about twice what they had been when the Bretton Woods agreement was signed, and three times what they had been when Franklin Roosevelt set the price of gold at $35 an ounce in 1934. It would have been pretty surprising if the free-market price of gold hadn't increased too by 1968. In March 1968 the quickening U.S.

* Actually, an increase in the official dollar price of gold was mostly resisted because speculators and Soviet and South African gold producers would have profited, and because President Lyndon Johnson would have felt personally embarrassed.

inflation and the flow of dollars abroad to pay for the Vietnam War finally blew off the \$35 lid. Between September, 1967, and March, 1968, the gold pool had been forced to sell \$4 billion in gold. With a 60% share in the pool, the United States supplied \$2.5 billion of it.

There now seemed to be only three options: The central banks could sell off the rest of their gold, the United States could submit to a domestic deflation, or the market price of gold could be allowed to rise. Wisely, the pool chose the later option. An emergency "two-tier" system was established. One tier of this was the private gold market, the second tier was the "monetary" gold market, in which governments traded gold with each other at the official fixed price. The United States continued to sell gold for "legitimate monetary uses" at \$35 an ounce, and continued to lose gold reserves. Undoubtedly many governments thought gold was a bargain at this price, and a few probably succumbed to the temptation to sell their monetary gold in the forbidden private market.

In the fall of 1971, the free-market gold price shot upward and the U.S. Treasury suspended gold sales to foreign governments. After an emergency conference at the Smithsonian Institution, the official U.S. price of gold was raised to \$38 an ounce, though the United States would still not sell gold. In February, 1973, the dollar had to be devalued again (by raising the official gold price to \$42.22 an ounce) and in March, 1973, fixed exchange rates were finally dropped. Since then, the major exchange rates have been determined in the open market. (Most small countries have kept their currencies pegged to major currencies.) However, governments do intervene in exchange markets to stabilize their currency, to raise its value, or to devalue it to encourage exports. This official intervention is called a "managed" or "dirty" float.

FLEXIBLE EXCHANGE RATES

The prime advantage of floating exchange rates is that they break the impasse created by inconsistent domestic economic policies. Recalling again purchasing-power parity, $P_d = eP_f$, if the domestic country (say the United States) has more rapid inflation than the foreign country (say Germany), parity can be preserved by a simple market devaluation of the first nation's currency. If P_d increases faster than P_f, then e will tend to increase, meaning that the dollar price of the mark rises. Specifically, according to Equation 17.2, $\Delta e/e = \pi_d - \pi_f$.

There has, in fact, been a good correlation between rates of inflation and exchange-rate changes since 1973, as shown in Figure 17.3. These data are longer-run averages; the relationship is much looser when annual or monthly data are used. In addition, the comparison in Figure 17.3 is not quite right because the price list includes nontraded goods while ignoring the prices of bonds and other assets, because domestic inflations are never evenhanded, and because central banks do intervene in exchange markets. Nonetheless, the indicated correlation is striking.

Flexible exchange rates have, so far, worked tolerably well. In a decade of enormous financial upheaval, with Eurodollars, petrodollars, and lightning capital mobility, foreign-exchange adjustments have been rather smoothly accomplished.

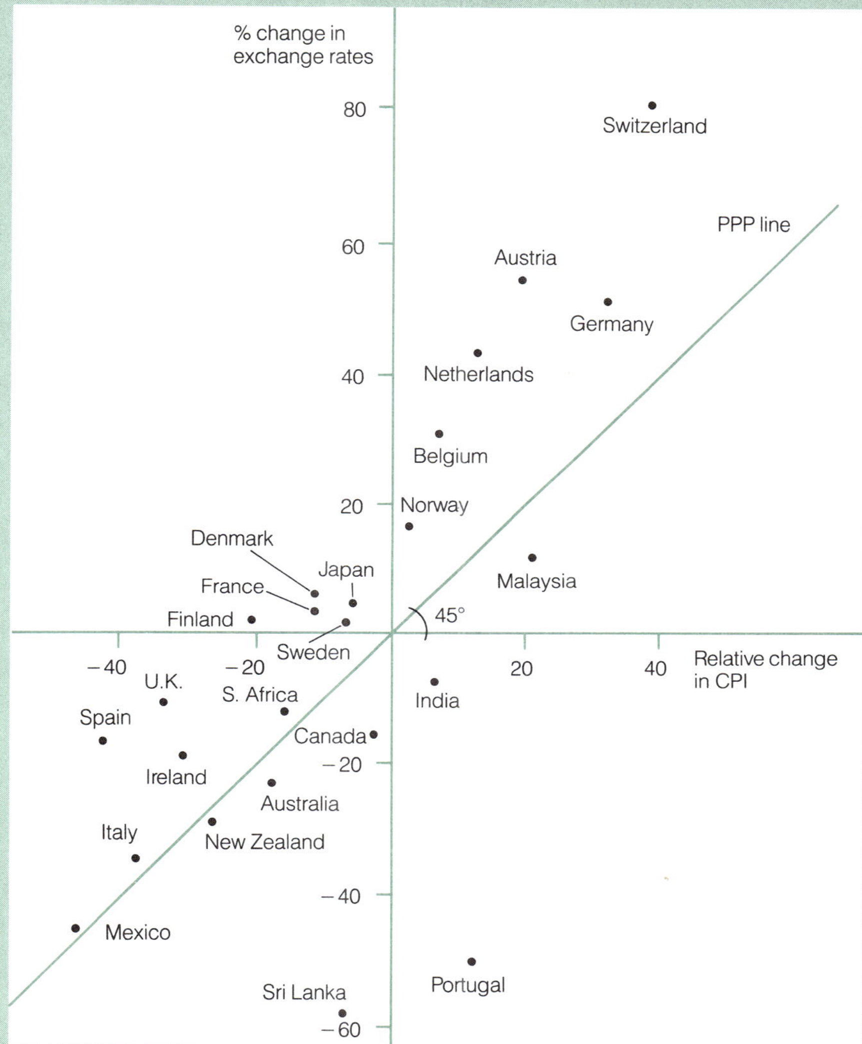

FIGURE 17.3 **CHANGES IN EXCHANGE RATES AND CPIs RELATIVE TO THE UNITED STATES, MARCH 1973 to MARCH 1980.** **If purchasing-power parity holds, the percentage change in an exchange rate would equal the relative change in prices—that is, the difference between the two inflation rates. In practice, although there is a relation between the two, it is not perfect. (Source: *Federal Reserve Bulletins* and *United Nations Monthly Bulletins.*)**

The petrodollar disruptions have been particularly challenging. Unprecedented increases in oil prices have created hundreds of billions of dollars of balance-of-payments surpluses and deficits. The economies of many poorer countries might easily have been crumpled by an inability to pay for oil and oil-related imports. The IMF and private banks have so far averted such national collapses by loaning funds implicitly from trade-surplus nations to trade-deficit nations.

The IMF has done this directly, borrowing heavily from Arab oil-exporting countries and lending to oil-importing nations. Private banks have also recycled petrodollars since the OPEC nations have invested large amounts in Eurocurrency deposits in Western banks, which have simultaneously lent hundreds of billions of dollars to oil-importing nations. It remains to be seen whether these loans can be repaid. If they cannot, the potential financial default could have staggering consequences. Critics of the IMF and Eurocurrency markets argue that it is dangerous to postpone the day of reckoning. Fundamental balance-of-payments disequilibria need to be corrected soon.

The other lingering international-finance nightmare is that speculative bubbles or panics will develop, with adverse effects on real economic activity. Tens of trillions of dollars worth of foreign-exchange trades are now made annually.* This is far, far more than needed to carry out international transactions. Like the stock market, most of these trades are for investment or speculative purposes, for buying currencies that are expected to appreciate and selling those that are expected to depreciate. The speculative excesses in financial markets in the 1920s and the financial collapse in the 1930s had quite real economic effects. The world's economies are now even more interdependent, and a contagious international financial panic could be an economic disaster.

A TWO-COUNTRY MACRO MODEL

Sometimes it is said that floating exchange rates free nations to follow their own separate economic objectives. This is true in the sense that each nation's price level (P_d and P_f) can move separately, with the exchange rate adjusting to maintain purchasing-power parity. But it is also true that each nation's economic policies affect other nations.

In order to analyze the international transmission of economic events, we will examine a macro model of a world economy consisting of two large nations. We can think of the domestic country as the United States and the foreign country as either a large trading partner or as the entire rest of the world. I will focus on the international consequences of U.S. monetary and fiscal policies. Since the two nations are modeled symmetrically, we can infer that the United States is similarly affected by foreign economic policies. Our analysis also applies to the international consequences of private economic events.

The model has two separate labor markets, one in each country. People work

* A 1980 Fed survey of 90 United States banks found that their foreign-currency trades totaled about $20 billion a day. Only 8% of these trades were for corporate accounts; 92% were trades between banks. Also in 1980, the volume of foreign-exchange futures contracts traded on the Chicago Mercantile Exchange frequently approached a billion dollars a day.

in the country in which they live, for a real wage equal to the nominal wage divided by the price level:

$$w_d = W_d/P_d$$
$$w_f = W_f/P_f \tag{17.4}$$

where w_d and w_f are real wages; W_d and W_f, nominal wages; and P_d and P_f, the price levels in the domestic and foreign countries, respectively.

There is a single, worldwide *IS* equation:

$$e_0 + e_d y_d + e_f y_f + e_r r = y_d + y_f \tag{17.5}$$

because the commodities produced in the two countries are assumed to be perfect substitutes. This assumption implies that purchasing-power parity ($P_d = eP_f$) holds. Purchasing-power parity is an extreme assumption that, as was explained earlier, is not quite accurate. We use it as a simplifying approximation. The actual *IS* equation (17.5) is analogous to our earlier model of a single, closed economy: World income is equal to world spending. World spending, in turn, is positively related to income in each nation and negatively related to the interest rate.

The nations' two moneys are not perfect substitutes, in that private citizens hold only their own domestic currency. Thus there are two separate *LM* equations:

$$l_0 + l_y y_d + l_R(r + \pi_d^e) = (M_d - F_f)/P_d \tag{17.6}$$

$$h_0 + h_y y_f + h_R(r + \pi_f^e) = (M_f - F_d)/P_f. \tag{17.7}$$

These private money demands (l and h) correspond to those of the closed-economy model. Both state that the demand for money is positively related to output and negatively related to the yield on securities. Governments hold foreign exchange, denoted by F. M is the total supply of money, and $M - F$ is the amount available to private citizens. An increase in the domestic price level reduces the real money supply.

Domestic and foreign securities are considered to be perfect substitutes,* and thus are priced to yield a common real rate of return, r. In each country, the difference between the real yield on securities (r) and the real yield on money ($-\pi^e$) is the nominal interest rate ($r + \pi^e$), and it is this rate that appears in the money demand equations.

The supply side

First, consider the special case of full employment. The two national labor markets are separated from each other, with labor demands, d, and supplies, s,

* Foreign currency is a poor substitute for domestic currency because it cannot be used for domestic transactions. Speculators who anticipate a currency appreciation will buy foreign securities rather than foreign currency. Thus, foreign securities are a viable alternative to domestic securities.

depending only on the domestic real wage rate. If these two markets are in equilibrium,

$$n_d[\overset{-}{w_d}] = s_d[\overset{+}{w_d}]$$

$$n_f[\overset{-}{w_f}] = s_f[\overset{+}{w_f}]$$

then real wages, employment, and output (via the national production functions) in both countries are unaffected by demand-side events at home or abroad. Spending decisions and financial markets determine only the world interest rate, prices in the two countries, and the exchange rate.

What if there are, instead, excess labor supplies because of sticky nominal wages and/or prices? As in the earlier closed-economy case, employment is assumed to be determined by labor demand. If nominal wages are not as flexible as prices, then an increase in the price level reduces real wages, thereby increasing labor demand, employment, and output. Thus there are positive supply-side relationships between each country's output and its price level:

$$y_d = y_d[\overset{+}{P_d}]$$

$$y_f = y_f[\overset{+}{P_f}]. \tag{17.8}$$

Alternatively, we can interpret these positive supply-side relationships as saying that, as each nation's output expands, upward pressures are exerted on production costs and prices.

The demand side

There are two *LM* equations (17.6 and 17.7), one for each country. The present model is more complicated than our earlier closed-economy model, in that there are now two outputs and two price levels to take into account. To deal with this we will use a somewhat different graphical apparatus. In particular, the supply-side equation (17.8) can be used to eliminate prices from our *LM* equations.

First, consider the domestic *LM* curve (Equation 17.6). Money demand is positively related to domestic output, while the real money supply is inversely related to the domestic price level. Since there is a positive supply-side relationship between output and the price level, these effects are reinforcing. When output increases, money demand increases. The accompanying increase in the price level reduces the real money supply and widens the gap between money demand and supply. To restore equilibrium, money demand must be diminished by an increase in the interest rate. The implied *LM* curve is shown in Figure 17.4.* To repeat, the usual *LM* curve says that an increase in output requires an increase in the interest rate so as to keep money demand equal to

* There are separate nominal interest rates, R_d and R_f, but (because of purchasing-power parity) a single real interest rate: $r = R_d - \pi_d^e = R_f - \pi_f^e$. To simplify the graphics the real interest rate is on the vertical axis in our figures.

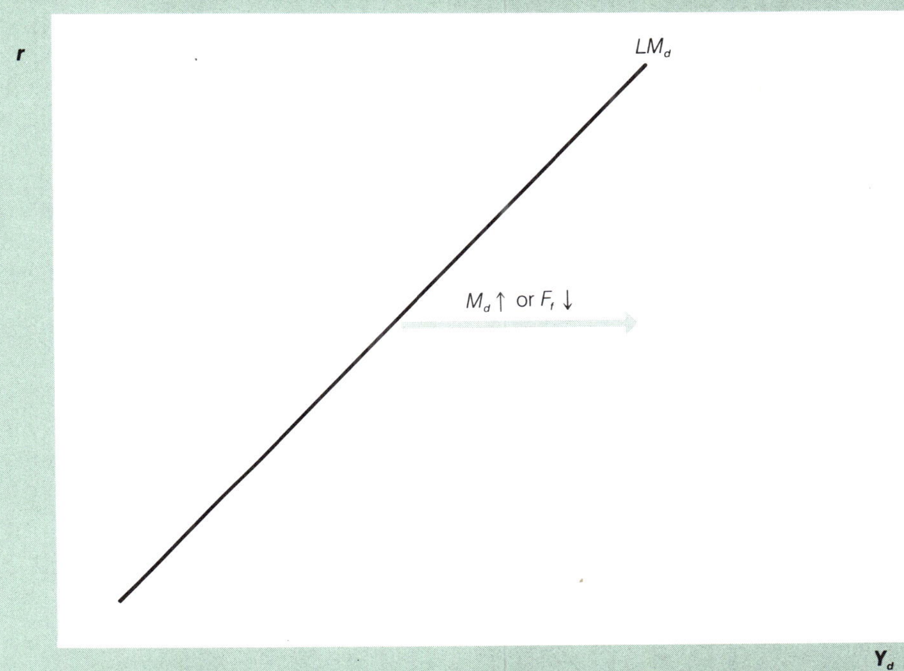

FIGURE 17.4 THE DOMESTIC *LM* CURVE. **This curve is positively sloped and shifted rightward by an increase in the amount of money supplied to private citizens through either monetary expansion by the domestic government or reduced holdings by foreign governments.**

supply. The somewhat more complicated *LM* curve in Figure 17.4 takes into account the fact that, not only does an increase in output raise money demand, but the accompanying increase in the price level also reduces the real money supply.

One additional new wrinkle is that the domestic money supply is equal to the amount of money the government has outstanding less the amount held by the foreign government. Thus the amount of money in private circulation can be increased either by the domestic government printing more money or by the foreign government using some of its foreign exchange. Either way, increases in the money supply shift the LM_d curve rightward.

The very same logic can be applied to the foreign *LM* equation (17.7). With the positive supply-side relationship between output and prices taken into account, an increase in foreign output requires a higher interest rate so as to keep the demand for foreign currency equal to the supply. So far, so good. But now, in order to put these two *LM* curves in the same figure, we are going to graph the foreign *LM* curve with domestic rather than foreign output on the horizontal axis.

Figure 17.5 shows the result. Since domestic output does not affect the demand for foreign money, this *LM* curve is horizontal. Any level of domestic output is consistent with equality between the demand and supply of foreign currency. Changes in foreign output shift this *LM* curve about. In particular, a decline in foreign output reduces the foreign nation's demand for money, putting downward pressure on the world interest rate, just as if the foreign nation had switched to an expansionary monetary policy.

The *IS* equation (17.5) states that world spending is positively related to output in each country and inversely related to the world interest rate. These assumptions imply an *IS* curve as drawn in Figure 17.6. Again, I have put the interest rate and domestic output on the axes. Changes in foreign output shift this world *IS* curve. The slope of the *IS* curve can be explained as follows. An increase in the interest rate reduces world spending. Therefore, if foreign output is held constant, an increase in r requires a decline in y_d to keep world output equal to world spending. So the *IS* curve is negatively sloped.

At any given interest rate, a decrease in foreign output must be offset by an increase in domestic output. Otherwise, world output would not equal world spending. Thus a decrease in foreign output shifts the *IS* curve rightward. Any

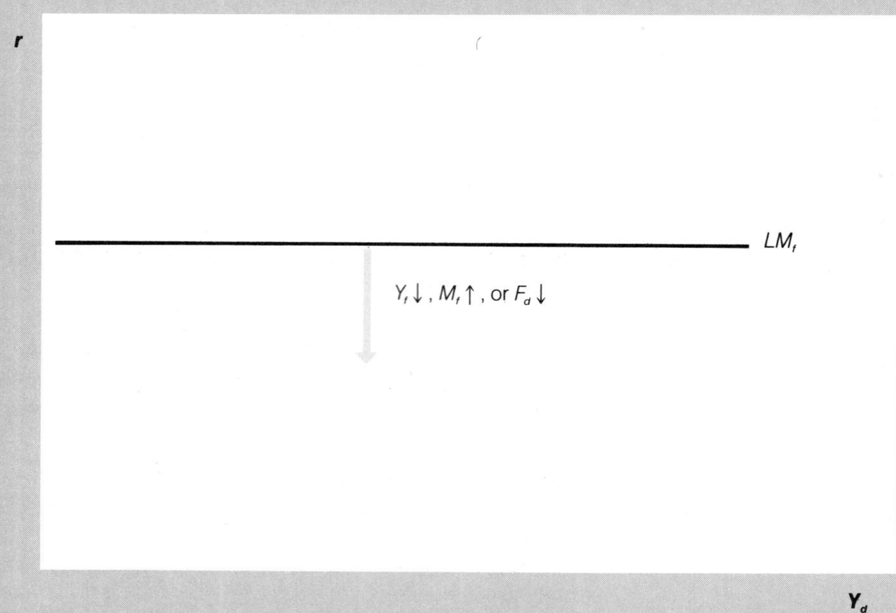

FIGURE 17.5 THE FOREIGN *LM* CURVE. **This curve is horizontal, since foreign money demand does not depend on domestic output. The curve is shifted downward by an increased supply (due to an enlarged supply by the foreign government or reduced demand by the domestic government) or a reduced demand (due to diminished foreign output).**

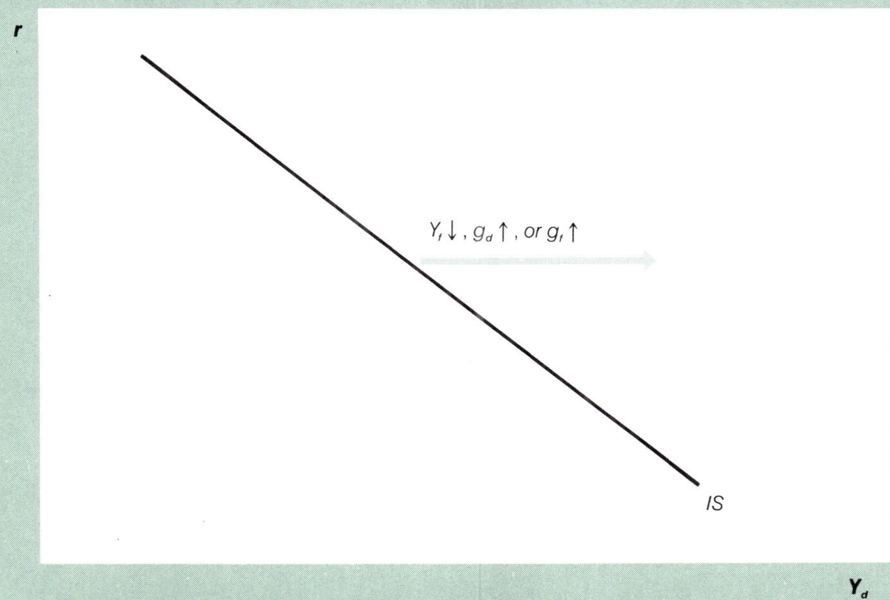

FIGURE 17.6 **THE WORLD *IS* CURVE is negatively sloped and shifted rightward by increased spending by either government or by higher foreign output (which increases private foreign spending).**

increase in government spending (g_d and g_f) or in private spending shifts the *IS* curve rightward, very much as in the earlier closed-economy *IS* curve.

Figure 17.7 puts the world *IS* curve and the two *LM* curves together. As explained, the *IS* curve and domestic *LM* curve have the usual appearances. The only added feature is that this is a world *IS* curve and it is shifted leftward by an increase in foreign output. The foreign *LM* curve is horizontal and is shifted upward by an increase in foreign output or by a decrease in the foreign money supply.

Foreign output, domestic output, and the world interest rate are determined by the intersection of these three curves. That is, the level of foreign output must be such that the *IS* curve and the foreign *LM* curve slide to a triple intersection with the domestic *LM* curve. We can then find domestic output and the interest rate at this intersection, too.

International effects of fiscal and monetary policies

Figure 17.8 shows the consequences of a bond-financed increase in government sending by either country. The *IS* curve shifts rightward from the initial point (Point 1). If only y_d and r rose (to Point 2) there would be insufficient demand

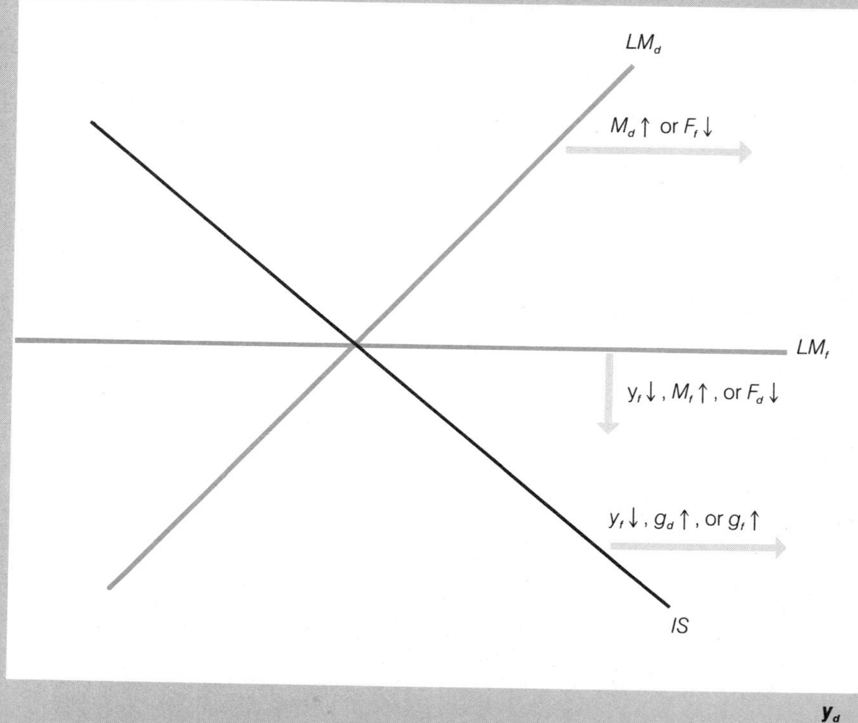

FIGURE 17.7 THE *IS* AND *LM* CURVES. **The triple intersection of the *IS* curve and the two *LM* curves determines foreign output, domestic output, and the world interest rate. The *IS* curve is shifted by fiscal policy, the *LM* curves by monetary policy.**

for the foreign country's currency (since the higher interest rate reduces money demand). To maintain foreign money demand foreign output must also rise. As foreign output increases, the *IS* curve shifts leftward, and the LM_f curve shifts upward. The new equilibrium is at the triple intersection (Point 3). Thus output increases in both countries, and the world interest rate is higher, too. Since the supply side tells us that prices move up with output, we also know that both price levels increase here. The exchange rate is determined by $e = P_d/P_f$ and may rise or fall, depending on whether P_d increases more or less than P_f.

These consequences of increased government spending are very similar to those for a closed economy. An increase in world spending expands output, employment, and prices in both countries. The enlarged output increases money demand, while the higher prices diminish real money supplies, pushing the world interest rate up. The signs of these effects are collected in Table 17.2. **An expansionary fiscal policy increases output, employment, and prices, both at home and abroad, and tightens world financial markets. The ef-**

fect on the exchange rate is uncertain because foreign prices may go up more or less than domestic prices.

Figure 17.9 shows the consequences of an open-market purchase by the domestic country, say the United States. The very same graph also applies to a decision by the foreign country to use some of its dollar holdings to purchase securities. As shown, the increased supply of U.S. currency shifts LM_d rightward, and a decline in foreign output, y_f, is required to give a triple intersection. The domestic consequences are the same as for a closed economy. An open-market purchase reduces the interest rate on securities, stimulating spending and thereby raising domestic output, employment, and prices.

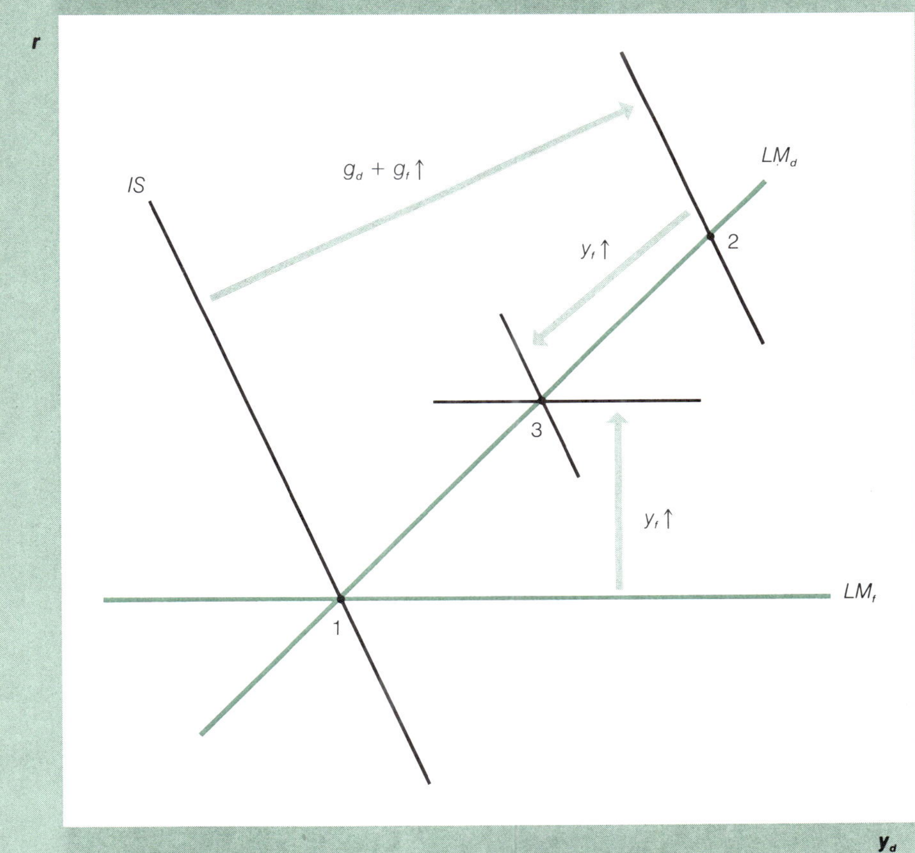

FIGURE 17.8 THE EFFECTS OF AN INCREASE IN GOVERNMENT SPENDING. **An increase in either nation's government spending shifts the *IS* curve rightward. An increase in foreign output restores a triple intersection, with the interest rate and domestic output also higher.**

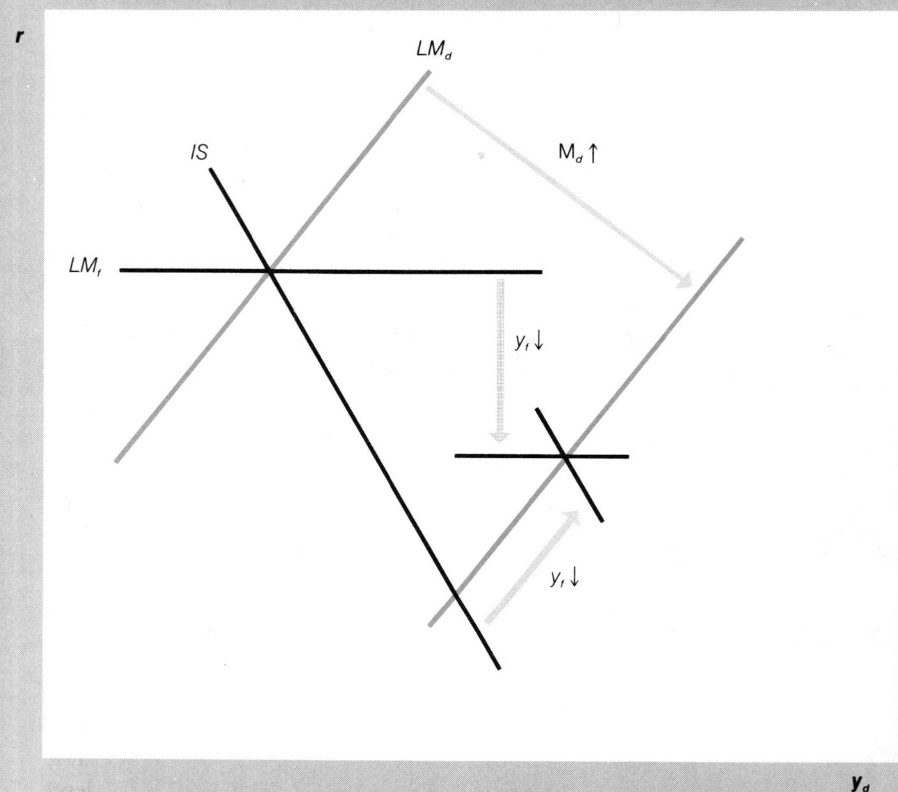

FIGURE 17.9 **AN OPEN-MARKET PURCHASE BY THE DOMESTIC COUNTRY shifts the domestic *LM* curve rightward. A decline in foreign output restores a triple intersection, with a lower interest rate and higher domestic output.**

But, surprisingly, foreign output, employment, and prices decline! This result is unexpected, but the logic is straightforward. An expansionary monetary policy reduces interest rates at home and abroad. This interest rate decline increases the demands for both domestic and foreign money. The increased U.S. demand is satisfied by the increased money supply. But if the foreign money supply is unchanged, then the increased money demand must be offset. A decline in foreign output reduces foreign money demand, while the accompanying decline in prices increases the real value of the foreign money supply, thereby restoring money equilibrium. Put somewhat differently, the lower interest rates brought about by U.S. monetary policies increase foreign money demand, which has the same effects on their economy as a contraction of the foreign money supply.

EXCHANGE-MARKET INTERVENTION

Fluctuations in exchange rates have concerned economic policymakers since the transition to widespread floating in 1973. There has been much debate about the feasibility and desirability of using intervention in foreign-exchange markets to limit movements in exchange rates.

Exchange-market intervention changes the currency composition of the financial instruments that the private sector can hold, making available, say, more dollar instruments and fewer Deutsche Mark instruments. There are two kinds of exchange-market intervention—unsterilized and sterilized. The difference between them is that unsterilized intervention affects the monetary instruments of the private sector but sterilized intervention does not.

Changes in the supplies of financial instruments available to the private sector are reflected in changes in the balance sheet of the financial authorities (the consolidated balance sheet of the central bank, the exchange stabilization fund, and general government). Consider the following stylized balance sheet for the financial authorities in a given country. It is conventional to divide the assets of the authorities into net domestic (currency) assets and net foreign (currency) assets. Net domestic assets are domestic bonds held minus domestic bonds issued; net foreign assets are foreign bonds held minus foreign bonds issued. Given these definitions, the only remaining liability of the authorities is the monetary base, which comprises currency and deposit liabilities to banks.

The net worth of the financial authorities increases whenever they run a current spending surplus, receive net interest payments, or experience a capital gain on their net assets.

Assets	**Liabilities**
Net domestic assets (NDA)	Monetary base (MB)
Net foreign assets (NFA)	Net worth (NW)

Financial policy actions including intervention operations can be represented by changes in the stylized balance sheet. Attention is focused on actions that cause the domestic currency to depreciate. The most familiar financial policy action is a domestic open-market operation. In an expansionary open-market operation the authorities increase the monetary base by purchasing domestic bonds ($\Delta\text{NDA} = \Delta\text{MB} > 0$). This operation causes the domestic interest rate to fall and the domestic currency to depreciate.

Intervention operations designed to cause the domestic currency to depreciate increase the supply of domestic financial instruments available to the private sector and decrease the supply of foreign financial instruments. In an unsterilized intervention operation the authorities increase the monetary base by purchasing foreign bonds ($\Delta\text{NFA} = \Delta\text{MB} > 0$). The operation is carried out in two steps. First, the authorities purchase a deposit at a foreign commercial bank; in paying for this deposit the authorities increase the monetary base. Second, the authorities use their deposit at a foreign commercial bank to purchase a foreign bond. The effects of an unsterilized intervention operation are similar to those of an open-market operation of equal magnitude. The two operations increase the monetary base by the same amount, so under reasonable assumptions they reduce the domestic interest rate by the same amount. However, following an unsterilized intervention operation, the supply of financial instruments available to the private sector contains more domestic instruments and fewer foreign instruments, so the depreciation of the domestic currency is somewhat greater.

In a sterilized intervention operation the authorities buy foreign bonds and sell domestic bonds (NFA $= -\Delta$NDA > 0). The operation is carried out in three steps. The first two are the same as the two steps in an unsterilized intervention operation. The third step is to sterilize the monetary base by selling a domestic bond; the payment for this bond made by the private sector to the authorities reduces the monetary base to its initial level. The effects of a sterilized intervention operation are quite different from those of an unsterilized intervention operation or an open-market operation of equal magnitude. A sterilized intervention operation leaves the monetary base unchanged, so it does not affect the domestic interest rate. However, following a sterilized intervention operation there are more domestic bonds and fewer foreign bonds available to the private sector, so the domestic currency depreciates.

Sterilized intervention has significant effects on the exchange rate if private agents regard home and foreign bonds as imperfect substitutes. However, if they regard home and foreign bonds as perfect substitutes, they require no inducement to change the currency composition of their bond holdings, so there is no reason for the exchange rate to change. Another implication of perfect substitutability is that open-market operations and unsterilized intervention operations have exactly the same effects on exchange rates.

The degree of substitutability between home and foreign securities has important consequences for economic policy. If home and foreign securities are imperfect substitutes, so that sterilized intervention has significant effects, the financial authorities can influence the exchange rate without changing their monetary policy, expressed in terms of the monetary base. With imperfect substitutability, a shift in private agents' bond demands away from home bonds and toward foreign bonds causes a depreciation of the home currency. The appropriate reaction to such a disturbance is sterilized intervention, a purchase of home bonds and sale of foreign bonds, to prevent depreciation of the home currency and induced changes in outputs and prices. This case is an illustration of the general principle that it is desirable to offset financial-sector disturbances so that they are not transmitted to the real sector.

Empirical tests for imperfect substitutability have yielded mixed results. Effort has been concentrated on tests of the joint hypothesis of perfect substitutability and rational expectations. If home and foreign bonds are perfect substitutes, the expected rate of return to speculation, the home interest rate minus the sum of the foreign interest rate and the expected rate of depreciation of the home currency, should be zero. If, in addition, expectations are rational, the actual rate of return to speculation, obtained by replacing the expected rate of depreciation by the actual rate of depreciation, should have a mean of zero and should be unrelated to all data available when expectations were formed.

In many tests the joint hypothesis is rejected; the actual rate of return to speculation is systematically related to some data that were readily available when expectations were formed. Of course, rejection of the joint hypothesis is consistent with either imperfect substitutability or nonrational expectations, or both.

A few tests of the joint hypothesis have been specifically designed to provide information on whether imperfect substitutability is the reason for rejection. The supply of home bonds is included in the data available when expectations were formed. If bonds are imperfect substitutes, the expected rate of return to speculation must rise in order to induce the private sector to hold a larger supply of home bonds. If, in addition, expectations are rational, the actual rate of return to speculation should be positively correlated with the supply of home securities. Almost no evidence of this relationship has been found in the data. Thus, available empirical work provides little support for the view that the joint hypothesis is being rejected because of imperfect substitutability. However, it is too soon to draw a firm conclusion about the degree of substitutability between home and foreign securities. (Dale W. Henderson)

Table 17.2.
International Effects of Fiscal and Monetary Policies

Parameter affected	Increase in government spending $(g_d + g_f)$	Increase in domestic money supply $(M_d - F_f)$	Increase in foreign money supply $(M_f - F_d)$
y_d	+	+	−
y_f	+	−	+
r	+	−	−
P_d	+	+	−
P_f	+	−	+
e	?	+	−

Since P_d is up and P_f is down, purchasing-power parity, $P_d = eP_f$, is maintained by an increase in the exchange rate, *e*. Table 17.2 shows these signs and those for the analogous case of an open-market purchase by the foreign country. **An expansionary monetary policy eases world financial markets; increases domestic output, employment, and prices; reduces foreign output, employment, and prices; and depreciates the domestic currency.**

Now, the foreign nation may not want the recession that is caused by U.S. monetary policies. If so, then they may be provoked into making their own open-market purchases to keep their output and employment from falling. Monetary policies may be internationally contagious! This economic epidemic could conceivably get out of hand, in that induced open-market purchases by the foreign nation will not only raise its output, but will also reduce the output of the first nation. The first country may make additional open-market purchases, thereby raising y_d, but again reducing y_f. By the time both nations are content, world money supplies may be enlarged considerably.

Some national objectives may be incompatible. For example, the United States may want low interest rates, while the foreign country wants high interest rates. The United States will then follow an easy-money policy, while the foreign nation follows a tight-money policy. As long as investors have international mobility in choosing securities, the two nations will quarrel and at least one will be frustrated.

Figure 17.10 analyzes one final example. Consider a situation in which the foreign country decides to use open-market operations to peg the exchange rate at some traditional value. Table 17.2 reminds us that this commitment means that the foreign country must make open-market sales if *e* starts to fall, and open-market purchases if *e* starts to rise. Figure 17.10 shows what now happens when the United States makes an open-market purchase. Again there is a rightward shift in LM_d, which, if unanswered, would (as in Figure 17.9) cause y_f and P_f to fall and cause *e* to rise. But now the foreign country responds with an open-market purchase to stabilize the exchange rate. Specifically, the foreign nation must put enough of its money into circulation to cause P_f to rise as much as P_d. Thus an expansionary domestic monetary policy induces expansionary monetary policies by foreign nations desiring stable exchange rates. Inflation is exported!

The general conclusion is that there are international consequences of economic events. Events in one country affect employment, output, and prices in

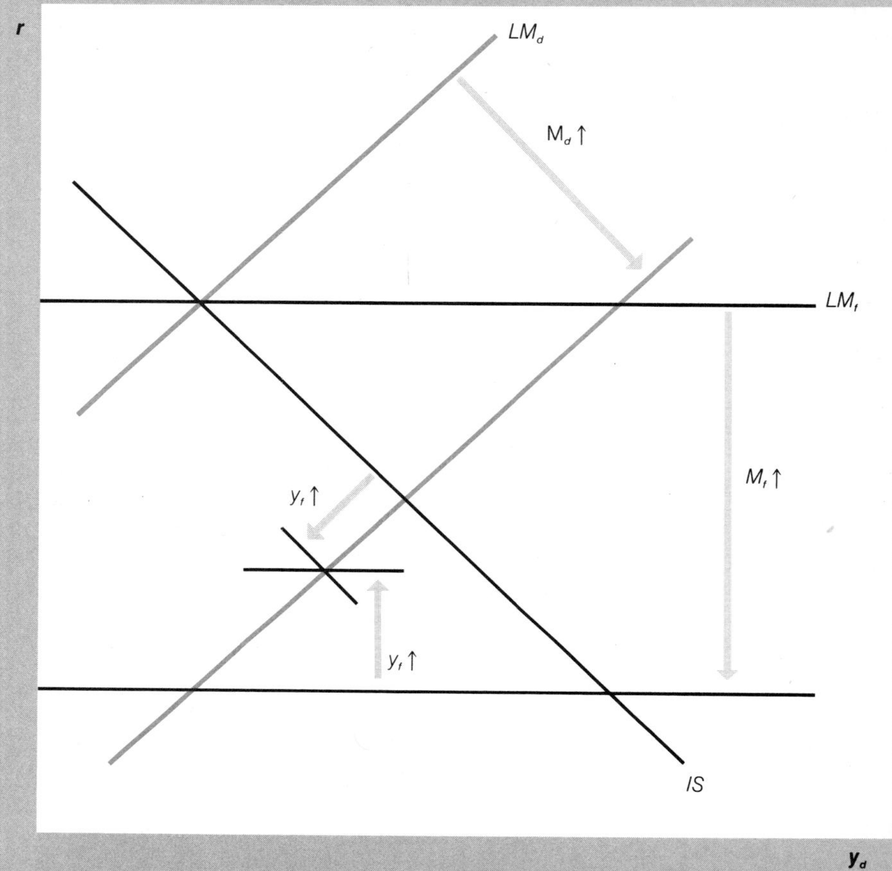

FIGURE 17.10 EFFECTS OF AN OPEN-MARKET PURCHASE BY THE DOMESTIC AND FOREIGN COUNTRIES. **A domestic open-market purchase shifts the domestic *LM* curve rightward. As Figure 17.9 shows, domestic output will then increase and foreign output fall. If prices move similarly, then the domestic currency will depreciate relative to the foreign currency. If the foreign government makes its own open-market purchase to stabilize the exchange rate, then foreign output will increase along with domestic outputs so that domestic and foreign prices increase equally.**

another. Specifically, an expansionary fiscal policy stimulates all countries, while an expansionary monetary policy depresses foreign economies. If foreign nations do not welcome these international economic ripples, then expansionary fiscal policies will tend to provoke contractionary policies abroad, while expansionary monetary policies will induce expansionary policies in response. In such a case there may well be international economic conflicts and a need for some coordination and cooperation.

IMPORTANT TERMS AND CONCEPTS

Closed economy
Open economy
Exchange rate
Devaluation
Purchasing-power parity
Trade balance
Goods-and-service balance
Current-account balance
Bretton Woods agreement
International Monetary Fund (IMF)
Special Drawing Rights (SDRs)

Domestic prices, foreign prices, and exchange rates are roughly linked through purchasing-power parity, or the "law of one price." While purchasing-power parity does not hold exactly, at least in the short run this concept is helpful in remembering the direction in which things will be moving. Purchasing-power parity is most appropriate for raw commodities and financial assets.

From data on international transactions specific details can be culled to measure such things as exports versus imports, borrowing and lending with foreign nations, and liquid international assets and liabilities. These various balances of trade and payment are useful and informative but are sometimes carelessly interpreted.

While the United States has been acquiring long-term claims against the rest of the world it has been selling gold and short-term liquid claims against the United States. The United States has been the world's banker, using its dollars as the world's money.

The international gold standard pegged exchange rates. This system, and the modified Bretton Woods plan, broke down because nations were unwilling to sacrifice domestic economic stabilization in order to hold exchange rates constant.

Flexible exchange rates have worked tolerably well, though there is some concern that speculative activity will disrupt international trade.

The domestic consequences of economic events correspond to those (described earlier) for a closed economy. Expansionary fiscal policies increase output, the price level, and the real interest rate. Expansionary monetary policies increase output and the price level, while reducing the real interest rate. If there is full employment, then output is not affected by fiscal and monetary policies.

Expansionary fiscal policies raise output and prices abroad and have an uncertain effect on exchange rates. Expansionary monetary policies reduce output and prices abroad and depreciate the domestic currency. Again, the output effects are absent if full employment prevails. In an interdependent world, each nation should take into account foreign economic events and foreign reactions to domestic economic events.

EXERCISES

1. Does a nation's balance of payments balance?

2. Recently the Fed announced an increase in the discount rate, and the stock market fell while the dollar rose on international exchange markets. Can theory explain this?

3. How would an open-market sale by the Fed act to "defend the dollar?"

4. In the early 1960s, the United States had high unemployment and balance-of-payments deficits. In the late 1960s, the United States had high inflation and balance-of-payments deficits. Why did the Fed find it easier to respond to the latter problem?

5. Comment on the following:

"International currency stabilization will, however, only be possible when national economies are stable—when the industrial countries have succeeded in combining reasonably high employment with tolerably stable prices. Until then all talk of international currency reform will be in a vacuum and can safely be ignored except by those whose employment depends on the discussion." (J. K. Galbraith, *Money,* p. 310.)

6. In "Official Intervention in the Foreign Exchange Market or, Bet Against the Central Bank" (UCLA working paper No. 185, October 1980), Dean Taylor has estimated that the central banks of France, Germany, Italy, Japan, Switzerland, the United Kingdom, and the United States have altogether lost more than $10 billion in foreign exchange transactions between 1973 and 1979. How did they do this? Should they stop this gambling in the foreign-exchange casino?

7. Explain the reasoning of the following:

The U.S. is doing surprisingly well lately with the current account in its international-payments book. That account covers trade in goods and services plus certain unilateral transfers . . . . this basic measure of international competitiveness has a moderating influence on both the price spiral and joblessness, and private analysts say it indicates that the White House incumbent probably won't be embarrassed by an acute weakness of the U.S. dollar any time soon . . . .

A relatively strong dollar helps restrain inflation, economists note, by making imported goods relatively cheap in dollar terms. Moreover, if the dollar stays fairly steady, the Federal Reserve Board won't have to jack up interest rates to make the dollar attractive for foreigners to hold. If a return to last spring's super-steep interest rates can be averted, then a sharp rise in unemployment might also be avoided. (Richard Janssen, *The Wall Street Journal,* August 22, 1980)

8. [U.S. Treasury Secretary G. William] Miller's message is that, because 25% of U.S. manufactured exports are purchased by developing nations, international aid to these nations eventually helps the U.S. "These purchases of U.S. goods and services have major beneficial effects on U.S. employment and profits—yielding gross-national-product growth of $3 for each dollar we pay to the banks (or agencies) [to distribute abroad]—and this in turn leads to increased tax receipts," which largely offset the U.S. contributions, Mr. Miller says. (*The Wall Street Journal,* September 17, 1980)

What's wrong with Mr. Miller's logic?

9. What is the economic logic behind the following news items:

The U.S. dollar plunged on a drop in U.S. and [Eurodollar] interest rates and the price of gold recovered some of its losses from earlier this week. (July 17, 1980)

The U.S. dollar spurted higher against most major currencies, carried aloft by higher American interest rates and speculation that the Federal Reserve System hadn't eased credit conditions as some analysts had believed.

Gold's price dipped $8 an ounce, to $618.40. *(The Wall Street Journal,* July 13, 1980)

10. Draw a graph like that of Figure 17.6 showing the effects of an open-market purchase by the foreign country.

11. Critically evaluate the following analysis:

Their leaders do not talk about it much, but a strong dollar carries some important benefits to the Europeans. While their imports cost more, their exports carry lower prices on foreign markets. That makes their goods more competitive around the world, and many economists believe Europe will gain in the end because increasing exports just as surely produces jobs as increasing domestic consumption. ("Why Europeans care about U.S. interest rates," *Boston Globe,* July 14, 1981)

12. A news article reported that "The Europeans, particularly the French, have complained that high U.S. interest rates force them to increase their own interest rates to

prevent an outflow of capital from Europe." (John M. Legeo, "U.S. Officials Contend European Policies Largely to Blame for High Interest Rates," *Wall Street Journal,* March 1, 1982) Why do Europeans object to high interest rates if these do, indeed, succeed in keeping investors at home?

13. Use Table 17.2 to determine the effects on employment, output, prices, interest rates, and the exchange rate of reduced government spending in one country, accompanied by open-market operations by a second nation designed to hold its output and prices steady.

REFERENCES

1. John Kenneth Galbraith, *Money,* Boston: Houghton Mifflin, 1975, p. 43.

2. Galbraith, p. 260.

SUGGESTIONS FOR FURTHER READING

For a discussion of fixed versus floating exchange rates, see Fritz Machlup, Gottfried Haberler, Henry C. Wallich, Peter B. Kenen, and Milton Friedman, "Round Table on Exchange Rate Policy," *American Economic Review, Papers and Proceedings* (1969), pp. 357–69. For more details on international monetary lulls and crises since World War II, read Robert Solomon, *The International Monetary System, 1945–1976,* New York: Harper and Row, 1977.

CHAPTER EIGHTEEN

LONG-RUN GROWTH AND PRODUCTIVITY

I see us free [eventually] to return to some of the most sure and certain principles of religion and traditional virtue—that avarice is a vice, that the exaction of usury is a misdemeanor, and the love of money is detestable . . . We shall once more value ends above means and prefer the good to the useful. We shall honor . . . those delightful people who are capable of taking direct enjoyment in things, the lilies of the field who toil not, neither do they spin. But beware! The time for all this is not yet. For at least another hundred years we must pretend to ourselves and to everyone that fair is foul and foul is fair; for foul is useful and fair is not. Avarice and usury and precaution must be our gods for a little longer still. For only they can lead us out of the tunnel of economic necessity into daylight.

JOHN MAYNARD KEYNES[1]

This chapter examines the factors that determine a nation's economic growth rate, and the reasons behind the productivity slowdown in the United States.

AT the very beginning of this book, we looked at the difference between actual output and potential full-employment output. A nation's output falls short of its potential when people are unemployed and factories stand idle. We also looked at some of the reasons for this shortfall. When the economy is buffeted by demand and supply events and there is no Walrasian auctioneer to keep wages and prices perpetually at general equilibrium full-employment levels, then households may be disappointed in their attempts to find jobs, and businesses may be disappointed in their efforts to sell output.

When sales slump, businesses reduce production. When businesses reduce production, households lose jobs. When households lose jobs, they cut back on their spending. When households spend less, sales slump. The economy can ride this nasty circle down into a brutal recession that everyone regrets, but that no individual can stop. There are similar circular multiplier effects when the economy rolls uphill.

Economic booms and busts are naturally of great interest to households, businesses, politicians, and professional economists. We can readily see year-to-year economic fluctuations. Businesses watch their sales go up and down. They see some companies falter and even fail. We see hardship inflicted on our friends. We fear for our own jobs.

But there is another important macroeconomic issue, which is not so easy to see. What determines a nation's full-employment output? Why is potential GNP higher in the United States than in England or Mexico? Why is U.S. potential GNP higher now than in 1950 or in 1850?

These are important and interesting questions, even though they are usually obscured by day-to-day economic events. This obscurity is partly due to the fact that potential GNP is a theoretical abstraction while economic fluctuations are very real. In addition, the growth of potential GNP is gradual and very easy to take for granted. And, indeed, at least in the short run, it is difficult to dramatically alter many of the factors that determine potential GNP, such as birth rates, education, and work habits.

On the other hand, small changes continued over many years do add up. Consider, for example, two countries whose real per capita GNPs grow by 1.25% and 2%, respectively, per year. There will be little change in their relative positions over any short period. But if these differing growth rates continue over many years, their relative positions will change dramatically. Assume that real per capita GNP in 1870 is $1800 in the first country and $1400 in the second. With their real annual per capita growth (1.25% and 2%), in 100 years, by 1970, real per capita GNP will be $7000 in the first country and $11,000 in the second. Their relative positions will have changed completely. The first country began with a real per capita GNP nearly 30% higher than the second, but 100 years later, the second had a real per capita GNP nearly 60% higher than did the first. This is the "miracle of compound interest." Incidentally, this is a real life story: The two countries are England and the United States.

BALANCED GROWTH PATHS

We begin our investigation of long-run growth by examining a hypothetical long-run *dynamic equilibrium,* in which population and output grow at constant rates, not necessarily the same.

Long-run output growth

Suppose that the labor force grows at a constant percentage rate, β, per year:

$$\frac{\Delta s_t}{s_t} = \beta \qquad (18.1)$$

where s_t is the labor supply in year t and Δs_t is the annual change in the labor supply.

A convenient way to model productivity growth is to assume that the production function has the specific form

$$y_t = ak_t^{\alpha}\,(n_t(1+\delta)^t)^{1-\alpha} \qquad (18.2)$$

where y_t, k_t, and n_t are output, capital, and employment in period t. Equation 18.2 is a specific production function, relating output, y_t, to the inputs of capital, k_t and of labor, n_t. The parameters α and $1-\alpha$ measure the extra output produced by additional capital and labor. The term $(1+\delta)^t$ reflects technological progress. If employment, n_t, is measured in hours, then (for a given capital output ratio k_t/y_t) output per hour grows at the rate δ.*

* Equation 18.2 can be rearranged as $y_t/n_t = (a(k_t/y_t)^{\alpha})^{1/(1-\alpha)}\,(1+\delta)^t$ to show that y_t/n_t grows at the rate of δ if k_t/y_t is constant.

Technological progress means that labor becomes more productive. If people can now produce as much in eight hours as they used to produce in ten, then, in essence, eight hours of work now is effectively equivalent to ten hours previously. Thus technological progress effectively enlarges the labor force. Having workers that are 25% more productive is like having 25% more workers. We can then speak of the *effective labor force*, $\hat{s}_t$, as being

$$\hat{s}_t = (1 + \delta)^t s_t. \tag{18.3}$$

The actual labor supply grows at a rate β. But, with productivity increasing at a rate δ, the effective labor supply grows at the rate $\beta + \delta$, which is called the economy's *natural growth rate.*

It is useful to suppress the time subscript whenever possible and to measure most economic quantities relative to the effective labor force. Thus I will define y, k, and n as, respectively, output, capital, and effective employment per effective supply of labor:

$$y = y_t/\hat{s}_t$$

$$k = k_t/\hat{s}_t$$

$$n = (1 + \delta)^t n_t/\hat{s}_t = n_t/s_t.$$

Variables y and k are basic measures of economic development: output and capital per effective labor unit, respectively. The variable n measures labor utilization, in that $1 - n$ is the unemployment rate.

The production function (Equation 18.2) can now be written as

$$y = ak^{\alpha}n^{1-\alpha}. \tag{18.4}$$

If there is full employment, then $n = 1$, and full employment output is:

$$y^* = ak^{\alpha}. \tag{18.5}$$

If capital grows at the same rate, $\beta + \delta$, as the effective labor supply, then k is constant and full-employment output will be growing at that same rate—$\beta + \delta$—too. This situation is called a *balanced growth path* in that output, capital, and the effective labor supply are all growing at the same rate.

For example, the labor supply might be growing by 1% a year. If productivity is increasing by 2% a year, then the effective labor force grows by 3% a year. Along a balanced growth path, output and capital will also grow by 3% a year.

Output, capital, and the real interest rate

Population growth and technological progress are both so little understood that it is typically assumed that these are predetermined factors, which are little affected by the state of the economy. Capital accumulation, on the other hand, is very much dependent on economic events. The demand for capital hinges on a comparison of the real profits yielded by capital and the real interest rates on

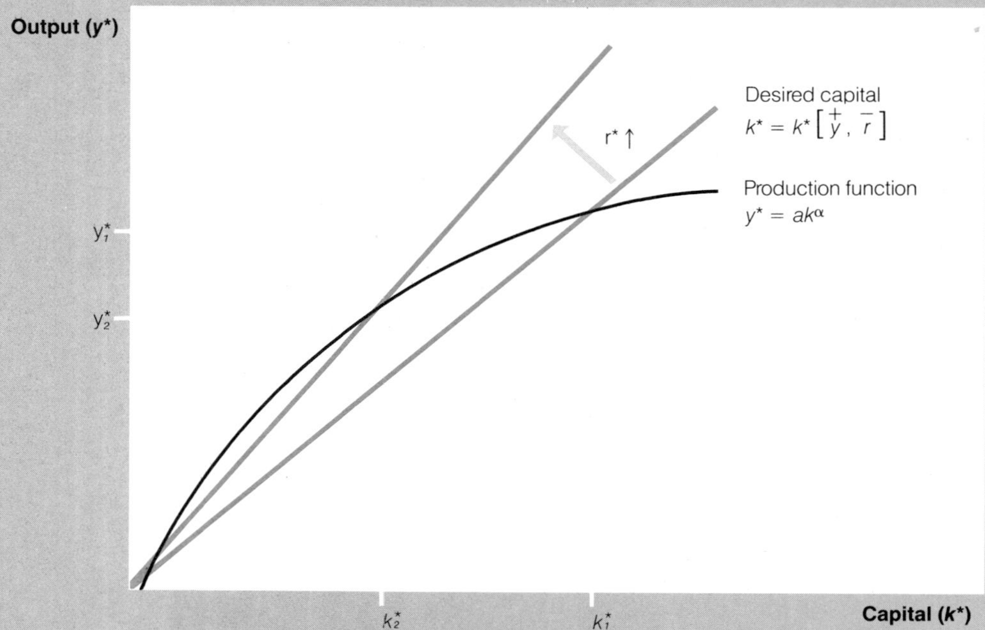

FIGURE 18.1 THE INVERSE RELATIONSHIP OF THE REAL INTEREST RATE AND LONG-RUN OUTPUT AND CAPITAL. When the real interest rate is higher, the dynamic equilibrium values of capital and output are diminished (from k_1^* and y_1^* to k_2^* and y_2^*).

financial assets. Capital's profitability, in turn, depends on real output. In sum, the long-run capital stock, k^*, is positively related to output and negatively related to the real interest rate,*

$$k^* = k[\overset{+}{y}, \overset{-}{r}]. \tag{18.6}$$

Equation 18.5 states that full-employment output depends on the capital stock. Equation 18.6 says that the long-run capital stock depends on output and the real interest rate. If we combine Equations 18.5 and 18.6, we find that, in the long run, there is an important interrelationship between output, capital, and the real interest rate. Figure 18.1, which graphs these two equations, shows

* Equation 18.5 implies that the marginal product of capital is $\Delta y/\Delta k = \alpha y/k$. If firms want to accumulate capital to the point where the marginal product of capital is equal to the real interest rate, r, then the equilibrium capital stock is $k^* = \alpha y/r$, a specific functional form for Equation 18.6.

that when the real interest rate is high, the dynamic equilibrium values of output and capital are both diminished.

Our growth model includes a variety of long-run growth paths, corresponding to different values of the real interest rate. In each case, real output and capital will be growing at the rate $\delta + \beta$, the rate of growth of the labor force plus that of productivity. Figure 18.2 shows some alternative growth paths for real output (using $\delta + \beta = 0.03$, $\alpha = 0.03$, and a scale $y_0 = 1000$ for $r = .05$). Which of the alternative growth paths is relevant? It depends on the demand side of the economy. Changes in private behavior or government policy that reduce the real interest rate will increase the steady-state levels of output and capital, but will not affect the rate of growth along this steady-state path. The rate of growth of the economy is independent of the real interest rate, but the scale of the economy is not. The lower the real interest rate, the higher the steady-state levels of output and capital.

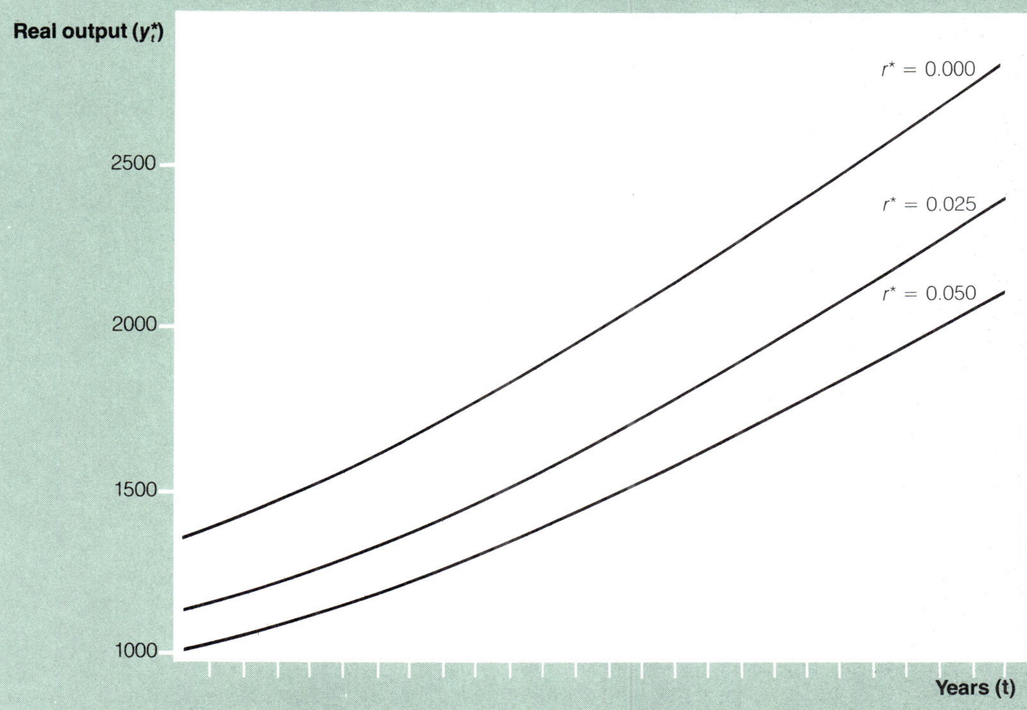

FIGURE 18.2 BALANCED GROWTH PATHS FOR OUTPUT AT DIFFERENT REAL INTEREST RATES. **Along a balanced growth path, output is higher the lower the real interest rate; but the rate of growth of output is constant, depending on the given rates of growth of population and technological progress.**

Asset stocks and government deficits

Along a balanced growth path, real financial assets will be growing at the same rate, $\beta + \delta$, as the capital stock. If the rate of inflation is π, then nominal assets must grow at the rate of $\beta + \delta + \pi$. A nondeflationary growing economy (with $\beta + \delta + \pi > 0$) will require continuing government deficits to keep government financial assets growing as fast as the economy.

We can formally show this important conclusion by letting m and b be, respectively, the real stocks of money and of government securities per effective labor unit; g and t, real government spending per effective labor unit; and Ψ, the fraction of government deficits financed by money issuance, and $1 - \Psi$ the fraction of government deficits financed by bond sales. The changes in the real (per effective labor unit) stocks of money and bonds are, consequently, as follows:

$$\Delta m = \Psi(g - t) - (\pi + \beta + \delta)m \tag{18.7}$$

$$\Delta b = (1 - \Psi)\,(g - t) - (\pi + \beta + \delta)b. \tag{18.8}$$

Government deficits increase the stocks of money and bonds. But inflation, population growth, and productivity improvements all reduce the size of these asset stocks in real terms, per effective labor unit.

In long-run dynamic equilibrium, both Δm and Δb must equal zero. The substitution of $\Delta m = \Delta b = 0$ into Equations 18.7 and 18.8 yields the long-run government budget constraint:

$$g - t = (\pi + \beta + \delta)\,(m + b) \tag{18.9}$$

This condition has very powerful and interesting implications. Along a balanced growth path, all nominal assets grow at the same rate—$\pi + \beta + \delta$—as nominal income. Equation 18.9 says that government-supplied assets will grow at this rate. The ratio $(g - t) / (m + b)$ is the percentage increase in the nominal supply of government money and bonds, and this rate of increase must equal $\pi + \beta + \delta$.

Equation 18.9 also implies that a steady-state balanced budget requires a persistent deflation, equal to $\pi = -(\beta + \delta)$. The labor force is growing at a rate β, and output per hour is growing at a rate δ, causing output and the demand for all real assets (including government money and bonds) to grow at a rate $\delta + \beta$. To meet this demand, either the government must issue more money and bonds by running persistent deficits, or there must be continual deflation in order to continually increase the real value of existing money and bonds. Specifically, for the government budget to be balanced, prices must fall as fast as real output is rising, thereby keeping nominal income constant, like the nominal supplies of money and bonds.

Repeating, in a dynamic growth equilibrium, a balanced government budget implies persistent deflation. A constant price level (or a steady inflation) requires persistent government deficits.

Summary

Along a balanced growth path, real output and capital will grow at the same rate as the effective labor supply. There are, however, several feasible balanced-growth paths, corresponding to different values of the real interest rate. The lower the real interest rate, the larger will be the size of the capital stock and output. The real interest rate that will prevail depends on the demand side of the economy.

In a full, long-run dynamic equilibrium, all assets will be growing at the same rate as income. Measured in effective labor units, real capital, money, and securities will all be constant. There will be a constant real interest rate and constant real output per effective labor unit. Inflation will be at a constant rate, π, and will be fully anticipated. Real per capita capital, output, and wealth will all be growing at the rate of productivity increase, δ. If the population is growing at the rate β, then the aggregate (not per capita) real capital, output, and wealth all grow at the rate $\delta + \beta$. In nominal terms, the dollar values of capital, output, and wealth all increase at the rate $\delta + \beta + \pi$.

The government budget may be balanced, with a steady deflation that holds nominal output constant, or unbalanced, with money and bonds both growing as fast as nominal output.

CONSUMPTION TODAY OR CONSUMPTION TOMORROW

It is tempting to think that a nation will always want to accumulate more capital in order to produce more. Figure 18.2 seems to imply that it is better to be on a higher output curve than on a lower output curve, and that the government should keep real interest rates very low so that we can have more and more output. Surprisingly, that is not necessarily the case.

More output does not automatically imply more consumption. More output per capita requires more capital per capita, which, in turn, requires more investment (and hence less consumption) to keep this larger capital stock growing as fast as the effective labor force. More output may, on balance, yield less consumption! We could find ourselves living as paupers while we use our machines to produce more machines that produce even more machines. While preparing for tomorrow we would never enjoy today. Keynes put it this way: "He does not love his cat, but his cat's kittens; nor, in truth, the kittens, but only the kittens' kittens, and so on forward for ever to the end of cat-dom. For him jam is not jam unless it is a case of jam tomorrow and never jam today."[3]

We can use our balanced-growth model to show how more output may yield less consumption. Figure 18.3 shows the production function $y = ak^{\alpha}$ together with the amount of investment, $i = (\beta + \delta)k$, required to sustain a balanced growth path.* The level of consumption is equal to the difference between output and investment.

The variables in Figure 18.3 are all measured relative to the effective labor supply. The specific plotted values are based on the following parameters: $a = 1000/(3000)^{0.3}$, $\alpha = 0.3$, $\beta + \delta = 0.05$. Table 18.1 shows several calculated values.

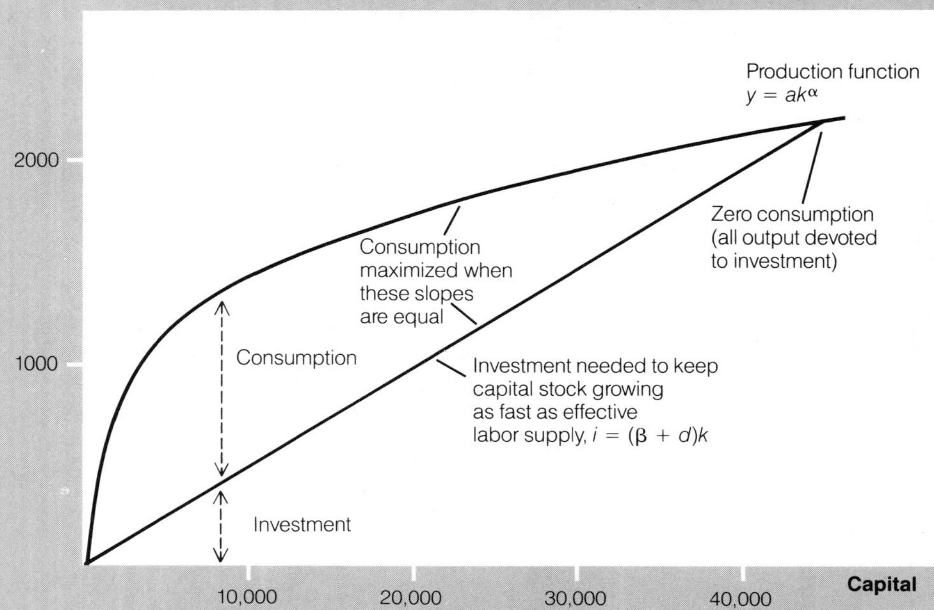

FIGURE 18.3 **LONG-RUN CONSUMPTION DEPENDS ON THE SIZE OF THE CAPITAL STOCK.** Both investment and output depend on the size of the capital stock, as does consumption, since it is the difference between output and investment. There comes a point—here with a capital stock of 8075—beyond which additional capital reduces consumption because the extra output is less than the additional investment needed to maintain the capital stock.

Table 18.1. Balanced-Growth Output, Investment, and Consumption Consistent with Various Capital Stocks*

Capital	Output	Investment	Consumption
3,000	1,000	150	850
5,000	1,166	250	916
8,075	1,346	404	942
10,000	1,435	500	935
20,000	1,767	1,000	767
45,096	2,255	2,255	0

* Real investment is $i_t = \Delta k_t = (\beta + \delta)k_t$. Real investment per effective labor unit is $i = \Delta k_t / \hat{s}_t = (\beta + \delta)k$.

As can be seen in Figure 18.3 and Table 18.1, there comes a point when investment increases more than output, causing consumption to fall. At a capital stock of 45,096, investment completely exhausts output; there is nothing left for consumption. A capital stock of 45,096 is the ultimate situation of "jam tomorrow and never jam today."

What is the maximum sustainable level of consumption? It is 942, with a capital stock of 8075. This maximum occurs when the two lines in Figure 18.3 are parallel—that is, when they have the same slopes. The slope of the production function is the marginal product of capital. The slope of the investment function is the rate of growth of the effective labor supply. Therefore, **the balanced growth path with the highest consumption level has a capital stock such that the marginal product of capital is equal to the economy's real rate of growth.** In this particular example, the economy's growth rate is 5%, and the marginal product of capital is 5% when the capital stock is 8075.

This maximum-consumption growth path is known as the *golden rule of economic growth,*[3] from the idea that each generation should do unto future ones what it would have hoped earlier generations had done for it. Balanced growth paths are infinite, while human life is all too brief. A selfish generation that did not give a whit for the future could consume everything and leave no capital for the next generation. Of course, this selfish generation would have hoped that the generation before had not played the same dirty trick on them. If all generations live by the golden rule, then none will be selfish.

There is, however, the further problem of what to do when society is not on a golden-rule path. What if the economy finds itself on a balanced growth path with a capital stock of 10,000 instead of 8,075? For some reason, society has stockpiled capital beyond the optimal point. In this situation of capital glut, the present generation can do future generations a favor by consuming more and investing less. If the current generation consumes more, then every future generation will be able to consume more.

What if the capital stock is instead too low—say only 5000? Now there is no solution that pleases everyone. Consumption and capital are both below golden-rule levels. And the golden-rule growth path can be attained only if one generation reduces its consumption even more. Earlier, we saw how households face a choice between consumption today and consumption tomorrow. Now we see that there is also an aggregate, intergenerational tradeoff in that future generations can consume more only if the current generation consumes less. Tobin put it this way: "How can an increase in the rate of growth of national output be achieved? The answer is straightforward and painful. We must devote more of our current capacity to uses that increase our future capacity, and correspondingly less to other uses."[4] Should policy makers encourage such capital accumulation? There is no objective answer, since we cannot say whether one generation's increased consumption is worth another's deprivation.

SOURCES OF ECONOMIC GROWTH

The model analyzed in the preceding section is a theoretical description of a balanced growth path. This growth path is a hypothetical long-run dynamic equilibrium the economy might reach if population growth and technological progress were steady and there were no changes in economic tastes and opportunities. The world we inhabit shows no signs of becoming so quiet and predictable.

Yet the model helps us think about a variety of interesting macroeconomic issues, including 1) the central role of real interest rates in determining long-run potential output; 2) the feasibility of a permanently balanced government budget; 3) how capital accumulation trades less consumption by the current generation for more consumption by future generations; and 4) how a society can have too much capital.

A balanced-growth model is also useful in explaining certain stylized historical "facts." Nicholas Kaldor has argued that in modern industrialized economies, output per hour and capital per hour have both tended to grow at roughly the same rate, so as to keep the capital-output ratio constant.[5] These general characteristics of the data are consistent with our balanced-growth model.

The balanced-growth model can also be used to identify the sources of long-run economic growth: how much of a nation's potential output growth is due to labor growth, to capital growth, and to productivity growth. Unfortunately, these sorts of tabulations can get bogged down in metaphysical debates about the extent to which technological progress is "disembodied" or "embodied."[6] Disembodied technical progress increases the productivity of all capital and labor; embodied technical progress increases the productivity of new capital and/or new labor. Disembodied progress includes organizational or procedural advances; embodied progress represents new and improved machines (for example, faster computers) or improvements in labor (better-educated people). It is obviously difficult to decide the extent to which increased output is due to better machines, to better people, and to better uses of machines and people. We won't fall into that sticky debate here, but instead, just report estimates of the overall sources of United States economic growth from a careful study by Edward Denison for the years 1929–69:[7]

Source of growth	Contribution in percentage points
Labor input	1.32
Capital input	0.50
Productivity	1.59
	3.41

Over the 40-year period (1929–69) real output grew by about $3\frac{1}{2}$% per year. Nearly half of this growth was due to increased productivity. The growth in the labor force was also important, while the growth in the size of the capital stock was less important.

This sort of cataloging of growth sources does not really tackle the even more difficult and much more interesting question of why nations grow. Why have some nations become rich while others remain poor? Why does a certain nation burst out of poverty and take off towards industrialization? Why does

IN THE NEWS

The Looming Impact of Population Changes

Economic forecasts are not usually noted for their accuracy. One exception, where a high degree of accuracy is possible, is in predicting the future age composition of the population. The reason for accuracy is simple. almost all the people who will be alive in the near future have already been born. To obtain reliable estimates you need only apply the appropriate mortality rates, which are very predictable, to each of the various age groups (or "cohorts") and add them up. And if we are focusing on the population over 10 years old, no estimates about birth rates are needed to project 10 years out.

Being able to project population age cohorts a decade ahead with great accuracy would be no more significant than an arithmetic parlor game were it not for the great importance of demographic trends in helping determine where an economy is headed.

Age structure has implications not only for what consumers will want but, more importantly, for the rate of productivity and total real growth and inflation. For example, to help create enough new jobs to absorb our swelling labor force during the 1970s, government policies were biased in favor of inflation. Jobs took preference over slowing inflation as a national priority.

Economic forecasters have tended to neglect the impact of population changes, concentrating instead on the twists of government policies, consumer attitudes and corporate decisions. These factors *are* important in assessing economic outlook and, indirectly, they reflect population changes themselves. But we need to pay more explicit attention to the powerful and predictable influence of population changes.

Consider the influence on economic performance of the changing age composition of the population during the 1970s. The essential facts can be gleaned from the following table:

Percentage increase in population by age groups, 1970–80

Ages	1970–75	1975–80	1970–80
Under 15	− 0.8%	− 6.7%	− 3.8%
15 to 17	7.7	− 4.0	3.4
18 to 24	10.0	11.4	22.5
25 to 34	22.1	19.1	45.4
35 to 44	− 2.6	14.2	11.3
45 to 54	2.6	− 4.6	− 2.2
55 to 65	5.9	7.6	14.0
Over 65	12.1	12.1	25.6

Just glancing down the columns shows the decline in the younger ages (under 15), and a tremendous bulge in the 18 to 34-year-group, where new job-seekers are concentrated. To briefly trace their effects: At first, enrollment in the elementary school grades thinned, followed, a bit later, by a decline in the nation's high-school population. By contrast, college enrollment soared, along with the ranks of the 18- to 34-year-olds.

No wonder our labor force grew rapidly. The absolute number of young people aged 18 to 34 swelled by one-third, from 49 million to 1970 to nearly 66 million in 1980—a net increase of almost 17 million individuals! As most of these people finished school, they looked for jobs and, for the most part, found them. An unsung miracle of the American economy in the 1970s is that it was a job-creating machine. True, unemployment also increased, but the system's ability to absorb a surging labor force was a major economic achievement.

At the same time, many of the young people entering the work force for the first time were inexperienced and relatively unproductive. The explosion of young unskilled workers was one factor dragging down our national productivity growth rate during the 1970s. In a sense, the economy absorbed workers by substituting workers for capital. The dimensions of that shift are not yet very clear.

While the ranks of young adults were expanding, the middle-age categories, between 35 and 54, showed little growth. The only significant growth was at the upper end of the age distribution—especially over 65. The number of individuals 65 and over surged from 20 to 25 million between 1970 and 1980, an increase of 25%. It is hardly surprising that the political strength of senior citizens grew, encouraging more generous Social Security and Medicare benefits. Moreover, these people were at a time of life when savings are typically dwindling, not accumulating.

The proliferation of young adults—a group that doesn't normally save much—also pushed down the personal saving rate. Our poor national saving rate inevitably reflected downward pressure from both ends of the age spectrum.

The 1980s appear destined to be quite different from the '70s, as a look at the prospective population changes for the next 10 years clearly shows.

Percentage increase in population by age groups, 1980–90

Ages	1980–85	1985–90	1980–90
Under 15	3.4%	7.0%	10.6%
15 to 17	−11.6	−10.3	−20.1
18 to 24	− 5.4	− 9.7	−14.6
25 to 34	10.2	3.0	13.5
35 to 44	22.2	16.6	42.4
45 to 54	− 0.9	12.4	11.5
55 to 65	2.4	− 4.1	− 1.9
Over 65	9.6	9.1	19.6

The only forecast in doubt is, of course, that for the under-15 group, which necessarily includes estimates of those not yet born. But we know that the total number of births will be up, even with a continuing low birth *rate,* because of an increase in the number of women in the prime child-bearing years.

A steep decline will occur among 15 to 24-year-olds, as will a sharp slowdown in the growth of the 25 to 34-year cohort. This is a drastic reversal of the trend of the 1970s. It means our labor force will grow only slowly. It means the supply of young, inexperienced, unskilled employes will dwindle. And it means that our productivity growth will not be diluted by a large influx of low-productivity entry-level workers. The result should be a gradual improvement in the nation's productivity performance.

It is not farfetched to predict the emergence of a relative shortage of unskilled workers in the U.S. as the 1980s unfold. The consequence is likely to be a boost for capital investment in an effort to substitute capital for labor—reversing the trend of the 1970s. The relative shortage of new labor force entrants may well give a desirable boost to the installation of robots to do the more tedious, repetitive factory chores.

People in their 30s and 40s can look forward to better prospects in the decade ahead. These, of course, are people who have been working for some years and have acquired experience and skills, the characteristics most needed to spur productivity growth.

No one can be certain about how changes in the age distribution of the population will affect our economic future. But based on past experience with population age shifts, the chances are good that savings, investment and productivity growth will benefit in the 1980s from a mature, more slowly growing labor force. (William C. Freund, *The Wall Street Journal,* April 6, 1982) this takeoff occur when it does, instead of a bit earlier or later? What can we do to improve living standards in less-developed nations?

These are important, provocative questions with no simple answers. The explanations for economic growth and stagnation involve resources, work attitudes, economic organization, laws, politics, historical accidents, and just about anything else one might add.

THE PRODUCTIVITY SLOWDOWN

It is equally difficult to explain precisely why, as we noted in Chapter 2, productivity growth has apparently slowed in the United States in recent years. We needn't go into the harmful effects attributed to television, rock music, alcohol, drugs, fluoridated water, and the new math; some other explanations follow.

Labor-force structure

As noted in earlier chapters, much of the labor force growth in the late 1960s and the 1970s consisted of inexperienced youths and females. These new labor force entrants were less productive than more experienced workers, and their influx has reduced average productivity. This does not mean that these new workers are less productive than new workers in the past, only that they are new workers with less-than-average experience. As the baby boom generation ages and work becomes more customary for women, the average experience of the work force and average productivity will both increase. Thus the changing age structure of the labor force has temporarily depressed average productivity, but this should soon be reversed.

Capital formation

Business investment in new plant and equipment rose slightly, from 9.7% of GNP in the 1960s, to 10% of GNP in the 1970s. But employment increased so much in the 1970s that capital per worker increased less than in earlier decades. Businesses increased output by hiring more labor instead of constructing more plant and equipment. This shortfall in capital per worker has slowed increases in worker productivity. In addition, businesses and government pared short-run costs by skimping on basic research that eventually increases productivity.

Some observers believe that U.S. firms have become too cautious and short-sighted. Instead of building modern, more productive facilities, firms have diverted their resources to cash management, inventory control, and acquisitions of other firms. These are safe strategies that enlarge current profits but may undermine future profits. This United States business myopia is, in turn, attributed to the fact that American managers flit from assignment to assignment, judged and rewarded at each stage by the current bottom line. Japanese firms are often touted for their contrasting willingness to look 10 years ahead and to invest in new technologies that are risky and that will take a while to return a profit.

Other observers believe that the problem in the United States is that confiscatory taxes have made capital unattractive and that excessive government borrowing has made it difficult for firms to finance new plant and equipment. It is argued that tax cuts and a balanced government budget will stimulate business investment and increase worker productivity. We have seen how taxes can be used to encourage investment, and how government deficits can reduce investment to the extent that government borrowing increases real interest rates. But we must remember that prosperity is crucial to investment. Tax breaks are a small consolation when there are no profits to pay taxes on. Cutting spending or increasing taxes to balance the government's budget may well reduce output and, with it, investment demand.

Energy costs

The increased costs and temporary shortages of oil, gas, and electricity in the 1970s encouraged the substitution of labor for energy. Farmers went back to cutting firewood; businesses increased their insulation, put in weather-stripping, and replaced leaky valves. People were hired simply to find ways to reduce energy costs. These sensible responses to the energy crisis reduced output per hour because some hours were spent reducing costs rather than producing output. Worker productivity also may have been reduced by the discomforts engendered by thermostats kept lower in the winter and higher in the summer. Some of these adjustments to high-priced energy appear to have been once-and-for-all changes that reduced the level of output per hour but may have little effect on future productivity growth.

Output structure

Worker productivity is low and grows slowly in most service jobs: salespeople, clerks, bureaucrats, teachers, barbers, and cooks. In the 1970s much of the employment increase was in service jobs, and this compositional shift reduced both the level and the rate of growth of productivity. This trend is expected to continue.

Regulation

Many businesses complain about the costs of complying with government laws and regulations. Measured productivity is reduced when resources are spent making jobs safer, reducing pollution, and sending reports to the government. These costs show up in the productivity data, while the benefits are neglected. If we included cleaner air, cleaner water, and safer jobs as part of output, measured productivity would be reduced less and might even be increased on balance.

Worker attitudes

The demise of labor's work ethic has been widely mourned. Many pundits believe that people no longer take pride in their work. Workers are lazy, products are shoddy, and nobody cares. This is an old lament that employers have always directed at employees and that each generation hurls at the next. But it is certainly easy to believe that things really have gotten worse. Affluent workers seem less willing to work hard to get ahead. There is little individual responsibility in large corporations, and correspondingly fewer opportunities to display one's talents and more chances to avoid work. In large, anonymous cities, there's little neighborly respect to be lost by being dishonest or incompetent.

Some observers believe that Japanese firms offer more incentives for employee pride and productivity improvements. Most Japanese workers have guaranteed lifetime jobs and do not move around as much as American workers. This lifelong identification with a firm encourages a worker to take pride in the firm's successes. In addition, employee compensation is based on the firm's profitability and the worker's productivity, rather than the job classification. Workers are rewarded for finding ways to cut costs and increase output. There is no danger that productivity improvements will eliminate the worker's job or the jobs of coworkers.

This grab bag of social, political, and economic explanations is a fitting place to end a textbook on macroeconomics. The great strength of macroeconomics is that it wrestles with large important questions, such as unemployment, inflation, and productivity. Macroeconomics injects a healthy dose of economic logic into these discussions. But it also recognizes that pure economic logic is not enough. We cannot fully understand the economy by writing down models of Walrasian auctioneers coordinating perfectly informed, competitive, rational maximizers. The world has a few uninformed, uncompetitive, irrational players. Legal restrictions, social psychology, and political decisions all shape economic outcomes. Macroeconomics has room for all this, and more.

IMPORTANT TERMS AND CONCEPTS

Dynamic equilibrium
Effective labor force
Natural growth rate
Balanced growth path
Golden rule of growth

The lower the real interest rate, the larger the capital stock and output. But, for any given real interest rate, real output and capital will grow at the same rate as the effective labor supply along a balanced growth path.

In dynamic equilibrium, the government budget may be balanced along with a steady deflation that holds nominal output constant while real output increases. Or the government budget may be unbalanced, with money and bonds growing as fast as nominal output.

When society accumulates capital it is generally trading less consumption by the current generation for more consumption by future generations. If, however, society has more than the golden-rule capital stock, then consumption can be increased for all generations.

EXERCISES

1. How can a society have too much capital?

2. Why did Tobin write that an increase in the rate of growth of output is "painful." Are there any painless ways to increase the growth rate?

3. A society's production function is $y = 100k^{0.25}$, the labor force is constant, and productivity is growing by 2% a year. What is the golden-rule capital stock? What is so golden about this capital stock?

4. Oil has just been discovered in Brooklyn, New York! What effects will this have on the level and rate of growth of potential output?

REFERENCES

1. J. M. Keynes, "Economic Possibilities for our Grandchildren," in *Essays in Persuasion,* London: Macmillan, 1931, pp. 371–2.

2. Keynes, p. 370.

3. E. S. Phelps, "The Golden Rule of Accumulation: A Fable for Growthmen," *American Economic Review,* September 1961, 638–43.

4. J. Tobin, "Growth Through Taxation," *New Republic,* July 25, 1960.

5. N. Kaldor, "A Model of Economic Growth," *Economic Journal,* December 1957, 591–624.

6. See R. M. Solow, "Investment and Technical Progress," in K. J. Arrow, S. Karlin, and P. Suppes, eds., *Mathematical Models in the Social Sciences,* Stanford University Press, 1960; E. F. Denison, "The Unimportance of the Embodied Question," *American Economic Review* (March 1964), pp. 90–93; and R. R. Nelson, "Aggregate Production Functions and Medium-Range Growth Projections," *American Economic Review* (September 1964), 576–606.

7. E. Denison, *Accounting for United States Economic Growth 1929–1969,* Washington, D.C., the Brookings Institution, 1974, p. 127.

GLOSSARY

accelerated depreciation See **depreciation.**

accelerator models Macro models in which capital depends on the level of output; hence, investment depends on the change in output, and an increase in investment requires an *acceleration* of output. (Ch. 13)

aggregate The sum, for an economy as a whole, of any quantifiable economic phenomenon.

aggregate demand curve The schedule of the combinations of price *(P)* and output *(y)* such that income equals expenditures and money demand equals money supply—that is, for various *P*, the *y* determined by the *IS-LM* intersections. (Ch. 4)

aggregate supply curve The schedule of the combinations of price and output determined by employment and production decisions. In a classical full-employment model, the aggregate supply curve is vertical, since, in that case, labor market equilibrium and full-employment output do not depend on the price level. (Ch. 5)

automatic stabilizer A factor, such as income taxes or unemployment compensation, that automatically reduces aggregate demand in a boom and bolsters demand during a slump. (Ch. 3)

balanced-budget multiplier See **multiplier.**

balance of payments See **trade balance, goods and service balance, current-account balance.**

balanced growth path Growth paths, (often the focus of long-run macro models) along which output, capital, and the effective labor supply (adjusted for productivity improvements) all grow at the same rate. (Ch. 18)

barter The trading of goods and services. (Ch. 14)

bracket creep In a progressive tax system in which rates depend on nominal income, the shift into higher tax brackets produced by inflation. This increases the taxpayer's average tax rate and reduces real, after-tax income. (Ch. 8)

Bretton Woods agreement Agreement made among the western nations in 1944 to maintain fixed exchange rates, subject only to periodic adjustments. Although there were occasional crises, the system lasted until the early 1970s, when it was replaced by one of flexible exchange rates. (Ch. 17)

capacity utilization A measure of how fully a nation's means of production are being utilized. Capacity utilization rates exceed 90% during economic booms and fall below 80% during slumps. (Ch. 2)

Chicago school The economists originally centered at the University of Chicago—and prominent among them, Milton Friedman—who emphasize the efficiency of competitive markets and have been skeptical of government intervention, including demand management policies. (Ch. 10)

closed-economy model A macro model that ignores exports, imports, and other international transactions; opposed to *open*-economy models. (Ch. 3)

commodity money Commodities—such as gold, tobacco, and sea shells—used as mediums of exchange. (Ch. 14)

consumer price index (CPI) The cost of a market basket of goods and services purchased by typical households relative to its cost in a base year. (Ch. 2)

consumption goods Goods such as food and clothing, that are consumed shortly after purchase. See **investment goods.** (Ch. 2)

crowding out Depression of private spending brought about by government borrowing and spending. In demand-side crowding out, government borrowing to finance expenditures (or tax cuts) raises interest rates and so discourages private spending. In supply-side crowding out, the economy is at full employment, with output a fixed pie, so that additional government spending necessitates less private spending. (Chs. 4, 5)

current-account balance A nation's exports and imports of goods and services, net of transfer payments, which must be financed by money, securities, and other claims. (Ch. 17)

demand management policies Government monetary and fiscal policies aimed at bolstering or restraining aggregate demand as needed to stimulate or cool the economy. (Chs. 6, 10)

demand side That side of the economy comprised of the financial markets and spending decisions that underlie the aggregate demand curve. (Ch. 4)

deposit multiplier See **multiplier.**

depreciation Decline in the value of tangible assets resulting from wear, aging, and/or technological obsolescence. (Ch. 2) Tax law allows firms to write off part of an asset's cost on the basis of depreciation. Provisions for **accelerated depreciation** permit a quicker write-off, and so encourage firms to acquire assets. (Ch. 11)

devaluation A drop in the value of a currency relative to other currencies. (Ch. 17)

discount rate of the Fed The interest rate that the Fed charges banks that borrow from it. (Ch. 9)

disequilibrium The state of a market in which demand and supply are not equal. Either buyers or sellers are then frustrated in their efforts to make transactions at the prevailing price. (Ch. 3)

disposable income The income of a household, net of taxes. (Ch. 3)

dual labor market A labor market hypothesized to consist of primary workers, with stable careers, and of secondary workers, whose only work options are undesirable dead-end jobs. (Ch. 16)

dynamic equilibrium A theoretical economic situation in which there are no inherent pressures for change. Output and prices are constant or grow at constant rates. (Ch. 3)

effective labor force How much a current labor force can produce relative to the labor force in some base period. (Ch. 18)

entitlements Government disbursements, such as Social Security payments, that rise automatically with the population, the cost of living, or other factors. (Ch. 9)

exchange rate The price of one nation's currency in terms of another. (Ch. 17)

expectational equilibrium A situation in which expectations (of inflation, for instance) have been fulfilled. (Ch. 7)

expectations hypothesis The hypothetical explanation of the structure of interest rates that postulates that any difference between long-term and short-term interest rates reflects anticipated changes in interest rates. When the former are above the latter, interest rates are expected to rise, and vice versa. (Ch. 15)

Federal Open Market Committee (FOMC) The seven Federal Reserve Board Governors and five of the twelve district presidents. At its deliberations the state of the economy is reviewed and monetary policies are determined. (Ch. 9)

Federal Reserve Board (Fed) The United States' central bank, with primary responsibility for the nation's monetary policies. The seven Fed governors are appointed by the President to overlapping fourteen-year terms. (Ch. 9)

fiat money Something with little intrinsic value that, because of law or custom, is used as money. In the United States, paper money and most coins are fiat money. (Ch. 14)

Fisher diagram An indifference curve analysis of the choice between consumption now or consumption later. Named for Irving Fisher, who recognized that the consumption-saving decision is really a choice between consumption now or consumption later and, as such, can be analyzed by the standard indifference curves used in microeconomics.

fiscal policy Government spending and revenue policy. These affect the *IS* curve, with increased spending or reduced taxes shifting it rightward. (Chs. 6, 9)

fixprice market A market (so designated by Sir John Hicks) in which the price does not adjust instantly to keep demand and supply equal. Labor markets are a prime example. (Ch. 3)

flexprice market Markets (so designated by Sir John Hicks) in which demand and supply are continually equated. Some financial and raw-commodities markets are the best examples. (Ch. 3)

flow data Data for an item over time; for instance, GNP data, which indicate the amount produced over a period of a year. (Ch. 2) See **stock data.**

flow-of-funds data Data on aggregate transactions among various sectors of the economy. Reported by the Fed, they are an especially good source of information on borrowing and lending by households, businesses, and a wide variety of financial institutions. (Ch. 2)

full-employment surplus An estimate of the federal government's budget balance (revenue less disbursements) were the economy at full employment. The actual budget, at less than full employment, has a smaller surplus or larger deficit, since tax revenue declines with output. (Ch. 3)

golden rule of growth The balanced growth path with the highest consumption has a capital stock such that the marginal product of capital is equal to the economy's real rate of growth. (Ch. 18)

goods and services balance A nation's international sales of goods and services, less its purchases. (Ch. 17)

gross national product (GNP) A nation's production of new goods and services, a measure of the strength of its economy. (Ch. 2)

Hicks' equation The argument that states that the compounded gross return on a long-term asset must equal the product of the anticipated gross returns from rolling over a sequence of one-year assets; for instance, the compounded gross return on a five-year asset is the product of the current one-year rate and the anticipated returns over the four succeeding years. See **expectations hypothesis.** (Ch. 15)

high-powered money The nation's monetary base, called high-powered because it can support much larger amounts of bank money. See **monetary base, deposit multiplier.** (Ch. 14)

indexing Automatic adjustment of laws, regulations, and contracts to a price index. For instance, Social Security payments automatically rise when the Consumer Price Index increases. (Ch. 8)

inflation rate The percentage increase in prices over some specified interval. (Ch. 7)

investment Long-lived tangible assets—such as goods, houses, factories, machines—that yield other goods and services. (Ch. 2)

investment tax credit A percentage (6–10%) of the cost of new plant and equipment businesses have been allowed to deduct from their taxes to encourage investment. (Ch. 11)

***IS* curve** Those combinations of output, *y*, and interest rate, *R*, such that aggregate expenditures are equal to aggregate income. The *IS* curve is negatively sloped and shifted rightward by increases in private or government spending. (Ch. 4)

Keynes effect The enlargment of the real money supply produced by a lower price level. Financial markets are consequently eased as surely as if the Fed had printed more money. To the extent interest rates fall and spending responds, this is a route by which falling prices automatically bolster aggregate demand. (Ch. 4)

Keynesian cross The graph showing income equals expenditures and spending depends on income, called so since Keynes emphasizes the macro implications of the interaction of spending and income. (Ch. 3)

labor hoarding The retention, when demand slumps, of employees, as well as capital, though neither may be fully utilized. This occurs because it is not costless to let them go and then replace them when demand resumes. (Ch. 3)

labor force Those who have jobs or are actively looking for jobs. The Bureau of Labor Statistics estimates the totals by means of household surveys. (Ch. 3)

life cycle model A model of consumption that assumes that people estimate their lifetime income and plan their spending patterns accordingly. (Ch. 12)

liquidity A measure of how readily an asset can be sold for its fair market value. (Ch. 15)

liquidity constraints Spending constraints imposed by available funds rather than estimates of lifetime income. Human capital is very illiquid. (Chs. 12, 13)

***LM* curve** Those combinations of output, *y*, and the interest rate, *R*, such that money demand is equal to supply. The *LM* curve is positively sloped and shifted rightward by an increase in money supply or decline in money demand. (Ch. 4)

M1 A popular measure of the money supply that includes currency, traveler's checks, and checkable deposits. (Ch. 14)

marginal propensity to consume (MPC) The response of consumer spending to income changes. A key element of Keynes' explanation of recessions is that when income declines, consumers reduce their spending sharply—leading businesses to reduce production and employment, in turn reducing household income even further. (Ch. 3)

marginal tax rate The fraction of additional income earned that is paid in taxes. Many economic decisions are influenced by how heavily certain actions are taxed. (Ch. 11)

market equilibrium The condition in which demand is equal to supply. See **disequilibrium.** (Ch. 3)

markup pricing The practice of setting prices as costs plus an amount that provides a normal profit. (Ch. 7)

marriage tax That aspect of a progressive tax system that results in a tax that is higher for married than unmarried working couples. (Ch. 11)

medium of exchange Any item—dollar bills, gold, parrot feathers—that is accepted in exchange for useful goods or services because it can be traded for other useful goods and services. (Ch. 14)

Modigliani-Brumberg model A simple macro model that illustrates many of the important implications of life-cycle consumption theories. (Ch. 12)

monetary base The amount of government-issued money outstanding, either outside banks (held by households and businesses) or inside banks (including their reserves deposited with the Fed). (Ch. 14)

monetary policy Government instigated changes in money supply or demand. These shift the *LM* curve—rightward if the money supply is enlarged or money demand diminished. (Chs. 6, 9)

money illusion Beliefs concerning wage rates, wealth, or other economic data that are based on nominal (rather than real) values. (Ch. 2)

money neutrality A classical proposition that holds that a change in the money supply will change prices proportionately, with no real effects on the economy. See **superneutrality.** (Chs. 6, 8)

multiplier The effect on one economic variable of a change in a predetermined variable, holding the other predetermined variables constant and allowing all other variables to adjust. In the simplest income-expenditure model, the income multiplier for an autonomous increase in spending is 1/(1 − marginal propensity to spend). (Ch. 3) In the income-expenditure model, the **balanced-budget multiplier** is the effect where an equal increase in government spending and in taxes raises output by the same amount as the increase in spending. (Ch. 3) The **deposit multiplier,** the size of bank deposits relative to the monetary base, depands on the fraction of deposits lent out by banks and the public's holdings of cash relative to deposits. (Ch. 14)

national income A nation's output before taxes and depreciation are taken into account. It can be derived from GNP by subtracting the taxes included in market prices and depreciation. (Ch. 2)

national income and product accounts The government's national income data used to monitor the nation's production and income. (Ch. 2)

natural growth rate In long-run macro models, the rate of increase of labor supply plus productivity. (Ch. 18)

natural rate of unemployment The unemployment rate where the long-run Phillips curve is vertical. (Ch. 7)

net present value The value of the cash flow (income less expenses) after future revenues have been discounted to the present, as in a long-lived investment project. (Ch. 13)

neutral policies Traditionally, government monetary and fiscal policies that do not interfere with the workings of competitive markets; current adherents favor policies that are determined by rules rather than discretion. (Ch. 10)

new classical macroeconomics The view that is classical in that it assumes market equilibria (so that all unemployment is voluntary) and new in that it assumes that price misperceptions explain temporary fluctuations in employment and production. See **surprise employment** and **surprise unemployment.** (Ch. 5)

neoclassical investment model A model that assumes a perfect market, in which capital can be bought or sold at production cost, so that firms can plan one period at a time—always choosing that capital stock such that the marginal product of capital is equal to the rate of return on financial assets plus depreciation, less any increase in the cost of producing capital. (Ch. 13)

nominal data Dollar values unadjusted for the purchasing power of the dollar. (Ch. 2)

Okun's law The estimate (by Arthur Okun) that each percentage point of unemployment represents about a 3% loss in real GNP. (Ch. 3)

open-economy model A macro model that takes exports, imports, and other international transactions into account; opposed to closed-economy models. (Ch. 17)

open-market operation The Fed's primary day-to-day tool for implementing its monetary policies by open-market purchases or sales of Treasury securities from private dealers. Purchases enlarge the monetary base, while sales contract it. (Chs. 4, 9)

permanent income The concept, devised by Milton Friedman, that a household's spending is influenced by a longer-run notion of its income. The main implication is that spending may not be responsive to temporary or unexpected income fluctuations. (Ch. 12)

Phillips curve The curve that expresses A. W. Phillips' view that both employment and prices are affected by fluctuations in aggregate demand. His empirical work suggested an inverse relationship between unemployment and inflation: Unemployment falls and inflation rises when the economy is strong, and the reverse occurs when the economy slumps. (Ch. 7)

Pigou effect The bolstering of aggregate demand by a lower price level. A. C. Pigou argued that the price level did so by increasing the real purchasing power of dollars and other nominal assets and, hence, real financial wealth. (Ch. 4)

political business cycle A cycle that reflects attempts by politicians to manipulate the economy to their political advantage. In particular, where a presidential candidate is the incumbent he may try to put the economy on a four-year political business cycle, cooling the economy after an election to pave the way for rapid improvement (and hence, voter approval) shortly before the next election. (Ch. 9)

potential output An estimate of aggregate production, were the economy at some specified full-employment level. The gap between actual and potential output measures the output lost through less than full employment. (Ch. 2)

predetermined variable In macro models, variables whose values are set outside the model (hence predetermined), either because they are little affected by the economy or because the model builder wants to see how changes in their values affect the economy. (Ch. 3)

purchasing-power parity The theory that the prices of identical items produced in different countries will be the same. This implies that the percentage change in an exchange rate equals the difference in the nations' rates of inflation. (Ch. 17)

quantity theory The theory that velocity is predetermined and, so, that changes in the money supply cause proportionate changes in nominal income (money supply times velocity equals aggregate nominal income). If velocity varies with interest rates, then matters are not so simple. (Chs. 4, 6)

rational expectations Expectations that take into account all available information, including that on government policies and their consequences. In new classical models, in which employment and output fluctuations are attributed to price misperceptions, rational expectations imply that only surprise government policies affect the economy. (Ch. 10)

real data Data measured in terms of purchasing power; for instance, the division of nominal income by the price level gives real income, a measure of how much that income can purchase. (Ch. 2)

required rate of return The rate of return by which future cash flows are discounted in making present-value calculations. For example, if the required rate of return is R, then the present value of \$ X received in t years is \$ $X/(1+R)^t$. (Ch. 13)

reservation wage In search models of unemployment, the minimum wage at which an unemployed person will accept a job. Reservations wages depend on such things as the dispersion of job offers across firms and the costs to the job seeker of additional search. (Ch. 16)

reserve requirements The fraction of their deposits that the Fed requires banks to hold as cash reserves, either in their own vaults or on deposit with the Fed. The rest can be loaned out. (Ch. 9)

Say's law Supply creates its own demand. This is a concise summary of the classical assumption that the economy is at full employment with output determined by available resources, regardless of demand. (Ch. 5)

search model of unemployment A model that postulates that some of the unemployed choose to be unemployed so that they can most easily collect information about the wages and working conditions offered by various employers. (Ch. 16)

shoe leather costs With respect to inflation, the time, energy, and other resources spent minimizing cash balances by constant shifting of invested funds not needed for spending. (Ch. 8)

stock data Data for an item at a particular moment; for example, the amount of outstanding debt. (Ch. 2) See **flow data**.

superneutrality A characteristic of money if its constant rate of increase does not affect real economic activity. See **money neutrality** and the **Tobin effect**. (Ch. 8)

supply side The side of the economy that encompasses employment and production decisions. Classical economists focused on how a nation's full-employment output depends upon labor demand, labor supply, and production. Keynes emphasized the *demand side*, arguing that for want of demand, actual output may fall short of its full-employment potential. (Ch. 5)

surprise employment In new classical models, temporary voluntary expansion of employment that occurs when workers underestimate prices and hence overestimate their real wages. (Ch. 10)

surprise unemployment In new classical models, temporary voluntary unemployment that occurs when workers overestimate prices and underestimate real wages. (Ch. 10)

term structure of interest rates The relationship among returns on assets of differing maturities. (Ch. 15)

Tobin effect The decline in the real return on cash (since the nominal return is fixed at zero) as inflation increases, which pulls down the real returns on assets that are substitutes for money. Thus, people will accept lower real returns on bonds during inflations to avoid holding cash, which earns even less. (Ch. 8)

Tobin's *q* The ratio of the market value of a firm to the replacement cost of its assets. Tobin argued that it is a useful barometer of investment spending. (Ch. 13)

trade balance A nation's exports of merchandise less its sales—an indicator of the competitiveness of its products. (Ch. 17)

transfer payments Gifts or fulfillments of obligations that do not involve the reciprocation of any goods or services. Government income taxes and Social Security payments are two examples, one a source of revenue and the other a disbursement. (Chs. 2, 3)

underground economy The illegal and other covert economic activity that is hidden to avoid taxes, prosecution or both. (Ch 11)

unemployment rate An estimate of the fraction of the labor force that is out of work, based on household surveys conducted by the government. (Ch. 2)

velocity The ratio of nominal output or transactions (during some interval) to the level of the money supply and, thus, a measure of how frequently money must be used to pay for output or transactions. See **quantity theory.** (Chs. 4, 14)

INDEX